Mastery and Drift

Mastery and Drift

PROFESSIONAL-CLASS LIBERALS
SINCE THE 1960S

*Edited by Brent Cebul
and Lily Geismer*

The University of Chicago Press   Chicago and London

The University of Chicago Press, Chicago 60637
The University of Chicago Press, Ltd., London
© 2025 by The University of Chicago
All rights reserved. No part of this book may be used or reproduced in any manner whatsoever without written permission, except in the case of brief quotations in critical articles and reviews. For more information, contact the University of Chicago Press, 1427 E. 60th St., Chicago, IL 60637.
Published 2025
Printed in the United States of America

34 33 32 31 30 29 28 27 26 25   1 2 3 4 5

ISBN-13: 978-0-226-83811-3 (cloth)
ISBN-13: 978-0-226-83813-7 (paper)
ISBN-13: 978-0-226-83812-0 (e-book)
DOI: https://doi.org/10.7208/chicago/9780226838120.001.0001

Library of Congress Cataloging-in-Publication Data

Names: Cebul, Brent, editor. | Geismer, Lily, editor.
Title: Mastery and drift : professional-class liberals since the 1960s / edited by Brent Cebul and Lily Geismer.
Description: Chicago : The University of Chicago Press, 2025. | Includes bibliographical references and index.
Identifiers: LCCN 2024021598 | ISBN 9780226838113 (cloth) | ISBN 9780226838137 (paperback) | ISBN 9780226838120 (ebook)
Subjects: LCSH: Liberalism—United States—History—20th century. | United States—Politics and government—20th century.
Classification: LCC JC574.2.U5 M37 2025 | DDC 320.510973/0904—dc23/eng/20240603
LC record available at https://lccn.loc.gov/2024021598

♾ This paper meets the requirements of ANSI/NISO Z39.48-1992 (Permanence of Paper).

To our mentors Brian Balogh and Matt Lassiter

. . . the fitting of government to the facts of the modern world is sure to be a very difficult task.

WALTER LIPPMAN, DRIFT AND
MASTERY: AN ATTEMPT TO DIAGNOSE
THE CURRENT UNREST (1914)

CONTENTS

INTRODUCTION
Professional-Class Liberalism 1
Brent Cebul and Lily Geismer

Part I: Generational Change and Continuity

1: HOW PHILANTHROPY MADE AND UNMADE AMERICAN LIBERALISM 19
Lila Corwin Berman

2: MANAGING GLOBAL DEVELOPMENT
Robert Nathan and the Liberal Roots of the Contract State in US Foreign Policy 35
Stephen Macekura

3: CREATING "INITIATORY DEMOCRACY"
Ralph Nader, the Center for the Study of Responsive Law, and the Shaping of Liberalism in the 1970s 53
Sarah Milov and Reuel Schiller

4: "WHAT IS A POPULIST APPROACH TO THIS CRISIS?"
ACORN's Liberalism and the 1980s Savings and Loan Crisis 73
Marisa Chappell

5: SURVIVAL PENDING CORPORATE SPONSORSHIP
The "Crisis" of the Black Family, Black State Skepticism, and the Evolution of Black Liberalism in the Post–Civil Rights Era 87
Danielle Wiggins

6: QUEER AUTONOMY AND THE AFTERLIFE OF THE FAMILY WAGE 107
B. Alex Beasley

7: MAKING THE LIBERAL MEDIA
Journalism's Class Transformation since the 1960s 125
Dylan Gottlieb

8: SEEING LIKE A STRATEGIST 145
Timothy Shenk

Part II: New Governance

9: THE PRESERVATION OF CONDITIONAL CITIZENSHIP AFTER THE 1965 VOTING RIGHTS ACT 167
Julilly Kohler-Hausmann

10: LIBERALISM'S LAST RIGHTS
Disability Inclusion and the Rise of the Cost-Benefit State 185
Karen M. Tani

11: COMPUTERIZING A COVENANT
Contract Liberalism and the Nationalization of Welfare Administration 201
Marc Aidinoff

12: LEFT IN LIMBO
The Fight for Temporary Protected Status and the Illiberal Effects of Liberal Policymaking 219
Adam Goodman

13: THE AUSTERITY IMPERATIVE
Democratic Deficit Hawks and the Crisis of Keynesianism 237
David Stein

14: THE PROFESSIONAL-CLASS PRESIDENCY OF BARACK OBAMA 259
Nicole Hemmer

15: STATE AGENCY
Social History with and beyond Institutionalism 277
Gabriel Winant

Acknowledgments 297   Notes 299
List of Contributors 379   Index 383

INTRODUCTION

Professional-Class Liberalism

BRENT CEBUL AND LILY GEISMER

For all the attention paid to partisan polarization over the last decade or more, the Right and a resurgent political Left largely agreed on a common adversary: professionally trained, elite, technocratic liberals. Democrats including Hillary Clinton, Pete Buttigieg, Rahm Emanuel, Kamala Harris, Barack Obama, and Elizabeth Warren embody many of the momentous transformations that have remade political liberalism since the 1960s. From one perspective, they symbolize liberalism's championing of equality of opportunity and diversity—a happily married gay man; the son of a single mother and Kenyan father; icons of second-wave feminism's successes; the daughter of Indian and Jamaican immigrants. But they also manifest the momentous professional-class transformations that have more subtly redefined liberal orientations to governance and popular politics. They were equally a former McKinsey and Company consultant; an attorney and long-standing member of Wal-Mart's board; an investment banker; a tough-on-crime prosecutor; and law professors.

To many on the right, these figures were high-flying examples of the "liberal elite": cosmopolitan, coastal, and contemptuous of the "Heartland" and its working-class (white) people—the so-called deplorables in Hillary Clinton's self-defeating formulation. On the left, when Clinton vanquished the social democrat Bernie Sanders in the 2016 Democratic Party presidential primary, many Sanders supporters dusted off an old concept to make sense of what had happened. By the 1970s, the "professional-managerial class," in Barbara Ehrenreich and John Ehrenreich's analysis, formed a novel managerial, bureaucratic, legal, and professional stratum that operated between working people and the highest echelons of corporate and finance capitalism.[1] With its ranks exploding in the 1970s, "the PMC" absorbed and moderated the era's radical politics, deflecting serious critiques of capitalist democracy. After Clinton and the liberal establishment rallied to defeat Sanders, "PMC" quickly became an epithet for a privileged *political* class's credulous commitments to capitalism and centrist moderation in the face of unfolding global economic, political, and ecological catastrophes.[2]

Rather than relitigate the PMC debates of the last decade, we conceived of this volume to better understand the significant transformations that remade liberalism and the Democratic Party after the 1960s, and which, we maintain, propels much of the recent frustration with liberal governance and electoral politics. Coming of age politically amidst these developments led us to wonder less about how momentary, strategic miscalculations by Democratic administrations or the cunning maneuverings of Republicans dashed potential moments of progressive opportunity. These episodes instead caused us to turn our attention to the limitations *internal* to liberalism, to examine its fraught relationship with the Left, and to clarify its relationship to neoliberalism.[3]

The essays that follow examine what we term "professional-class liberalism" and explore important conjunctures between professional-class formation, electoral politics, and liberal ideologies of governance. We employ the terms "professional class" and "liberal" to explain how emergent class formations and governing ideologies relate to a set of broader historical political, economic, and demographic transformations as well as to the deeper liberal political tradition.

This focus shifts attention to different sorts of developments than are the focus of most traditional histories of twentieth-century American politics. In particular, we emphasize the political effects of the expansion of graduate and professional training in the United States beginning in the 1960s and accelerating in the decades that followed. Some figures illustrate these remarkable demographic, educational, and professional developments. Between 1963 and 1979, the annual number of first-year law students doubled to more than forty thousand. Other professional schools and MA programs saw similarly explosive growth: between 1959 and 1980, the figure more than quadrupled to nearly three hundred thousand new students annually. During the 1970s and 1980s, formal training in public policy also grew substantially. By the mid-1970s, more than one hundred universities offered advanced degrees in public policy, and by 1990, these schools together graduated around a thousand new masters students annually.[4] The growth and diversification of professional and graduate training was particularly striking among women, whose enrollment in law school, for instance—which had accounted for just 9 percent of the total students in 1970—reached parity with that of men circa 2000 and eclipsed it two decades later.[5] The combination of civil rights legislation and the wide implementation of affirmative-action programs also expanded professional training opportunities for African Americans. In 1970, there were around four thousand African American lawyers in the United States; by 2005 there were more than forty thousand.[6]

As the essays suggest, from within the broader ranks of these professionally trained managers, lawyers, and expert bureaucrats of the 1960s and 1970s, there emerged a rising and increasingly diverse generation of political liberals. Their attitudes about governance were shaped not only by their professional training but also by their particular generational relationship to capitalism and the vast and necessarily complex bureaucratic state. These increasingly career-oriented political and policy-development professionals came to exert profound influence over the Democratic Party and the democratic process—as arbiters of political narratives, moderators of party politics, and essential actors in policy development and implementation.[7]

Rather than mark a decisive break with New Deal and mid-century liberalism, however, professional-class liberals' ideas about capitalism and democracy were in many ways adapted from mid-century and Cold War liberals, even as these younger liberals strove to define themselves as against their forebears' methods of state and market making. This volume, then, charts the causes and components of professional-class liberalisms' distinctive governing logics, which emerged in the economically and politically tumultuous 1970s and were theorized and formalized in the 1980s during liberalism's sojourn in the Reagan-era wilderness.

In emphasizing these political class developments, we also aim to bring a higher degree of clarity to discussions of the emergence of neoliberalism.[8] Many of the chapters that follow explore how professional-class liberals played important roles in constructing neoliberal forms of governance that prioritized capital formation, hollowed out the social safety net, discharged greater social and economic risk onto citizens, and resisted mass democratic organization and participation. The vast majority of actors in these pages, nevertheless, would not have used the term "neoliberal" to describe their worldview or politics and, in the main, believed uncynically in the distant horizon of social promise that informed their actions. It is important that they conceived of themselves as carrying forward a liberal or progressive tradition, and we seek to take seriously this self-conception. Understanding the idiosyncratic and contingent path professional-class liberals took toward embracing neoliberal logics is essential not only for a better grasp of our political past but also for envisioning alternative futures.

This specificity is also important for capturing the particular ways that professional-class liberals reflected and shaped momentous changes in the liberal-Democratic electoral coalition. In recent decades, of course, the Democratic Party has become the exclusive vessel for political liberalism, a marked change from the 1930s through the 1960s when liberal Republicans supported causes such as civil rights. During those decades, the Democratic Party's electoral prospects depended upon the New Deal coalition, a motley array of plural and locally rooted interests: white-ethnic urban machines; Jim Crow segregationists; union members; white, first-time suburban homeowners; and growing numbers of Black voters. The dissolution of this variegated coalition has been the subject of vast scholarly cottage industries. Yet, far from marking the end of liberalism as a political force, the crack-up of the New Deal coalition propelled liberalism's evolution by giving the lawyers, economists, and others who had shaped liberal governance since the Progressive Era and New Deal much freer hands to formulate public policies and electoral strategies.[9] Partisan and ideological polarization as well as the increasing nationalization of US electoral politics further empowered professional-class liberals by blunting minority coalition members' leverage within liberal electoral coalitions and governing priorities.[10] Meanwhile, the demographic growth of the professional middle class also meant that professional-class liberals' life experiences, political cultures, and professional outlooks were reflected back to them by an increasingly vocal and well-resourced plurality within the Democratic Party's base and from within institutions of profound social, economic, and political influence, chiefly philanthropy, media, and universities.[11] Professional-class liberals, then, emerged as political and state actors whose training, instincts, and social worlds were increasingly embedded in and defined by the globalized, financial, legalistic, and managerial capitalist systems they imagined themselves reforming.

These transformations reached their political zenith in the Clinton and Obama administrations. Yet, the acute economic and political crises that have unfolded since 2008—which professional-class liberals themselves helped author—firmly exposed professional-class liberalism's contradictions and limitations. With renewed contestations over the meanings of liberalism, the content of its governance, and its relationship with a resurgent Left, the moment is ripe to consider modern liberalism's historical evolution and enduring impact on contemporary politics and society.

* * *

Grappling with liberalism since the 1960s presents distinctive challenges. For instance, over the last half-century, durable majorities of Americans have consistently supported key liberal causes and social aspirations such as a public health-insurance option; more robust family leave and child support; gun control; and environmental protection.[12] Yet liberal politicians, their political appeals, and their approach to policy and governance receive reliably lower approval ratings.[13] Even apparently clear-cut victories regularly become bogged down by popular discontent and political exhaustion—think of Obamacare and its Rube Goldberg–like market mechanisms, its mixed and rising costs, its state-by-state variations, its disastrous web rollout, and the fierce opposition it stoked.[14] Meanwhile, liberalism's aspirations toward equal rights and citizenship, inclusivity, and diversity have broad public support, but the public policies liberals implement to achieve them often fail to make lasting or broad-based change. Modern liberalism has the uncanny habit of appearing at once politically wan and culturally omnipresent.

This volume examines the development of these tensions by centering liberal approaches to governance. By governance, we mean the apparatus of state power as well as the broad practice of public authority by state actors and their partnerships with philanthropic, market, voluntary, and other non-state entities.[15] Indeed, much of the existing literatures on modern liberalism and neoliberalism fails to take seriously the centrality of governance in the liberal imagination and the ways in which technocracy, expertise, and pragmatism themselves were both cause and consequence of the vast, complex machinery of the modern state. Grappling with such intricacies only ratified liberals' celebration of new technologies, faith in data-based evidence, and deep satisfaction at finding sophisticated and, for citizens, difficult-to-comprehend legal and technical policy fixes.[16] In modern governing and market apparatuses, of course, technical and legal expertise, finely tuned policy knowledge, and an appreciation for incremental, reformist, pragmatism are not merely understandable but rather essential. Following the 1960s, however, such technocratic and legalistic rationalities came to define not merely the means of liberal governance but also its ends, drawing ever more narrowly the limits of liberal social aspirations.

The volume's contributors explore the perspectives of many figures and groups included in the category of professional-class liberals—public-interest lawyers and philanthropic foundation officers, journalists and academics, Democratic politicians, policy experts, and political strategists. Perhaps the defining professional-cultural characteristic stitching members of these professions into the fabric of contemporary liberalism has been, to borrow the Ehrenreichs' words, the "persistent" faith that their professional training, "high ethical standards," and "class interests are identical to the interests of society at large."[17] Indeed, many professional-class liberals prioritized visions of the public good in their career choices, sacrificing earnings on behalf of what they might describe as vocational callings rather than mere careers. Yet there are obvious risks with too closely associating one's particular worldview with that of the public writ large, not least of which could be moods of "contempt and paternalism" in response to alternative or opposing visions.[18] Such attitudes also reflected professional-class liberals' class blindness and, for many, racial privilege, which was rooted in their shared life experiences: their internalization of meritocracy, their education and training, their careerism. The essays compiled here are less directly focused on such affective politics or on professional-class liberals' "emotional tone."[19] But their close attention to key actors, ideas about the state, and electoral strategies offer critical context for exploring these more affective dimensions of liberal politics and thus also the disaffection with liberalism that has taken hold among the working class, people of color, and rural voters.

Our contributors highlight well-known figures including Ralph Nader, Robert Rubin, and Cass Sunstein, as well as lesser-known actors such as political strategist Stan Greenberg, economic-development consultant Robert Nathan, Atlanta's Fulton County commissioner Michael Lomax, and state welfare administrators in Louisiana and Mississippi. They also explore the perspectives of those who challenged professional-class liberals from the left or who advanced alternative visions of liberalism—housing activists in the Association of Community Organizations for Reform Now (ACORN), LGBTQ and disability rights activists, and Central American asylum seekers who sought more capacious visions of individual rights.

What emerges in these pages, then, is a liberalism in perpetual tension and in perpetual flux: one that continued to hold individual opportunity, security, and a certain egalitarian impulse as essential to its self-conception and vision of a good society, but whose ideas about the state, democracy, and the market were increasingly cost-conscious, technocratic, and particularistic rather than grounded in populist or universal appeals. The key, we argue, to unraveling modern liberalism's seeming disjointedness and discontents lies in capturing the growing distance between professional-class liberals' rhetorical and social aspirations and their actual relationship to governance, capitalism, and democracy.

* * *

Though this volume seeks to make sense of contemporary liberalism's evolution, it is not meant to be an apologia, much less champion of these developments. The assembled authors manifest an analytical and critical detachment from liberalism shaped by shared generational experiences and, in many cases, political orientations on the left. Yet we all have received PhDs and currently hold positions at colleges and universities. That is to say, we have been shaped by and operate within professional-class institutions and worldviews and so may inadvertently reproduce certain blind spots or latent assumptions. But this shared position also gives us unique insight into these developments, their antecedents, and their contemporary manifestations.

Our contributors came of age politically and intellectually after the Cold War had ended and during the presidencies of Bill Clinton and Barack Obama. We saw firsthand the possibilities and limitations of liberal approaches to policymaking and political strategy as they confronted crises of governance, asymmetrical political polarization, mounting extremism, and a protracted global war on terror. Social and political divisions, meanwhile, were fueled by widening economic inequality driven by the reorientation of national political economy toward real estate, global financial capitalism, and increasingly precarious service employment. Yet, rather than seek to reign in or reform these sectors, professional-class liberals more often bolstered and partnered with them.

As they did so, liberal politicians and the policymakers and professionals who circulated around them updated longer-lived Progressive Era and mid-century values of efficient public administration, technocratic managerialism, and elite definitions of "good governance."[20] Indeed, in his 1914 book, *Drift and Mastery*, the progressive public intellectual Walter Lippmann lamented the nation's social drift—its inequality, social fragmentation, and ineffectual governance. The solution, he believed, would be found in the emerging professional classes of social scientists and business and government bureaucrats. These "new type[s] of administrators, the specialist[s]," he averred, would bring order to "complexity"; would "distinguish fact from fancy"; and would "shap[e] . . . fact to a chastened and honest dream."[21] In many respects, the presidency of Barack Obama, roughly a century later, epitomized Lippman's ideal. In the face of mounting Republican extremism, inequality, and social discontent, President Obama celebrated "smart" governance as somehow the first step to renewing American democracy's social promise and restoring bipartisan consensus—bipartisanship itself offering evidence of the moral rectitude and rationality of liberal governance. According to one account, during his two terms Obama publicly promoted his policies using the word "smart" more than nine hundred times.[22] This example reinforces how liberals like Obama genuinely believed that centering expert-led, technocratic governance itself offered the best way to solve social problems and "do good" in ways that might preclude more thoroughgoing structural economic, constitutional, or democratic reform. Despite such technical mastery, however, Obama's promise of hope and change failed to arrest societal drift.

Other dynamics beyond the rise of professional-class liberals, of course, also shaped liberalism's narrowing social imagination. The post-1970s era saw the Left and labor politically weakened and internally fragmented. The rise of professional-class liberals was not the cause of labor's decline—deindustrialization, capital flight, and unions' internal discontents were structural realities dating to the 1940s. But big labor's waning power enabled professional-class liberals to operate with greater autonomy and, by the 1980s, to openly disparage political partnerships with labor or the Left. Ironically, however, such enervation on the left could also make the left-liberal coalition seem more coherent and stable than it was. Indeed, the historical absence of a true labor party in the United States as well as the particularities of the American two-party, majoritarian system has consistently made the Left and labor junior partners within broader liberal coalitions. Whereas in a parliamentary system a left bloc might extract specific concessions, claim clear political victories, and in the process maintain a certain independence and coherence, in the majoritarian US system, particularly after the 1970s, professional-class liberals' enduring quest to capture the support of the "center" only further obscured and marginalized the Left's role in American politics.

And, as Gabriel Winant suggests in the volume's concluding essay, similar dynamics played out within the historical profession itself. Following Reagan's landslide reelection in 1984, a cohort of labor and social historians abandoned radical analysis and subjects in favor of an analytical and political rapprochement with liberalism. In the process they made a strong case for institutional historical analysis and the political promise of state-centered rather than populist social reform—grasping the influence of bureaucrats, in other words, held greater political promise than did excavating the social worlds of the masses who, in Reagan's elections, seemed to be abandoning liberalism or the Left in any event.[23] Like liberalism writ large in the 1990s and early in the first decade of the 2000s, these intellectual developments both obscured and discounted the ongoing evolution of the Left. The unexpected popularity of Ralph Nader's third-party presidential bid in 2000, the sharp and sustained opposition to the War on Terror, the rise of Occupy Wall Street, the Black Lives Matter movements, and Bernie Sanders's strong bids for the 2016 and 2020 presidential nominations all suggest significant fissures not only within liberalism's base but also within the broader left-liberal coalition.

But this volume also emerges at a moment of renewed tensions *and* partnerships between the Left and liberalism. These contemporary dynamics might remind us of an important historical truth: liberalism has most often achieved its highest social aspirations—the victories, in other words, liberals are most likely to celebrate—when pushed from the left and by movements for labor, civil rights, welfare rights, women's liberation, and LBGTQ rights.[24] Such disagreements among liberals and the Left, then, are not new but have been core features of American politics since the emergence of political liberalism in the nineteenth century. Against conservatives' or the media's tendency to apply a "left-liberal" label to the contemporary Democratic coalition, then, these meaningful distinctions underscore how liberalism and the Left have had and continue to have markedly distinctive ideologies of governance, rights construction, and social change.

This volume is divided into two parts organized around its two major ideas and themes: first, the emergence of a new *generation* of professional-class liberals; and second, the ways in which their ideas about and approaches to *governance* became implemented through policy. Part I, Generational Change and Continuity, examines the emergence of this new generation of professional-class liberals: these were lawyers, economists, policy practitioners, nonprofit and philanthropy staffers and executives, political consultants and pollsters, and journalists. The chapters in part I also emphasize how this generational shift was not without contestations from within the liberal-left coalition, as advocates for economic justice, civil rights, and LGBTQ rights sought to challenge the version of professional-class liberalism taking shape or to remake it on their own terms. Part II, New Governance, focuses on how the technocratic, high-tech, pragmatic, and purportedly nonideological worldview of professional-class liberals directly shaped their diagnoses of and solutions for problems of governance and democracy. It interrogates the policies that flowed from this generation of liberals' fetishization of new technologies and strategies of governance, which became one of the main avenues through which professional-class liberals defined themselves, their coalition, and their politics.

Liberalism's Governing Ideologies

It was over the course of the twentieth century that American liberalism became an ideology chiefly defined by its approach to governance. Nineteenth-century liberalism was largely animated by two warring tendencies: faith in individual autonomy, human progress, and perfectibility; and a tendency to "serve as an apologia for *laissez-faire* economic policy."[25] The Great Depression exposed the fundamental irreconcilability of these positions, and so New Dealers began constructing the liberal state to moderate between them. Liberalism as an ideology of democratic governance, then, emerged as an enduring effort to use the state as an independent agent balancing individual opportunity and market capitalism.

At least two generations of social, political, and urban historians along with multidisciplinary scholars of race, gender, ethnicity, and historical institutionalism have excavated the successes, limitations, compromises, frustrations, and inequalities associated with the quest to strike this precarious balance.[26] From rich accounts of specific liberal policies and social politics in action, one could sketch a synthesis or typology of twentieth-century liberal governance and rights delivery. It would underscore just how much of liberal statecraft relied upon publicly structured markets, finance capital, and the maintenance of the heteronormative and normatively white nuclear family. It would emphasize how the highly porous liberal state empowered local elites and private-sector partners to distribute the social benefits essential for shoring up individual opportunity—and so regularly saw its social aspirations limited by the primacy of private profit, the vicissitudes of markets, and the persistence of Jim Crow segregation.[27] Beginning in the 1960s, critics also described how "corporate liberalism" had invited the capitalist fox into the regulatory henhouse, hobbling the regulatory state and producing significant dangers for citizens and the environment.[28] Perhaps the most infamous example of private interests enriching themselves at the expense of taxpayers—and at the cost of millions of lives lost around the world—was the military-industrial complex, whose grip on democratic institutions became hotly contested in the Vietnam War era.[29] The many mainstream and radical social movements of the 1960s and 1970s, then, were a potent expression of the liberal state's compounding legitimacy crisis rather than a symbol of its purported excesses.[30]

Taken together, the flourishing literature on New Deal and midcentury liberalism suggests that the passive language of "contradictions" or "paradoxes" obscures liberals' numerous, repeated, and deliberate policy choices that made equitable distributions of wealth, wages, housing, educational opportunity, and health and retirement benefits not simply out of reach for many marginalized Americans but also highly contingent even for fortunate insiders. These dynamics propelled the 1960s' rights-based movements *and* a base for the resurgent Right among disgruntled white workers and middle-class homeowners.[31]

Rather than signal the end of liberalism as a coherent political force, however, these discontents drove its ongoing evolution. The emerging professional class of liberals largely opposed the Vietnam War and the draft, supported the broad goals if not always the modes of expression of the era's social movements and rights revolutions, and were deeply anxious about the state of American democracy and political institutions. In fact, the threat posed to individual flourishing and the efficacy of democracy by the highly bureaucratized liberal state itself—and to a somewhat lesser degree its adjuncts in large unions and corporations—was the most obvious source of their generation's dissatisfaction. Liberalism's evolution continued in the 1960s and 1970s, in part because the younger baby-boom generation, like the young law students who went to work at Ralph Nader's Public Citizens, as illustrated in Sarah Milov and Reuel Schiller's chapter, or the journalists joining news desks and magazines, as Dylan Gottlieb's chapter explores, shared many of the Left's critiques of the undemocratic qualities of the mid-century state and bureaucracies.

Yet professional-class liberals did not reject their liberal legacy wholesale. This younger generation carried forward essential political instincts and orientations shared with their mid-century, Cold War–era forebears. If New Dealers had often operated in creative tension with leftist movements like the Popular Front, by mid-century, avowedly anti-communist liberals such as Arthur Schlesinger Jr. expressed mounting skepticism for such idealistic and ideological forms of mass politics even as he worried that liberalism itself was failing as a "fighting faith."[32] For professional-class liberals, similar skepticism for idealistic, mass politics was only reinforced by the seeming excesses and exhaustion of the radicalism of the 1960s and 1970s. This skepticism for mass ideological movements was bolstered as well by incremental victories secured through legal action, the administrative state, and the courts led by a rising generation of public-interest lawyers and other professionals.[33] Failing to democratize the bureaucratic state from without, they would earn the credentials to enable them to reform it from within.

Professional-class liberalism, then, had significant genealogical ties to Cold War–era liberals, whose vision of society, politics, and political economy viewed the overt exercise of state power, partisan ideologies, and popular movements with considerable suspicion.[34] State bureaucracies and regulatory oversight certainly grew in these years, but Cold War–era liberals demonstrated a hesitancy to use direct funding authority or pursue constitutional reform to guarantee new "rights."[35] Coming of age amidst the social and governing crises of the 1970s, then, professional-class liberals would often exceed their predecessors' wariness for the overt exercise of state power, in some cases embracing overt anti-statism.

Professional-class liberals also came to champion an expert-led democracy—one that, to paraphrase Daniel Rodgers's characterization of Progressive Era reformers, emphasized not so much a democracy of *form* but rather a democracy of *outcomes*. In this vision, so long as enough people voted to keep liberals in power, popular democratic or civic capacities were increasingly irrelevant to the content of governance and the substance of rights.[36] The social and political contradictions compounded: by the 1990s, many professional-class liberals believed that technocratic, elite-driven governance could be bolstered by growth in high-tech and finance sectors, which, David Stein's chapter reveals, allied liberals with bond traders and finance capitalists' deficit hawk agendas. The potential excesses of those markets, meanwhile, would be tempered with demographically targeted, technologically efficient, apolitical, and noncontroversial social-welfare provisions, which, as Marc Aidinoff's chapter illustrates, relied upon new computing capacities that also enabled the welfare state to offset the costs of welfare entitlements by extracting resources from "deadbeat dads." Liberals also pursued the delivery of social benefits through creative uses of the tax code and legal proceduralism and sought to legitimize spending through the use of cost-benefit analysis—key limitations facing the 1970s' disability rights movement, as Karen Tani shows in her chapter. And throughout, liberal politicians sold these ideas about governance and social rights to the electorate as distinctly nonideological, fiscally frugal, fundamentally rational, and, above all, as evidence of professional-class liberals' pragmatism and smarts. In the process, however, liberals played a central role in further eroding and delegitimizing the New Deal's limited welfare state.[37]

The reality that the American population was growing exponentially—it nearly doubled in size between 1930 and 1980—and, along with it, the varieties and scale of market and state interpenetration only accelerated liberals' retreat from the New Deal's populism and their embrace of techno-optimism.[38] Facing such financial and technological complexities, professional-class liberals often trusted these emergent sectors to self-regulate and relied upon them to innovate and administer emergent public-private policies.[39] Indeed, Lila Corwin Berman's chapter suggests how liberals' long-standing reliance upon philanthropic sectors offers a crucial site for tracing these developments, revealing how philanthropic governance fundamentally transformed liberalism and the state. Similarly, the rise of for-profit consultants and contractors also shaped how the federal government carried out its domestic and foreign policy agendas, and, as Stephen Macekura reveals, those practices, which certainly accelerated after the 1960s, had deep roots in the New Deal. Throughout, democratic accountability over the provision of public authority—always a tenuous proposition—became further attenuated.

Legal expertise, economic and policy training, and professional-class orientations also shaped liberals' emerging arguments against more universal or redistributionist modes of reform or rights. Indeed, professionals offered solutions for liberals' wariness about mass politics, which many political elites associated with the Right's claims of a range of "interest groups" whose demands they blamed for the governing and fiscal crises of the 1970s as well as liberalism's declining electoral fortunes in the 1980s. Julilly Kohler-Hausmann's chapter exposes profound liberal anxieties about mass democracy as promised in the Voting Rights Act of 1965 and the increasingly intricate efforts elites pursued to more carefully "sculpt the electorate." Likewise, in his chapter, Timothy Shenk examines the role campaign strategists and pollsters played in crafting highly targeted electoral outreach to what they called a "coalition of the ascendant" or, in practice, a coalition of the predominantly white center. This focus blunted professional-class liberals' interest in the more collective-oriented politics and universal policy ideas of the labor movement, the poor people's campaign, or the welfare rights movement, which—as Marisa Chappell's chapter demonstrates—remained critical to the version of liberalism articulated by groups like ACORN in the 1980s and beyond.

As chapters by Alex Beasley and Adam Goodman reveal, professional-class liberals' turn away from universalism as well as their more austere vision of rights shaped the more limited and liminal opportunities afforded to LBGTQ citizens, immigrants, and refugees. And, as Danielle Wiggins reveals in her chapter, the long history of racialized state violence and unfulfilled promises led many Black liberals to mirror professional-class liberals' wariness for robust state action and to advocate for private-sector approaches and forms of opportunity. For very different reasons, then, diverse strands of liberals shared commitments to professional-class opportunities and versions of "state skepticism."

Modern Liberalism—and Its Historians

Earlier waves of scholarship struggled to make sense of many of the key continuities and disjunctures within liberal thought, governance, and neoliberalism that are the subjects of this volume. In part, this challenge emerges because scholarship on twentieth-century liberalism has only just begun to explore developments beyond the 1970s, and this history's sheer recency has made it difficult to trace continuities and divergences. Moreover, the first drafts of the post-1960s period understandably tend to reflect the perspectives of political actors and observers who were involved in struggles within liberalism—most notably many of the professional-class alumni of the Clinton administration and the Democratic Leadership Council.[40] The tendency to gravitate toward historical actors' categories and narratives is not unique to this topic; it is a common problem of writing recent history. In the case of twentieth-century liberalism, however, these dynamics risk reproducing caricatured versions of the relationships between New Deal and Great Society liberalism and its more modern successors precisely because professional-class liberals so often overdrew those distinctions as part of their own strategies and worldviews.[41]

The other dominant trend among scholars and pundits has been to frame liberalism's evolution after the 1960s as emblematic of a rightward shift among liberals themselves and the country writ large.[42] Instead, the essays collected here make the case that professional-class liberals' governing ideology in fact comes into sharper focus when contrasted with conservatism and its own versions of and paths toward neoliberalism. While the conservative movement is composed of differing and often contradictory threads, a search for raw political power, the rollback of liberal governance, and the defense of received hierarchies (defined somewhat differently by its populist and plutocratic wings) has consistently unified conservatism's varied ideological forms.[43] For liberalism, meanwhile, strategies of "good governance" increasingly served as its unifying force, its primary proving ground, and its source of ideological continuity and internal debate across decades of momentous change.

Rather than signal a convergence with or capitulation to conservatism, over the 1970s and 1980s liberalism's shifting class-orientation and its turn toward managerial, technocratic governance grew not only from deep continuities with earlier modes of liberal approaches but in response to the increasingly globalized political economy.[44] Indeed, the transformations we trace in domestic liberalism were not unique to the United States. Many of the same structural, economic, and demographic factors—including the rise of globalization, financialization, new generations of professionally trained, technocratic policymakers who supported market-oriented approaches and shoring up nonunionized sectors—reshaped a number of Western democracies and their political landscapes, all of which, by the late twentieth century, earned the moniker "neoliberal." The parallel developments in nations such as Great Britain and Germany make clear that the shifts we trace in US liberalism were hardly reducible to domestic partisan dynamics and fleeting campaign strategies of "triangulation."[45]

In arguing that liberalism's transformations were not primarily to do with ideas or strategies borrowed from the right, we also advance the claim that there was a coherent and distinctively *liberal* path toward neoliberal governance—one that converged at key points with conservative preferences but that depended upon recognizably liberal political logics and motivations. Rationality, efficiency, growth, faith in markets, and commitment to individual opportunity and autonomy had been key components of liberal governance since at least the New Deal, were updated by the Kennedy and Johnson administrations, and, by the 1970s, were reanimated, transformed, and newly ascendant in new political contexts and alongside shifting economic and technological capacities. Put another way, since at least the New Deal, liberals have sought to moderate and rationalize capitalism in ways that emphasize individual opportunity—one generation's support for labor organizing (unions, Schlesinger Jr., wrote, were "as clearly indigenous to the capitalist system as the corporation itself") becomes a later generation's support for affirmative action or, as Alex Beasley's chapter emphasizes, the expansion of marriage rights.[46]

To be sure, the growing political and social power of conservatism and the Republican Party has always imposed important constraints on the liberal imagination and governance. The Reagan administration's domestic austerity, the Gingrich Congress's legislative brinksmanship, increasingly aggressive modes of pro-life and business conservatism, and Fox News' fixation on real and imagined scandals all hemmed in liberal ambitions. They also created governing problems liberals felt called to solve—these included the perceived need among liberals to balance budgets busted by Republicans or to offer bipartisan solutions and watered-down compromises as evidence of liberal rationality and the triumph of good governance. Against Republicans' strategic antistatism, "liberalism" increasingly meant sober governance.

These dynamics, then, also shaped many of the compromises Democratic policymakers from the 1970s onward did "accomplish"—from promoting free trade, expanding the carceral state, ending "welfare as we know it," and shifting the party and the economy away from industrial manufacturing and unions and toward Wall Street and Silicon Valley.[47] At the same time, engaging with the Right on the floor of Congress, on the campaign trail, and in the courts also had the effect of replacing or equating visions of the social good with procedural aspects of the liberal approach to governance: its aversion to ideological zeal, its emphasis on rationality and procedural norms, its search for common ground, and its commitment to the ideals of equality and individual rights. Though liberal politicians' efforts to secure bipartisan common ground on signature policies like health care, immigration, or infrastructure have often been read as a capitulation to the right, that impulse, as Nicole Hemmer's chapter suggests, reflected a long-standing liberal faith in bipartisanship. Indeed, the quest for responsible conservative partners has been a characteristic trait of liberal governance since at least the Cold War, when liberal scholars and commentators presented the health of the two-party system as evidence of the essential soundness of American democracy versus the dangers of one-party states.[48] And this understanding further captures key distinctions between liberalism and the Left, which has rarely shown the same commitment to cooperation or compromise when fundamental social values are at stake.

In total, then, we insist that particular ideas about the social and political primacy of the state and practices of governance and an ongoing but contextually specific search for social rapprochement with capitalism are the foundational characteristics of liberalism's historical and generational evolution. They explain not only the yawning gaps between liberalism's egalitarian aspirations and approaches to policymaking and politics, but, more recently, the ways in which the intricacies of contemporary governance have tended to bolster professional-class liberals' power at the expense of the less empowered. In the process, professional-class liberals became key architects of the neoliberal age. Examining their history, we hope, suggests that technical expertise, savvy policy design, or appreciation for legal and constitutional nuance are necessary and inevitable components of any democratic governing apparatus as complex as that of the United States. But this history might also suggest that in a just society, governance must be made a servant of the people, subordinated to and marshaled on behalf of abiding moral and social visions.

PART I

Generational Change and Continuity

CHAPTER 1

How Philanthropy Made and Unmade American Liberalism

LILA CORWIN BERMAN

In the spring of 2017, six Republican senators requested that Secretary of State Rex W. Tillerson open an investigation into George Soros's philanthropy. The lawmakers alleged that the Hungarian-born hedge funder was interfering with America's "bilateral relationships" by supporting leftist political movements abroad with "our tax dollars." Hardly a stranger to Republican animus, Soros had cameoed in Donald Trump's final campaign advertisement just a few months earlier. As the soon-to-be president railed against "the global special interests ... that don't have your good in mind," Soros's face flashed across the screen. An exemplum of the threats posed by elite and putatively un-American forces, the foreign-born Jewish billionaire who used his personal wealth to exercise political power made an easy target.[1]

While Republicans pilloried Soros, two books gained attention for shedding light on the "dark money" that propelled a far-right takeover of the Republican Party. One written by a journalist and the other by a historian, both books detailed how fossil-fuel billionaires Charles and David Koch clandestinely deployed their wealth to fund conservative and libertarian think tanks, academic departments, and policy campaigns, all focused on advancing a right-wing agenda that undermined American democracy. Alongside investigations into the Kochs' outsized political influence were public campaigns to pressure universities and arts and culture institutions to break their dependency on the wealthy benefactors and expel them from boards.[2]

By the early years of the Trump presidency, portraits of philanthropy gone awry abounded. Whether Soros, the Koch brothers, or a handful of others like Bill Gates, the Sackler family, or Mark Zuckerberg, the figure of the string-pulling and purse-wielding philanthropist loomed large in efforts to diagnose America's political turmoil. No matter from which side of the political aisle the hit came, it was driven by a similar assessment: that elite private interests posturing as operating for the public good were, in fact, destroying it.

The vilification of philanthropy might be dismissed as the political fallout of a hyper-polarized era that nonetheless cohered around populist pronouncements, yet it signified a far deeper story about how American liberalism had been made and unmade in the twentieth century. Behind the headlines and the exposés rested a history of philanthropy's remarkable rise into a form of governance that first bolstered liberalism before hollowing it out. Throughout most of the twentieth century, political leaders from both parties envisioned progress as the result of successful efforts to balance the rights of private property and capitalism with the public good and the state. This vision was both the heart and the seeming irresolvable tension of political liberalism. Persistent efforts to determine what constituted adequate private-property rights versus sufficient public good reshaped the American state many times over and formed the basis of state agents' attraction to philanthropy. Resting at the intersection of private wealth and public benefit, philanthropy held out the promise of perfecting liberalism by resolving its inner tension.[3]

The era from the New Deal through the Great Society gestated philanthropic governance by fostering a quiet but clear relationship between statecraft and philanthropy. So long as state agents believed they could use philanthropy as a tool to achieve public ends, it appeared a perfect enactment of the liberal ideal and, thus, a worthy recipient of state support through tax exemptions, direct grants, and legal permissiveness. In these years, state agents called upon private foundations and other philanthropic bodies to conduct research, pilot policies, and experiment with global development projects. Often working in tandem with state officials and at their behest, philanthropic leaders helped channel state energies to solve problems at home and abroad that challenged American stability. The American government could hedge its risk by encouraging a private foundation to conduct an experimental policy in India or inner-city Philadelphia, while it could also glean information about how to expand its global development or urban-renewal efforts. With few visible resources on the line, the state nonetheless tested out new ideas that might eventually be incorporated into official policies. Key components of postwar urban policy and international humanitarian assistance projects had their roots in these partnerships and advanced liberal visions for balancing private freedoms with the common good.[4]

Philanthropy's role began to transform in the 1970s as it moved from an incubator for state policy to a stand-in for state power and gradually expanded into a mode of governance that steadily overwhelmed other governing strategies. Philanthropic governance prioritized private power over public decision-making in a move that promised to resolve liberalism's fundamental tension between private-property rights and the public good. Acting as a proxy for state power, philanthropic governance used the instruments of the state, including its democratic structure of public consent and its revenue-generating capabilities, to empower private actors to take the helm of public policy creation, delivery, and reform. A bevy of anti-regulatory, pro-market, and state-shrinking measures endorsed across party lines from the 1970s through the 1990s smoothed the way for the rise of philanthropic governance. Together, they directed public funds and plaudits toward private foundations and other philanthropic bodies.[5]

By the final decades of the twentieth century, the logic and structure of philanthropy had permeated every realm of American power, from domestic and foreign policies to corporate practices to grassroots politics. In other words, no domain of American power operated bereft of the capital and logic of philanthropy. This fact served to lash together disparate political actors from the left and the right, who no matter their policy divisions all conceded to—and often lauded—philanthropic governance. Still, the old wisdom of regarding it as small stakes, a laboratory for statecraft and a way of taming the excesses of capitalism, remained intact in the laws applicable to it, and influenced historians' tendency to marginalize philanthropy from the central narratives of American politics.[6]

Philanthropic governance revolutionized American liberalism by vesting the weight and wealth of the state in private entities, but it launched softly—even imperceptibly—into power. Because the centralized American state re-formed itself over the twentieth century, because the line between state and private power remained fuzzy, and, finally, because the public's reliance on philanthropy made it difficult, even perilous, to speak of it as anything other than the generous acts of individuals, this truly revolutionary transformation in American governance went largely unmarked. Instead of announcing itself as a new political mode, something for an electorate to endorse or not, philanthropic governance expanded inconspicuously in the shadows of the headline-grabbing partisan divisions. By the end of the twentieth century, its substantial power appeared natural, making it difficult for observers to account for it other than in grand pronouncements or ad hominem attacks.[7]

To recognize philanthropy as essential to the history of modern American liberalism is to make visible a force that gained governing power through its own inscrutability and divergence from well-worn plotlines of American liberal politics. The historical development of philanthropy into a mode of governance cannot be explained through the left-right binary, even as it is irrefutable that certain philanthropic endeavors fueled materially disparate political ideologies. Rather, philanthropy attracted policymakers precisely because it seemed to skate above the partisan fray and resolve the liberal tension between private property and the public good. Absent historical contextualization, the fire under which philanthropy has come over the last decade may appear as just another flare-up of political polarization and the culture wars. But sensationalized scandals and takedowns obscure the far more seismic role that philanthropy has played in making and unmaking American liberalism. In its bid to solve liberalism's most fundamental tension between private property and the public good, philanthropy made liberalism appear perfectible, but it did so by destroying liberalism's lifeblood: the vital tension between the private and the public.

State Growth and the Logic of Philanthropy

Charitable institutions long existed on the North American continent, but they only concatenated into a philanthropic system in tandem with the formation of American state power. As legal historian Sarah Barringer Gordon explains, nineteenth-century states "simultaneously supported and disciplined" non-state associations, from churches to universities to fraternal organizations and other collective institutions. A state could wield property-tax exemptions and the rights of incorporation as carrots and sticks, offering charitable entities legal protections and full coffers but only in return for these entities' consent to state regulation. Mandates to appoint governing boards, limitations on property ownership, and state reporting requirements all gave states authority over private organizations, drawing them into the space between public control and private power.[8]

By the late nineteenth and early twentieth centuries, large private foundations and mass charitable organizations played an instrumental role in the consolidation of American state power away from individual states and toward a more nationalized set of domestic and international policies. American global expansion, critical to a budding sense of national unity and strength, significantly overlapped with Protestant missionary work in places like Cuba, Puerto Rico, and the Philippines. On-the-ground assistance from American evangelicals, who raised funds at home to bring "Christian civilization" to new American territories, linked philanthropic efforts to America's global ambitions. Likewise on the domestic front, Progressive Era benevolent associations provided social-welfare services to assimilate newcomers into American life and create a productive and "Americanized" citizenry. Even as they provisioned for the needs of many Americans, these organizations also helped make the case for expanding and nationalizing a public infrastructure to meet health, education, and welfare demands that might exceed private actors' capacity.[9]

As the landscape of philanthropic organizations grew more complex so did the puzzle of how to stitch them into the evolving nature of American liberal governance. With the advent of a national income tax, state policymakers drew upon the paradigm of discipline and support that had guided individual states' approach to non-state associations. In 1913, when the federal income tax finally became law after the passage of the Sixteenth Amendment, it reflected the logic of exempting organizations defined as operating for the public good. The government's power to define and provision for public-benefit associations by relieving their tax burden grew broader in 1917, when individuals who donated to those associations were similarly released from taxation on income equivalent to that contribution (up to a specified percentage of income). Through its power of taxation, the American state forced its conceptions of the public good into its citizens' private expenditures.[10]

Political theorist Rob Reich describes philanthropy as an "artifact of the state," part and parcel of the state's laws and policies, yet as it developed philanthropy also served to counterbalance the very state that nurtured it. State sanction and subsidy followed upon the state's evaluation of whether a private entity met the threshold for advancing the public good. Once the bar was cleared, funds that would have otherwise been captured as public revenue remained in the hands of non-elected actors who retained substantial decision-making power about how to achieve a public benefit. The fact that the Carnegie Corporation tended to support educational programs and libraries or that the Rockefeller Foundation funded public-health measures represented the determinations of private individuals, not necessarily the priorities of the state, even though each of these entities used public resources to advance its agenda.[11] Evidence of the substantial power that philanthropy exercised, even in this state-crafted system, could be found in Congress's persistent anxiety about abuses that might occur under the cover of philanthropy. Its reluctance to grant a federal charter to the Rockefeller Foundation in the early twentieth century, for example, reflected Congress's concern that the foundation acted as a veil for avaricious and self-aggrandizing corporate schemes.[12]

Even so, in the early decades of the twentieth century, suspicion of philanthropy paled in comparison to the benefits that politicians and policymakers perceived in allying themselves with wealthy philanthropists and charitable organizations. Philanthropic actors' centrality to solving large social problems was so broadly accepted as consistent with liberal ideals that by the end of the 1920s President Hoover responded to the Great Depression by immediately turning to the Rockefeller Foundation, the Russell Sage Foundation, and a handful of others to help solve the crisis. His move made perfect sense given the government's growing reliance on private foundations to guide the way in testing and crafting policies to ameliorate big social problems. For example, the Social Science Research Council, established in 1923 and funded by most of the largest private foundations, had steadily attracted many political leaders who relied on it for research and policy ideas. Yet the magnitude of human distress caused by the Depression overwhelmed the philanthropic resources the president could marshal, and Hoover's inadequate response to the Depression led voters to elect his Democratic rival, Franklin Delano Roosevelt.[13]

Roosevelt's New Deal programs sidelined private charitable-relief efforts in favor of nationalized ones financed by public revenue and centrally coordinated. As if to amplify the difference between philanthropy and government, Congress under Roosevelt's watch also sought to curb philanthropic organizations' political power, legislating in its 1934 Revenue Act that "no substantial part of the activities" of philanthropic organizations could be directed toward "carrying on of propaganda, or otherwise attempting to influence legislation." The law reflected an undercurrent of concern—evident in earlier controversies—that philanthropy might undermine the liberal balance between public and private by placing its gilded thumb on partisan scales for its own private gains.[14]

As the Roosevelt administration instituted the New Deal, state relief work appeared to overshadow philanthropy, now subject to a new form of political regulation. However, in the shadows of the state, liberals relied on philanthropy to offset what might have appeared as anticapitalist, centralized, and isolationist trends. A contradiction built into the income tax helped bolster this counterbalancing effect. Although initially only levied on the highest earners, the federal income tax had expanded apace of state growth, first to help finance America's involvement in World War I, then to fund New Deal programs and US involvement in World War II. The progressive nature of the tax guaranteed that even as more earners were subject to it, those at the lower income levels paid a proportionally smaller share of public revenue. Yet on the flipside of a progressive income-tax system was a regressive philanthropic system that drew public revenue away from the state and toward the private actors with the highest incomes and, thus, most to gain from tax deductions and exemptions. The American state effectively subsidized the private holdings of those who promised to dedicate a portion of their property to the public good, in this way placing philanthropy at the heart of liberalism's twinned commitment and counterbalancing the state's growing power.[15]

Even Roosevelt, who had recoiled from his predecessor's courtship with philanthropy, integrated it into his vision of national recovery, with its "novel combinations" of public and private resources. His administration's strategic compromise with private philanthropic and business interests was evident in Roosevelt's embrace of a new corporate charitable deduction as part of his 1935 Wealth Tax and his refusal to modify the regressive logic of charitable tax exemptions despite the New Deal's revenue-raising pressures.[16] Furthermore, his signature social-welfare policies bore the imprint of philanthropy. The Rockefeller and Carnegie foundations, which had both helped fund the expansion of medical education and services in the United States since the end of World War I, remained key partners in researching New Deal health-care policies and enacting state-subsidized private health insurance and Social Security. Finally, even as the Roosevelt administration focused its efforts on domestic concerns and studiously attempted to avoid international entanglements, philanthropic ventures underwritten by the Carnegie Foundation in the 1930s to Africa and other holdings of the British Empire bolstered an American presence in arenas of global power.[17]

An expanded philanthropic arena—eventually termed the nonprofit sector—emerged as a tangible outgrowth of Roosevelt's state-building policies, almost in spite of themselves. Philanthropic organizations in the 1940s were more professionalized, better capitalized, and more state-enmeshed than ever before. As they developed, they also expanded their international horizons, forging a pathway for American global power that placed private capital and actors at its center and laid the foundation for enriching the power of philanthropy to balance liberalism's private and public commitments.[18]

The Philanthropic Center of Cold War Liberalism

In 1954, Senator Lyndon B. Johnson introduced an amendment on the Senate floor seemingly to constrain philanthropic groups' political activities. In practice, however, his proposal ushered in a new political calculus for liberating philanthropic power to shape American Cold War liberalism. The amendment, which passed without any debate, restricted tax-exempt organizations from campaigning for political candidates, a limitation added to the already-prohibited practice of substantial legislative lobbying. The day before Johnson succeeded in advancing his amendment, one of his colleagues had suggested giving government the broad power to strip the tax-exempt status from any organization that engaged in "subversive" activities. A congressional committee had similarly recommended "the complete exclusion of political activity" from all such organizations. In distinction to these proposals for unfettered and potentially McCarthyite state regulation, Johnson's amendment deftly freed philanthropic organizations from statist modes of control by employing a narrowly precise definition of political activity and excluding the rest from governmental oversight. Indeed, by the time he became president, Johnson's bid to protect philanthropic power resulted in multiple foreign and domestic programs incubated by private foundations and then adopted into state policy.[19]

Over the next decades, Congress fell into a pattern of giving lip service to concerns about unchecked philanthropic power while effectively facilitating its steady growth as an instrument of liberal statecraft. Although some politicians expressed grave concerns about the threat philanthropy posed to state sovereignty, most regarded philanthropy as a useful arm of their power and an object lesson in the remarkable power of American liberalism's public-private hybridity. A handmaiden in the effort to spread democracy and capitalism across the globe and to ensure stability at home, philanthropy showcased the value of private property and non-statist goods, while also advancing key American interests.[20]

A series of investigations conducted by Representative Wright Patman, a populist Democrat from Texas, throughout the 1960s highlighted the enfeebled efforts to wean American state leaders from philanthropic riches. At the center of Patman's investigation was the Ford Foundation, which after a massive bequest in 1948 was the largest private foundation in the world, holding a $3.3 billion endowment by the 1960s.[21] One practically tripped over the evidence of Ford's ties to American state officials. Already by the early 1950s, Ford exercised significant diplomatic power in so-called Third World nations such as India, where it piloted community development projects staffed by personnel who moved seamlessly between the foundation and the US State Department. In the early 1960s, an open—and often revolving—door existed between the Kennedy administration and Ford. The "Gray Areas" program, named for the urban neighborhoods that experienced demographic transition from white to black residents, began as a Ford project and then served to inform federal urban policy, just as Ford's international programs shaped American foreign-development programs and also wove their way back into domestic policies. In addition to this evidence in plain sight, Patman also discovered CIA efforts to commandeer the Ford Foundation to assist its anti-communist operations in Eastern Europe in the 1950s. Although Ford reportedly declined the CIA's entreaties, Patman bristled hard at potential cases of unaccountable governance, whether in counterintelligence programs, global development, or urban renewal.[22]

The more proof Patman amassed about the close links between Ford and the American government, the steeper the challenges his committee faced mustering support to regulate philanthropy. Evidence of the government's intimacy with philanthropy, after all, revealed a dependency that only intensified during the years of Patman's investigation, especially as President Johnson rolled out the War on Poverty. From its research and development phase, which was largely conducted through foreign-aid work funded by Rockefeller, Carnegie, and Ford, to its delivery mechanisms that awarded a mix of government and private philanthropic grants to nonprofits and newly created community development corporations, the War on Poverty tied state policy to philanthropic institutions.[23]

In 1969, when Congress passed a long-awaited tax reform bill, Patman's tireless investigations received a nod in the form of modest regulations over philanthropy, but the populist spirit of his critique had been all but crushed. Organizations like Ford that were classified by the terms of the new law as private foundations took on perfunctory reporting requirements and an annual spend-out rate of 5 percent of their corpus, which generally grew annually at a far faster clip, and were subject to basic anti-abuse measures to prevent self-dealing and business gains. (So-called public charities, like churches, hospitals, universities, and broad-based charities, were exempt from many of these regulations.) Far from dialing back philanthropic power, Congress's meager regulations primarily served to invigorate philanthropy with new tax strategies to raise capital and with a redoubled expression of its value to the American state.[24]

True populists like Patman, who sought to empower the mass electorate by restraining elite institutions, were a fading breed, gradually replaced by professional-class liberals with resumes and governing philosophies that dulled the distinction between popular and elite interests. Instead of concerning themselves with separating philanthropy from other modes of public governance, these new leaders perceived utility in blurring the lines, just as their own positions straddled the different realms. Decades of state reliance on philanthropic entities to incubate policies and fund research primed politicians and the public to expect philanthropy to be wherever the state was, whether in domestic or global locations.[25]

This existing pattern of the state's dependency on philanthropy and its minimal regulations over it offered a new template for how to govern. Operating well beyond the world of private foundations and public charities, philanthropic governance subordinated both sides of liberalism—its commitment to private-property rights and its investment in the public good—to a singular presumption that private entities were best equipped to define and safeguard the public good.

Philanthropic Governance beyond Philanthropy

Philanthropy became a mode of governance when its logic infused the operations of power at almost every level of American politics, from the governmental to the grassroots to the corporate to the global. Never a one-way street, the very mode of philanthropic governance incorporated traces from each of these arenas, yet as state agents, grassroots activists, businesspeople, and international communities became increasingly reliant on philanthropy's capital and rationale, they validated its norms and naturalized its practices. Spreading the ideal that private power should be determinative of the public good, philanthropic governance seeped into almost every realm of American life by the end of the twentieth century, narrowing the space from which one might resist it and bending the will of partisan opponents to accept it as a governing strategy. While ideological divisions between liberal and conservative politicians, especially around "family values," preoccupied the media and political pundits (and historians) from the 1970s through the end of the century, these occluded a striking consensus around the logic of philanthropic governance.[26]

The threads of philanthropic governance already visible in prior decades were woven into a clear system of political rule first most visibly in American international-development policies, conforming to the imperial pattern of testing governing strategies abroad and then importing them back home. In 1973, Nixon signed into law the Foreign Assistance Act, which set the course of American global aid efforts for the coming decades as, by law, reliant on philanthropic energies. The act restructured the Kennedy-era United States Agency for International Development around the dictate that programs "should be carried out to the maximum extent possible through private sector, including... voluntary agencies."[27] This policy was less a change of course than a codification and regimentation of regnant practices. However, the new law signified the American government's desideratum to empower nongovernmental organizations (NGOs) to create American global networks of power and not simply to serve as pragmatic tools to build inroads into foreign arenas.[28]

Even as philanthropic governance carved out pathways for American tax dollars to flow into global development projects, it absented the American state by channeling those dollars through non-state agents. This withdrawal was by design. As historian Joanne Meyerowitz explains, NGO-led global development could "cleanse foreign assistance of the taint of national self-interest, military intervention, and bureaucratic bungling" while still giving the United States strategic international footholds. Philanthropic efforts helped the American government shore up its global presence without running afoul of burgeoning anti-colonial movements or being hamstrung by the significant backlash it faced from the Vietnam War.[29] Still providing government grants and tax exemptions to international assistance efforts, the American state did not so much recede as it submerged itself in philanthropic and humanitarian efforts that doubled as global capitalist and neocolonial ventures.[30]

Mirroring the transition away from state-based to philanthropic global development, the sight line of international assistance projects shifted from foreign governments to foreign private actors. Instead of trying to work within existing governments or empowering new ones to meet the needs of their citizens, humanitarian activists suggested that direct aid to needy people would be more efficacious. This proposition was a clear extension of the logic of philanthropic governance, that the public good was best served through private means. Reflecting a localized and on-the-ground approach, American feminists lobbied Congress to include in the 1973 Foreign Assistance Act a clear commitment to directing global development funds to women. By drawing focus away from reconstructing the public political process of foreign nations and toward funding private actors, feminists and others in the avant-garde of American development work led the way for American NGOs to designate their nongovernmental counterparts in a growingly privatized system of foreign aid.[31]

The significant presence of liberal and leftist voices in efforts to bolster the role of NGOs and private actors in American global development hinted at rising bipartisan disenchantment with the American social-welfare state. Activists on the left and the right steadily pinned the failures of the New Deal and Great Society on the government and sought to find a new governing strategy to meet the needs of the country's citizenry. Despite their clear differences on social values, many across the political spectrum cohered around authorizing private efforts to drive the public good. A group of fresh-faced and well-educated Democrats, the so-called New Democrats, crafted the case for expanding the work that private foundations like Carnegie and Ford had been doing around social policy and transferring power to them and other private entities to stand in for public social services. Whereas New Deal political leaders had relied on philanthropic foundations as policy incubators, New Democrat politicians and their technocratic, professional class analogues in nonprofits and think tanks envisioned delegating policy creation and implementation (including funding) to non-state actors, from private foundations to churches to nonprofits and, eventually, to private corporations.[32]

Throughout the 1980s, at the behest of philanthropic funders and government mandates to partner with nonprofits, community-development corporations (CDCs) flooded American cities. With roots in the Ford Foundation's urban work in the 1960s, CDCs served as a proxy for city government. Regular citizens who wanted affordable housing or updated infrastructure to keep their neighborhoods livable learned to turn to them. Local activists became skilled in grant writing and crafting neighborhood initiatives to attract private investors. These efforts resembled those of grassroots actors in the 1960s, who had been backed by Ford and other private foundations to fund even some of the most radical civil rights efforts.[33] However, by the final decades of the twentieth century, the routinization of philanthropic governance foreclosed some of the most flexible and radical ways that philanthropic dollars had been used at earlier moments. As neighborhood-based movements grew dependent on private investments and nonprofit structures, their members witnessed governance through private not public means, even as those private efforts were often underwritten by public dollars. The erosion of trust in government to get things done seemed only logical, as public parks, schools, streets, and even prisons fell to the rule of largely ungovernable private forces and funders.[34]

New Democrats' policy goals varied from those of their Republican opponents, but the political foes increasingly followed a similar playbook, validated by hundreds of local initiatives, for how to govern. Pro-market and deregulatory measures passed under Ronald Reagan and George H. W. Bush helped create the capital conditions to foster the New Democrats' vision of protecting the public good with the privatized and financialized logic of philanthropic governance. Bush's "thousand points of light" simile, through which he described voluntary actors illuminating the world with their private resources, was hardly so different from Bill Clinton's vision—and perhaps this similarity helps account for Clinton's success in upending a dozen years of Republican rule when he won the White House in 1992. He promised to build something new but set upon a foundation of private power over public goods that had come to seem more natural and effective than relying on public channels to apportion public goods.[35]

As he entered office, Clinton pledged to reform the American welfare system, the most enduring vestige of the New Deal state, in the image of philanthropy. As if a private foundation, the government would disburse modest grants to neighborhoods and communities, leverage those grants to attract private funders, and then require grantees to wean themselves off funding by becoming their own capital generators. Far from a plan for economic redistribution, his vision prioritized economic independence as an outcome. It vacated state management of economic goods by linking the private-sector rule that every expenditure should be met with a clear return on investment to a philanthropic logic that private entities could serve the public good best when the state freed them from regulation but enriched them through tax subsidies. Thus, the Clinton administration adopted the model of philanthropic governance while further eroding the distinctions that had demarcated philanthropic governance from the state or from the private sector. Instead of serving as a fulcrum to balance the tension between these sectors, philanthropy bled across them all and blurred profit-seeking and public-serving logics. Obliterated in this model that prized economic independence over redistribution was a sustainable method for redressing structural inequalities entangled with long histories of neglect and exclusion.[36]

Yet philanthropic governance's hold over Americans' sense of moral, political, and economic possibilities restructured political movements long committed to seeking public remedy and resources. For example, feminist collectives that had operated on shoestring budgets and volunteer energies suddenly had the opportunity in the late 1980s and 1990s to win grants from philanthropic foundations. In those decades, major foundations such as Rockefeller and Ford created "Women's Funds." Aligning with the wisdom that guided global development programs to invest their funds in individuals, not political processes, and reinforcing the evisceration of public-welfare programs in the United States, these funds shaped a new kind of feminism that conformed to philanthropic governance. Grants to working-class and minority women in the United States and to women living in poverty in foreign countries reflected the ideals of economic independence, not systemic reform and redistribution.[37]

Unsurprisingly, as soon as Clinton left office, he established a charitable foundation to channel grants from corporations, foreign governments, and wealthy donors to meet humanitarian needs at home and abroad and staffed by technocrats, many of whom had backgrounds in management consulting. From his time in office, he had learned that one need not be elected to office to govern. Extending an animating (if floundering) goal of his presidential administration, Clinton's foundation focused immediate attention on health care and especially the global fight against HIV/AIDS. Working from its worldwide offices and leveraging Clinton's reputation, the foundation brokered agreements with political and business leaders for the distribution of antiretroviral drugs. Like the much larger Gates Foundation, the Clinton Foundation supplanted state-based political processes, some of which were clearly failing to address pressing health-care needs. Instead, it enticed private entities to donate goods and services often in return for access to new markets to eventually sell their drugs and other products.[38]

When the Clinton Foundation came under scrutiny for its lack of transparency about donors and disbursements early in the first decade of the 2000s, critics had little ground to stand on. More than two decades of state policy under Republican and Democratic administrations had fashioned a political order that steadily moved against private regulation and accountability in the name of the public good. Imported from philanthropy, the logic of assuming that private entities, whether designated as philanthropies or simply market-oriented firms, should be treated as generators of the public good had become the governing strategy of American life. So expansive were philanthropic governance's reaches that for many Americans and international actors it was hard to imagine a different order.[39]

In line with Clinton-era welfare policies, women were encouraged to form their own businesses and to integrate into the global economy as individual entrepreneurs who needed neither public nor private assistance but could become their own self-sustaining economic units. Hitting a crescendo in Sheryl Sandberg's prescription to "lean in," a new brand of American feminism was inseparable from the assumption that private efforts and markets if rightly deployed could solve all varieties of public inequities. By the early decades of the new millennium, the very mechanics of fundraising devolved responsibility to the individual in need, as websites like GoFundMe made crowdfunding just the latest iteration of a public good sold to those private entities that promised to steward it toward greater and greater profitability. Philanthropic governance was seemingly everywhere, cosplaying liberalism while slackening its fundamental tension between the public and private.[40]

The Revolution Will Not Be Funded[41]—Or Has It Already Been?

In the frenzy to explain how Trump had won the presidency in 2016, public commentators thrust philanthropists into the limelight. These wealthy individuals and entities were blamed (or praised) for enabling Trumpism, and the very existence of a billionaire class, so far beyond the control or contemplation of most Americans, preoccupied conversations across the political spectrum about what was wrong with American democracy. With changes to campaign finance law effectuated by a 2010 Supreme Court decision and with a steady stream of tax avoidance schemes that allowed the wealthy to classify their assets as non–income bearing, the power of a select few Americans to tip the scales of democracy seemed unfettered.

Stories of prominent philanthropists' indiscretions, misconduct, and criminal behavior (think, for example, of allegations that the Sackler family used its philanthropy to obscure their role in driving the opioid crisis) only heightened the sense that far from committing their private property to the advancement of the public good, the very wealthy had only their own pockets and egos on their minds. In a book emblematic of a new genre, journalist and former business consultant Anand Giridharadas characterized philanthropists and their handlers as selling the false promise of a "win-win" to Americans. In truth, these elites were taking wins while saddling the American public with profound losses.[42]

To blame the crises in democratic liberalism on philanthropists may be a percussive populist rallying cry, but it offers a perilously narrow diagnosis of the current state of American political life. Over the course of the twentieth century, philanthropy provided a great utility to liberalism. It made liberalism possible by offering a solution to liberalism's intractable claim that private-property rights and the collective good could coexist. State agents relied on philanthropy to make a case for the enterprise they were defending. Whatever the specific project, the notion that philanthropy transformed private earnings into public goods without the heavy hand of state regulation girded liberalism against its strongest foes and advanced a theory of American progress and perfectibility.

So adept were policymakers and philanthropists at proving the value of non-state resources to state goals that philanthropy steadily moved from the periphery of American political life to its very center. In this way, it became a mode of governance. What had once made liberalism appear possible now encroached on liberalism. If private funds and actors not only incubated but implemented policy, then how could an American public be imagined as anything other than beholden to them? And if state policy left philanthropy unregulated as a testament to the sanctity of private-property rights, then how could an American public demand to understand what private actors did in its name?

The spasms of indignation against philanthropy coming from across the political spectrum by the early decades of the twenty-first century revealed just how effectively it had become a proxy for a government of, by, or for the people. Instead of preserving liberalism's tautness—held in place by the poles of private-property rights and the public good—state agents who helped empower philanthropy insisted that the two poles were improbably one and the same. With nothing left to balance, liberalism was obsolete. After all, liberalism's irresolvable dilemma had also been its lifeblood.

For much of the twentieth century, philanthropy had helped make liberalism possible, but by the early twenty-first century philanthropic governance unmade it. Whether a revolution or a program of political recovery would follow, the vaunted and minimally regulated position of philanthropy seemed unlikely to remain intact. Without liberalism to safeguard its primacy, the case for empowering private dollars to act in the stead of the public was seriously weakened. What mode of governance might step into the breach remains an open question, as political voices trumpet diverse ideologies of populism, reactionism, authoritarianism, and socialism. It is conceivable that philanthropy will weather the changes—or, even, that it is already funding them—but if it continues to serve as a governing strategy, it will almost surely be absent the liberal vision that crowned it king of the last century.

CHAPTER 2

Managing Global Development

Robert Nathan and the Liberal Roots of the Contract State in US Foreign Policy

STEPHEN MACEKURA

Robert Nathan was not the most prominent figure in Franklin Roosevelt's wartime cabinet, but he got a taste of the public spotlight in April 1942 when he was the subject of a *Life* magazine profile. The journalist Joseph Thorndike Jr. followed Nathan through a typical week in Washington, DC, lauding Nathan's jocular personality and modest lifestyle. Photographs accompanying the article showed Nathan preparing a pancake breakfast and exercising in a boxing ring. What most impressed Thorndike, though, was the thirty-five-year-old economist's statistical analysis and planning work for the US government. Nathan, an ardent New Dealer, had contributed to the first national income estimates during the 1930s. In January 1942, he joined the War Production Board, the federal agency that managed wartime production. Wielding charts and graphs as weapons in fierce debates over how best to mobilize for the war, he estimated how to boost defense production while preventing another domestic depression. In Thorndike's telling, Nathan was a patriotic public servant who used his statistical acumen to help fight the Great Depression and World War II.[1]

Bob Nathan, however, had ambitions beyond a career in public service. In 1946, less than a year after leaving the government, Nathan created one of the country's first for-profit economic consulting firms. During the following decades, Nathan's globe-spanning company, Robert R. Nathan Associates Inc., won contracts from the United States Agency for International Development (USAID) and international organizations such as the United Nations, the World Bank, and the Asian

Development Bank to advise national governments from Burma to Israel and Afghanistan to El Salvador. By the 1970s, Nathan Associates was one of the most successful economic consulting firms in the world. As he had done during the Roosevelt administration, Bob Nathan used statistical analysis to craft economic plans. But throughout his career, he made plans for other governments—and much profit for himself and his firm.

The history of Bob Nathan and his company illuminates the origins and evolution of what I call the "contract state" in US foreign policy. For much of the twentieth century, but especially during and after World War II, the US government outsourced many core public functions to private actors. Through this "contract state," US government officials used private-sector contractors to expand their administrative capacity, and in turn, for-profit companies such as Nathan's earned significant revenue from the state. The best-known result of this relationship was the military-industrial complex, but the wider contract state enabled US leaders in the second half of the twentieth century to pursue a foreign policy of military primacy and wage the Cold War without overt centralized planning or major expansions of the federal workforce.[2]

The contract state and Nathan Associates' role in it have at least three important implications for the history of US foreign policy and the origins and evolution of professional-class liberalism. First, the liberal architects of US international-development policy during the 1940s and 1950s relied upon and worked through the private sector from its very inception; the so-called "New Directions" reforms of the 1970s, which reemphasized private contracting, thus represented an extension of midcentury practices rather than a rupture, as often assumed.[3] Bob Nathan was an ardent Cold War liberal who admired the New Deal and supported an aggressive anti-communist foreign policy.[4] He defended the US mixed economy and its contracting functions as a model of liberal governance that embraced the best of public purpose and private-sector management. A technocrat with a deep faith in economic and managerial expertise, Nathan and his colleagues contributed to a broader intellectual culture that centered both market development and private contractors as brokers and practitioners within the field of international development. Consultants proffered schematic expertise that they believed could be replicated from country to country. Yet they did so without substantive cultural or historical knowledge of the people, places, and landscapes they sought to develop.[5] This blinkered and chauvinistic approach ultimately limited the effectiveness of the consultants' work, just as an overreliance on contracting starved US foreign-aid agencies of in-house expertise and created byzantine networks of subcontractors that defied effective oversight.

Second, Nathan's career reveals deep continuities between seemingly distinct periods in twentieth-century US political economy. Scholars have long distinguished two discrete economic eras: a mid-century liberalism shaped by New Deal Keynesianism and then a late twentieth-century neoliberalism influenced by Milton Friedman, Ronald Reagan, and Bill Clinton. Nathan's seamless transition from dedicated public servant to millionaire CEO of a consulting firm, however, marks a great deal of institutional, personnel, and ideological continuity. Historians have recently revealed how mid-century liberal state-building methods often muddied the distinction between public good and private interests.[6] Nathan Associates encapsulated this dynamic as a for-profit consulting firm that relied on government grants for its financing and that shaped public policy in the United States and for foreign governments. Similar to the philanthropic governance Lila Corwin Berman analyzes in this volume, the contract state developed "inconspicuously in the shadows of headline-grabbing partisan divisions," sustained by a bipartisan consensus about the virtues of using private means to pursue public goals. Because Nathan never held a prominent role in government after World War II ended, it would be easy to dismiss his policy influence as minimal. But focusing on the contract state reveals how private-sector professionals shaped US foreign policy and how US foreign policy worked through the private sector.

Finally, Nathan's career also shows how professionalization influenced the firms that worked with the contract state. When Nathan founded his company, it was a small organization of just a few employees. A prodigious networker with many friends in the liberal establishment, Nathan won contracts for his company in its early years largely through his personal connections with high-level government officials. As the contract state expanded through the 1960s, personal relationships became less significant for contracting firms than their organizational capabilities and past work for the state. What mattered by the 1970s was less Nathan's personal relationship than the firm's professional reputation for navigating the increasingly byzantine world of contracting rules and regulations. In 1950, US and foreign officials hired Nathan Associates because of Robert Nathan; by 1980, they hired the company because of its record of winning past contracts.

Over time, the contract state became what its advocates claimed it would prevent: a government plagued by inefficiency and wasteful spending and devoid of meaningful accountability. But US foreign policy officials' continued dependence on the private sector—and the assumption that hiring private contractors offered an efficient means to advance public goals—meant the contract state continued to grow. In the 2019 fiscal year, USAID obligated over 31 percent of its funding to contractors, totaling over $5 billion.[7] The history of Bob Nathan's work with Nathan Associates exposes the liberal origins of the contract state and its many pitfalls.

Nathan Associates and the Transformation of US Foreign Policy

Bob Nathan spent his childhood as he did much of his adult life: in pursuit of business opportunities. Born in Dayton, Ohio, on Christmas Day in 1908, he grew up poor, the son of Jewish immigrants from Galicia. From a young age, he started many small businesses, from paper delivery to advanced tutoring. His strong academic performance won him admission to the University of Pennsylvania, where he earned a Master of Science degree in economics.[8] Yet his first job after graduation was not in business but in government. Upon graduating in 1933, Nathan went to work for his old professor Simon Kuznets at the Commerce Department to construct the country's first official national income and product accounts (which later became the first official Gross National Product, or GNP, estimates). He also constructed unemployment tables for the President's Committee on Economic Security and compiled much of the data for policymaker Harry Hopkins's popular 1935 book, *Spending to Save*.[9] Nathan then worked extensively for the war mobilization efforts, overseeing feasibility studies and rising in early 1942 to become chairman of the War Production Board's Planning Committee. He helped to engineer a productive juggernaut of a state that "relied heavily on public investment, public management of industrial supply chains, and robust regulation."[10]

Nathan's government work directly influenced his postwar professional trajectory. He had become well known and well connected among liberal elites. He was a regular in the Georgetown social set, joining the self-styled goon squad of DC luminaries including Joe Rauh, a popular young civil rights lawyer; Phil Graham, publisher of the *Washington Post* (then just beginning to rise in stature); and key policymakers in the Roosevelt administration including Lauchlin Currie and Leon Henderson. In his official capacity, Nathan worked with Roosevelt's closest advisors and often met important foreign dignitaries and luminaries. During the war, for instance, Nathan befriended French politician Jean Monnet, who was impressed by how Nathan's statistical acumen translated to effective planning.[11] Nathan's personal and professional worlds meshed rather seamlessly: "Bob knows everybody in Washington and they all like him," claimed one of Nathan's associates in 1942. "If the town had a mayor, Bob could be elected in any year."[12]

Nathan interpreted the New Deal and wartime mobilization as evidence that government and business worked best together when guided by technocrats. "I think that anybody who ever had fear that the New Deal was anything but a moderate free enterprise institution should have seen what's happened in the war and the immediate postwar, and how well it was done," Nathan recalled. "It was a blend, as I say, of Government control, Government vigilance, Government review on the one hand, and the inducement of the private sector on the other."[13] Nathan's work with the board impressed upon him the virtues of empowering managers (such as himself) and achieving public goals through privatized means. The war mobilization effort, Nathan said, "achieved a fairly good balance of relying on human greed and acquisition instincts on the one hand, and taking away the excess profits on the other hand, and watching against favoritism and corruption."[14] Economists took a starring role in Nathan's telling. "Washington got loaded with economists" during the war, he later recalled, "figuring out how to finance the war, how to divert resources, how to use economics as a way to keep neutral countries neutral. It was basically a planned economy, so naturally it took a lot of economists."[15] Along with economists, many early management consultants also served in the wartime state, reorganizing military and civilian agencies to promote greater efficiency.[16] Nathan worked alongside these types of technocratic managers to guide national economic activity in a way that balanced liberal goals of pursuing the public good and protecting private profits. He soon fashioned a new business around making such expertise exportable by bringing private consulting into government planning around the world.

Nathan founded Nathan Associates, Inc., in January 1946. He had developed strong differences of opinion with Truman administration officials over the speed and nature of domestic reconversion, and so he left government to start a business.[17] He also recognized that his dozen years working for the Roosevelt administration gave him many contacts to pursue for government contracts.[18] While the degree of centralized oversight and planning during the war effort did not persist in the postwar years, one crucial element did: the integration of professional consultants, especially management consultants, as contractors who advised and guided government agencies. Consultants played an important role in what historian Brian Balogh has termed the "proministrative state"—the merger between professional experts and increasingly expansive administrative apparatus—that reformulated the associational state-building practices of Herbert Hoover and the New Deal.[19] The wartime experience generated a national political culture that accepted the growth of state capacity and the fusion of corporate capitalism with statist intervention, a "warfare state," in historian James Sparrow's words, that the subsequent Cold War sustained.[20]

After World War II ended, conservative politicians criticized the large size of the federal civilian workforce, which counted over two million employees even after demobilization. Congressmen from the Republican Party likened the New Deal to Soviet communism and conflated "antistatism with anti-communism" as part of an effort to curtail federal spending.[21] Facing a Republican-controlled Congress after 1948, President Truman tasked former president Herbert Hoover to study the possibilities of governmental reorganization. Hoover hired management consultants to conduct the research. They highlighted the valuable role that private-sector experts could play in managing federal responsibilities. Spurred on by a series of legislative amendments led by Congressman Jamie Whitten, Truman and his successors henceforth chose to cap the expansion of the federal civilian workforce and instead increase the number of private-sector contractors.[22] By the early 1950s, then, the character of the American state had changed and changed forever. The New Deal and wartime states generated the contract state.

The contract state shaped how the US government pursued its new foreign-policy commitments. During the late 1940s, the Truman administration launched a series of new foreign-policy initiatives, including $400 million for aid to Greece and Turkey in 1947 and nearly $14 billion for the Marshall Plan.[23] In 1949, the administration created the Point Four program to extend foreign aid to promote the economic development of the noncommunist world. Point Four received a relatively small budget (Congress authorized just $35 million initially), but Truman and his closest advisors saw the program as one of many tools to facilitate private sector–led development abroad.[24] Believing private capital would finance large-scale projects, the administration extended guarantees from the Export-Import Bank and provisions against expropriation in bilateral commercial treaties to reduce risks for corporations working abroad.[25] The Point Four program complemented these policies by dedicating 60 percent of its budget to "technical assistance": sending "expert technicians," public and private, abroad to advise governments and businesses about modern engineering and management techniques to make overseas investment more likely.[26] Point Four, after all, was "never meant to be just a Government program," Secretary of State Dean Acheson explained. "The entire effort that the government agency carries out here is really carried out through private organizations. We do not have in the Government sufficient people to staff these operations, sufficient people to give us all the ideas, to give us all the working groups which are necessary."[27] Acheson's comments reflected political realities in Congress and the ideological affinities of administration officials who envisioned the private sector as a necessary partner for global prosperity and national security. This approach cemented the contract state in US foreign aid. By early 1955, the US government had signed 198 contracts with private entities worth $98 million dedicated to technical assistance and economic aid abroad.[28]

Using foreign aid to promote economic development abroad during the Cold War captured many liberals' imagination. Foreign assistance yoked two overarching liberal policy goals together into a unified policy. First, it would spark a "modernization" process to uplift much of the "traditional" world out of poverty and contain the spread of more radical ideologies (such as communism) that promised rapid economic and social change through centralized state planning and ownership. Second, liberals saw modernization of the so-called Third World as a morally edifying and strategically necessary process through which they could transform distant countries to comport with liberal American values such as individual autonomy, the protection of private property, and, ideally, democratic forms of government. Modernization allowed liberals such as Bob Nathan to wage Cold War action in countries from South Vietnam to Guatemala to Iran and feel as though they were doing good in the process.[29]

In 1951, Bob Nathan's personal connections and reputation led Nathan Associates to receive its first major US government contract to provide planning assistance to Burma, a country that the US saw as a key part of its Cold War project in Asia. U Hla Maung, a Burmese official and economist, admired Nathan's work in the New Deal, and Nathan's State Department friends wanted to provide technical assistance to Burma's socialist prime minister, U Nu, in the hopes that consultants could guide the revolutionary nationalist government away from Soviet or Chinese communist influence. Nathan personally hired a small group of economists to assist him in Burma.[30]

In country, Nathan Associates technocrats embedded in the Planning Ministry, where they quickly clashed with skeptical Burmese officials. Nathan noted that many Burmese officials "thought socialism was a good way" to development, which Nathan dismissed because of their "lack of sophistication of economic policies and approaches." He accepted that many countries had socialist policies, but in Burma there was neither the "competence" nor "managerial ability" to warrant granting the government such power. Instead, Nathan sought to "encourage small, private business."[31] The consultants, however, would soon wear out their welcome. Their salaries were as much as ten times higher than those of Burmese officials (to say nothing of the income of the average

Burmese farmer).[32] The Burmese ambassador to the UN called them "white elephants" because of their ostentatious lifestyle.[33] And in the eyes of U Nu's opponents, the consultants were the epitome of wasteful spending and neocolonial intrusion. U Nu narrowly survived a no-confidence vote against his government by parliament in early 1958, but he stepped down anyway. His departure ushered in a period of instability, culminating in a coup by General Ne Win in the fall of 1958. Shortly after taking office, Ne Win denounced American experts and terminated Nathan Associates' contract.[34]

The end of Nathan's work in Burma presaged a political ritual that shaped the history of the contract state. Contractors explained away their past struggles in ways that only served to justify granting them more funding in the future, often by blaming public authorities for the disappointing results. Lou Walinsky, who served as chief economist for Nathan Associates in Burma from 1953 to 1959, blamed the consultants' failure on the shock of Ne Win's seizure of power. He claimed that it came just as the consultants were finally getting everything right. The political crisis, Walinsky later wrote, "had occurred just when the accumulated experience of the previous years gave promise that the Government would be more receptive to action along these necessary lines."[35] Bob Nathan told a similar tale. "We kept selling them on the idea of private, small enterprises as a way to develop, and we succeeded," Nathan recalled about his time working with U Nu. When Ne Win took over in 1958, "that was the end of that progress."[36] This narrative offered the consultants a way to justify the intellectual value of their work and the necessity of contracting by placing the burden of success on public authorities and a country's political circumstances. The consultants thus presented their past failures in one place as potential future successes in another. The result of telling such stories in memoirs, official reports, and congressional testimony was to enable Nathan Associates to win more contracts in the future.

Although Nathan lacked the same depth of personal ties to the Eisenhower administration, he became a vocal public advocate for foreign aid while crafting a narrative about the specific need for the services his company provided. He frequently lobbied Congress for increased aid expenditures by connecting technical assistance, business interest, and international security. "The Communists obviously have decided our aid techniques are effective" since they, too, had started to send experts worldwide, he claimed in 1955. "It is nonsensical for us to run from these techniques now, when we need to use them most."[37] Before a joint committee on economic policy in 1955, Nathan explained, "Unless the experience of the more industrialized countries is somehow transmitted or somehow made available to the underdeveloped countries in much larger degree than heretofore, the disparity between the have and have-not nations of the world will grow . . . Material assistance to underdeveloped countries through loans, grants, and investments will not accomplish its purpose unless there is the know-how to use it productively."[38] Management and economic expertise—rather than capital investment, political independence, or anything else—was an urgent necessity. "What the underdeveloped counties need most of all is management," Nathan wrote in 1959 for the *Washington Post*. He called for the US government to increase its support of businessmen to "manage" the development process.[39] Foreign aid linked Nathan's ideological commitments with his business interests.

The Professionalization of the Contract State and Nathan Associates

Nathan Associates grew in size and scope during the 1960s and 1970s, for two main reasons. One related to Bob Nathan's extensive personal networks and public lobbying, which only grew once John F. Kennedy came into office in 1961. Nathan had led Americans for Democratic Action (ADA), a staunchly anti-communist advocacy group that supported liberal social policies at home and an aggressive foreign policy abroad, from 1957 to 1959, through which he forged close contacts with Democratic Party leaders. With Democrats back in control of the federal government, Nathan Associates grew their operations. Gross revenues doubled during the mid-1960s, and the full-time staff expanded to eighty (with sixty working in the United States on contract management and twenty working abroad full-time on various projects).[40] Nathan's close relationship with the White House sustained his firm's fortunes, with Kennedy himself vouching for Nathan to foreign leaders. The president sang Nathan's praises to the king of Afghanistan, Mohammed Zahir Shah, which Nathan identified as a "helpful" act for his company's efforts to win further contracts in the country.[41] He also maintained personal friendships with congressional Democrats. In one instance, at a Senate hearing in 1964, Senator Paul Douglas called Nathan an "old friend" and described hearing positive reports of Nathan's work in El Salvador during a family vacation.[42] Nathan's personal connections and public advocacy aligned with his firm's material interests.

The second reason for Nathan Associates' expansion during and after the 1960s stemmed from a transformation of the United States' foreign-aid bureaucracy. In 1961, the Kennedy administration created the US Agency for International Development (USAID) to centralize and strengthen US foreign-aid policy amid rapid global decolonization and increasing Cold War tensions.[43] Privatization was a key element of the new agency long before the "New Directions" reforms took place. Section 601 of the 1961 Foreign Assistance Act, the legislation that created USAID, included a provision "to encourage the contribution of United States enterprise toward economic strength of less developed friendly countries, through private participation in programs carried out under this Act."[44] By 1964, for technical-assistance projects alone, USAID had committed over $400 million through over 1,200 separate contracts to for-profit firms, universities, and nonprofits.[45] In 1967, USAID made its commitment to the private sector even more explicit, establishing a new policy for obtaining skilled personnel. The directive required that the agency first give priority to "contract with non-governmental organizations," then by "participating agency agreement (or contract) with other federal, state or local government agencies," and only then by direct hire.[46] By 1968, over half of the agency's American personnel working abroad were not direct hires.[47]

Contractors such as Nathan Associates became even more important to the conduct of US foreign aid just as foreign aid was becoming more important to US foreign policy. The 1961 Act and its subsequent amendments codified the informal role contracting consultants such as Nathan Associates had already established by limiting USAID's ability to build out its own administrative capacity and incorporate private enterprise in project implementation. As had been the case when the Truman administration created the Point Four program, liberals in the Kennedy and Johnson administrations designed new policy initiatives to rely on the private sector.[48]

Nathan Associates benefited greatly from these changes. The company expanded its advisory operations, conducting studies and writing reports for countries such as El Salvador, Costa Rica, Ghana, Nigeria, Turkey, and Iran.[49] In many places, Nathan Associates worked as a de facto extension of USAID. In El Salvador, the lines between private and public blurred to an extent that would even surprise Nathan. Salvadoran officials asked his team members to act beyond the terms of their contract to help write loan proposals to USAID officials back in Washington.[50] In Costa Rica, local officials appeared less than enthusiastic at their contract with Nathan Associates. Nathan suspected that Costa Rican officials did not initially request his firm's services, but rather that USAID officials had encouraged them to oversee the implementation of foreign assistance.[51] In these situations, Nathan acted as a diplomat and contractor, offering the US government insights into events abroad and providing advice to foreign governments about what they could expect from Washington. The distinction between US government officials and private contractors became largely nonexistent, save for the fact that the contractors received higher, tax-exempt salaries than their governmental counterparts did.[52]

In the era of big development projects, Cold War rivalry, and global decolonization, consulting for the government was becoming a highly lucrative profession. In March 1966, the *Washington Post* ran a two-part series on what it termed the "bull market in brainpower" as government demand for economic consultants soared. Nathan Associates was the "largest and oldest" organization solely focused on economic management abroad, but many others had joined the business. The *Post* reporters calculated, using data from the National Science Foundation, that approximately one-tenth of all "qualified" economists lived in the Washington, DC, metropolitan area. In Washington, DC, alone, annual billings had reached about $12 million for top firms. While private companies had to compete with universities and nonprofits for government contracts, there were plenty of opportunities available to all.[53] As a sign of the times, in 1971 Nathan moved his company's Washington, DC, headquarters from an old converted doctor's office to an entire floor in the "Ring Building," a large commercial space conveniently located in between Dupont Circle and the White House.[54]

With the growth of the contract state, personal networks began to matter less for winning contracts compared to whether one's firm had long-standing institutional ties to the government. Contracts begat contracts. Contractors then developed the administrative capacity to deliver public goods that the US foreign-policy state lacked by design. That capacity enabled contractors to position themselves to win ever more contracts and take on more stately functions: not only carrying out projects, but, by the 1960s, designing and assessing development projects, too. The growing complexity and time-consuming tedium of grant reporting requirements created major overhead costs for contracting firms and so created barriers to entry for smaller firms. Only large, well-resourced firms could stand to win and complete major multi-million-dollar grants. Taken together, these forces propelled contracting firms such as Nathan Associates to rapid growth in size and capabilities. That growth, in turn, solidified their place within the broader amalgamated structure of public/private partnerships that represented the US government in its myriad international-development endeavors.

The Evolution of the Contract State during the 1970s

USAID underwent a series of reforms in the 1970s. Often lumped under the nickname "New Directions" or the turn to "Basic Human Needs,"

USAID began to promote smaller-scale development initiatives, with an emphasis on localism, minimal US government action, and private-sector partnerships (with for-profit and nonprofit organizations).[55] Liberals in Congress, such as Senator Frank Church (D-ID), criticized the failures of past development interventions, the tendency of US officials to favor authoritarian anti-communists over democratic-socialist movements, and the extent to which American firms had profited excessively from public funding designed to reduce poverty abroad.[56] The ensuing shifts have often been treated as revolutionary. In some ways, such characterizations are warranted. Indeed, the number of direct hires at USAID plummeted. In 1968, during the Vietnam War, the direct-hire workforce reached a peak around 17,500. By 1980 the number decreased to six thousand, plunging to just under two thousand by 2000.[57] But in terms of *how* USAID designed and carried out policies, the changes were evolutionary. The reliance on contractors, fundamental to USAID at its creation, continued during the 1970s. The primary change, however, was that private actors became at once less accountable and more deeply intertwined with USAID.

New Directions' advocates hoped to democratize USAID by promoting smaller-scale projects and bringing more participants into foreign aid. In practice the opposite happened. Liberals such as Senator Church had lamented that most foreign-aid funding had gone to authoritarian governments abroad or wealthy contractors at home, but the congressional response was to enroll ever-greater numbers of non-state actors in development assistance.

Greater reliance on private actors meant that USAID officials had to track and assess far more contractors' work without adding full-time staff. Contractors, too, faced extensive reporting and oversight requirements under federal law and USAID policy, which required greater time and resources to prepare proposals, submit regular updates, and produce detailed concluding reports. USAID officials responded to these challenges by privatizing and contracting project evaluations. Nathan Associates, like many other well-established firms, began winning new contracts as project evaluators. For example, in 1976 Nathan Associates reviewed USAID's agricultural development work in Liberia. Nathan Associates staff, with assistance from the Liberia mission evaluation director, reviewed existing initiatives and pointed to directions for future support. This review was but one of many such internal evaluations that relied on external actors. Though USAID had repurposed many of its technical staff from implementation positions to evaluation ones (largely because of the increasing use of contractors as implementors), the agency still lacked the technical competency and sufficient in-house staff to conduct the detailed analyses final assessments required.[58] Far from creating the clarity necessary for greater public accountability, the New Directions reforms just expanded the contract state.

The growth of contracting during the 1970s created other opportunities for large contractors to coevolve with USAID. One small shift that proved especially lucrative involved the increased use of indefinite quantity contracts (IQC). IQCs were contracts created by government agencies that covered a fixed period (usually three years for USAID during the 1970s) and included a negotiated minimum cost. IQCs left it to the contractors to decide exactly how much and in what ways a particular service needed to be delivered. In other words, the "indefinite" part of the IQC essentially meant transferring project design and implementation entirely to the judgment of a private organization that received a guaranteed payment. The IQC further displaced public responsibilities to private enterprise, creating little risk for the recipient while simultaneously granting the public agency less oversight of the contractors' choices.[59] It allowed USAID missions to access contractors quickly to meet the demands from Congress for increased use of the private sector and more-detailed program evaluations, since firms working an IQC already had approval to conduct work for USAID. And it lowered oversight requirements for USAID staff since the agency could give out fewer contracts.[60]

Nathan Associates' IQCs mirrored much of their earlier advisory work, with greater leeway over deciding the content of their interventions abroad. The firm won a major IQC in 1975–1976 for work in agriculture and rural development worldwide.[61] The firm divided the contract into a series of small research projects. They conducted assessments of the viability of crop insurance as an "instrument of development policy" for small farmers in countries across Latin America; a general overview of the social, economic, and environmental conditions in Zambia; and a feasibility study of multinational industrial-development projects in multiple Middle Eastern countries.[62] This contracting format allowed the firm to work with more governments. By 1978, Nathan Associates had staffers employed in thirty-five different countries around the world.[63]

By the end of the 1970s, a company's reputation and its established relationship with USAID had become more important traits for securing contracts. These shifts during the 1970s further professionalized the firm as it hired a new generation of executives to win the larger and larger contracts that USAID and other granting agencies doled out. The changes also revealed that the contract state had evolved in such a way that personal friendships and reputations mattered far less for winning contracts than did the nature, size, and history of the contracting organizations themselves.

Robert Nathan and Professional-Class Liberalism

Nathan's personal and professional life track this shift in the contract state. Yet that does not mean that Nathan abandoned his liberal commitments. Rather, Nathan's executive responsibilities and his faith in managerial expertise led him to embrace values that resonated with the emerging professional-class liberalism. Nathan emphasized the pragmatic need to focus on his business's growth over ideological consistency and the virtues of technocratic governance over mass politics.

For example, through much of his early career, Nathan was a vocal supporter of antitrust policies. In both domestic and foreign consulting, he emphasized the virtues of competition and the dangers of monopoly. He was also a supporter of labor unions: one of the firm's earliest contracts came in 1946 when, for his friend Phil Murray, head of the Congress of Industrial Organizations (CIO), Nathan prepared a report and recommendations on a national wage policy favorable to workers.[64] But by the 1960s as Nathan strove for contracts lucrative enough to support his growing firm, he accepted jobs as an expert witness and consultant for businesses such as AT&T, major electric utilities, the Japanese Automobile Manufacturer's Association, and manufacturers working in the United States and Mexico seeking to change tax laws to their benefit.[65] Nathan's corporate gigs surprised many colleagues and journalists who found it a stark contrast to the old New Dealer's reputation. His defense of AT&T's monopolistic power "raised old-line New Deal eyebrows," according to the *Washington Post*.[66] It was not that Nathan had undergone a personal ideological shift; during this era, Nathan still publicly advocated for other antitrust policies and Nathan Associates won contracts to that end. Rather, Nathan the business owner had a responsibility to help generate revenue for his company. Professional obligation trumped personal ideology.

Nathan brushed away critics who claimed he had betrayed his liberal bona fides by pointing to his technocratic empiricism. "When we take a project, we go where our research leads us," he told *Business Week* in 1977.[67] Supporters who leapt to his defense likewise used high-minded arguments about the liberal tradition's support for freedom of choice. Economist Leon Keyserling, an influential technocrat in the Democratic Party orbit and Nathan's friend, defended Nathan publicly by asserting that "the very essence of liberalism includes that independence of mind an action which prompts an individual on an ad hoc basis to defend the cause he believes right." In this line of argument, liberal principles reinforced material interests. After all, Keyserling could easily have been describing himself, as the celebrated liberal economist did contract-based consulting for corporate clients in the natural gas industry.[68] For such wealthy liberal capitalists, determining what was "right" had become less a matter of absolute moral conviction than a business decision.

For Nathan, managerial skill and expertise provided the framework to decide who could make valid claims on the state and to determine the appropriate balance between public and private interests rather than moral principles such as fairness or equality. He criticized the Eisenhower administration, for example, for its perceived neglect of expertise. "If you had a high IQ, the Eisenhower team thought something was wrong with you," he wrote. In contrast, Nathan praised the Kennedy administration's embrace of technocrats. "A respect for intellectuals came out of the Kennedy Administration, and it helped the liberal cause."[69] In response to urban poverty and blight during the 1960s, Nathan said that "what we can do in this fight is limited only by what we can mobilize in the way of manpower and competent administrators."[70] In a 1976 interview, he claimed that sluggish growth and high inflation meant that "if we don't move toward more effective competition, then we may have to move toward some degree of regulation. I have great doubts about this, because I've been in and out of government, and I'm not always impressed by the quality of government talent."[71] Nathan prized a politics that celebrated respectability and perceived seriousness but often served to bolster the status quo of an unequal political economy. Valorizing managerial competence and technocratic fixes to social problems, Nathan presaged a younger generation of professional-class liberals that would rise in prominence over the following decades.

By this point, the firm did not depend on Bob Nathan's personal networks for business. As he approached his seventieth birthday in the late 1970s, Nathan's personal involvement with the firm gradually declined.[72] But even as Nathan's role in the company faded during the 1980s and 1990s (he continued to work in a limited capacity during the 1980s and died in 2001 at the age of ninety-two), the firm's close relationship with the contract state ensured its ongoing success. Whereas Nathan and his firm often saw their fortunes decline when Democrats left the White House during the 1950s, by the 1980s that was no longer the case. The Reagan and Bush administrations championed the use of private enterprise and the promotion of small businesses in development, two hallmarks of the kind of programs liberals had promoted since Nathan Associates first encouraged socialist Burma to boost small businesses as part of the country's development plans.[73] One 1983 study estimated that by that year the government annually awarded more than eighteen million contracts totaling over $150 billion and that more than 130,000 federal employees worked just on contract and grant administration.[74] By 1992, Nathan Associates held fifteen active USAID contracts totaling over $26 million (making it one of the twenty largest USAID contractors).[75]

These trends continued during the Clinton administration. President Clinton and his advisers, a vanguard of professional-class liberals organized under the banner of "New Democrats," advocated for "market-oriented, entrepreneurial techniques" in government policy.[76] The administration treated USAID as a "reinvention laboratory," in part to make privatization in the agency "more effective."[77] In practice, under Clinton USAID's use of IQCs increased. The agency, largely shorn of its internal technical expertise, relied on large firms holding vast IQCs to carry out many aspects of its work. Between 1996 and 2005, a Government Accountability Office report found that the amount of funds going to the largest five contractors went from $57 million to $1.25 billion, with the proportion of total contracts to those five rising from 33 percent to 46 percent of the total.[78] By the end of 1995, Nathan Associates alone held over $60 million in USAID contracts. Many larger firms secured even larger IQCs. Chemonics International and KPMG Peat Marwick, for example, held over $200 million in active USAID contracts by that time.[79]

With more and larger contracts to administer, Nathan Associates continued its professionalization and expanded far beyond its founders' personal network. During the 1980s and the 1990s, Nathan Associates recruited near-retirement or recently retired government officials to staff their upper management with individuals well known to the contracting agencies.[80] The firm also increased its ability to furnish economic advice in legal cases. By 1998 the firm set up an affiliation system with leading economists and finance professors whom Nathan Associates paid as much as $300 per hour for "weighing in for corporations in need of an opinion."[81] These changes enabled the company to continue its government contracting and expand its private-sector consulting far outside US borders. By the 2021 fiscal year, Nathan Associates held dozens of federal contracts totaling over $43 million.[82] But the US government is not its primary source of revenue. The company now maintains hundreds of full-time employees in offices in Arlington, VA; London, UK; and Chennai, India (in addition to many smaller program offices around the world), working on hundreds of contracts from governments, international organizations, and private clients.[83]

Conclusion

Bob Nathan's career and his company's evolution make clear that the US foreign policy agencies' reliance on private, for-profit contractors was not just a product of neoliberalism but rather extended a core feature of earlier liberal state-building forged in the New Deal and wartime state. Even at the high tide of "big development" and "modernization theory" during the 1950s and 1960s—when faith in statist development approaches was at its peak—private companies, working through governments, wrote five-year plans, conducted myriad surveys, implemented myriad development projects, and evaluated many more. Likewise, it was liberal presidents—Truman and Kennedy in particular—working collaboratively with Congress and the private sector that created and expanded the contract state for foreign aid.

The story of Nathan Associates also illuminates the contract state as a problem not only in terms of oversight and accountability but also in terms of the effectiveness of democratic governance. While the contract state permitted the government to gain administrative capacity that it lacked, the record of its many contractors is far from stellar. One remarkable aspect of Nathan Associates' contract work is that it was often marginal, incomplete, or ignored. Searching for some evidence of the company's influence in Burma, Lou Walinsky, Nathan Associates' lead on the project, wrote in late 1959 of trying to gain from Burmese officials "some understanding of the process by which some of the recommendations made by us were adopted," but in return he "only got a vague reply."[84] In El Salvador during the 1960s, Nathan's suggestions, which emphasized the need to raise taxes modestly to boost revenues, foundered because of Salvadoran officials' "ultra conservatism" on fiscal policy and so never became policy.[85] Elsewhere, the consultants' reports went nowhere. In one case, one USAID official who worked extensively in Turkey during the 1970s and 1980s, when Nathan Associates had a major contract to assess the country's state-owned enterprises, lamented the lack of accomplishments: "Much of the [USAID] money went to paying Robert Nathan to put together a bookshelf full of volumes on what each individual state economic enterprise ought to do to fix itself." But in the end, the Turkish government "didn't do many of those things."[86] Projects often remained mere plans on a page, but contractors received their payments just the same.

Rather than democratizing or enhancing the efficiency of foreign policymaking, as so many liberals and conservatives alike have long claimed, the contract state insulated for-profit companies from meaningful public accountability. Rather than conserving resources and promoting entrepreneurial energies as professional-class liberals celebrated, the state's reliance on the private sector led to wasteful spending, unproductive projects, and a vast and convoluted parastatal bureaucracy far removed from meaningful public oversight. Investigative journalism and congressional hearings during the 1980s and 1990s revealed many instances of inefficiency, waste, and fraud. But these exposés inspired only minor reforms designed to limit funding for the largest contractors and establish a more competitive bidding process—solutions about who could participate in the contract state rather than the pitfalls of the system as whole.[87]

The twenty-first-century contract state is a legacy of the twentieth-century international-development policy and the tensions inherent within liberals' attempts to sustain capitalist development while constructing a state capable of managing its worst social and political consequences. US foreign-aid policy could not exist and function without private contractors. Nathan Associates would not have evolved in the way that it did without the agency and other governments dependent upon them for their services. The liberals who created and sustained US foreign aid built not only many dams and factories abroad but also a large network of for-profit consulting firms selling their expertise and earning large profits at home.

CHAPTER 3

Creating "Initiatory Democracy"

Ralph Nader, the Center for the Study of Responsive Law, and the Shaping of Liberalism in the 1970s

SARAH MILOV AND REUEL SCHILLER

Ralph Nader was one of the most famous political activists of the 1960s and 1970s. For much of this period, he was routinely named in Gallup's rankings of "most admired Americans." He was a fixture of the college lecture circuit and even sparked popular demands to run for president in 1972.[1] Young and austere, he cut a singular figure in the Democrat-dominated Washington of the era, calling out the failings of liberalism for its capitulation to big business. His brand of earnest reformism brought thousands of young people to the nation's capital to expose the bureaucratic corruption and incompetence that endangered the public welfare. In 1969, Nader created the Center for the Study of Responsive Law ("the Center") as an institutional home for his acolytes—the law students, graduate students, and undergrads who wished to spend a summer working for him. Dubbed "Nader's Raiders" by a captivated press corps, the vast majority of these idealistic new recruits to DC's political ecology were white, male, expensively educated, well-connected, and at least comfortably middle class. The Center provided them an opportunity to be part of the great youth-fueled movements remaking politics the world over—at least for the duration of their summer vacations. For a brief but influential half-dozen years, the Raiders produced muckraking investigative reports on regulatory agencies, Congress, and corporations under the auspices of the Center. Published with attention-grabbing titles like *The Interstate Commerce Omission*, *The Closed Enterprise System*, and *The Vanishing Air*, the trade books resulting from these reports were a hit with their intended audience—the Washington press corps, congressional staffers, and other Beltway insiders.[2]

This strategy of packaging a technocratic critique of powerful institutions as a muckraking, mass-market paperback drew directly from Nader's own first brush with the political spotlight. In late 1965, Nader published, with little fanfare, *Unsafe at Any Speed: The Designed-In Dangers of the American Automobile*, a dense indictment of automakers' profit-driven disregard of the safety hazards in the cars they manufactured.[3] Few expected this novice effort of a recent Harvard Law School graduate to be of interest to anyone other than actuaries and, perhaps, cautious motorheads. Yet, General Motors' paranoid response to its publication made Nader a household name. The company had Nader followed by private investigators, questioned his associates about possible "homosexual tendencies," and allegedly used female "sex lures" in vain attempts to embarrass and discredit him. When GM's foul play came to light during congressional hearings on motor-vehicle safety legislation in 1966, a near-mythological figure was born.[4] The press—eager for both the primary revelations about rollover-prone cars and the secondary intrigue that followed—obligingly cast Nader in a familiar cultural script. "GM's Goliath Bows to David," read the headline of the *Washington Post*'s analysis. Claiming to be "shocked and outraged," the president of General Motors, the largest corporation in the world at the time, later appeared before a Senate subcommittee and apologized to the thirty-two-year-old for the harassment he endured. The hearings pushed *Unsafe at Any Speed* to the top the bestseller charts and catapulted Nader to a rare position in American life: a figure revered for being assertively virtuous.[5] General Motor's harassment built not only Nader's reputation but also his institutional footprint. Nader sued General Motors in 1970 for invasion of privacy, and was awarded $425,000, which he used to fund the Center.

Nader's name appears frequently in historical accounts of postwar politics and political culture, and liberal political institutions like the public-interest bar and left-leaning think tanks have been populated by ambitious former Raiders for decades. But the substance of Nader's thought and the actions of the Raiders have been understudied by historians. Indeed, even as scholars have begun to focus on the antagonistic relationship between public-interest lawyers and the administrative manifestations of postwar liberalism, few have engaged in a sustained reading of the monographs produced by the Center.[6] These materials as well as the Center's recruitment tactics paint a surprising picture of Naderite reform—one discordant with much of the activism of the late 1960s and early 1970s. Nader, of course, is well known for his hostility toward consolidated corporate power and its domination of the state through agency capture. As such, he is mostly closely associated with liberal and left participatory political movements—the consumer movement and the environmental movement, in particular.

Yet, a close examination of his approach to activism reveals it to be anything but inclusive or based on mass participation. Instead, Nader called for "initiatory" activism, wherein a small number of highly educated, professional elites would act as a "countervailing force" to the organized interests that perpetuated social and political pathologies like corruption, incompetence, and bureaucratic inefficiency. In this vision of liberalism, highly educated, poorly paid interns would keep continuous watch on institutions. Indebted to mid-century pluralist ideas about interest group organizing, Nader's "initiatory democracy" imagined that the Center would itself serve as a public-interest counterweight to the private pressures and entropic pull that enervated government agencies. This essay examines this resolute elitism that rejected popular, participatory politics. In doing so, it illuminates a neglected source of liberalism's technocratic turn in the 1970s.

Nader is no stranger to historians of American liberalism. Historical examinations of the social movements and policy initiatives that typified liberalism in the 1970s—consumerism, environmentalism, governmental reform—all dutifully recount Nader's involvement.[7] Similarly, his name frequently appears in studies of the resurgent Right during this period. These works argue that opposition to Nader-supported, anticorporate initiatives served as a catalyst for conservative interests as they fashioned a political juggernaut that ultimately resulted in the election of Ronald Reagan.[8] Yet, while Nader's fingerprints seem to be everywhere in the histories of 1970s, his ideas are curiously absent. He often appears as little more than a symbol in these narratives: a totem of the energetic liberalism that was deeply contested in the 1970s and ultimately defeated in 1980. By focusing on the thought and practice of Naderism at the apogee of its influence, we illuminate a strand of professional middle-class liberalism too often lost in narratives of backlash and decline.

Scholarship on the public-interest movement has come the closest to identifying the distinctive political vision of post–New Deal liberalism—one that was critical and adversarial, but also optimistic about the possibility of reform from within. This scholarship focuses largely on the actions of the founders of public-interest law organizations, which promoted novel, legalistic responses to the problems of the mid-century American administrative state.[9] Our essay contributes to these examinations of public-interest liberalism of the 1970s but departs from them in two important respects. First, by focusing on the young people working for Nader, we illuminate the social contours of Nader's political vision. Nader recruited wealthy Ivy League students because they were cheap to employ, garnered media attention, and came with an assumption of competence. In contrast to many contemporary activists, Nader's was a class project, creating a cadre of professional-class liberals drawn from prestigious law schools and colleges.

Secondly, a sustained reading of the reports issued by the Center and an analysis of the tactics used to advance Nader's agenda similarly reveals a belief system at odds with scholarly and popular conceptions of the "consumer crusader." Far from taking "very seriously democratic politics as both an end and a means of liberal reform"—as one early and influential account of the public interest movement put it—Naderite liberalism was elitist.[10] We demonstrate that Nader was philosophically indebted to a pluralist vision of politics forged in the heyday of the postwar liberalism he so savagely assailed. We then describe how Nader developed and implemented a vision of political reform appropriate for a time when distrust of the state was widespread, but which was also explicitly antipopulist. "Historical changes, including the American revolution, have always come through minorities," Nader explained in an introduction to a monograph on how to establish student-run political organizations.[11] Accordingly, taking Naderite liberalism seriously means attending to the ways it promoted reform indifferent to both the grassroots organizing and the coalition-building necessary to sustain the electoral majorities that had reliably delivered Democrats to office since the New Deal. Having eschewed mass politics, Nader's strategy could not build an enduring movement from the peripatetic energies of students or the intense but fleeting curiosity of the media.

The First Raid on the Federal Trade Commission

Student interns are now a summertime commonplace at DC nonprofits, but they were rare in the late 1960s.[12] Indeed, Ralph Nader helped pioneer the use of college and graduate school students from elite institutions. In the summer of 1968, he put them to work uncovering misbehavior in government agencies. His first target was the much-maligned Federal Trade Commission (FTC), for decades the subject of withering criticism.[13] Nader's celebrity recruited student investigators.[14] All came from Harvard, Yale, or Princeton. They included William Howard Taft IV (the great-grandson of the president), Edward Cox (soon to be Richard Nixon's son-in-law), Peter Bradford (a descendant of the Rothschilds and the son of the former managing editor of the *New York Times*), and Judith Areen, the group's only woman, whose father was a high-ranking Chrysler executive. While future cohorts of summer recruits would not include the relatives of presidents, the first summer's students set a template for the kinds of educational and social backgrounds for which Nader selected: Ivy-educated, white, and possessed of social capital that generated media attention. At a time when less than a third of twenty- and twenty-one-year-olds were enrolled in any form of higher education, Nader drew from an especially rarefied group.[15]

The FTC project was a stunning success. The publicity that resulted from the January 1969 release of the *Nader Report on the Federal Trade Commission* vindicated Nader's recruitment strategy: the educational backgrounds of the students suggested competence, and their social standing garnered publicity. The *Washington Post*, the prime outlet for reportage on DC's federal workforce, lauded the report as a "penetrating book of quiet horror" that pulled back the curtain on the capture of the agency from without and the indolence within. In a separate editorial, the paper suggested that the "totally devastating" portrait of the agency meant that Congress and the new Nixon administration ought to "abolish the FTC and build a new agency, or perhaps two, on its ashes."[16] And it was the *Post*'s William Greider who dubbed the student investigators "Nader's Raiders," giving politicians, the public, and would-be recruits a memorable way to refer to the youthful crusaders, the mere mention of whom could "make some Federal bureaucrats quiver."[17]

The students' class status—and their proximity to the highest echelons of politics and business—assured the report's publicity. Connecticut senator Abraham Ribicoff, who had worked with Nader to pass the 1966 Motor Vehicle Highway Safety Act, held hearings on consumer protection at which five of the report's investigators testified.[18] Taft and Cox, as well three other Raiders—Robert Fellmeth, Andrew Egendorf, and John Schulz—were introduced by the senator as "three law students from Harvard, a student at Yale, and an assistant professor of law at the University of Southern California" (where Schulz had begun teaching).[19] The professional-class background of the investigators was as much on display as their critique of the FTC. After the five Raiders recapitulated the central findings of the report, Ribicoff's questioning focused entirely on the ways in which "bright young students use their talents in constructive ways," working within "the system"—a constructive rejoinder to the "impression that all students are interested in revolt."[20]

Ribicoff was especially impressed by the fact that that none of the summer investigators were paid, save for a $500 grant that Schulz received from Yale. "In other words, your room and board and various expenses were paid by you gentlemen individually?" Ribicoff queried. "That is correct," Schulz replied. "Or by our parents," Taft clarified.

"I would say your respective parents probably felt it was a very worthwhile investment," Ribicoff observed, connecting the students' ambitions to their class backgrounds. He picked out Taft for particular praise: "You are following in a great tradition of the Taft family, which has, generation after generation, dedicated their lives and their energies to public service."[21] As young people across the world launched demonstrations, occupied university buildings, and held vigils to protest capitalism, imperialism, and racism that very same summer, the authors of the FTC report suggested, at least to some members of the political establishment, that critical youthful energies could be harnessed by the system itself.

The following year, Nader founded the Center to direct those energies. The summer interns he recruited would be supervised by a smaller number of law and professional school graduates. These older, full-time employees continued the students' research and prepared the reports for publication in non-summer months, after the interns had departed. The first five supervisors were all young white men with advanced degrees—JDs from Harvard, Yale, Michigan, and Ohio State, and a PhD candidate in government at Harvard. Four were under thirty; the eldest was thirty-three. The organization's expenses—staff salaries and the overhead on its headquarters in a decrepit Victorian mansion on Q-Street—were funded by philanthropy, the bulk of which came from a $55,000 Carnegie Foundation grant.[22] Institutionally, the Center ran on the energies of the rich, while cultivating the talents of liberalism's emerging professional class.

Nowhere was this dynamic more evident than in the Center's recruitment for the bulk of its labor force: the interns. The publicity received by the *FTC Report*—including coverage in the *Harvard Crimson* and *Daily Princetonian*—set scores of students in search of summer employment with Nader. Nader explicitly recruited from the Ivy League networks with which he was familiar, sending a recruiter to Princeton, his undergraduate alma mater, in March of 1969 to find "technically minded upperclassmen and graduate students."[23] Nader was a frequent visitor to Princeton, giving speeches and guest lectures for a fee that went toward the operating budget of the Center. At Harvard, too, Nader loomed large—in spite of (or because of) his stated contempt for the institution where he received his law degree. In a speech at the Law School attended by four hundred students, Nader slammed the school for failing to inculcate a "sense of injustice" among its students, while inviting them to join him in creating public-interest law firms to redress the balance of power in Washington. "Official Washington would never be the same again," Nader vowed, "if you had several hundred lawyers working the other side of the fence—working to force disclosure, ripping aside curtains of secrecy to instill a professional quality of representation of the public in the administrative process."[24] Not long after, the *Harvard Law Record* announced the availability of summer positions with the Center.[25]

By the summer of 1969, the Center had expanded rapidly, recruiting nearly one hundred interns to pursue critical investigations of the Interstate Commerce Commission, the National Air Pollution Control Administration, the Federal Water Quality Office, the Department of Agriculture, and the Food and Drug Administration.[26] These investigations generated agency-focused "task force reports" that were later published as *The Interstate Commerce Omission, Vanishing Air, Sowing the Wind, The Chemical Feast,* and *Water Wasteland*. The demographics of these Raiders mirrored those of the FTC cohort, except there was a broader representation of the professions. The plurality were law students, but medical students, engineering students, and graduate students in the arts and sciences were also selected for their technical knowledge of the subjects under investigation. Two were Black. Ten were women.[27]

Like his first cohort of interns, the class background of many of these students enabled Nader's organization to run cheaply.[28] Nader paid his Raiders a pittance—between $35 and $100 a week, depending on need. Nader dubbed these poverty wages "motivational screening."[29] Indeed, when the Nader organization established a permanent presence on university campuses through the creation of Public Interest Research Groups (PIRGs), it instructed leaders to keep the salaries of professional staff members low to ensure that they "would harmonize their jobs with their values systems."[30] He also recognized that free labor from wealthy summer interns formed an in-kind donation to the organization. "If someone will come in and work for room and board, fine, or if his family will support him, fine," Nader explained in a 1971 *New York Times* profile. "That's the same as a $4,000 or $5,000 contribution right there."[31] For this reason, Raiders were encouraged to forgo any compensation if they did not need it.[32] Nader imagined the activated and young "citizen-consumers" in his employ to have the leisure, education, and networks of social connections to organize a technically sophisticated, socially connected citizens group.[33] This was no mass, broadly participatory movement.

Thus, by the beginning of 1970, Nader had hit upon a novel institutional mechanism to facilitate social change. He had constructed the Center out of the materials of postwar affluence: educated, financially secure white college and professional-school students who were willing to deploy their social capital on behalf of legal liberal reform. And, despite the creature comforts the Raiders forsook, a summer investigating an agency was more professionally valuable (and safer) than one spent protesting segregation in the South or marching to stop the American bombing of Vietnam and Cambodia. When combined with Nader's unique charisma, the alchemy of this combination was undeniable. Thirty-five hundred people applied to spend the summer of 1970 working at the Center for next to no money.[34]

Yet Nader's approach to institution-building was not merely a tactic designed to advance the public interest as cheaply as possible. His personnel choices—building the Center around liberal, affluent, white men—also reflected a particular belief about what the public interest was, who best understood its contours, and how it should be achieved. The identity and behavior of Nader's Raiders were supposed to embody a critique of postwar society and forge a response. A corrupt, incompetent political system flourished because of deadening consumer culture and political cronyism. The public interest required a cadre of abstemious experts to serve as a countervailing force.

The Problems: Power Elites, Consumer Culture

When student interns arrived at the Center at the beginning of the summer, they were introduced to a diagnosis of the problems with contemporary American society animated by a specific vision of institutional corruption. As Nader's recruitment speech at Harvard intimated, this diagnosis was rooted in a set of assumptions about the relationship between the state and private institutions that was increasingly common on the left in the 1960s and 1970s. Left-leaning thinkers such as C. Wright Mills, Gabriel Kolko, and Theodore Lowi described a society run by intertwined corporations and government bureaucracies, acting in the interests of a rarefied "power elite." For these thinkers, business and government were barely distinct institutions. They were a single entity, run by an elite class bound together by economic interests as well as social and psychological affinities nurtured in a wide variety of elite institutions. Meanwhile, the public's ability to resist this leviathan had been destroyed by a deadening mass culture and an oppressive bureaucracy that turned the people into passive consumers of elite opinion—"inactionary," in Mills's words.[35]

These ideas made their way into the Center's publications largely unchanged.[36] The Center's mission was to uncover the corrupt relationships among politicians, government agencies, and private industry. Parroting these thinkers, the Center's monographs emphasized that America's existing political economy bore little resemblance to an imagined world of free enterprise and democratic political participation.

Instead, the United States operated under a "closed enterprise system," in which giant corporations were "so deeply insinuated into the politico-economic fabric of society that a veritable revolution against citizens has occurred."[37] Corporations had nothing but "contempt" for genuine competition and "the productive work ethic."[38] Instead, they allied themselves with government agencies that furthered their interests, creating an economy that Nader described as "corporate socialism."[39]

Each monograph described the ties between corporations and the state by exposing the mechanisms of agency capture: the frequent exchange of personnel between agencies and the corporations they were supposed to regulate; the agency advisory councils made up entirely of corporate officials; the industry lobbyists dispensing campaign contributions to politicians who oversaw agency action; the boondoggle trips to luxury resorts that agency officials took, generously provided by corporations.[40] The result of this capture was not surprising. Agency "regulation" was either a mechanism that allowed for the creation of state-sanctioned monopolies, or a fig leaf that allowed politicians and administrative officials to assert that they were acting in the public interest, when, in fact, they were allowing corporations to profit at the expense of the environment, public health, and consumer safety. This "regulatory-industrial complex" was so pervasive, Nader wrote, that "one can look at the regulators and then at the regulatees and be unable to distinguish them."[41]

Nader and his staff at the Center also subscribed to the assertion by contemporary critical thinkers that mass communications, advertising, and consumer culture had created a population that was incapable of governing itself.[42] Indeed, central to Nader's public persona was the ironic image of the consumer advocate who disdained consumption. Scarcely an article about him failed to mention his "rumpled suits," "scuffed shoes," "monklike" social life, and preference for plain food and drink.[43] He never seemed to miss an opportunity to lecture the public—waitresses, flight attendants, journalists—about the perversions of consumer society, be they processed foods or plate-glass windows.[44] Pollution, junk food, and corporate monopolies were bad, but symptoms rather than causes of the era's political malaise. The root of the problem lay in consumer culture itself. "Ralph is not a consumer champion," a friend once said, "he is just plain against consumption."[45]

The Center's monographs provided a framework for Nader's refusal to engage in the pleasures of consumer society. They were replete with assertions familiar to any student of mass society. Advertising had rendered humans manipulable, nearly devoid of free will. Consumers no longer had the power to make rational choices—or any choices at all. Instead, their desires were manufactured by what one report cryptically referred to as "the communications revolution," which included "mass data-handling techniques to attack the privacy and autonomy of the consumer." Consumers stupefied by "overpowering appeals to strongly irrational elements of the human psyche" poisoned themselves with cheap products sold at high profit margins.[46]

This critique rested on the assumption that emotional and rational decision-making processes were distinct and that most Americans had little capacity for the latter. The market preyed upon the weaknesses of the psyche. Politics, by contrast, ought to be the domain of reasoned assessment exercised through formal channels. "Many Americans know far more about entertainers and football players than about their representative in Congress," Nader complained to *Ladies' Home Journal*. "[This] is a major factor underlying the problems that confront us."[47] Consumer society distracted Americans into political submission. Young people—the target of Nader's recruitment efforts—were the demographic group most susceptible to the siren song of the culture industry and the least likely to hold political power. "They are urged to drink cola, buy luxury or frilly clothes, cars, and records, and to attend movies," explained a report on student organizing. "Over and over the ceaseless message to consume, consume, consume is repeated, and beneath the words whispers the subliminal message that the problem of skin blemishes is more important than hunger in Appalachia or that a good breath mint will solve a problem more serious than air pollution."[48]

Against this theoretical background, Nader made explicit demands of the Raiders. Because consumption deadened reform impulses, he required that they emulate his lifestyle. He welcomed his summer staff to DC with an injunction against "weed" and "partying."[49] He bemoaned the fact that many of his young recruits seemed to imagine that their summer experience would include an occasional softball game to break up the monotony of days spent reading agency reports and tracking down disgruntled government employees who might be willing to discuss food additives. According to Nader, such desires in the face of the enormity of contemporary social problems was a sign of just how alienated consumer culture had rendered people.[50] No wonder a nineteen-year-old Michael Kinsley, the future editor of the *New Republic* and *Slate*, described the dominant feeling of his summer spent at the Center as one of "guilt."[51] Gestures of "sensual deprivation"—such as avoiding junk food and sleeping in—were one way to guard against the guilt that came with knowing that "someone's kid somewhere was eating a poisoned hamburger or watching a radioactive television."[52]

The Solution: Initiatory Democracy

While the Center's diagnosis of the problems with contemporary society—agency capture, a population inactivated by consumer culture—echoed critiques common among the 1960s Left, its solutions did not. For many on the left, dysfunctional politics and unjust social policies were to be remedied by promoting participatory democracy.[53] Thus, many young radicals placed their hope in grassroots organization and the assertion of "people power," either through new mass organizations—Students for Democratic Society, the National Welfare Rights Organization, the Student Nonviolent Coordinating Committee—or by revivifying older, somnolent populist institutions, particularly within the labor movement.[54]

Nader had very different ideas about who should be mobilized and the tactics they should use. The foot soldiers in his campaign against corporate interests and captured government agencies would not be "the people," writ large. Instead, Nader extolled the virtues not of participatory democracy, but of "Initiatory Democracy" in which "college and professional school" students and recent graduates, as well as "young lawyers and other specialists," acted as a vanguard for "a new class of public citizens."[55] This faith in the professional class stemmed from a belief in the congenital passivity of most members of society. Apathy, he claimed, was pervasive in democracy—"98 percent of people who know of a certain abuse are not going to say anything." But political integrity could be redeemed if "2 percent or 1 percent [will] speak out."[56] This 1 or 2 percent would be drawn from elite institutions and professions.

For Nader, the nature of the problems the country faced—corrupt institutions, environmental degradation, unhealthy foods, complex price-fixing schemes—demanded a new, intellectualized form of activism that only the educated and disciplined were capable of. "Expertise, lengthy and often arduous research, and tedious interviews with minor bureaucrats" were the truly efficacious forms of activism.[57] Thus, he dismissed the tactics of "mass demonstrations, highly publicized confrontations with authorities, and summer projects such as the Mississippi voter registration drives and freedom marches."[58] These "easy paths of sloganeering" had to be replaced with "lonely hours in the library and inglorious confrontations with low-level officials," tasks that affluent, educated young people were suited for if they could shake off the sedating influence of consumer culture.[59] Whereas New Left community organizers sought to empower the "oppressed and exploited" to advocate for themselves, Naderites sought technocratic fixes in the interstices of the administrative state: "professional citizens" within "a steadfast, public-interest Commission" or "professional advocates" pressuring agencies from the outside.[60]

Even Naderite activists who would engage in traditional political activities were expected to cultivate expertise, money, and time. Being a victim of poor regulation was not enough to grant a movement legitimacy. Nor was it enough for would-be citizen reformers to write their representatives. Instead, citizens should deploy knowledge: a "thoroughly documented, expert report"[61] and support from a "'disinterested source'—another congressman, a respected columnist, or experts."[62] In fact, even substantive expertise was not enough. Citizens had to develop expertise on the legislative process, lest they be nothing more than "unprepared citizen lobbyist[s]." They should read printed hearings and the *Congressional Record*, contact the Congressional Reference Service, and file Freedom of Information Act requests. Nor should they simply rely on the government to supply them with information. They should conduct their own investigations. A "building-by-building search" to find polluters conducted by the Upper West Side Air Pollution Campaign was cited as inspiration.[63] According to Nader, effective advocacy was the province of the exceptionally well-informed, not the exceptionally affected.

Deploying expertise and cultivating insider connections thus required extensive social capital: time, resources, and connections—to serve as a counterweight to the corrupt, captured agency's own crafting of its message. Citizen activists should enlist the support not of those poisoned by pollution or displaced by a highway, but those "known for involvement in civic affairs" like "the president of your neighborhood association, the lawyer who headed the fundraising drive for the reform candidate, or the ex-director of the free breakfast program for Model Cities."[64] Politics was, for Nader, a fundamentally legalistic endeavor, so groups of activists should have a "legal adviser," who could be "useful for taxes, lobbying, demonstration permits, unraveling bureaucratic regulations, spotting congressional lawlessness, and knowing when to bring suit." Similarly, they should enlist "sympathetic wealthy individuals who can underwrite you with thousands of dollars."[65] Such funding was especially important because "to be effective citizen lobbyists, group organizing should not stop at the local level." It should maintain some type of presence in Washington—a member of the group might even need to register as a lobbyist.[66] When the Center sought to illustrate these tactics, its examples suggested rarefied citizens: doctors, engineers, nuclear physicists, media executives.[67] Given the realities of agency capture and the complexities of the regulatory process, initiatory democracy thus imagined reform driven by educated elites both outside and inside of government.

Just how far removed this approach was from mass-movement politics was illustrated by Nader's thinking about the civil rights movement. In an interview with *Playboy* shortly after the assassination of Martin Luther King Jr., Nader was asked whether the "problems of the black ghetto" seemed "more urgent" than the consumer problems of the "affluent middle class." While conceding that many times "Negroes are far more exploited than the white population," Nader insisted that consumer concerns "are related as much to the quality of life in the ghetto as to the quality of life in Scarsdale or Grosse Pointe." Yet, for all his insistence that civil rights and economic rights were intertwined, Nader saw his movement as separate from—and a precondition to—racial justice: "The people in the slums are aspiring to a society I would like to make worthy of their aspirations."[68] Although many young white people who worked for Nader were shaped by—and occasionally involved in—the civil rights and antiwar movements, the Center's operations were philosophically, demographically, and organizationally distinct from the era's mass-protest movements. In fact, Nader believed that mass-movement tactics, which he characterized as "publicity campaigns," might alienate important constituencies from the reform institutions he wished to create.[69] Somebody had to push back against the overwhelming power of intertwined corporate and political elites, but it would not be "the people" writ large. Instead it would be members of the professional classes, possessed of expertise and inculcated with a Naderite world view.

Tactics: Social Capital as a Countervailing Force

The tactics that Nader dictated for his newly mobilized professionals were substantially different from those of mass movements. To roll back corporate power, he turned to strategies suggested by postwar pluralist thinkers writing a decade before the emergence of the idea of participatory reform that animated so many on the left in the 1960s and 1970s. American society worked best, these thinkers suggested, when a wide variety of interest groups balanced each other, ensuring that no single interest predominated.[70]

John Kenneth Galbraith, the iconoclastic Harvard economist and Kennedy confidant, espoused a brand of pluralism particularly appealing to Nader and the staff of the Center. Galbraith argued that, in a modern, mass society, it was unreasonable to assume that traditional, atomistic modes of economic and political competition would operate to generate desirable outcomes. Instead, these outcomes could only be achieved when large institutions with divergent interests pushed against each other in a manner that created an equilibrium. "Countervailing power" produced stable oppositions: unions balanced employers, retail groups balanced associations of manufacturers, agricultural cooperatives balanced monopolistic food distributors. The solution to economic and political monopoly was a parallel concentration of opposed economic and political power, not a futile struggle to promote popular participation in the political process.[71]

Nader admired Galbraith, whose intellectual fingerprints are all over the work of the Center.[72] Indeed, Nader believed the cadres at the Center and the PIRGs represented an accessible, cheap, and media-generating labor force that would act as a "countervailing force in the private sector against the special interests and the lobbyists."[73] They were "instruments of civic action" that would "galvaniz[e] governmental and non-governmental institutions, such as Congress and the media," thereby forcing them to act in the public interest.[74] These groups would accomplish this end by amassing expertise and coordinating the actions of otherwise atomized elite citizens "to make the commanding institutions of our society respond to needs that they have repudiated or rejected."[75] The Center, PIRGs, and other citizens' groups were thus designed to be "countervailing powers of response," revealing the "linkages" between malevolent actions of "regulators [and] industries and the public's plight."[76]

Nader believed that these groups of elite citizens should not be the only locus of countervailing power. Unlike Galbraith, other pluralist intellectuals, and later critics of the postwar political order, he believed that the administrative state could *itself* serve as a countervailing power if the bureaucracy itself could overcome its own enervation and rot. Thus, while the pluralists believed the administrative state simply brokered group interests, Nader's vision was one in which activist agencies themselves could become a countervailing force if they were staffed by highly educated, vigorous young people—young people who had become acculturated into "active citizenship," perhaps as they passed through one of Nader's organizations.[77] The key, then, was fostering bureaucratic regeneration through agency staffing.

The Center's studies suggested that most agencies had a long way to go. They presented a portrait of demoralized, incompetent, compromised agency officials at every level of the bureaucracy, resulting in an administrative state that did next to nothing for regular citizens. This regulatory somnolence was generated by political appointees beholden to corporate interests, and the lazy, incompetent staff that these appointees preferred. Thus, the Justice Department's Antitrust Division was "a home for the aged" and a place where "attorneys, happily homeostatic in a government sinecure, have lost their zeal for public service or the law."[78] According to the Center's investigators, the Federal Trade Commission purposely avoided recruiting top-flight lawyers. "Given a choice between a bright one and one who is merely good, take the good man. He'll stay longer."[79] The result of this recruiting strategy, the Center caustically concluded, was a backwater agency filled with southern, rural lawyers from second-rate law schools.[80] Nor was it just lawyers who were prevented from exercising their professional expertise to turn agencies into a countervailing power. In agency after agency, staff economists and scientists frequently came from jobs at the very companies the agency was supposed to regulate. Consequently, their research often served as a cover for industry, usually concluding that "more study is needed" for any pollution control initiative.[81] Thus, the Center sought to make the agencies more potent, thereby freeing them from the thrall of corporate America. Translated into pluralist terms, the purpose of regulation was to serve as a "a corporate counterweight."[82]

That counterweight had several components. First and foremost, agency leaders needed to be appointed who were not beholden to industry.[83] Second, agencies needed to get rid of lethargic staff and replace them with zealous lawyers and other experts who were committed to the public rather than corporate interests.[84] Third, Congress ought to provide agencies with sufficient resources to actually enforce the statutes that empowered them.[85] The Center's prescription for every agency it assessed—the Food and Drug Administration, the National Pollution Control Administration, Federal Trade Commission, and the Department of Justice's Antitrust Division, for example—was that it use its enforcement powers more aggressively than it had done in the past.[86] The reports urged Congress to provide the agencies with additional such powers.[87] Finally, the Center demanded that the administrative state itself become an active muckraker. After all, the exercise of countervailing power was done not simply through specific legal sanctions but also through publicity and negative political attention. Accurate information was itself a "countervailing force" to deceptive industry propaganda. When agencies stopped parroting industry talking points and instead described industry depredations, they would be advancing the public interest in a manner consistent with pluralist assumptions.[88] Indeed, pluralism demanded that agencies adopt such a forceful stance toward industry.

Lawyers and legal tactics were central to generating this countervailing power both inside and outside the administrative state. These tactics fell into two broad categories: using agency power or private litigation to break up monopolies or increasing agency enforcement powers to prevent or deter corporate malfeasance.[89] Most of the Center's studies suggested that breaking up large corporations was the prerequisite to creating some form of countervailing power. Such legalist, technocratic processes could only be carried out by lawyers and other professionals. Thus, the Center's studies of corporate concentration—*The Closed Enterprise System* and *The Monopoly Makers*—were permeated with technical explanations of the problems of interlocking directorates, delivered pricing, and retail price maintenance.[90] Entire chapters covered the pros and con of the Robinson-Patman Act and the benefits of per se antitrust rules.[91] Should corporations be taxed as partnerships? (Yes.)[92] Was the partial-divestiture remedy in the *Textron* case a satisfactory outcome? (No.)[93] These directions were aimed at internal agency actors who, the Center hoped, would be persuaded by rational, legalistic, countervailing expertise. Nader also envisioned a cadre of citizen-lawyers bringing antitrust actions independent of the Justice Department or the FTC. This strategy would, in turn, necessitate the "growth of a professional antitrust constituency outside of the federal government."[94] Within the growing ranks of professional-class liberals would emerge "lawyers and economists to work systematically for operational strategies in antitrust application."[95]

A similar legal, professional class focus permeated the Center's other studies. The use of aggressive antitrust enforcement to break up large energy producers, automobile companies, drug corporations, and agricultural conglomerates was the first step in creating a clean environment, wholesome food, and safe, reliable consumer products.[96] In addition, the Center's studies dug into the details of agency attempts at direct command-and-control regulation, advocating for more intense enforcement either by agency actors or by the public. The monographs spent hundreds of pages explaining the arcana of "abatement conferences," rulemaking versus adjudicatory approaches to standard setting, and the appropriate mechanisms for determining the correct quotas for residual fuel oil.[97] As with antitrust enforcement, the monographs went out of their way to highlight and praise legal mechanisms that allowed private enforcement of statutory or regulatory requirements. While the Center pilloried the proposed legislation that would become the Clean Air Act and the Clean Water Act ("One is hard put to imagine a more ineffective measure"[98]), it praised the proposed provisions of each act that allowed citizens to sue agencies to get them to enforce the laws, as well as other sections that would aid "citizen professionals," such as whistleblower provisions and the requirement of public hearings when the agency set pollution standards.[99] Even with otherwise disappointing legislation, lawyers could force legal change on recalcitrant agencies regardless of whether the public at large had the ability to mobilize against them. Here was the essence of initiatory, rather than participatory, democracy.

These were not the only "insider" tactics suggested by the Center's monographs. Each of the books that Center published combined mind-numbing technical details of regulatory regimes with inside-the-Beltway, gossipy takedowns of politicians and agency officials the Center disliked, and praise for the few it admired. The result was sometimes disorienting shifts in tone where, within a single chapter, a study would transition from sarcastically excoriating Edmund Muskie (viewed by the Center as a paper-tiger environmentalist) to describing the applicability of the fuel substitution rule with respect to sulfur oxides.[100] This focus on naming names suggested that one of the main audiences for the Center's publications were other Washington insiders: the DC press corps, congressional staffers, agency deputy commissioners, high-profile lawyers with government practices, and the editorial board of the *Washington Post*.

While the Center may have insisted that hard, boring work was the central ingredient of technocratic reform, it was adept at exercising power in other ways familiar to Washington insiders. The FTC Report again set the template for mobilizing traditional Beltway institutions to affect change.[101] Nader and his staff may have appeared to be crusading muckrakers from outside the district, but, in fact, their investigation of the FTC was done in coordination with allies in Congress, the staff of the agency, and an extremely cooperative press corps. Dissident agency personnel, including commission member Philip Elman, passed information to Nader's staff. The Raiders fed reporters information about the agency's depredations while they were investigating it, generating the political momentum that their allies in Congress and at the agency wanted. Nader timed the release of the report with the arrival of the Nixon administration in Washington and then handed the legislative work to his longtime ally Senator Ribicoff. When the agency's chair, Paul Rand Dixon, lashed out at the Raiders, attacking them in the press and restricting their access to agency personnel, Nader and his staff fed compromising evidence of corruption to Jerry Landauer at the *Wall Street Journal*. This tactic yielded unflattering coverage of Dixon in that paper as well as in *Time*, *Advertising Age*, *Forbes*, and the *Post*. Within weeks of assuming office, Nixon asked the American Bar Association to investigate the FTC. Ribicoff started oversight hearings on the agency in March of that year. By the end of the year, Dixon was replaced as chair, leading to a series of chairs who were credited with revivifying the agency. By 1975, Congress passed the Moss-Magnuson Act, ratifying the actions of Dixon's replacements and extending the agency's powers to protect consumers from shoddy products and deceptive warranties.

When Nader scaled up operations in the summer of 1969, he sought to replicate the success of the initial FTC investigation, using publicity and disgruntled informants to expose agency malaise.[102] Feeding the press ready-made, scandalous articles, Nader cultivated journalists in a manner that generated positive coverage for the Center and its priorities.[103] At the same time, Nader identified and worked with sympathetic politicians including Ribicoff, Warren Magnuson, Walter Mondale, and Philip Burton. More importantly, he also advised the Center's staff to concentrate their attention and flattery on congressional staff and agency actors, the people who actually drafted legislation and formulated regulations.[104] Consequently, the Center was involved with writing legislation from the ground up, including Moss-Magnuson, the Occupational Safety and Health Act, the Clean Air Act, the Toxic Substances Control Act, and the Freedom of Information Act amendments of 1974.[105] These tactics were effective, but they were hardly *Rules for Radicals*. Instead, Nader's conception of countervailing power dictated that he would use the same tactics as the corporations he was seeking to geld—pulling the levers of powers by establishing mutually beneficial relations with the consummate DC insiders: the press, agency officials, politicians, and their staff.

Conclusion

Despite their large cultural footprint, Nader's Raiders collapsed under their own weight by the middle of the 1970s. Nader was a poor manager. Disgruntled Raiders complained bitterly of "dictatorial treatment, poor supervision, [and a] lack of meaningful assignments." Nader and the Center's other leaders' expectation that every student would be a driven, ascetic "mini-Nader" was unreasonable to say the least.[106] Even more damaging was Nader's inability to distinguish between implacable opponents and flawed allies. His caustic attacks on congressional allies for even slight deviations from Naderite purity demonstrated that he lacked the pragmatism that sat at the center of even elitist pluralism.[107] A commitment to compromise and alliance building—the sine qua non of pluralist theory—was not part of Nader's character.

That said, Nader's influence endured long after the dust settled on the last of the agency raids. The institutions he created—the Center, PIRGs, and the good government group Public Citizen—are still active. Even today, visitors to PIRG's website are greeted with a historically significant slogan—"Action for a Change," the title of Nader's 1971 student manual for public interest organizing.[108] The redoubts of Democratic Washington—the public-interest bar, government agencies, and liberal think tanks—have been well populated with ambitious and well-educated former Raiders since the 1970s. They achieved quick prominence in the Carter administration, where alums worked as a speechwriter, as the head of the National Highway Transportation Safety Administration, and within the Office of Management and Budget, the Nuclear Regulatory Commission, and the EPA, among other posts.[109] Others remained within the public-interest orbit as law professors, practicing attorneys, and lifelong advocates of causes such as consumer and environmental protection.[110] Still others had notable careers in publishing and journalism, defining the sensibility of fin de siècle liberalism.[111] Beyond the Center's immediate institutions and alums, its mode of legalistic, technocratic, elite-driven liberal reform would come to define liberalism into the opening decades of the twenty-first century.

Despite these successes, however, the trajectory of American politics since the 1970s suggests that Naderite reform strategies were not particularly effective either as a countervailing force on behalf of the public interest or as a political alternative to genuinely participatory liberalism. Indeed, despite the Raiders' idealism and hard work, initiatory democracy only served to further impoverish liberalism. Politics that valued expertise above experience and viewed mass political participation as obsolete and counterproductive could not withstand the onslaught of Reagan-era conservatism. Its potent blend of corporate-financed populism, evangelical social revanchism, and hawkish patriotism easily bested a vision of politics that imagined social change brought about by ascetic young men wading through agency reports, writing monographs with clever titles, and earnestly lobbying legislators to make technical improvements on behalf of the anesthetized masses.

In the age of "Morning in America," abandoning mass politics and the populist touch in favor of technocratic reform was never likely to succeed. Rather, Nader promoted a form of liberalism that identified genuine social and political problems, raged furiously against them, and then offered up solutions so impractical that many of those outside the elite might be forgiven for wondering if it had much to offer them at all. For those within Nader's targeted demographic of the young and the educated, his vision was generative—inspiring them to spend their time working on pressing issues far removed from their own lives. To solve those problems, however, they would have to find a different strategy than the one he bequeathed them.

CHAPTER 4

"What Is a Populist Approach to This Crisis?"
ACORN's Liberalism and the 1980s Savings and Loan Crisis

MARISA CHAPPELL

The lesson of the 1980's is that the aspirations of the financial services industry can and often do run counter to the needs and interests of working Americans.

GEORGE BUTTS, PHILADELPHIA ACORN, 1991

Let's get citizens more directly involved in both the government and private decisions that affect money and its institutions—so that those decisions are genuinely democratic.

FINANCIAL DEMOCRACY CAMPAIGN
TALKING POINTS, 1989

In March 1989, Mildred Brown testified before the Senate Banking Committee in Washington, DC, about a proposed bailout for the collapsed savings and loan industry. Brown was a national leader of the Association of Community Organizations for Reform Now (ACORN), a multiracial organization of seventy-five thousand working-class families in twenty-six states. She claimed to represent "the viewpoint of average citizens," the "broad, solid foundation of the country and the economy" whose quality of life would be most affected by how Congress handled the crisis.[1] She insisted that Congress fund any bailout with increased taxes on the beneficiaries of deregulation—financial institutions and wealthy investors. She demanded reregulation to return the industry to its historic mission of making homeownership accessible and affordable to first-time homebuyers. And she proposed measures to ensure that the public-private financial system facilitate homeownership for those who had been excluded from that twentieth-century liberal promise—non-white and lower-income people and the majority-minority urban neighborhoods that had been redlined for decades.[2]

A working-class African American woman, Brown was not the typical participant in policy debates about financial regulation. Her presence was a result of nearly two decades of organizing. Her organization, ACORN, began as an experiment by National Welfare Rights Organization (NWRO) staff, who became convinced that welfare recipients were too narrow and stigmatized a constituency upon which to build a progressive movement. In 1970, the NWRO sent Wade Rathke to Little Rock, Arkansas, where he convinced local welfare-rights leaders to organize more broadly. Looking to the histories of organized labor, the Black Freedom Movement, and Saul Alinsky's community organizing model, ACORN's mostly college-educated organizers set out to build a class-based movement akin to the Populist uprising of the late nineteenth century. ACORN used community organizing to engage residents of "low- and moderate-income" neighborhoods in campaigns to tackle dangerous intersections, vacant lots, and other community problems. Members also joined in citywide and eventually national campaigns focused on jobs, housing, and community development. In the 1970s, a decade that one historian has characterized as "the last days of the working class," ACORN was building a new, politically efficacious working class, one that was self-consciously broad-based, multiracial, and committed to building political power.[3] Even as the dominant historical narrative frames the last three decades of the twentieth century as an era of liberal collapse and conservative ascendancy, then, ACORN's history suggests a much richer, more complicated, and more contingent story about American politics and liberalism's fate.

Brown's testimony captures the aspirations and political vision of ACORN's multiracial working-class membership in the 1970s and 1980s—their own version of liberalism. ACORN members had seen mid-century liberal policymakers wield government's redistributive and regulatory powers to fulfill the American Dream for tens of millions of mostly white American families. Federal policies subsidized white access to homeownership in well-resourced neighborhoods and the economic security and generational mobility that came with it. At the same time, these policies shut out people of color and facilitated urban disinvestment that left ACORN members' neighborhoods starved of private capital and public investment. Sometimes, ACORN's professional organizers, most of them college-educated progressives, wished members would reject the liberal regime that had created these racial, geographic, and economic disparities and demand a wholesale transformation of the American political economy. Instead, ACORN members built their political vision from the tools at hand: the promises and policies of New Deal liberalism. They envisioned a fairer and more equitable public-private financial regime in which working-class people like themselves had access to the private capital necessary to become homeowners and the public resources to rebuild their neighborhoods. And they insisted this outcome would only happen when working-class urban residents won their fair share of political power.

ACORN members articulated this vision in the 1970s and 1980s, the very moment that Democratic strategists were redefining the party's brand of liberalism.[4] White support for public policies that broadly distributed wealth and well-being had always been contingent on the exclusion of African Americans and other people of color. As civil rights activists won greater access to the liberal state's promises, white support faltered.[5] Then, in response to the challenges of an increasingly globalized financial system, policymakers began to direct the state's redistributive and regulatory authority in new directions. Some were free-market ideologues who were building new centers of power in organizations such as the Business Roundtable, the Heritage Foundation, and the Republican Party. But many, including Democratic mayors of struggling cities and the so-called New Democrats associated with the Democratic Leadership Council, were liberals who were looking for ways to restore economic growth and deliver on liberalism's promises.[6] And some of these New Democrats joined with congressional Republicans to cut taxes on the wealthy and corporations, reduce safety net programs, and dismantle New Deal regulations, including financial regulations that had delivered on the promise of homeownership and intergenerational mobility to so many white Americans in the postwar decades.[7]

The collapse of the savings and loan, or thrift, industry, in the late 1980s opened space for ACORN members to critique financial deregulation and mobilize public support for their own version of liberalism. But policymakers and financial industry lobbyists hoped to design a bailout behind closed doors. They viewed financial policymaking as the province of industry insiders and highly educated technocrats.[8] ACORN members disagreed. Financial regulations profoundly affected the ability of ordinary Americans to access decent and affordable housing, achieve economic security and upward mobility, and inhabit safe and well-resourced neighborhoods. ACORN members demanded that policymakers seek "democratic input into the big decisions which set the course of the country's financial institutions" and implement "thoroughgoing changes in the relationships among financial institutions, government agencies, and citizens."[9] They championed a grassroots, egalitarian liberalism rooted in their understanding of the New Deal promise: a democratically regulated system of public-private housing finance that would counteract racial, gender, and geographical inequities and make homeownership and economic security a reality for working-class Americans. Their political vision and activism suggest the long reach and continuing relevance of New Deal liberalism in the late twentieth century. Indeed, while ACORN's critics frequently denounced the organization as an advocate of socialism, communism, or other varieties of radical leftist ideology, its members' demands to bolster the redistributive and regulatory state—if not their demand for greater democratic control over that state or their insistence that its benefits be shared by people of color—had for decades represented the very center of American politics and governance.

ACORN's Case for Financial Democracy

The mid-twentieth-century thrift industry played an important role in ACORN members' liberalism. In the 1930s and 1940s, Congress created the Federal Home Loan Bank Board (FHLBB) to charter, regulate, and provide capital to savings and loans through twelve district banks and created the Federal Savings and Loan Insurance Corporation (FSLIC) to insure thrift deposits. Federal chartering and regulation ensured that thrifts served the needs of consumers in their communities by restricting lending to specific geographical areas, limiting interest rates, and requiring that most lending go toward residential mortgages. The system, which premised creditworthiness on whiteness, provided many white Americans access to homeownership, wealth accumulation, and well-resourced neighborhoods. It excluded people of color from those benefits and facilitated private and public disinvestment from their neighborhoods. In the 1970s, ACORN members and other urban reinvestment activists won new federal regulations to increase regulated mortgage lending in working-class urban neighborhoods, including Black neighborhoods. The Home Mortgage Disclosure Act (HMDA) required lenders to disclose the geographic distribution of mortgage loans. The Community Reinvestment Act (CRA) asserted depository institutions' "affirmative obligation" to "meet the credit needs" of their communities, including the "low- and moderate-income neighborhoods" that had long been redlined. ACORN and other activists used this legislation to win millions of dollars of mortgages for working-class homebuyers, most of them people of color.

Just as working-class urban residents gained some access to the New Deal housing finance regime, policymakers began to dismantle it. When high inflation and interest rates in the 1970s created competition for deposits, bipartisan majorities in Congress allowed commercial banks to create higher-interest investment products to attract capital. Then, to enable thrifts to compete with commercial banks, Congress removed interest rate ceilings, increased the size of insured deposits, and authorized thrifts to offer new kinds of loans. The result was catastrophic. By the mid-1980s, savings and loans had transformed "from quiet little neighborhood banks paying three percent interest on large numbers of small accounts to junk-bond dealers where [wealthy] people . . . could get huge loans with almost no paperwork."[10] By 1987, FSLIC, the federal insurance fund, was bankrupt, and the Federal Home Loan Banks began to sell failed thrifts to wealthy investors in secret auctions. These "assisted acquisitions" were a boon to buyers like billionaire investor and Democratic Party donor Ron Perelman. In a typical deal, Perelman paid $161 million for five Texas thrifts. The federal government took on those thrifts' riskiest assets and gave Perelman a $1.2 billion tax break and a host of regulatory concessions, hoping he would successfully manage the thrifts' remaining assets and obligations.[11] Regulators also loosened the rules to hide the extent of the problem. By 1988, more than a third of the country's savings and loans were insolvent. The Bush administration hoped Congress would listen to the wisdom of industry-connected "experts" and quickly bail out the industry. Bush's proposed bailout legislation saddled taxpayers with the bulk of the bailout bill and offered only minor reforms to address the structural causes of the crisis.[12]

ACORN members had other ideas. As the administration wrote its bailout bill, ACORN launched the Financial Democracy Campaign (FDC), a "progressive, citizen-based response to the S&L crisis." Four hundred civic, religious, labor, farm, and consumer organizations soon joined, as did a few high-profile spokespersons such as the Reverend Jesse Jackson and Texas progressive Jim Hightower. But ACORN was always the FDC's prime mover, with strategist Steve Kest serving as co-director and ACORN members providing most of the grassroots action.[13] As Congress debated Bush's bailout, ACORN members held press conferences, testified before congressional committees, and staged protests on regulators, industry lobbyists, and thrift managers. They expressed their vision of the role that private finance should play in a democracy and proposed widely popular proposals for a fair resolution to the crisis.

The FDC had little trouble articulating a populist narrative of the crisis. A typical FDC flyer portrayed thrift managers and investors as obese white men in business suits with party hats, party horns, and confetti. "For the past eight years it's been party time at many of the nation's largest savings and loan associations," the flyer declared. Managers and investors had "wrecked an industry that was formed expressly to provide access to homeownership for ordinary taxpayers—the American Dream."[14] Another FDC publication described "embezzlers, swindlers and greedy incompetents who have robbed our S&Ls," who "gambled on horses, Eurobonds, and luxury high rises . . . rather than make home loans to our families."[15] Bolstered by media coverage of criminal activity by wealthy investors such as billionaire Charles Keating, the FDC's narrative of financial elites profiting at the expense of ordinary savers, homeowners, and taxpayers resonated with a broad swathe of the American public.

But to ACORN members, the crisis was not a result of individual greed; it was fundamentally *political*, created by an undemocratic system of deregulatory policymaking that put the interests of financial elites above those of ordinary Americans. FDC literature highlighted close connections between the thrift industry and the Reagan and Bush administrations. Richard Pratt, who helped engineer thrift deregulation as Reagan's FHLBB chair, was an executive in the investment firm Merrill Lynch, which had been "a leader in marketing risky brokered deposits and junk bonds to S&Ls." While serving as treasury secretary and then White House chief of staff, another Merrill Lynch executive, Don Regan, had blocked measures to outlaw brokered deposits.[16]

ACORN members charged industry lobbyists with using campaign contributions to subvert democracy. Arkansas ACORN chair Rommie Sauls, a middle-aged African American Army veteran and ROTC teacher, denounced "the present campaign finance system where wealthy contributors and big corporate PACs get special favors at the expense of the average taxpayer."[17] At an FDC kickoff event in April 1989, more than two hundred ACORN members rallied at the headquarters of the US League of Savings Institutions, the industry's chief lobbying group and a frequent FDC target.[18] Campaign literature charged that the industry had used massive campaign contributions to win deregulation, lax oversight, and several years of inaction, which allowed the crisis to grow large enough to require a taxpayer bailout. ACORN members also targeted individual members of Congress—both Republicans and Democrats—who took money from the industry and insisted that the League "accept responsibility for causing the savings and loan crisis."[19]

ACORN members ultimately blamed the crisis less on individual politicians than on the destruction of a long-standing social compact between financial institutions and the American people, a compact codified by the New Deal regulatory regime. In an op-ed, Mildred Brown pointed out that financial institutions received "an unparalleled set of public protections" in exchange for providing "safety, soundness, and a healthy economy." Bush's bailout bill, she charged, omitted any "clear definition of [this] public obligation."[20] George Butts of Philadelphia ACORN likewise defined federal deposit insurance as "a social contract between taxpayers and the financial services industry to meet the public needs of the nation's economy."[21] The specific role that thrifts played in the New Deal regime made their public purpose particularly significant. In contrast to commercial banks, thrifts were expected to "help provide affordable housing for all citizens" through low-interest, long-term mortgages to working- and middle-class Americans.[22] Arkansas ACORN member Arthur Cross, a sixty-year-old Black man and Army veteran, claimed that "the only justification for maintaining a separate thrift industry" was if thrifts met this "important public need."[23] After Congress removed many New Deal–era regulations in the early 1980s, thrifts no longer committed the bulk of their lending to residential mortgages, investing instead in a wide range of commercial ventures, many of them high-risk.[24] Homeownership rates in the United States fell for the first time since the 1930s. Boston ACORN member Maude Hurd, a middle-aged Black woman, laid-off clerical worker, and urban homeowner, called that decline the "most visible and shocking legacy of deregulated finance." Homeownership, Hurd insisted, was "the most basic component of the social contract we call the 'American Dream.'" Congress broke that contract when it "backed away from its longstanding role as public steward of the private financial system."[25]

Because thrifts played such an important public role, ACORN members insisted that the public policies that governed them should be subject to broader and more substantive democratic governance. They harkened back to a model in which thrifts were not only highly regulated but also locally rooted, operating in and responsible to a specific localized community of depositors and borrowers. In Arkansas ACORN's "Sunshine, Safety and Service" campaign, members criticized the Federal Home Loan Bank of Dallas for selling insolvent thrifts in a secret auction and demanded the chance to interview prospective buyers to assess their commitment to serving working-class Arkansans. Arthur Cross acknowledged that "tax money is routinely spent without citizen participation" but saw a chance to "set a precedent for a more democratic mechanism of deciding how to allocate public funds." When ACORN members "call policymakers on these matters," he reported, "the people on the other end of the phone have tried to brush us off, to convince us that we couldn't understand these technical matters." But ownership and operation of thrifts shaped "our communities, home mortgages, which will or will not be available to our sons and daughters," and "opportunities for revitalizing our communities." Therefore, he argued, such decisions should be subject to broad democratic discussion. ACORN members thanked Congressman Henry Gonzalez (D-TX) for holding public hearings on the crisis, a "topic over which a small, elite group of people have tried to claim exclusive expertise."[26] They claimed that they, too, were "experts on the housing crisis" who should participate in designing "strategies to re-regulate the industry."[27] In fact, ACORN members envisioned an ongoing role for the public in overseeing the public-private housing finance system. They advocated creation of "powerful, independent and lasting organizations that represent the financial interests of ordinary citizens" playing "a watchdog role vis-à-vis financial regulators."[28]

ACORN members wanted the public to oversee thrifts, but they wanted financial elites to pay for the bailout.[29] The Bush administration, meanwhile, proposed funding the bailout with long-term bonds issued by a new agency, the Resolution Trust Corporation. This way, policymakers could avoid accounting for the cost of the bailout in the federal budget, which was subject to limits imposed by deficit reduction legislation. But bond funding would significantly increase the bailout's overall cost, saddling taxpayers with interest payments that enriched bond brokers and buyers. The FDC charged that bond financing would more than triple the bailout's price tag, costing each taxpayer $1,000.[30] ACORN member Elena Hanggi, a white housewife-turned-activist from Little Rock, Arkansas, proclaimed that Bush's plan would "dig deeply into the pocket of the overalls worn by the farmer in Iowa, the uniform worn by the policewoman in Pennsylvania . . . [and] the pinafore worn by the third grader in Oregon" to "bail out crooks and incompetents."[31] Instead, ACORN proposed that Congress pay for the bailout "on budget," with "new revenues collected from wealth holders and financial firms who reaped windfall benefits from financial deregulation."[32] At an FDC rally outside the Chicago FSLIC office, Illinois ACORN member Ernestine Whiting put the matter bluntly: "We didn't cause the crisis, we certainly didn't benefit from it, and we are not going to bail the rich folks out of this mess."[33]

The FDC articulated populist arguments designed to appeal to white Americans. While African Americans had a long history of making claims as taxpayers, scholar Camille Walsh has argued that in American political culture, the figure of the taxpayer was "always already code for whiteness in the political imagination of those in power."[34] Certainly in the 1980s, taxpayer politics in the United States was firmly associated with conservative politics, which no doubt shaped how audiences responded to the FDC's populist rhetoric.[35] FDC literature portrayed the victimized taxpayer as a deracialized or implicitly white "taxpayer."[36] It helped that Elena Hanggi, one of ACORN's few white leaders, played a prominent role in the campaign. The prominence of a white spokesperson likely contributed to the FDC's success in generating support for its demands.[37] Polls in February and March 1989 showed widespread opposition to a taxpayer-funded bailout, but that opposition reached a new level in May 1989, when television presenter Phil Donahue devoted an entire episode of his popular daytime show to the savings and loan crisis. FHLBB head Lawrence White and Representative Steve Bartlett (R-TX) defended Bush's bailout bill while Hanggi and Representative Joseph Kennedy (D-MA) offered the FDC's critique. An industry publication reported that Hanggi and Kennedy "won the hearts and applause" of the live audience and "clearly carried the day."[38] More than ten thousand viewers called the toll-free phone number that connected them to ACORN's Brooklyn office to volunteer their time and resources to the FDC.[39]

When ACORN members spoke about "the rights of . . . taxpayers," though, they meant working-class people of color as much as middle-class whites. Throughout the post–World War II decades, many white Americans responded to Black and Latinx demands for desegregation and a fair share of public resources by moving to all-white suburbs and withdrawing political and financial support from any public goods or services to which they did not have exclusive access—a complex process often referred to as "white flight."[40] They justified this withdrawal by ignoring or erasing the substantial and disproportionate share of tax dollars contributed by people of color. In the second half of the twentieth century, then, white taxpayer movements, which culminated in the tax revolts of the 1970s, contributed to infrastructural inequality and an overall erosion of public services and the public sector. ACORN members rejected this individualistic and baldly transactional version of taxpayer politics that served to protect white racial and middle-class advantage.

To ACORN members, "taxpayer rights" meant rights to redistributive tax and spending policies that would reduce economic inequality and provide all residents of the United States a decent standard of living. They charged that the cost of Bush's bailout would provide legislators with an excuse to further reduce public services and safety net programs that served working-class people of color and others who had been left out of the liberal promise of economic security. Legislators' decision to burden taxpayers with the bailout, Arthur Cross insisted, was "a decision not to spend money on a thousand other projects," many of which "directly benefit people and relieve human suffering."[41] Mildred Brown warned legislators that the bailout "cannot be funded... by raiding the school lunch program."[42] ACORN members' liberalism demanded a robust and broadly accessible safety net funded by progressive taxation.

In fact, ACORN members saw the crisis as an opportunity to grow the liberal safety net by expanding access to decent and affordable housing, another element of the liberal promise.[43] Never fulfilled, the promise receded in the 1980s, as growing income inequality, high interest rates, and a sharp reduction in federal aid made housing unaffordable to growing numbers of Americans.[44] But the bailout created an opportunity. The federal government (and therefore the American people) acquired the assets of insolvent thrifts and could use them to provide affordable housing and homeownership opportunities. ACORN members proposed turning over acquired residential properties to public and private nonprofit entities to use for affordable rental housing. They also proposed turning proceeds from the sale of nonresidential assets into low-cost financing for affordable-housing developers and first-time homebuyers. They also wanted the Federal Home Loan Banks to offer thrifts low-interest capital specifically for investment in affordable housing.[45] Most ambitiously, ACORN members proposed the creation of a Housing Opportunity Fund to provide below-market financing for affordable housing, capitalized by a small tax on the investment portfolios of all financial intermediaries. "The obligatory participation... by all financial players," Mildred Brown declared, "would firmly establish the principle that institutions which enjoy massive public benefits and protections have an obligation to give back, to promote important public values."[46] ACORN members viewed affordable-housing proposals as "the least [thrifts] can do to atone for their sins"—that is, their history of redlining and disinvestment.[47]

ACORN members also insisted on regulatory mechanisms to ensure that thrifts serve working-class urban residents. ACORN staff imagined far-reaching policy innovations like turning insolvent thrifts into "people's banks"—publicly owned credit unions serving working-class communities. The FDC's eventual demand was more modest: require thrifts to fulfill their existing "affirmative legal obligation to meet the credit needs of low- and moderate-income people in their service area." Anti-redlining activists won that mandate in 1977, in the Community Reinvestment Act. More than a decade later, though, journalists and researchers continued to document rampant geographic and racial redlining. Mildred Brown denounced the "national disgrace that S&Ls on average make half as many loans to black and Hispanic applicants controlling for income, as for white applicants." She concluded that it would be a "national outrage to deduct money every week from the paychecks of Hispanics and blacks to pay to bail out an industry with a shocking record of illegal discrimination."[48] ACORN members demanded that Congress expand the CRA's anti-redlining provisions and strengthen enforcement. ACORN convinced its political allies Joseph Kennedy and Henry Gonzalez to incorporate these demands in a proposed amendment to the bailout bill. They called it the Fair Lending Oversight and Enforcement Act. Among other provisions, it required lenders to identify the race, gender, and income of all mortgage borrowers and applicants. This provision would make it easier to document discrimination and "much more difficult for financial institutions to claim that their poor [lending] performance in certain areas is due to minimal demand for mortgage credit."[49] ACORN's demands thus accepted that private finance would continue to play a central role in the housing regime. But they insisted that the federal government use its redistributive and regulatory authority to make that system fairer to ordinary taxpayers and working-class people. And by revealing the devastating consequences of financial deregulation, the savings and loan crisis gave ACORN's vision broad appeal.

Wins and Losses for ACORN's Liberalism

ACORN succeeded in transforming the politics of the savings and loan crisis. The administration and Congress hoped to insulate financial policymaking from public debate. In doing so, they presented a massive taxpayer subsidy to wealthy investors and financial industry elites as the only logical response to the crisis, obscuring significant political questions about the role of finance in a democratic society. ACORN members' activism pierced through their technocratic façade and sparked public debate on these very questions. In late May 1989, Steve Kest reported that "tapes of the *Donahue Show* [on the S&L crisis] are being shown all over the Hill, apparently to great effect." Insiders reported that legislators had begun to "fear the political consequences of a vote for the bailout" and were cooling on Bush's bill.[50] Representative Chuck Schumer (D-NY) reported that congressional discussions of the bailout were affected by "a strong populist wind sweeping across the House."[51]

The House incorporated all three FDC demands—"on budget" financing, affordable-housing provisions, and strengthened anti-redlining measures—into the House bill. Widespread taxpayer outrage convinced a majority of Democrats to support an amendment, sponsored by FDC supporters Joseph Kennedy and Bruce Morrison (D-CT), to pay for the bailout "on budget." Fewer Democrats supported ACORN's antiredlining and affordable-housing provisions. Democratic policymakers' commitment to progressive redistributive and regulatory measures had never matched the liberalism of ACORN members; it had always been partial and racialized. ACORN overcame resistance by framing the matter as a "civil rights" issue. When the Banking Committee rejected the Fair Lending Oversight and Enforcement Act, ACORN mobilized allies in "DC-based housing and civil rights organizations" and the Reverend Jesse Jackson to contact House liberals, especially members of the Black and Hispanic Caucuses, and urge them to "actively participate in the debate and speak out on these measures." The strategy worked. Steve Kest reported that "turning CRA/HMDA into a civil rights issue helped force the ... Democratic leadership to impose some party discipline on their troops."[52] Of course, mandating a "civil right to borrow," as Jesse Jackson put it at an FDC rally, could easily benefit lenders at the expense of working-class people.[53] That may be why the tactic also won support from some Republicans. Jim Leach (R-IA) reported that the anti-redlining provisions "all of a sudden became a vote that dealt with civil rights and decency," which "put many members on notice." Forty-one House Republicans voted for the measure.[54] In the Democratic Party's evolving liberalism, the moral weight of "civil rights" remained strong but limited to a kind of equal-opportunity capitalism rather than to more robust visions of economic justice so central to the Black Freedom Movement. Here, Democratic legislators championed a right to go into debt rather than the right to decent and affordable housing. The commitment to using public policy to counter the economic and political power of private capital, a central tenet of ACORN's liberalism, was a harder sell.

The Senate's version of the bill illustrates even more starkly the distance between ACORN members' liberalism and the liberalism of the Democratic Party.[55] Despite a Democratic majority, the Senate agreed to Bush's taxpayer-funded financing and rejected the FDC's affordable-housing and anti-redlining provisions. Some Democratic senators were probably sympathetic to Phil Gramm (R-TX)'s argument, which framed ACORN's demands to save taxpayer dollars as a *threat* to those very taxpayers. Gramm, a former Democrat, insisted that financing the bailout "on budget," which everyone admitted would save taxpayers billions of dollars, was a ruse to win "a major tax increase." Gramm was onto something, of course. The Kennedy-Morrison amendment was "widely understood on the Hill to be a vehicle for forcing a tax surcharge on the wealthy to pay for the bailout."[56] In other words, advocates of "on budget" financing *did* want to increase taxes, but not on the ordinary taxpayers whose interests Gramm claimed to champion. Gramm portrayed the FDC's affordable-housing measures as a "theft of taxpayer assets," since they would give "repossessed housing owned by broke S&Ls" to affordable-housing developers at "flea-market prices" rather than to the highest bidder. In Gramm's telling, the beneficiaries were not working-class families desperate for decent and affordable housing but "a privileged class of special housing interest groups" who would create "government-subsidized housing" for their own profit. Gramm thus countered ACORN members' taxpayer populism with a conservative white taxpayer populism. He implied that the interests of urban, working-class families and communities of color were at odds with the interests of "taxpayers" and the "general public."[57] This framing reflected a white suburban politics that shaped the views of many Democratic policymakers. It also hid the true beneficiaries of a debt-funded bailout, who would be financial elites.[58]

In one sense, the final bill, the Financial Institutions Reform, Recovery, and Enforcement Act of 1989 (FIRREA), was a clear victory for ACORN and the FDC. It strengthened the HMDA and the CRA. It gave public agencies, nonprofit developers, and low- and moderate-income people first crack at purchasing residential assets acquired from failed thrifts at below-market prices. These were impressive wins. They depended on Democratic policymakers, such as Henry Gonzalez and Joseph Kennedy, who shared ACORN members' working-class liberalism. Like ACORN members, they believed that financial institutions chartered, subsidized, and insured by the government had an obligation to serve the public interest; that the country's public-private system of housing finance should be mobilized to expand affordable housing and facilitate homeownership for people who had been disadvantaged in the New Deal regime; and that the federal government should use its redistributive and regulatory authority to reduce economic and racial inequality. Another, broader group of Democratic policymakers could be persuaded to support measures designed to enact those principles, particularly when they were framed as protecting ordinary taxpayers or promoting civil rights.

But if ACORN members won these battles, they lost the larger war over financial deregulation and progressive funding. Despite the broad appeal of their political vision, ACORN members were simply outgunned by the vast financial and political power of the financial industry. The FIRREA funded the bailout by creating a semipublic entity, the Resolution Trust Corporation, to issue thirty-year bonds, which it then turned over to the federal government. This spending could be accounted for "off budget," sparing Congress the headache of either raising taxes or making an exception to the spending limits mandated by deficit reduction legislation. ACORN and the FDC denounced this funding mechanism. Referring to conservative operative Lee Atwater, an FDC summary bestowed "The Atwater Trophy signifying Honorary Membership in the RNC" on congressional Democrats, who "despite constituent pressure, polls, common sense, and common decency" had "worked overtime" to preserve Bush's bill.[59] In 1990 and 1991, as the Bush administration returned to Congress to request additional bailout funds, ACORN members and FDC allies continued to insist that Congress reregulate the industry and shift the cost of the bailout to wealthy investors and financial corporations. Indeed, in 1991, despite opposition from House Speaker Tom Foley (D-WA), ACORN's proposal for "a fair pay-as-you-go" funding mechanism came within twenty-five votes of passing in the House. Steve Kest was elated. "We took an issue that wasn't even on the Congressional agenda, one that was at best the extremely marginalized concern of some cranks like Joe Kennedy," he told supporters, and "pushed it into the mainstream of public debate."[60]

In the end, the American public paid $130 billion for the bailout.[61] Most of the cost was borne by working- and middle-class people, who contributed a disproportionate share of the country's tax burden. Meanwhile, Democratic policymakers continued to support financial deregulation, which became a signature goal and achievement of the Clinton administration. Rather than expand access to safe, affordable mortgage credit to working-class people of color, the new regime of housing finance enabled exploitive lending practices that enriched investors, bankrupted working-class families, destroyed working-class neighborhoods, and, in 2007, catalyzed the deepest and most protracted economic recession since the 1930s. It wasn't what ACORN members imagined when they sought inclusion. If, as ACORN members insisted, "a money system ... expresses the public values of a democratic society," then by the turn of the century, the values of the United States, and of the Democratic Party, diverged dramatically from ACORN members' version of liberalism.[62]

CHAPTER 5

Survival Pending Corporate Sponsorship

The "Crisis" of the Black Family, Black State Skepticism, and the Evolution of Black Liberalism in the Post–Civil Rights Era

DANIELLE WIGGINS

Late in the summer of 1986, thousands of black families gathered on the National Mall to celebrate the "heritage, tradition, and values" of "the black family." The National Black Family Reunion celebration was the brainchild of National Council of Negro Women (NCNW) chair Dorothy Height. She was inspired to organize the event after watching a troubling CBS special entitled "The Vanishing Black Family" in January 1986. Hosted by former Johnson administration press secretary Bill Moyers, the special followed several black female-headed families whose purported deviance was driving the growth of the urban "underclass."[1] It echoed a much longer and fraught discourse surrounding the pathological black family and the problems it supposedly wrought. Although civil rights leaders had been privately discussing the purported crisis for much of the 1980s, they were dismayed that the CBS special brought to national attention, once again, the so-called crisis of the black family. According to Height, the special "accelerated the amount of negativity about the black family."[2] She decided that in celebration of the NCNW's fiftieth anniversary, the organization would host a "positive demonstration, something that would bring people out to act on their own behalf."[3] The reunion would not only showcase the strengths of the black family but demonstrate black Americans' willingness to help themselves at a moment—the height of Reagan's presidency—when doing so increasingly appeared to be the only option.

But the National Black Family Reunion would not be an entirely self-driven or self-funded affair. The event was organized by Height and "national family values heroes" Bill and Camille Cosby but sponsored by Procter and Gamble. As the number of family reunions grew into regional variations around the country over the next several years, so too did the number of corporate partners. These corporate-sponsored black family reunions were illustrative of a turn to the private realm—both to the private sphere of the family and home and to the private sector—in black politics in the post–civil rights era. And this turn was not just coming from the few "lonely" black conservatives. Contemporary commentators noted the growing number of calls for self-help and responsibility coming from ostensibly liberal black elected officials and leaders of civil rights organizations. The *Wall Street Journal*, for example, celebrated the revival of self-help discourses that emanated not from "Thomas Sowell, Glenn Loury or another of that small but increasingly influential band of conservative black intellectuals." Rather, they came from people like Roger Wilkins, nephew of former National Association for the Advancement of Colored People (NAACP) head Roy Wilkins, who the *Journal* described as "an eloquent spokesman for the liberals who have dominated black civil rights organizations and traditionally stressed government intervention, not self-help, as the key to black progress."[4] Michael Lomax, an ambitious county commissioner from Atlanta, surmised that black Americans had a "new" attitude, "a stronger attitude that in part our solutions are found in a new perspective on ourselves: a sense of personal responsibility and empowerment."[5] This new attitude, embodied most potently by a new generation of post–civil rights black leaders, would enable black Americans to thrive in a political and economic landscape of austerity that offered fewer federal promises of security. The growing black political class was not alone in embracing the funds and tools of the private sector. They were in alignment with the new generation of professional-class liberals who sought to trade the bureaucracy of New Deal and Cold War–era liberalism for more decentralized, flexible, and cost-effective governing solutions.

Yet this "new" approach embraced by the post–civil rights black political class was not very new at all. More accurately, their shift toward the private sector signaled a return to a very old strategy forged for a century before Reagan came to office. Black Americans had, of course, long embraced private solutions in response to the organized public abandonment of their communities. In the ruins of Reconstruction, black communities turned inward, relying on black institutions. Through the politics of racial uplift, black reformers also devolved responsibility to black families and individuals in an effort not only to counter racist stereotypes and prove their worthiness for citizenship but also to fortify black communities against white supremacist violence. Black nationalist organizations such as Marcus Garvey's Universal Negro Improvement Association and the Nation of Islam also engaged in the politics of racial uplift in their nation-building, seeking to build up independent black economic, social, and cultural institutions with self-determination rather than eventual integration as the driving goal.

Even in the mid-twentieth century, when the federal government began taking more active measures to include black Americans in the American political and economic order, black activists continued to fortify black institutions. They often did so with the support of the white private sector. Even black leftist organizations sometimes funded their initiatives with white private money, albeit with more trepidation. The Black Panther Party initially funded their survival programs with support from "White philanthropists, humanitarians, and the heirs to the corporate monopolies" to fund the programs that ensured black "survival pending revolution," as Black Panther Party co-founder Huey P. Newton described the purpose and initial funding of their many survival programs.[6] While the Panthers would later eschew the support of white capitalists, other radical activists and their counterparts in liberal organizations accepted white corporate and nonprofit support in addition to federal funding.[7]

Given this tradition, it is unsurprising, then, that liberal black political and civic leaders would once again call for a return to private means of withstanding the evisceration of the welfare state and concomitant intensification of the carceral state in the 1980s. Their approach represented not quite an embrace of conservatism, as commentators suggested at the time, nor simply the adoption of novel neoliberal strategies, as scholars have suggested since.[8] Instead, these calls for self-help and corporate partnership reflected the resurgence of foundational strategies in the black liberal tradition. Black liberals understood that although the poor law tradition of social welfare—in which public assistance was offered to only the neediest and only when their families could not provide support—may have been supplanted by a welfare state (however inadequate) for white Americans, it didn't end for black Americans with the New Deal or even the Great Society.[9] Austerity, for black folks, was a familiar condition.[10] In the 1980s, black liberals' strategies for surviving austerity happened to dovetail with the conservative talking points and the neoliberal solutions advanced by both Republicans and the New Democrats.

Placing corporate-sponsored family reunions within the black liberal tradition also reveals a long-standing tension within black liberalism between an interventionist imperative and an impulse characterized by state skepticism. Black liberals have long demanded a more robust and interventionist state, insisting upon the expansion of state power to protect black Americans from racial violence, robust antidiscrimination laws, and the protection of voting and civil rights. With the advent of the New Deal and the gradual incorporation of black Americans into the Democratic Party, black liberals pushed at the bounds of New Deal liberalism to demand protection, security, and inclusion into the liberal democratic order. By the 1960s, the interventionist imperative was advanced by both black political brokers and more radical grassroots activists who organized for full employment, welfare rights, and a redistributionist Freedom Budget. As those power brokers moved from protest to politics, they carried these demands to the new halls of power.

Yet, alongside this interventionist imperative existed a state skeptic impulse that reflected a necessary recognition of the limits of the liberal state, a pragmatic awareness of the harms of its abandonment, its overt forms of violence, and its interventions to uphold Jim Crow capitalism. The black liberals who headed local civic organizations administered New Deal and Great Society programs and, eventually, entered elected office clearly weren't anti-statist. But they were rightfully skeptical of the state. Black state skepticism differed from the anti-statist impulse of liberalism writ large. Their distrust of the state functioned as a mechanism of community survival rather than as a means to protect individual liberty. It reflected not the imagined fear of an overreaching, totalitarian state but the reality of the exclusion, neglect, and violence of white supremacy. Black liberals believed state power needed to be mobilized to address exclusion and inequality. Yet, they recognized that it could rarely be trusted or relied upon.

Black liberals were not alone in their reservations about the American state and critiques of its interventions (and noninterventions) into black communities. Since the end of Reconstruction, black activists calling themselves conservatives, progressives, nationalists, and radicals sought to develop black communities' capacity for self-reliance through various strategies ranging from investing in black enterprises and black property ownership to creating cooperatives and community survival programs.[11] Yet, black liberals' state skepticism differed from those on the left and right of the black political spectrum. Unlike black nationalists and leftists, black liberals were liberals, meaning they did not fundamentally reject the American liberal state and its principles. Instead, they demanded equal opportunity, nondiscrimination, and full inclusion into America's liberal institutions, such as the democratic process and market capitalism. Furthermore, unlike anti-statist black conservatives and neoconservatives, who were often critical of social-welfare programs and affirmative action, black liberals believed that a strong central state was necessary to guarantee inclusion, equality, and economic security. And unlike those to the left and right, they felt the state had the potential to empower black communities and families rather than weaken them. Black liberals adopted what could be described as a *both-and* perspective, believing both state intervention and black private action were necessary for black collective advancement.

Since emancipation, this *both-and* perspective—grounded in a recognition of the insufficiency of the private sector alone and the unreliability of state intervention—guided black liberal politics for much of the twentieth century: organizing for a federal job guarantee, for instance, existed alongside collaborations with private foundations like the Ford Foundation, both understood as necessary in the struggle for economic justice and inclusion. But the 1980s represented "a turn" in black American history, as Elizabeth Hinton has suggested.[12] This period was marked by a cruel irony: the ascension of a new black political class to public office at the very moment when the notion of "a public" was being undermined by the emergent neoliberalism of both political parties. In the "Black 1980s," as scholars are beginning to call it, black liberals were growing increasingly pessimistic about the capacity of an increasingly parsimonious and reactionary federal state to address racial inequality. Ironically, this skepticism was growing among many of those elected to be representatives of the state. In the Black 1980s, black liberals once again prioritized private-sector solutions and questioned the feasibility of more expansive interventionist public-sector strategies. The *both-and* impulse that had long underscored black liberal strategy was supplanted by a *yes-but* perspective in which liberals still recognized that, yes, obviously, massive state action was necessary to address deepening racial inequality but doubted the state's ability to do so.

Black liberals' *yes-but* approach was grounded not only in the black liberal tradition of state skepticism but also in their recognition of the tensions within post-1960s liberalism, particularly the incongruity between professional-class liberals' stated ideals of equal opportunity, social justice, and multicultural pluralism and their actual modes of governance, which historically were piecemeal, contingent, and constrained by federalism. In other words, the *yes-but* perspective reflected how black liberals, particularly those in positions of political power, mediated what the editors of the volume call "the growing distance between liberals' rhetorical and social aspirations and their actual existing approaches to governance and democracy."[13] *Yes-but* represented both a rhetorical move and a governing strategy that legitimated a narrowed black political agenda and obscured black liberal elites' role in sustaining the distance between expectation and reality. Black liberals' response to the perennial "crisis" of the black family in the post–civil rights era exemplified their *yes-but* approach. It underscored civil rights organizations' corporate-sponsored family reunions and, eventually, the "responsible fatherhood" efforts of Barack Obama. Obama's corporatist and communitarian approach to the problem of the black family sprouted where black liberals' pragmatic turn to black institutions and corporate support in the absence of a strong public sector converged with white liberals' enthusiastic embrace of the private sector in governance—the crossroads of two distinctly liberal paths to neoliberalism.

The Scope of Black Liberalism in the Modern Black Political Age

To say that African Americans have had a fraught relationship with the state would be an understatement. The very same federal state whose power emancipated the enslaved, promised equal protection and due process, granted black men the franchise, and expanded its capacity to provide for the social welfare of the emancipated through the Freedman's Bureau, withdrew its protections in the late nineteenth century. During what has been called the "nadir of American race relations," African American civic participation was hemmed in by the emergent Jim Crow racial order, buttressed by state and local governments working in concert to reconfigure white supremacy in light of emancipation.[14]

In light of their marginalization within the broader civil society, black Americans in the late nineteenth century turned inward "in their efforts to preserve themselves."[15] In the last decades of the nineteenth century and the first decades of the twentieth, black Americans created a robust civil society behind the veil.[16] They established churches, mutual-aid societies, women's clubs and fraternal orders, schools, banks and insurance companies, and other institutions through which the emergent black elite coalesced as a class of race managers. As "the leaders of the race," they pursued the collective survival and advancement of the race on behalf of black people as a whole. Black Americans' ability to make a way out of no way and to survive despite the exploitations and brutalities of the period served as a source of pride.

Yet not all self-help was entirely community-funded. Though much of their development was funded through the pooling of resources, community fundraising, and donated time, black institutions such as schools and hospitals also received support from missionary societies and corporate philanthropic organizations such as the Carnegie Corporation, the Rockefeller Foundation, the Rosenwald Fund, and the Peabody Fund among others.[17] Thus, from the beginnings of the modern black political age, "self-help" was often bolstered by (usually) white corporate and philanthropic support.

Foundation support was not without its constraints, however. While foundations provided much-needed resources for black institutions when federal and state governments refused, donations often limited black institutions' autonomy and self-determination. As scholars have shown, funders such as the Peabody Fund, the Carnegie Foundation, and the Phelps Stokes Fund, for example, imposed a narrow vision of black education on its recipients by prioritizing institutions that instructed in the "Tuskegee Model" of agricultural and industrial education over liberal arts institutions. The Tuskegee Model, touted widely by the late nineteenth century's foremost black spokesman, Booker T. Washington, "[emphasized] the training of black southerners for jobs that would not challenge white supremacy and anti-Black subordination in the region and would thus favor the economic and political interests of white people."[18] Even after corporate philanthropy supplanted foundation funding after the 1960s, white funders continued to have a hand in shaping black schools' priorities.[19]

Black schools were not the only institutions disciplined by white donor control. Civil rights organizations also found their agendas informed by white philanthropic organizations. Megan Ming Francis has shown how the Garland Fund pushed the NAACP, who were financially struggling in the 1920s, to sideline their fight against racial violence and instead prioritize a legal battle against segregated education. Francis describes the Garland Fund's efforts as movement capture, or "the process by which private funders leverage their financial resources to apply pressure and influence the decision-making process of civil rights organizations."[20] While black activists turned to corporations out of a pragmatic skepticism of the state, they also had to remain suspicious of foundations that often sought to use their donations to maintain the white-supremacist social order.

Given the limits of relying on the private sector, whether white foundations or impoverished black communities, black liberal activists continued to advance a both-and approach, a strategy enhanced by shifts in federal governance. By the late 1930s, the New Deal had transformed how black liberals conceived of state capacity and expanded their visions of what the federal government could do for black Americans. Of course, New Deal legislation did not fundamentally transform the Jim Crow racial order; many New Deal programs deepened the color line and further codified white supremacy.[21] Nonetheless, its expansiveness and potential emboldened black liberals throughout the mid-century to continue to push at the limits of federal state power through each branch of government. The civil rights movement reflected this new credence in the federal power to override state and local segregation laws and not only to include but expand the rights and privileges of full citizenship. Yet, the black private sector remained robust at the height of mid-century liberalism. The continued work of black civic organizations, NAACP and National Urban League (NUL) chapters, church groups, women's clubs, neighborhood groups, student organizations, and political associations carried out the mass movement for civil rights. They often worked with the support of white nonprofits, foundations, local businesses, and corporations.[22]

Black liberals' struggle against poverty perhaps represented the height of their credence in the capacity of the federal government and the power of liberal institutions. Anti-poverty activists sought to mobilize federal power to provide decent housing, better schools, decent medical care, expanded welfare benefits, and, perhaps most centrally, more jobs for poor people. In endorsing the Freedom Budget in 1965, for example, black liberals such as Roy Wilkins of the NAACP, Vernon Jordan and Whitney Young of the NUL, and Dorothy Height of the NCNW joined forces with leftist allies to call for "full and fair employment for all." The document's authors Bayard Rustin and A. Philip Randolph argued, "We can all recognize that the major cause of poverty could be eliminated, if enough decently paying jobs were available for everyone willing and able to work."[23] By the 1970s, even after the federal government had abandoned the most ambitious goals of the War on Poverty, black liberals in civil rights organizations, anti-poverty groups, and newly elected positions in the halls of Congress sustained the spirit of the 1960s by organizing for a federal job guarantee that would not only address intransigent poverty but also one of poverty's most troubling symbols: the broken black family.

The Perpetual Problem of the Black Family

In 1965, the "problem" of the broken black family became a topic of national concern and federal policy following the leak of the Moynihan Report, or "The Negro Family: A Case for National Action," a controversial report by then–assistant secretary of labor Daniel Patrick Moynihan that rooted black poverty in black Americans' purportedly pathological matriarchal family structures. But well before the Moynihan Report, the black family had been a site of contestation in the black public sphere.[24] Black thinkers across the political spectrum held different ideas about the black family and the extent and nature of its purported brokenness. From the Marcus Garvey movement in the 1910s and 1920s to the Nation of Islam in the 1950s and beyond, black nationalists believed that, like the black nation, the family needed to be redeemed by strengthening the nuclear family unit, empowering the black patriarch, and protecting but often subordinating the black mother.[25] In the 1960s, black-power activists also decried the supposedly emasculated black patriarch and argued that the reassertion of black manhood was essential in the revolutionary struggle for self-determination.[26] For the most part, black nationalists sought to redeem the black man and the black nation broadly through self-help and black economic development rather than through state support, which they, like black conservatives, believed was a source of the black family's brokenness to begin with.

Black liberals also understood the "problem" of the black family to be grounded in the absence of heteronormativity that thwarted black men and women from the roles of breadwinner and household manager respectively, due to the history of slavery and the present realities of discrimination and poverty. Black liberals had long treated the black family as a site to be reformed through the guidance of elite experts. During the Progressive Era, black clubwomen worked to improve black home life by helping working-class and poor black folks learn their proper gender roles in the household.[27] They entered poor homes to model proper home economics and appropriate marriage dynamics and sometimes surveilled their households, keeping tabs on their transgressions. Their somewhat invasive practices of racial uplift were motivated by their recognition of the violence of state intervention. Indeed, the state did intervene in black home life through morals policing, arresting and incarcerating black men, women, and children in state penitentiaries, prison farms, and group homes.[28] State intervention into black family life had proven violent and disruptive; thus, black reformers turned toward the private realm to address the family's inadequacies. Black elites sought to encourage two-parent families, fortified to withstand both the neglect and violent intrusion of the state.[29]

Nonetheless, as American liberalism evolved, black liberal elites' prescriptions for black family stability also changed. Though they still understood the black family as a problem to be explained and fixed, midcentury black sociologists such as E. Franklin Frazier and Kenneth Clark advanced different methods for repairing it. Unlike their Progressive Era predecessors, the mid-century social scientists and activists did not prioritize self-help and elite-led family-strengthening initiatives as primary solutions. But like the reformers who preceded them, they also focused on gender, framing family instability as a crisis of black matriarchy and male joblessness.[30] Reflecting black liberals' expanded belief in the capacity of a federal state transformed by the New Deal, social scientists and the activists who cited their work in their campaigns called for federal programs to address black men's unemployment.

Black liberals' fight for full employment in the 1960s and 1970s reflected a widespread faith in the state's capacity to fortify black families against the vagaries of the market. Yet, the political-economic ground upon which black liberals waged their battle was shifting. Ironically, just as black Americans were entering the very same federal apparatus whose power they hoped to wield, a recession, inflation, and the crisis of Keynesian liberalism that the two provoked, as well as the growing reactionary conservative movement, altered the logics by which the state operated, shifting governing priorities and capacities across all levels.[31]

These shifts were revealed starkly in the campaign for full employment, which became increasingly urgent as black unemployment rates escalated during the recession. By the mid-1970s, black liberals in elected positions and civil rights organizations had organized to pass the Humphrey-Hawkins Full Employment Act. The bill, first proposed by former vice president and then-senator Hubert Humphrey and Congressional Black Caucus member Augustus Hawkins in 1974, sought to instate a federal job guarantee, create a job guarantee office and a Standby Job Corps, and change the name of the US Employment Service to the US Full Employment Service.[32] The bill became one of the central issues in the 1976 Democratic primaries, and Democratic nominee Jimmy Carter expressed tepid support. Nonetheless, once Carter won the nomination, the bill was revised to reflect Carter's priorities: curbing inflation and balancing the budget. The bill he eventually signed in 1978 as president was significantly weaker, outlining goals for unemployment but not a federal job guarantee. By 1980, Carter had largely abandoned the goal of full employment.[33] The election of Ronald Reagan later that year signaled the end of the federal government's commitment to full employment along with the death of mid-century liberalism.

Ultimately, the federal government's priorities shifted from addressing the sources of poverty through public assistance and employment programs toward containing poverty's ramifications through policing and incarceration. These shifts shook black liberals' faith in the willingness and capacity of federal power to address the deepening crises of poverty and inequality. On the local level, black political representation increasingly appeared to be a hollow prize to the majority of black residents, as capital flight, federal cuts to urban programs, and white hostility to black leadership hamstrung black elected officials' ability to redistribute power and resources to their black constituencies.[34] Re-emergent state skepticism was reflected in the pessimistic tone that marked much black liberal discourse in the 1980s. In 1982, NUL executive director John

E. Jacobs portended, "The 1980s are a potentially disastrous decade for blacks." Describing the shifting political-economic landscape of the period, he contended, "With the rug of federal programs and national sympathy pulled out from under us, black organizations and individuals will have to directly confront the internal problems of the community to a greater degree than in the past."[35] Yet, Jacobs was quick to recognize the limits of privatism, arguing, "Let us not fool ourselves that voluntary activity can solve our problems or even significantly reduce them . . . Only strong federal and private sector actions can overcome society's heritage of black disadvantage." The task for black liberals in the 1980s, then, would be to maintain the *both-and* approach, to balance making demands of an increasingly stingy and punishing state with strengthening the black private realm. Black liberals' response to increasing black family instability would reveal the difficulty of maintaining this balance.

The "Crisis of the Black Family" and the (Re)Turn Inward in the 1980s

As the impact of recession, inflation, rising unemployment, and federal spending cuts became visible in black communities around the country in the late 1970s, concerns about the state of the black family began to circulate once again. After the publication of the Moynihan Report, black liberals closed ranks to defend the black family. Black social scientists such as Andrew Billingsley and Joyce Ladner and cultural commentators in the pages of black periodicals spent much of the decade following the report's release highlighting the resiliency of the black family, particularly women-headed households.[36]

But perhaps more than the Moynihan Report, black feminists shifted the discourse on the black family. Theorists such as Frances Beale, Toni Cade Bambara, and Audre Lorde challenged the heteronormative metrics by which both liberals and black nationalists measured the state of the black family. They challenged the notion of pathological matriarchy and the assumption that women-headed households were inherently inferior. Radical black feminists acknowledged the "double jeopardy" of black women, oppressed by their race and gender and thus doubly exploited in the capitalist economy.[37] So while they agreed with liberals that single mothers were vulnerable to poverty, black feminists argued that the solution was not more investment in men's employment but more support for black women whether they worked or not. Thus, as liberal and leftist black activists were fighting for full employment, feminist activists in the welfare rights movement struggled for increased benefits for recipients of Aid to Families with Dependent Children, expanded eligibility for entitlements, a guaranteed income, and an end to paternalistic and invasive rules and requirements for assistance.[38] The welfare rights movement gained support from black activists across the political spectrum, who embraced the expansive vision of the rights of citizenship the movement's leaders imagined.

Yet, in the late 1970s, as the movements for both full employment and welfare rights encountered setbacks, concern mounted once again about the "sheer survivability of the black family in the face of so many odds."[39] As Andrew Billingsley surmised in 1977, "It (the black family) is in deep trouble precisely because the nation itself is in deep trouble."[40] Billingsley's concern reflected broader concerns about the American family in the 1970s, whose nuclear ideal was destabilized by declining wages, increasing numbers of mothers in the workforce, and rising divorce rates.[41] But if shifting political-economic conditions and changing social mores shook the foundation of the white family, these changes seemingly upended the already fragile black family. By the early 1980s, the so-called crisis of the black family, often defined by rising numbers of single-female-headed households, unemployed fathers, and teenage pregnancies, had the potential to, as NAACP director Benjamin Hooks put it, "negate the gains we have won over the years."[42] And, the interventionist solutions that black liberals had embraced in the 1960s seemed less feasible in the era of inflation and spending cuts.

As the crisis seemingly worsened, black liberal political and civic leaders began to organize among each other to address the problem. In May 1984, the NUL and the NAACP convened a joint "Summit on the Black Family" at Fisk University in Nashville. Over 175 representatives from black civil rights and political organizations spent a weekend having "full and frank discussions" in which they "examine[d] the various crises facing black families, and most important, ... map[ped] strategies to support and strengthen families."[43] The conference proceedings reflected the pragmatic skepticism of the state's will to address the needs of the black poor that had undergirded black liberal organizing in the age of Reagan. In his opening statement, the NUL's John Jacobs acknowledged that even at their most dysfunctional, black families' struggles were a "response to a society that practices discrimination and inflicts poverty on masses of black people through denial of opportunity and the refusal to institute even the most basic programs that foster independence and opportunity."[44] The conference proceeded from the assumption that massive federal intervention was necessary.

Yet, there was often a "but," a "while," or another contrasting conjunction in their framing; black liberals would consistently recognize the need for state power but would also demand black Americans to look inward and take responsibility for addressing the problem. Jacobs, for instance, contended, "The problems of the black family relate to black problems in jobs, in housing, in health care, in education and a host of other fields. *But at the same time,* we have to recognize that some of our problems may be self-inflicted, that we may have allowed our just anger at what America has done to obscure our own need for self-discipline and strengthened community values" [emphasis added]. Ultimately, Jacobs conceded, "It's up to us. Washington couldn't care less about black people and black families."[45]

The workshops reflected the tension at the heart of black liberalism. In each session, participants addressed the extent of the issue and its structural and "cultural" roots before brainstorming potential solutions. The recommendations were divided into three categories of responsibility: public policy, the private sector, and black organizations and institutions. In the jobs and economic security session, the participants discussed rising unemployment exacerbated by the decline of manufacturing. But they also sought to address the questions: "How do you get individuals, families, and institutions within the black community to stop complaining about external forces and take greater control of their destiny? In short, how do you 'manage' racism?"[46] In many of the sessions, the recommendations reflected the impulse of state skepticism among black liberals with many more solutions that helped black communities "manage racism" and state neglect than solutions that sought to address the "external forces." Public policy recommendations included demanding that the Reagan administration enforce the Humphrey-Hawkins Act, support vocational training, create a national industrial policy, and expand Aid to Families with Dependent Children. However, these recommendations were often vague and included few details about how black Americans could mobilize once again to organize for full employment or welfare reform or the role those present would play in coordinating these movements.

In contrast to these relatively limited public-sector solutions, the list of recommendations for the private sector and black institutions was more robust and detailed. These included the creation of a black business network, support for black-owned businesses, and research into venture capital. In the workshop on single families, no federal public policy recommendations were explicitly proposed. Instead, the recommendations for black institutions included parental education focused on "teaching children values and values clarification," improved sex education, more youth programs in churches, better sex education, and a "return to and/or development recognized ceremonial 'rites of passage' designed to give the young a sense of development, worth, richness, and anticipation," among other recommendations.[47] Though conference participants may have tried to balance interventionist approaches that addressed the structural foundations of the crisis of the black families with those that managed their purported cultural roots through privatism, the solutions that prioritized self-help quite literally overwhelmed those that involved federal action.

The "Black Leadership Family Plan for the Unity, Survival, and Progress of Black People" released the following year extended this emphasis on self-help, buttressed by private-sector support. The plan was created by members of the Congressional Black Caucus, heads of civil rights organizations, and other prominent black figures who christened themselves the "Black Leadership Family." The Family's call for participation in a planning session in 1985 reflected black liberals' attempt to balance calls for federal responsibility with calls for black community responsibility. Black Leader Family head Walter Fauntroy wrote, "While we reject the notion that government should be absolved of its responsibility to ensure the equitable allocation of our national resources, we also reject the notion that it is the sole responsibility of the government. We reject the idea that black people cannot or will not assume responsibility for their own survival and progress. In fact, we believe that we must accept a substantial responsibility for our survival and progress."[48] Again, evoking the contrasting "while," he continued, "While acknowledging that Black people have been denied full and unfettered access to the nation's resources; and acknowledging that we continue to suffer the dehumanizing effects of vestigial discrimination, we submit that our frequent misdirection of those resources and institutions which we do control has also contributed to our plight."[49]

The Family Plan thus called for black Americans to re-embrace the inward-facing community development strategies of the first nadir. It sketched a plan to redirect internal resources and coordinate voluntarism among black institutions. It outlined a role for nearly every segment of the black community, from churches and civil rights organizations to elected officials, entertainers and athletes, law enforcement, youth, and senior citizens. Liberal social scientists, most prominent among them sociologist William Julius Wilson, argued that the capital flight left the inner-city underclass without work just as the exodus of stable middle- and working-class families left the underclass without appropriate role models and systems of community surveillance. In the absence of the stabilizing power of employment and, as significantly, the watchful guidance of community leaders who, Wilson described, "help keep alive the perception that education is meaningful, that steady employment is a viable alternative to welfare, and that family stability is the norm, not the exception," aberrant behavior and dysfunctional structures proliferated unchecked.[50] Thus, the plan encouraged the black middle and professional classes to reconnect with the brothers and sisters they had purportedly left behind.

The plan also sought to mobilize individuals to take responsibility for developing themselves, calling on black workers to "establish yourself as employed, proficient, productive, and equitably compensated."[51] It called for every black citizen to assume responsibility for developing the black private sector by donating monthly to one different type of black organization each month (for example, to a civil rights organization in February or to an HBCU in March) and investing 1 percent of their income to a Black Development Fund. These fundraising initiatives, the plan explained, "operated under a self-help concept, encourages greater trust, self-support, self-reliance and accountability among Black people. It makes a break with the traditional dependency of Black people on the unpredictable benevolence of non-Blacks with power and wealth."[52]

But black liberals still relied on the supposedly unpredictable "benevolence of non-Blacks" for their purported self-help initiatives. Foundations and corporations, some of whom had complicated relationships with black America, were quick to get involved in the movement to renew and rebuild the black family. This was not the first time corporations used a crisis in black America as an opportunity to build their brand in black communities; as Marcia Chatelain has shown, McDonald's capitalized on urban unrest in the 1960s, opening profitable black-owned franchises in neighborhoods damaged in the rebellions.[53] Other corporations like Xerox and Eastman-Kodak and corporate foundations like the Ford Foundation also co-opted demands for black economic power by investing in a black entrepreneurial class they hoped would serve as a check on more radical forces.[54] Following the Black Family Summit, sponsored in part by the Rockefeller Foundation and Carnegie Foundation, corporations and foundations including Philip Morris, Coca-Cola, Xerox, IBM, and the MacArthur Foundation each donated $1 million to support the NAACP and NUL's fight against black family breakdown. The Ford Foundation, longtime supporter of civil rights organizations, donated $4.5 million.[55] Other corporations waded into the black family crisis discourse to repair their brand's relationship with black Americans. The Coors Brewing Company, which faced an NAACP-led boycott in February 1984 after their director William Coors made a racist remark, provided funding for a Black Family Awareness conference hosted by the Nashville Urban League in October 1984. The conference featured workshops on single parenthood, extended family relationships, and unemployment as well as a Coors-sponsored reception where Ossie Davis was honored. The controversial Adolph Coors IV was even in attendance. Coors described the company's support as an "example of the Coors corporate commitment" to black communities.[56]

The National Black Family Reunion represented a pinnacle of corporate-sponsored self-help in the 1980s. Procter and Gamble was one of the earliest sponsors. The company had a long history of supporting civil rights organizations and black causes. James Norris Gamble, son of founder James Gamble, was one of the founding donors of Bethune-Cookman College in 1905 and had been donating to the United Negro College Fund since 1945.[57] The family reunion was thus a natural next step for the brand in the post–civil rights era. Procter and Gamble provided funding for the initial national reunion in 1986 and national and regional affairs around the country in subsequent years. They also "loaned" an executive to help Dorothy Height and the NCNW plan and expand the reunions. At the reunions, Procter and Gamble's products were on full display, with different brands sponsoring themed pavilions. Charmin, for example, sponsored a roundtable analyzing youth unemployment in the young adults' pavilion and distributed free guides on how to find a job in the private sector, while the Crest-sponsored pavilion provided free dental checkups for children.

As the reunions spread to cities like Atlanta, Los Angeles, Philadelphia, Detroit, Cincinnati, and Memphis, more corporations got involved. In 1989, several more corporate partners had signed on to support the reunion including Pringle's, Coca-Cola, Cover Girl, Folgers Coffee, the Adolph Coors Company, Anheuser-Busch, AT&T, Burger King, and IBM. Other corporations got involved in the black family reunion industry by funding genealogy workshops for black families interested in discovering their roots, sponsoring traveling photo exhibits that celebrated black family life, and organizing sweepstakes for free family portrait sessions and fully funded family reunion packages.[58] The black family reunions and other family-strengthening initiatives provided a relatively uncontroversial way for corporations to signal their support for black communities and grow their brands among black consumers. The reunions, then, represented a product of the convergence between expanding practices of corporate social responsibility and broader shifts in black politics in the 1980s.

For the attendees, the family reunions provided more than simply an opportunity to snag some free P&G products or hear top R&B artists like Melba Moore and James Ingram perform. For many, the reunions provided a chance to show off and celebrate their own families, to show that, as Melba Moore put it, "the black family is alive, healthy, strong, well."[59] Garnett Huguley, who brought his wife and two young daughters to the Atlanta reunion in 1987, contended, "I think it's important for us to come out today and show there is still some vitality in the black family. And with my family being here today, that is a statement." Countering negative stereotypes was particularly important to Huguley who explained, "On the evening news, you see a lot of black-on-black crime. But there are other sides, a lot of vital families that are together and have perpetuated each other."[60] Organizers and attendees suggested the family-friendly positivity was particularly important for black children to experience. Philadelphia attendee Guy Wallace brought his eight-year-old son to "expose him to as much culture as possible." He explained, "It's good to be around when people are reacting to each other in a positive way."[61] The reunions, then, served as a vehicle through which black Americans could reveal to the onlookers and, more significantly, prove to themselves their own strength, resiliency, and resources. Attendees could walk away feeling that black people could, in fact, rely upon themselves—with a bit of corporate support.

But the corporations and the liberals who championed private-sector solutions to public issues might have gained much more than the reunion attendees. The partnership between Procter and Gamble and the NCNW—and between American corporations and the black family more generally—was precisely the sort of innovative, market-friendly, and cost-efficient solution that professional liberals (and their collaborators in the Democratic Party eager to the party's "big government" reputation) heralded as the future of social-welfare provisioning. While black organizations turned to corporations largely out of necessity, they unintentionally legitimatized and provided positive publicity to a corporate-centered approach. That private sector–led method of addressing structural problems only further undermined the legitimacy of public solutions whose limitations, ironically, necessitated the corporate-sponsored reunions in the first place.

The Legacy of "Yes-But" Black Liberalism in the Post–Civil Rights Era

Black liberals' responses to the purported crisis of the black family conspicuously resembled those of black neoconservatives, like those of Robert Woodson's National Center for Neighborhood Enterprise, whose initiatives were funded by conservative foundations such as the John M. Olin Foundation and the Sarah Scaife Foundation.[62] Yet, black liberals were quick to distinguish their tactics from those of black conservatives. Conservatives, they argued, focused almost exclusively on the pathologies of the black family and often "blamed the victim." As John Jacobs contended, any assessment that focused on the pathologies of black families "must be totally rejected because it ignores the context in which black families struggle for survival."[63] And black liberals, unlike conservatives, consistently called attention to that context, citing unemployment rates, funding cuts, threats to welfare, attacks on affirmative action and set-aside programs, incidents of police brutality and rising rates of incarcerations, failing schools, and other metrics of decline in the post–civil rights era in their assessments of the problem. Unlike black conservatives, who in the 1980s were not only skeptical of federal spending on social policy but hostile to it, black liberals continued to demand federal intervention to address these structural problems. The Congressional Black Caucus released alternative budgets, and its members advanced legislation that sought to expand the capacity of the state to address poverty.

Despite their intentions, black liberals' renewed focus on self-help, corporate partnerships, and voluntarism dovetailed rather neatly with the imperatives of austerity and the Reagan administration's push to devolve responsibility for social policy to communities, families, and individuals. And by the late 1980s, their "yes-but" liberal strategies also reflected the shifting governing priorities of the Democratic Party. As Lily Geismer has shown, the New Democrats, whose ascension to party dominance was epitomized by the election of Bill Clinton in 1992, sought to use "the tools of the private sector rather than direct governmental assistance as a main means to address persistent poverty and structural racism."[64] The New Democrats, then, too, were skeptical of state action to address inequality. Their skepticism was not grounded in the lived experience of the exclusion, exploitation, and violence of white supremacy but instead emerged from their professional-class, technocratic critiques of bureaucratic inefficiency and long-held liberal concerns about welfare dependency. Bill Clinton's claim in 1996 that the "era of big government was over" reflected a reality black Americans knew intimately long before Clinton entered office. Yet, in governing amidst austerity, black liberals forged new partnerships with Clinton and the Democratic Leadership Council (DLC) and revived established approaches to black community survival, ultimately providing legitimacy to the ideologies prevailing in both parties that they claimed to challenge.

Scholars have explained black liberals' propensity to advance or accommodate policies that further weakened the public sector, undercut welfare, or expanded police power by arguing that they embraced "an-all-of-the-above" or a "both-and" approach. In unpacking why black liberals in the post–civil rights era consistently voted to "lock up their own," James Forman Jr., for example, argued that black liberals advanced both punitive policies that would address the immediate problem of crime and long-term policies that would address crime's structural foundations. They were more successful, however, in winning funding and support for more (yet diversified) police and longer and more punitive sentences.[65]

Yet, in their response to the crisis of the black family, black liberals also advanced the "yes-but" approach that reflected the pragmatic state skepticism impulse in the post–civil rights era. They acknowledged that, yes, the black family was being destabilized by various structural forces largely outside of their control and, yes, state intervention on the scale of a Marshall Plan for inner cities would be necessary. But that state intervention was unlikely to come anytime soon. Thus, black folks had to once again turn to the private realm, to their own families and institutions, to foundations that had long supported black communities when the public sector refused to do so, and to corporations looking for new ways to engage black consumers in their brand.

The *yes-but* approach has been most clearly reflected in how black liberals have approached the "problem" of the black family since the 1980s. In the first decade of the 2000s and the early 2010s, Barack Obama's solution to this seeming perpetual crisis focused on "healthy marriage," an initiative he carried over from the Bush administration, and "responsible fatherhood."[66] Working from the assumption that family instability was not only a problem of economic precarity but a crisis of responsibility among fathers in particular, Obama's Responsible Fatherhood Initiative sought to repair broken values and shift parents' priorities. Obama himself acknowledged the limits of government to address a problem that was rooted, in part, in culture. In a 2009 town hall in which he announced the initiative, Obama claimed:

> Our government can build the best schools with the best teachers on Earth, but we still need fathers to ensure that the kids are coming home and doing their homework, and having a book instead of the TV remote every once in a while. Government can put more cops on the streets, but only fathers can make sure that those kids aren't on the streets in the first place. Government can create good jobs, but we need fathers to train for these jobs and hold down these jobs and provide for their families.[67]

The state, Obama surmised, "can't legislate fatherhood."[68] Although he didn't host massive reunions on the White House lawn, Obama's initiative employed many of the same strategies black liberals had utilized for decades: voluntarism, faith-based initiatives, and partnerships with corporations and nonprofits. Even in the highest positions in the federal apparatus, black liberals remain deeply skeptical of that state's capacity to address the roots of black precarity.

Tracing the evolution of black liberalism's state skeptic strain illuminates one of the many "distinctively liberal paths toward neoliberal governance."[69] Ultimately, many black liberals walked in rhythm with their white counterparts in media, the nonprofit sector, state agencies, and elected office. However, their path to neoliberalism differed from that of white liberals. Their turn toward the private realm reflected not solely a generational rejection of mid-century liberal values and governance strategies or a fetishization of rationality, efficiency, and procedure. Indeed, black liberals' path was informed less by a critique of the excesses of mid-century liberalism and driven more by a disappointment in its timidness as well as rightful concern about the cruelty of New Right revanchism. Their state skepticism was informed by a recognition of the violence of the state, which shored up white citizenship through the exclusion and exploitation of black people. Ironically, then, the black path to neoliberalism was grounded in historical knowledge of the limits of liberalism, whose privileging of the individual, meritocracy, and racial capitalism both necessitated and perpetuated inequality.

CHAPTER 6

Queer Autonomy and the Afterlife of the Family Wage

B. ALEX BEASLEY

On May 9, 2012, President Barack Obama made headlines when he became the first American president to publicly voice support for same-sex marriage. Coming just months before Obama's election for a second term, the decision shocked observers who expected the president to withhold any controversial proclamations until after the ballots were counted. Yet the announcement was, in another sense, unsurprising and overdue. Years of evidence suggested that Obama's public opposition to same-sex marriage reflected political concerns rather than personal objection. More importantly, a steadily increasing proportion of Americans now indicated their support for same-sex marriage in public polling—according to some polls, even a majority.[1]

Polls and political calculation aside, Obama framed his sentiments about same-sex marriage in profoundly personal terms. On television, Obama cited intimate discussions with "friends and family and neighbors" as key determinants in his "evolution" on the issue. Press Secretary Josh Earnest's written summary of the news described the president's "soul-searching," the long conversations with his wife and daughters "around his kitchen table." The thought of having to explain his opposition to same-sex marriage to his children was, in this depiction, a catalyst for his changing views: "It wouldn't dawn on them that somehow their friends' parents would be treated differently." Ultimately, Obama asserted that it was these close friends and family—including "members of [his] own staff who are in incredibly committed monogamous relationships, same-sex relationships, who are raising kids together"—who inspired him to change his mind.[2]

Since the 1960s, the incorporation of LGBTQ rights[3] into American citizenship represented a dramatic shift in the national understanding of liberalism and the platform of the Democratic Party. This incorporation has by no means been steady, equally distributed, or uncontested. But Obama's public support marked a major milestone in this longer story. It also reflected a sea change in the public understanding of the relationship between liberalism and queer identity. Through the tireless work of activists at the grassroots, in schools, in courtrooms, in public office, in health clinics and doctors' offices, in boardrooms, and in the marketplace, the subject of queer rights and queer citizenship had become impossible for liberal heavyweights to ignore.[4]

This iconic moment in 2012 was the culmination of a *liberal* definition of queer citizenship that became hegemonic in the first decade of the twenty-first century.[5] Obama's careful framing of his "evolution" emphasized his intimate acquaintance with the kinds of gay men and lesbians who were engaged in "committed monogamous relationships . . . who are raising kids together"—whose lives were familiar, intelligible, and respectable. His new position was not a political commitment in an abstract, general, or universal sense but rather a moral judgment that hinged on particular, personalized cases. The problem was that good, kind people were unable to be part of a rights-bearing institution that would have been available to them if only they were not queer. The clear answer to such a conundrum was to make that institution open to them.

This vision of queer citizenship assumed that "queer" was an existing and static category of people that the state was excluding from key components of liberal citizenship. For Obama, the liberal state had a responsibility to grant that group the *opportunity* to enjoy those components of citizenship. Ensuring queer citizenship and protecting queer rights depended on opening doors to existing institutions—in this case, access to the benefits and protections of marriage. In other words, the version of queer citizenship suggested in Obama's announcement, and in the subsequent (and now imperiled) *Obergefell v. Hodges* Supreme Court decision, prioritized asking what existing components of liberal citizenship queer people *could not access*. It thus resisted taking seriously the full range of queer lives and so avoided a more capacious reimagining what *kinds of lives* liberal citizenship makes possible.

This definition of justice combined two political objectives that previous generations of liberals would have understood to be quite distinct. The first concerns the role of the state in protecting and advocating for marginalized groups, in particular the question of what actions the state should take to ensure inclusion across lines of race, gender, class, and, now, sexuality. The second concerns the role of the state in promoting, protecting, and supporting families. Each of these two threads carries its own complex and debated history in liberal political thought, but over the past several decades the national debate on gay marriage effectively merged them. Framing *the freedom to marry* as a crucial policy position thus obscured other questions that once lay at the heart of liberalism.

Perhaps the most glaring of those questions is this: Why does marriage have anything to do with citizenship—or with liberalism—at all? Typically, Americans tend to think about marriage as a profoundly private matter. In fact, we often discuss our "public lives" and "private lives" as foundational polar opposites, with marriage and family being relegated clearly to the latter. As historian Nancy Cott has argued, this understanding of marriage has even been "enshrined in legal doctrine" via a 1944 Supreme Court decision that found "that the U.S. Constitution protected a 'private realm of family life which the state cannot enter.'"[6] Yet liberalism has a long-standing interest in sanctioning, demarcating, and managing marriages and families, and the family has in fact been a primary institution through which liberals have attempted to achieve their broader social and political goals.

Moreover, the relationship between the liberal state and the institution of marriage marks a significant difference in liberalism between the New Deal and postwar era and our own post-1970s period. At multiple scales, New Deal liberal policy sought to support, subsidize, and sanction the white, heteronormative family. Liberals discussed *families* as the victims of economic dislocation, and their proposed solutions often focused on promoting family stability and well-being.[7] Mid-century liberals championed the family wage, a bargain struck between capital and organized labor to ensure that male (and disproportionately white) workers employed in much of the industrial sector earned a high enough wage to support a housewife and children. This gendered division of labor represented "the good life," celebrated in popular culture and officially promoted in state policy. For these same workers, the state promised to make the dream of single-family homeownership achievable through rapid state-subsidized suburban development. Throughout the postwar era, the rising fortunes of straight, white families became a benchmark of liberalism's success. It did not hurt that many liberals believed that stable and secure families were also less likely to be inclined toward disruption or political radicalism.[8]

The Left *did* push back against this vision of the family and this model of citizenship, and this resistance reached its apex in the 1970s, when numerous movements demanded an end to liberalism's gendered and racial exclusions. A range of leftist activists—among them feminists, gay and lesbian activists, and Black women activists in movements like the Welfare Rights Organization—decried how liberalism's vision of "the family" reinscribed and deepened the marginalization of people who did not inhabit the white heteronormative nuclear family. Importantly, these movements did not only demand providing formerly excluded groups access to these liberal programs. Rather, they challenged a foundational principle of the New Deal bargain: namely, the equation of citizenship with marriage and the state's use of the family as a primary mechanism through which to bestow rights and protections.

The way these movements discussed marriage was almost irreconcilable with the gay rights movement to which Obama responded in 2012. Take, for instance, Wilmette Brown, a Black lesbian activist leader of Black Women for Wages for Housework, an organization to which I will return. Brown identified a major obstacle stopping other Black lesbians from coming out: they were "trapped in [straight] marriages by dependence on a male wage."[9] For leftist activists, the gendered dynamic of marriage, nurtured by liberals, was itself an enemy of queer freedom.

But just as these political movements emerged, the economic status quo was undergoing radical change. During the 1970s, ordinary Americans became aware that the political economy they had grown to expect—marked by persistent growth, high employment, a robust industrial sector, relatively strong unionization, and a strong export market—seemed suddenly unstable. Just as leftist activists grew influential enough to sway liberals, liberalism itself was poised to make its own metamorphosis. This moment is often narrated as a sad coincidence: when social movements reached their height of power, they faced insurmountable structural obstacles from a contracting economy and a resurgent Right.[10] But more than coincidence, this moment marked a fundamental *realignment*, the crumbling of one set of ideals about the family, developed to serve a particular political economy, and the emergence of a new liberalism struggling to reconcile marriage and the family with a new economic context.

These profound changes in what marriage and the family represented mean that it is not sufficient to ask *why* queer rights have become a core component of American liberalism since the 1970s. Rather, we need to identify what we even *mean* when we say "queer rights."

Taking our lead from Wilmette Brown, we might turn our attention from the language of rights to track instead something at once more precise and more nebulous: the demand for viable queer autonomy. Defining the goal of queer citizenship in this way demands that we gauge queer freedom by the *ability of individuals to live queer lives*. Living a queer life might require an individual to sever ties with a family or community of origin, with an institution or network, or even with a spouse—meaning that queer autonomy necessitates some ability for individuals to support themselves financially *as individuals*. Simultaneously, queer autonomy also might involve the ability of queer communities to operate somewhat independently of non-queer institutions of power. In this reframing of the objective of queer politics, the necessity of non-queer citizens to tolerate, support, or advocate for queer rights does not disappear, but it is decentered. Rather than prioritizing convincing outsiders to support an excluded group, this framework reorients broader political objectives around engendering the *ability*—not just the opportunity—for all people to enjoy meaningful autonomy.

My aim here is not to write about queer autonomy as a normative demand—something I think the state or activists *should* prioritize—or, by contrast, that they *shouldn't*. Instead, I use autonomy as a lens to show continuities and ruptures between New Deal liberalism and post-1960s liberalism that aren't fully captured in narratives that trace debates over rights, opportunity, meritocracy, or democracy. And marriage is an ideal place to begin, even though *marriage* and *autonomy* as concepts are not obvious bedfellows.

* * *

As American liberalism was forced to grapple with demands for queer inclusion over the past several decades, activists and policymakers debated how they should define *inclusion* itself. Despite the circulation of a diverse and complex range of ideas, post-1970s liberal political and legislative priorities have tended toward integration, equal opportunity, and nondiscrimination approaches at the local, state, and federal levels. Just as crucially, the political work of extending these opportunities has hinged on convincing the public of the legitimacy of this *particular* category—queer people—and of queer claims to equal access and opportunity. Likewise, political opponents have argued that queer people are not or should not be eligible for rights and protections because being queer should be understood as illegitimate or, more recently, because acknowledging queer rights impinges on the sincerely held religious beliefs of those who categorically oppose queer inclusion.[11] When same-sex marriage emerged as a central political question in American politics, it fit easily within these assumptions.

In examining the origins and implications of the coalescing of queer politics around same-sex marriage during the Obama era, some scholars have traced the push for same-sex marriage to longer histories of formal legal and political rights for sexual minorities, emphasizing the radical potential of redefining the boundaries of an institution so enshrined in modern law and culture.[12] Others have drawn a stark contrast between the liberal focus on marriage and the more radical parameters of leftist queer organizing in previous decades, arguing that neoliberalism has relied on reframing queer politics as an effort to include select classes of queer people while excluding others, without ever disrupting broader structures of economic, racial, gender, and sexual oppression.[13] In its broadest strokes, the former story suggests a coherent twentieth-century liberalism grounded in the right to privacy and recognition of minority rights.

The second, on the other hand, traces a quite different story. In this version, the liberalism of the New Deal and the Great Society, while fundamentally limited in its imagination of justice, held the capacity to be pushed leftward on bread-and-butter issues. Movements that considered identity to be inextricable from class, wages, or labor rights stood a chance under this version of liberalism, it seemed. But those hopes were dashed by the Democratic Party's shift toward neoliberalism, which recast identity—including queer identity—as a floating signifier that served primarily to usher a select few into a reworked ruling class while justifying continued exploitation of the rest. At stake is the question of whether gay marriage or other forms of queer citizenship have been liberatory or coercive—whether they have functioned primarily to expand queer rights or to contain them.

Focusing on how *marriage* mattered to liberals and to liberalism, I argue, offers a third, more overlooked genealogy to trace the push for marriage equality. As a legal, social, and cultural institution, marriage has been a crucial component of how liberals have defined and negotiated the promises, obligations, and limits of their political philosophy. Even before the consolidation of New Deal liberalism, Americans understood the character of individual freedom, the nature of property rights, and the boundaries of the market to be defined by the marriage contract. At the same time, the ability to marry connoted who was and was not a free person, and the balance of power within that marriage was both dictated by and helped to determine the power differential between men and women on a larger scale. After the Civil War, marriage helped to mark the contours of meaningful freedom in the aftermath of slavery and as industrial capitalism took hold of more Americans' lives. Freedom to marry was a marker, for Black Americans, of no longer being enslaved. It was also a property right bestowed to men over the women they married. It promised to demarcate realms—the home, the family—that the market could not penetrate. But it was simultaneously an unequal agreement that bound wives to husbands and compelled their labor in the home while subsuming their legal rights.[14] During the Progressive Era, a diverse set of policymakers saw marriage as a means to insulate Americans from the dislocations of modern life; to establish the boundaries of whiteness via eugenic and anti-immigrant restrictions; and to expand and standardize state power by granting state authority to deny marriage applications if one party was deemed unable to consent, again relying on eugenic understandings of mental capacity and disability.[15] In each of these cases, defining the boundaries of marriage was at the core of defining the contours of the liberal state and liberal citizenship.

Marriage and the heterosexual family became cornerstones of New Deal liberalism, too. Feminist legal triumphs succeeded in reshaping marriage law in the late nineteenth and early twentieth centuries, ousting most of the tenets of coverture and crafting marriage, legally and socially, into a more companionate institution. But New Deal policy, for all its complexities and contradictions, iteratively built a vision of marriage that would be an enduring bedrock of American cultural, political, and economic life: one characterized by a male breadwinner and his dependent wife and children. This arrangement reflected the bargain that industrial capitalism had offered, in its ideal form, anyway: work and home were separate spheres; men controlled one, and women the other; labor was for sale at work, but work performed at home was private and so done for free. Unlike coverture, though, this vision of marriage could coexist with an ideal of companionship between spouses rather than husbands' domination of wives. "This economic emphasis ... operated more through incentives than through ultimatums," historian Nancy Cott explains. "Yet because the economic figuration of marriage blurred lines between public policy, economy, and society, it was inescapable." And while a male breadwinner plus an unpaid female homemaker was never a universally *attainable* model in any period in American history, it became a social *ideal* deeply embedded in and reinforced by public policy.[16]

The crucial change that the New Deal made to the function of marriage was to tie this particular economic relationship between spouses into core components of citizenship and state-making. In determining what the state owed to its citizens and what standard of living should define the nation, New Dealers prioritized ensuring that men earned a family wage, defined as a wage sufficient to support himself and his dependent wife and children. The concept was an old one, but it had never before been the object of robust public or federal interest. Women workers, or women-coded job categories, lay completely beyond the expectation or requirement to provide a family wage. And if a woman found herself with children and without a husband, she did not become entitled to a family wage herself. Instead, the state provided aid in the form of financial support she might otherwise have received from a spouse.[17]

Judged on the basis of autonomy for its participants, the New Deal definition of marriage was limiting, particularly for women. What marriage *did* purport to promise was access to a family wage—the exchange of a single adult's labor for a price deemed sufficient to support the lives of two adults and their children. The family wage quietly acknowledged the economic value of reproductive labor performed by women. Yet it paid men, not women, for that labor and granted men authority over the distribution of those funds. Marriages were difficult to leave, but when they ended, legally the state expected men to continue to take care of their ex-wives economically—though in practice, it often fell short of upholding this standard.

A defining feature of the New Deal state, which held in some way in American political culture until the 1970s, was its equation of family-based economic security with modern American citizenship. Of course, even at the heyday of the family wage, it was never universally available to all Americans. Married couples who were not white were disproportionately excluded from the family wage, and unmarried women had limited options to make enough money to support themselves, let alone children. While the state made clear that access to the family wage through heterosexual marriage was the proper path to economic security, public support in the form of welfare was intended to provide for those who could not tap into private patriarchal compensation. But welfare came with strings attached. Suspicion, surveillance, policing, and the strict enforcement of rules governing morality, sexual propriety, and comportment were the costs of any semblance of economic security outside the family wage system.[18]

Moreover, liberal policy emphasis on marriage, gender normativity, and whiteness did not only have the power to *exclude* people from its protections; it also *created* categories of vulnerable people whose vulnerability could be exploited to help the system run more efficiently. As historian Margot Canaday has shown, queer workers excluded from liberalism's family bargain were a prime example. While we might assume that queer employees were uniformly deeply closeted before the era of gay liberation, Canaday shows that many employers seemed to agree to "look the other way" as long as their employees did not "flaunt" their sexuality too overtly. This dynamic, Canaday argues, worked alongside the family wage to maintain queer employees as "a vulnerable labor force—*one . . . who commonly knew of other queer people who had lost jobs.*" This comparative vulnerability drove down their wages and blunted bargaining power. Moreover, unlike male breadwinners, employers were able to treat them as mobile and untethered from family ties.[19] Unwillingness or inability to take part in the family wage system came at a profound *cost* to queer workers, while their vulnerability advantaged employers.

Indeed, this role of queer employees within American capitalism before the 1970s reinforces feminist theorist Gayle Rubin's understanding of what she called the "sex/gender system," or "the set of arrangements by which a society transforms biological sexuality into products of human activity, and in which these transformed sexual needs are satisfied."[20] Throughout much of the twentieth century, being "queer" did not just signify sexual or gender difference; it was also an unstable category that is not "an idealized position or a prescription but . . . a *relation* produced by uneven and shifting dynamics of power" entwined with "non normative expressions of kinship, gender, and pleasure."[21] And as queer theorist Cathy Cohen has demonstrated, these transgressions have also been inextricable from constructions of race.[22] In this context, being queer meant, definitionally, standing outside the sex/gender system—in stark contrast to the contemporary notion that the right to *queer marriages* is a cornerstone of contemporary liberalism.

On the level of the individual, then, this pre-1970s vision of marriage provided little room for autonomy. Indeed, this is a key point that many scholars and queer activists make to critique the tremendous expenditure of political resources on the fight for gay marriage: marriage has been as much a tool of oppression and resource-hoarding as it has been something we might understand as a right. In a sense, marriage and autonomy might even seem like antonyms.

I linger on this evolution of the role of marriage within state policy precisely because marriage, like Obama's views on it, has *evolved*. And the movement for same-sex marriage emerged in the midst of a crucial transitional point in this history. Social, political, and legal revolutions in the 1960s and 1970s transformed many aspects of the institution of marriage. Women secured new rights within marriage, including property rights, access to independent credit, and the introduction of the no-fault divorce. Greater numbers of women, especially more affluent and white women, entered the workforce in their own careers, and many of these women found marriage to be both less socially and economically obligatory than it had previously been.[23] The strict gender rules within marriage codified during the New Deal relaxed in both de jure and de facto senses. And, landmark legal decisions forbade some of the most egregious sex-typing of jobs and differentials in pay between men and women. In the process of becoming a less starkly gender stratified institution legally, socially, and economically (though not, of course, an entirely equal one), marriage was becoming something that *could* incorporate same-sex couples.

At first glance, marriage's evolution, including the incorporation of same-sex marriages, seems to be transparently more aligned with autonomy. But contemporary marriage has also developed in the context of the dissolution of the family wage and its replacement with the increasing necessity of dual-earner households. Real wages have, on average, fallen or stagnated since the 1970s. Worse, March 2019 marked the highest average hourly wage *since* February 1973, meaning that during each year in the previous forty-six, workers had earned *less* in real wages than in that high-point month fifty years ago.[24] At the same time, policymakers, spurred by bondholders and consultants, have attacked and dismantled social provisions intended to meet the gap between incomes and the cost of living.[25] Citizens have used consumer credit to fill the gap, propping up spending while forcing them to hustle all the harder to pay bills.[26] In the atrophied welfare programs that remain, morality surveillance has only strengthened, sharpening the association between poverty and the policing of private life.[27]

Simultaneously, increased queer visibility and the movement to "come out" disrupted the old economic arrangement between queer employees and their bosses. Indeed, queer people became somewhat less vulnerable as a class thanks to shifting social attitudes and emergent if limited civil rights protections. The end of the family wage, then, coincided with the decline of gay employees providing a form of precarious labor performed by vulnerable workers. Yet, at the same time that gay workers became less vulnerable as a class, the end of the family wage meant that essentially *all* American workers became more precarious, accustomed to being treated as mobile and untethered. As Canaday puts it, gay "employees . . . had prefigured the employment regime of late capitalism," one that left all Americans, married or not, more vulnerable.[28]

* * *

If we consider autonomy not simply as the *opportunity* to live a certain life but as the meaningful *ability* to do so, how should we understand the dissolution of the family wage and its replacement with precarity and exhaustion? In the era of the family wage, economic security was understood as simultaneously a public commitment and a private affair governed by men. In addition to the heralded victories that cast households as having a right to privacy that the state should not overstep—Justice William O. Douglas explained the Court's ruling in *Griswold v. Connecticut* by referencing "the sacred precincts of marital bedrooms" and "the notions of privacy surrounding the marriage relationship"—the family wage itself made household autonomy a reality for millions of white and middle-class families.²⁹ And while the patriarchal arrangement of the family wage subjected women to their husbands' domination, as historian Lauren Gutterman has found, sometimes these marriages allowed room for extramarital same-sex relationships without dissolving their heterosexual marriage bonds.³⁰

The circumscribed autonomy of married people, especially married women, during the era of the family wage is certainly not an ideal to which to aspire. But it helps to illustrate what is and is not different in our current era's version of marriage. Historians Canaday, Nancy Cott, and Robert Self have argued that one of the most profound continuities in the history of marriage is the state's effort "to minimize any drain on public coffers by assigning economic support to the private household."³¹ Since the 1970s, this tendency has certainly persisted—but in the absence of significant government investment in economic security.

Instead of pursuing new standards of economic justice, however, liberals have been instrumental in constructing a revised version of marriage. This model is less gendered and easier to dissolve, but it remains an institution with an essential function of privatizing economic survival and assigning caretaking responsibilities absent public support. Liberals have been at the forefront of these shifts, most demonstrably in President Bill Clinton's campaign promise and ultimate success in "end[ing] welfare as we know it." The 1996 Personal Responsibility and Work Opportunity Reconciliation Act required recipients to work and limited the time that they could receive public assistance. For Clinton, the problem that his policy aimed to solve was "intergenerational dependency." Adults—even if they were single parents of children—should not be "dependent" on state support for long, because state support should be "a second chance, not a way of life."³² If the family-wage marriage model privatized a public commitment to economic security, the post-family-wage marriage model privately distributes economic risk that might otherwise be borne publicly or collectively.

Moreover, the value of reproductive labor has fallen off the balance sheets. The expectation and growing necessity of a dual-income household has jettisoned the family wage's recognition of reproductive labor. The ideal of a single income supporting a family of five has been replaced with two incomes, each often downsized to support a single adult. Care work, meanwhile, must be performed in the "leisure" time of a full-time worker—and almost always by a woman worker—or, for the luckier few, by hiring nannies, home cleaners, daycares, and, more recently, Instacart shoppers.³³

Commentators have thoroughly documented these transformations but have largely overlooked their impact on queer life. Indeed, the economic transformation of marriage was markedly absent from the majority opinion to grant a federal right to same-sex marriage in *Obergefell v. Hodges*. Justice Anthony Kennedy's written decision relied exclusively on noneconomic arguments: "the right to personal choice . . . inherent in the concept of individual autonomy"; "the right . . . to enjoy intimate association" in "a two-person union unlike any other in its importance to committed individuals"; the necessity to "safeguard . . . children and families"; and to grant same-sex couples access to "a keystone of the Nation's social order." Famously, Kennedy closed his opinion declaring that, "No union is more profound than marriage, for it embodies the highest ideals of love, fidelity, devotion, sacrifice, and family."[34]

Yet many of the arguments for gay marriage in the years predating the decision relied not only on the consecration of love, but on the economic and legal uncertainty befalling same-sex couples who did not have access to marriage. In 2009, *New York Times* financial reporters estimated that exclusion from the ability to marry would cost a same-sex couple earning an "average" income as much as half a million dollars over a fifty-year relationship. "Nearly all the extra costs that gay couples face would be erased if the federal government legalized same-sex marriage," they wrote, emphasizing expanding access to publicly regulated private benefits or to direct federal payments such as health insurance, retirement benefits, and Social Security.[35] Indeed, economists estimated that members of unmarried couples were "two to three times more likely to be uninsured" than married people, costing them both their financial and physical health.[36]

These arguments rarely considered the costs of *deciding* to remain unmarried, or the ways in which these economic incentives for marriage constrained the kinds of queer lives that were feasible, particularly in a post-family-wage world. A debate over the freedom *to* marry masked the various means by which marriage had been reasserted as a profound necessity, a means to survive under austerity. And if same-sex couples felt compelled to *enter* marriage, they might find it even more difficult to *leave* those marriages—if access to health insurance or funds saved collectively for retirement hung in the balance. To be sure, exclusion from marriage was an expensive injustice, but *why* was marriage such a cost-saving bargain to begin with?

* * *

This question is not a new one. At the moment when the family wage was in crisis during the 1970s, many leftist queer activists recognized the relationship between economic security and queer autonomy. One profound example lies in the work of lesbian activists within the Wages for Housework movement. An international movement most active between 1972 and 1977, Wages for Housework (WfH) developed a Marxist critique of the role of the nuclear family within capitalism.[37] Advocates rarely demanded literal wages for housewives within heterosexual marriages, as the name might misleadingly suggest. Rather, WfH articulated a complex critique of unpaid reproductive labor and women's subjugation within that system. In this framework, "housework" was a broad term that referred to "a political-economic modality that regulated radicalized, gendered, and sexual labor across multiple sites that included, but was not confined to, the heteronormative familial household." Ultimately, WfH activists fought against the liberal status quo to establish "an altogether different organization of sexuality and social reproduction."[38]

At the core of this political perspective was meaningful autonomy for women. This autonomy involved access to money, yes. But it also required undoing the conflation of *women* and *housework* on a larger scale. For Marxist feminist Silvia Federici, a key theorist with the WfH movement, the very demand for a wage itself made visible the labor that the capitalist order relied upon and thus denaturalized the relationship between women's nature and that labor. As she explained:

> not only has housework been imposed on women, but it has been transformed into a natural attribute of our female physique and personality, an internal need, an aspiration, supposedly coming from the depths of our female character. Housework had to be transformed into a natural attribute rather than be recognized as a social contract because from the beginning of capital's scheme for women this work was destined to be unwaged.[39]

This demystification, for Federici, would make it possible "so that eventually we might rediscover what is love and create what will be our sexuality which we have never known"—a project rooted in a profound quest for autonomy.[40]

Within the WfH movement, some argued that *lesbian* sexuality represented a foundational refusal of the capitalist order rooted in women's unrecognized reproductive labor and men's family wage. For Federici, "coming out is like going on strike," and "a direct attack on the work-sexual discipline imposed on women in capitalist society."[41] Lesbian perspectives on Wages for Housework also held that queer autonomy *relied* on disentangling economic survival from familial relationships—and that this objective was necessarily interlinked with movements for racial and gender equality as well.

Wilmette Brown of Black Women for Wages for Housework made this point very clear. For Brown, queer autonomy was inextricable from women's liberation and from Black freedom. Wages for housework, in her framework, would make autonomous lesbian lives possible for Black women and would also liberate Black women more broadly. "Black women with ten children who are on welfare are struggling as much against their heterosexual work as I am struggling against my heterosexual work," she pointed out; "those women in making the demand on the state, on the government, to give them money ... are making the same struggle I am making, which is *for* money *against* dependency on the power of men." And, crucially, Brown's objective was not to declare absolute individualism for women, an embrace of the liberal subject severed from all social ties. Instead, reallocating financial resources was a means to "give us the power to begin to define and discover our own possibilities," a project that would build *collective* power through *individual* autonomy.[42]

Liberal policymakers overwhelmingly rejected the demands of Wages for Housework, and many of those demands were not reducible to policy interventions anyway. But their political ambitions live on. As historian Ryan Patrick Murphy has shown, flight attendants joined the labor movement in part through recognizing that women and gay men held "full-time jobs in a heavily unionized industry that was recognized for high wages," yet did not enjoy those benefits themselves. In a job associated with women and femininity, flight attendants—regardless of their gender or sexuality—were presumed to be future wives who did not require their own high wages or benefits. For Beth Skrondal, president of her Transport Workers Union local in the early 1970s, this presumption was not only a problem of gender; it was directly connected to her location outside the bonds of the nuclear family. As an activist, she explained, "My little thing has always been single people ... No 'rights' are ever discussed for single people."[43] Their movement won crucial legal battles and wrought concessions from employers during the 1970s and 1980s before their efforts faced devastating opposition in the form of airline deregulation and anti-worker mobilization.[44] Their example also hints at the ability of more mainstream institutions, like labor unions, to push different understandings of the family and autonomy in the absence of other institutional liberal support.

In the intervening years, scholars, policymakers, and activists have continued to document the problem from multiple political perspectives. In the 1990s, social-work scholar Diana Pearce pointed to a phenomenon she called the "feminization of poverty" and developed the Self-Sufficiency Standard, an alternative to the federal poverty line that better accounted for the costs of reproductive labor, including health care, and that held women's autonomy as a primary goal in determining adequate income.[45] More recently, scholars have highlighted a "crisis of care" at the core of the present and future prospects of US and global political economy.[46] When Senator and presidential candidate Elizabeth Warren demanded attention to "the two-income trap" during the 2020 presidential primaries, the issue gained even more widespread attention.[47] But it has been challenging for any of these critiques to gain traction in policy.

Our contemporary marriage status quo relies on individuals to think of their survival as a fundamentally private affair—while also considering their familial entanglements as at-will.[48] This requirement, in fact, has represented a crucial difference between the era of the family wage and our post-family-wage model of marriage. In the old order, marriage was a relationship of reciprocity and obligation that was definitionally unequal. The lasting nature of marriage and the legal, economic, and social compulsions to preserve it at any cost were all forms of policing intended to maintain the social order.

By contrast, *Obergefell* made apparent that structuring marriage as an at-will relationship could *also* carry regulatory force. In our current era, state policy privileges marriage while the dominant cultural and legal regime imagines marriage as primarily a matter of personal taste, an optional relationship structure that carries certain benefits to those who choose it. In the context of austerity and a withering infrastructure to ensure economic rights, this new definition of marriage is less invested in maintaining *marriage*, or individual *marriages*. Instead, marriage functions as part of a larger project of framing all responsibilities as *individual* responsibilities. The ability to share resources with a spouse through marriage is no longer an expected or naturalized outcome but rather a *bonus* for which to be grateful. Each spouse enjoys the right to leave a marriage, but doing so imperils that special status. Contemporary marital coercion comes not from making spouses stay but from making them believe that they *chose* to stay. In this way, same-sex marriage has been a means *both* to expand queer autonomy—by reducing the economic costs involved in a partnership with a same-sex partner versus a heterosexual marriage—while also *restricting* that autonomy, by relegating the means for economic survival to the private world of the married household. Thus, the new framework of marriage resurrects old questions about the problem of *choice* within liberal thought: What sorts of choices are meaningful? And when do *choices* themselves become a means to police, regulate, and restrict?

The current assemblage of marriage carries implications for all forms of autonomy, regardless of sexuality. The perverse insistence that we marry purely at will—mirrored in the workplace by a similar fiction, that we labor at will—has reinforced the importance and the governing power of marriage at precisely the historical moment that large numbers of Americans became open to marriage's alternatives.[49] And marriage has served as this bulwark of survival, cornerstone of citizenship, and implement of exclusion for even the most heteronormative of Americans.

But centering the kinds of limits marriage places on queer autonomy reveals, unsurprisingly, that these costs are not evenly distributed. What kind of queer autonomy functionally exists if economic survival depends on family ties—either through a family of origin or through a spouse? Securing financial support outside of state-recognized family systems is, of course, possible. But in the context of the expectation of a two-income household and the disappearance of any economic accounting for reproductive labor and the costs of care, the cost savings represented by familial forms accorded state recognition are hardly negligible. Despite unprecedented legal rights and social acceptance for queer people in the United States—though, of course, the Right mounts ever increasing threats to this status quo—queer people often find themselves choosing between severing themselves from harmful relationships and making next month's rent.

* * *

In his essay "Capitalism and Gay Identity," historian John D'Emilio famously argued that homosexual identity was only able to emerge in the context of the industrial revolution, "when *individuals* began to make their living through wage labor, instead of as parts of an interdependent family unit." This form of individual autonomy could only be even imagined because of workers' "ability to remain outside the heterosexual family and to construct a personal life based on attraction to one's own sex."[50] This process, for D'Emilio, was a foundational feature of capitalism: as a system, it "has gradually undermined the material basis of the nuclear family" over time, "taking away the economic functions that cemented the ties between family members" and relocating those ties in the labor market. On the other hand, capitalism has "enshrined the family as the source of love, affection, and emotional security," as a bulwark against capitalism's dislocations but also to justify the privatization of reproductive labor and risks even while "socializing production" to the primary benefit of capitalists. "Ideologically," D'Emilio argues, "capitalism drives people into heterosexual families," while "materially, capitalism weakens the bonds that once kept families together."[51]

Our current marriage bargain complicates this division between the material and the ideological. *Economic* limits have become one of the most powerful tools to constrain queer autonomy. Indeed, the most effective limits on the kind of queer life one might lead stem from asking, *What kind of queer life can I afford*?

Perhaps the most chilling implication of this conceptualization of queer citizenship—grounded in the distinctively liberal freedom to chart any number of queer lives but constrained by profound economic limits placed on that freedom—is that it is deeply vulnerable to attack. Right-wing opposition to queer gains in the American polity has grown increasingly comfortable with authoritarianism and appeals to religious authority. An "aggressively conservative" Supreme Court has repeatedly ruled that the religious belief of a corporation—which is, perplexingly, determined to be capable of religious belief—is grounds for denying queer Americans health care benefits, consumer access, and employment.[52] And the recent Republican attacks on transgender minors' access to standard medical treatment, now extended to take aim at transgender adults in a number of states, plays a similar game without the religious rhetoric. Most of the proposed bills take aim at insurance coverage and medical malpractice policy, hoping, on the one hand, to force transgender patients to pay out of pocket for care, and, on the other, to drive up the cost of protective insurance so high for physicians that few will continue to offer transition treatment.[53] The goal is to make this kind of queer life impossible by making pursuing transition not just dangerous but also economically prohibitive.

Legislative victories like the *Obergefell* decision relied on a basic liberal demand that same-sex couples were a worthy minority group who deserved inclusion in the sacred institution of marriage. This logic struggles to withstand the objection that another ostensibly worthy group of Americans deserves the right to *oppose* that inclusion—particularly since opponents can now point to the many other arenas of American life where queer people *may* participate. A sense of justice based, instead, on queer autonomy demands not acceptance, tolerance, or inclusion, but simply the right to be able to chart a different path, regardless of the opposition of hostile forces. And to be meaningful, that right must include an economic ability to live without those forces being able to coerce the shape that life takes.

CHAPTER 7

Making the Liberal Media
Journalism's Class Transformation since the 1960s

DYLAN GOTTLIEB

In the weeks after November 8, 2016, journalists found themselves gripped by paroxysms of self-doubt. How could their entire industry have failed to anticipate Donald Trump's Electoral College victory? Who exactly were his supporters, and where did they live? Had the media become so cloistered—too educated, too metropolitan, too self-satisfied—that they had lost touch with those "real" Americans? After decades of fending off conservative accusations of the media's elite and liberal bias, some journalists were ready to admit that, just maybe, those critiques had a ring of truth. Margaret Sullivan, media columnist for the *Washington Post*, anatomized the profession's near-sightedness on the morning after the election. "College-educated, urban" journalists, Sullivan wrote, may have "touched down in the big red states for a few days, or interviewed some coal miners or unemployed autoworkers in the Rust Belt. [But] we didn't take them seriously. Or not seriously enough."[1]

What those mea culpas were missing, however, was a sense of history that predated Trump's arrival on the political landscape. Even now it remains unclear how print journalism had changed since its mid-century apogee, when its relevance was nearly universal and its cultural authority almost unquestioned. What sort of social transformations had rendered the news and newsrooms so out of touch with the main currents of American life in the twenty-first century? And could those shifts in journalism tell us something about how liberalism itself evolved over those decades, as it was remade by and for an emerging professional class?

This chapter reveals how material and social changes remade the newspaper and magazine industries since the 1960s, giving rise to a media infrastructure that can, in fact, be fairly characterized as elite and liberal in its institutional, demographic, and geographic base—and, to an extent, in the content of its coverage.[2] Throughout the twentieth century, print journalism's trajectory mirrored the changing face of American political economy. From the 1930s through the 1960s, the metropolitan newspaper had hewed to a Fordist business model, with large numbers of unionized employees from diverse class backgrounds earning robust wages in large, centralized workplaces. Papers sought to appeal to the broadest possible audience, as advertisers hoped to capture the buying power of a growing American mass market.

This arrangement began to break down in the 1960s. To pursue affluent readers and advertisers, who were moving in increasing numbers to the suburbs, publishers and editors ramped up their service and consumer coverage while cutting back on the labor beat. Newsrooms changed, too: college-educated journalists began to crowd out an older generation from more varied backgrounds. By the 1970s, traditional papers and news magazines were joined by a suite of new "lifestyle" publications wholly devoted to the tastes of metropolitan professionals. In the pages of magazines like *New York*, working-class people were less often fully-realized subjects—folks just like "us"—and more often the objects of anthropological curiosity. Even the most radical publications, like the New Left's underground press, undertook a similar process of embourgeoisement as their publishers and readers grew older and more professionally established. Those trends accelerated as inequality deepened after the 1970s. By the 1980s, avowedly liberal publications, from *Washington Monthly* to the *New Republic*, revamped their coverage to speak to the concerns of an upscale readership—just as that same demographic was remaking the Democratic Party in its image. That choice would have profound consequences for the political common sense of professional-class liberals.

The advent of Internet journalism in the mid-1990s only deepened journalism's class divide. It hastened the fall of the Fordist model of media, as large, hierarchical, unionized, nationally distributed, and class-integrated newspaper operations gave way to small, flexible, non-unionized, coastal-city-based, elite-dominated outlets. In the case of the 1994 San Francisco newspaper strike, the transition was literal: striking *San Francisco Examiner* journalists launched one of the first online-only news websites. That experience inspired one *Examiner* alum, David Talbot, to found the "militantly centrist" Salon.com the following year. Freed from the constraints of physical publishing—along with the need for expensive fixed investments in craft labor and printing infrastructure—the news media and its political vantage grew more elite and more parochial as the century drew to a close.

Ultimately, journalism's class transformation echoed, and indeed contributed to, the remaking of liberalism that the chapters in this volume explore. Beginning in the 1960s, the media industry was at the vanguard of new forms of labor relations that were more flexible and more technologically advanced than the Fordist newspapers of earlier decades. Yet that reconfigured newsroom also offered less stability, lower wages, and employed fewer people—particularly those without elite credentials. As journalism shed its craft workers and less educated lifers, its class base narrowed and the range of voices in the newsroom shrank. In time, so would its political perspective. By the 1980s, magazines like the *New Republic* proffered a constrained and technocratic vision for liberalism that accorded with the foreshortened horizons of its professional-class authors and readers. By the end of the twentieth century, the attenuated politics that the "liberal media" championed was stripped of nearly all idealism. Even if it remained committed, at least in the abstract, to ideas of equality, its menu of political possibilities had dwindled to a list of legalistic, developmental, or technocratic fixes. Above all else, the liberal media in this era aimed to gratify its upper-middle-class readership—an audience that felt self-satisfied with their "smarts," political savvy, and cultural centrality. In the early decades of the twenty-first century, as liberalism itself grew culturally all-powerful but politically wan—as Brent Cebul and Lily Geismer argue in the introduction—so too would the stories it told about itself, in the pages of America's newspapers, magazines, and websites.[3]

* * *

The rise of the large metropolitan newspaper is a story of class and organizational consolidation. At the start of the twentieth century, major cities counted dozens of daily papers, with different publications for each political party and ethnic, language, and racial group. The most significant dividing line, though, was social class. Working-class evening papers ran horse-racing reports and poked fun at the city's elites. Middle-class papers dispensed etiquette tips along with news to their "respectable" (or at least aspirationally respectable) readers. Elite papers reported on national and global events along with a healthy dose of society gossip.[4] But those class distinctions started to blur as the industry consolidated. Beginning in the 1920s, chains like Hearst, Scripps, and Gannett began buying up competing dailies. In 1923, the United States had five hundred cities with two or more daily papers. After the Depression, that number fell to just over a hundred. In the 1930s, one chain published both the leading morning and evening editions in San

Francisco, Los Angeles, New York, and Chicago. Most of the surviving major papers adapted their content to court the broadest possible readership, with separate sections or columnists appealing to readers from different class (if rarely racial) backgrounds.[5]

By the 1930s, metropolitan newspapers were increasingly hierarchical, automated, unionized, and class-integrated institutions—assuming the Fordist structure that characterized much of the industrial economy after the New Deal. At some papers, literal conveyor belts carried stories from reporters through to the copydesk and on into the composing and layout rooms.[6] In the automated newsroom, just as on the industrial shop floor, seniority counted for more than educational credentials. Mid- and senior-level reporters had more of the former than the latter: except for the top papers' global and national desks, many journalists in the 1920s and 1930s did not have college degrees, and even fewer had experience via undergraduate internships. Fewer still attended journalism programs. When Morton Sontheimer worked as a reporter in Philadelphia in the late 1920s, he "didn't dare let on" that he was taking college classes in the morning, since "city editors didn't want anyone who had been contaminated by a school of journalism."[7] Aspiring writers usually began their career on the copydesk, learning the ropes by ferrying photographic plates, writing boilerplate stories, or running errands for reporters. Arthur Gelb, who worked his way up to become managing editor at the *New York Times*, began his career as a $16-per-week night copyboy after dropping out of City College. A plucky charmer, Gelb convinced editors to let him write: first an internal newsletter on the *Times*, then short stories as a cub reporter. Gelb's trajectory, with on-the-job promotions outweighing internships or diplomas, remained typical into the 1950s.[8]

In the 1930s, as organized labor strengthened across industries due in part to New Deal legislation, newspapers' white-collar and craft workers joined, for the first time, under the umbrella of a shared union. Papers had long observed a division between industrial jobs, like typesetters and printing, and desk jobs, like reporters and salespeople. Manual laborers were almost always organized in craft unions, such as the powerful International Typographical Union. Meanwhile, management underpaid and overworked the putative "professionals" in the newsroom. By the early 1930s, it was not uncommon for a printer to be paid double the wages of a mid-level editor. In response, newsroom workers joined craft workers in 1933 to form the American Newspaper Guild (ANG), over the objections of some journalists who argued that joining a union would degrade whatever remained of their professional status. (The "Guild" appellation was a concession to this constituency.)⁹ In 1937, the ANG joined the CIO. By the end of the 1930s, most metropolitan newspaper workers—from editors to drivers to elevator operators to copyboys to typographers—were organized. Many journalists, even those long-resistant to the idea of industrial unions, joined the ANG. Somewhere between one-third to one-half of journalists were members of the guild in the 1940s, with even higher concentrations in large cities.[10]

By mid-century, large metropolitan newspapers resembled most other corporations in the heyday of twentieth-century American liberalism. They were huge, bureaucratic, and hierarchical. Most workers were unionized. Salaries, hours, and job descriptions were stable and comparable across the entire industry. Male journalists could expect to earn a family wage and enjoy the perquisites of a middle-class life. The postwar capital-labor accord, however tenuous, had come to the news business.[11] These arrangements held in spite of the fact that almost every paper owner and most editorial boards remained aligned with Republican business interests, and many urban tabloids espoused a conservative populist politics.[12] Yet this push to make journalism resemble other white-collar professions set in motion a class transformation that would render the industry unrecognizable by the 1980s.

* * *

The social transformation of journalism began in the late 1950s, as college-educated journalists began to supplant working-class writers in newsrooms. It began, ironically, with the ANG. As the union improved pay and conditions, journalism became respectable—an appealing alternative to other white-collar professions. The ANG also helped formalize formerly ad-hoc hiring practices, emphasizing a college education as a prerequisite for entry-level positions. During the 1950s, many publications changed the hiring rules for copy boy and copy girl positions, requiring that they be filled by interns who were either enrolled in or had just graduated from college. The ANG encouraged newspapers to create formal training courses for interns, exposing them to all aspects of the editorial and reporting process. By the 1960s, most editors came to expect new hires to have experience at a campus newspaper.[13] Each spring, college papers ran ads for summer internships at leading publications, and editors visited campuses to recruit aspiring reporters. But those internships, however attractive, offered little or no salary. In effect, newsrooms offloaded the cost of training apprentices onto students and their families. Together, the reliance on poorly paid internships and the new prerequisite of a college degree tended to favor young trainees from well-off backgrounds—the same sort of class upscaling that Sarah Milov and Reuel Schiller trace in Ralph Nader's legal team.[14]

During the 1960s and especially the 1970s, college became an ever-more-important qualification for work in a newsroom. This shift was, of course, part of a wider surge in the number of Americans pursuing higher education, a trend launched by massive federal investments during liberalism's mid-century heyday. As late as 1971, only 58 percent of journalists possessed a bachelor's degree. In 1982, that figure had crept upward to 70 percent. By the start of the first decade of the 2000s, 93 percent of journalists were college educated. Over the same period, enrollment in graduate journalism schools also rose, if more slowly. (One in five newsroom workers had a master's degree by the 2010s.)[15]

Newspapers' content evolved along with their newsrooms, as journalists hewed to issues that mattered to middle- and upper-middle-class readers. In the immediate post–World War II period, publishers had pursued the widest possible audience, since advertisers hoped to harness the buying power of a growing mass market. Circulation—the total number of readers—was what mattered, even if that mass audience was almost always coded white.[16] But as prosperous readers abandoned central cities for suburbs, the metropolitan newspaper was refashioned to follow them. By the late 1960s, newspapers transformed their existing "women's pages" into stand-alone sections that were heavy on consumer, style, and service-oriented stories. Newspapers also launched suburban sections. In 1968, the *Los Angeles Times* added an Orange County edition. Under pressure from suburban retail advertisers, the *New York Times* followed suit the following year with weekly sections on northern New Jersey and Long Island.[17] John Mount, a *Los Angeles Times* marketing specialist, explained that the new lifestyle sections would appeal to readers with a "high demographic profile." And it "just happens," Mount said, "that the more affluent and educated people tend to be white and live in suburban communities."[18]

In politics, papers gratified a more educated liberal audience by shifting their emphasis from daily coverage of bureaucratic goings-on to more complex analytical articles that took a critical stance toward government and large corporations. To appeal to good-government liberals—a constituency that grew with the rising mistrust of institutions during the Vietnam War—papers launched desks to investigate self-dealing officials. The *Boston Globe's Spotlight* team, which exposed corruption in local government and the Catholic church, was a leading example. Both the New York and Los Angeles *Times* assumed a more adversarial position vis-à-vis the NYPD and LAPD. In a more Naderite vein, David Horowitz pioneered the first consumer-awareness news segments on NBC's Los Angeles TV affiliate.[19]

Chasing suburban tastes, newspapers cut back on their coverage of labor and working-class issues. As chains continued to buy competing papers and trim editorial budgets, fewer papers kept a reporter on the labor beat. There had been some two dozen daily labor reporters in the 1950s. In the early 1960s, there were at least five on staff at the *New York Times* alone. By the 1970s, though, the *Times* was down to two labor reporters, and most other papers had abandoned the beat.[20] Meanwhile, the *Times*, along with the *Washington Post*, *Boston Globe*, and *Chicago Tribune* all added stand-alone business sections in the late 1970s.

When stories did address organized labor, they were less sympathetic to workers' perspectives than in earlier decades. Since the Depression, stories about strikes had mostly quoted workers, union leaders, or government officials. When New York bus drivers struck in 1941, the *New York Times* coverage was generally supportive. Stories asked readers to identify with the bus drivers, who were quoted and photographed. But by the early 1980s, when New York–area transit workers launched another strike, the emphasis had shifted to its impact on suburban consumers. The *Times*' lead headline read: "Rail Strike Clogs Traffic on Roads in New York Area." The paper ran a front-page photo of three disgruntled executives from Westchester, forced to commute by subway through the Bronx.[21]

It wasn't just editorial: newspapers' sales and marketing departments intensified their pursuit of upscale demographics while abandoning poorer and minority readers. Overall readership had slipped since the late 1960s, battered by economic recessions and the rising popularity of television, particularly among less educated Americans. From 1967 to 1977, newspaper consumption fell by over 15 percent among those with less than a high school degree, but only by 4 percent among college graduates.[22] Across the industry, newspapers turned to consultants to help them boost sagging circulation and ad sales. Their recommendation? Instead of attempting to recapture working-class readers, papers should try even harder to chase the professional class—the one market segment that saw its buying power increase during the 1970s.[23] That meant more service-oriented lifestyle journalism, more personal-finance columns, and more suburban-centric consumer guides. It also meant that marketing departments worked even harder to inform potential advertisers just how wealthy and sophisticated their subscribers were. A 1970 *New York Times* ad campaign that ran in newspaper trade journals featured photos of their ideal reader: white well-to-do people engaged in upmarket leisure activities, from squash to high-end shopping. Below, in the *Times*' signature Gothic font, was the cheeky tagline: "The New York Smarties" or "The New York Spenders," depending on the ad. "More than 500,000 of them hold post-graduate degrees," it continued. "They're the people who read The New York Times."[24] As marketing departments sought to "improve" the class makeup of their readership, thereby boosting their advertising revenue, they also abandoned poor and minority audiences. The *Los Angeles Times* considered adding Spanish-language content—until a 1977 internal report found that Latinos were "suffering from economic deprivation" and would make a bad business bet.[25] The *Washington Post* cut print distribution in Black neighborhoods to "upgrade the quality of its demographic audience profile." Across the Southeast and Midwest, chain-owned papers dropped rural white subscribers. Total circulation—a mass market—mattered less than the "quality" of the dwindling number of readers who remained.[26]

* * *

Just as the daily paper was being remade by and for the college-educated, another group of journalists started a movement that aimed to radically reinvent the news: the underground press of the New Left. These papers, which by the late 1960s would number in the several hundreds and boast a readership in the millions, were everything the establishment press was not. They were lean operations, with writers often doing the editing, compositing, printing, and distribution without help from the usual team of craft workers. Their content was profane, visually avant-garde, and politically militant.[27] Opening a representative issue of Atlanta's *Great Speckled Bird*, a paper founded in 1967 by members of the local Students for a Democratic Society chapter, readers would find editorials attacking the "straight" press headlong. *Life* magazine and the *New York Times*, wrote one syndicated columnist, failed to cover the issues important to young radicals: from "full-scale rebellion" on the streets of Berkeley to the subversive music of the Doors. Mainstream journalists, supine to the interests of the corporate and Washington elite, were keeping radical art from the masses. Real change, he argued, would require the overthrow of those interests. And young people could hasten that revolution through the consumption of the right kind of cultural products.[28]

In that respect, underground papers like the *Bird* embodied a tension within the 1960s New Left. Their politics may have been avowedly radical. But from the start, they leavened their anti-imperialist and anti-capitalist viewpoints with a healthy dose of hip consumer advice. Ads for local countercultural businesses flanked scathing antiwar editorials.

Record reviews sat beside articles attacking Georgia's segregationist governor, Lester Maddox. Readers may have wished, or even agitated for, the overthrow of capitalism. Yet most were, after all, the children of the white middle-class postwar suburbs—the heartland of America's Consumer's Republic. They understood that consumption was an arena for politics, and that politics could be pursued through consumption. Even after the New Left ebbed in the 1970s, veterans of the movement, many now in professional careers, retained the sense that they could continue to pursue their political goals through their consumer choices. A host of businesses with countercultural or activist roots—including Ben & Jerry's in Vermont, Whole Foods in Austin, and the LGBT bookstore Giovanni's Room in Philadelphia—emerged to fulfill this impulse.[29]

The underground press evolved to serve its increasingly upscale readership. In 1978, the publishers of thirty alternative papers met in Seattle to form a trade organization whose name, the National Association of Newsweeklies, was intended to distance it from what reporter Calvin Trillin called the "incense and marijuana smoke" of the underground press. These so-called alternative weeklies still hewed to a left-wing perspective—albeit a more polite and less movement-oriented one. Some, like the Chicago *Reader* and San Francisco *Bay Guardian*, boasted serious editorial and investigative teams. But above all else, alt-weeklies amplified the consumerist strain of the 1960s press. At the Seattle meeting, publishers talked about reaching educated "urban sophisticates" whose purchasing power would attract upscale advertisers.[30] As the papers professionalized along with their readers, they grew even more committed to consumer and lifestyle coverage. And their writers began to look the part. At the association's 1987 meeting in Portland, Maine, most attendees came dressed, one witness reported, "as if they all bought their clothes at the same store: Benetton or The Limited or one of those other yuppie chains." Instead of awakening the proletariat, alt-weeklies had become a way for comfortable, left-leaning journalists to reach an audience of liberal yuppies.[31]

In the 1970s, the alternative press, as well as traditional dailies, faced competition for that bourgeois audience from a new wave of lifestyle magazines. Led by Clay Felker's *New York*, these publications applied the libidinous spirit, spiky prose style, and graphical flair of the sixties alternative press to the terrain of upscale consumption. If the New Left had seen consumption as a means for political action, lifestyle magazines viewed consumption as an end in itself. As Michael Wolff wrote in a commemoration of *New York* on its thirty-fifth anniversary, Felker had the "crass but revolutionary . . . notion that you are what you buy." Like other urban lifestyle magazines launched in this era, *New York* was "not so much a guide to the city," Wolff continued, "as it was a guide to being cleverer, hipper, more in-the-know"—a handbook for young metropolitan professionals looking to distinguish themselves via their consumer savvy.[32]

This "in-the-know" spirit also extended to politics, which the magazine treated as yet another arena for connoisseurship. Beginning in 1967, *New York* compiled an annual list of the "ten most powerful men" in the city. Politics, these articles implied, wasn't a terrain for moral or material struggles. It was more like a stage where celebrity personalities performed. And *New York* promised its shrewd readers a peek behind the curtain, into the offstage area where experts actually got things done.[33] *New York*, which shared this insider tone with similar publications like *Atlanta Magazine* and *New Times*, proved remarkably popular. *New York* saw its circulation soar from fifty thousand to 335,000 over its first five years.[34] The success of these lifestyle magazines spurred old-guard newspapers to try to emulate them. In the early 1970s, Abe Rosenthal, managing editor of the sober *New York Times*, pressed his editors to mimic *New York*'s style of service journalism. Rosenthal even hired several former *New York* journalists, one as a restaurant critic and another as editor of a new "Home" section. As the metropolitan upper-middle class assumed greater power, all manner of publications vied for their attention.[35]

In the 1970s and particularly the 1980s, a string of high-end consumer magazines sought to capture emerging demographic segments within the ascendant professional elite. Deepening economic inequality and the diversification of America's corporate and managerial workforce drove this trend. From the mid-1970s to the mid-1980s, households headed by college graduates saw their real wages rise some 20 percent as the postindustrial economy paid ever-greater dividends to educated men and women, particularly in high-wage metropolitan areas. In contrast, blue-collar and lower-level corporate workers—even those who hadn't been laid off in waves of plant and branch closures—saw their buying power fall as inflation, soaring mortgage interest rates, and rising energy costs ate into their pay.[36] Meanwhile, women and African Americans entered the professional workforce in ever-larger numbers. Flush with disposable income, both groups tantalized advertisers. Publications soon sprang up to target them. A half-dozen magazines targeting Black professionals were launched in a span of a decade: from *Black Enterprise* to *Emerge*, *Upscale*, *Excel*, and *Black Collegian*. (*Jive* was the only new publication aimed at working-class Black readers. Meanwhile, many longtime Black newspapers, suffering from plummeting urban readerships and advertising, shuttered in this era.) And while women across the economic spectrum joined the workforce during the 1970s, most new publications pursued the career woman, with *Savvy, Working Mother, Self,* and *Working Woman* among the most notable titles. Unlike mid-century women's service magazines (*Good Housekeeping, Redbook*), they explicitly targeted the top of the class ladder. As the editor of *Working Woman* confessed in 1985, "cashiers in supermarket checkout lines ... should not be part of our audience."[37]

Even though these urban and high-end lifestyle magazines were designed to reach an upscale audience, they still published their share of journalists from blue-collar backgrounds. Those writers assumed an important role as cultural intermediaries for their readers. They embodied, and helped yuppies to decode, the perspectives of the white-ethnic urban villagers that they lived alongside in gentrifying neighborhoods like Park Slope or the Back Bay. Beginning in the late 1960s, as a portion of the white working class began to turn against liberalism and depart the New Deal coalition, metropolitan liberals depended on these journalists for perspective on the "common man" and his shifting political allegiances—just as Democrats turned to envoys from the rural white working class to make sense of Donald Trump's election in 2016.

Take the case of Pete Hamill, the consummate Brooklyn newspaperman and columnist. The oldest of seven children born to Irish immigrant parents, Hamill abandoned a sheet metal worker apprenticeship to take a job on the rewrite desk at the New York *Post* in 1960. By the end of the decade, he was writing long pieces for the *Village Voice, New York,* and *Esquire,* essential outlets for his New Journalism peers.[38] Hamill's writing was peppered with urban working-class argot: knowing references to stickball and the Myrtle Avenue El that validated his streetwise credentials.[39] But Hamill and his contemporaries could move seamlessly between worlds—he did, after all, date both Shirley MacLaine and Jacqueline Kennedy Onassis. And so his most important articles in lifestyle magazines were missives from what he called the "White Lower Middle Class"—the prototypical Archie Bunker type who was "in revolt" against rising taxes, street crime, and, above all, liberal elites' sanctimonious sympathy for Black Americans.[40]

At his best, Hamill did vital translational work for his educated audience. His articles provided economic and sociological context for his subjects' seemingly irrational resentments. But by ventriloquizing an imagined blue-collar viewpoint, Hamill could also find himself defending some of their most reactionary claims, particularly on the terrain of race and sexuality. In his later columns for *Esquire,* he justified anti-Black racism as having "a certain validity," based as it was on street-level encounters with "the virtually permanent welfare-supported underclass," the people "sitting on the stoop while they go to work."[41] In a long essay addressed to an imaginary Black friend, Hamill exhorted the same "underclass" to follow the upward course of his own immigrant parents, people who were too proud for the dole and "too busy for self pity."[42] Hamill, like many of his working-class male peers—Jimmy Breslin, Gay Talese, and particularly Norman Mailer—also bristled at the feminist and gay rights movements.[43] In a 1990 column—at the height of the AIDS crisis—Hamill admitted that he felt an "uncomfortable sympathy" with gay baiters and was "bored" by homosexual protesters' "theatrical rage" and "self-pitying aura of victimhood." "I am tired," he continued, "of listening to people who identify themselves exclusively by what they do with their cocks."[44] Hamill's everyman persona allowed him to indulge, if vicariously, in what he imagined to be the white working class's disdain for racial and sexual minorities. Worse still, he validated those latent sentiments among his liberal professional-class readers—underwriting some of the punitive policies the Democratic Party would endorse and enact in the 1980s and 1990s.

* * *

Pete Hamill represented only one part of a wider ideological shift within the liberal magazine commentariat. Established publications like the *New Republic* and self-declared neoliberal magazines like *Washington Monthly* punctured, with no small dose of contrarianism and sarcasm, what they saw as the exhausted tenets of New Deal–era liberalism. After Marty Peretz assumed ownership and editorial control of the *New Republic* in 1974, it charted an upscale direction for the Democratic Party.[45] It began with its elite readership, which comprised, Peretz crowed, "the opinion class, the policy class, the university professors, lawyers and legislators." It may have only counted a circulation of a hundred thousand. But as Peretz frequently joked, it was "the right 100,000."[46] In its pages, it dispensed disdain for the Democrats' traditional constituencies, now lumped together as "special interests": labor unions, urban ethnics, and above all, the Black poor. In column after column, the *New Republic* attacked the putative African American underclass, blaming the excesses of the welfare state for its perpetuation. Columns by Charles Murray and Hendrik Hertzberg assailed affirmative action; unsigned editorials blamed mid-century liberalism for deepening "social pathologies."[47] (The 1980s *New Republic*, from its policy positions to its author bylines, had substantial overlap with the neoconservative *Public Interest* and *Commentary*.) Looking abroad, the magazine advocated for an intelligent but muscular foreign policy that rejected the rigid orthodoxies of the "doves" on the left and "hawks" on the right. A 1986 editorial (likely penned by Charles Krauthammer) made the counterintuitive "Case for the Contras." Without American aid, it argued, the Sandinistas would quash democracy in Nicaragua. One by one, it debunked doves' ethical arguments for neutrality.[48]

Ultimately, the *New Republic* insisted that any a priori political or moral commitments—what literary editor Leon Wieseltier called "extravagant ideological entailments"—were themselves the problem.[49] What was needed instead were "smarts": the protean intelligence to navigate an increasingly complicated world. Conveniently, smarts were something that America's educated elite believed they had in spades. In this respect, the *New Republic* (along with *Washington Monthly* and *George*, and later, *Politico*, *Vox*, and *Pod Save America*) forged a new form of reportage: what media scholar Jay Rosen calls the "savvy style" of political journalism. Reporters and pundits, many of them with experience inside Democratic administrations, aspired to be "hyper-informed, perceptive, ironic, 'with it,' and unsentimental" above all else. Winning the political horse race or wonky policy argument was their highest aim. Savvy journalists (David Riesman called them "inside dopesters") let readers in on the game, too. Instead of mass politics, they offered a glimpse of the way that power "really" works in Washington, DC—a peek behind the curtain, where smart operators not unlike themselves play the game. Participatory politics yields to savvy spectatorship and scorekeeping.[50] Seven decades after Walter Lippmann founded the *New Republic*, it appeared that his vision for democracy, mediated by a "specialized class" of disinterested experts, had won the day.[51]

The ascendance of that technocratic faction was not without its critics, however. As publications pivoted toward upscale readers and journalists themselves grew more educated and cosmopolitan, they faced mounting accusations of elitism and liberal bias. In the 1970s, neoconservatives, particularly Irving Kristol, took aim at journalists for belonging to and advancing the interests of a "New Class" of cultural elites. Along with their peers in universities, public-interest nonprofits, and government regulatory agencies, neoconservatives argued, media professionals were disproportionately liberal, expensively educated, urban, secular, and white.[52] They wanted to upend free enterprise and traditional morality. They remained unduly sympathetic to African Americans and the poor (even if these sympathies had begun to wane, as evidenced by the editorial evolution at the *New Republic*.) The New Class, Kristol wrote, believed "that they can do a better job of running our society and feel entitled to have the opportunity."[53] In the 1970s and 1980s, a series of right-wing books and conferences took aim at the so-called media elite within the New Class. They anatomized journalists' expensive educations (93 percent had graduated college), narrow geographic base (over two-thirds came from a small number of northeastern states), and liberal politics (81 percent had voted for Senator George McGovern in the 1972 presidential election).[54]

To be sure, this critique of the elite liberal media came from a group of New York intellectuals who were themselves part of an adjacent elite. After all, Kristol's broadsides were published in his column in the *Wall Street Journal*. And their attacks were tinged with no small amount of personal animosity and racial resentment. But neoconservatives' diagnosis did contain a shred of truth, particularly to the white working-class Americans who felt left behind by journalism's class transformation. Metropolitan newspapers had indeed abandoned poor, rural, blue-collar, and urban white-ethnic audiences since the 1960s. The "savvy" style was for educated insiders—and it openly condescended to less-informed outsiders.

Political coverage had taken an adversarial and interpretive turn in the wake of Vietnam and Watergate, a shift that historian Matthew Pressman locates in the hegemony of "liberal values" in the newsroom.[55] Lifestyle magazines adopted the cultural politics of the New Left, even as they slavishly targeted upscale readers. The bevy of new consumer magazines largely ignored inflation-strapped, downwardly mobile Americans. Journalists themselves were drawn from a small handful of colleges and graduate programs, particularly at top national publications. And journalists' politics in fact diverged from most rank-and-file white union members. Tellingly, at the 1972 Democratic convention, the ANG's executive committee, dominated by white-collar journalists, endorsed George McGovern. Meanwhile, the AFL-CIO—along with most of the ANG's non-journalist membership—declined to endorse him, even in the general election against President Richard Nixon.[56] For neoconservatives, along with the white silent majority they claimed to speak for, journalism had become incontrovertibly more elite and more liberal since the 1960s.

* * *

In the early and mid-1990s, the advent of the Internet deepened journalism's long-term structural, social, and ideological transformation. But new technology was only partly responsible for this shift. Online publishing accelerated a decades-long decline for the Fordist model for media, with its large, unionized newspaper operations that dotted nearly every town and city across the United States. In the 1990s, those structures began to yield to small, nonunion web outlets, which were staffed and managed by highly educated professionals in a small number of coastal cities. Ownership passed from family-owned firms to conglomerates to private-equity firms. Expectations for profits rose; journalists' wages and job security worsened. Craft workers were replaced by typesetting computers. Staff reporters and career pressmen were laid off and replaced by nonunion freelancers, stringers, and third-party production firms.[57] Even as work conditions deteriorated, publications demanded ever-more-elite degree and internship credentials for new hires, further narrowing newsrooms' class makeup. And publishers—in print and online—intensified their pursuit of high-income audiences, the one bright spot in a consumer economy that grew more unequal with each passing year. As the sun set on the twentieth-century liberal order, the news industry was subject to many of the same changes that were remaking American life.[58]

Ironically, the sharpest blow to the Fordist media resulted from a strike, with the Newspaper Guild playing a key role. In November 1994, 2,600 employees from eight allied unions walked out of San Francisco's two daily newspapers, the *Examiner* and the *Chronicle*, to protest wage freezes, planned layoffs, and the replacement of 150 Teamster-affiliated delivery drivers with independent contractors.[59] Ownership retained a union-busting law firm that had broken similar actions at the *New York Daily News* and *Chicago Tribune*. For twelve days, editors, composers, and pressmen marched together outside the papers' headquarters, attacking delivery trucks that attempted to cross the picket line.

But even as the presses sat dormant, the papers' editorial staff were busy publishing their own online-only news daily, the *San Francisco Free Press*—one of the first sites of its kind.[60] The *Free Press* wasn't ornate: striking editors sketched its layout on a bar napkin, and it rented server space from WELL, the local computer network with roots in the *Whole Earth Catalog*, a 1960s print emporium for ecologically minded countercultural products. However shambolic, the *Free Press* proved that news and opinions could be delivered effectively on the World Wide Web. It broke at least one national-level story, and it counted some hundred thousand daily readers, most of them affluent and tech-savvy.[61] The *Free Press*, like the countless websites it inspired, promised journalists a seemingly frictionless medium to convey their ideas. The Internet required no expensive newsprint, no printing presses, and, importantly, no expensive blue-collar employees to make and deliver the news. "It was a traditional newspaper strike, traditional union issues," remembered Bruce Koon, co-editor of the *Free Press*. "Here the strike was being supported by a medium bypassing it. There was a certain irony at the time." Even as guild members struck in solidarity with craft workers, they pioneered the technological form that would undermine the very institutions that employed them both. Eight unions went on strike together. The success of the *Free Press* hinted that all but the guild might soon be obsolete.[62]

The *Free Press*, which emerged at nearly the same moment as the pioneering Netscape web browser, inspired a surge of interest and investment in Internet news. In 1995, *USA Today* began to put out free online content. The *New York Times* would follow less than a year later. By the middle of 1995, 150 newspapers worldwide ran Web editions.[63] Many of the first Internet journalists were former *Examiner* and *Chronicle* employees. In the span of a year, the papers lost a publisher, multiple section and desk editors, several reporters, three culture critics, and even their editorial cartoonist to Internet publications.[64] In 1995, David Talbot and several other *Examiner* journalists used money from Apple and Adobe to launch Salon.com in San Francisco. *Salon*, whose founding manifesto boasted of its "militantly centrist" politics, would elevate the "savvy style" to new heights, running regular pieces by DC insider journalists Jake Tapper and Jonathan Broder and neoconservative gadfly David Horowitz. By 1996, the former factory buildings in San Francisco's South of Market neighborhood were so chockablock with Internet newsrooms that locals took to calling the area "Multimedia Gulch."[65]

These small, scrappy publications styled themselves in opposition to the large mid-century newspaper. Their newsrooms were open and informal, with little physical infrastructure besides clusters of desks and rows of humming computer towers. Reporters' wages and benefits were low. Except for a handful of technical and janitorial staff (usually third-party contractors), there were no craft workers on staff: no librarians, no typesetters, no delivery drivers. No one belonged to a union. Even if compensation lagged, what Internet publications could promise journalists was a workplace that was informal, hip, and nonhierarchical—a far cry from the layers of often-overbearing management at old-school dailies. At HotWired, *Wired* magazine's website, journalists pecked out stories under posters listing their Ten Commandments: "Invent New Words," one read. "We're Not in Newspapers Anymore."[66]

That swashbuckling atmosphere, however, concealed trends that made journalism even more cloistered by geography and class. Internet publications, unlike the local newspapers they replaced, were concentrated in a tiny number of high-cost American cities. By 2015, the moment when the number of web journalists surpassed the number working at newspapers, nearly three-quarters of Internet news jobs were located in either the Boston–New York–Washington–Richmond megalopolis or the Seattle-to–San Diego corridor. Another 5 percent were based in Chicago.[67] Journalists headed to those outlets were increasingly well educated. Most editors expected entry-level writers to possess technical computing skills; almost all required college-level internship experience. And without a union to set a livable starting wage, young journalists regularly drew on family wealth to survive. One editor offered a Chicago journalist a job with a salary under $10,000. "Can't your parents help you out?" he asked her.[68] Even affirmative-action efforts, which marginally increased racial diversity starting in the 1970s, did little to broaden the industry's class base. By the 1980s, one internal *Los Angeles Times* report found that its affirmative-action program mostly recruited from Ivy League universities and paid wages that could not cover the high cost of living in LA.[69] Well into the 1990s, leading magazines continued to hire entry-level editors primarily from their ranks of unpaid interns. Those interns were overwhelmingly well-to-do and white. For example, William Whitworth, the editor of the *Atlantic*, had only two Black interns among the hundreds who passed through the program between 1981 and 1995. Despite finding that fact "unfortunate," Whitworth confessed that the diversity of the internship pool had "not been at the top of my agenda." The *Atlantic* wasn't alone. In 1995, the *New Yorker* had fewer than seven non-white editors on a staff of over one hundred. Both *Harper's* and the *New York Review of Books* were entirely white.[70]

As layoffs and wage cuts spread across the industry during the wave of corporate consolidation in the 1990s and the first decade of the 2000s, journalism grew only more elite. While the field retained much of its cultural capital, it offered employees a slimmer path to a secure, well-paying career. Increasingly, only those with familial wealth, or at the very least, a wealth of marketable credentials, decided to join the profession—trusting that they'd remain secure in the (likely) event they lost their job. By the 2010s, journalists were more likely to have graduated from a top university than members of the federal judiciary, CEOs of Fortune 500 companies, or even US senators. Fully half of the masthead at the *New Republic*—the magazine that had served as an intellectual engine for the newly upscale Democratic Party in the 1980s—boasted an Ivy League degree.[71]

* * *

In 1996, only months apart, two new media outlets emerged that embodied the fruits of journalism's widening class divide. The first, Slate.com, was founded as a joint venture between Microsoft and Michael Kinsley, a key force at the *New Republic* in the 1980s. *Slate* was the post-Fordist publication par excellence. Its three bureaus—in Seattle, New York, and Washington—spoke to its tripartite investment in the worlds of technology, magazine publishing, and politics. Instead of hiring an expensive roll of reporters, it made several high-profile hires (Paul Krugman,

Nicholas Lemann, Michael Lewis, and James Fallows) and filled out the rest of its staff with freelancers and interns.

Slate's content was oriented toward affluent, highly educated readers—the "politically and culturally engaged people," Kinsley said, who also subscribed to the *Economist* and the *New Republic*. (Initially, *Slate* was also sold in print form at Starbucks locations.) Its audience didn't visit the weekly online magazine for up-to-the-minute reporting. They came for political analysis that gratified their insider knowledge of the Washington scene. Each week, *Slate* ran a column by a consultant that deconstructed election-season TV ads. Its recurring "Horse Race" feature promised to "track the presidential candidates like stocks, as priced by the opinion polls [and] the pundits."[72] Even though most of its readers were self-described liberals, *Slate* prided itself on partisan promiscuity: it rented DC office space from the American Enterprise Institute, and its first advice columnist was Herbert Stein, chairman of President Nixon's Council of Economic Advisors.[73] In 2002, in the lead-up to the invasion of Iraq, *Slate* ran a debate featuring pro-war takes from a range of hawks, from Andrew Sullivan to John McWhorter to Gregg Easterbrook.[74] That feature, like much of *Slate* in those years, typified the orientation of many professional-class liberals toward politics at the close of the twentieth century. Instead of an urgent democratic contest for power, politics had become a domain for intellectual swordplay, where experts—some with dangerously reactionary views—offered "takes" whose counterintuitiveness was taken as a sign of their perspicacity. Smarts and smarm were coins of this realm.

Just a few months after *Slate*'s debut, Rupert Murdoch, the Australian publishing magnate, launched the Fox News network. The cable channel targeted a culturally blue-collar audience—precisely the demographic that print media had neglected since the 1960s. Fox News offered a muscular, populist conservative take on the news. Murdoch had pioneered this approach in the 1980s with *Sky News* in the UK and, even earlier, with the *New York Post*, which he purchased in 1976 and transformed from a left-leaning broadsheet into a sensationalist, racially reactionary tabloid. The formula was fantastically successful: by 1980, the *Post*'s circulation had risen by nearly a third, making it the best-selling afternoon paper in the United States.[75]

Fox News fused the tabloid flair of the *Post* with a biting critique of America's elites. It also pulled off a deft sleight of hand when it came to its class positioning. Fox's populism wasn't aimed at economic titans; the network actively refrained from attacking Wall Street during the 2008 financial crisis. Instead, Fox directed its ire at supercilious cultural elites who disdained the values and degraded the status of an "authentic" blue-collar white majority. In the postindustrial era, that identity had more to do with education than income. Fox News was fantastically successful at reaching that demographic: 76 percent of Fox News viewers did not possess a college degree, by far the highest proportion among cable news networks.[76] Fox's style was essential to communicating its sympathy for this audience. The network's mastermind, Roger Ailes, recruited hosts from a variety of regional white identities, directing them to play up their blue-collar bona fides. "Shep" Smith spoke with a folksy southern drawl; Sean Hannity reminded viewers he had worked in construction; Bill O'Reilly leaned into his everyman Long Island accent. In true tabloid style, the network's graphics and title cards were bold and combative. As media scholar Reece Peck argues, Fox's style *was* its politics.[77]

Fox News' popularity reflected the rising salience of a blue-collar identity among a swath of white Americans since the 1960s. Regardless of their actual economic standing, they tended to value the same qualities: toughness, religiosity, hard work, respect for tradition, and masculine authority. Above all else, blue-collar conservatives resented the perceived snobbery and condescension of the New Class of liberal, professional-managerial, and technocratic workers.[78] Mainstream journalists were among the most hated avatars of that cosmopolitan class.

By the end of the twentieth century, this long-running conservative critique of the elite media had become even more salient. And as we have seen, it had real material origins—this was no case of fake news. Since the 1960s, the industry had abandoned working-class readers and subjects in favor of high-income audiences. Journalists themselves were also drawn from an ever-thinner educational stratum. In the 1990s, under pressure to boost profits in an age of corporate ownership, the last vestiges of the large, unionized Fordist newspaper finally gave way, suffering a similar fate as the New Deal political coalition writ large. By the first decade of the 2000s, the United States was left with the media landscape we are familiar with today: a coterie of expensively educated reporters, concentrated in a few metropolitan areas, struggling to understand how they could have missed the groundswell of blue-collar conservatism that drove Donald Trump's victory. Far from accidental, their failure was the culmination of five decades of institutional and social change that had entirely remade American news.

But it wasn't just media, of course. Journalism was only one part of a much broader process of class polarization in the United States. That fracture, often narrated as a story of a widening political gulf between left and right, was in fact just as much the product of other divides: between cities and their exurban or rural hinterlands; between cosmopolitan professionals and businesspeople heading regional or family businesses; between highly educated technocrats and those without a college degree; between upwardly mobile knowledge workers and a downwardly mobile tranche of the former middle class.[79] Journalism alone did not create those fissures. But it remained one of the few arenas where liberals could work out potential solutions. In the very decades where they might have imagined new and more egalitarian visions for a divided nation, liberals lost the mediating influence of a press that reflected the true diversity of American experience. With it, they lost the imagination needed for a more capacious, more democratic, and more popular political movement.

CHAPTER 8

Seeing Like a Strategist

TIMOTHY SHENK

Sifting through election returns in the autumn of 1966, Kevin Phillips caught a glimpse of the future. Born in 1940, Phillips was a Republican operative who had been drawing up maps of voting patterns since he was fifteen years old. He had spent his young life in the shadow of the New Deal coalition, an electoral majority linking blue-collar families around the country with the Solid South. Examining the results of the 1966 midterms, where Republicans gained ground in both the House and Senate just two years after Lyndon Johnson's 1964 landslide, Phillips saw the Democratic Party cracking under the combined force of the backlash to the civil rights movement, opposition to the emerging counterculture, and the rise of the Sun Belt. By 1968, Phillips thought the results were undeniable. Richard Nixon's victory and George Wallace's impressive showing as a third-party candidate—the two pulled in a combined 57 percent of the vote—marked the arrival of what he called, in a 1969 book of the same name, *The Emerging Republican Majority*.[1]

Not bad, as prophecy-making goes. The GOP never assembled a proper successor to FDR's majority, but it won six of the next nine presidential elections, took back the South for the first time since Reconstruction, and broke Democrats' iron grip on the House of Representatives. By the 1980s, Democrats had fallen into what historians have described as a kind of civil war. On one side, self-described neoliberals urged the party to give up on the hard-hat politics of the industrial age and focus on courting younger and more educated white-collar voters in a postindustrial economy.[2] On the other, Jesse Jackson stood at the head of a movement exhorting Democrats to rally behind a principled left-wing platform that would summon a rainbow coalition made up of "the damned, the disinherited, the disrespected, and the despised."[3]

With the benefit of hindsight, it is now clear that the agonies of the Democratic Party fit into a larger pattern.[4] Across wealthy Western democracies, electorates that had previously split along economic lines were increasingly divided by identity, a process referred to as class dealignment. Even as income and wealth inequality spiked, left-wing parties were transformed by the infusion of highly educated voters often motivated by what political scientist Ronald Inglehart described as "postmaterialist values," including tolerance, diversity, and expanding rights for the oppressed.[5] At the same time, ideological polarization linked American liberalism to the fortunes of the Democratic Party. Liberals consolidated within the Democratic coalition, and liberalism underwent transformations chronicled elsewhere in this volume.

In the United States, the intra-Democratic feud between neoliberals and the rainbow coalition ended with a surprise marriage between the two during the Obama years, with journalists announcing the birth of a "coalition of the ascendant" made up of racial minorities, the college-educated, and the young.[6] But the path from Franklin Roosevelt to Barack Obama was filled with twists. And there was a time—quite a long time, in fact—when it seemed as if both Democrats and liberals might head in different directions.

Understanding this alternative history requires taking a closer look at how Democrats tried to stitch together electoral majorities during the political winter that followed Nixon's victory. Think of it as seeing like a political strategist.

By the end of the twentieth century, these strategists—pollsters, media consultants, direct-mail gurus, digital whiz kids—had become essential actors in and interpreters of the democratic process. With billions of dollars cycling through political consulting firms each election cycle, campaign operatives pursued two interrelated goals: first, determining the boundaries of public opinion; then, producing messages and policies that could build majorities for their clients.[7] Strategists, therefore, understood politics differently than policymakers or even politicians. They begin with the assumption that public opinion is a real force. Determining its exact outlines might require a mix of art and science, but strategists must believe that their assessments of the electorate—typically based on a mix of polls and focus groups—are not just projections of their own biases. Although strategists acknowledge that voter sentiment can shift radically over time, they are usually skeptical about how much those views are likely to change during a single campaign. The most effective candidates, therefore, focus on the issues that are of greatest concern to the electorate and then figure out a way to get on the right side of public opinion.

Whether or not this approach is a useful way of thinking about politics—and it has plenty of critics across the ideological spectrum—what matters for our purposes is that it was taken quite seriously indeed by politicians. Which means that no history of either the Democratic Party and American liberalism is complete without taking into account the small group of people who made careers trying to win elections for Democrats.

Of particular relevance are the strategists behind the only Democrat in the second half of the twentieth century to win two terms in the White House. The key members in Bill Clinton's political team were not just some of the most influential figures in Democratic politics. They were also textbook examples of seeing like a strategist.

But those points of overlap didn't stop a fundamental debate from breaking this tiny world in two. Eventually, this conflict spilled into the pages of newspapers, where journalists reported on a battle tearing Democratic consultants apart.[8] One camp, associated with Stan Greenberg, lead pollster for Clinton's 1992 presidential campaign, argued that populist economics and cultural moderation could build a lasting majority by drawing white working-class voters back into the Democratic coalition. The other, led by Mark Penn and Douglass Schoen, who took over as chief pollsters for Clinton's reelection bid, insisted that class politics had lost its punch. According to Penn and Schoen, Democrats were competing in a center-right nation where they couldn't afford to give up on *any* potential swing voters, whether they were upwardly mobile soccer moms or angry white men. Where Greenberg said that Democrats could bring back the economically divided politics of the New Deal years, Penn and Schoen told Democrats to accept that they were living in Reagan's America.

In the long run, both sides lost this war. During the Obama years, a new generation of political operatives rose to prominence, and with them came a different vision for the Democratic Party. With the country becoming more racially diverse, young people supporting Obama by landslide numbers, and college-educated voters moving into the Democratic column, it seemed as if a new majority was springing to life—a majority that Greenberg, Penn, and Schoen had all dismissed as a fantasy not long before.

What both sides were fighting over, how their debate influenced Democratic politics, and why it was so easy to leave them behind—these questions are more than just footnotes in recent history. They cut to the center of the Democratic Party, American liberalism, and democracy itself.

But before getting to this history, there's another question to answer first: how did political consultants become so important in the first place?

The Rise of Political Consulting

While the old Democratic coalition was falling apart in the late 1960s, a new industry was taking shape. Credit for coining the term "political consultant" goes to Joseph Napolitan, a Democratic politico with a resume that included stints on campaigns for John Kennedy in 1960, LBJ in 1964, and Hubert Humphrey in 1968.[9] With the wounds from Humphrey's defeat still fresh, Napolitan helped organize the inaugural meeting in 1969 of the American Association of Political Consultants (AAPC). By its twentieth anniversary, the AAPC's membership had ballooned from just a handful of people to over eight hundred. Today, its more than 1600 members are part of a multibillion-dollar industry that controls virtually every part of a campaign, from rounding up signatures to get candidates on the ballot down to writing victory and concession speeches. In between, they produce ads, analyze data, map out fundraising strategies, oversee social media presences, target potential voters, and send out swarms of volunteers to knock on doors. American politics is, to a significant degree, what the consultant class has made it.

Political consultants were a bridge between the outgoing world of party bosses and the new regime of professionalized partisan crusaders. They might have gone to college with the head of Planned Parenthood or a senior fellow at the American Enterprise Institute, but they made their reputations by running successful campaigns, or at least by telling plausible stories about how they trounced the other side, typically by specializing in one of three areas: polling, messaging, and turning out the vote.

Despite a few high-profile exceptions—California-based Campaigns Inc., for instance, which helped sink Upton Sinclair's bid for governor in 1934—political consultants did not establish themselves as a proper industry until the 1970s. Partly, that's because their calling cards were often recent inventions. Although bringing voters to the ballot box was a time-tested art, public-opinion surveys and mass-media campaigns were both thoroughly modern endeavors. Message gurus only became a valued commodity when radio and television made well-crafted advertisements into an expected part of electioneering. Reliable polls combining large sample sizes with statistical rigor first began appearing in the 1930s, and it took decades for prices to fall low enough that candidates could afford to make them a routine part of campaigning.

Money, too, was a factor. When campaign finance laws tightened after the Watergate scandals, political consulting remained a legitimate source of expenditures. The drive to clean up campaign funding took place at the same time that businesses were ratcheting up their investment in politics and direct-mail fundraising was turning small-dollar donations into a major source of revenue. With more cash flooding to fewer targets, consultants reaped the rewards.

Which did not always sit well with Democrats. Into the 1970s, Republicans were more likely to employ professional consultants, Democrats to rely on labor unions and grassroots activists. As diversity was becoming a prized ideal within the party, consultants remained overwhelmingly white and male.[10] They were also tied up with the business world. Overseeing high-profile campaigns was the best kind of publicity, but the private sector was a much larger market, and corporate work paid the bills between election cycles.

Then there was the huckster dilemma. Consultants could spin compelling stories about the single ad that turned around a campaign, or the candidate who doomed a race by refusing to follow sound advice. But these stories were anecdotal evidence from people who paid the bills with good storytelling. Meanwhile, political scientists churned out research demonstrating that most elections turned on forces outside a candidate's control, chiefly the state of the economy and the popularity of the incumbent president. Studies repeatedly showed that most television advertising had a tiny and fleeting impact on a race, yet spending on TV was usually the largest item on a campaign's balance sheet—and a hefty portion of the consultant's paycheck. Plunging response rates for polls made it even more difficult to produce accurate readings of public opinion. And it didn't take a graduate course in statistics to see that wealthy candidates could hire the most celebrated talent in the business and still get walloped on election day.

Not until the George W. Bush years did campaigns begin systematically studying which parts of the campaign actually delivered votes. The results were not encouraging. "Eighty percent of what they did in the old days didn't work," one longtime Democratic consultant observed, and the evidence for buzzy techniques combining big data with microtargeting was just as mixed.[11] The day when cutting-edge research would finally turn campaigning into a science kept slipping into the future. In a profession rife with uncertainty, it could seem like the only abiding truth was that a candidate's check had to clear.

But there were good reasons the money kept flowing. In competitive races, a well-run campaign could boost turnout by just enough to make the difference between victory and defeat. Even if most elections were determined by the broader political climate, candidates still had to explain why they were running. That choice—the message to voters—was the single most important decision candidates would make. No wonder they wanted help from professionals.

Here is where the history of political consulting links back up with the struggles of Democrats to put together a new majority. The structural forces transforming left-wing parties around the world—rising income levels, increasing education rates, heightened salience of social issues—were not going to change drastically between elections. Wages weren't going to fall back to Depression standards, and Republicans weren't going to seek a truce in the culture war. Even if organized labor reversed its prolonged decline, the question of why union members were attracted to candidates like Richard Nixon and George Wallace still had to be answered. Campaign strategy was pushed to the center of a raging battle over the future of the Democratic Party and the meaning of liberalism.

Polarization was at the heart of the debate. It is often argued that ideological polarization is the central fact of modern American politics. It is less often noted how much of a danger this polarization posed to Democrats. Going into the 1960s, Democrats significantly outnumbered Republicans, but only a minority of Americans considered themselves *liberals*. Even today, just a quarter of Americans call themselves liberals, compared to over 70 percent who say they are either moderate or conservative.[12]

There are limits to how much can be concluded from ideological self-definition, and a number of policies associated with liberalism—from abortion rights to Social Security—have solid support with voters who say they are conservative. But as memories of the New Deal faded, and liberalism became increasingly associated with the movements of the 1960s, the once formidable Democratic coalition disintegrated. Although Democrats picked up support with college-educated professionals, those gains were more than offset by losses elsewhere—most dramatically in the South, but also with white working-class voters across the nation.

The question for Democrats was whether the class-based voting that gave the party its majorities under FDR could be restored. Among Democratic operatives, the case for hope was most closely associated with one name.

The Class Project

Stan Greenberg always had a plan. It was how the son of a family teetering on the border between working and middle class found himself on the tenure track in Yale's political science department while still in his twenties.[13] Born in 1945, Greenberg spent much of his childhood living in a majority-Black neighborhood in Washington, DC. He was drawn to politics by the civil rights movement, then pushed leftward by the turmoil of the 1960s. He came to New Haven straight out of graduate school at Harvard, where he had supervised a national survey of attitudes in a hundred poor neighborhoods for the Office of Economic Opportunity. The survey provided the starting point for a dissertation examining why broadly similar economic conditions produced starkly diverging political cultures in five of those communities (Mexican Americans in San Jose; Appalachian whites in Hamilton, Ohio; and African Americans in Philadelphia, Detroit, and Atlanta).[14]

The subject was a natural one for a thinker of Greenberg's radical sympathies. He used his time in graduate school to immerse himself in the Marxist canon, where he was particularly struck by Antonio Gramsci's writings on hegemony—the ways that capitalist elites secured their legitimacy with the wider public, including key sections of the working class.

Fascination with the mechanics of hegemony provided the point of departure for Greenberg's enquiry into the politics of the poor. Next it took him to Johannesburg for an ambitious comparative study in the making of "racial orders"—that is, societies built around formalized and pervasive racial hierarchies.[15] Published in 1980, *Race and State in Capitalist Development* grew out of dozens of interviews conducted with representatives for business and labor groups in South Africa and Alabama, supplemented by additional work in Israel and Northern Ireland. Rejecting stark binaries between material and cultural forces, Greenberg sought to understand the lives of "actors who live simultaneously in a class and racial milieu."[16]

Racism, Greenberg believed, could not be reduced simply to economics, but it also did not need to be accepted as a permanent fact of life. "White steelworkers in Alabama and the white mineworkers in South Africa, whatever their awful role in excluding blacks," he later observed, "were not without social democratic impulses."[17] The trick was to coax buried egalitarian sentiments to the surface, which required careful maneuvering around the intersecting questions of class and race, along with sympathy for the people you were trying to persuade. The project was not, however, enough to secure its author tenure at Yale. Although Greenberg remained an adjunct professor at the university until 1987, the prospect of life in the academic precariat quickly shunted him onto an alternative career path.

Participation in formal politics had long been a sideline for Greenberg. He interned on Capitol Hill while in college, worked for the Young

Democrats, and attended the 1964 Democratic National Convention. In graduate school, he volunteered on Robert Kennedy's 1968 presidential run, joining a team that developed a computer program using results from the primaries to determine where an appearance from the candidate would turn out the most votes. At Yale, he became active in state and local politics. In 1980, he took over polling for Chris Dodd's Senate campaign, which, as it happened, was being managed by Greenberg's wife, future congresswoman Rosa DeLauro.

Dodd won the race, leading to more clients for Greenberg—including, in the wake of Ronald Reagan's 1984 landslide reelection, a request from the Michigan Democratic Party and the United Auto Workers for a study into what had gone wrong. Greenberg focused on white middle- and working-class voters, once loyal Democrats, who had voted overwhelmingly for Reagan. In focus groups with residents of Macomb County, just outside Detroit, he encountered sentiments with more than a passing resemblance to the views he heard in South Africa and Alabama. "Distaste for black Americans," he found, "pervaded almost everything they thought about government and politics." After hearing a defense of the nation's historic obligations to African Americans, attributed to Robert Kennedy, one focus group member replied, "That's bullshit." Another added, "No wonder they killed him."[18]

Yet Greenberg did not believe that racism was the only factor at play in Macomb's transformation. "Even though I was writing about people who were racist," he said, "I wrote about what decisions they made as rational decisions that drew on their lives, their history, their needs, interests."[19] These onetime Democrats were driven to the GOP by a mixture of cultural anxiety, economic grievance, and wide-ranging frustration with the political establishment, especially with a Democratic Party they felt had betrayed them. And Greenberg thought they had a point. The Democratic Party, he later said, had become an "elitist and suburban party with contempt for working Americans," at least if they were white.[20] He wasn't surprised that voters noticed.

This, paradoxically, was the good news. If the white working class had been pushed away by Democratic mistakes, then it wasn't lost for good. Just like his subjects in South Africa and Alabama, the citizens of Macomb harbored latent egalitarian impulses that could be tapped into with the right message. They believed that corporations had too much influence over politics, thought blue-collar families deserved government support, and wanted a strong labor movement. These people weren't monsters. In fact, they weren't even Republicans, at least not yet. They were "Reagan Democrats"—a term Greenberg popularized—who had not found a secure home with the GOP and might once again become part of a progressive, multiracial majority, if Democrats embraced economic populism while staking a middle ground in the culture war.

The Democratic National Committee did not share Greenberg's sunny assessment. With memories of Jesse Jackson's unexpectedly strong performance in the 1984 primaries still fresh, DNC chair Paul Kirk was not looking to kick-start a debate over racial politics.[21] But members of the newly founded Democratic Leadership Council were eager to hear more. Greenberg began polling for the group, helping ease his transition out of academia—he quit for good in 1987—as he set up his own firm in Washington.

Greenberg's partnership with the New Democrats wasn't exactly a natural union. It is safe to assume that he was the rare DLC affiliate who started off the Reagan years contemplating the finer points of Lenin's writings on nationalism. And, in an abstract sense, his goals were the same as Jesse Jackson's—a rainbow coalition uniting working Americans of all races. Except Greenberg believed there was no way that Macomb County would support a party led by Jesse Jackson. Although his patrons at the DLC might have different political visions when it came to class politics, they shared a common set of enemies: liberal activists blind to the electoral damage they caused the party; a Democratic establishment unwilling to pick necessary fights with the party base; and, ultimately, Republicans. For the moment, that would do.

In a 1991 essay for the *American Prospect*, Greenberg laid out his strategy for rebuilding the Democratic majority. He began from the premise that the breakdown of the New Deal coalition had not done away with the underlying clash of interests between capital and labor. Class conflict was real, and it could fuel an electoral realignment. "A party that can speak expansively of broad, cross-class issues, such as full employment tax relief, and health care," could, he maintained, forge a "bottom-up coalition—a mass party, encompassing the needs of the have-nots and working Americans." But disillusioned white voters would not listen to this economic message until Democrats showed respect for their values. Although Greenberg recognized that cultural polarization had brought some gains to Democrats—especially, he noted, "among younger, better-educated, and women voters"—he insisted that moving to the center on social issues was the price of admission for "a new class politics."[22]

The article quickly made its way into the hands of the chairman of the DLC, who also happened to be Greenberg's savviest client. Bill Clinton had brought Greenberg on for his 1990 reelection campaign in Arkansas, and he soon recruited him as the chief pollster for his presidential bid. Greenberg believed Clinton was a kindred soul, describing him as a believer in the moral and practical imperative of making Democrats a party of the multiracial working class. He dubbed it the "class project."[23]

Greenberg's academic Marxism had evolved into a class-forward liberalism intent on turning the Democratic Party into a vehicle for social-democratic change with a coalition drawing support from working people of all races. An electoral realignment driven by the resurrection of class politics would be, if not the full expression of left-wing hegemony, then an essential first step.

On the campaign trail, Clinton put Greenberg's strategy into action, with early speeches promising to "honor the values and promote the interests"—a neat interweaving of moral and material concerns—down to a post-election pledge to "focus like a laser beam on this economy."[24] He denounced Reaganite greed, supported universal health insurance, and called for raising taxes on the rich. He also endorsed welfare reform, called for Democrats to get tough on crime, and publicly distanced himself from Jesse Jackson, at the time the most prominent Black activist in the country. Democrats responded by giving him a clean majority during the primaries, a winning coalition that—just as Greenberg predicted—drew support from working-class voters of all races.

Not that Clinton was Greenberg's ideal candidate in every respect. A career politician with degrees from Oxford and Yale was a tough sell as a populist outsider, and Clinton was dogged by scandals—allegations of extramarital affairs, illicit drug use, dodging the draft—that marked him as product of the sixties. Although he could play the part of class warrior, Clinton worried about alienating his peers (and potential donors) in the elite. Greenberg watched Clinton schmooze bankers at a private meeting on Wall Street, a meeting that left him with, as he delicately put it, "some appreciation for the conflicting pressures on the candidate."[25]

Whatever doubts Greenberg might have harbored about Clinton's concessions paled in comparison to his exhilaration after Clinton's victory in the general election—confirmation, he said, "of my life's work as well as Clinton's."[26] Democrats were heading back to the White House, and, with Stan Greenberg as the new president's favorite pollster, the class project was coming too.

"We Do Not Have the Natural Majority"

It didn't stay there for long. Greenberg's fall from Clinton's graces was almost as precipitous as his rise. He spent much of Clinton's first two years in office warning that the president was drifting away from the populist program that had won him the election. After the 1994 midterm debacle, Clinton needed a scapegoat. Greenberg's reputation as one of the administration's leading liberal voices—he had urged the White House to go big on universal health care—made him a convenient sacrifice. He was eased out of Clinton's inner circle.

This change in personnel signaled a larger strategic shift—not a pivot to the center, exactly, but a new attempt to define the middle ground. The populist language, left-leaning elements, and realigning ambitions of Clinton's 1992 campaign gave way to new themes. Clinton became more comfortable with chastising government and celebrating markets, eager to defend Medicare without dwelling on universal health care and reconciled to fighting on an electoral battlefield dominated by the right. He wasn't going back to FDR. He was building a bridge to the twenty-first century—and to a different kind of Democratic Party.[27]

The ascent of Dick Morris provided an early marker of this transition. A longtime friend of Clinton's with a track record advising candidates in both parties, Morris quickly took over Greenberg's role as Clinton's favorite pollster. But Morris made enemies in the White House thanks to his penchant for self-aggrandizement and vicious office politicking. When news broke that Morris had been seeing a prostitute, he was dumped.[28]

Mark Penn and Doug Schoen filled the vacuum left by Morris's hasty departure. The consulting duo's entrée into Clinton's world came through Schoen, whose relationship with Morris stretched back to 1969.[29] Morris, a recent Columbia graduate, recruited Schoen, then a teenaged student at the prestigious Horace Mann School, to canvass for a young reformer campaigning for a seat in the New York State Assembly. Morris urged Schoen to join his burgeoning crew of "West Side Kids," promising an unmatched education in the arts of political organizing. Instead, Schoen enrolled at Harvard, but he stayed in touch with Morris, and he soon established his own consulting career in partnership with Mark Penn.

Throughout the 1970s and 1980s, Schoen and Penn had established a reputation for winning tough races by marrying centrist messaging with cutting-edge tactics. Penn was the technical wizard who in 1977 assembled a computer with a take-home kit, then used it to conduct daily polls for Ed Koch's mayoral campaign, a previously unheard-of luxury.[30] Schoen was the more penetrating political thinker, an Oxford DPhil who published his first book—an incisive study of right-wing populism in Britain—the same year that he and Penn helped guide Koch to a surprise victory. Unlike Greenberg, the erstwhile academic, Penn and Schoen from the outset sought to make their professions in pursuit of political power.

As an undergrad at Harvard, Schoen devoured Kevin Phillips's *The Emerging Republican Majority* and its Democratic rejoinder, Richard

Scammon and Ben Wattenberg's *The Real Majority*. Both documented the crack-up of the New Deal coalition, driven by the flight to the GOP of voters that Scammon and Wattenberg described as the "unyoung, unpoor, and unblack."[31] Although Phillips's work is better remembered today, Schoen preferred Scammon and Wattenberg, later calling it "the single most important book that I read."[32] Where Phillips depicted the coming age of Republican dominance as a historical inevitability, Scammon and Wattenberg, both veterans of LBJ's administration, insisted that Democrats could hold onto their majority by lowering the temperature around divisive cultural debates. "That the electorate is unyoung, unpoor, and unblack," they wrote, "does *not* mean they are antiyoung, antipoor, or antiblack."[33] The space between "un" and "anti" was the site where majorities were made—and the place where Schoen planned to stake his career.

That career took off when Schoen and Penn helped guide Koch to victory in 1977. Word spread in Democratic circles of the whiz kids from Harvard dragging campaigns into the computer age. But the technical innovations only mattered because they fit inside a larger political framework that Schoen had cobbled together. Treating voter preferences as stable, at least for the duration of a campaign, Penn and Schoen promised to weave real-time estimates of public opinion into a coherent message that put candidates' positions at the center of the electorate, where campaigns could still be won.

Although their specific recommendations varied from campaign to campaign, the duo eventually settled on a handful of guiding principles. Polarization around hot-button social issues had killed off the FDR coalition, and no viable successor had emerged to replace it. In a 1986 editorial for the *New York Times*, they announced that "an anti-New Deal consensus" had become the dominant force in American politics. The only hope for Democrats was to "demonstrat[e] that they shared the Republicans' basic position on fiscal issues" and then pivot to "local issues and personality differences."[34] Diligent constituent service and running on policies that cut across the usual partisan divide—cleaning up nuclear waste in Nevada, for instance—could be a winning strategy, but only if voters believed that a candidate wasn't just another tax-and-spend liberal. Polling and local contacts would indicate which type of liberal (if any) it was most safe to be.

In states leaning toward the GOP, running on "local issues" might require moving well to the right of the national party. (When the *Wall Street Journal* said that one of their clients, Indiana's Evan Bayh, "often sounds more Republican than his Republican opponent," Schoen and Penn took it as a compliment.[35]) Where Democrats were gaining ground, candidates could take bolder positions on the cultural front. Looking at the nation as a whole, Schoen and Penn believed they had outlined a blueprint for making the next Democratic majority. This coalition would only come into being if the party broke its dependence on the politics of class and resisted the pull of the culture war.

The argument had credibility because they had put together a track record of winning races in wildly different political climates. They helped elect Democrats in New York City and Alabama, New Jersey, and West Virginia. Ted Kennedy used their polls early in his 1980 presidential campaign (which nevertheless made a strong class appeal), and Donald Trump brought them on when he was contemplating a White House run in 1988. They had a special talent for guiding wealthy candidates successfully transition from business into politics, not always the easiest career switch. This corporate-friendly reputation also led to consulting in the private sector, with a roster that included Texaco, Eli Lilly, and AT&T.

Schoen and Penn brought all the lessons they took from this distinctive mix of experiences to their work for Clinton's 1996 reelection campaign. It was their first time overseeing a US presidential race, and it required making some tweaks to their usual playbook. There was no hiding from national issues, and Clinton's troubled personal life meant they couldn't run on character alone. But they stuck to the central tenets of their formula—constant polling with an eye toward claiming the middle ground. They imported techniques from the corporate world into politics, running focus groups in malls and conducting "neuro-personality polls" based on an adapted Meyers-Briggs test. After slicing the electorate into eight political-cum-personality types, they zeroed in on two key demographics, labeling them "Swing 1" and "Swing 2." Swing 1 voters leaned to the right on economics and to the left on culture. Often well-educated women in dual-income families, they fell squarely into the middle and upper-middle class but worried about keeping what they had. Swing 2 was more blue-collar and male, hostile to Washington and uncomfortable with social change.[36]

Despite the flashy techniques that went into their creation, "Swing 1" and "Swing 2" were rebranded versions of political types that were already familiar characters in punditry on the campaign—soccer moms in the first case, angry white men in the second. And both of those categories were updates of those old standbys, well-educated suburbanites and the white working class.

For a generation, Democrats had struggled over how to balance gains with the former against their losses with the latter. Now Schoen and Penn argued that Clinton couldn't afford to choose between the two. They gave a slight preference to Swing 1 voters, who polls showed were more gettable, but warned that a blowout with Swing 2 would be fatal. There wasn't one "center" to the electorate, but two, and Democrats had to contest both fronts.

The Clinton team set out to bring these two very different camps into their coalition. They did so armed with Penn and Schoen's political strategies and policy prescriptions. On culture, the campaign depicted Clinton as the moderate alternative to a reactionary GOP that would drag the country back to the 1950s; on economics, a champion of sensible government who would protect Social Security and Medicare without busting the budget. At Schoen and Penn's urging, Clinton supplemented this central message with programs aimed at their target audiences—initiatives against teen smoking for Swing 1, tough talk on trade for Swing 2. The policies were kept small-bore to avoid triggering suspicions of big government that were common in both groups. So, too, was an emotion their data indicated was coursing through the electorate—fear. "They were worried about crime, retirement, technology, pressure at work, and illness," Schoen said. "How they reacted politically to those fears was what made our work so challenging."[37]

Clinton secured a clear victory on election day. But the win came with asterisks. Ross Perot's third-party bid drew enough votes to keep the president under 50 percent of the popular vote. Republicans held onto the House while adding two seats to their majority in the Senate. Meanwhile, turnout slumped to 49 percent, the lowest level since the 1920s.[38]

Critics pounced, including Greenberg. "Rather than ushering in a new progressive era the current period seems to reflect the exhaustion of political forces that have battled to an inclusive and ugly draw," Greenberg observed while passing judgment—not without a sense of vindication—on his old boss's "incomplete victory."[39]

But to the brains behind this incomplete victory, Clinton's slender margin proved that they had made the right choice. "Democrats must face a hard truth," Schoen said. "We do not have the natural majority coalition in American politics."[40] Schoen thought his former mentor Dick Morris's preferred term for Clinton's strategy, "triangulation," was sugarcoating the issue. Most voters said they didn't want an activist government, and populist appeals weren't resonating with the electorate. "The country," in short, "was trending to the Right."[41]

Which left Democrats with few options. "Wishing for a mass conversion is not a political strategy. Neither is rallying the base," Schoen said. All of the fancy polls and microtargeted policies were just ways of maneuvering around these unpalatable facts, tools for making it through a hostile environment with a bare majority of the vote. (Or, in Clinton's case, an even less impressive plurality.) "For Democrats to win elections they must come up with a compelling broad-based vision that . . . must be moderate—even conservative—in tone," Schoen explained.[42]

When critics lambasted the president for not using bold leadership to transform public opinion, Schoen said they were living in a fantasy. You could question the results of his polling with Penn. Greenberg certainly did, accusing the pair of rigging the surveys to support corporate-friendly politics. But Democrats still had to build majorities out of the electorate as it existed, and independent pollsters confirmed that landslide majorities wanted lower taxes, reduced immigration, and a tougher approach on crime.[43] Liberals might ignore those inconvenient facts, but if Democrats refused to give voters what they wanted, then Republicans would be happy to oblige.

The New Era

The battle lines were drawn. Conflict versus consensus, class polarization versus owning the center, a politics pitched at Macomb County versus one stitched together out of focus groups—or, as it was shorthanded by Democratic operatives, Greenberg versus Penn and Schoen. Although Greenberg was on the outs with the Clintons, he reestablished his credibility at home by turning himself into a guru for the global center-left, assembling a list of clients that included Nelson Mandela in South Africa, Tony Blair in the United Kingdom, Gerhard Schröder in Germany, and Ehud Barak in Israel.

Where Greenberg traveled, Penn and Schoen were often close behind. Following Clinton's example, Blair relied on Greenberg's advice to help win a first term but grew weary of playacting populism. "I just don't believe the problem with Britain is the few at the top," he told Greenberg.[44] At Clinton's recommendation, Blair turned to Penn, who designed a campaign more to his client's liking, casting Blair as the leader of a modernizing, inclusive Britain.

Back in the United States, Al Gore joined the 2000 presidential race with Penn and Schoen as his main pollsters, only to fire them a few months into the race, frustrated with Penn's repeated suggestion that he wrap himself around the Clinton legacy. Gore thrashed his way through the primaries, and then, shortly before his formal nomination, brought Greenberg onto the campaign. The vice president was soon campaigning on a new slogan—"The people, not the powerful"—as he moved ahead of George W. Bush in the polls for the first time.[45]

The election's messy denouement gave both factions evidence for their respective cases. Greenberg claimed that Gore's populist conversion had saved the campaign, arguing that a better performance in the debates would have given Democrats a majority in the Electoral College. Schoen told the *Washington Post* that if Gore had stuck to the center, "I'm very confident he would be president-elect today."[46] Meanwhile, the partners at Penn, Schoen, and Berland congratulated themselves on shepherding Hillary Clinton to her Senate victory in New York.

Seven years later, Clinton entered her first presidential bid with Penn at her side. The campaign put Penn in an odd position. In a book released to coincide with the election, Penn touted his role in moving Democrats beyond their fixation with "downscale, noncollege workers" while bringing well-educated suburbanites into the coalition.[47] Penn fit this transformation into a larger story about the reinvention of the Democratic Party as a leading force in "the global Third Way movement—the triumph of pragmatic, independent thinking over left- or right-wing ideology."[48]

Political commentators John Judis and Ruy Teixeira went even farther. In a much-discussed 2002 book, *The Emerging Democratic Majority*, they announced that an impending realignment was about to launch a new era in American politics.[49] Economic, demographic, and cultural shifts would give Democrats the opportunity to forge an enduring majority built around educated professionals, racial minorities, and the young—groups whose numbers were going to expand in the years ahead. The analysis mixed together previously distinct strains in progressive thought, offering a bit of Jesse Jackson's rainbow coalition here, a dash of New Democratic enthusiasm for knowledge workers there. It also pointed a way beyond the battles of the Clinton years. Judis and Teixeira accepted that there was no going back to the economically polarized coalitions of the New Deal years, but they did not believe Democrats were condemned to chase the center in a country that was trending right—because, finally, demographic changes were pushing the center to the left.

Little wonder, then, that Hillary Clinton wasn't the natural favorite for the emerging Democratic majority. That honor went to Barack Obama, whose biography—summed up in the phrase "first Black editor of the *Harvard Law Review*"—could have been drawn up in a lab to satisfy the demands of a Democratic coalition where African Americans had been an essential voting bloc for decades and college-educated liberals were growing stronger by the day.[50]

Penn was not worried. In private memos, he told Clinton that Obama was the candidate of the future—not the present. Young voters were unreliable, affluent suburbanites were not a majority, and working-class voters of all races were up for grabs. Penn urged Clinton to exploit

Obama's strengths "with the high class Democrats" by casting herself as "the candidate of people with needs," rooting her coalition in a "lower and middle class constituency." "He may be the JFK in the race," Penn told Clinton, "but you are the Bobby."[51]

The irony was not lost on Greenberg. Under Bill Clinton, he noted, Democrats had become "the natural party of young people, virtually all racial and immigrant minorities, the best-educated women, the most cosmopolitan and global regions, and increasingly, suburban America."[52] When those voters delivered the Democratic nomination to Obama, Greenberg admitted, "I was not unhappy to see Hillary lose."[53]

Obama's victory offered powerful evidence in favor of Judis and Teixeira's thesis. It also pushed both camps in the Clinton wars farther away from the center of Democratic politics. Penn kept a lower profile after the implosion of Clinton's 2008 campaign, taking shelter in a high-ranking position at Microsoft, a fitting symbol for a career that had peaked in the nineties. Schoen became a regular contributor on Fox News, where he regularly scolded Democrats for abandoning the center.

Greenberg was more welcome in Obama's Washington, which quickly became a problem of its own. Just a few weeks into the new administration, it was revealed that, before joining the White House as chief of staff, then-congressman Rahm Emanuel had spent five years living rent free in a DC apartment owned by Greenberg and his wife, Congresswoman Rosa DeLauro. That Emanuel had funneled over half a million dollars to Greenberg's firm when he ran the Democratic Congressional Campaign Committee would have been headache enough for the Obama team. More troubling still was the light it cast on Greenberg's extensive list of corporate clients, including Monsanto, Boeing, and British Petroleum. A number of these companies also worked with Penn, evidence that parties of the center-left weren't the only groups with their pick of the Democratic consultant class.[54]

But as he reflected on his own career, Greenberg was struck by a different set of ironies. In a memoir published shortly after Obama was sworn into the White House, Greenberg noted a recurring pattern in his work. First, even getting candidates to see that running against economic inequality might be in their political self-interest required enough proof to make the case beyond a reasonable doubt. "I have come to appreciate that in virtually all these countries that there are forces at play not always visible and direct, that work to preclude messages and strategies that highlight class, equity, or fairness," he wrote, "even when the survey tests well, [and] 'the facts' repeatedly take you to that message or choice."[55]

And it was all downhill from there. Time and again, he helped politicians on the center-left win by running on a vaguely populist platform, only to see them take a neoliberal turn after the campaign—Clinton, Blair, Ehud Barak, even Nelson Mandela. "After every one of these elections, these big, sometimes historic, leaders had a 'come-to-Jesus' meeting with the principal managers of the economy," Greenberg said. "Without even being in the meeting, I knew the content: 'That was all well and good for the campaign, but you need to understand that the economy is at great risk, deficits are out of control, investment will not be forthcoming, austerity and fiscal balance has to be your first priority.'"[56] The people had spoken at the ballot box, and now they were expected to sit quietly while their government bowed to the dictates of a global marketplace.

Then came the tragic conclusion. Economic growth might pick up over the long run, but as the gap between populist campaigns and neoliberal governance widened, so too did the economic gap between the many and the few. Defensive politicians turned into apologists for the status quo, asserting in public that things were getting better, then grumbling in private about ungrateful voters. Disillusionment settled over their former supporters, especially among the working class and young people just starting their work lives. Frustration might curdle into apathy. Or it could mutate into toxic grievances, with consequences that were not pleasant to contemplate.

The question for Greenberg, in 2009, was whether Obama could break the pattern—and, if he couldn't, what would happen next.

Democrats looking forward to hope and change did not have much appetite for doubt. It was easier to dismiss both sides of the Clinton wars as relics of the before times. Which in a real way they were. The electorate was becoming more racially diverse and the tactics to reach them ever more technically demanding. Public opinion was shifting to the left on issues ranging from same-sex marriage to support for unions. The percentage of self-identified liberals in the overall electorate was inching upward, and within the Democratic coalition the total was exploding. According to Gallup, in 2008 about equal numbers of Democrats considered themselves liberal or moderate—just under 40 percent each—while conservatives took up the remaining fifth. That was already a departure from the Clinton years, when moderates had been the dominant faction, while liberals and conservatives battled for second place. And the change was even more stark by the end of Obama's second term, when 48 percent of Democrats identified as liberal, 35 percent as moderate, and just 15 percent as conservative.[57]

But there was a catch. Democrats and the public might have been moving in the same direction, but Democrats were heading there faster. The more consistently liberal Democratic coalition of 2016 was also a more educated and affluent coalition that was bleeding support with blue-collar whites and struggling to maintain enthusiasm with Black and brown working-class voters.

Yet as signs piled up that the optimism of 2008 was premature—the Tea Party backlash of 2010, the grinding 2012 campaign, the shocking election of 2016—a rising generation of Democratic strategists was not inclined to go ransacking the past for advice on what to do next. A new era was supposed to be dawning.

They had new polls to run, electorates to slice and dice, data to parse—and no time for looking backward.

PART II
New Governance

CHAPTER 9

The Preservation of Conditional Citizenship after the 1965 Voting Rights Act

JULILLY KOHLER-HAUSMANN

When President Johnson signed the Voting Rights Act on August 6, 1965, he declared that the country had finally aligned its practice with its liberal democratic ideals. Until that day, he explained, the nation had been "two rivers—one shining with promise, the other dark-stained with oppression" flowing along "divided channels." Johnson declared that the Voting Rights Act would finally "strike away the last major shackle of those fierce and ancient bonds. Today the Negro story and the American story fuse and blend."[1]

In the decades since 1965, politicians and pundits have often echoed Johnson's celebratory narrative about the progressive realization of the nation's principles. Many present the Voting Rights Act as the nation's democratic apotheosis and the culmination of mid-century liberalism's successful civil rights project. Others, however, insisted that the struggle to build an egalitarian multiracial citizenship had only just begun. And, in the decades to come, Americans endeavored to explain why—as the starkest barriers to the franchise fell—political participation plummeted, inequality soared, and faith in government plunged.

This chapter uses battles over voter registration to illuminate the trepidation and contestation about American democracy that shadowed the triumphalist rhetoric after 1965. It argues that liberals' legitimation of conditions on citizenship—where rights and benefits were earned privileges, not guarantees—combined with post-1960s Democrats' wariness about an expanded, empowered electorate to help restrain the era's more emancipatory democratic visions. Liberals' acceptance of qualifications for full civic standing ceded important strategic ground that conservatives leveraged to resist and, in some cases, roll back the expansion, protections, and simplification of voting. The broad acquiescence to conditional citizenship inhibited both the enactment of a robust social citizenship and a fully unencumbered franchise.

Narratives about recent voting-rights struggles have rightly highlighted conservative efforts to preserve racial hierarchy, limit participation, and suppress opponents' votes. Liberals have, for understandable reasons, received less scrutiny. After all, it was liberal politicians of both parties, under pressure from the civil rights movement, who championed the most profound extensions of the franchise in the post–World War II period. And liberals' ambivalence toward expanding the electorate diverged in profound ways from explicitly illiberal, ethnonationalist, or antidemocratic strains in conservative politics.[2]

Yet liberals were not mere foils for conservatives. Indeed, in the decades after the Voting Rights Act, they did not uniformly or unequivocally champion fuller participation and an unrestricted franchise. While it was typically liberal Democrats who advanced legislation to expand the electorate, others actively opposed or passively inhibited them. The issue was rarely prioritized. This ambivalence toward new voters can be explained in large part through simple electoral calculations. After all, entrenched party elites are only incentivized to enlist unpredictable voting blocs under limited conditions.[3] Reforms that profoundly destabilize the status quo are often responses to pressure from outside the party. After the Voting Rights Act enlisted tens of thousands of new Black voters, Southern Democrats collaborated with Republicans to obstruct policy that would further ease registration. They were often abetted by other established Democrat Party officials who were also threatened by mobilized groups, particularly African Americans.

The social upheavals of the 1960s compounded the fiscal and political costs of accommodating new voting blocs, intensifying some Democrats' ambivalence toward mass politics.[4] With the party navigating demands for everything from a universal minimum income to a job guarantee to an end to US imperialism, many Democrats saw newly galvanized constituencies as threats to the existing leadership and the party's fragile coalition. As economic conditions deteriorated in the 1970s, many liberals feared that accommodating "special interests" and burgeoning social-welfare commitments could derail the economy and permanently impair the party's electoral prospects. As we'll see, members of the Democratic Leadership Council (DLC) organized in the 1980s explicitly to counter these perceived risks. Meanwhile, the burgeoning political-consultant industry incubated an increasingly sophisticated science of voter mobilization. More and more, party leaders used professionalized and technocratic tools (such as microtargeting, polling, and direct-mail communications) to target voters as individuals, thereby minimizing their reliance on organized collectives or other grassroots political formations to deliver votes and funds.[5]

Where electoral incentives contributed to Democrats' ambivalence toward mass politics, liberalism's governing logic helped provide the rationale for a limited franchise with onerous qualifications. Liberals regularly conceded and thus legitimized understandings of citizenship where rights and benefits were contingent upon fulfilling civic responsibilities or possessing certain capacities. In an era of colorblind celebrations of equal rights, this conditional understanding of citizenship became an increasingly powerful idiom to adjudicate between legitimate voices and the "undeserving" or "special interests." Both conservatives and liberals tended to operate within this logic, foreclosing more universal visions and confining debates to *which* constraints on the franchise or conditions for benefits were appropriate.

Voter registration requirements and qualification procedures may at first appear to be a highly technocratic, even tedious, focus. Yet it is precisely election administration's ability to masquerade as bureaucratic, procedural, and apolitical that makes it such a lucrative site to pursue electoral advantage. As a historical lens, it brings our attention to the ongoing struggles to define the borders of the electorate and the terms of full citizenship. Indeed, debates in the late twentieth century were rarely fought over democracy per se.[6] Everyone claimed to be defending "free and fair elections," even as they struggled bitterly to shape election administration and to demarcate legitimate and illegitimate participants in the democratic process. Despite rhetoric celebrating the nation's democratic fruition, these fights are best understood as part of the long, ongoing struggle over the norms of American democracy.

Examining registration requires that our political analysis not just focus *within* the electorate. Centering voters makes sense when analyzing election returns, but it has profound limitations for understanding political culture more broadly. When commentators conflate "voters" with the "public," they draw conclusions about the entire nation based on elections with turnout only rarely exceeding 60 percent in presidential races (and considerably lower in other elections) and skewed in favor of older, white, and middle- and upper-class citizens. Widening the perspective to include nonvoters allows scrutiny of the varied forces that demobilize, deflect, and alienate certain groups from electoral politics.[7]

While writers regularly note how participation rates influenced particular elections, they often treat turnout as dictated by haphazard surges, natural currents, or charismatic candidates. In doing so, they elide the blunt regulations and increasingly sophisticated professional expertise, technology, and machinery dedicated to sculpting the electorate. Focusing within the electorate also risks erasing from our narratives those groups that remain barred from the process. The implications are particularly stark in the late twentieth century when two of the most important groups in the political economy and social imagination—resident noncitizens and people disenfranchised due to criminal convictions—were formally excluded from the electorate. And their percentage of the voting-age population actually increased dramatically throughout the twentieth century. In 1972, noncitizens and felons were only about 2 percent of the voting-age population. By 2004, nearly 10 percent of the voting-age population were ineligible.[8]

The seemingly mundane battles over voter registration during the late twentieth century broaden the lens beyond the electorate by bringing into the frame the fierce struggles to define its borders. These battles reveal that Democrats wavered about expanding their own coalition, a wavering that in turn helped limit the electorate as a whole. And they illuminate the ongoing liberal acceptance of conditional citizenship that persisted alongside (and compromised) their commitments to an egalitarian, multiracial democracy.

Liberalism and Conditional Citizenship

Conditional citizenship is deeply rooted in the nation's intellectual traditions, particularly liberalism. By *conditional citizenship*, I refer to the long tradition of creating hierarchy within formal citizenship through imposing screens for civic virtue and capacity. Classical liberalism has a long, uneasy relationship with democracy—marked especially by fears that tyrannical majorities threaten individual rights and private property.[9] Despite the insistence on universalism in liberal theory, equality in practice was often reserved for those already understood as equals.

This logic, of course, rationalized white supremacy, patriarchy, and colonialism by insisting that subordinated groups did not have the competency to "contract in" to liberal citizenship. Philosophers have identified the ways that the liberal social contract actually entailed a "sexual contract" and a "racial contract" that delimited who was a full political person capable of freedom and of independently entering contracts. Gender or race supposedly betrayed a person's intellectual and moral competency to qualify for social and political equality. At different historical moments, the ability to claim the full rights and benefits of citizenship was also contingent upon—among other things—ethnicity, sexuality, intelligence, mental competency, proper behavior, age, or fulfillment of civic responsibilities such as working, paying taxes, and abiding by laws. Broader participation was either blatantly undesirable or carefully subordinated to protecting the purity of the electorate. According to this reasoning, the pollution of the ballot box with unworthy, fraudulent, or unqualified votes was an overriding threat to US democratic integrity. The very definition of a full citizen was historically constructed through contrast with those defined as incapable, unprepared, or undeserving.[10] The hierarchies within citizenship were also produced dialogically through contrast with noncitizens, such as legal residents, "illegal aliens," or refugees.[11]

Conditional citizenship persisted even after the Fifteenth and Nineteenth Amendments prohibited disenfranchisement based on race or gender. Since the law did not prohibit all conditions, election regulators simply deployed different qualifications to preserve hierarchy and white supremacy. The mass disenfranchisement of African Americans under Jim Crow was mostly accomplished through ostensibly race-neutral policies (that were nevertheless enforced by explicit racial terrorism). White southern elites took the conditions society had imposed on the majority of African Americans—illiteracy, poverty—and made those the criteria by which people were forbidden to vote.[12]

Conditional understandings of citizenship also shaped the construction of the American welfare state. During the New Deal era, liberal architects designed few truly universal programs and instead crafted benefits that were earned, means- and morals-tested, contingent, and forfeitable. Women, people of color, and homosexuals were offered restricted or inferior benefits, if they were not denied benefits altogether. Policymakers reserved the most robust programs for "deserving" full citizens who had earned their benefits through being defined as "taxpayers" or "workers."[13]

Conditional citizenship endured after the Voting Rights Act alongside the triumphalist language of universal enfranchisement. The 1965 law targeted qualifications for the franchise—the tests and devices requiring the ability to read, interpret, or possess good moral character—that were used to abridge the right to vote *on the basis of race*. It did not reject conditions on the franchise per se, assuming some could be applied in a non–racially discriminatory manner. For example, the Voting Rights Act left many literacy tests, pauper exclusions, and poll taxes on the books in northern states undisturbed.

Yet as the legitimacy of some conditions eroded, the whole structure was destabilized, forcing courts and legislators to re-evaluate the standards for political participation. In 1966, the Supreme Court outlawed the poll tax, arguing that "wealth or fee paying has, in our view, no relation to voting qualifications."[14] The Supreme Court's ruling in *Oregon v. Mitchell* upheld Congress's 1970 ban on literacy tests.[15] The rejection of these particular tests did not, however, represent the total repudiation of devices designed to cultivate an engaged, informed, virtuous or intellectually competent electorate.

By the early 1970s, qualifications for the franchise were renegotiated but not abandoned. The vote remained a right that could be forfeited (though law breaking or pauperism) or a privilege that had to be earned by clearing explicit bars (such as registration or a certain duration of residency). Felon disenfranchisement was arguably the most overt remaining expression of this normative commitment.[16] But the vote also remained contingent upon reading materials in English, mental competency, or living in certain territories, such as Puerto Rico or Guam. All these limitations rested on the logic that immoral, fraudulent, or uninformed voters posed a greater risk to democracy than a limited, unrepresentative electorate.

The Bipartisan Reluctance to Ease Voter Registration

The ongoing commitment to a conditional franchise persisted alongside a growing anxiety about low voter turnout in the post–World War II era. While some interpreted nonparticipation as reflecting popular satisfaction, most political elites in the 1960s interpreted the levels of political participation in the US as a grave problem that reflected an unvital or deteriorating civic body. Declining participation took on special urgency in the Cold War context, as Soviet officials could be trusted to exploit any shortcoming to bolster their critiques of bourgeois democracy.[17]

When a spate of commissions, journalists, and researchers set out to unravel the mystery of the "vanishing voters," they usually turned to explanations of "voter apathy." Yet, upon deeper study, these investigations often ended up indicting structural features of the US system. President Kennedy—alarmed that less than 65 percent of the voting-age population had participated in the 1960 election—impaneled a commission to study the causes of low turnout. Its members expressed surprise to discover that a key difference between the United States and other democracies was not in the civic dedication of its populace but in the mundane details of election administration.[18] In many countries with higher participation rates, the government was responsible for maintaining accurate voter rolls. In the US, the burden was on individuals to register (and reregister if they moved), and that hurdle was riddled with bureaucratic impediments.[19]

The passage of the Voting Rights Act foregrounded debates over who should (and could) have responsibility for voter registration. Indeed, registration escalated in importance precisely because courts and Congress had confiscated the other tools elites long used to sculpt the electorate. Civil rights organizers, southern election officials, and the federal government fought over who should bear the new immense costs of enlisting the tens of thousands of unregistered Black citizens. Although civil rights leaders condemned the anemic federal protection and assistance, the number of registered African Americans still more than doubled between 1962 and 1968. More than half of voting-age Black citizens were registered in every southern state by 1968. Black registration rates still lagged behind those of whites, but these new voters radically transformed national politics and endangered southern segregationists' privileged position in the Democratic coalition.[20]

Voter registration drives threatened the status quo in the North as well. In the wake of the profound economic and demographic shifts wrought by "deindustrialization," African American politicians challenged white-dominated Democratic Party organizations for control of urban municipal governments. Black activists saw registration campaigns as a prerequisite for seizing power. And, in response, incumbent politicians in both parties moved to encumber or defund registration campaigns. Local Community Action Agencies generated particular ire, as Southern Democrats and big-city Democratic officials alleged that they used federal money to fund targeted registration efforts, often in communities of color, that had partisan implications. Democratic senator Robert Byrd of West Virginia complained that the Community Action leaders in his state were "social misfits and malcontents" determined to upend the existing order. Congress hurriedly squashed this threat in 1967, passing amendments that put community action programs under the direct control of local officials and prohibited the use of federal antipoverty funds for voter registration.[21]

Lawmakers also moved to choke off the funding to voter registration that flowed from private foundations. White Southern lawmakers resented the Voter Education Project, a foundation-supported organization that funded many registration campaigns in Black communities across the region. And in the North, scrutiny followed the 1967 election of Cleveland's Carl Stokes, who was hailed as the first African American elected to lead a major US city.[22] Stokes defeated the white Democratic Party establishment in the primary and then a seasoned Republican opponent in the general election. Critics fixated on a Ford Foundation grant to the Cleveland chapter of CORE that helped fund a registration drive conducted in predominantly Black communities.[23] To impede what they saw as targeted political interference, congressional members proposed an amendment to the Tax Reform Act of 1969 that largely prohibited foundations from funding voter registration work. Civil rights leaders charged that the proposal was a transparent ploy to constrain Black political power.[24] Their organizing helped block a complete ban, but Congress still enacted significant restrictions on foundations' ability to fund voter registration.[25]

While bipartisan coalitions constricted various avenues of support for registration campaigns, others attempted to expand the electorate with procedural and constitutional reforms. Lawmakers amended the constitution to lower the voting age to eighteen years old and almost passed the Equal Rights Amendment. Others pushed to ease the procedural hurdles to voting. Between 1971 and 1976, Democratic lawmakers continually reintroduced a plan to allow postcard registration for all federal elections. The policy enabled citizens to submit their registration through the mail, thereby reducing the need to travel to often far-flung registration offices during their limited hours. Opponents of easing registration, principally Republicans and Southern Democrats, argued that mail-in registration was an invitation to fraud and recruited contractarian understandings of citizenship to rationalize preserving procedural barriers to voting.

Lawmakers connected easing registration to the profound renegotiations over the rights and responsibilities of citizenship catalyzed by civil rights activists. In 1973, the lieutenant governor of Alaska told the congressional committee that "citizens must no longer be forced to earn the 'privilege' to vote. But rather they must be insured the right to vote."[26] When Senator James B. Allen (D-AL) joined with other Southern Democrats to obstruct the legislation, he defended procedural hassles on normative grounds, implying they increased the value of the franchise. He asked his colleagues, "Why should we spend millions of dollars to hand the franchise, this priceless gift, this right that a person ought to be willing to fight for, and just present it to a disinterested person on a silver platter?"[27] Although the Senate passed the postcard registration bill in 1973, a coalition of Republicans and southern Democrats defeated the House version in spring of 1974. The House passed a more diluted version of postcard registration in 1976, but it died again after encountering threats of a bipartisan filibuster in the Senate and a veto by President Ford.[28]

Jimmy Carter made the next aggressive bid to reverse plummeting turnout rates. Upon taking office, he tapped Vice President Walter Mondale to spearhead comprehensive election reform. Carter's statement introducing the 1977 legislative package explained that he was "deeply concerned that our country ranks behind at least twenty other democracies in its level of voter participation."[29] In addition to the president's personal commitment to promoting democratic norms and election integrity, his staff probably also recognized an overlapping partisan incentive. Pat Caddell, Carter's political consultant, warned in a 1976 memo that turnout declines jeopardized Democrats' ability to win nationwide elections and recommended registration reform as one of the necessary responses.[30]

The administration proposed a series of wide-ranging reforms: making federal matching funds available for House and Senate campaigns, the abolition of the Electoral College, and the loosening of the Hatch Act restrictions on the political activity of federal employees. However, election-day registration was the cornerstone of the administration's package. A policy enacted with considerable success in Mondale's home state of Minnesota, it allowed citizens to register and vote at the polls on election day, bypassing the need for previous paperwork or visits to the registrar's office. Recognizing that the risk of fraud would be the principal objection to the law, Carter's plan required registrants on election day to present identification to prove eligibility, a higher threshold than was required in other registration procedures. They also included harsh penalties for voter fraud, authorizing up to $10,000 fines and five years in prison for a first offense.[31]

The initial response to the proposal was encouraging. With Democratic majorities in both houses of Congress, pundits and politicians alike assumed the time was ripe to standardize registration procedures. The plan secured key endorsements from Republicans, including members of party leadership. But opposition arose quickly. In an article titled "Voting Plan: Has the GOP Gone Crazy?" the columnist David Broder wrote, "The leadership of the Republican Party has just taken one of the larger gambles in the long history of the GOP. It has committed its support to a proposal by President Carter that could change the composition of the American electorate more profoundly than anything since the enfranchisement of women."[32]

It was soon clear that election-day registration was a gamble Republicans were unwilling to take. Most GOP support fell away during the ensuing months, and lawmakers stalled the bill with familiar arguments about fraud, cost, and administrative complications. Meanwhile, journalists openly acknowledged that simple electoral math animated much of the antagonism to the plan. Article after article paired opponents' concerns about fraud with the assumption that the reform would recruit more poor and minority voters into the electorate.[33] Republican strategist Kevin Phillips warned that same-day registration was "a satchel of pure political dynamite that could blow the Republican party sky high."[34]

Conservative critics often conflated illegal voting and stigmatized groups voting for the Democratic Party. A *Human Events* article by Victor Riesel linked voter fraud to archetypes in the pantheon of racialized threats: the "welfare queen" and the immigrant "aliens." Riesel warned that in New York City had "enough adult aliens, some carrying the legal green card and some who are here against the law, to swing an election for President of the U.S." He also invoked tropes about welfare fraud by rehashing sensationalistic stories circulating about the infamous Chicago "welfare queen," whom he claimed had amassed 250 aliases, thirty-one addresses, three Social Security numbers, and eight "deceased husbands," all presumably to defraud the welfare program. "Why wouldn't she vote 10 or 20 times?" he asked.[35] Such rhetoric corroborated the menace of voter fraud by linking to assumptions about Black and Latinx criminality. It rested on the notion, largely unchallenged in both parties, that suspect groups, such as criminals or welfare recipients, should have diminished civic standing and voice in the polity.

By summer of 1977, it became increasingly obvious that same-day registration did not have the votes to move forward in Congress. Skepticism was not limited to Republicans. One reporter's sketch of the opposition suggested it covered virtually the entire political map: "Opponents of the bill include Republicans, southern Democrats, freshman and sophomore house members of both parties and democratic congressman from Northern cities with massive party organizations."[36] Vice President Mondale wrote a memo to Carter explaining the bill's dismal prognosis and laying out the options moving forward. In a revealing statement, Mondale wrote, "There is, unfortunately, no real constituency for this bill." He went on to explain the lack of enthusiasm within the Democratic Party: "All the members got elected without it and they don't see how it will help them . . . while they don't always say so, they are very suspicious of the effect it will have."[37] Faced with this dismal political landscape, the Carter administration abandoned the bill altogether in summer of 1977.[38]

Democrats' Ambivalence in the Registration Wars of the 1980s

The defeat of Carter's reforms was not the end of struggles to shape the US electorate. Fights over voter registration raged throughout the 1980s, becoming key forums for debates among Democrats over how to respond to Reaganism and, more fundamentally, which principles and constituencies should anchor the party. Through debates over voter registration, Democrats clashed over whether to make the party's social base the "new" working class (increasingly nonunionized, multiracial, female, and employed in precarious service and care-work sectors) or some combination of middle-class professionals (suburb dwellers, knowledge workers) and the "old" working class (imagined to be headed by white, male, industrial workers harboring racial and cultural grievance with 1960s liberalism).

Interpreting Reagan's 1980 victory became a proxy for these longstanding battles over the DNC's direction. Many centrist Democrats charged that the party had become *too* democratic, *too* liberal, and beholden to organized "special interests"—by which they meant not corporations but youth, African Americans, women, Latinx, gay and lesbian groups, and organized labor. They felt that these groups—once mobilized and registered to vote—made demands for resources and power that threatened to overload the system, alienate Democrats' "traditional constituencies," and tank the party's electoral prospects.

Critics on the left inverted this interpretation of Reagan's victory, arguing that the Democratic Party had done *too little*, not too much, for the most marginalized, particularly the poor, the working class, and communities of color suffering from the economic dislocations of the 1970s. Some of these commentators attributed Republican victories as much to turnout declines as any rightward turn of the electorate, pointing out that the 1980 race marked yet another decline in voter participation. Frances Fox Piven and Richard Cloward were influential proponents of this analysis. As both activists and academics, they were well-known figures on the left and veteran tacticians of the welfare rights movement. They joined with other activists who saw mass registration as a strategy to resist Reaganism and push the Democratic Party left. Groups such as Operation Big Vote, Project Vote, and ACORN initiated widescale registration drives targeting the poor, the unemployed, communities of color, and others affected by Reagan's assault on the New Deal welfare state. Fueled by grassroots energy, these person-to-person operations were massive undertakings, requiring intense volunteer mobilization, coordination, and resources. And they quickly crashed against the institutional barriers to mass mobilizations. Tedious bureaucratic hurdles—such as securing registration forms or certifying volunteer registrars—continually hindered their efforts.[39]

To circumvent these impediments, Piven and Cloward began advocating in the mid-1980s for an alternative to person-by-person registration drives. They helped form Human Service Employees Registration and Voter Education Fund (Human SERVE) in 1984 to champion "agency registration," a policy requiring state agencies to offer people applying for a driver's license or social services the opportunity to register to vote.[40] Because most of the registration was implemented at motor vehicle departments, these policies would become popularly known as "motor voter laws." Piven and Cloward, however, were primarily invested in registering low-income people at human-services offices, which they hoped would offset the class and racial skew of the electorate. With social movements more quiescent, they proposed that injecting a huge number of low-income voters into the Democratic Party could generate pressure on Democrats to better represent the multiracial working class and "might well force a party realignment along class lines."[41]

As they predicted, efforts to register welfare beneficiaries encountered fierce obstruction from election officials and both parties. Advocates had to sue repeatedly to gain volunteers' access to public agencies to register poor people. Officials refused to deputize registrants, blocked entrance to public buildings, and barred volunteers from welfare, unemployment offices, and surplus-cheese distribution lines. In Ohio, a volunteer was arrested and strip-searched after refusing to leave a welfare office where she was registering voters.[42] In 1984, the Reagan administration threatened to cut all federal grants-in-aid to states where governors had issued executive orders authorizing human-services workers to register clients.[43] Activists interpreted this obstruction (along with all the convoluted registration regulations) as a continuation of the nation's disenfranchising tradition. Thomas Edsall explained in a *Washington Post* article that "across the nation, liberal to radical organizations are attempting to make barriers to registration the political cause of the 1980s."[44]

This grassroots energy intertwined with Jesse Jackson's insurgent primary campaigns for the Democratic presidential nomination in 1984. A veteran of the civil rights movement, Jackson was a chief proponent of making the party's class basis the oppressed, exploited Americans of all races. To serve them, he championed, for example, a robust social safety net, universal single-payer health care, and economic redistribution. Tactically, Jackson's campaign aimed to ensure that Black voters would not be an inert, hostage force within the Democratic Party coalition.[45] Expanding the electorate was central to his strategy for mobilizing an interracial "Rainbow Coalition." He offered registration at his events and, in his speeches, he attributed Ronald Reagan's 1980 victory to a demobilized, unrepresentative, and shrunken electorate. At a rally, Jackson explained: "[Reagan] won by the margin of despair, the fracture of our coalition, he won by the margin of racial division, he won by default." To illustrate his point, he cataloged a long list of states and cities where Reagan's narrow margin of victory was dwarfed by a vast pool of unregistered students or African Americans.[46]

Threatened by these efforts, Republicans initiated countermobilizations that were ultimately better funded and more technologically sophisticated. The Christian Right undertook huge registration campaigns, often using the specter of Jackson to rouse their own supporters.[47] Meanwhile, the Republican Party itself funded massive, expensive, hi-tech targeted voter registration efforts. The party devoted around $8 million to register between 1.7 and two million people. In some states, they spent five to seven dollars for every new registrant.[48]

Democrats did not match the Republican investment. After Walter Mondale won the party's nomination in 1984, the party declined to prioritize voter registration, despite publicly declaring support for a robust campaign. Democrats were aware of the massive Republican spending but claimed they could rely on the volunteer registration drives and the magnitude of their demographic advantage.[49] Even so, following Mondale's loss, many commentators, and growing numbers of liberals, too, declared that the 1984 election proved recruiting nonvoters was a tried and failed strategy for the Democratic Party. Reagan had won reelection in a historic landslide. The voter registration campaigns had produced the first increases in national turnout rates since 1960, but the significant gains by the volunteer, grassroots efforts were largely offset by Republicans' better-funded, computer-targeted registration drives.

The Democratic Party's financial duress may have discouraged significant investment in voter registration, but left-wing critics hypothesized that party elites also harbored concerns about a more representative electorate.[50] Joel Rogers discussed the risk new voters posed to incumbent Democrats in the *Nation*: "If millions of voters join the Democratic Party, they will not join as mere election fodder but as people with expectations, interests and demands of their own." Critics suspected that many Democratic leaders and the growing ranks of professional strategists who advised them preferred competing on constricted but familiar terrain. As Rogers put it, "They seek a controlled mobilization, or none at all."[51]

Sometimes party elites acknowledged the appeal of a limited electorate outright. In 1984, prominent Democratic consultant Robert Squier told a gathering of political scientists that "[w]e would rather have a few voters we can deal with in an effective way" than a larger but less manageable electorate. He detailed how campaigns often pursue messaging or advertisements that do not aim to convince undecided voters or mobilize supporters. Instead, they are calculated to discourage opponents' votes. "We call it chloroforming or deep-freezing," he explained.[52]

The "New Democrats," a new coalition marshaling within the Democratic Party, explicitly spurned the strategy of mobilizing nonvoters. This loose alliance of suburban, professional-class liberals, neoliberals, southern Democrats, and social conservatives founded the Democratic Leadership Council (DLC) in 1985 to reinvigorate the party: cultivate new leadership, diagnose the party's ills, and reverse unfavorable electoral trends. They advocated realigning the party away from the marginalized, poor, and communities of color targeted by Jackson. In their orienting documents, the New Democrats rebuffed the "Mobilization Myth"—the notion that the party could win electorally by registering new voters.[53] They rejected the premise that nonvoters were more liberal than voters in general and warned that targeted registration drives—particularly among African Americans—would trigger Republican countermobilizations. To recruit moderate white voters, their main priority, they insisted it was critical to signal the party leadership's independence from the "Jackson wing," not expand it. DLC-aligned strategists advocated more punitive postures on racially coded social issues, particularly welfare and crime. They advanced market-friendly pro-business strategies to mitigate inequality, and the promise of the new tech economy—growth, in other words, rather than redistribution or new programs for "special interests." Less focused on equal outcomes, the DLC instead championed economic opportunity and embraced familiar social-contract language about mutual reciprocal responsibility that avoided (and often explicitly rejected) commitments to universal entitlements and social supports.[54]

As the DLC consolidated power within the Democratic Party throughout the 1980s, proponents of registration reform worked at the local level to establish motor voter programs. Encouraged by the success of the state-level experiments, a coalition of civil and voting rights organizations, such as Human SERVE, the NAACP, and the League of Women Voters, resolved in 1988 to push again for registration reform at the federal level. Advocates hoped agency registration would be insulated from the concern about voter fraud because officials at DMVs and welfare offices would be registering people already affirmatively identified by the state. But the specter of fraud continued to haunt the debate. It rationalized opposition to the law, as well as justified the inclusion of new voter-list maintenance requirements and the elimination of election-day registration from the proposed legislation.[55]

Republican lawmakers overwhelmingly opposed the law.[56] Senator Mitch McConnell (R-KY) campaigned tirelessly against it throughout the early 1990s, sarcastically dubbing it "auto-fraudo" and arguing that "relatively low voter turnout is a sign of a content democracy." McConnell also recycled bromides about the dangers of undesirable voters, warning that the law would "make voting so extremely easy that even political couch potatoes will roll out and vote."[57] Many Republicans saw the policy as a flagrantly partisan ruse to smuggle Democratic voters into the electorate. And they denigrated unregistered voters with the racialized claim that they had not fulfilled their civic obligations and were therefore undeserving. "Why are you helping the people in the wagon, and not the people pulling the wagon?" Phil Gramm (R-TX) asked during the Senate floor debates.[58] McConnell and others successfully stalled the bill's passage in the Senate until 1992, when three Republicans broke ranks to defeat the filibuster. President George H. W. Bush vetoed the legislation on the grounds that it was "an open invitation to fraud and corruption."[59]

However, unlike past registration reforms that encountered opposition from within the Democratic Party, Bill Clinton championed, and most Democrats supported, the federal motor voter reforms. Clinton proudly signed the bill after lawmakers broke another Republican filibuster in 1993. His backing might seem contradictory, considering the DLC's historic skepticism about mobilizing nonvoters. But Democratic support congealed in part because the policy did not immediately threaten incumbents or risk reorganizing the social bases of either party. Analysts suspected that registrations from motor vehicle offices could benefit both parties, and they wavered between predicting the law would boost Democrats electorally and predicting it would have negligible effects.[60] With grassroots mobilization quieted, the motor voter reforms offered bureaucratic rationalization but not political disruption. The Democratic Party continued to refine its capacity to target voters individually using increasingly sophisticated technological tools.[61]

Piven and Cloward suspected that elites were not fundamentally threatened by motor voter reforms in the short term, but they hoped that clearing away structural impediments to the franchise would ease the path for when social movements again organized collectives to wrangle state power. "Since protest will once more politicize people," they explained, "it could matter a great deal that access to the franchise will, for the first time in history, be unencumbered. That's what we all hope. Time will tell."[62] Whatever the laws' ultimate electoral implications, the history of the motor voter law illuminates the profound hurdles to democratizing reforms. After passage, advocates encountered years of legal and bureaucratic obstruction in implementing the 1993 law. Although most motor vehicle offices ultimately complied, many state officials remained intransigent in their refusal to register clients at social-welfare offices.[63] As Piven explained in a 2017 interview, "after a while, it became clear that no one really wanted to register people of color who were poor."[64]

The Broader Stakes and Stubborn Persistence of Conditional Citizenship

This reticence toward full participation and an unfettered franchise persisted despite the momentum toward expanding the franchise in the late twentieth century. Politicians preserved hierarchies within citizenship. Limitations on suffrage, such as "mental competency" bars and the disenfranchisement of voters in Washington, DC, and US territories, remained lodged in law.[65] Felon disenfranchisement became a particularly conspicuous testament to the nation's fealty to a conditional citizenship. Although many states lifted the prohibition on voting by people after incarceration or release from parole throughout the 1960s and 1970s, the pace of reforms stalled during the following decades as incarceration rates skyrocketed. Lawmakers from both parties championed increasingly draconian sentencing regimes that incarcerated millions, ballooning the numbers of people formally stripped of voting rights. As prisons and jails filled with Black and brown citizens popularly depicted as incapable of "integration," the penal system's commitment to rehabilitation eroded, undermining a principal justification for restoring voting rights post-conviction.[66]

Efforts to restore felon voting rights after incarceration roused opposition within both parties. In 2002, senators defeated a bill that would have allowed people to vote in federal elections after leaving prison and completing parole. Twenty-three Democrats including then-senator Joe Biden joined with forty Republicans to defeat the measure.[67] Politicians deployed classic liberal arguments about the purity of the electorate, the unconditionally irredeemable status of felons, and the social contract to explain their opposition to the law. Senator Mitch McConnell (R-KY) declared, "Those who break our laws should not have a voice in electing those who make and enforce our laws. Those who break our laws should not dilute the vote of law-abiding citizens."[68] The number of states disenfranchising people while incarcerated actually increased at the end of the century. Massachusetts amended their constitution to disenfranchise prisoners in 2000, leaving only two states—Maine and Vermont—that allowed their entire incarcerated population to vote.[69]

The custom of conditioning rights and benefits had consequences beyond the ballot box.[70] Civil death—the idea that a person sacrificed the benefits of citizenship when breaking the law—undergirded the harsh economic and social "collateral consequences" that continue long after release from prison and parole.[71] It justified the slew of social liabilities that lawmakers from both parties attached to criminal convictions throughout the 1990s, such as the withdrawal of access to credit, housing, education, jobs, and welfare supports.

This determination to reserve full political rights for "deserving" citizens facilitated (and was facilitated by) the evisceration of the US welfare state and the abandonment of vulnerable groups to market dictates. The penchant for a socially stratified safety net intensified among centrist Democrats with the ascendancy of neoliberalism and the end of the Cold War.[72] Building on the market-oriented and exclusionary traditions that had always been strains within US liberalism, the New Democrat wing distanced the party from a commitment to social rights, unions, and a multiracial working-class social base. They emphasized the importance of "reciprocal responsibility" where social standing and benefits were earned through work and service.[73]

These logics structured the contentious debates over welfare that raged throughout the late twentieth century. Opponents of Aid to Families with Dependent Children (AFDC), often deploying racist and sexist stereotypes of Black mothers, aimed to transform welfare from an entitlement to a benefit contingent upon fulfilling civic responsibilities, such as wage work. Congress and President Clinton articulated an updated compact in 1996, when they replaced AFDC with Temporary Assistance for Needy Families (TANF). The policy mandated work requirements in exchange for benefits and implemented lifetime limits on aid. TANF relied heavily on "sanctions"—the reduction or eliminations of benefits—to punish recipients for noncompliance with work and reporting requirements.

Various facets of these long-running battles over registration restrictions and the terms of citizenship collided during the contested presidential race in 2000. With the entire election hinging on the outcome in Florida, a national spotlight swung onto the democratic processes in the state, illuminating the consequences of byzantine election regulation, voter-roll purges, and felon disenfranchisement. With videos of election officials examining hanging chads in the background, television pundits debated whether people who failed to ballot properly should forfeit their voice in a democracy. Florida, the nation learned, was one of seven states that permanently disenfranchised people with felony convictions, even after the completion of their sentence and release from supervision. Newspapers reported that in the run-up to the election, contractors hired to "clean" the voting rolls had purged an unknown number of legal voters whose names were mistakenly identified as matches from list of disenfranchised felons. Any combination of these factors could have erased the 537-vote margin that delivered the state—and therefore the presidency—to George W. Bush.[74]

My point—however—is not only that seemingly mundane election mechanics have profound electoral consequences. Nor is it simply that liberals have often joined conservatives to contain mass mobilization and limit political participation. Instead, I hope to bring attention to the features of the broader democratic culture that make such postures palatable. A conditional understanding of citizenship, with firm roots in liberalism, assumes that full civic standing is contingent rather than universal, a privilege rather than a right. In earlier periods, citizens established their capacity for self-governance through military service, whiteness, owning property, literacy, tax-paying, or being a man. After movements forced the state to stop using ascriptive characteristics—such as race or gender—to construct formal civic hierarchies, this liberal logic of conditional citizenship still perpetuated racial, gender, and class subordination. In the late twentieth century, qualification for political and social rights was more frequently established through "working," "mental competency," enduring the procedural hassle of registration, producing identification, or not being incarcerated for crime. Even if these conditions were applied uniformly—liberalism's much-vaunted promise of equality before the law—they inevitably fall most heavily on the most vulnerable and precarious. For as long as the country is marked by profound social and racial inequality, even the most seemingly mundane conditions on citizenship will repress the most subordinated and insulate the most powerful.

CHAPTER 10

Liberalism's Last Rights

Disability Inclusion and the Rise of the Cost-Benefit State

KAREN M. TANI

No longer dare we live with the hypocrisy that the promise of America should have one major exception: Millions of children, youth, and adults with mental or physical handicaps. We must now firmly establish their right to share in that promise.

SENATOR HUBERT HUMPHREY, 1972

Everybody wants disabled people to have what they deserve except if it's going to cost them money.

DISABILITY RIGHTS ORGANIZER
JUDITH HEUMANN, 1979

At the core of modern US liberalism was a belief that members of the polity deserved a modicum of social security and economic opportunity. Also central was the belief that government—working within the parameters of capitalism—had a fundamental role in guaranteeing this baseline. By the 1940s, the language of individual rights became the norm for expressing these twin principles, both in political rhetoric and in law.[1] This chapter is about liberal policymakers' extension of rights to disabled Americans in the 1960s and 1970s, in recognition of a long history of exclusion.[2] Following a pattern set vis-à-vis racialized minorities, liberal policymakers made no guarantee that disabled people *as a group* would enjoy an equal share of the nation's resources; rather, they used the government's rights-conferring power to enable what Naomi Murakawa (referencing racial civil rights) has called "the meritocratic pursuit of the good life."[3]

These efforts to acknowledge and remedy disability-based exclusion have not received much attention from scholars of US political history, despite abundant research on liberal policymakers' other inclusionary endeavors.[4] To be sure, disability-focused scholars, advocates, and organizers have produced insightful interpretations of relevant laws and policies, but liberalism per se has not been their main concern.[5] Building on scholars who have tried to bring disability from the margins to the center of US history, this chapter shows how attention to disability alters and enriches our understanding of the history of modern liberal governance.[6]

Specifically, I place liberal efforts at disability inclusion at the center of an important shift: from a political order structured around the right to equal opportunity to a political order that, while still valorizing rights, treated efficiency in governance as the highest goal of all. Were this focus on efficiency simply about the professional, non-wasteful pursuit of governmental goals, it would be no great innovation; after all, the valorization of efficiency was a defining characteristic of progressive reformers, among others.[7] What was distinct about the late twentieth-century notion of efficiency in governance was its heavy reliance on welfare economics to decide which governmental goals may be pursued and which may not. "Neoliberal" is one descriptor of this latter political order. Also apt is the "cost-benefit state," to borrow the celebratory phrasing of the prolific legal scholar and former "regulatory czar" Cass Sunstein.[8]

That Sunstein's words feel apt is no coincidence. Born in 1954, educated at Harvard College and Harvard Law School during the 1970s, and shaped subsequently through a mix of government and academic positions, Sunstein is the kind of "professional-class liberal" this volume highlights. But Sunstein is particularly relevant to this chapter, for not only did he venerate cost-benefit analysis, he also revered President Franklin Delano Roosevelt's "Second Bill of Rights," describing it in 2004 as an "unfinished revolution" of critical contemporary importance.[9] Tethering these two impulses together was the notion that all "rights have costs."[10]

The corollary of "all rights have costs"—in a political economy that assumes scarcity—is that not all rights have *value*; some people's rights may be explicitly traded off, in service of wealth-maximizing uses of resources. This notion, I argue, became Americans' common sense, and tracing the history of disability rights helps explain that trajectory. Through the aperture of disability, this chapter suggests, liberal notions of equality rights came to coexist comfortably with an all-encompassing imperative of efficiency.

Disability and Law in the Long 1960s

Starting in the early 1960s and continuing into the 1970s, Americans witnessed a flurry of disability-related legislation and policymaking.

Some impetus came from the Kennedy family, liberal standard-bearers for whom intellectual disability was both a personal concern and a philanthropic focus.[11] Also vital was a mid-century polio epidemic, which spurred parents of disabled survivors to organize with parents of other disabled children and fight for the futures they believed their children deserved.[12] Inspired by *Brown v. Board of Education* and buoyed by the economic prosperity of the post–World War II period, these parents envisioned a "bill of rights" for their disabled children and an "equal right to training."[13] Underlying these campaigns were earlier organizing efforts by disabled veterans and wartime workers, who made disability "legible" to policymakers and challenged assumptions about whether disabled people could be productive citizens.[14] By the early 1970s, disability was both visible enough to the public and salient enough to a new cohort of organizers that a "disability rights movement" could take shape. Led by disabled people, representing a range of disabling conditions, the movement encouraged lawmakers to embrace an even more robust vision of inclusion.[15]

The era's array of disability-related policies mapped onto core liberal agendas, such as providing social protection for the "deserving." In 1963, for example, Congress began directing funds to states to help care for people with intellectual disabilities, so that warehouse-like institutions would become less necessary.[16] Such policies expanded on liberal initiatives from the previous decade, including a federally subsidized income-support program for disabled people and the extension of social insurance to people who left work prematurely because of disability.[17]

Complementing these welfarist policies—all designed for people too disabled to work—were policies aimed at disabled people who *might* be able to work. Starting in 1954, the federal government (in partnership with the states) significantly expanded the funding and energies directed at vocational rehabilitation, with an eye not only on people with physical disabilities but also on those diagnosed with mental illness.[18] At the time, these programs were less about inclusion than they were about national social and economic health, but like other employment-related programs from the Kennedy and Johnson administrations, they suggested that neither poverty nor disconnection from the labor market need be accepted as facts of life; through modern medicine, education, and training, people on the economic margins could become what the labor market wanted.[19] As President Kennedy put it in a 1962 message to Congress, disabled people were "human resources" that could be "rehabilitated" into "self-supporting taxpayers."[20] Congress expanded the vocational rehabilitation program further in 1965.[21]

Finally, there were policies framed around equality. Lawmakers did not include disability in the landmark Civil Rights Act of 1964, which identified race, color, religion, national origin, and sex as protected categories, but an analogy to these categories existed within the liberal imagination.[22] In 1966, Congress incorporated disability into the Elementary and Secondary Education Act, a statute that policymakers understood in both anti-poverty and civil rights terms.[23] In 1975, in the wake of landmark "right to education" lawsuits and legal settlements involving disabled children, Congress expanded significantly on this law.[24] Still another example is the 1968 Architectural Barriers Act, which imposed an accessibility mandate on facilities designed, built, altered, or leased with federal funds.[25] Although crafted mainly with "rehabilitated" workers in mind, the Act also sent an "integrationist" message.[26] So did the 1970 transportation financing statute that declared the "right" of "handicapped persons" to "utilize mass transportation facilities and services."[27]

The era's most important disability law covered all of the above, and more: with the enactment of Section 504 of the Rehabilitation Act of 1973, receipt of federal funds became contingent on providing "qualified" disabled people with equal access to whatever benefit or program the federal funds were supporting.[28] Phrased differently, Section 504 appeared to do for disability some version of what Title VI of the Civil Rights Act of 1964 did for race and Title IX of the Educational Amendments of 1972 did for sex. These provisions targeted recipients of federal funds and made their funds contingent on nondiscrimination. At a time when federal money infused nearly every aspect of American governance, these "Spending Clause civil rights" functioned as antidiscrimination mandates for vast swaths of public activity.[29]

Administrative Interpretation of Section 504: Rights without Costs

For a provision of such broad potential significance, Section 504's legislative history is sparse: members of Congress did not debate it, nor did any visible constituency lobby for or against it.[30] According to the most exhaustive investigation into Section 504's origins, responsibility for the provision rests primarily with a handful of staffers associated with the House Committee on Education and Labor and the Senate Labor and Public Welfare Committee. Building on prior (unsuccessful) legislative efforts by Representative Charles Vanik (D-OH) and Senator Hubert Humphrey (D-MN), staffers inserted what would become Section 504 into a late-stage version of a 1972 bill, hoping the provision would escape notice.[31] At least one of these staffers was connected to the world of disability advocacy, but others acted simply from a sense that liberal Democrats should help people on the bottom—"disabled people, minorities, poor people, you name it," explained one staffer.[32] Section 504 seemed to advance this mission while also securing a symbolic victory over President Nixon, who had repeatedly outmaneuvered liberal legislators.

Implementing this liberal "win" proved far more complex. The spare text of the statute left ambiguous who fell under Section 504's protection or what it would mean for a federally funded entity to not discriminate on the basis of disability.[33] Administrators in the Department of Health, Education, and Welfare (HEW)—and, more specifically, in that agency's Office for Civil Rights (OCR)—were left to fill in the gaps.[34]

In doing so, OCR administrators made at least two momentous choices. First, drawing on their experiences with Title VI and Title IX, as well as on conversations with a small circle of disability rights activists, OCR lawyers drafted regulations for Section 504 that foregrounded inclusion and downplayed cost.[35] Money had been "a red herring in race discrimination issues," explained one OCR insider, referencing segregationist foot-dragging, so there was "reluctance" to dwell on issues of cost in the Section 504 context.[36]

Second, in drafting the regulations, OCR drew an important analogy: between disabled people seeking inclusion in public programs and non-English-speaking children seeking access to school.[37] The latter had been a deep concern in jurisdictions with large Spanish-speaking populations—to the point that, in 1968, Congress amended the Elementary and Secondary Education Act to incentivize bilingual schooling.[38] With no appropriated funding in fiscal year 1968 and only $7.5 million the following, however, the law remained ineffective, and concerned Latinx leaders turned to OCR, the go-to enforcer of Title VI. OCR responded by informing federally funded schools that, for non-English-speaking students, formally equal treatment might not meet schools' obligations under Title VI; sometimes, school districts must "take affirmative steps," such as adjusting the curriculum and hiring bilingual teachers.[39] Four years later, when working on the Section 504 regulations, OCR administrators drew on this precedent. According to the regulations they drafted in 1974–1975 (revised only modestly thereafter), Section 504 required more than evenhanded treatment; sometimes it required affirmative alterations to the status quo.[40]

On April 28, 1977, the secretary of HEW signed the regulations and the agency began developing guidelines for other federal agencies to follow as they devised their own, area-specific Section 504 regulations.[41] Anchoring this work was OCR's "rights-oriented full accessibility approach."[42]

A wide array of institutions and practices changed in response to Section 504 and related laws. Transit agencies installed wheelchair lifts on buses. Hospitals acquired teletypewriter equipment and hired sign-language interpreters. The physical landscape shifted, too. Curb cuts appeared in sidewalks; buildings gained elevators and ramps. Educational experiences changed, as disabled children mixed more freely with nondisabled children and accommodations became more routine. Around the country, meanwhile, disabled people increasingly organized *as disabled people* rather than as members of discrete groups (or not at all). This trend was probably overdetermined: many groups from this era organized around group-specific experiences of exclusion and subordination. But it also had a connection to law: Section 504 and related laws emphasized disability (not particular disabilities). HEW even funded pan-disability organizing and training, which spurred further change.[43]

There was also resistance, however—both from authorities who were subject to Section 504 and from people who perceived a negative impact on their own well-being. Often this resistance used the language of cost, alongside accusations of illegitimate redistribution. In the early years of Section 504, federal financial aid was not broadly available to cover the expense of legal compliance, creating the perception that public service providers might have to divert precious resources to fulfill this new mandate.[44] As important, long-standing social and cultural understandings of disability framed disabled people as *already* a drain on society, because of their perceived inability to produce economic value.[45] Disability activists and theorists had begun articulating a rejoinder—arguing that disablement flowed as much from societal choices and biases as from the limitations of particular bodies—but the broader public was unfamiliar with this view.[46] Cost critiques abounded as disability rights entered the implementation phase.

Disability Rights in Practice: The Rise of Cost Narratives

To be sure, cost arguments were never completely foreign to civil rights discourse, but before roughly 1980 and outside of the disability rights context, such arguments had limited traction. A critic might attack a particular remedial order as overbroad, as occurred sometimes in the desegregation context,[47] but it was less permissible and less advantageous to say, "inclusion is too expensive."[48] When alleged discriminators tried this line in formal legal proceedings, they did not fare well. Surveying the situation in 1983, law professor Judith Wegner found that courts had been particularly hostile to cost arguments in cases involving constitutionally protected civil rights: "economic considerations pale when invaluable civil rights are violated."[49]

The "priceless rights" idea also occasionally prevailed in a disability context, but as disabled rights–claimers made greater use of new statutes, the trend went the other way. Despite liberalism's openness to analogies from race-based exclusion to other types of exclusion, the American public was primed to see disability as a negative trait, rationally connected to a person's worth and status. This perspective, in turn, made disability-based discrimination appear different in kind from race- or sex-based discrimination—and also made cost arguments more legitimate in the disability context, especially as Americans absorbed political messaging about fiscal limits and hard choices.

One place to see this trend is in the upper echelons of the administrative state. Before HEW's leadership (reluctantly) signed the Section 504 regulations, agency secretary Forrest David Matthews commissioned an "inflationary impact analysis" on the proposed regulations, which meant asking an outside consultant whether the costs of OCR's interpretation of this civil rights law outweighed its benefits. Impelling him, he claimed, was an executive order by President Gerald Ford requiring that executive branch agencies evaluate the "inflationary impact" of "[m]ajor proposals . . . for the promulgation of regulations or rules."[50] But many significant proposals escaped such review in the mid-1970s, raising questions about whether Matthews was required to subject the Section 504 regulations to this process.[51] Ultimately, the extra analysis did not stop the draft regulations from becoming law, but the mere fact that it was done—with so few apparent objections—suggests the vulnerability of disability rights to cost critiques.[52]

Cost arguments were also prominent in disability rights litigation from this era. Within just five years of Section 504's enactment, multiple disabled citizens sued state, regional, and local transit authorities for failing to provide equal access to public transportation.[53] Other lawsuits targeted school boards, institutions of higher education, healthcare facilities, and public employers.[54] Often, defendants raised cost concerns—in ways that made the costs seem absurdly high or unfairly uncertain. For instance, when faced with the prospect of having to make transportation systems more accessible, defendants sometimes estimated how many potential transit users shared the plaintiff's specific disability-related accessibility needs and then calculated a cost per disabled transit user. Following this method, Cuyahoga County's Regional Transit Authority informed a federal court that it was being asked to spend $54,400 *per disabled user, per year* in operating costs and $334,000 *per disabled user* on capital expenditures.[55] This kind of costing-out was not a prominent feature of disputes over racial desegregation. Rarely, however, did judges in disability cases critique this cost-focused argumentation. Some amplified it. "If the federal government, in all its wisdom, decides that money should be spent to provide opportunities for a particular group of people," wrote a federal court judge in South Carolina in 1977 in a disability case, "that government should be willing to spend its own money (i.e., our taxes) for such purposes."[56]

When the Supreme Court finally heard a dispute involving Section 504, in the 1979 case *Southeastern Community College v. Davis*, cost arguments played a crucial role. Frances Davis was a licensed practical nurse who applied to Southeastern's nursing program, but Southeastern rejected her application because of a hearing impairment. After a court of appeals ruled that Section 504 required Southeastern to reconsider Davis's application "without regard to her hearing ability"—and that Southeastern might have to accommodate Davis's disability—Southeastern sought Supreme Court review.[57] The American Council on Education and attorneys general from twenty-seven states joined Southeastern in urging the Court to take the case. These parties argued that "administrative excess and judicial inventiveness" had transformed Section 504's spare language "into a tool of oppression not contemplated by Congress," and sought the Court's guidance.[58] The Court responded by declaring that not only was there no violation of Section 504 in this case, but also that Section 504 did not require institutions to make "extensive modifications," nor did it impose "any affirmative-action obligation."[59]

Cost framings of disability rights received further legitimacy several months later, when disability-inclusion mandates entered the domain of the Congressional Budget Office (CBO), an agency that sociologist Elizabeth Popp Berman has characterized as "a key site for institutionalizing" a new "economic style" of reasoning within the national government.[60] In 1979, a team of economists at the CBO prepared a report on alternative ways of interpreting statutory disability-inclusion mandates in transit.[61] The report concluded that the Department of Transportation's interpretation of Section 504 (which was based on HEW's earlier interpretation) "would be very expensive," costing an estimated $6.8 billion over thirty years. The report further found that "relatively few handicapped persons would benefit from it." Throughout, the report adopted cost-benefit methodology while questioning whether statutory language had to be interpreted in terms of civil rights.[62]

Such conclusions allowed the media to be even more blunt. "Must every bus kneel to the disabled?" the *New York Times* editorial board memorably asked in 1979, after the CBO released its report. As the notoriously cash-strapped city contemplated its legal responsibilities under

Section 504 and related legislation, the *Times* editorial board framed the discussion in stark terms—a "vocal segment of the handicapped" versus everyone else. "Do the 30 million Americans afflicted with physical or mental handicaps have a right of access, no matter what the cost, to all publicly sponsored activities?" The answer must be "no," the editorial board suggested, especially when "separate-but-better" options were available.[63] *Washington Post* syndicated columnist Neal Pierce likewise portrayed the situation as a "multibillion-dollar adventure in regulation-writing-run-amok" and accused Washington of getting run over by "the wheelchair lobby."[64]

Rights as Burdens in the Reagan Era

After the election of President Ronald Reagan, the cost narratives within disability civil rights law merged with the Reagan administration's more general enthusiasm for cost-benefit analysis and efficiency. One of Reagan's campaign promises was to roll back the regulatory excesses that he associated with liberal policymakers, and key to his mission was executive branch cost-benefit review of administrative output. Reagan directed agencies to conduct "Regulatory Impact Analyses" (defined as, essentially, cost-benefit analysis) for all "major rules." The Order also directed that, "to the extent permitted by law," agencies "shall not" undertake regulatory action "unless the potential benefits to society for the regulation outweigh the potential costs to society."[65] A new Regulatory Relief task force had a mandate to "study past regulations with an eye toward revising them."[66] The Section 504 regulations were among the task force's targets.[67]

As early as February 1981, "roundtable discussions" had begun at the executive branch's Office of Management and Budget (OMB) on how to avoid "the adverse administrative and economic consequences" of Section 504's implementation.[68] Meanwhile, the US Department of Justice, which had taken over HEW's civil rights enforcement work, began its own revision of the Section 504 regulations. Leaked drafts of the new OMB and DOJ guidelines in early 1982 made clear how fragile disability rights were.[69] Proposed changes removed some federally funded programs from Section 504's reach and limited the types of actions that could be considered discriminatory.[70] The draft guidelines also made cost the crucial determinant of which disabled people qualified for protection.[71]

Through political pressure, and with the help of allies inside the Reagan administration, disability rights advocates thwarted the proposed revision, but the lesson was clear: proponents of disability rights must be prepared to defend themselves on cost-benefit terms.[72] Staff members at the Disability Rights Education and Defense Fund, a leading disability rights organization, expressed outrage while also circulating internal memos on how to talk about costs and benefits in the most advantageous way. These memos also offered a more profound observation: *all* civil rights laws had costs. Previewing a point that Cass Sunstein would later articulate, albeit to different ends, they noted that it was "never costless" to eliminate race- or sex-based discrimination.[73] Why were only disability rights translated into societal burden?

Meanwhile, in the courts, the cost-conscious language from the Supreme Court's *Davis* opinion hung over every Section 504 case. For instance, siding with transit operators, the Court of Appeals for the DC Circuit found a disputed set of transit regulations mandated precisely what *Davis* found "beyond the scope of Section 504," because they "required extensive modifications of existing systems and imposed extremely heavy financial burdens on local transit authorities." Nowhere did the decision discuss the benefits that the regulations might bring to disabled people, nor did the decision engage the concept of civil rights, other than to note that HEW preferred to frame Section 504 in that way.[74] As one observer astutely noted, such decisions diminished the power of "the language of rights" and emphasized instead "the politics of resource allocation."[75]

In the 1985 case *Alexander v. Choate*, a more generous Supreme Court interpretation of Section 504 finally emerged—acknowledging that Section 504 promised "meaningful access"—and yet the decision is most salient in retrospect for translating disability rights claims into demands for resources.[76] Evaluating the allegation that state-level Medicaid cutbacks discriminated against disabled patients, the Court characterized this civil rights claim as, at bottom, an attempt to tilt a difficult allocation decision in favor of one needy group over another.[77] The opinion's author was none other than Thurgood Marshall, the Court's leading liberal. Like the Reagan administration officials who tried to roll back the Section 504 regulations, Marshall seemed to accept the notion that disability rights claimants were prone to asking too much, at the expense of everyone else.

Rights as Redistribution in the ADA Era

Given enduring skepticism of disability rights, the enactment of the Americans with Disabilities Act of 1990—a landmark civil rights law—might seem surprising. But, in fact, it is consistent with the history this chapter has chronicled. In the wake of the ADA, elite discussions of disability law and policy would continue to normalize and expand cost-benefit thinking—such that, by the turn of the twenty-first century, many self-identified political liberals could both revere civil rights and have no objections to a style of cost-benefit analysis that threatened to attenuate those very commitments.

As numerous disability scholars have now noted, the ADA was a legislative bargain with a particular quid pro quo at its heart: disabled Americans secured recognition for their essential dignity, while society gained a tool for shrinking the welfare state. Reprising what had become a familiar argument, proponents of the ADA claimed that a nondiscrimination mandate would lower barriers to employment and thereby reduce the need for government support. In a context in which public income-support programs were under attack by liberals and conservatives, the ADA-as-welfare-reform framing had broad appeal.[78] Other language in the ADA, meanwhile, made clear that disability rights would never be radically redistributive, because alleged discriminators could cite cost and burden as valid reasons for rejecting rights claims.[79] Put another way, this law accepted the notion that disabled people were costly and framed their civil rights as either cost-savers (as compared to welfare spending) or necessarily limited.

But if scholars and activists have long understood the forces that enabled the ADA's passage and contained its reach, they have been less alert to how the discourse informing this landmark law seeped into the realm of civil rights more generally. A good example of this phenomenon is the work of law professor Richard Epstein, who famously made a libertarian case for the repeal of Title VII of the 1964 Civil Rights Act and other employment discrimination laws. Thinking about *disability*-based discrimination helped him develop his argument, as seen in his 1988 article on employment protections for people with AIDS.[80] Employer discrimination against people with AIDS was rational, Epstein argued, because they represented significant health-care costs. If the law barred employers from discriminating, they would simply pursue "second-best solution[s]," leading to "substantial social losses."[81] Epstein thus urged the repeal of Section 504 and similar laws—previewing an argument he would make more forcefully in his 1992 (post-ADA) book *Forbidden Grounds*.[82]

This expanded version of Epstein's argument, which went beyond disability law to criticize employment discrimination laws more generally ("capricious," "expensive," "wasteful"), attracted national notice, and sometimes praise, in leading outlets.[83] Soon non-libertarian and more mainstream legal scholars also began questioning the distributive consequences of civil rights laws and deploying explicitly utilitarian arguments.[84] Within a decade, one could find in the pages of prestigious law journals the argument that, at least in the business context, nondiscrimination should only be recognized as a "right" when the alleged discriminator accorded different treatment to people who were "equivalent sources of money" ("a worker is essentially just her embodied net marginal product, a customer no more than a source of net receipts"). Discrimination claims that did not fit that description should be treated as "claims on social resources," law professor Mark Kelman explained, and they should compete in the policy space with other such claims.[85] By 2004, this interpretation had become the "canonical paradigm" of employment discrimination, according to one scholar.[86] Familiar language of equal opportunity endured, but was now shot through with the language of economics and the logic of the market—thanks, in part, to ideas that had circulated first and most freely in the disability context.

Meanwhile, scholars who were sympathetic to disability rights seemed to feel compelled to engage with notions of cost and efficiency—in ways that, again, spilled over into discussions of civil rights more generally.[87] Writings from this period emphasized the functional and aspirational similarity between the ADA, which included an accommodation requirement, and older civil rights laws that did not use that language. *All* these laws might impose costs on alleged discriminators (such as by depriving them of expected profits), these articles noted; that the ADA's costs seemed more obvious did not make that law different in kind.[88] Some of these scholars also took pains to frame the ADA as efficient: its provisions could prevent unfair cost distributions while maximizing overall welfare.[89]

To be sure, there remained other ways of discussing disability civil rights laws, including the language of justice and morality. But what these scholars recognized is that moral or ethical justifications were not enough—not for the ADA and not even, perhaps, for more established civil rights protections. As Samuel Bagenstos warned in 2003, "civil rights supporters will increasingly be called upon to defend antidiscrimination laws as regulatory measures that, despite their moral goals, have costs and benefits that must be factored into the decision of whether these laws are worthwhile."[90] His words proved prescient—as Obama-era technocrats like Cass Sunstein would soon show. Trying to move beyond "morals without technique," as Sunstein once described the New Deal, an ascendant generation desacralized rights and placed faith instead in cost-benefit calculation.[91]

Civil Rights in the Cost-Benefit State

In the late twentieth and early twenty-first centuries, the arena of executive-branch regulatory review (where Sunstein exerted influence) is perhaps the best place to see the steady expansion of cost-benefit analysis (CBA)—including, quietly, into the realm of civil rights.[92] Regulatory review is, of course, just one aspect of American governance, but it is a vital one. Polarized politics and congressional dysfunction have meant that much policymaking in the last several decades has occurred via administrative interpretation, the domain over which regulatory review hangs.[93]

Returning briefly to 1981, when the Reagan administration adopted a robust form of CBA for evaluating government regulation, disability rights regulations were a clear target, and yet observers did not see CBA as a threat to civil rights more generally.[94] Sunstein, then a law professor, put it this way in a 1981 article written shortly after his clerkship for Justice Thurgood Marshall and a brief stint in Reagan's Department of Justice: the cost-benefit requirement was simply not "properly applicable" to laws other than those aimed at "remedy[ing] 'market failure' in the economic sense." Certain environmental regulations were clearly subject to this kind of review, but not regulations interpreting public benefits laws, "civil rights provisions," or "provisions protecting the handicapped."[95]

Over the next two decades, what had once seemed obviously off-limits became less so. Rather than reject CBA, President Bill Clinton adopted his own version of Reagan's famous executive order.[96] Clinton was not about to give up a font of presidential power, nor was this form of regulatory review inconsistent with his New Democrat style.[97] Sunstein, meanwhile, was amassing the CV that would eventually lead him to the Obama administration's Office of Information and Regulatory Affairs (OIRA), the subdivision of OMB charged with effectuating presidential CBA mandates. In as-yet aspirational terms, Sunstein's writings from the 1990s described the rise of the "cost-benefit state."[98] He continued to concede the inappropriateness of a rigid form of CBA for some situations (such as statutes "designed to eliminate illegitimate discrimination"), but he also took pains to sketch out varieties of CBA, one of which brought a modest form of cost-benefit "balancing" to statutes "that had formerly been thought to be absolutist."[99] Around the same time, Sunstein's work garnered praise for recognizing what "liberals ... often need reminding": "that rights are not free," in the words of one reviewer.[100]

President Obama, too, embraced CBA—in Sunstein's softer proposed form—and, at Sunstein's urging, issued his own executive order to this effect.[101] For his part, Sunstein emerged from his stint at OIRA (2009–2012) unwilling to concede that CBA had any subject-matter limits—even in the face of dubious applications. In one memorable example, law professor Lisa Heinzerling highlighted the "labored, distasteful, and gratuitous essay on the economics of rape and sexual abuse" that a federal agency produced as part of a Regulatory Impact Analysis of a proposed interpretation of the Prison Rape Elimination Act.[102] Sunstein maintained that "you should monetize everything you can" and that his method of CBA was entirely consistent with humane policymaking. As an example, he cited the Obama administration's application of CBA in the disability rights context: administrators treated as "justificatory" (that is, potentially worth the costs) "the dignitary benefits of being able to use a bathroom if you're in a wheelchair."[103]

By this time, it was hardly surprising to see cost arguments mapped onto disability rights—but one does not need to look hard to find other civil rights examples. Consider the Department of Education's 2022 proposed amendment to the regulations implementing Title IX (newly controversial in the Obama years, when federal officials deployed this law against campus sexual assault): in a "costs and benefits" section of the Notice of Proposed Rulemaking, the Department circumspectly declined to quantify "in monetary terms" the benefits of being free from sex discrimination in educational settings, but it nonetheless applied the CBA framework.[104] Or consider the more extensive analysis that the Department of Housing and Urban Development (HUD) offered in 2013 when it proposed a rulemaking to give teeth to its mandate to "affirmatively . . . further" the antidiscrimination policies at the heart of the Fair Housing Act: HUD duly estimated net annual compliance costs and offered several nonquantifiable benefits.[105] The claim here is not that CBA dictated the fate of these policies. It is that federal officials translated *civil rights guarantees* into the decisional language of economics, and relatively few people noticed or objected.

How should we understand this trajectory, from Reagan's aggressive but limited executive order to the less rigid but more expansive CBA of Obama's OIRA, from a framework that seemed clearly inapplicable to "civil rights provisions" to one that conceded no bounds? And how do we reconcile the creep of CBA with the continued pursuit and valorization of rights, as evidenced, for example, by the movement for LGBTQ equality claims in the late twentieth century? Without advancing a strong causal argument, this chapter has called attention to the expansion and elaboration of disability rights during this period and to the significance of a type of civil right that, from almost the very beginning, was supposed to "pay its own way."[106] Disability rights were in this sense *not* liberalism's "last rights" but rather the door to their neoliberal future.

* * *

Emerging from World War II, the pursuit of equality was a pillar of modern liberalism in the US. When liberal policymakers set out to "secure the rights" of Black Americans—and thereby built a template for other marginalized groups—that effort was bounded in many ways, but cost was not the most important constraint, nor was efficiency the primary goal. By the turn of the twenty-first century, many liberal policy choices and aspirations from that crucial mid-century period continued to structure American life, including a commitment to rights—but cost had become much more salient, and efficiency had become the metric by which to judge virtually all policies.

This "enthusiasm for efficiency" had dark consequences for people on the left, as Duncan Kennedy predicted back in 1981, because it made their "hopes of reconciling social justice with material plenty" appear "inconsistent with elementary economic laws."[107] Likewise, it boded poorly for many people living at the "borders of belonging," whom liberal policymakers imagined they might help.[108] Two decades into the twenty-first century, to "belong" in the American polity depends on being recognizable as a past, present, or future contributor to the nation's economic well-being, and the quality of one's belonging is contingent on the perceived substantiality of one's contribution. This state of affairs, in itself, is not so different from the "breadwinner liberalism" that animated the New Deal or the Great Society.[109] But policymakers' imaginations have narrowed rather than expanded as to what it means to contribute—such that only individual participation in a thinly regulated formal labor market now seems to count—and there is little sense of obligation to those who are counted out. Advancing a different vision of citizenship is possible, and urgently important. But this history suggests looking beyond liberalism's "rights revolution" to find it.

CHAPTER 11

Computerizing a Covenant
Contract Liberalism and the Nationalization of Welfare Administration

MARC AIDINOFF

There are few things liberal politicians claim to hate as much as politics. And, throughout the second half of the twentieth century in the United States, there were few issues more politicized than welfare. Welfare was politicized because in the 1960s poor people, led by Black women, organized to make it so, as a strategy to access basic entitlements. In response, elected officials, policy professionals, and campaign strategists increasingly crafted a politics of welfare designed to inflame and mobilize white resentment. Across the political spectrum, Aid to Families with Dependent Children (AFDC), which most Americans simply called "welfare," became a representative example of political failure—a publicly elevated manifestation of how the electoral process had failed to produce a sufficient, let alone popular, welfare state. With a stated goal of modernizing welfare, and a complementary goal of preserving their political futures, the great aspiration of many liberals then was to *depoliticize* welfare by turning a contested and deeply politicized social policy into a technical problem of good governance.

So, in response to racialized rights claims of the 1960s, and the racist tropes of the "welfare queen" in the 1970s and of the "deadbeat dad" in the 1980s, liberals worked to automate, professionalize, and nationalize welfare. Liberals believed that they could diminish the political potency of welfare as an inflammatory political issue by computerizing welfare administration. By the 1980s, for welfare recipients, computers were everywhere. With these networked technologies, liberals constructed a specific social contract in which anti-poverty payments would be tracked as debts using the seemingly objective mechanisms of computerized accounting. In their attempt to bound the politics of welfare, liberals transformed welfare's underling logic from a rights-based liberalism to contract-based liberalism. Computerization animated this ideological shift.

If caseworkers once came to the homes of welfare claimants or interviewed them face-to-face in local offices, they increasingly spent their time entering claimants' data into networked computing systems.[1] In Wisconsin, parents receiving AFDC told their Social Security numbers to caseworkers who entered the number into Wisconsin's Computer Reporting Network (CRN) and recorded which jobs or job-training programs recipients sought as a condition of receiving payments.[2] In North Dakota, the state's Technical Eligibility Computer System (TECS) produced summary reports of state benefits and asked welfare recipients to identify absent parents who might be sought out to offset the cost of those benefits. Using the Mississippi Application Verification Eligibility Reporting and Information Control System (MAVERICS), caseworkers in Mississippi entered two-letter marital-status codes into a database to automatically trigger child support collection processes. Through California's Uniform Welfare Information System (UWIS), more than one hundred thousand poor noncustodial fathers felt the effects of a tax-refund intercept program that automatically deducted child support payments from tax refunds before anti-poverty checks ever arrived in mailboxes.[3]

These computerized tools not only reformulated the locally administered system of welfare, they also nationalized it. Citizens could be tracked and surveilled across jurisdictions because computer systems themselves were similar or interoperable using common standards. Wisconsin's CRN resembled California's UWIS, while North Dakota's TECS and Mississippi's MAVERICS were practically indistinguishable. Indeed, a limited network of private vendors had sold and resold analogous digital tools.[4] In a distinct manifestation of federalism, states shared and repurposed hardware and software. Interoperable computer systems, especially those designed and sold by private-sector contractors, determined public-sector administrative capacity and practices.[5] By the 1980s, the result was steady convergence upon a set of integrated, interstate administrative tools and strategies. Such technological federalism created a shared national infrastructure for welfare administration, an area long the purview of states.[6] Nationally policymakers came to assume that extraordinary levels of individualized tracking, sorting, monitoring, wage garnishing, and accounting were operationally straightforward.

The widespread availability of these technologies was particularly appealing to a liberal professional class that embraced computers as the quintessential symbol of their modern policy perspective.[7]

Computerized government systems, they hoped, would be and feel professional, offering both a metaphor and the mechanism for new projects of modern liberal governance. Guided by a "pragmatic idealism," these liberals saw the horizon of political possibility through the lens of what they deemed technologically achievable.[8] Computerization, as sold by contractors, imagined by reformers, and actualized in numerous state agencies as a tool for surveilling individuals and recouping costs, determined the bounds of what the idealized "functional" welfare system could be, and therefore the contours of what many liberals hoped it should do.[9] Computing networks powered a specific theory of operational modernization in which the federal government would become more popular, with a centrist white electorate if administrative systems became more efficient and discerning through technological innovation. Crucially, liberals also believed that with the digitally automated mechanism of contract, AFDC could be discussed without reference to race or rights.

This mutual reinforcement of the technology of computerized case management and the idea of welfare as a contract was the foundation for the "new consensus" articulated in the spring of 1987, by the old stalwart of liberal governance, New York senator Daniel Patrick Moynihan, and the prominent advocate for updating liberalism, Arkansas governor Bill Clinton.[10] At a Senate hearing on welfare, Clinton touted the new welfare case-management technologies for enforcing a reciprocal contract. Moynihan was thrilled, elevating Clinton's language of contract to the loftier language of covenant: "Governor Clinton spoke about 'contract,' that you owe the society something, and the society owes you something . . . And that is what the whole notion of American Democracy is about, that notion of 'covenant.' It is a powerful idea."[11] That idea led to more federal funding for case management systems to account for AFDC payments as debt, primarily as sums owed by noncustodial parents through child support payments. Digitally tracked child support payments went directly to the state coffers to offset any AFDC payments the custodial parent received. Instead of AFDC operating as an entitlement that ostensibly underwrote independence, it had become a strange type of contracted loan that noncustodial parents paid off.[12]

Computerization therefore enabled an update to a nineteenth-century story, the move from status to contract. Late nineteenth-century liberals believed that the status of citizenship offered poor citizens, especially Black women, few protections against poverty, but a marriage or labor contract could.[13] Late twentieth-century liberals again sought to move from status-based entitlements (for being a citizen or for being a mother) to now-automated contracts. Again, they sought to privatize responsibility and anti-poverty efforts. This computerized covenant was similar to a marriage contract; it privatized the cost associated with children to parents. But crucially, the debt relationship enabled by the child support enforcement system was not a marriage contract. It joined people who in most cases had actively chosen *not* to be joined in marriage, in an ongoing relationship.[14] The computerized debt contract functioned as an alternative to marriage by preserving some of the perceived benefits of privatized financial responsibility, while acknowledging that the state could no longer, or would not, mandate marriage. The state was again facilitator and enforcer of privatized contract, but also a party to the contract—actively intervening to collect debt payments. Gone was the covenant sanctified by God and county clerk, and in its place was a debt contract, legitimatized, liberals hoped, by nationally interoperable state computers.

The work of computerizing the welfare state and contracting its rights, then, was distributed and prolonged: linking records like Louisiana and Texas's welfare databases in 1980, passing the Family Support Act of 1988, and operating a suite of the child support enforcement tools in states like Mississippi in the 1990s. The result was a national welfare system remade as an automated reciprocal obligation, all before the passage of Clinton's famed 1996 welfare bill. As an extractive force, this networked national welfare state proved robust, able to collect debts across all fifty states. As a political entity the national welfare state was weak, its opacity and newly nationalized status leaving it vulnerable to the very national reforms that would end liberal welfare entitlements altogether.

Welfare as We Knew It

Computerization and New Deal liberalism emerged together. Title II of the Social Security Act of 1935 established "Federal Old-Age Benefits"— the program still called "Social Security"—as retirement income for a tightly bounded class of disproportionately white male citizens. Social Security relied on nationalized accounting and computing from the start. The work of tabulating each citizen in a national system through a numeric identifier fell to International Business Machines (IBM). By 1937, the federal government had issued Social Security numbers to twenty-six million workers that required four hundred IBM accounting machines and more than eight hundred keypunches.[15] These machines kept a careful ledger of what citizens had "paid" into the system through payroll taxes to determine future retirement payments. As historian Linda Gordon described it, Social Security relied on "a legal fiction that contracts had been established between government and citizen, or more specifically between government and worker."[16] Computerization recorded and transacted that contract.[17]

Title IV of the Social Security Act established "Grants to States for Aid to Dependent Children" (ADC), the precursor to AFDC welfare. In sharp contrast to Social Security, ADC administration relied on paper notes written longhand and the human judgment of state and local welfare administrators. Those subnational officers guided caseworkers who assessed a poor family's deservingness of cash payments. While Social Security retirement checks proved a reliable source of middle-class stability, welfare checks did not. Welfare administration was stingy, stigmatizing, and disciplinary. It was a project of controlling poor women in exchange for meager support.[18] By the 1960s both the Left and Right attacked the welfare system. Contrary to Social Security's contract-based respectability, welfare was ensnared in a negative feedback loop, in which, as Gordon puts it, "the modern pejorative meaning of 'welfare' results from the debasing conditions of receiving public assistance, but it also causes them."[19]

Nevertheless, welfare as a status-based entitlement in which certain Americans received cash payments was a historic accomplishment, setting important social and fiscal precedents even as its benefits were limited.[20] Unlike many state or federal anti-poverty programs that relied on annual discretionary appropriations legislation, Congress authorized funds for welfare to be "appropriated for each fiscal year thereafter" to be treated as mandatory funding.[21] Situating welfare as an entitlement was an operational achievement. As historian Karen Tani has shown, it was federal administrators who, following the passage of the Social Security Act, used the framework of a welfare entitlement or welfare rights to enforce adherence to national standards for economic relief.[22] By the 1960s, rights claims were the explicit language of political organizing, resulting in the successful establishment of local minimum standards and procedural safeguards.[23]

As the entitlement expanded and welfare recipients were increasingly non-white and not widows, broader political support for a right to welfare weakened.[24] Conservatives were committed to dismantling welfare while making the program more punitive, and they sharpened their ability to leverage the issue of welfare, along with racist tropes, for political gain. Liberals undermined welfare with both earnest and cynical reforms.[25] They developed policy and political critiques of welfare as a threat to traditional two-parent households. After the failure in 1972 of a guaranteed minimum income—President Nixon's Family Assistance Program, spearheaded by Moynihan—most liberals stopped defending welfare altogether. They feared the issue was too racialized and risked associating the entire liberal project with inflammatory rhetoric around "entitled" single Black mothers.[26]

Instead of defending the idea of entitlement or the citizens accused of "being entitled," liberal policymakers sought to reform program administration. They turned again to bureaucratic regulations and legal proceduralism.[27] During the late 1970s and into the 1980s, those new regulatory codes and procedures were increasingly expressed as computer code.[28] If computerization had helped create the contractual insurance of Social Security, in the case of AFDC welfare it would ultimately dismantle an entitlement.

Constructing a National Infrastructure of Individualized Calculation

While national actors debated welfare as an abstraction, state-level civil servants were responsible for making the welfare state function. In Louisiana that task fell to Herb Sumrall, who became the administrator of the Office of Economic Security in 1979 as the national welfare debate intensified.[29] Sumrall had previously worked in state information services where he fielded complaints when new technologies designed to collect revenue displayed a "very human habit" of "starting to act generally cranky, followed by outright refusal to work."[30] More than sluggish computers, Sumrall struggled with the federated, state-by-state structure of the welfare system in which the federal government maintained some regulatory standards of national uniformity and each state operated its own welfare department. Sumrall's programmatic responsibilities had ended at the borders of the state, but national and local politics of welfare put increasing pressure on administrators like Sumrall to expand their purview.

Sumrall and state agency colleagues worried that state autonomy weakened its welfare system, particularly as politicians led by his senator, Russell Long (D-LA), encouraged administrators to root out welfare fraud.[31] Sumrall focused on hypothetical citizens double-dipping by receiving welfare benefits in multiple states and workers who underreported their income, sometimes by working in multiple states. Under the federated system, Louisiana and Texas maintained separate administrative apparatuses to manage national welfare programs—the Louisiana Department of Labor and the Texas Department of Human Resources each processed their state's payments. If a Louisianan moved to Texas, that person might have a national Social Security card, but the rest of the paperwork required starting from scratch to access federal entitlements. The former Louisianan would go to a county office in Texas and sit for an intake interview. After recording that person's information, a caseworker would extend or deny financial support to Texas's newest resident. Although that caseworker could place a call to the neighboring state, information rarely crossed the Sabine River, even as families regularly did.

States compared strategies about how they might use computing and internal databases to better manage case files and track claimants. Despite the incredible mathematical ability of 1970s and 1980s computing (the reason why states signed large computing contracts for engineers building roads and bridges) and the rise of the personal computer (the dominant historiographic story for the period), for a state administrator like Sumrall, a computer was a tool for accounting welfare payments over time and across jurisdictions. Sumrall would have known how in the spring of 1980 the Arkansas Social Services Division matched state welfare rolls against state employment records. As a result, they cut off cash support for 2,439 welfare recipient and reduced payments for 510 more. Arkansas governor Clinton heralded this accomplishment as just the beginning of an effort that "could save millions and millions of dollars."[32] That winter, Louisiana and Texas began sharing an integrated computer system for tracking welfare expenditures. In theory, according to one journalist, integrating systems meant that a complete history of the claimant's past aid would be "available at a push of a button." Sumrall promised the integrated approach would "help stop welfare fraud or tax fraud." The "hookup" was "touted as the first of its kind in the nation."[33]

Welfare agencies did not simply "hook" into each other—these connections required significant investments in hardware and software. Literal wires, mostly copper, connected states with distinct case-management procedures. Even with physical linkages, states had incommensurable data sets. County records were rarely uniform throughout the state. How would the accounting problem be possible? One approach drew on the model and infrastructure of Social Security to use computing technologies to tally outlays and associate those figures with a government-issued number. Administrators like Sumrall tried to repurpose Social Security numbers, but many AFDC recipients did not have or did not want to share Social Security numbers, nor did the state did trust applicants to report their numbers honestly.[34] Instead, states relied on systems of name-matching, which were technologically more sophisticated, correspondingly less reliable, and legally tenuous.[35] By associating ever more information with each individual name, an increasingly robust capacity was emerging to enable individualized welfare accounting.

State interoperability depended upon not just geographic proximity and hardwired connections, but also the flow of software and computer professionals. The Mississippi Central Data Processing Authority, the agency charged with computerizing welfare administration in Mississippi, also prioritized interconnectivity with Louisiana and Texas, and considered repurposing Texas's System for Application and Verification Eligibility Reporting and Referral (SAVERR). Despite the acronym, Texas's system saved neither time nor money; the software had overwhelmed the outdated UNIVAC equipment, so Mississippi had to turn to North Dakota for a model.[36] As one manager put it, Mississippi "basically lifted North Dakota's program."[37]

A network of professional private-sector technicians, consultants, and salespeople, primarily associated with IBM, made these exchanges and adaptations possible. The Mississippi Data Processing Authority intended "to transfer both concept and code and agreed to limit modifications" to accommodate regional administrative idiosyncrasies, like Mississippi's two-month budget cycle. Contractors submitted bids in the fall of 1985 to assist with efforts to transfer the North Dakota Technical Eligibility Computer System (TECS) to Mississippi.[38] TECS, it turned out, was not even native to North Dakota—its underlying code was originally crafted for Alaska. The analogous or interoperable hardware and software contractors sold and installed formed the connective tissue among public-sector agencies and with the federal government.[39] For decades, IBM's business model relied on an army of aggressive salespeople working to navigate the public sector.[40] North Dakota acquired Alaska's welfare administration system after a helpful call from a contractor who suggested repurposing Alaska's welfare eligibility system.[41] Indeed, IBM's network of consultants and salespeople helped states navigate federal approval processes, the prerequisites for federal funding. As the federated, procedurally complex, but increasingly interoperable national welfare system emerged, contracts begat contractors who begat more contracts.

Common technical standards unified these systems, and because of its market dominance, IBM often determined those standards.[42] Occasionally a state chose to contract with a different vendor, but rarely did the state reject IBM-compatible standards.[43] IBM standards enabled a common technical infrastructure—Systems Network Architecture, or SNA—to facilitate sales across states as well as additions to existing systems. This architectural choice, according to IBM, was a "logical structure, formats, protocols (rules), and operational sequences for transmitting information through networks and controlling their configuration and operation." IBM recognized that "SNA needs to be understood in a larger sense. Not only is SNA a specification, it is also a means for structuring a network and a set of products with which to assemble such a network."[44] In other words, IBM set a standard for interoperability, and interoperability was the means to overcome the limitations of a federated welfare system. With each new contract, IBM and its allied vendors were making a national welfare state. Indeed, administrators felt they needed SNA for fear that opening the door to multiple standards could lead to "chaos." One state official in Mississippi explained that a commitment to IBM "provides guidelines for tactical decisions that promote consistency and compatibility as the pieces of the puzzle come together."[45] IBM's SNA was in practice a nationalizing network of networks—making distinct state apparatuses compatible and interoperable across various databases and programs.

IBM also sold a professionalized ethos which was particularly meaningful for besieged welfare administrators and professional-class liberal policymakers alike. Contemporaneous studies showed that the most important feature of a computerized welfare system for state or local welfare offices trying to manage federal auditors was making civil servants appear "competent." Case-management technologies were especially valuable. The true worth of these tools, the information scholar Rob Kling argued, was "administrative attractiveness," not "administrative efficiency."[46] One internal state-agency evaluation reported that "automation has added a professional dimension" to determining eligibility.[47] In the face of compounding political critiques of the nation's welfare system, computerization promised to brand welfare administration as modern, efficient, and professional—a liberal's dream, regardless of how well it worked. Indeed, if the rising liberal professional class shaped momentous transformations of American governance after the 1970s, computers held the promise of turning anyone, even a government caseworker, into a professional.

With new professional capacities came new governing possibilities. TECS and MAVERICS were case management software with which case workers translated information from potential welfare recipients into machine-recognizable codes. Initially, the system collected self-reported income, number of children, and employment status, and new modules were continuously added. By 1985, as figure 11.1 shows, computerized accompaniment techniques for anti-poverty technologies were being deployed in the majority of states. The result was an accounting system that not only worked across state lines and recorded the amount of AFDC money issued but also held the potential to locate funds that could offset costs. These technical updates would prove particularly appealing as welfare reform again moved to the center of national political debates.

CHAPTER 11

LOCATION OF WELFARE TECHNIQUES *

☒ One or more AFDC, Food Stamp or Medicaid Techniques in Operation or Under Development

☐ No AFDC, Food Stamp or Medicaid Techniques Reported. (This category includes survey nonrespondents.)

* Alaska and Hawaii each reported one or more AFDC, Food Stamp or Medicaid techniques. No welfare techniques were reported in Guam, Puerto Rico or the Virgin Islands.

11.1. A map of automated technologies for eligibility verification based on state self-reporting. Inspector General Richard P. Kusserow, *Catalog of Automated Front-End Eligibility and Verification Techniques* (Washington, DC: US Department of Health and Human Services, September 1985): 6.

Fathers of Liberal Reform

Daniel Patrick Moynihan had spent most of his career trying, with limited success, to reform welfare. Since 1955, when he began work on New York State's poverty programs, through domestic-policy leadership positions in the Kennedy, Johnson, and Nixon administrations, and in the Senate, Moynihan hewed to a centrist liberalism marked by a defense of government support constrained by what he saw as pragmatic concern for creating dependency.[48] By the spring of 1987, the sixty-year-old senator was closer than ever to shepherding a "new consensus" on welfare reform. He was aided by the work of the National Governors Association led by Bill Clinton. Over the previous two decades, as economic growth slowed and budgets tightened, states like Clinton's Arkansas had become increasingly both laboratories for punitive approaches to welfare administration and sites of resistance to those restrictive and incipiently carceral regimes.[49] Learning from these state-level experiments, Clinton asserted that all welfare recipients "should sign a contract with the State, making a personal commitment in return for benefits to pursue an individually developed path to independence."[50] This commitment to treat welfare as a reciprocal agreement "in exchange for benefits" formed the foundation of Clinton and Moynihan's agreement.

Clinton and Moynihan's accord corresponded to a strong underlying belief shared by many liberals and conservatives that the breakdown of the family structure explained poverty generally, and Black poverty in particular. Moynihan spoke of the "18-year contract" between a parent and child. Speaking from the Senate dais to an imagined noncustodial parent not paying the costs of raising a child, Moynihan scolded: "You just have to understand that if you are going to bring children into the world, you are going to have to support them for 18 years."[51] Moynihan had been chastising that imagined parent his whole career. Moynihan's name had become synonymous with his infamous 1965 diagnosis that, in simplified form, the absence of Black fathers was largely the cause of persistent Black poverty.[52] Armed with the latest social science, liberals cyclically rediscovered the problem of poverty and routinely blamed one-parent households and, particularly in the 1980s, the absent Black father.[53] Indeed, if the "welfare queen" was the primary rhetorical villain of 1970s welfare politics, by the 1980s she was joined or overtaken by the figure of the "deadbeat dad" whose libidinous irresponsibility cost dutiful taxpayers.[54]

At that 1987 Senate hearing on welfare, Governor Clinton testified that the contractual approach to reforming welfare required investments in technical infrastructure. "This contract," he explained, "has to be enforced not only on the part of the recipient but on the part of the State, through a case-management system."[55] Technological infrastructure, even more than a culture of responsibility or a new legal regime, would enforce a welfare contract. Clinton's assumptions were shaped by the computerized IBM infrastructure already deployed in states including Arkansas. Governors believed that with the right technology, a local welfare office could track and record a person's income, number of children, work history, welfare payments received, potential enrollment in a worker training program, and, when there was a child, former sexual partners.

Liberals saw in absent fathers not only a root cause of poverty, but also the appropriate source of funding to offset the state's fiscal burdens for supporting mothers and children. As historian Marissa Chappell has shown, conservatives were not alone in pushing to hold fathers responsible, as liberal feminists also worked to "reprivatize the cost of childbearing."[56] Noncustodial parents, in this vision, owed the state for supporting the custodial parent. For liberal welfare reformers, enforcing a strict regime of child support payments promised an efficient anti-poverty model that offset public costs with private dollars.[57] The arrangement depended on public-sector intervention and increased surveillance. Starting in 1975, Congress required AFDC applicants to assign their child support rights to the welfare administering agency. In contrast, for middle-class families, child support was a private arrangement. For families on welfare, networked computing made state welfare agencies a party to what were otherwise private marriage and alimony contracts. At the time, President Gerald Ford worried, as Moynihan remembered it, "about the unnecessary intrusion of the Federal Government into domestic relations."[58] By the 1980s, liberals and moderates were eager to plunge ahead.

In the 1987 Senate committee hearing on welfare reform, alongside Clinton, Delaware governor Mike Castle, a moderate Republican, bragged of "extensive computer networking" that tracked parents across states. Think about a father who would "just get in a car" or "get on a boat in the outgoing tide," said Castle.[59] Castle detailed how Delaware shared data with New Jersey. To find fathers, the governors explained, states could also compare the names of parents with department of motor vehicles records and labor data. They might find hidden income, which the state could then collect as part of its revised and expanded welfare "contract."

Still, the narrative and operational logic of a contract could not get a bill passed without political salesmanship. As he championed the Family Support Act, Moynihan likely saw in Clinton a shared commitment to professionalized liberalism. But in Clinton, Moynihan must have recognized something the academic policymaker lacked: savvy political charisma rooted in glad-handing southern politics. Clinton, an avatar of both another New South and a new generation of liberals, offered a model to national legislators. The southern governor promised them a path through the thicket of racialized welfare politics, by committing to addressing poverty while blunting the contested politics of entitlements though technological and technocratic practices of pragmatic reform. While senators credited Moynihan's diligence, it was Clinton who would get credit, even begrudgingly from Moynihan, for rallying bipartisan support for a welfare reform bill.[60] On the House side, co-sponsor Harold Ford Sr., the young Black congressman from Tennessee with an MBA from Howard University, even invited Clinton to mark up the bill.[61]

With Clinton's support, Moynihan's Family Support Act of 1988 became law in a short-lived moment of liberal consensus. The Act mandated that all states implement "comprehensive and statewide automated data processing and information retrieval systems" for child support enforcement and, crucially, committed the federal government to covering 90 percent of the costs of these systems.[62] The act itself did not redirect the evolution of welfare in the United States so much as accelerate the state-level mechanisms that made the bill's programmatic goals possible. Through open-ended federal matching funds, the Family Support Act further incentivized case-management technologies, interstate information sharing, and aggressive tools for child support enforcement.

Technologies of Contract Enforcement

In 1991, incentivized by the Family Support Act's funding, Mississippi submitted a proposal to fully automate their child support enforcement program. An expanding array of digital tools would enhance the state's ability to identify who owed child support and to collect those funds. The plan cost $32 million for fifty-one months of hardware installation and software development.[63] Even with knowledgeable contractors repurposing code and federal funds, the promise of debt collection as an expanding source of revenue did not self-evidently justify the multimillion-dollar costs of new computing systems. Put another way, if the moral or contractual cases had adherents, the economic or fiscal case remained to be made. Mississippi officials claimed that their new system would increase revenue by automating targeting and collection of child support cases. One internal tally promised $32 million in "savings" from a child support system upgrade.[64] To at least one member of the Mississippi oversight board assessing these expenses, the figures did not add up. He scrawled the math in the margins of official assessments. If child support cost approximately $2,400 per month per child, this funding could support 2,713 children for five years. Doubtful that there would be $32 million of additional revenue or cost savings, he was "having a problem with the business case for this." His underlined conclusion was clear: "A computer is not going to collect child support."[65] But computers had, in fact, begun collecting child support in states across the country. In Mississippi child support payments collected by the state drastically increased from $50 million in 1992, to $84 million in 1995, and to $104 million in 1996.[66]

With these technological tools, states worked to collect child support differently from other types of fines, fees, or recouped costs. All states required employers to withhold income directly from payroll. Using techniques developed as for Social Security administration, employers garnished child support payments directly from the paychecks of employed parents. Additional subsystems from different states, which matched parental names against new-hire reports, automatically notified employers to remove funds from a paycheck. The Tax Offset Program allowed states to "intercept state and federal taxes from noncustodial parents delinquent in making their child support benefits."[67] For poor families, this policy meant that state or federal tax benefits, intended to support food or housing, could instead end up back in state coffers when they were garnished to offset the cost of child support.[68]

As more parents were identified who owed the state money, Mississippi automatically referred many noncustodial parents to child support enforcement officers.[69] The system wasn't perfectly efficient. Bulletins laid out the difficulties of reconciling collection data (child support payments received by the state) and public-assistance data (welfare funds distributed by the state) without the precision of a Social Security number. Instead, case workers might call the help desk in Jackson to ensure accounting was in order.[70] Such bureaucratic hacks allowed case workers to enter a summary of custody payments and record them as income even when the parent's identifiers were uncertain.[71]

States implemented increasingly data-intensive tools to surveil and punish those who failed to pay, including seizing funds directly. By the late 1990s, the Financial Institution Data Match program relied on name-matching to compare the names of noncustodial parents who had overdue child support payments with clients at all financial institutions (local and national banks) doing business in the state. To follow the computerized path: if, according to calculations from the case management system, welfare payments were distributed, and if the noncustodial parent as digitally documented had not paid the state, that parent's name was sent to their bank. That bank account might be frozen or funds automatically withdrawn. The minimum amount owed to trigger this process automatically was just $250.[72]

If no matches were found, or if the account held insufficient funds, the state used additional enforcement tools. Again, relying on name-matching, the noncustodial parent's information was sent to various state agencies, including the Mississippi Department of Public Safety which could suspend various state-issued licenses for failure to pay, or failure to comply with warrants to participate in paternity testing or child support hearings.[73] Most consequentially, hundreds of Mississippians were briefly incarcerated for failure to pay or for compounding offenses like driving without a license suspended because of earlier enforcement measures.[74] Technology helped the state become more adept at surveilling the poor and extracting payments with the threat of punishment. Interoperable computer systems championed by liberal reformers thus unified an increasingly extractive carceral state and an ostensibly beneficent welfare state.

From Contract to Covenant to Contract

In October 1991, as he launched his presidential campaign, Bill Clinton borrowed Moynihan's phrase for effective welfare administration. Rather than use the more transactional language of a contract, Clinton offered the aspirational language of a "New Covenant." This idea would become a central motif of his campaign—a promise to remake the relationship between citizen and state. A voter could hear that Clinton wanted to update and reform the New Deal compact, and a claim that Clinton was at once FDR's heir and something fundamentally new. With "covenant" not "contract," Clinton would not fully disenchant liberal citizenship with the language of the market, but he would sanctify it with technocratic reforms that promised less contestable means of distributing and funding social programs.

With the campaign's first major policy address at Georgetown, his Jesuit alma mater, Clinton fleshed out his covenant. It was an attempt to preserve some core commitments of what voters called liberalism while expanding the Democrat's electoral coalition. Clinton, the modernizing Arkansas Baptist, adopted the framing of Catholic social commitments associated with liberals like Ted Kennedy, Tip O'Neill, and Moynihan to sell policies that undermined those very commitments. Clinton's New Covenant paradoxically promised both collectivity and individuality. "That's what our hope is today: A New Covenant to shoulder our common load. When people assume responsibility and shoulder that common load, they acquire a dignity they never knew before." That new dawn would come "when fathers pay their child support." The state was defining, brokering, and enforcing these obligations technologically. No matter how powerful though, the New Covenant only truly mattered, Clinton reminded his audience, if it could help win elections. "This New Covenant can only be ratified by the people," Clinton reminded the audience, and then specified, "in the 1992 election."[75]

By 1994, after the legislative failure of the Clinton administration's health-care plan and limited administrative welfare reforms, Congressman Newt Gingrich responded with an alternative "contract." The Republican Party's *Contract with America* was a concise set of commitments, ten bills to pass if they took control of Congress. While the Clinton administration envisioned dramatic welfare reforms through its proposed Work and Responsibility Act, Gingrich outflanked Democrats with a straightforward repeal of AFDC through the Personal Responsibility Act. Moynihan was disgusted by both by the Republican proposal and the Clinton administration's capitulation. The Republican welfare reform plan, in Moynihan's assessment, "would be the most regressive event in social policy of the 20th century."[76] Following Gingrich's sweeping success in the 1994 midterms and his elevation to Speaker of the House, Moynihan was frustrated by Clinton's submission: "Determined to go along," the Clinton administration developed a tactic where "Democrats would *demand* that Republicans add *a little* extra money for various services" but the core commitments to ongoing financial support would end.[77]

Many, including Moynihan's own staff, thought the senator should take responsibility for not only articulating a liberal position on welfare but also drafting a bill and whipping the necessary votes. Indeed, Moynihan's aides were "baffled, even horrified" that their boss did not forcefully offer a liberal counter to Gingrich's welfare reform taken up by Clinton.[78] For liberals aligned with Moynihan, the Personal Responsibility and Work Opportunity Act (the very name of the 1996 welfare law hybridized Clinton's and Gingrich's proposals) was a fundamental rupture from the sorts of incremental reforms in the Family Support Act of 1988. Lawrence O'Donnell Jr., Moynihan's committee staff leader, was shocked by the pace at which welfare was gutted. O'Donnell told the *Washington Post*, "Very little has changed in our knowledge about what to do to help the welfare population. The only thing that's changed is our politics."[79]

By 1996, the Clinton and Moynihan camps agreed on very little, except that the problem was politics. The technical success of welfare administration systems had not neutralized the conservative political power of attacking welfare. By signing a bill that transformed the national welfare system into state block grants, Clinton ended "welfare as we know it." As part of the package, he promised "the most sweeping crackdown on deadbeat parents in history."[80] Many of the operational and even legislative tools for that crackdown, nevertheless, were already in place with interoperable databases humming along and state agencies garnishing paychecks. Indeed, both Clinton and Moynihan had been instrumental in ensuring that child support enforcement had grown, as Libby Adler and Janet Halley note, "from a feeble and disconnected array of judicial orders into a nationalized, computerized, and (at least for wage earners) nearly seamless collection apparatus."[81] The former governor surely knew that "nearly seamless" extraction was a technological accomplishment.

In the White House Rose Garden for the bill signing, in the full swing of his 1996 reelection campaign, President Clinton promised an end to the politics of welfare. "Welfare will no longer be a political issue. The two parties cannot attack each other over it. Politicians cannot attack poor people over it." The press followed up, asking if the president had not betrayed core constituents of the liberal coalition. Clinton promised to closely monitor the implementation and fix whatever glitches arose. One reporter pushed further: "What guarantees are there that these things will be fixed, Mr. President, especially if Republicans remain in control of Congress?" Clinton responded crisply: "That's what we have elections for."[82]

CHAPTER 12

Left in Limbo

The Fight for Temporary Protected Status and the Illiberal Effects of Liberal Policymaking

ADAM GOODMAN

In December 1990, El Rescate, an organization that provided social and legal services to Central Americans in Los Angeles, threw a Christmas party for families in the community. There was much to celebrate. Less than a month earlier, President George H. W. Bush had signed into law legislation providing Temporary Protected Status (TPS), including work authorization and relief from deportation for up to eighteen months, to Salvadorans who had lived in the United States continuously since September 19, 1990.[1] Advocacy groups had tirelessly—and unsuccessfully—lobbied for TPS for years. When Congress passed the act, Frank Sharry, director of the National Immigration, Refugee, and Citizenship Forum, described people as "stunned, shocked and thrilled."[2]

Representative Joe Moakley, a Massachusetts Democrat and the proud sponsor of the TPS provision, was among those rejoicing. Though he couldn't make it to the Christmas party, he sent a statement for actors Edward James Olmos and Esai Morales to read in English and Spanish. "The New Year will begin with the much fought for and needed recognition that the Salvadoran community here in the United States are refugees fleeing generalized violence of civil-war and thus deserve our protection," Moakley wrote. "The struggle to secure protective status for Salvadorans has been a long and difficult one, but the courage and commitment of your community both here and in El Salvador . . . has always served to guide me and fuel my work for reforms in immigration and foreign policy." TPS was "a fitting Christmas gift."[3]

Moakley's assessment of TPS's impact was only partially accurate. The new status certainly did have immediate and long-term benefits. The day after Bush signed the law, some immigration judges began granting stays of deportation to Salvadorans, even though the provision didn't go into effect until January 1991.[4] In the years and decades ahead, TPS would shield hundreds of thousands of people from removal, becoming a policy that liberal Democrats championed and fought to defend.

Yet, right after Congress created TPS, potential beneficiaries found themselves in the difficult position of needing to choose, in the words of an El Rescate lawyer, "between continuing to live with the security they have known as undocumented refugees or to venture into a system historically hostile to their plight."[5] And, over time, as TPS became a fixture of the US immigration system, it left an increasing number of people in a precarious, prolonged state of limbo. In 2001, Óscar Chacón, then head of the DC-based Salvadoran National Network, called for an end to the "'temporary' nightmare that separates families and keeps a permanent cloud of fear over so many Central Americans."[6] A few years later, Salvadoran activist and educator Roberto Lovato described TPS recipients as being "on a legal and emotional roller coaster, not knowing if [they] will be deported or legalized, because no president has kept the promise to end the legal purgatory that 'temporary' legalization became."[7] This remains true today. TPS has now existed for more than three decades, during which time Salvadoran beneficiaries have lived with the ever-present threat that US authorities could terminate the program and seek to expel them. TPS for Salvadorans has been set to expire more than two dozen times and has ended more than once, only to be reinstated later.

This chapter traces the decades-long history of the fight for a provision that has offered crucial protections to Salvadorans and others, while also exacting considerable material costs and psychological violence on them over time. I show how Joe Moakley, a provincial, liberal congressman from a Catholic family, became a leader in the Central American solidarity movement, and I examine the long-term illiberal effects of the bargain he struck to defend Salvadorans.

The history of TPS offers important insights into the relationship between liberal policymakers and left-wing activists since the 1960s and into how both play instrumental, often intertwined roles in bringing about political change. The durable legacy of the Vietnam War profoundly shaped the politics of the leftists and liberals who forged alliances throughout the 1980s to challenge the Reagan administration's conservative agenda. The seeds of Central American solidarity organizations, including local groups in Moakley's district, such as the Jamaica Plain Committee on Central America (JPCOCA), can be found in the antiwar movement of the 1960s. And after Vietnam, liberal Democrats like Moakley became increasingly skeptical of Cold War approaches to US foreign policy and embraced the turn, spurred by President Jimmy Carter, to protecting people's human rights.[8]

But the story of TPS also exposes the limits of liberal policymaking to ensure the well-being, equality, and human rights of all. This reality only became clearer in the years and decades after its enactment, as New Democrats increasingly employed technocratic modes of governance that often hurt, rather than helped, the most marginalized. Throughout the 1980s, Central Americans fleeing civil wars sought permanent legal status in the United States through asylum. The Reagan administration, for its part, consistently refused to recognize Salvadorans as refugees, largely because of Cold War geopolitics and the fact that the US government had sent billions of dollars in aid to the right-wing Salvadoran government people were fleeing. Temporary protection emerged as a politically viable middle ground. However, when Moakley forced recalcitrant Senate Republicans and the Bush administration to include TPS in the Immigration Act of 1990, the possibility of Salvadorans receiving asylum became more remote, pointing to the compromises and contradictions inherent to the liberal legislative process. Soon, Central American refugees and their allies found themselves fighting just to defend these imperfect half measures, arguably making it more challenging to achieve the ultimate goal of winning permanent protection.

Historians have written extensively about immigration policy and the so-called immigrant experience. Many classic works framed migration as a linear process in which people left their countries of origin, settled in the United States, and made new lives for themselves.[9] Other studies have focused on how laws, the growth of the bureaucratic state, and the hardening of borders during the twentieth century have changed the country by controlling who can enter and who can remain.[10] Yet, many migrants' experiences have been defined by neither assimilation and integration nor exclusion and deportation. In recent decades, liberal US immigration policies and a deep-seated belief in technocratic proceduralism have produced widespread liminal legality that now shapes the lives and defines the precarious subjectivities of millions of people—from asylum seekers and applicants for permanent residence or citizenship waiting as their cases wind their way through labyrinthine bureaucracies, to individuals with provisional protections such as TPS or Deferred Action for Childhood Arrivals (DACA) that could be stripped away at a moment's notice.[11] Since 1965, the combination of technocratic liberal statecraft and conservative intransigence have created an expanding number of tenuous legal statuses that provide contingent rights but little-to-no hope of ever gaining full citizenship.

TPS offers a paradigmatic example of these dynamics. Although most studies of TPS focus on its implementation, we should not take its existence for granted. Understanding how the provision came into being requires us to grapple with the intersecting histories of the Salvadoran civil war of the 1980s, US politics and policies during the last decade of the Cold War, asylum seekers' fight for permanent legal status in the United States, the influence of religion in politics, and the roles grassroots organizers and legislative entrepreneurs play in bringing about transformative change. Our story begins in neither San Salvador nor Washington, DC, but in Boston.

A Politician of and for the People

John Joseph Moakley was an unlikely champion for Salvadoran refugees. Born in 1927 to an Irish American father and an Italian American mother, Moakley, the oldest of three brothers, grew up during the Great Depression in an apartment over a hardware store in the South Boston projects. The family lived just down the street from the Bulgers, including sons William, or Billy, the future president of the Massachusetts Senate, and James Joseph, or Whitey, the future gangster and FBI informant. Moakley trained to be a sheet metal worker in high school, but dropped out at age fifteen and forged papers so that he could enlist in the US Navy and serve in World War II. After the war, he returned to school, then became involved in local and state politics while earning a law degree from Suffolk University at night. He won a seat in the US House of Representatives in 1972, beating incumbent Louise Day Hicks, and represented Massachusetts' 9th District for the next twenty-eight years, rising to become chairman of the House Rules Committee. Both the New Deal and the Great Society influenced Moakley, who believed that government played an important role in bettering people's lives. However, he was far from a social liberal on some issues, including his opposition to school integration through busing. Above all, he cared about and concentrated his energies on serving his constituents. Moakley was, in his own words, "strictly a bread and butter democrat, domestic type. A foreign affair to me," the congressman from Southie quipped, "was going to East Boston and getting an Italian sandwich."[12]

Although the link is perhaps not immediately apparent, Moakley's upbringing in a white working-class family from South Boston helps explain his later involvement in El Salvador and advocacy on behalf of Salvadoran refugees. He was a fighter, both literally and figuratively. Known as the "Boston Bull" during his days as a light heavyweight boxer, Moakley liked to tell a story from his childhood about driving in the neighborhood one day with his father when they came across a scuffle between two kids, one much larger than the other. His father stopped the car and told him to intervene on behalf of the smaller child. Young

Joe got out of the car and beat up the bigger kid, later crediting this experience as contributing to a lifelong hatred of bullies. By the 1980s, that hatred extended to the Salvadoran government officials and military authorities (and their backers in the United States) responsible for murdering innocent civilians and even clergy.[13]

Moakley's Catholic upbringing and the strong presence of the Church in Boston also played a role in why he first spoke out about El Salvador. By the early 1980s, the Salvadoran government had come to view Catholic clergy as subversives aligned with the poor and the Frente Farabundo Martí para la Liberación Nacional (FMLN). "Be a patriot, kill a priest" became a common slogan on the Salvadoran right. On March 24, 1980, a gunman assassinated Archbishop Óscar Romero, a figure beloved by the poor and despised by the powerful, while he celebrated mass in the chapel of a San Salvador hospital. He was not the first priest to be killed in the country. Fewer than nine months later, a group of Salvadoran National Guardsmen acting on "orders from above" raped and murdered nuns Ita Ford, Maura Clarke, and Dorothy Kazel, and lay missionary Jean Donovan—all US citizens.[14]

The horrific killings of the four churchwomen shocked people in the United States and led then-president Jimmy Carter to suspend military aid to El Salvador. The Reagan administration reversed that decision. Jeane Kirkpatrick, who would soon become Reagan's ambassador to the United Nations, went as far as to imply that the women themselves, rather than the Salvadoran government, might have been to blame. "The nuns were not just nuns; they were political activists" who supported the FMLN, she told a reporter a couple of weeks after their murder.[15]

Such acts and sentiments did not sit well with Moakley, who came from a place where people treated clergy with reverence. He took to the floor of the House of Representatives on December 8, 1981, less than a week after the one-year anniversary of the brutal crimes against the slain churchwomen. "What has the Salvadoran Government done to right this gross injustice?" he asked, before denouncing the Reagan administration's failure to act and decision to increase military aid to El Salvador. "The four women who were murdered in El Salvador were carrying out their religious convictions of aiding the poor and helpless. Let us remember them for their courage and determination in carrying the banner for social justice. And let us have the foresight and commonsense to not let their deaths have been in vain."[16]

Yet the Salvadoran military and right-wing death squads continued to kidnap, rape, torture, and kill. Just three days after Moakley's speech, Salvadoran soldiers in the US-trained Atlacátl Battalion murdered nearly a thousand innocent men, women, and children in and around the village of El Mozote in the eastern province of Morazán. Journalists for the *New York Times* and *Washington Post* traveled to El Mozote and reported on the massacre in January 1982, but the Reagan administration dismissed their stories as propaganda and sent $81 million in additional military support plus another $100 million in economic aid to the Salvadoran government.[17] Moakley denounced the decision. "By militarily propping up a regime that oppressed and terrorizes its people, we, too, are contributing to that oppression." He signed onto a congressional resolution to suspend all US military aid to El Salvador and sent a letter to President Reagan. "The parallels between our involvement in Vietnam and our present policy toward El Salvador are uncanny," he wrote. "I am fearful that in the not too distant future we will see the first American soldier come home from El Salvador in a coffin."[18]

Reagan paid no mind to Moakley's warning. Jim McGovern, Moakley's then-aide and a future Massachusetts congressman, later explained why. The administration viewed Central America as a "fight between the United States and the Soviet Union" in which "the revolutionary currents in El Salvador were somehow . . . masterminded in Havana or in the Kremlin." However, McGovern pointed out what a generation of Cold War liberals had learned from the war in Vietnam: "You can't export revolution like you export a foreign car or something." The Salvadoran civil war stemmed from a combination of long-standing problems, including poverty, inequality, impunity, and violence. Rather than addressing these underlying issues, the United States "just shoveled all this military aid down there," McGovern continued. Instead of siding with the campesinos, students, Catholic Church, organized labor, or opposition political parties, "we sided with the most antidemocratic force in El Salvador: the armed forces." The United States stood "with some of the biggest creeps of the hemisphere, and we did so because we were under the illusion that we were fighting communism."[19]

Ongoing US support in the face of such blatant, widespread human rights violations emboldened the Salvadoran military to continue to kill at will. By the end of 1982, Salvadoran security forces and allied paramilitary groups had murdered at least 33,473 people, disappeared 1,874 more, and forced hundreds of thousands to flee the country and seek refuge elsewhere within a period of just three years.[20]

The Reagan administration's policies toward El Salvador and Central America outraged many people, including several of Moakley's young, liberal, college-educated constituents who pushed him to act. Salvadoran refugees also shared their testimonies directly with the congressman, which deeply disturbed and moved him. He proved receptive to such pressure from below. Whereas his mentor, legendary House

Speaker Tip O'Neill, liked to say that "all politics is local," Moakley "took that one step further," according to McGovern. "For him, all politics was personal. He responded to individual requests. He was moved most by someone's personal story."[21] During his first years in Congress, Moakley traveled around his district in a Winnebago, publicizing his itinerary in advance and warmly greeting people who lined up to speak with him, to share their problems, and to request his assistance. After retiring the Winnebago, he visited the post office in each town in his district at least once a year, installed himself in the manager's office, and continued his open-door policy.[22] Such an approach stood in stark contrast to modes of constituent relations—relying on pollsters and consultants, "activating" voters along nationally salient partisan lines—that New Democrats would embrace in the years ahead.

Moakley's brand of retail politics played a critical role in him becoming a leading figure in the fight for TPS. In mid-December 1982, the Jamaica Plain Committee on Central America (JPCOCA), whose members had come of age during the mass anti–Vietnam War protests of the late 1960s, organized a group of nine activists, clergy, and community leaders to send a letter to the congressman requesting a meeting about US policy in Central America. They also planned strategic visits to his post office forums and packed the lines with people who shared their concerns. A month later, in late January 1983, a handful of the signatories—Felix Arroyo of the Massachusetts Latin American Brotherhood; Ed Crotty of Citizens for Participation in Political Action; Miguel Satut, the Executive Director of Oficina Hispana; and Carol Pryor and Virginia Vogel Zanger of JPCOCA—met with Moakley in his Boston office and gave him a petition signed by 450 local residents calling for stopping US military aid to the region. They also planned to push him to take a stronger public stance on El Salvador. After reviewing his record, however, they realized that Moakley was already on their side of the issues, including ending US aid to repressive Central American governments. Still, they hoped Moakley would commit to one of four action items included in an advocacy statement drafted by Oxfam America. Number three caught Moakley's attention: "to provide extended voluntary departure status and political asylum for Salvadoran and Guatemalan refugees in the United States until circumstances permit their safe repatriation."[23]

Moakley's most engaged colleagues on Central America focused their energies on US policy toward the region, rather than on the domestic consequences of the conflicts. Taking up the refugee issue made sense for the bread-and-butter congressman from Southie, since it meant helping people in his district who lived in fear and under threat of deportation to a place where the military killed priests and nuns with impunity. In the years ahead, fighting on behalf of Salvadoran refugees became key to Moakley's local constituent services and dedication to protecting international human rights.[24]

The Fight to Protect Salvadoran Refugees

Soon after the meeting with the activists, Moakley began organizing. He and his staff drafted a letter to Reagan's secretary of state, George Schultz, and attorney general, William French Smith, urging them to temporarily halt deportations of Salvadorans "until such time as it is safe for them to return to their homeland." They also circulated a "Dear Colleague" letter in hopes of rallying widespread support in the Democrat-controlled House of Representatives.[25] Jim McGovern took the lead. Born and raised in Worcester, McGovern was only twenty-three years old when he became a driving force behind Moakley's efforts to protect Central American refugees. One JPCOCA activist doubted that the congressman would have taken up the issue without his young legislative aide's encouragement. McGovern conducted original research about the challenges Salvadoran refugees faced in the United States, gathered signatures from other members of Congress, met with constituents, and made clear that nothing would happen without significant, sustained political pressure from below. JPCOCA members responded by contacting local and national media and reaching out to advocacy groups across the country, including Church World Services, the Committee in Solidarity with the People of El Salvador, the Washington Office on Latin America, Interreligious Task Force, the American Friends Service Committee, and the National Immigration, Refugee, and Citizenship Forum. Their collective efforts raised awareness about the issue among politicians and the public. When Moakley sent the letter to Schultz and Smith at the end of April 1983, a bipartisan group of eighty-eight members of Congress had signed on.[26]

The Reagan administration, committed to Cold War geopolitics, rebuffed Moakley's campaign. Schultz claimed that granting extended voluntary departure to Salvadorans would spur additional unauthorized migration. He also argued that people could seek refuge in the countries they passed through before arriving in the United States. Such reasoning didn't sit well with Moakley. "The vast majority of Salvadoran refugees are not economic aliens, but persons who have been displaced by violence. It is no easy journey to the United States, and there is no reason to believe that allowing Extended Voluntary Departure will make that journey easier, or encourage more people to take it," he and a colleague argued. Moreover, "to suggest that Salvadorans seek shelter in the already overcrowded refugee camps expanding throughout Central America is an abdication of our responsibility to those refugees presently in the United States."[27]

The executive branch's unwillingness to act led Moakley to seek a legislative solution. During four consecutive congressional sessions in the 1980s he and Senator Dennis DeConcini (D-AZ) introduced and advocated for bills to temporarily protect Salvadorans from deportation and, in turn, political violence and civil unrest in El Salvador.[28] Central American social-service and legal-aid organizations such as El Rescate and the Central American Refugee Center (CARECEN), formed in the early 1980s in response to the growing refugee crisis, kept pressure on the legislators. And national lobby groups such as the American Civil Liberties Union; Church World Service; National Immigration, Refugee, and Citizenship Forum; and the National Council on La Raza activated their networks and pushed Congress to pass the Moakley-DeConcini bills.[29]

Providing people with some form of safe haven became more urgent over time, since Salvadorans had little-to-no chance of winning asylum. Although authorities technically adjudicated asylum cases on an individual basis, US foreign relations influenced their decisions. People fleeing so-called enemy (which often meant Communist) governments received the highest approval rates, while those fleeing right-wing anti-Communist regimes had the lowest. From June 1983 to September 1989, US authorities approved just 2.5 percent of Salvadoran asylum cases—compared to 72.6 percent for the Soviet Union, 61.5 percent for Iran, and 41.8 percent from China.[30] By the middle of the decade, some immigration lawyers simply stopped encouraging Central Americans to apply.[31] Moakley joined refugees and their allies in denouncing the biased asylum adjudication system. He also pointed out that, since 1960, the United States had granted extended voluntary departure fifteen times to people from countries he believed were "comparable to El Salvador."[32]

The Reagan administration and Republicans in Congress remained unmoved, offering divergent, specious explanations for their repeated opposition to the Moakley-DeConcini bills. One argument centered on the misleading claim that the proposed legislation failed to protect Salvadoran nationals from war-related violence, since it only applied to people in the United States and "ignore[d] nationals of other violence affected countries." A second argument, reiterated by numerous officials, reasoned that under US law "generalized conditions of poverty and civil unrest do not entitle people who leave their homelands to settle here."

Adherents of this view, including Deputy Assistant Secretary of State for Human Rights and Humanitarian Affairs Laura J. Dietrich, warned that "if this were our test, half the 100 million people living between the Rio Grande and Panama would meet it, as would hundreds of millions more people in other parts of the world."[33] "Where and on what basis do you draw the line?" Senator Alan Simpson (R-WY) asked during a 1987 congressional hearing. "Should we then grant this extraordinary grace to Afghanistan, Sudan, Mozambique, Angola, Cambodia, Iran, Iraq, Lebanon?" Although Simpson claimed to understand the impulse to want to help people in need, he insisted that "the citizens of the United States would find it indigestible."[34] A third argument, which seemingly overlooked the frequent use of extended voluntary departure for other countries, claimed that the Massachusetts congressman's proposals undermined the nation's immigration laws. Alan Nelson, commissioner of the INS, went as far as to say that Moakley's bill would leave the Refugee Act of 1980 "emasculated."[35]

Even in the face of such staunch opposition, Moakley never stopped fighting. But by the late 1980s, his patience with the Reagan administration and his congressional colleagues was wearing thin. "I am tired of the double talk, I am tired of the politics and I am tired of the games," he wrote in a statement embodying former president Jimmy Carter's call to center people's human rights when crafting policy. "The bottom line on this issue is the protection of human life. And, quite frankly, it is unconscionable that this administration and this Congress have yet to offer protection to these refugees."[36] In 1987, the House passed Moakley's bill, which would have shielded Salvadorans and Nicaraguans from deportation, but the legislation died in the Senate. Moakley had failed for a third time.

Two crucial things happened in 1989 that presented Moakley with an opportunity to finally break the congressional impasse. In June, he became chairman of the House Rules Committee after the previous chair, eighty-eight-year-old Claude Pepper (D-FL), died. This influential position gave Moakley the power to determine which bills made it to the House floor for votes—a power he would soon leverage to great effect.[37] Then, on November 16, 1989, just weeks after Moakley introduced the latest version of his bill and only days after the FLMN launched its "final offensive," six Jesuit priests were brutally murdered at the Universidad Centroamericana in San Salvador, along with their housekeeper and her daughter. The killings sparked outrage and reignited debates about US support of the Salvadoran government and military. Moakley chaired a special congressional task force to investigate the murders and conducted extensive fact-finding missions. He also co-sponsored legislation to cut US military aid to El Salvador in half. "Enough is enough," he declared during the floor debate. "The time to act has come."[38]

Moakley's role on the task force and renewed attention to widespread human rights abuses and military impunity in El Salvador helped him make the case to protect people seeking refuge from state-sponsored violence. As Frank Sharry, president of the National Immigration, Refugee, and Citizenship Forum, told asylum advocates at the time, Moakley's "gloves are off." In October 1990, members of the two houses met in conference committee to hammer out a final version of an immigration bill that included temporary protected status for Salvadorans. Influential senators from both parties opposed the provision halting deportations, but Moakley put his foot down. His colleagues knew that, as chairman of the House Rules Committee, he had the power to kill the bill, though some questioned whether he actually would. The senators called a recess and conferred with President Bush. When they returned, they agreed to offer Salvadorans temporary protected status for eighteen months. The provision became law when President Bush signed the Immigration Act of 1990.[39]

Moakley had played hardball and won. He understood how legislative politics worked and used his position as chairman of a powerful committee to great effect. "The one difference [between TPS and other bills] is that someone able to carry out threats maintained an interest," said Michael Meyers, staff member of the Senate Subcommittee on Immigration and Refugee Affairs. Moakley "never gave up, though it took eight years. When everybody else was willing to give up, he did not."[40] TPS also never would have been created if not for the broad coalition of activists, advocates, and Central American solidarity groups that engaged in sustained organizing. "You needed a person on the inside to really do the work and have the commitment," JPCOCA activist Virginia Zanger later explained. "And you needed the pressure from the outside, to give him the excuse to move forward with it."[41] Her comment underscored how much TPS's passage depended not only on the movement's inside-outside strategy, but also on the mutual dependency of left activists and liberal policymakers to achieve change, particularly within the constrained political landscape of the post-1960s era.

The Challenges of Implementing TPS

The creation of temporary protected status represented a significant political victory for hundreds of thousands of Salvadorans and their allies. Rossana Pérez, a Salvadoran refugee who came to Los Angeles in 1983 after her husband was disappeared and she herself spent ten months in prison, later described TPS as a cornerstone for the community. "People were feeling safer, and the idea of going back to El Salvador was at kind of a distance."[42] Yet, implementing the program proved challenging, and over time, many came to question its long-term impact and legacy.

Even in the short term, not everyone greeted TPS with unbridled enthusiasm. Many Salvadorans worried about what would happen if the attorney general failed to extend TPS after eighteen months. The idea of voluntarily providing information about where they lived and worked, which the Immigration and Naturalization Service (INS) could later use to apprehend them, concerned potential beneficiaries.[43] One woman told sociologist Cecilia Menjívar, who interviewed Salvadorans living in the United States in the early 1990s, that "once the INS obtained your name and address, you were practically signing your own deportation orders."[44] People had good reason to distrust US authorities, given the Reagan and Bush administrations' ongoing support of the right-wing Salvadoran government and the years of INS harassment they had experienced since arriving in the United States. Although the possibility of gaining a liminal legal status offered a glimmer of hope to some Salvadorans, Central American service organizations urged people to "proceed with caution and consider well the benefits and risks."[45] Few people registered for TPS at first. "What stuck in people's mind[s]," according to then-CARECEN executive director Madeline Janis, "was deportation, deportation, deportation."[46]

Moakley and his Democratic colleagues in Congress may have won the battle to create TPS, but the Republican-controlled executive branch decided how to implement it. As a result, prohibitively high registration fees discouraged people from applying. During the eighteen-month grant period, the INS required Salvadorans to reregister every six months, each time filling out several forms and paying fees for TPS and work authorization. The total cost for an individual came to $405 ($940 today), which meant that a family of four would need to come up with as much as $1,620 (more than $3,750 today). Outraged advocates claimed that excessive government fees threatened to undermine the entire program. Joe Moakley and Dennis DeConcini, the congressional sponsors of TPS, began lobbying the INS before the law went into effect in hopes of keeping fees down. "Registration for TPS was intended to be a simple, efficient, one-step process in which the registrants receive work authorization at the time of registration," DeConcini wrote to INS Commissioner Gene McNary. "In addition, the cost of registration and obtaining work permission was intended to be reasonable." INS officials blamed the high fees on Congress, since the legislation specified that the beneficiaries, rather than taxpayers, would cover the costs of the program. However, the substantial fees stood out even more—and pointed to the executive branch's politicized singling out of Salvadorans—when considered alongside the fact that officials only charged $50 to Kuwaitis, Libyans, Somalis, and people from other countries who registered for TPS under the general provision. For Guillermo Rodezno, the executive director of El Rescate, the INS's requirements for Salvadorans undermined the "good intentions" of the legislation.[47]

All the while, and despite these considerable challenges, a broad coalition of refugees and their allies fought to protect Central Americans. They won a significant victory in the courts just weeks after TPS started. At the end of January 1991, the US District Court for the Northern District of California approved a settlement in *American Baptist Churches v. Thornburgh (ABC)*, a class-action lawsuit originally filed in 1985 by more than eighty religious, refugee, and legal-aid organizations that challenged the US government's systemic discrimination against Salvadorans and Guatemalan asylum seekers. The landmark settlement provided new asylum hearings to hundreds of thousands of people and offered work authorization and protection from deportation to individuals with pending cases. It also specified that any Salvadoran who registered for TPS would qualify for a new asylum hearing under *ABC*. This stipulation, in turn, led activists to re-evaluate their tepid stance on TPS. "We think now that [TPS] is a good opportunity," Rodezno told a reporter. "One, two or three more years of protection could make a big difference to someone."[48]

Although the *ABC* settlement may have alleviated some people's fears of being deported after TPS ended, most Salvadorans remained hesitant or unable to take advantage of these new legal protections. Only thirty-three thousand of the three hundred to five hundred thousand eligible beneficiaries had applied by early April, halfway through the six-month registration period. And just eighty-five thousand people had registered by late June, despite dozens of local and national groups redoubling their outreach efforts and a lawsuit pushing the INS to lower the TPS registration fee to $255 per person ($587 today). At the same time, advocates had been working with Moakley on a bill to extend the registration deadline to midnight on October 31, 1991. They succeeded. During the next four months, El Rescate, CARECEN, and other Central American social-service and legal-aid organizations worked tirelessly to help more than a hundred thousand additional people apply. One of them was Gloria Argueta, a seventeen-year-old high school student who had lived in Los Angeles with her family for three years and registered two days before the cutoff. "I waited until now because I didn't have the money to apply," she said. "I'm a little afraid. This could have been a trick to deport us all, but I think it's a good deal."[49]

Living in Limbo

What would happen to the nearly two hundred thousand Salvadorans with TPS when the program expired on June 30, 1992? Ongoing uncertainty fed people's fears, especially since most beneficiaries had lived in the United States for years by that point and had no plans of leaving. The January 1992 Salvadoran peace agreement marked an end to the twelve-year civil war, but it also raised questions about whether and for how long US authorities would allow TPS beneficiaries to remain in the country. Around the same time, Salvadorans who renewed their six-month work permits received notices from the INS about their impending deportation. As people frantically sought out information about the fate of TPS, the executive branch's decision to postpone any announcement about the program's future until late spring only heightened anxiety levels.[50]

Refugee advocates and politicians in El Salvador and the United States urged the administration of George H. W. Bush to act, for both humanitarian and geopolitical reasons. Mass deportations, they warned, would have a devastating impact on individuals and families, in addition to threatening El Salvador's political and economic stability just as the nation began to rebuild. "Sending back so many people is like sending a bomb," said Jorge Ruiz, El Rescate's TPS coordinator. "If the President of the United States wishes to ensure peace in El Salvador, the best way to demonstrate his dedication is to extend TPS." Salvadoran president Alfredo Cristiani wrote a personal plea to his US counterpart, and Moakley wrote to Attorney General William P. Barr and Secretary of State James A. Baker, asking the administration to renew TPS for another eighteen months. Doing so would "reassure the Government of El Salvador" and "calm the fears of refugees in the United States."[51]

For four months, Bush failed to respond to activists' calls, further amplifying TPS beneficiaries' feelings of uncertainty. The administration's plans only became clear in mid-May, when President Cristiani revealed them, unexpectedly, during a press conference in San Salvador. The United States would extend work authorization and protections from deportation for Salvadorans for another year, until June 30, 1993—but not under TPS. Instead, the Bush administration created a new program: Deferred Enforced Departure (DED). Although the rhetorical shift from an initiative focused on protecting people to one ensuring that they leave seemed ominous, DED resembled TPS in substance. It also served to extend people's asylum benefits under *ABC*. To apply for DED, Salvadorans who qualified had to fill out additional paperwork and pay $60 (more than $133 today). Salvadoran TPS holders and their advocates had succeeded in winning another twelve months of legal protections.[52]

Any relief people felt did not last long. With the new expiration date fast approaching, anxieties returned as Salvadorans, with support from the service and advocacy groups that had become essential to their cause, organized yet again to extend DED. This pattern became a familiar one, and Salvadorans found themselves living in a precarious, prolonged state of limbo. They had to fight ad infinitum to maintain the tenuous legal status that allowed them to remain in the country but did not provide a pathway to citizenship. They had to consistently navigate complex government bureaucracies, grasp technical and often confusing policies, keep track of ever-changing application deadlines and expiration dates, and come up with the money to pay significant fees—all while being keenly aware that their presence in the country depended on the whims of whomever occupied the White House.

In May 1993, Bill Clinton extended DED for eighteen months. Amid rising anti-immigrant sentiment, he refused to do so a second time. "They can't deport all of us who are here, can they?" asked a twenty-five-year-old woman who worked in a warehouse in Orange County, California. After DED expired, on December 31, 1994, most Salvadorans' only option to maintain some kind of legal status was to apply for asylum under *ABC*. But by the time the INS started hearing people's cases, in April 1997, the landscape of immigration politics had shifted. The previous year, Clinton had signed the Illegal Immigration Reform and Immigrant Responsibility Act of 1996, a draconian law drafted by Republicans and supported by law-and-order Democrats that drastically restricted relief from deportation. This act, along with the militarization of the border, expansion of immigration detention, and crackdown on asylum seekers, marked a punitive turn in US immigration policy ushered in—and furthered in the years ahead—by both Democrats and Republicans. Activists, meanwhile, continued to organize and won an important victory in November 1997, when the Nicaraguan Adjustment and Central American Relief Act restored the rights of some Salvadorans (and Guatemalans) to apply for suspension of removal. Many people did not qualify, though, and remained in a liminal status. Their liminality reflects the limits of liberal policymaking to ensure the well-being of all people. Indeed, the Clinton administration's technocratic and pragmatic mode of governing harmed rather than helped many of the most

TABLE 12.1. Tracing Temporary Protected Status for Salvadorans

#	Date	Event
1.	11/29/1990	President George H. W. Bush signs the Immigration Act of 1990, creating TPS
2.	1/1/1991	TPS goes into effect (18 months)
3.	1/31/1991	*ABC* settlement; Salvadorans in US as of 9/19/1990 can apply for asylum; people with TPS can apply after status expires
4.	6/30/1992	DED replaces TPS for Salvadorans (12 months)
5.	6/8/1993	DED extension (18 months)
6.	12/31/1994	DED terminated; work authorization extended until 9/30/1995; Salvadorans must apply for asylum under *ABC*
7.	1/31/1996	Extended deadline to apply for asylum under *ABC* for those with DED/work permits. Extended early August 1995, instead of ending 9/30/1995. In late August, INS also announced an automatic extension of work permits until 1/31/1996, avoiding a four-month gap between asylum deadline and work authorization
8.	4/30/1996	Late December 1995, INS announces three-month extension of work permits while people seek asylum. But the deadline for filing for asylum is still 1/31/1996, creating confusion
9.	9/10/1996	TPS for Salvadorans removed from 1990 Act (Sec. 303)
10.	9/30/1996	President Bill Clinton signs the Illegal Immigration Reform and Immigrant Responsibility Act, repealing suspension of deportation as means of relief from removal, in addition to dramatically expanding the number and types of deportable offenses
11.	11/19/1997	President Bill Clinton signs the Nicaraguan Adjustment and Central American Relief Act (NACARA), offering amnesty to some Nicaraguans and reinstating suspension of deportation for certain Salvadorans and Guatemalans
12.	3/9/2001	George W. Bush announces new TPS designation for Salvadorans after two massive earthquakes and a powerful aftershock in January and February (18 months)
13.	7/11/2002	TPS extension (12 months)
14.	7/16/2003	TPS extension (18 months)
15.	1/7/2005	TPS extension (18 months)
16.	6/15/2006	TPS extension (12 months)
17.	8/21/2007	TPS extension (18 months)
18.	10/1/2008	TPS extension (18 months)
19.	7/9/2010	TPS extension (18 months)
20.	1/11/2012	TPS extension (18 months)
21.	5/30/2013	TPS extension (18 months)
22.	1/7/2015	TPS extension (18 months)
23.	7/8/2016	TPS extension (18 months)
24.	1/18/2018	President Donald J. Trump announces the termination of TPS for El Salvador, Haiti, Nicaragua, and Sudan, effective 9/9/2018

25.	10/3/2018	A judge in the Northern District of California issues an injunction in *Ramos v. Nielsen*, blocking Trump's attempt to end TPS
26.	10/31/2018	Continuation of TPS in compliance with *Ramos v. Nielsen* injunction (6 months, through 4/2/2019)
27.	3/1/2019	Continuation of TPS in compliance with *Ramos v. Nielsen* injunction (9 months, through 1/2/2020)
28.	11/4/2019	Continuation of TPS in compliance with *Ramos v. Nielsen* injunction (12 months, through 1/4/2021)
29.	12/9/2020	Continuation of TPS in compliance with *Ramos v. Nielsen* injunction (9 months, through 10/4/2021)
30.	9/10/2021	Continuation of TPS in compliance with *Ramos v. Nielsen* injunction (15 months, through 12/31/2022)
31.	11/10/2022	Continuation of TPS in compliance with *Ramos v. Nielsen* injunction (18 months, through 6/30/2024)
32.	6/21/2023	President Joe Biden's DHS rescinds President Trump's termination of TPS for Salvadorans and issues an extension (18 months, through 3/9/2025)

Source: *Federal Register* 1990–2023; compiled by author

vulnerable. It was not until March 2001, after Clinton left office, that the United States redesignated El Salvador for TPS—only because two powerful earthquakes struck the nation and displaced more than one million people. Since then, Democratic and Republican presidents have extended TPS for Salvadorans nearly twenty times.[53]

However, TPS has become a highly polarized political issue in recent years, particularly after President Donald J. Trump attempted to end it in 2018. Had he succeeded, more than 402,000 people, including around two hundred thousand Salvadorans, many of them long-term residents, would have faced removal. Democrats, by contrast, defended TPS and denounced Trump's cruelty. In June 2023, President Joe Biden rescinded his predecessor's termination order and extended protections for Salvadorans through March 9, 2025. But Democrats have not spoken out about the costs of living in liminality. The material and psychological toll TPS has exacted over time amounts to what sociologists Cecilia Menjívar and Leisy Abrego have described as a form of legal violence. Neither liberal nor conservative politicians have addressed this violence, let alone pushed for a permanent solution to the seemingly endless limbo in which some Salvadorans have been trapped for more than three decades.[54]

The long-term negative effects of TPS are undeniable. So is the fact that TPS's creation in 1990 was a major victory for Salvadorans in the

United States and all who fought to protect them from the uncertain fates awaiting them back in El Salvador if deported. TPS would not exist if not for the persistent pressure from below that refugees and solidarity activists applied throughout the 1980s. Nor would it exist without Joe Moakley, a receptive and dogged ally in Congress. TPS's early advocates could not foresee the various factors that would shape the provision's history in the decades ahead. Yet the benefit of hindsight and careful historical analysis illuminate these contingencies and underscore the often-fraught compromises inherent to liberal policymaking, especially since the 1960s.

CHAPTER 13

The Austerity Imperative

Democratic Deficit Hawks and the Crisis of Keynesianism

DAVID STEIN

In late April 2022, as President Joe Biden's legislative agenda stagnated in the face of congressional gridlock, White House chief of staff Ron Klain sought to focus attention on what he considered a great victory of the administration: deficit reduction. "Just a quick fact," he wrote on Twitter. "After the deficit went UP each year that Trump was President, it is going DOWN each year that @JoeBiden is @POTUS . . . with the country on track to see the largest one-year decline in the deficit in US history in 2022."[1] Klain was pilloried. As one Twitter user wrote sarcastically, "oh thank god. Housing is unaffordable and the climate crisis is accelerating, but at least this abstract economic indicator has shifted slightly."[2] The replies illuminated the limits of the deficit as a metric for economic or social well-being, as well as its fraught role in partisan politics.

Even as Congress passed the Inflation Reduction Act, which included urgent environmental priorities, Democrats' framing remained preoccupied with the deficit. "This bill tackles inflation by lowering the deficit," Biden touted in his signing statement.[3] Here Democrats were especially influenced by the need for centrist senator Joe Manchin's vote. But by linking inflation and the deficit together, Biden risked undermining the case for ambitious public investment regardless of its impacts on the deficit.[4] Nevertheless, more than one year after the legislation, the law has facilitated even more ambitious spending than some initial hopes.[5] Beneath his rhetoric, Biden's policies suggested the weakening power of deficit hawk politics.

The relative wane of Democratic deficit hawk power also prompts the question of how it arose in the first place. How did the party most associated with the New Deal, Keynesianism, and countercyclical, fiscal-directed economic management become the party that sought to adhere to balanced-budget fiscal orthodoxy? By 2003, former treasury secretary and Wall Street executive Robert Rubin—one of the key architects of this conversion in party priorities—marveled at the transformation he had helped establish. "One of the ironies of this period is that today those policies [of fiscal discipline] are opposed by many leading conservatives and supported by many Democrats," he noted in his memoir.[6]

This chapter details how Rubin and a broader constellation of deficit hawk economists and policymakers shaped this conversion within the Democratic Party and liberal economic governance since the 1970s. Rubin played a pivotal role in Democratic policy circles, first as a key fundraiser for candidates from his leadership position at Goldman Sachs, and later as head of President Clinton's National Economic Council and then treasury secretary. Throughout, Rubin championed a framework that demonized deficits, and he sought their reduction as a means to lower interest rates and facilitate private-sector investment.[7] But by prioritizing private-sector investment, liberal fiscal policy tolerated the organized abandonment of the population to the market.[8]

Rubin and his allies—including the economist Larry Summers—cultivated the growing orthodoxy within the Democratic Party that balanced budgets were the necessary, market-friendly salve to inflation problems, and were also politically necessary to what they considered sound fiscal stewardship. In their ideal conception, shrinking the deficit would encourage the Federal Reserve to lower interest rates, which would catalyze private investment and ultimately create new jobs.[9] Under this perspective, good economic policymaking was no longer about what the policy did for constituencies directly to produce a public good or service. Instead, its cost-effectiveness or impact on the deficit took precedence. The government's role was thus mainly to create a climate that pleased private businesses and investors, upon whom, they believed, the social and economic vitality of society overall now rested.

As this form of politics became entrenched within the Democratic Party, the deficit hawks constrained social-spending proposals at all times, even in recessions. In the 1940s, liberals debated various means of direct and indirect government investment, but they took as a given that the private sector was ill-equipped for the task of stabilizing investment across business cycles (and thus stabilizing the production of needed goods and services).[10] The ascent of Democratic deficit hawks ratcheted down the expectations of governments, suggesting that the most important thing policymakers could do was to satisfy private investors.

The deficit is important to economic policy, though not in the way that deficit hawk rhetoric represented it. According to sectoral-balance analysis developed by British post-Keynesian economist Wynne Godley, a federal government deficit will be offset with a surplus in the nongovernmental sector and vice versa; and a government surplus will be counterbalanced with a nongovernmental or private deficit.[11] Sectoral-balance analysis emphasizes governmental and nongovernmental sectors as different accounting identities. As former chief economist to the Senate Budget Committee and leading Modern Monetary Theory economist Stephanie Kelton has explained, "for every deficit that exists in one part of the economy, there is an equal and opposite surplus in some other part."[12]

Versions of this viewpoint were influential in New Deal–era economic debates. When he was at the Treasury Department in 1934, economist Lauchlin Currie developed a series called the "Net Contribution of the Federal Government to National Buying Power." Economist Alan Sweezy, Currie's Keynesian compatriot, emphasized the importance of Currie's innovation. "This was both a technical improvement on the official deficit as a measure of the impact of the government's fiscal operations on the economy, and even more important a semantic triumph of the first magnitude," he stressed.[13] Yet, this perspective was never able to become hegemonic in the administration or beyond, as treasury secretary Henry Morgenthau adhered to more traditional fiscal conservatism.[14]

Instead, relative intellectual incoherence would become a hallmark of post–New Deal economic policy, with the disjointedness on the issue of public debt a particularly salient feature of this general dynamic.[15] Considered from the perspective of sectoral-balance analysis, or that of the "net federal contribution to buying power" framework, the famed fiscal surpluses that President Bill Clinton attained were not the achievement that many touted them to be.[16] Rather, they created household budget deficits in the place of government ones. During the Clinton era, household debt increased, alongside a decline in the personal savings rate (see figure 13.1).[17] But the sectoral-balance or "net contribution" perspective would differ. As Kelton has emphasized, "[governmental] fiscal surpluses rip financial wealth away from the rest of us, leaving us with less purchasing power to support the spending that keeps the economy going."[18] By curtailing government support for family purchasing power, deficit reduction compelled working people to make ends meet by borrowing from an increasingly powerful finance sector. Whatever the short-term political advantages Clinton's deficit reduction

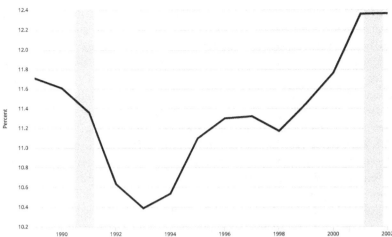

13.1. As the federal government balanced its budget during the Clinton administration, household indebtedness increased. Board of Governors of the Federal Reserve System (US), "Financial Soundness Indicator, Households; Debt Service and Principal Payments as a Percent of Income, Level [BOGZ1FL010000346A]," FRED, Federal Reserve Bank of St. Louis, accessed February 23, 2024, https://fred.stlouisfed.org/series/BOGZ1FL010000346A.

offered—and those are debatable—they structured a personal-debt crisis across society.

Deficit hawk politics reflected a broader transformation in the Democratic Party's political priorities as well. This policy pivot was about catering to "Reagan Democrats" and suburban white voters at the expense of the labor and civil rights movements. It was about reordering public policy to prize private-sector jobs. And it placed wealthy investors, venture capital funds, and banks fully in the driver's seat of what goods and services were created—a retreat from the more ambitious aspirations of New Deal liberalism.[19] From the deficit hawk view, the public sector existed to do things like assist capital formation via tax incentives and accelerated depreciation schedules, and to train workers for whatever the private market foresaw as profitable. But the public sector's role in creating economic stability for households would be shrunk.

While the political language of sound finance and deficit reduction was often shrouded in circumlocutions, it also had profound implications for the social, economic, and employment security of historically marginalized groups.[20] In this sense, it was closely connected to the racialized anti-statism and producerist politics that disparaged public-sector workers, and the public goods their labor helped produce.[21]

Whether deficit hawks recognized it or not, debates over the role of deficits were fundamentally about whose life chances were worthy of governmental support. Al From, the foundational figure behind the Democratic Leadership Council (DLC), stressed that deficit reduction was the essential opening move in the broader transformation of the Democratic Party's agenda away from what they considered "special interests"—the base of organized labor, African American, feminist, and environmental organizations. "The key thing for us [in the DLC], I believe, was the shift of the thrust of Democratic economic policy from redistribution to growth. We believed that fiscal discipline and having a sound fiscal policy, tax policy, was critical. It was the critical first step for that," he reflected in 2006.[22] The DLC merged deficit hawk politics with culture war politics.[23] Such a stance tilted the party's policy agenda away from debtors and the social-welfare state and toward creditors.[24] If the choice was between public-sector programs to support marginalized and disempowered people, or creating efficient, frugal, and deficit neutral policies, the DLC and the deficit hawks pursued that latter. It is easy to lose sight amidst these seemingly dry debates over the budget of the real harm these policy choices wrought on the nation's most vulnerable groups, as well as on millions of debt-saddled and downwardly mobile Americans. But these debates about the deficit were fundamentally debates over state design, state capacity, and democratic governance.[25]

While the New Deal's social compact had imagined—if never fully realized—employing deficit spending to ensure economic stability, the commitment to balanced-budget orthodoxy heralded a retreat from these aspirations and techniques. The Democrats' official platforms track this transformation in the party's policy priorities, from full employment's rise in the 1940s to the dominance of balanced budgets after the 1980s. Reflecting the power of the full-employment agenda, the 1972 Democratic Party platform emphasized that "full employment—a guaranteed job for all—is the primary economic objective of the Democratic Party."[26] Such a view was echoed again in 1976 and 1980, as it had been in prior decades. But by 1984, full employment barely warranted a mention in the platform, while the federal budget deficit drew thirty-seven references (see figure 13.2).[27] That shift in focus would persist during the Clinton years and beyond. This stance was not just an effort to score political points in election years. At a core level, deficit hawk politics were about reordering governmental priorities, constraining the ambitions and achievements of the public sector. These policies would eventually undermine efforts to ameliorate the harms of the 2008 recession, and they continue to curtail the prospect for adequately addressing climate change.

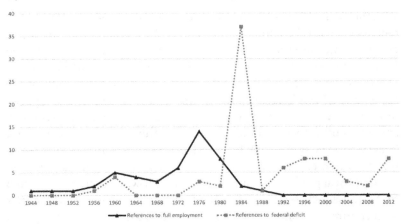

13.2. Author's calculations from Democratic Party platforms.

Rethinking Keynesianism and Political Struggle

The global economic turmoil of the 1970s shook every facet of social life—from daily diets to wait times for gasoline—and would reshape economic ideas. In the first half of the decade, two significant supply shocks pushed up the rate of inflation. The first shock came to food systems in 1973–1974 due to bad harvests and crop failures, among other factors. The second and more famous shock to energy markets was directly political in nature—in response to the US support for Israel in the 1973 October War, Arab oil producers in the Organization of Petroleum Exporting Countries (OPEC) declared an embargo of the US. Producer states in OPEC then used their market power to raise its price, which soon quadrupled. In the later part of the decade, another supply shock drove up food prices thanks to the idiosyncrasies of weather and agriculture. Each year between 1978 and 1980 saw food's share of the Consumer Price Index (CPI) grow by over 10.3 percent.[28] These shocks to supply produced a difficult mix of economic impacts—recession combined with inflation.

These economic challenges brought a new word into the public lexicon: *stagflation* (stagnation plus inflation). Conservative policymakers in the Nixon and Ford administration used a variety of techniques—including relatively successful wage and price controls—to try to balance the economic turmoil with Nixon's 1972 reelection ambitions.[29] But after his 1972 election victory, Nixon's administration turned toward what they called the "old-time religion" of fiscal and monetary austerity—a far cry from Keynesian policies.[30] During this moment—when loosely

Keynesian economics dominated intellectually—policymakers groped for answers that could accord with their broader ideological principles, were politically actionable and popular, and could be economically successful. They did not find much durable success.

The lack of policy success to manage stagflation led many to claim that Keynesianism could not answer the problems of the 1970s, a point commonly echoed by many historians.[31] Yet it was not that Keynesianism was unable to understand or address the economic turbulence of the 1970s.[32] Rather, neo-Keynesianism, the dominant form of Keynesianism at the time—which grafted a limited version of Keynesian macroeconomics onto neoclassical microeconomic foundations to forge the famed "neoclassical synthesis"—had difficulty creating remedies that policymakers found politically efficacious.

Indeed, a group of post-Keynesianism economists such as Joan Robinson and Alfred Eichner *did* have sound and even cutting-edge analyses and ideas of creating stability, but the core challenges they faced were political, not intellectual.[33] In contrast to the neo-Keynesian school, Robinson famously dubbed the neoclassical synthesis as "bastard Keynesianism . . . [that] never even pretended to discuss the use of resources." In general, it was not that either neo-Keynesian or post-Keynesian analysts lacked an intellectual understanding of simultaneous inflation and unemployment. What they lacked in the 1970s was the political power to actualize their solutions. Robinson further stressed this point regarding the inflation of the early 1970s. "So-called Keynesian policy was not really applied in such a way as to maintain stability," she emphasized.[34] Robinson's former student, economist Gar Alperovitz, was a leader of an organization, Consumers Opposed to Inflation in the Necessities (COIN), which put forward innovative strategies for managing inflation. These strategies included incomes policies like wage and price controls, credit controls, and economic planning.[35] Some of COIN's proposals even received support from the AFL-CIO leader George Meany and the labor movement. But COIN's post-Keynesian solutions were not tried in any serious way. As Alperovitz later reflected, "we got meetings with the president . . . that was a symbolic achievement . . . but there was no successful legislative achievement at all."[36] The fact that policymaking is rarely steered by optimal solutions should not be taken by analysts as the failure of Keynesianism. Accepting such assessments risks perpetuating the idea that there was no alternative to neoliberalism.

One outcome of the melee over economic policy in the 1970s was a growing rejection of deficits by policymakers who blamed deficits for the decade's inflation. Faulting deficits in this way signaled a shift underway since the early 1960s. In 1962, President Kennedy devoted a portion of his Yale commencement address to the Keynesian economics of deficits—representing a high point for presidential leadership on the issue of public spending. "The myth persists that Federal deficits create inflation and budget surpluses prevent it," he said. "But honest assessment plainly requires a more sophisticated view than the old and automatic cliché that deficits automatically bring inflation." At least on that day, Kennedy wanted to focus on different questions—those concerned with full implementation of resources. "How can we generate the buying power which can consume what we produce on our farms and in our factories?" he asked.[37] But these sorts of questions receded in the following decades as "old and automatic cliches" reemerged.

Kennedy's questions were actually at the heart of the post-Keynesian analytic Robinson and Eichner had outlined. While many at the time—and still today—view inflation as resulting from an overheated economy, Eichner and the post-Keynesian milieu differed. Inflation was not due simply to excess demand. It was not, as the famed cliché usually says, "too much money chasing too few goods." For Eichner, inflation was about resources and their distribution in relation to consumer demand for them. Accordingly, slowing the economy and inhibiting production via high interest rates was counterproductive, since it inhibited output. Nor was reducing aggregate demand a socially just option, since doing so would likely add increased unemployment atop rising prices.[38] "The conventional policy instruments, by curtailing the level of economic activity, simply reduce the amount of income and output available for distribution, thereby heightening the social conflict underlying the inflationary process," Eichner noted in 1979.[39] In the years that followed, however, overemphasis on the deficit occluded more fundamental questions about resources—what they are, how they are made, and how the government could direct their creation and distribution.[40] Such nuanced viewpoints regarding deficits, inflation, and resource distribution would become relatively obsolete within the Democratic policy establishment, in favor of deficit hawk politics.

Abandoning Deficits in the 1970s

Although deficit hawk politics did not begin in the 1970s, they took on rising salience because of the stagflation crisis and Jimmy Carter's political ascent. In the late 1950s, even a historically hostile organization like the Chamber of Commerce had softened its stance toward deficit spending, explicitly opposing any effort to mandate a balanced budget.[41] But during Carter's presidency—and alongside a shift in economic thinking that sought to use the state to protect the market—the Democrats' relative embrace of deficit spending began to be undone.[42]

Despite President Ford having governed via austerity, Carter homed in on the deficit to one-up his opponent. Carter's disdain for deficit spending put him out of step with his Democratic colleagues like House Majority Leader Tip O'Neill and provoked conflict within the Democratic caucus. But he drew on an alternative historical lineage than those who admired the party of President Roosevelt or the economic theories of Keynes. "I had pledged during my campaign to emphasize fiscal responsibility and strive for a balanced budget," he later wrote. "This had not been a popular stand with some members of my party, but it was compatible with the beliefs of Southern Democrats and of Democratic Presidents I admired, like Jefferson, Madison, Jackson, and Wilson."[43] Appealing to middle-class and suburban constituencies without union contracts and cost-of-living-adjustments, Carter linked budget deficits and inflation and framed reducing inflation as more important than reducing unemployment.[44]

President Carter's scorn for deficits prompted repeated clashes with members of his party, many of whom still held New Deal-style aspirations. In the spring of 1977, soon after being elected, Carter met with Ford, and they bonded over their shared concern for what Carter described in his diary as "spending getting out hand." By contrast, a few weeks later, Carter had a rough and memorable meeting with the Democratic leaders. "The congressional leadership breakfast was devoted almost entirely to expressions on the part of the liberal members (Tip O'Neill, Shirley Chisholm, and John Brademas) that we were neglecting social programs in order to try to balance the budget in four years," he commented in his diary. For Carter, the meeting demonstrated a fundamental divergence with his party. He would later criticize O'Neill in his diary, writing that "his measure of success is passage of new or expanded social programs."[45] Carter noted that O'Neill "flinched visibly whenever we talked about balancing the federal budget or constraining the any of the Great Society programs"—perhaps anticipating the hardships that would result if such policies were enacted.[46]

While Carter's background was in state and local politics, where balanced budgets were far more necessary, he expressed a seemingly overarching moral philosophy that federal deficit spending was sinful. Carter's assessments put him closer in alignment with that of Gerald Ford's former treasury secretary William Simon, who in 1978 and 1980 published widely read books attacking social spending and deficits as sources of inflation. While not speaking in Simon's culture war frames,

Carter essentially accepted the terms of debate presented by Simon and Republicans. Accordingly, Carter criticized fellow Democrats like O'Neill and Chisholm, "to whom the phrase 'balanced budget' coming from a Democratic President was almost blasphemous."[47]

As Carter tried to develop a strategy to manage inflation, deficit reduction became even more critical. This strategy emerged partly due to the removal of other options to manage inflation, like utilizing forceful price controls—such as those applied during World War II under the Office of Price Administration, or Nixon's initial experiment with them. Organized business lobbies like the Business Roundtable had successfully forced these techniques off the political table.[48] Without adequate political tools at his disposal and an economically conservative inclination, Carter fumbled toward a strategy to manage inflation.[49] He thus appointed Federal Reserve chair Paul Volcker, who sought to deflate the economy by any means necessary: a harsh recession—the worst since the 1930s. At the same time, many economists and pundits blamed inflation on deficits and what they construed as disproportionate money in circulation, under the belief that inflation simply resulted from excess demand. Volcker too, like others at the Fed, promoted the theory that deficits accelerated inflation. As political scientist James Savage has emphasized, "the loss of legitimacy [for deficits] was largely caused by Democratic leaders who failed to defend the policy of deficit spending when it most needed defending, during the mid and late 1970s."[50] This trend would intensify in the 1980s under the leadership of an influential set of New Democrats and their advisors.

The Political Entry of Robert Rubin

Jimmy Carter's vice president, Walter Mondale, would further entrench Carter's deficit hawk stance during his 1984 run for the presidency. Despite jobs and unemployment being among the top concerns in the country after years of grinding recessions, Mondale eschewed running on a significant program to address unemployment. Instead, he focused on the deficit. Accepting the party nomination for president, Mondale told the American people that he would raise taxes. "By the end of my first term, I will reduce the Reagan budget deficit by two-thirds ... Mr. Reagan will raise taxes, and so will I. He won't tell you. I just did." At the time, almost nine million people were unemployed—they were still awaiting the economic recovery that had supposedly already begun. Yet, Mondale told his audience that there would be no significant public spending to counteract Reagan's domestic austerity or mollify their pain. Mondale warned Congress not to even try him. "We must cut spending and pay as we go. If you don't hold the line, I will. That is what the veto is for."[51]

Mondale's views on this subject were hardly a shared assumption among the Democratic Party or its milieu of economists. A few months earlier, at a hearing of the Joint Economic Committee, Democratic representative Augustus Hawkins had described this economic framework as a setup. "In placing deficits as the big issue that we go into this discussion revolving around, we get into the trap of using that as merely an excuse for cutting domestic spending," he said.[52] At the hearing, leading economist Robert Eisner underscored that federal deficits were stimulative. "The debt of the Government is an asset to private individuals," Eisner had written a few months earlier in the *New York Times*—a view he echoed in the Joint Economic Committee hearings.[53] Economist Leon Keyserling, a New Deal stalwart who had served as head of President Truman's Council of Economic Advisors, also stressed that private debt—not public debt—was the issue to be preoccupied by. "I do not see how anybody can deny that this kind of increase in the consumer debt burden is more serious and less manageable than the increase in the Federal deficit," he said.[54] After all, private individuals—unlike the federal government—do not control the currency; private individuals—unlike Congress—do not direct the Federal Reserve's policy mandates. Despite rhetorical appeals from politicians that the federal government needed to tighten its belt, the federal government was not a household.

But Mondale had been prodded along on his deficit phobia by his business council of some three hundred executives. Especially prominent was Goldman Sachs' Robert Rubin, who operated as Mondale's finance chairman in New York. Rubin was joined by other leading investment bankers in visiting Mondale's home the month of the convention to discuss his deficit-reduction plans, pushing him to balance the budget and increase taxes. As one explained, "It's very important to have senior officers of financial firms who are Democrats ... Democrats, as a matter of business policy, need to take a strong and aggressive position on curbing deficits."[55] Rubin shared this view. And his perspective on federal deficits, and influence on the Democratic Party, would only increase over the coming years. Soon, it earned its own moniker—Rubinomics.

At the core of Rubinomics was deficit reduction as a strategy to lower interest rates to stimulate private investment. For Rubin, high deficits ineluctably led to high interest rates, which curtailed borrowing, investment, and economic activity. As Rubin explained in his memoir, his disdain for Reagan's budget deficits propelled him into deeper involvement with the Democratic Party. While Rubin did not eschew deficits wholesale, especially not in a recession, he feared the long-term fiscal and economic situation for the US. When questioned on the shaky empirical veracity of the matter, however, Rubin would appeal to "the laws of economics" or "Introductory Economics," under the notion that—at some point or another—what he considered the precarious budgetary position of the federal government would provoke a crisis. "The first thing you learn in Introductory Economics," Rubin argued, "is that supply and demand determine price." Under this thinking, as long as US government debt was in ample supply, bond traders would demand a higher premium in order to buy it.[56] But, in the 1980s, the candidates who backed Rubinomics—including Mondale and in 1988 Michael Dukakis—lost their elections, partly due to their focus on the issue. Mondale later lamented to Rubin that he failed to make the perceived direness of the fiscal situation relevant to voters' lives.[57]

Nonetheless, there was a different audience in mind for deficit hawk politics. Geared as it was toward ephemeral ideas of business confidence, deficit hawk politics helped fuse Democrats to the finance sector and Wall Street.[58] By the 1990s, however, the deficit hawk framework would receive some degree of electoral validation during the Clinton administration.

The Triumph of Rubinomics

As Bill Clinton transitioned into the presidency, he was caught between two visions for economic policy. There was, on the one hand, an industrial policy and public-investment agenda championed by his future labor secretary, Robert Reich. On the other hand, Rubin embodied the faction most concerned with deficit reduction. Though deficit reduction was present as a campaign agenda item, it was not necessarily dominant. It was only during the post-election transition period that shrinking the deficit became the key economic-policy lodestar.

Clinton's deficit reduction agenda was also bolstered by the third-party candidacy of Ross Perot, who made it the heart of his campaign. As Bruce Reed, Clinton's deputy campaign manager, later reflected, "[Perot] was concerned about the deficit. He had tapped into Americans' concerns about how Washington was broken. Clinton's natural instincts were in that direction."[59] This view was echoed by Rubin and others in the campaign.[60] DLC leader Al From considered cutting the deficit and reducing public-sector jobs to be a crucial factor in demonstrating that Clinton had the "toughness to govern, the ability to stand up to interest groups."[61] For From and the DLC, the interest groups they wanted to defy were members of the Democrats' traditional coalition: civil rights organizations and labor unions.

For Rubin, this robust, multi-angled attack against the deficit was essential to shaping public attitudes. "You had relatively high unemployment and there was a broad feeling, among the American people, that this was associated in some way, in some causal way, with our fiscal deficits and that became a broadly held view," he said. If it took a popular front against fascism in the 1930s to construct an agenda hospitable to deficits, it took a kindred one to unmake it. "I do think that that [anti-deficit attitude] was a product of a lot of different voices," Rubin stressed, highlighting the role of Clinton's opponents, Perot and Democrat Paul Tsongas.[62] While overturning the Keynesian agenda had many components, the abandonment of deficits by Democrats was a critical one.

When constructing the team for the White House, Clinton continued that trajectory, surrounding himself with fiscal hawks who would ultimately undermine his public-investment agenda. As treasury secretary, Clinton appointed Lloyd Bentsen, a DLC member and former head of the Senate Finance Committee.[63] At the Office of Management and Budget, he placed another DLC member, former congressman and deficit hawk Leon Panetta. As Panetta's deputy director, Clinton appointed Alice Rivlin, an economist and arch-deficit hawk, who had been the first director of the Congressional Budget Office (CBO). Rivlin had established the CBO as a key institution of ostensibly nonpartisan, anti-deficit politics focused on cost-effectiveness.

Clinton placed Rubin in charge of the newly created National Economic Council, which was intended to elevate economics and its leitmotif of efficiency as an overarching style of reasoning in policymaking.[64] While the Council of Economic Advisors had existed since 1946, after its creation as part of a broader Keynesian agenda under the 1946 Employment Act, its role had grown to focus more on economic analysis than policy. In Rubin and Clinton's vision, the NEC would have a more robust role in policymaking. As Rubin recalled, Clinton wanted the NEC "to do for economic policy what the National Security Council did to coordinate foreign policy."[65] Clinton had pledged to reduce the White House staff by 25 percent and the federal government by at least a hundred thousand workers.[66] But Rubin sought to ensure he had a well-staffed army for the budget war to come. "I told [the incoming White House chief of staff] that the NEC wouldn't work without an adequate staff, which I judged to be at least twenty people."[67] Just as Rivlin had built the CBO into a well-staffed battalion of budget hawks, Rubin would do something similar at the NEC.

Powerful as Rubin was, the deficit hawk attitude went far beyond him. Chris Edley, a senior economic policy advisor on the transition team and associate director at OMB, stressed how deficit phobia was a relatively natural issue for Clinton. "I don't think it's fair to portray [Rubin] as some kind of a Svengali who captured Clinton's imagination," he said. "[Clinton] came to the Presidency as certainly a fiscal moderate, if not a fiscal conservative." Having worked on domestic policy in the Carter administration and for the Dukakis campaign, Edley thought this point was crucial in the wider shift in the party agenda that DLC members sought to catalyze. A critical element of this policy matrix, Edley believed, was the shifting rationales for the deficit hawkery. He understood Carter's anti-deficit attitude to be morally based. By contrast, the ascent of the NEC and the rising prestige of the economics profession framed the issue differently. "The creation of the National Economic Council by Clinton created a mechanism for both collecting and amplifying the perspectives of economists and economoids," Edley emphasized.[68] By handing such issues of public debt and its use over to economists, the Clinton administration silenced political debates about what the role of government should be.[69]

But despite all the performative sophistication of the economics profession and the NEC, there was not necessarily coherent science undergirding the assumptions about deficits that so governed their choices. Alice Rivlin was asked in an oral history, "As an economist, how do you determine, say, what is an acceptable and unacceptable level of debt and deficit would be. What is the science and mathematics that go into something like that?" She replied, "Oh, there isn't science and mathematics."[70] Rubin made a similar point. "I was concerned that creating credibility with financial markets might take longer than one would hope," he noted, regarding the lag time between deficit reduction action and its effective impact. This variable was a critical one in economic policymaking, since it could influence electoral outcomes. If—as intended— deficit reduction yielded lower interest rates but wasn't timed with an electoral cycle, it could make for bad politics. "I remember saying that there was nothing scientific about how much deficit reduction would have credibility and create a real economic impact," Rubin said.[71]

Nonetheless, these performances had an audience in mind, as Edley and Rubin stressed Wall Street's approval. They believed Wall Street demanded deficit reduction and that such reduction was necessary to enable lower interest rates and thus needed investment. Some have suggested that Federal Reserve chairman Alan Greenspan was the key figure pushing Clinton's deficit reduction. But others within the Clinton administration have questioned this notion. "Greenspan's role was very marginal," Rivlin recalled. "I'm sure he had a couple of conversations with Clinton, but at the time he wasn't a player."[72] More important was the widely shared understanding that both Greenspan's Fed and Wall Street would react favorably to deficit reduction. "For us to achieve those lower interest rates . . . financial markets would have to believe that the administration was serious about deficit reduction," Rubin said.[73] Edley similarly recalled, "[They believed] deficit reduction was intrinsically important for economic health. But probably even more important was the effect that a policy of deficit reduction had on Wall Street perceptions."[74] Rather than debating the future of public investment and rethinking economic governance after the Cold War, the Clinton administration's economic policy sought to please the Fed, create lower long-term interest rates, and facilitate private investment in the sectors that investors deemed most likely to be profitable.

Rubin further stressed the economic case for deficit reduction in a 2004 paper written with Peter Orszag, future head of President Obama's Office of Management and Budget. "If financial markets begin to doubt that commitment [to avoiding substantial inflation], investor confidence would be reduced and an additional premium would be added to the required return on federal government debt," they wrote.[75] While this assertion guided the Clinton administration, empirical verification for the belief has been mixed. As Orszag himself reported in another paper, "the effects of fiscal policy on interest rates have proved difficult to pin down statistically."[76] Nonetheless, because of this belief, Rubin insisted that Clinton focus on deficit reduction in order to ensure investor confidence.[77] These emphases helped harden the importance of deficit reduction to the first Clinton budget. Such a view—pushed by OMB and the NEC—meant that others in the administration struggled to win arguments that deficit reduction was less urgent and could be moderated.

Reflecting on the Clinton administration's deficit reduction, economist Joseph Stiglitz—a former chairman of Clinton's Council of Economic Advisors—provided something of a mea culpa on deficit reduction. He noted that the New Democrats went overboard on cutting the deficit, seeking to eradicate the idea of the "tax and spend" liberal. He also believed that many of his colleagues and others misattributed the reasons for the relative economic recovery in the Clinton years. "We cannot simply observe that the deficit was reduced and the economy recovered, and say that the deficit reduction *caused* the recovery . . . interest rates would have fallen anyway." As he explained, "the forces taming inflation—weaker unions, increased international competition, increasing productivity—were already at play, and it was the lower inflation as well as the deficit reduction that lowered long-term interest rates." Meanwhile, Stiglitz observed, the Clinton Treasury Department's preoccupation with deficit reduction prevented the administration from taking advantage of lower rates to steer public investment into areas of need. "When the Council of Economic Advisers proposed a modest program to improve the dilapidated conditions of some of our inner-city schools, Treasury, with its fixation on deficit reduction, spoke against the idea," he recalled. Such an example, again, reveals the racial, gendered, and class politics of deficit reduction.[78] Given the choice between deficit reduction or investments and governmental support for marginalized and oppressed people, the cost-benefit calculus of deficit hawk policymakers consistently tilted toward the former.

This retreat from deficit spending signaled an abandonment of the public sector and meant ceding investment decisions to private actors, with all their attendant discriminatory practices and choices. Completing a campaign promise that angered organized labor but was a core component of the deficit reduction agenda, Clinton sought to reduce the federal workforce by a hundred thousand people as part of a broader push to reinvent government. By the end of Clinton's presidency, with the federal workforce cut by 426,000 workers, Clinton's lieutenant in the operation, DLC stalwart Elaine Kamarck, boasted of producing "the smallest government since Dwight D. Eisenhower was president."[79] This boast highlighted the shift that Clinton's presidency had consolidated. Rather than seeking to advance the public sector and develop public goods, they prioritized private-sector jobs, irrespective of quality or industry.

A sectoral-balance perspective puts even harsher light on the Clinton surpluses that resulted from these choices. Under Clinton, the personal savings rate plummeted and household debt spiked—this outcome was the other side of policies of "Rubinomics" geared at federal deficit reduction. As economists Dimitri Papadimitriou and Randall Wray noted in 1998, "deficit reduction ... played a significant role in depressing aggregate demand, which was offset only by unsustainable private sector borrowing."[80] As the Clinton surpluses dragged down the buying power of consumers, families increasingly turned to credit to make ends meet. When Clinton took office in January 1993, the personal savings rate was 8.6 percent. But the rate had fallen to 4.9 percent upon his exit in January 2001. Similarly, debt service payments as a percentage of disposable income also increased during this time, from 10.4 percent in the first quarter of 1993 to 12.1 percent in the first quarter of 2001.[81] Reviewing the 2000 Economic Report of the President, economist James Galbraith emphasized similar conclusions. "Thus we have the Keynesian devolution," he wrote. "Debts have gone private." Presciently, Galbraith warned that "these debts, at roughly four times that of the federal government, have the collective power to keep fiscal drag in check, at least for a time."[82] And it was those private debts, particularly in housing, that blew up the world economy in 2007–2008 and helped usher into office Barack Obama.

Barack Obama and the Hegemony of Rubinomics

As Obama entered office during a historic recession and housing crisis, he relied on many of Clinton's economists and staffers and on their policy playbook that overemphasized fiscal discipline. By doing so, his administration constricted their own ambitions about what kinds of economic-recovery policies should be even proposed. In the summer of 2008, after securing the Democratic Party nomination, Obama added Jason Furman as the key economist on his staff. Almost immediately, however, his selection raised red flags from organized labor and progressives. Furman arrived after directing Rubin's anti-deficit Hamilton Project at the Brookings Institution.[83] Over the ensuing weeks, Senator Obama began regular conference calls with Larry Summers (Rubin's successor as Clinton's treasury secretary), former Fed chair and sound-money enthusiast Paul Volcker, Warren Buffet, and others to evaluate the economic environment and consider policy responses.[84] As Reed Hundt, a colleague of Rubin and Summers in the Clinton administration and member of the Obama transition team described the thinking among this group: "The big risk was that excessive deficit spending might cause the private sector to demand higher interest rates out of fear of inflation."[85] Despite the economic crisis, the Rubinomics framework that dominated the Clinton administration was poised to do the same in the Obama presidency.

With unemployment at 6.8 percent in November 2008 and rapidly rising, President-Elect Obama began to formulate a plan for a stimulus.[86] Incoming head of his Council of Economic Advisors Christina Romer calculated that a $1.7–1.8 trillion fiscal package was needed. But Obama's team could not figure out what to put in such a legislative package without including tax cuts—a strategy they disliked since they were hoping to later balance the budget.[87] Infamously, Summers, who was incoming head of Obama's NEC, dismissed Romer's proposed figure as politically, though not economically, unattainable. He thus excluded it from the memo he sent Obama for the meeting.[88] Reflecting on this crucial choice, journalist Ryan Grim commented, "Summers was out of his lane, play-acting as a pundit, guessing what was politically feasible."[89] Summers recalled "I did tell Christy [Romer] that we don't know how to spend $1.7 trillion and it will just freak the room out, so it's better to leave this out." Summers's assessment was also constrained by which economists were in the room and their attitude toward deficits. Romer remembered the transition team eschewing her proposals for a stimulus of around $1.2 trillion—which she deemed necessary to achieve an unemployment rate below 7 percent. "Peter Orszag . . . didn't want to go that big [because the deficit would be so large]," she said.[90] By December, the unemployment rate had already risen half a percentage point to 7.3 percent. In the month after the election, another 750,000 people had lost their jobs.[91]

The questions Summers had raised about the ability to pass the type of economic plan that Romer deemed needed were real. But they were also circumscribed by strategic choices. Obama chose not to lobby Congress with the political and economic urgency that the moment demanded.[92] So, instead of focusing on what was needed, the Obama administration—hamstrung by a deficit hawk economic team—curtailed their request to a limited, $800 billion stimulus.

In February 2009, Obama opened his first message to Congress by acknowledging the pain of everyday people in the recession. "It's the worry you wake up with and the source of sleepless nights," he said. "It's the job you thought you'd retire from but now have lost." But then he reiterated the fear of large deficits and announced that a Rubinomics framework would follow the recently passed American Recovery and Reinvestment Act. "I asked this Congress to send me a recovery plan by President's Day that would put people back to work and put money in their pockets. Not because I believe in bigger government—I don't. Not because I'm not mindful of the massive debt we've inherited—I am. I called for action because the failure to do so would have cost more jobs and caused more hardships. In fact, a failure to act would have worsened our long-term deficit by assuring weak economic growth for years." The president promised that "over the next two years, this plan will save or create 3.5 million jobs."[93] But there were thirteen million people unemployed at the time.[94] By assuaging the fears of deficit hawks, endorsing Rubinomics orthodoxy, and failing to pursue the robust stimulus that Romer and others suggested was needed, Obama and his administration ensured that the impact of the recession would stretch on.

Unemployment kept rising for more than a year after the speech, peaking above fifteen million people and 10 percent of the labor force in October 2009. Unemployment remained above fourteen million people until January 2011. But during his January 2010 State of the Union address, Obama doubled down on deficit phobia. He affirmed the necessity of the stimulus from eleven months prior, but then pivoted. "Families across the country are tightening their belts and making tough decisions. The federal government should do the same," he said. "Starting in 2011, we are prepared to freeze government spending for three years ... Like any cash-strapped family, we will work within a budget to invest in what we need and sacrifice what we don't. And if I have to enforce this discipline by veto, I will."[95] Just as Mondale had issued Congress a veto threat with almost nine million people unemployed as he accepted the Democratic nomination, President Obama made a similar move. This time, however, it was to a Democratic Congress, ten months before a midterm election, with the unemployment rate at 10 percent—fifteen million people were actively searching for work. Who knows how many more had quit looking? Unemployment would not return to February 2009 levels for another three years.[96]

Partly because of inadequate federal support, state budgets were ravaged, as losses of income, sales, and property taxes all dropped. States have far less debt-bearing capacity than the federal government because they do not control the currency. Additionally, almost all states have balanced-budget laws and consequently cut their budgets as they managed the crisis. Although insufficient, the stimulus did help, just not enough. In the fourth quarter of 2009, with unemployment hovering around 10 percent and fifteen million people looking for work, combined local, state, and federal government spending declined. By 2012, forty-six states were cutting services and more than thirty states had raised taxes—a policy response that would deepen the economic slump.[97] This effect was predicted in the Summers memo on the stimulus. As he explained, "these [state-level] steps would not only be macroeconomically contractionary, but would also damage health and education systems." But, Summers warned, "state fiscal relief is likely to be unpopular with some, especially Republicans, who view it as letting states off the hook for their profligacy."[98] But state spending had not been extravagant. It had little to do with the 2008 recession and housing crisis. Nonetheless, as Romer recalled, "[Larry] thought of himself as a political person who could figure out the most Congress would go for. So he didn't start with what the numbers said about how big [the stimulus policy] should be. It was immediately tempered by what he thought we could possibly get through Congress."[99] While Summers may have been wrong about that assessment, he was right that the recession would devastate state budgets. The plodding recovery from the recession meant that states lost hundreds of billions in possible tax revenue, leading to the shrinking of the public sector.[100]

Constrained in their own policy ambitions by their deficit hawk principles, the social and economic effects of the 2008 recession stretched far into the 2010s, shaping what many have called a "lost decade." It took almost the entirety of Obama's presidency until unemployment got below 5 percent, first hitting that mark in January 2016. In contrast, the rapid economic recovery from the COVID-induced recession has provided support for the hypothesis that much more could have been done to help the economy after 2008, had policymakers overcome their fear of deficits. Further, the strong showing for Democrats in the 2022 midterm election has added weight to the theory that deficit hawk politics contributed to the rise of the Tea Party, the poor showing in the 2010 midterm election, and the ascent of Donald Trump.[101] Democratic policy choices hamstrung Democratic political fortunes—and did material harm to millions of Americans in the process.

Beyond the Deficit Hawk Paradigm

In one moment of clarity during the early days of his administration, President Clinton recognized the vexed position of being a Democratic deficit hawk. As his public investment program sputtered in the spring of 1993, he raged and wondered what had become of the Democratic Party. "Where are all the Democrats?" he asked sarcastically. "We're Eisenhower Republicans here, and we are fighting the Reagan Republicans. We stand for lower deficits and free trade and the bond market. Isn't that great?" Earlier in the day, when news of the failed plan for public investment hit Clinton, he was despondent. "We're losing our soul," he said.[102] Clinton, however, could have looked inward for answers. While he was not the inaugural Democratic deficit hawk, in many ways he was confronting the success of the vision of governance that he had empowered.[103] After all, he had selected deficit hawks like Rubin, Bentsen, Panetta, Rivlin, and Summers for his administration. In that brief moment, however, Clinton worried whether deficit reduction was a winning political strategy.

While Clinton was wondering about such priorities, activists in Los Angeles were trying to steer an alternative path beyond deficit hawk politics. In the aftermath of the 1992 uprising, a coalition led by the Labor/Community Strategy Center (LCSC) and featuring scholars like Mike Davis and Laura Pulido looked out on the city's smoldering ashes. Assessing the past few decades of public policies, they saw the active construction of dry kindling awaiting its spark. "During [the 1970s], the backlash against social programs for people of color led to the end of the government's explicit commitment to fight, let alone end, unemployment and poverty," the group wrote. It noted that Carter's retreat from public-sector employment in the name of inflation presaged more cuts under Reagan and Bush. Extending that trajectory, they stressed, "the Clinton administration is obsessed with the middle class, deficit reduction, and business incentives." By contrast, the activists called for "integrated economic development for South L.A. and other low-income, high-unemployment areas of L.A. . . . [and] their reconstruction as *centers of environmentally-sound production of technologies of the future*, focusing on solar electricity, non-polluting prefabricated housing materials, electric car components, and public transportation vehicles, both buses and trains."[104] Although their focus was the future of Los Angeles in the 1990s, this policy vision would have been at home with that of left-Keynesian economists in the 1930s and 40s, Coretta Scott King and Congressman Augustus Hawkins in the 1970s, and the Green New Deal framework pursued by the Sunrise Movement and Congresswoman Alexandria Ocasio-Cortez after 2019.

But in 1993, this vision of public investment in environmentally sustainable jobs was cast aside, one of many victims of deficit hawk politics. As the activists noted, "the [Clinton] administration has completely embraced the arguments of Ross Perot and the right wing of the Democratic Party that 'deficit reduction' is a major national priority—code for further cuts in already depleted essential social programs."[105] As LCSC knew, the private sector had scant interest in weatherizing homes for low-income renters, for youth arts programming, for mass bus service. The focus on reducing deficits thus silenced a vibrant debate about what the public sector could and should be.

The Biden administration's unfolding green industrial strategy therefore poses questions for the future of deficit hawk politics, the form public investment can take, and of the role of the public sector more broadly.[106] While Biden staffed his administration with many veterans of the Clinton and Obama years, he also reached beyond the traditional circuit of policymakers and economists and included a group to the left of those mainstays, while excluding those like Larry Summers. As Biden proposed a large fiscal agenda, including industrial policies, some analysts began to wonder whether Rubinomics was dead—even hazarding that such shifts were evidence of a "economic policy revolution."[107]

Indeed, despite Biden touting the deficit reduction portion of the Inflation Reduction Act, the new law still demonstrated a different trajectory than the traditional Rubinomics policy matrix. Under the law, the Biden administration recognized that supply-side public investments and government regulation each have a role to play in managing inflation and the broader economy. This recognition was a tremendous policy development and a shift away from a four-decade paradigm that prioritized deficit reduction and monetary policy as main tools of economic management, and fiscal discipline as an essential metric of good economic policy. In several ways Biden's presidency put him more in line with Clinton's early ambitions for public investment, the hopes of which were dashed by his cabinet of deficit hawks. While it is too soon to fully evaluate whether the era of the deficit hawk Democrat is dead or merely dormant, such a moment of change should prompt questions about what kind of society—and what constituency—liberal policies should cultivate. These are debates that proponents of a Green New Deal and a high-care, low-carbon economy have forced onto the party agenda.[108] To fulfill their promise, liberals must eradicate the deficit hawk paradigm for good.

CHAPTER 14

The Professional-Class Presidency of Barack Obama

NICOLE HEMMER

Barack Obama's path to the presidency began at Boston's Fleet Center in the summer of 2004. Tapped as the keynote speaker for the Democratic National Convention, he wrestled for weeks over how to introduce himself to the nation, to knit together his unconventional biography in a way that felt distinctly familiar to the millions of Americans watching his national debut.

But the speech was not just biography, nor just a hype speech for Massachusetts senator John Kerry, the Democratic presidential nominee. It was also an introduction to Obama's theory of politics. Americans, he argued, truly embodied the notion of the nation's motto, "E pluribus unum," united by an ideological commitment to "a belief that we are connected as one people." Division, polarization, rancor—these things only existed as a political project of "those who are preparing to divide us, the spin masters and negative ad peddlers who embrace the politics of anything goes." Those dividers disrupted the natural order of American politics, a consensus-building project of a people who shared far more in common than even they believed.[1]

Obama's keynote at the 2004 Democratic National Convention resonated with many Americans in a bitterly divided moment, when the idea that there was not a Red America or a Blue America seemed, if not true, then a worthwhile aspiration. The contentiousness and conspiracy-mongering of the 2008 presidential campaign did not shake Obama from this understanding of politics. Even as he ran into a wall of Republican obstruction, Obama stuck with his belief in government by consensus, one that defined bipartisanship as the measure of good legislative work.

As Republican obstruction ground legislation to a halt during the Obama administration, there was also a burst of bipartisan myth-making, the construction of a halcyon bygone era when comity ruled

Washington. Nothing exemplified this mythmaking more than the bestselling book *Tip and the Gipper*, written by MSNBC host Chris Matthews in 2013. The subtitle was telling: *When Politics Worked*. Perhaps even more telling was that one of the most popular hosts on the most liberal cable news network during the Obama years wrote a book celebrating Ronald Reagan's approach to politics, not because he had been won over to Reagan's politics but because he admired Reagan's process. That message of process over politics fit neatly into the Obama era, and assured that throughout his eight years in office, Obama would always start negotiations at the halfway point, abandoning the broader vision of progressive change before he even reached the bargaining table.[2]

That lack of a broader vision—the failure to articulate a "new New Deal" that liberal commentators hoped the Obama presidency would deliver—defined Obama's politics. True, he shepherded through significant spending for economic-recovery programs, successfully passed health-care reform, withdrew US troops from Iraq, and, by hiring more women, Latinx, and Black appointees than any previous president, transformed the face of the federal government. But revolutionary governance it was not: the administration had little appetite for prosecuting those responsible for the financial collapse or for war crimes, dropped both the public option and abortion coverage from the health-care bill, and showed little interest in the growing economic redistribution movement Occupy Wall Street.[3]

The Obama administration was a bit more successful in advancing progressive governance than the Clinton administration had been; in that sense, it did offer a break from the past. But its successes made it the fulfillment of post-1960s liberalism rather than a rejection of it; its failures made it a foil for a resurgent Left and a more visionary liberalism rather than a font of them.

The constraints of professional-class liberalism have rarely been the main explanation for the limited achievements of the Obama administration. The more popular explanation, from both the administration and contemporary observers, focused instead on the obstacles thrown up by the Republican Party. From deep within the battles of the Obama years and the presidency of Donald Trump that followed, it made sense that scholars were preoccupied with Republicans, tracing their radicalization through the Obama years as a way of making sense of the crisis of democratic governance that marked the Trump years. Many analysts attributed the limits of the Obama administration to those political circumstances: a polarized country with a rapidly radicalizing right narrowed the space for political change, forcing the administration to tweak the economic system rather than remake it.[4]

And fair enough. Such constraints did exist. But viewing the Obama years with some historical distance, and with the insights offered throughout this volume, allows us to also understand the way this particular form of liberalism, born in the twentieth century and sustained well into the twenty-first, also constrained the Obama administration. Pragmatic, technocratic, and institutionalist, the Obama administration made clear the limits of professional-class liberalism in the post–Cold War era and helped spur grassroots activists to pressure the Democrats for far more change than the Obama years offered. It also allows us to more clearly see that the administration's understanding of conservatism and the Republican Party, an understanding first forged by liberals in the Cold War era, likewise constrained the Obama administration's vision and achievements.

Cold War Liberalism and the Search for a "Responsible Right"

"Should any political party attempt to abolish Social Security, unemployment insurance, and eliminate labor laws and farm programs, you would not hear of that party again in our political history," President Dwight Eisenhower wrote in 1954. The observation, now much quoted, succinctly captured both the new liberal consensus of the post–World War II era and the centrality of bipartisanship to that consensus. Working across the aisle would become a central feature of national governance in the decades that followed, predicated on the understanding that, while Democrats and Republicans might have a difference in emphasis, they shared a common set of beliefs and values that allowed them to build consensus and govern responsibly. And while many activists and politicians in the 1950s and 1960s criticized bipartisanship, seeing it as a force that constrained reform and limited policy options, by the end of the twentieth century, it would be understood almost exclusively as a force for functional governance.[5]

Though Republicans were nearly always in the minority in Congress during the Cold War, consensus politics kept them relevant in an era of Democratic dominance. Because neither party was ideologically sorted—there were liberal, moderate, and conservative Republicans, and liberal, moderate, and conservative Democrats—cross-party alliances were common. Most of the liberal legislative achievements during the Cold War era, including the core economic and civil rights victories of the Great Society, were achieved with a significant number of Republican votes. Over 80 percent of Senate Republicans voted for the Civil Rights Act of 1964, compared with 69 percent of Democrats; 94 percent of Senate Republicans voted for the Voting Rights Act of 1965, compared with 73 percent of Democrats. In each case, Republican votes were necessary for final passage of the bills.[6]

If Republicans were vital to the liberal project in the Cold War era, liberals understood conservatives to be opponents: political actors operating outside this bipartisan consensus. The new right-wing activists organizing during the Cold War in groups like the John Birch Society—the ultraright, as many journalists dubbed them—were not just opposed to New Deal liberalism but seemed to reject liberal society more broadly. The early 1960s were awash in panicked dispatches from journalists covering the Far Right, and the rise of Barry Goldwater as the Republican Party's presidential nominee in 1964 seemed to suggest the bipartisan liberal consensus had fractured. But with Goldwater's defeat, and with the disavowal of the Birch Society by editors at the conservative magazine *National Review*, it seemed that there was once again room for what was then known as "the responsible right" in the liberal political vision.[7]

Even as liberals were making space for "the responsible right," the consensus they hoped to shore up was shattering. The challenges were coming from both the left and the right: white male voters had begun to look skeptically at a party that had created space for Black civil rights and second-wave feminism, and while they had not fled the party en masse, their loyalties were weakening. At the same time, left-wing activists saw the Democratic Party as corrupt, corporatist, authoritarian, and imperialist, a conflict that boiled over in an orgy of police violence against protesters at the 1968 Democratic convention. In 1960, social scientist Daniel Bell had written one of the core texts of the liberal consensus, *The End of Ideology*. Within a decade, it looked as though it was consensus rather than ideology that was at an end.[8]

As the liberal consensus crumbled, the Republican Party was both growing increasingly conservative and making a play for disaffected white Democrats. Those who categorized themselves as part of the responsible right, like *National Review* founder William F. Buckley Jr., tempered their electoral expectations, at least temporarily, arguing that the Right should support the rightmost *viable* candidate. At the same time, Richard Nixon, running for president in 1968, courted conservatives as an essential part of his electoral and governing coalition. Once elected, Nixon touted the "silent majority" as the successor to the "liberal consensus," a more conservative and punitive vision of bipartisan consensus than what came before.[9]

This evolution of ideology and compromise continued through the Reagan presidency in the 1980s. Ronald Reagan represented the victory of the Right within the Republican Party, and a serious blow to

New Deal liberalism. He clashed regularly with Democrats in Congress, though they maintained space for negotiation when possible. Journalist David Broder noted that after a deep rivalry formed between Reagan and Democratic Speaker Tip O'Neill in the first two years of Reagan's presidency, the two came to find space for compromise, or at least to carry out their agendas as best they could. Rather than a post-ideological or technocratic bipartisanship, this approach was an older model of bipartisanship cooperation predicated on collegiality between elite white men. The men "have defined a relationship of mutual respect that allows each of them room to do his own vital political business without foreclosing cooperation on other issues," Broder wrote in late 1983. But he warned that détente between Reagan and O'Neill could come at a cost, allowing them to work together on small things while leaving the more pressing issues of the day, from immigration to entitlements to defense spending, unresolved. This observation would prove prescient.[10]

The end of the Cold War also saw the end of Democratic dominance in Congress as well as a new era of conservative politics. The emergence of a firebrand Speaker in Republican Newt Gingrich promised a new era of polarization and partisanship. Gingrich had, after all, spent the 1980s building a conservative agenda and teaching Republicans to use powerful, punchy language to denigrate and demonize Democrats. As political scientist Thomas Schaller explained, Gingrich's philosophy in the 1980s was simple: "Do not cooperate, do not compromise, do not seek bipartisan solutions—ever, on anything." That philosophy helped him become Speaker of the most conservative Congress in modern US history, one that was laser-focused on damaging Democratic president Bill Clinton.[11]

Yet for Clinton, Republican leadership was both a foil and an opportunity. Though Gingrich rose to power by bashing Democrats, he also believed there were deals to be made. Clinton, after all, touted a "third way" in US politics, an approach that he believed could circumvent ideological divisions by stiff-arming the Left, criticizing the Right, and building a nimble, public-private government that safeguarded capitalism while using it to sand down the rough edges of growing inequality. It was an approach that would provide ample opportunities to work with the right-wing Republicans who took over the House in the 1994 midterm elections.

That bipartisan approach was underway even before Gingrich became Speaker. During Clinton's first year in office, he relied on Gingrich to find the votes to pass the North American Free Trade Agreement (NAFTA) through the House. Negotiated under George

H. W. Bush, NAFTA was a Republican priority that fit into Clinton's third-way vision: favoring markets over regulation while breaking with a traditional Democratic constituency, labor. The omnibus crime bill, negotiated a year later, likewise relied on Gingrich to whip Republican votes for a bill that gave Clinton tough-on-crime cred while also instituting an assault weapons ban. Gingrich, who fought hard against the ban, nonetheless provided the necessary votes. After Gingrich became Speaker, the two men plotted together to work on cuts to Social Security and Medicare, until impeachment drove both men away from the bargaining table.[12]

That history is worth rehashing because it played an important role in underscoring the importance of bipartisanship to the Democratic Party under Clinton, but one that looked quite different than in the 1950s and 1960s. It was one not in thrall to its base, but rather one that favored an appearance of toughness and independence. It also showed that the growing radicalism in the Republican Party did not necessarily spell the end of bipartisan governance. Even as the rhetoric grew more heated and the tactics more extreme, compromise remained possible—and remained a central value of post–Cold War liberalism. Obama may have criticized the Clinton approach at times, but he would not deviate from Clinton's ideas about the value of bipartisan compromise.

The rise of the grand compromise also conformed with the professionalization of the Democratic Party and liberalism more broadly: these bills were technically complex, designed to navigate but also create legal and constitutional thickets, and made use of Congress's authority over the subtleties of the tax code to pursue an expanding range of domestic social agendas. It served the interests of both the professionals who understood how to navigate the new infrastructures and the liberals who sought to build social programs in a conservative era. This "submerged state," as political scientist Susan Mettler described it, grew rapidly in the 1990s and the first decade of the 2000s, developing programs that expanded state power, accelerated economic inequality, and functioned largely out of sight.[13]

The George W. Bush presidency furnished even more evidence of the feasibility of bipartisanship, despite deepening ideological division and even more radical tactics employed by the right. Following the 2000 election, which had featured the use of force to halt ballot-counting in Florida and an ideologically split Supreme Court ruling to decide the outcome, Democrats nonetheless continued reaching out to the Republican Party to achieve their legislative aims. Senator Ted Kennedy worked with Bush to pass education reform, Democrats fell in line to provide votes authorizing the invasion of Iraq, and legislators worked with the Bush administration on immigration reform before the right wing of the party killed it. That was one of the warning signs Obama might have attended to as he ran for president.

Obama and Elite Diversification

As the first Black president, Obama embodied change. He carried with him not only an unusual presidential biography—son of a white mother from Kansas and a Black father from Kenya, who grew up in Hawaii and Indonesia before becoming a community organizer in Chicago—but a sense that his election could shake up a political system that had become stagnant and irrelevant to so many Americans. Even before the financial crisis engulfed the 2008 presidential campaign, Obama positioned himself as the outsider running against an establishment too sclerotic to appeal to most Americans. The failures of George W. Bush's administration were obvious enough: Americans had long since turned on the incumbent, whose approval ratings had been dragged to near-record lows by unpopular wars, a shaky economy, and widespread frustration at government inaction in places like hurricane-wrecked New Orleans. The presidential nomination of Senator John McCain, who had been in Congress for a quarter-century and was already in his seventies, made it easy for the Obama campaign to argue that a vote for McCain was a vote for more of the same. But Obama also applied those arguments to his primary opponent, Hillary Clinton, who through both politics and marriage seemed to be a continuation of the last century's Democratic Party. Obama argued, and clearly believed, that his election would mark a clean break from the politics of the past for both parties.

What he did not believe was that his election would usher in a new "post-racial" era. Though often seen as separate from the Black political tradition in the United States, Obama carried on the tradition of "yes, but" Black liberalism that historian Danielle Wiggins explores in this volume: yes, there were significant structural inequalities that needed to be addressed by the federal government, but given the unlikelihood that such help would be coming, work would have to carry on in the private sphere. Having a "yes-but" Black liberal as president created a profound tension: Obama understood that structural inequities required targeted intervention, precisely the kind of governance that the liberal quest for bipartisan compromise made politically improbable.[14]

Indeed, he understood that pursuing programs targeted toward Black Americans could evaporate white support. On the cusp of the Clinton years in 1991, Obama explained his decision to embrace universalist policies that made no reference to race in an unpublished manuscript that he wrote with Robert Fisher, a friend at Harvard University. "Within an admittedly racist culture, we can design and pursue strategies that either align the interests of the white majority in ways that blunt the influence of racism, or instead isolate blacks from potential allies and make blacks more vulnerable to racist sentiments." Liberalism, Obama believed, would have to avoid targeted interventions for people of color, or it would lead to more conservatism, more retrenchment.[15]

Avoiding such interventions did not require a retreat from civil rights, one of Obama's main critiques of the moderate liberalism of the Clinton administration. But it did place limits to how frontally a politician, especially a Black politician, could address racial inequality. In that sense, bringing a "yes-but" Black liberalism to the White House as president meant that Obama's skepticism about the ability of the federal government to directly aid Black people—lest such aid blow apart his electoral majority—would bound his governing philosophy.[16]

Yet it was also the case that one of the signature achievements of late twentieth-century liberalism and the Obama administration itself was the embrace of the values of diversity and inclusion among an elite set of Americans—in culture, in politics, and in the corporate sector, especially. If one needed any evidence of the emergence of elite diversification, the Obama administration's staff and political appointments were living, breathing examples. Yet such diversification—along lines of race, gender, and sexuality—also created an opportunity for right-wing politicians and activists to activate profound anxieties and antagonism within their base. This dynamic was one Obama had studied carefully as a law student, and fears of backlash and the loss of responsible conservative governing partners shaped his incremental approach to civil rights and reform. And despite the increasing radicalism and political intransigence on the right, these instincts also informed the administration's increasingly fruitless search for any bipartisan partner—which would provide evidence, they believed, of the merits of their smart, commonsense approach to governing.

The people surrounding Obama reflected the triumph of elite diversification: Janet Napolitano went from being the first woman governor of Arizona to the first woman secretary of homeland security. Sonia Sotomayor became the first Latina Supreme Court justice. Eric Holder became first Black attorney general in the nation's history. More broadly, the administration had moved past barrier-breaking to create a federal government in which there was a critical mass of women, people of color, and LGBTQ people in leadership roles, unlike any other administration in history. The Obama administration was, thus, far more diverse than previous administrations. But the new people in those roles were also a reflection of the president's own view of change: incremental, bipartisan, low-drama, meritocratic. The change they were asked to effect would not be radical or even aggressively liberal. It would be gradual and technocratic, aimed at winning over moderate voters and Republicans even at the cost of liberal goals.[17]

These dynamics would become especially apparent on the terrain of gender. The rise of professional women to the upper echelons of government coincided with the publication of Sheryl Sandberg's best-selling book, written with Nell Scovell, *Lean In: Women, Work, and the Will to Lead*. Prior to writing *Lean In*, Sandberg had worked at the World Bank and the Clinton administration Treasury Department before making millions as an executive at Google and Facebook. Her biography aligned neatly with the contours of liberalism in the first decade of the 2000s: a woman working in elite leadership positions, amassing power and wealth as she floated between public service and private industry with the belief that both types of work helped make the world a better, fairer place. In *Lean In*, she assured other women that they too could conquer the corporate world, if they just tweaked their behaviors in order to succeed. Sandberg saw the barriers to women's success in corporate spaces as one of individual actions, not structural discrimination. In this conception, corporations were essentially meritocratic places, and women simply had to learn how to legibly display and amplify their merit within those systems.[18]

The Obama White House operated under a similar set of assumptions about the staff. Having the right people in place meant that while there might be some vestigial structural problems—there were not enough women's restrooms, for instance, and none of the facilities had tampon dispensers—but a good liberal staff, designed with an eye toward diversification and lifting up underrepresented groups, would not have to deal with issues like sexism. It was a logic that placed the Obama staff outside the structures they sought to overturn. And it is why Obama appeared caught by surprise when his senior adviser (and close friend) Valerie Jarrett informed him that the senior women on staff were chafing under the "general macho atmosphere" of the White House. At a meeting convened to allow those women to explain their experiences, the president offered Sandbergian advice: "I handpicked each of you. This is the White House. I expect you to fight to make your voices heard." He expected them, in other words, to lean in.[19]

If Obama succeeded in modeling the promise of diversity through his political appointments, there was, however, even less tolerance for talking about racism as president than he had anticipated. After commenting on the arrest of Henry Louis Gates, a Black Harvard professor arrested for disorderly conduct upon suspicions that he had broken into his own home, Obama saw his support with white voters slump from 53 percent to 46 percent—a significant downward swing from which he would not rebound. The administration's growing wariness about racism led it to overreact to any stories that might trigger reactionary white voters. In 2009, the Department of Labor, backed by the White House, fired Shirley Sherrod, Georgia's state director of rural development, after the release of a deceptively edited video that suggested she discriminated against white farmers. The president simply backed away from discussions of race—so much so that one political scientist found that he spoke about race less in his first two years than any president since John Kennedy.[20]

That reticence began to erode with the emergence of Black Lives Matter as a racial-justice movement. The acquittal of George Zimmerman for the murder of 17-year-old Trayvon Martin led Obama to speak frankly and emotionally about the cost of anti-Black racism; the attention to police brutality enabled the Justice Department under Attorney General Eric Holder, already committed to the broader project of criminal-justice reform, to enter into more consent decrees with police departments around the country.

Yet the administration's actions on policing and criminal-justice reform showed how thoroughly it had become a creature of post-1960s professional-class liberalism, especially its commitments to pragmatism, technocracy, and professionalization. Better-trained officers, better data, better community-feedback systems: these tweaks could solve, or at least mostly mitigate, the problem of racist policing and police brutality. The Obama team was, by and large, a team of lawyers, heirs to the Naderite tradition, who saw the potential for change in some blend of targeted political action and legal maneuvering. Obama, having himself worked as a law professor, was perhaps the most skeptical member of his team when it came to the law as a tool of generational change. In his 2006 book *The Audacity of Hope*, he wrote, "I wondered if, in our reliance on the courts to vindicate not only our rights but our values, progressives have lost too much faith in democracy." Finding the law too constraining, he entered politics instead. Yet, Obama, too, embraced such technical, incremental reform: technocratic, legalistic approaches ultimately seemed the safest path between the thickets of racial reaction and the realities of such vast and complex governing structures and congressional politicking.[21] Perhaps smart governance itself, Obama seemed to hope, might begin to revive faith in democracy.

Policing also revealed the administration's commitment to technocracy and, relatedly, techno-utopianism. In response to the protests in Ferguson,

Missouri, following the police killing of Michael Brown, Obama created the Task Force on 21st Century Policing. He was following a path carved out by presidents since the 1960s, when the federal government took more interest in policing in response to the increased visibility of police brutality. With the advent of the War on Drugs, that federal role became more and more punitive, focused on creating and raising mandatory minimums, strengthening federal statutes, and adopting, in both Democratic and Republican administrations, a "tough-on-crime" approach to federal law enforcement. The ties between local and federal police grew stronger starting in the 1990s with the modern 1033 Program, which delivered surplus military equipment to police departments for domestic enforcement, including drug and counterterrorism programs.[22]

In that sense, the Obama administration represented a significant change. Where previous administrations had sought to take a more aggressive approach to law enforcement, Obama believed that incarceration rates were far too high, that the legal system unfairly targeted Black men, and that those who had been convicted of felonies faced systemic discrimination that made their reentry after incarceration unnecessarily difficult. And at least at first, the administration found governing partners among Republicans, many of whom had grown more open to criminal-justice reform in the twenty-first century. While seeking legislation to rectify inequality in sentencing for crack and cocaine—a move so popular it was passed by voice vote in the House and unanimous consent in the Senate—the administration also worked to limit racial profiling in policing, offer de-escalation training to police departments, and highlight prison reform efforts. The administration did not move to reschedule marijuana, but it did limit actions against states that had begun legalizing the drug for recreational use. After Ferguson, Obama issued an executive order that limited the 1033 Program, and in his final year in office, oversaw a massive push to offer clemency and commutations to those convicted of nonviolent drug offenses.[23]

When it came to on-the-ground policing, the administration's approach could be seen in the Task Force on 21st Century Policing, which drew together police officers including Charles Ramsey, the former Philadelphia police commissioner, and Roberto Villaseñor, the Tucson chief of police; activists like Brittney Packnett of Teach for America and Bryan Stevenson of the Equal Justice Initiative; and academics like Laurie Robinson of George Mason University and Tracey L. Mears of Yale Law School. The idea was to get a mix of perspectives from reasonable representatives of various stakeholders and create a plan that would modernize policing and, in the process, address racism and inequity in law enforcement.[24]

In response to the task force's recommendations, in May 2015, the White House launched its Police Data Initiative (PDI). As the administration described it, the PDI was comprised of experts and practitioners "committed to improving the relationship between citizens and police through uses of data that increase transparency, build community trust, and strengthen accountability." The new initiative enlisted private companies like Safe Software and Nextdoor to help collect and maintain data as part of its program. These commitments to the private sector would begin to have purchase with Republicans as well. It was the only way the administration could move forward with any sense of bipartisanship. The Republican Party was radicalizing throughout the Obama years, abandoning criminal-justice reform for broadsides against Black Lives Matter and more aggressive pro-police politics. A major criminal-justice reform bill that seemed likely to pass with significant bipartisan support in 2015 collapsed as Donald Trump made tough-on-crime rhetoric central to his presidential campaign. Nor was it just criminal justice. Across policy areas, conservative reaction clipped the administration's ambitions, not only through obstruction but through increasingly conspiratorial claims.[25]

In the face of such seemingly irrational attacks on his citizenship and the very legitimacy of the Obama presidency, the administration offered "smart" governance.

"Smart" Governance, Gridlock, and Professional-Class Liberalism's Discontents

"Smart" governance—data-driven, technology-enabled policy—was the watchword of the Obama administration. It stemmed from their belief that technology would not only streamline government but deliver significant social improvements—and it would do so without anyone being any the wiser. Government out of sight, stripped of ideological markers, would appeal both to the public and to a restive opposition party.

That notion, that modernization and reform were largely interchangeable, had been a core liberal philosophy for decades. Expertise and technology offered a way out from seemingly intractable political and social conflicts: they required no institutional reparations, no resolution of incompatible values, no major structural change.

Smart governance also fit well with Obama's approach to bipartisanship. But for the Obama administration, bipartisanship meant not just reaching across the aisle but meeting Republicans halfway at the start of any negotiation. Efforts at immigration reform would only follow efforts to appear tough on deportations; minimum-wage targets would settle around $9 an hour, even in the middle of the Fight for 15 movement. The federal government could work toward liberal goals, but its vision of generational change was change that might take a generation to achieve. And, on all fronts, the concede-in-advance strategy failed to win over Republican allies.

The reality of the situation, one that never quite hit home with the Obama team, was that the technocratic, consensus-driven, bipartisan approach to government favored by the president and by professional-class liberals simply was no match for Republican obstruction. It wasn't that Republicans were stronger or more powerful than Democrats; they were simply employing a different mode of politics. Obama had a critique of this approach, one he laid out in his 2004 convention speech about "those who seek to divide us" with a "politics of anything goes" (though he seemed to think such a politics was a function of campaigns rather than governance). What he did not have, and what his fellow professional-class liberals lacked, was an effective way to counter it.

In the press, this new era of gridlock was explained as a problem of polarization, evidence that, contra Obama, there *was* a Red American and a Blue America, and they were rapidly moving apart, becoming not just different but alienated from one another. Polls showed that his presidency marked historic highs in polarization as measured by presidential approval ratings; throughout his time in office, he recorded the highest gap between partisan approval ratings in modern history. He lamented that despite his efforts to the contrary, the "singular regret" of his presidency was that "our body politic has become more polarized."[26]

That passive language signaled that both Obama and the press thought of polarization as a descriptor of a process, rather than a political strategy of its own. If the US had become more polarized, it was because Republicans had actively worked to make it so. But that analysis still leaves out the role of professional-class liberals in polarization: not as drivers of polarization but as anemic political forces unable to counter it, primarily because they had neither the framework to understand it nor the ideological tools to oppose it.

But these flaws rarely garnered much attention, especially in the early days of the Obama presidency. Obama's embrace of new technology had been a selling point of his campaign, part of the newness and change he promised to bring with him into office. While the campaign was still finding its footing in Iowa in the long slog of the 2007 phase of the campaign, Chris Hughes, one of the founders of Facebook, traded his job in Silicon Valley to take charge of social media for the Obama campaign. He joined a scrappy tech team that was building out new communications strategies, new fundraising strategies, new microtargeting strategies. And when Obama won, he was eager to bring these young tech gurus and their revolutionary technologies into the administration, to enhance communication, transparency, and, above all, the efficacy of government programs.[27]

In seeing only upsides in this new technology, the Obama administration tapped into a techno-utopian spirit that touched most US institutions circa 2010. This was the era of MOOCs, massive online open courses that promised to make higher education cheap and accessible; the era of digital disruptors that promised to democratize media by opening the door to a new generation of citizen-journalists; the era of e-tail shopping that would bring down prices while expanding options for consumers around the country; the era of digital banking that would bring financial opportunities to the poorest and least connected parts of the world; the era of the Arab Spring, when social media would bring revolution and democracy to countries that had languished under (often US-backed) dictatorships.

In that atmosphere, the *values* of these new technology corporations seldom came up for debate. The idea of public-private partnerships with Silicon Valley seemed to have only upsides, and the administration was keen to highlight efforts that showed the potential of new technologies. For instance, as part of their efforts on labor and unions, they hosted Michelle Miller, co-founder of Coworker.org, which allowed workers to engage in labor activity without unionization. And so many administration officials cycled out of government and into these new tech corporations that the *Washington Post* called Silicon Valley "the new revolving door for Obama staffers." Even as the administration began to come into conflict with tech companies, as it did with Apple over efforts to decrypt the iPhones of the attackers who carried out the 2015 San Bernardino terror attack, there was little sense that the administration was at war with Apple. Tim Cook's Silicon Valley and Barack Obama's Washington had too much in common: both believed in elite diversification and do-good billionaires, and both believed that technology and technocracy could make the world a better place—and make their leaders wealthy in the process.[28]

At nearly every level of governance, across policy issues, the administration highlighted the need for more and better data, processed by newer technologies and expert analysis. This notion that data made for good governance was not new to the Obama era; Progressives in the early twentieth century and liberals during the Cold War also saw value in number crunching, and the Atari Democrats and Clinton administration had touted how technology could make government more efficient. But the obsessive use of data as both a value and a brand, along with the belief that data could drive policy, or even be a substitute for politics, set the administration apart. The Data-Driven Justice Initiative, Climate Data Initiative, and Precision Medicine Initiative joined efforts across the executive branch—in defense, public health, education—to not only gather more and better data, but to allow data to lead the way in setting priorities and policy. The administration's attraction to behavioral science came from the same impulse. Obama found the idea of choice architecture, the idea that people could be "nudged" into making better choices by simple, noninvasive environmental cues, so appealing that he appointed Cass Sunstein, the co-author of a book on the subject, to run the Office of Information and Regulatory Affairs. Goodbye, welfare state, hello, nudges.[29]

The nudge came with the we-know-better-than-you attitude that professional-class liberals brought to much of governance. Consider the working-class tax cuts the administration passed to help stimulate the economy in 2009. When President Bush sent out tax rebate checks during his presidency, Americans stashed the money in savings rather than spending it. But for stimulus purposes, the Obama administration wanted people to spend. So rather than cutting checks, they cut payroll taxes. People had more money and spent it, which the administration wanted, but they had no idea that they were benefactors of a government program. That was the trade-off of the tax tweak: the administration could manipulate behavior but would not get credit for raising the net income of working-class Americans.[30]

Professional-class liberals had little interest in big, showy, costly government, so these hidden programs held great appeal. As did their low cost. In fact, in Sunstein's definition, a nudge *had* to be "cheap," or else it was not a nudge. This emphasis on frugality also became part of the administration's strategy, to foreground economic or fiscal arguments to demonstrate that good liberal policies could come with low price tags. This point was especially important to Sunstein, who, as Karen Tani reveals in her chapter in this volume, was one of the main proponents of the cost-benefit approach to government. When it came to criminal-justice reform, for instance, the administration underscored that cost-benefit analyses lined up with its preference for less incarceration and stronger civil rights protections. A 2016 study of the economics of criminal-justice reform created by Obama's Council of Economic Advisors studied three approaches to reform using a cost-benefit analysis and found that increased incarceration failed the test. Increased funding for police and a higher minimum wage both passed.[31]

But if low-cost, out-of-sight programs were meant to appease, or at least not provoke, conservatives, the nudgers had misjudged their opposition. Sunstein became one of the primary targets of right-wing radio and television host Glenn Beck, who reached the height of his influence during the Obama years. Calling Sunstein "the most dangerous man in America," Beck argued that nudges were the first step on the road to the transformation of the United States into a police state. "They are treating you like a lab rat," he told his audience as he talked about Sunstein's nudges. "That's how they look at you." It was, Beck explained, part of a system of "manipulation and control by the federal government," even more insidious for happening out of sight, embedded deep in the layers of federal bureaucracy.[32]

Nudges reflected modern liberalism's particularly risk-averse, poll-tested approach to political leadership. That approach to political leadership would be strained to the breaking point by the increasing radicalization of American conservatism and the Republican Party. While the Republican Party still boasted a group of leaders that shared a commitment to technocracy, reform, and political wonkery, those officeholders found themselves at war with a new generation of tea-party insurgents who had little interest in disguising their ideological goals in dry budgetary and procedural language. Often, they had little interest in policy at all. The party's new right flank left Obama-era Republicans like Paul Ryan and Eric Cantor, the self-styled young guns of the House leadership, wedged. On one hand, they saw a path toward greater conservative dominance that followed the Obama model: policy buried in the tax code or smuggled into an omnibus bill, grand bargains to reform immigration policy or downsize Social Security and other safety net programs, diversification of the party along lines of race, gender, and ethnicity, with targeted outreach to Black and Latino voters.[33]

But such policies, favored by Ryan, Cantor, and a short-lived group of reform conservatives (known in the press by the unfortunate label "Reformicons"), stood little chance in a conference filled with Tea Party members. When Cantor attempted to pass a conservative modification to the Affordable Care Act (ACA), which involved diverting funds from disease-prevention efforts to create high-risk pools for difficult-to-insure Americans, he met stiff opposition from his right. Tea Party members preferred to vote to repeal the ACA in its entirety instead. Any attempt to modify the ACA, they believed, would legitimate it. Obstruction and repeal were the only options. The same held true for immigration reform. When Senator Marco Rubio threw his weight behind a reform effort in 2013, he ran headlong into right-wing opposition. There would be no half measures on the issue, only calls to close the borders, deport all undocumented immigrants, and build a wall. When offered an option between something and nothing, the Tea Party Right chose nothing. And they would keep choosing it throughout the Obama administration.[34]

Like the Reformicons, the administration constantly misjudged the politics of the Republican Party, continuing to pursue compromise politics in order to forge an elusive bipartisan agenda built on professional-class technocratic solutions. The failure to fundamentally rethink this commitment landed the Obama administration in a difficult spot with supporters, in large part because it had misjudged them as well. The energy and enthusiasm that flowed through the "coalition of the ascendant" during the 2008 campaign was real; the tears and cheers that greeted his election were genuine. But the coalition wanted more than Obama was willing to deliver: not just accountability for the financial crimes and war crimes that accompanied the global economic crisis and the wars in Afghanistan and Iraq, but a demolition of the limits that had defined professional-class liberalism.

Though Obama had himself been a community organizer who worked closely with activists and residents on the South Side of Chicago, he seemed to be caught flatfooted by the eruption of the national and global movements that began breaking out in the first term of his presidency. Occupy Wall Street, the call to rethink the financial system and commit to sweeping income redistribution and debt forgiveness, demonstrated the hunger for more systemic change. Though the movement was not greeted with much seriousness within the White House, the themes that fueled Occupy would become the framework for the 2012 reelection campaign against Mitt Romney. Obama's speech in Osawatomie, Kansas, in December 2011, echoed Occupy's critique of income inequality, focusing on the gains made by the top 1 percent of earners—though the policy Obama was promoting, a payroll tax cut, lacked the movement's revolutionary verve.

Likewise, the emergence of Black Lives Matter during the administration of the first Black US president makes sense not only as a reaction to police brutality but to the administration's embrace of universalist rhetoric and wariness of direct discussions of racism. Historian Keeanga-Yamahtta Taylor, writing about the rise of Black Lives Matter in the age of Obama, traced the movement to the way Obama's election had raised hopes among Black Americans, only to have those hopes shattered by the president's tepid response to anti-Black racism. When Obama failed to intervene in the death penalty case of Troy David, who many believed had been wrongly convicted, Black activists reeled at his lack of action— and lack of comment. "President Obama gives opinions on everything that's safe and what he thinks America wants to hear," Michael Rushing, a Black man from Atlanta, told the *Washington Post*, "but he straddles the fence on issues important to African Americans." While Obama began speaking more openly about race in his second term, his commitment to non-targeted policies remained in place—as did the Black-white wealth gap. Frustration with the limits of the administration's actions to aid Black Americans became a source of continued strain through the end of the Obama years.[35]

The administration was also caught off-guard by the rapid shift in attitudes toward immigration policy occurring among the party's base. In the early years of Obama's presidency, the administration focused on boosting its deportation numbers, part of an effort to demonstrate a commitment to border security in advance of negotiations on immigration reform. But as reform floundered—first with the failure of the DREAM Act in 2010 and then with the failed congressional negotiations of 2013–2014—activists began to see the administration as an inherently moderate, if not conservative, force.

The administration left behind other limits for liberalism and the Democratic Party as well. Having put forward Obama as an instrument of generational change, the White House set aside the work of investing in the broader party infrastructure. Over the eight years of the Obama administration, Democrats would lose more than a thousand seats nationwide, and the party infrastructure seemed moribund. The DNC took another major blow during the 2016 campaign, when it seemed to protect Hillary Clinton from left-wing challenges, rather than creating a robust space for debate about the future of the party—a particular problem at a time when the base was surging left. As a result, the Obama era did not construct a new New Deal or create a stable Democratic majority that relegated the Republicans to a generation of minority politics. It instead exposed the impoverished vision and political impotence of professional-class liberalism, a tired and ineffectual approach to politics that held little appeal for a new generation of political activists.

Those activists, frustrated with the Obama administration in its closing years and furious with the prospect of a Clinton presidency, found voice in Bernie Sanders's campaigns. Their criticisms of professional-class liberalism would broaden and deepen during the Trump administration, which called attention not only to the need for robust civil rights protections and policing reforms, but also to the need for a strong government safety net. Growing inequality, coupled with the emergency measures of the COVID-19 pandemic, created a clear example for many Americans that intense government intervention was both valuable and possible, and had to be pursued in the face of a radical, obstructionist Republican Party, no matter how difficult such a pursuit might be. In pursuing that vision, the party's progressives would not be acting in the Obama tradition, but rather would have to break from it decisively.

CHAPTER 15

State Agency
Social History with and beyond Institutionalism

GABRIEL WINANT

If a historian of the United States entered the public square in the 1960s or 1970s, it was often for reason of radical commitments. Eugene Genovese became a lightning rod after offering his "welcome" to the possibility of a Viet Cong victory; Staughton Lynd emerged as an icon of conscience thanks to Yale's denial of his tenure over his antiwar activities; Lawrence Goodwyn's writing on populism served as a historical bible for movement activists; Christopher Lasch was even read by Jimmy Carter in the White House, although he later castigated the president for missing his point. The profession seems to play this role less frequently today—despite celebrated exceptions such as Keeanga-Yamahtta Taylor. Today the most prominent "historians in public" are in different ways, and for good or ill, mainly working within liberalism, seeking to defend its institutions and norms against attack.[1] Lasch's brief moment in the sun notwithstanding, this latter group has a wider audience and even a kind of access to state power.[2]

Tracing the fall of radical history and ascent of liberalism in the historical profession offers a chance to consider historians' own place in the consolidation of professional-class liberalism, a process negotiated in part through a new relationship between social history and the tradition I call institutionalism: the approach that emphasizes political actors—policymakers, parties and their leaders, and the intellectuals who inform them—as first movers. What makes this approach specifically liberal is its emphasis on the autonomy of political ideology and action from social forces.

As our profession both accesses the halls of power at its upper reaches and collapses in its internal economic structure, it is undergoing significant intergenerational ideological polarization. This development prompts reassessment of the renewed relationship between historiography and liberalism, through which historians drew closer analytically and practically to the institutions of state power—and so became institutionalists both in method and in politics. In the process, they gained new powers. But we may have lost something too. This ambiguity is written across the scholarship of the 1980s and 1990s—for example, generating internal tension within the classic volume *The Rise and Fall of the New Deal Order*. Perhaps enough time now has gone by to sort it out.

To place historians within the development of history is a useful exercise in two ways. First, of course, it is central to the project of historiography, the intergenerational dialogue by which we become self-conscious of how our angle of retrospective view has changed as we have moved forward in time. More ambitiously though, it is sometimes possible to say something meaningful about a historical event or process by reading contemporary historical work symptomatically. To push historiography from its traditional place as a secondary source and treat it as primary material might turn over fresh layers from familiar episodes. In particular, it is in relation to debates about method that historians often disclose some truth of their era.

In the years after 1980, the US historical profession fell into intense internal debate—reaching a peak in the 1990s but not fully resolved today—as the lines of inquiry established by social history seemed increasingly alien in a more conservative historical moment.[3] Theoretical and methodological strife ricocheted through historical scholarship, a branch of the "theory wars" occurring simultaneously across disciplines. The intellectual-historical context, the collapse of the horizon of possibility glimpsed by the New Left and the decline in scholarly belief in the potentiality of social activism, corresponded to the political context of the defeat of the postwar welfare state. Within US history, a debate ensued about how to absorb the meaning of Reaganism—and ultimately, more broadly, neoliberalism—into scholars' account of the past, for which social historians' core concept of "agency" no longer seemed adequate given these political results. The political event had to be digested not only at the empirical level of substantive historical arguments, but also at the more abstract level where historical concepts are forged.

Social history in particular, the engine of historiographical transformation since the 1970s, faced critiques from within and without implicating the "agency" concept. Agency, a humanist idea, aimed to describe the capacity of ordinary people to influence historical events: at each juncture, the historical presence of women, the enslaved, African Americans, immigrants, and the working class could be established and their efforts shown to have contributed to the outcome. Yet the disappointing political outcomes of the 1980s cast doubt on such an approach.[4]

As the debate developed, it emerged that the reasons that some categories of human experience coagulated into "agents" of a particular kind—social-movement actors, especially—had largely been taken for granted by the "new social history."[5] What made a machinist an agentive worker and his union struggles a subject for labor history, asked Nell Painter, but the racism of his exclusionary union something less analytically significant? Surely one had to ask how race and class were constructed to reach an answer. Such critiques formed the basis of the "cultural turn" in history.[6]

It was also here that the second critique, arising from social science, made its impact. Social history's original maneuver—a critique of consensus liberalism—seemed ill-placed in a world where consensus liberalism had been defeated not from the left but from the right. As Alan Brinkley put it in his classic 1994 essay on conservatism, "New Left political scholarship has ... generally been more interested in discrediting liberalism—and, within the academic world, in wresting leadership and initiative from liberal scholars—than in confronting what it has generally considered a less formidable foe: the self-proclaimed Right." In his first footnote, Brinkley observed that social scientists have done a far better job than historians of tracking conservatism.[7]

While those influenced by both cultural history and social science can be characterized as "post-Marxist," they exited social history's vaguely Marxist encampment heading in almost opposite theoretical directions: one group into the interpretive and hermeneutic, the other into positivism. Yet only the first, the cultural turn, has attracted sustained disciplinary reflection. The rise of cultural history has been widely debated, celebrated, and criticized. (Reader, imagine a colleague describing a talk or paper as "very 1990s." What you envision probably involved discourse analysis, performativity, postcoloniality, the carnivalesque, or similar.)[8] But what came of this second, social-scientific line of argument, which often emanated from a more avowedly politically and methodologically liberal position? We must remain in some sense within it, since we have not yet looked backward at it.

Brinkley, however, was part of a broader historical phenomenon. The call for social historians in crisis to reunite with liberalism—against which the field initially had emerged in revolt—was widespread. "The once-passionate impulse to recapture working-class struggles and commitments to anticapitalist imperatives now risks creating sentimental reminders of times lost and aspirations disappointed," wrote Ira Katznelson in the same year, 1994, pointing to the failure of socialist dreams.

His proposed alternative was to engage what he called "liberal theory," in particular "to reincorporate at the center of the discipline the subjects of state-focused politics, institutions, and law."[9] What the US history field has not yet made explicit in its own self-narrative is how successful this call was.

This reentry into liberalism in the end produced a generation of "new political historians," whose method was "institutionalism." (Something closely related occurred in the next decade with another off-ramp from social history, this one into the history of capitalism.) The purpose here is not to attempt to vindicate or disprove institutionalism—neither of which could be done even at book length—but to illustrate and historicize it. For a new generation of scholars, this method has been in continuous ascendancy for most of our lifetimes. What results has it yielded and what limits has it met?

Social history's exhaustion by the 1990s had real sources, and institutionalism offered something significant in response. But institutionalism also aimed to suppress some animating elements of social history that might prove useful in the discontented, unequal period beginning around 2010. Many of us, including the contributors to this volume, who have been shaped profoundly by institutionalism—arguably its third generation in the field of US history—also lack the memories and scars that inspired it. We have different ones instead, which we can understand and to which we can assign meaning only partly through concepts developed in the 1980s and 1990s. This generational difference corresponds to a wider one among professionals, the younger cohorts of whom have drifted leftward, bypassing lessons of moderation learned and exemplified in the 1980s and 1990s by professional-class liberals. Since this period, political conditions have changed for the worse, possibly quite drastically. Such deterioration poses questions for any method of political analysis.

Broadly, scholarly institutionalism can be classed into three groups. They are the "organizational synthesis" of the 1970s and 1980s in business and political history, the substantivist economic sociology of Karl Polanyi, and most significantly the "state-centered approach" that arose in the 1980s in political science (often itself called "neo-institutionalist" or "neo-Weberian").[10] These traditions have their own intersecting but distinct histories, but they share some personnel, as well as three fundamental features.

First, institutionalists have been concerned with market structure. As was repeatedly argued by center-left reformers in the 1980s and 1990s, it is easier and more effective to regulate markets than to infringe directly on investment decisions and property rights: progressive reform might instrumentalize the power of markets rather than set itself against them hopelessly.[11] These instincts shaped scholarly agendas. In the 1990s and the first decade of the 2000s especially, production tended to fall out somewhat as sites of social antagonism or historical analysis as it ceased to be a site of political possibility. Instead, market behavior signalized social class—consumer politics or antimonopoly.[12]

Second, institutionalists share a particular interest in the specific and contingent organizational forms of economic and political life, to which they give causal priority over more abstract formalisms or determinisms. Politics and markets happen only through formation of organizations, and these organizations have particular histories. A populist focus on specific mechanisms and actors rather than structural determinants of elite power—corporate forms, elite networks—emerged here.[13]

And third, institutionalists see political power as irreducible to socioeconomic power. Instead, they trace it to organizational form, most importantly the state form. The modern bureaucratic state depends on expert knowledge and civil society organization, including party organization—a common feature of all modern societies. Finally, for this reason, the political party in general—and for US scholars, the Democratic Party in particular—have distinct historical importance. Politics must be done through parties. They are—and in the modern US the Democratic Party exclusively is—the indispensable vehicles of social progress.[14] In this view, liberal electoral success is analytically prior to, and ultimately politically more imperative than, any other political program. Generational efforts at political change, such as go into great social movements, and which often demand sacrifices of liberal politicians, diminish in importance.

The rest of this chapter considers why and how these resources in institutionalism offered a possible solution to the crisis of social history, inquiring into both the origins and consequences of this pact. In some sense, the alliance was natural: if the social history revolution emerged out of the New Left to excavate suppressed patterns of solidarity, agency, and contentious politics in US history, then institutionalism represented first an attempt to reckon with the durability of state structures against democratic challenge. To understand the fate of radical social movements, it was obviously necessary to try to grasp the specificity of institutions of state—as was widely understood on the New Left by the mid-1960s. As antiwar activist Paul Potter asked in his famous "name the system" speech of 1965, "How do you stop a war then? If the war has its roots deep in the institutions of American society, how do you stop it? Do you march to Washington? Is that enough? Who will hear us?"[15]

On the other hand, institutionalism had at its heart a profound commitment to historical contingency. As Richard John put it, "It is, for example, no longer as intuitively plausible as it had been in 1980 to posit that the major changes in American public life bubbled up from below." Importantly, John drew a distinction between "society" and "political economy" as units of analysis: "Not only individuals and groups, but also institutions, can be agents of change." What marks this position as the historical methodology of political liberalism is the analytic removal of "society" and "political economy" into separate spheres: over here are citizens going about their lives; over there are markets and the state institutions that govern them. The relationship between the spheres has no necessary shape—it is, as John emphasizes, "contingent."[16]

Historians appreciate contingency, of course. Benignly, such a method of contingency allows for the possibility that the state might actually represent the people: if politics is not reducible to the social, then the inequalities in society might be counteracted by the equalities of democracy. As Gary Gerstle, a 1980s labor historian par excellence who became a prominent political historian, concluded his synthesis of American state development, *Liberty and Coercion*, "Fixing the system does mean giving Americans the tools and flexibility to fashion a government that works, and one that as members of a polity in which the people are meant to be sovereign, they deserve."[17] Such neo-Progressivism does not dismiss the reality of social inequality. Indeed, it laments it. But it dispenses with social inequality as a direct cause of historical effects. It is in its method rather than its ethics that institutionalism diverges most from the traditional commitments of social history. Divergence being only partial—methodological more than ethical—encounter and affiliation were possible.

But it is also historians' task to explain obdurate continuities of social hierarchy. And as those continuities have reasserted themselves over recent decades, the shortcomings of this methodological liaison have shown more clearly. How can it be that each discrete outcome appears contingent and non-inevitable on close examination; yet at the same time, when we pull back the frame, so many events seem to align toward the reproduction of social inequality? Answering this question requires a move up the ladder of abstraction, a resort to structural explanation. To the extent that such moves fell out of historians' repertoire, then the meeting of the two traditions seems less an alliance of equals and more an assertion of liberal hegemony over a defeated Left—tracking closely with developments going on in American politics writ large. After all, institutionalism's particular origins were interwoven with a critique of the New Left's perceived neo-Marxist and identitarian excesses—ideological phenomena that, described more sympathetically, were fundamental to social history.

Still, "hegemonizing is hard work," as Stuart Hall once put it. The master is transformed alongside the subaltern, and the outcome always departs from conscious designs of participants. Whatever else it was, the liaison did prove generative.[18]

Origins of Institutionalism

The turmoil of the 1960s accelerated critiques of the dominant pluralist paradigm in American social science, which represented the state as a more or less passive clearinghouse of competing interests. From the New Left, several tributaries combined to supply an alternative: first the "corporate liberalism" scholarship; then comparative historical sociology, particularly Barrington Moore's *Social Origins of Dictatorship and Democracy*; and most critically, the 1971 translation and subsequent diffusion of Antonio Gramsci's prison writings.[19] By the mid-1970s, this approach became an international theoretical discourse at a high level of sophistication.[20]

While there was a wide range of debate within the tradition of Marxist state theory, it generally shared the idea that the capitalist state discovers and enacts the common interests of the ruling class, including negotiating necessary concessions to subordinate classes. When a ruling bloc succeeds at this task, it establishes what Gramsci called "hegemony." Such material and ideological coordination between ruling class and subordinate classes is always contingent and contested, but also represented the characteristic political success of liberal democracies.

One central intellectual accomplishment of this New Left tradition of state theory was to consolidate the paradoxical concept of the "relative autonomy" of the capitalist state. Against both pluralist accounts of the state as relatively fair "polyarchy," and against reductionist Marxist views of the state as immediately subservient to capitalist interests, this approach proposed that the successful capitalist state did secure the common interests of the ruling class—but its ability to do so rested on its capacity to transcend the interests of particular capitalists. While subordinate to bourgeois class interests in the final analysis, the state could ignore or defy them on particular questions arising in the day-to-day management of society, responding instead to political pressure from all directions. Limited but real contingency is thus introduced into the relationship between class and state—"relative autonomy."

Indeed, the ruling class did not need to rule, as sociologist Fred Block put it in 1977. It did not even need to be conscious of itself. "In a capitalist economy the level of economic activity is largely determined by the private investment decisions of capitalists," wrote Block. Thus "state managers have a direct interest in using their power to facilitate investment, since their own continued power rests on a healthy economy."[21] Continuing with this illustration, some factions in society might organize to demand fiscal or monetary policies that would impinge on investment allocation—for example, full employment. But this battle is an uphill one given the preexisting dependency of the capitalist state on favorable private investment decisions.[22] The allocation of investment authority away from the state to the capitalist class thus both embodies and enacts the political power of the capitalist class, redrawing the line between public and private.

Because the state-society distinction is itself an effect of political struggles, social and economic conflicts always take on some political character and implicate state institutions—more than this, they produce state institutions. In political sociologist Nicos Poulantzas's preferred metaphor, social conflict "condenses" contending forces into the state. The state, constructed in this emergent, structural, and contested way, is somewhat acephalous and porous. Social struggles traverse it and, in so doing, lodge themselves in its institutional elements. Different institutions of state power are imprinted by and correspond to different elements of society, and there is in turn a hierarchy among these different institutions corresponding to the hierarchy in society at large: it is harder for civil rights activists to win full employment (and accordingly state direction of investment) than for bankers to secure bailouts. As Leo Panitch observes, this hierarchy is easy to grasp when one contemplates the likely outcome of a disagreement between the Federal Reserve and the Department of Labor.[23] This issue is one of the major departures of a pure neo-institutionalism, which would argue that no state organ is a priori more powerful for social reasons, and that power inequalities among them are effects of differences in knowledge and organization rather than of social inequality.[24]

In the neo-Marxist account, the achievement of hegemony appears as structural effect rather than a necessary outcome, arising from the negotiated resolutions of political and social struggles and the state institutions that preside over and result from these resolutions. A state that could not enact this effect would not last. As Poulantzas sums up, "The State organizes and reproduces class hegemony by establishing a variable field of compromises between the dominant and dominated classes." Such compromises depend on popular mobilization but, Poulantzas emphasizes, there are not "*over here* state functions in favour of, and imposed by, the popular masses and *over there* pro-capital economic functions. All measures taken by the capitalist State, even those imposed by the popular masses, are in the last analysis inserted in a pro-capitalist strategy or are compatible with the expanded reproduction of capital." If such compatibility is not evident right away, it will become so over time, as the initial impetus of popular pressure fades and "'popular gains' can be progressively stripped of their initial content and character."[25] What political scientists have often called path dependency can be seen as this principle in action: for example, in cases where earlier compromises to extend social insurance in some partial form become obstacles to new forms of social policy, as historian Colin Gordon has shown for the politics of health care reform.[26]

Neo-institutionalism emerged in political science from a direct critical dialogue with this neo-Marxist "relative autonomy" scholarship. Its key advocates sprang up along the rightmost edge of the New Left. While there was intellectual fraternization, the neo-institutionalists were always self-consciously more politically moderate. Theda Skocpol, for example—preeminent in this milieu—was involved in civil rights and antiwar activity in the 1960s but found herself alienated by perceived excesses of radical movements. As early as 1973, she was developing a critique of Moore, her doctoral advisor, for his Marxist emphasis on the social determination of political outcomes, arguing instead that states themselves could impose new socioeconomic regimes.[27] Similarly Ira Katznelson described himself as "a person who identified strongly with what, in retrospect, was the most assertively liberal moment of the New Left in struggles about racial justice and opposition to the war in Vietnam, also put off by the late-decade turn to sectarian political stringency."[28] Neo-institutionalism articulated this disapproving response to the left turn of the late 1960s and early 1970s at the level of social theory, abstracting a way of thinking about politics generally from what historian Paul Buhle later described as the normative distinction between the "good sixties" and the "bad sixties."[29]

The radical turn at the end of the decade developed in reaction to the failure of mass mobilizations to end the war or dislodge the power elite from its perch. The response on the radicalizing Left was to deduce that such a resistant ruling bloc must be at some level incapable of adjusting, a problem which called for a structural explanation and a revolutionary solution. But such a solution was not forthcoming. In reaction to the failure of revolutionary politics, institutionalists then argued that there exists no certain correspondence between class interest on one side and state formation on the other. States behave how they do because of who has power within them, not because of the structure of society: understanding state behavior demands more specific political analysis.

Neo-institutionalism itself was the product of institutional support, having been incubated by the Committee on States and Social Structures, a project with the Social Science Research Council (SSRC) led by Skocpol, Dietrich Rueschemeyer, and Peter Evans beginning from 1979. As Rafael Khachaturian demonstrates, drawing on research in the SSRC archives, the committee began its life in direct conversation with neo-Marxism: Katznelson was a relatively unambiguous inheritor and participant in this tradition across the 1970s, and Skocpol was certainly in conversation with it. But the connection broke in the 1980s. Khachaturian observes in the emerging emphasis on autonomous state action a "defense of the ongoing role of public institutions" in the dawning neoliberal moment.[30] This context helps explain the enormous resonance of the two volumes produced by this project, *Bringing the State Back In*, which served as neo-institutionalism's collective manifesto, and *The Political Power of Economic Ideas*, which marked the launch of the "varieties of capitalism" school of comparative politics—reiterating the idea, and for some, the promise, that states could direct economies rather than the other way around.[31]

This mode of analysis enabled an account of policy change as the result of political ideology and organization rather than social processes. Analyzing the mixed outcomes of the first New Deal, for example, Skocpol and her co-author Kenneth Finegold emphasized uneven state capacity over social causes, enjoining that "we must go beyond the social-determinist proclivities of conventional pluralism and conventional Marxism alike."[32] In retrospect, we can see how this intervention presents a dispute over rhetorical emphasis and analytic scale as a more totalizing social theory: this maneuver is what marks it as a political intervention at the level of social theory.

In this case, Skocpol and Finegold attribute the differential outcomes of first New Deal policies to the greater state capacity of the federal government in the agricultural arena than the industrial. But why did the federal government have greater capacity for the regulation of agriculture? The article presents a litany of specific events that had strengthened the Department of Agriculture over preceding decades, but analytically this presentation only begs the question: we still see only how, not why. The accumulation of such occurrences is not explored from any higher position of abstraction. Doing so would compel the question of why agricultural problems and interests in general became so deeply lodged in state institutions. And this question would point ultimately back to some form of social explanation, presumably related to the class interests of farmers.[33]

In fact, however, such an insight was available already in Marxist historiography. In his early 1980s essays in *New Left Review*, for instance,

Mike Davis had argued, "The existence in the United States of a numerically dominant class of small capitalist farmers... provided secure social anchorage for an explicitly bourgeois politics celebrating the sanctity of private property and the virtue of capital accumulation." This secure social anchorage for bourgeois politics was, he argues, ultimately decisive for the failed social democracy of the New Deal.[34] The significance is not that Davis is right and Skocpol and Finegold are wrong; it is that the institutionalist empirical claim does not sustain the methodological intervention, because the same empirical insight can be pointed in either direction theoretically.

Skocpol and Finegold obliquely acknowledge this problem when they pursue their methodological claim—that "conventional pluralism" and "conventional Marxism" are unable to "directly explain" the result in question. "Conventional" and "directly" smuggle in an unstated and undefended argument about the proper scale of inquiry and form of empirical presentation at which a political explanation becomes satisfactory. While the empirical, substantive argument about the first New Deal does not rest on this undefended methodological argument, the accompanying theoretical intervention, regarding how to think about the state more generally, rests on it entirely.[35]

If direct causation cannot be shown between the economic interest of a social class and the transformation of a state institution, then in the neo-institutionalist account, a class effect cannot be claimed: Marxist causality is disproven. As Skocpol put it on another occasion, "Political outcomes are attributed [by Marxist theory] to the abstract needs of the capitalist system, or to the will of the dominant class, or to the naked political side-effects of working-class struggles."[36] This maneuver defines Marxism down into implausibility, while claiming any explanation that is more complex and indeterminate as proof for neo-institutionalism. Skocpol eventually indirectly acknowledged this pattern in her work by revising the name of her approach from "state-centric" to the vaguer "polity-centric," broadening the concept to include society—an unacknowledged partial concession of the fundamental theoretical issue.[37]

Institutionalism, that is, represented a political program as well as an intellectual one, and it maneuvered and compromised to advance that program. In doing so, it was not unique. All intellectual programs embody some politics of method and construct coalitions around themselves with uneasiness and instrumentality on their margins. By these compromises, staged between Marx and Weber theoretically and the New Left and the Democratic Party politically, institutionalists accomplished a scholarly sea change. They insisted that the state had to be understood empirically, not abstractly. And this the Marxists had bothered to do only intermittently—rarely filling in the mediating empirical layers between the ultimate causal power of class forces and the messy reality of governance. In principle, as Katznelson observed in 1981, this rapprochement should have posed no conceptual problem for neo-Marxism: the whole thrust of "relative autonomy" after all was to allow for particular and contingent episodes of struggle out of which hegemony arises as an effect.[38] Few would argue that this process could be understood only in the abstract, even if in practice Marxist state theory was too rarely an empirical affair. Institutionalism bent the stick the other way and insisted that state formation could only be understood in its specifics. In this sense, there was perhaps an available common ground in the late 1970s and 1980s, which was despoiled by the polemical polarization of the field of debate.

Sharp distinctions against proximate rivals are often useful in building influence for a new program. And institutionalism sought intellectual and political influence simultaneously. Indeed, its express content was the proposition that liberalism succeeds politically when professional producers of liberal ideas—that is, liberal professors—are listened to in the public sphere. The political effect of the theoretical intervention in the end was to confront the missing mass base for left-wing politics, by arguing for shedding connections to problematic social-movement allies in favor of a wider but shallower connection to a popular majority that could install liberal experts into power.

By the mid-1990s, the faction that institutionalist scholars assembled, encompassing historians as well as social scientists, found an alignment with intellectuals and policy entrepreneurs on the left wing of the Democratic Party policy apparatus. Particularly after they lost their struggle within the Clinton administration to the finance-aligned Treasury, this latter group—advocates of industrial policy, market regulation, and managed globalization—discovered the institutionalists as a possible source for deeper thinking about how states could direct markets and push back neoliberalism.[39]

Free mingling went on over the 1990s between the ascendant progressive social scientists and the defeated progressive policymakers. The *American Prospect*, the public home for this interchange, was founded in 1990, distinguishing its position from both conservative and left-wing critiques of reform. "Our view is different," the founders declared. "We look on the capacities of democratic government and public deliberation with neither faith nor contempt, but rather a conviction that they are worth the struggle: we have no alternative but to make them work."[40] Core personnel—Robert Kuttner, Paul Starr, Robert Reich, William Julius Wilson, Alan Brinkley, Todd Gitlin—generally shared the critique of the New Left's betrayal of a vision of the common good in favor of parochial sectarianism. (Kuttner, for example, broke the 1960s down into a "sweet, idealistic part" and then later "acid trips and nihilism."[41]) Their program rested on the idea that a political opening existed for a new liberal politics. They identified neoliberalism as a bad idea rather than a structural dynamic, and hoped the Reagan-Bush years might prove an aberration. Their politics aimed to step into this gap, to apply the progressive spirit to a new moment. The return of Democrats to power in the Clinton administration itself revealed the possibility of an alternative: Clinton himself seemed attuned to a communitarian, neo-Progressive politics.[42]

In 1996, this alliance was consummated at a conference in rural Virginia, organized by Skocpol and Stanley Greenberg. Greenberg, a political scientist turned pollster, was the campaign politico among the defeated left wing of the Clinton administration (as described in Timothy Shenk's chapter in this volume). His strategic proposal demanded that the Democrats "rediscover broad-based social policy that sends a larger message: Democrats are for 'everybody,' not just the 'have-nots.'"[43]

In this communitarian spirit, the 1996 gathering endorsed welfare reform and the 1990s crackdown on crime, on the theory that such measures would bring Democrats into alignment with popular common sense and sever ties to unpopular "special interests." At the same time, they wished to rebuild the labor movement and regulate campaign finance. The congregants, who included many of the stars of the world of the *American Prospect* and the new institutionalism, shared the view of the Democratic Leadership Council that Republican ascent was due to backlash against the excessive power of parochial narrow interests on the left, even if they preferred different policy responses. To achieve progressive political change, they reasoned, Democrats first needed to win.[44]

The Social History Connection

It was to this intellectual and political formation that numerous social historians looked to resolve their crisis in the 1990s. Alan Brinkley himself provides an excellent example: his first book moved to Americanize the insights of European social history, rescuing Charles Coughlin, Francis Townsend, and Huey Long from the enormous condescension of posterity; he cites E. P. Thompson and Eric Hobsbawm in his third footnote.[45] His turn to more methodologically state-centric political history in his contribution to *The Rise and Fall of the New Deal Order*, his 1994 essay on conservatism, and then in *The End of Reform* marks this transition perfectly, and indeed Brinkley would be a founding board member of the *American Prospect* and a participant in the 1996 Virginia conference.[46]

The paradoxes of this choice, exemplified by Brinkley but made by many social historians, appear right on the surface. One tradition, derived ultimately from Marxism, emphasizes the necessity of social conflict as the essence of democratic life and engine of political change; its heroes are rebels and agitators. The other, arising from liberal reaction against the excesses of radical politics, emphasizes the possibility of a consensual common good and the necessity of suppressing extremist political demands of unpopular minorities.

And yet these positions turned out not to be so far apart; something clicked. First, of course, there was the political disorientation on the academic Left and the evident need for rethinking. Even at the beginning of the 1980s, complaints had arisen from within or nearby social history that it ignored politics.[47] By the 1990s, the crisis of traditional forms of class analysis was a topic of constant discussion.[48] "All too often, the 'new' labor history exaggerated the power of working people and sentimentalized their subcultures," wrote Melvyn Dubofsky in 1994. "The stress on the private rather than the public, the cultural rather than the political, the discursive rather than the policy-making aspects of the past has made it more difficult for us." Although social historians proceeded with hesitation—Dubofsky for example insisted that the state "did not act autonomously"—institutionalism still offered something attractive: a way to imagine egalitarian political advance without bringing the arduous sequence of class formation to completion.[49]

One can see this unequal but cooperative relationship negotiated within the pages of the classic collection *The Rise and Fall of the New Deal Order, 1930–1980*. In an intellectual case of ontogeny recapitulating phylogeny, the volume rehearses the entire arc from social history to institutionalism: its early chapters, drawing mainly from labor history and neo-Marxism, are heavily dependent on social analysis to explain the rise of the New Deal. Its middle—beginning with Alan Brinkley's preview of *The End of Reform*—turns more to institutional explanations of the New Deal order's limits: Brinkley's account pivots on maneuvering within networks of policy thinkers and entrepreneurs, for example. Katznelson then infers the failure of the Great Society from the limits described by Brinkley. This collective account remains critical of liberalism, but the method of the critique has shifted. By the end of the book, Michael Kazin, Maurice Isserman, Jonathan Rieder, and Thomas Byrne Edsall are arguing that the rise of a new, culturally liberal elite faction within the Democratic Party, aligned with an unpopular underclass, has opened the way for the politics of backlash. By the 1990s, the project was to figure out how Democrats could stop the bleeding. Altogether, the volume both announced a consolidated consensus and inaugurated a distinction: Marxism for back then, liberalism for right now.

Electing Democrats was easier, after all, than organizing millions. It happened a little less than half the time, whereas the CIO had only happened once and had required the Great Depression. The contingency of the crash itself became an increasingly important source of explanation for the New Deal, which began to look anomalous rather than structural. "These transforming events," as David Brody wrote of the New Deal in *Dissent* in 1991, "were not of labor's making. Nor can we expect that they will be when—if—another historic moment like the 1930s arrives." (The next article in the issue was by Robert Reich, on the subject of workforce development.)[50]

Unnoticed congruency occurred at the theoretical level as well. Social history's theoretical wellspring had been humanist Marxism, which emphasized agency and lacked a theory of the state—rather than the anti-humanist structural Marxism, out of which most state theory arose. In an abstract way, social historians and institutionalists even tacitly shared a concept of how historical events happen: agents, whether revolutionary agitators or skilled bureaucrats, think and then act upon their thoughts. States must "puzzle before they power," in the famous formulation of political scientist Hugh Heclo, quoted ubiquitously in neo-institutionalist political science.[51] Oppressed social groups must similarly develop consciousness of their situation in order to contribute "by conscious efforts, to the making of history," as E. P. Thompson put it.[52] While structural explanation emphasizes the fragmentary, partial nature of individual consciousness and its complex, incidental relation to historical outcomes, humanism prefers to see actors making choices and pursuing goals deliberately. We thus find Thompson and Skocpol on the same side of this distinction.

Finally, the relative recency of the decline of labor and liberalism meant that these processes were barely subjects of social history by the 1990s. They were ongoing, and in this sense they remained the province of social science. It was thus difficult for social historians to answer the challenge by means of their characteristic maneuver—the unearthing of overlooked sources of popular agency. If possibility was to be found, it was going to have to come from more traditional sources in the political process.

This new alignment proved generative very quickly. As Gary Gerstle narrates the 1996 founding of the "Politics and Society in

Twentieth-Century America" series at Princeton University Press, "Our interest in power meant that we were ourselves political historians of a sort. But only in the 1990s did we begin to think of ourselves in such terms."[53] In much of the work that resulted, the institutionalist-social history axis was an explicit influence. Margot Canaday, for example, writes in *The Straight State*, "Ignoring the state is less of an option than it once was, largely because social scientists working outside of history have made the case for its significance so powerfully."[54]

One common expression of this influence was methodological. Many of the resulting studies focused on a federal agency: the Federal Civil Defense Administration was at the heart of Laura McEnaney's *Civil Defense Begins at Home*; the Office of Price Administration the same for Meg Jacobs's *Pocketbook Politics*; the Immigration and Naturalization Service for Mae Ngai's *Impossible Subjects*; the Committee on Economic Security and then the Social Security Board in Jennifer Klein's *For All These Rights*.[55] Such studies all made broader arguments based on wide and deep research, but their core method was close examination of bureaucracy—similar to the role that community studies had played for social history a generation earlier.

Although in some sense institutionalism mastered social history, this resulting body of historical inquiry has not straightforwardly replicated neo-institutionalism's own precepts. At the analytic level, most such scholarship does treat social actors, rather than state actors, as prime movers: capital or labor or social movements, or the struggles among them. This approach marks a significant departure from institutionalism in its uncompromised form. At the same time, however, bureaucracy is the primary object of attention. In this approach, state institutions become the medium where more fundamental causal forces make themselves felt and clash against each other. But institutions are not merely a passive medium like the pluralist state of old. Rather, they generate friction, inertia, and resistance (most often); unexpected alignments and opportunities (sometimes); and aleatory moments of open possibility (occasionally). Ngai's *Impossible Subjects* is replete with employers seeking to procure and dispose of labor as cheaply as possible. Yet Ngai does not reduce the development of immigration policy and bureaucracy to this source in any mechanical way, although it is in a minimal sense causally primary; nor is the operation of labor markets themselves her specific focus. Rather she traces a complex interaction between legacies of empire, racial ideologies, bureaucrats, and courts—as well as the immigrants and employers navigating them.[56] The labor movement's demand for "security" functions the same way in Klein's *For All These Rights*: it stimulates and shapes the action but does not explain every outcome.

In both cases, the requirements of capital do not directly translate into a particular historical outcome but rather set parameters that historical actors are unable to escape; in this sense, such work is far closer to Poulantzas than to Skocpol theoretically, even if it is genealogically nearer to neo-institutionalism than neo-Marxism.

Nowhere is this adaptive mutation clearer than in the historiography of mass incarceration. In the milieu of the 1990s alliance between neo-institutionalist political science and liberal policymakers, it was taken for granted that crime had to be "fought"—an uncomplicated example of what strong state capacity could do for the common interest. "Clinton proved that a Democratic leader could be tough on crime," wrote Greenberg in *The New Majority*. "That is a major accomplishment for the Democratic Party."[57] Crime is invoked in later chapters of *The Rise and Fall of the New Deal Order* exclusively in relation to its capacity to stimulate backlash. Down to the present, voices from this milieu warn against anti-police activism as likely to marginalize the Democratic Party.[58]

But the burgeoning historiography of mass incarceration indicts the Democratic Party as much as the Republicans for the construction of the carceral state, seeing this horrifying institutional growth as a bipartisan political solution to powerful social and economic forces. Deindustrialization, fiscal crisis, and the challenge to white supremacy made anti-crime politics an attractive strategy for policymakers.[59] Here the incorporation of social-historical possibilities for "bottom-up" pressures transforms not only the analysis but the political significance it carries. And here the influence of black Marxism has been most powerful, particularly the work of Ruth Wilson Gilmore: her concept of an "antistate state" is exactly a device for explaining how state institutions that prove serviceable for capital accumulation exert power and expand capacity at the expense of ones that are less so.[60] A useful comparison can be drawn to the later work of Katznelson, who also explores the racialization of social policy, but attributes it to the political limits imposed by southern Jim Crow without a clear account of how such limits relate to capitalist strategies.[61] What separates *Golden Gulag* from *Fear Itself* is the much stronger sense in the former that the state is condensing and managing social forces, rather than expressing the ideas of those who rule.

Indeed, consideration of the history of white supremacy more generally brings out how far the social history of politics has come from any institutionalist theoretical origin point—and, in this journey, how much it implicates liberalism as well as conservatism. Recent work in urban history, such as Kim Phillips-Fein's *Fear City*, Keeanga-Yamahtta Taylor's *Race for Profit*, and Destin Jenkins's *The Bonds of Inequality*, in some sense fits the institutionalist mold methodologically: all are bureaucracy studies par excellence. Yet they are quite incompatible with the institutionalist hypothesis of political, rather than social, determination. In these books the real estate and financial industries drive the action, reshaping the state around their economic interests. In all cases, it is the existing social landscape of class hierarchy and white supremacy that creates channels for capital accumulation with state assistance. Each shows that the core concept of institutionalism—state capacity—is not socially neutral. Capacity for what, and for whom? In Jenkins's analysis, for example, lenders "came to rule over cities" through the bond issues that expanded the capacity of municipal government. This rule enacted the dominance of white citizens over black. Here the hierarchy among institutions, corresponding to the hierarchy in society, returns as access to credit becomes the decisive question for local political power.[62]

Prodigal Children, Contested Inheritance

It stands to reason that mass incarceration and financialized racial and social inequality—characteristic developments of the neoliberal period—would usher the historical study of political institutions onto new ground. These phenomena epitomize how the American state is an instrument of unequal, coercive rule. Neo-institutionalism arose to explore the possibility of progressive governance in the face of the neoliberal challenge, arguing that social and economic forces did not give any irresistible logic to the upward redistribution of wealth and power. But the 2020s present a harder environment for this view than the 1980s and 1990s did, as even figures from within the orbit of neo-institutionalist political science have recognized.[63]

Within the intellectual sphere, forty years of worsening inequality have given rise to an increasingly radicalized layer of younger scholars who are disinclined to suppress the mechanisms of social determination as the special pleading of parochial interests, and unwilling to accept that what is most needed to achieve appropriate and coherent governance is for competent liberal technocrats to hold power. Mass incarceration, US imperialism, unchecked climate catastrophe, the privatized welfare state, the financialization and deregulation of the economy, the illegalization and deportation of immigrants—liberals have their fingerprints on all these phenomena, as the chapters in this volume document; just as they do on the crisis of the university itself, which has forged the unequal institutional environments in which we ourselves work. Yet the discovery of these fingerprints has itself been made possible by the fusion of institutionalist social science with social history, which generated a reservoir of historical knowledge we can draw on to explore the darker, less democratic threads of our history—and the possible social bases for resistance and transformation.

Although all historians are shaped by the moments in which we write, we first learn how to look at the world historically through the eyes of scholars shaped by an earlier moment. Tensions in historical discourse must develop from this sliding contradiction. But we can learn from this paradox if we will allow it its own historical meaning, in which we are necessarily implicated politically. Doing so is not antithetical to learning from previous generations: it is how we do it. As E. P. Thompson once observed, historians "are as much subject to our own time's formation and determinations as any others. If our work is continued by others, it will be continued differently."[64]

ACKNOWLEDGMENTS

This project emerged in the depths of the pandemic out of a deeply felt need for intellectual community. First and foremost, then, we extend our gratitude to the fantastic community of scholars who worked so hard and expertly and with such good humor through numerous rounds of discussions, workshops, and chapter revisions.

The volume itself began coming together at a conference hosted by the Jefferson Scholars Foundation at the University of Virginia in May 2022. For many of us, this was our first in-person scholarly event since the onset of the pandemic. It would be hard to overstate the sheer pleasure and intellectual energy generated by engaging together around a big table after so many months and then years of Zoom fatigue (with apologies to the few participants who needed to Zoom in!). We are tremendously grateful to Jim Sparrow, Linda Winecoff, and the entire team at the Jefferson Scholars Foundation for their generous financial and logistical support. In addition to many of the volume's contributors, we also thank others who traveled to Charlottesville and took an active and instrumental part in the workshop: Salonee Bhaman, Brian Balogh, Bobby Cervantes, Nathan Connolly, Salem Elzway, Sarah Igo, Timothy Mennel, Tej Nagaraja, Trish Kahle, Jim Sparrow, Bruce Schulman, Thomas Sugrue, and Mason Williams.

We consider ourselves lucky to have had the chance to work once again with Tim Mennel, and we are profoundly grateful for his support for our work, considerable patience, and helpful motivation. We also thank Andrea Blatz, Lindsy Rice, Jessica Wilson, and the rest of the staff at the University of Chicago Press. We are very grateful to our two anonymous reviewers, who provided extensive and trenchant comments that strengthened the volume in general and our introduction in particular.

We owe our utmost gratitude to Mason Williams for playing a critical role in the early stages of this project's development. We extend our deepest thanks to Matt Lassiter and Bryant Simon who both read versions of the introduction and offered incisive comments that led us to reconceptualize key aspects of the framework and argument. We are also grateful to Henry Tonks and Abby Whitaker as well as Penn undergrads Mica Lin-Alves, Connor Nakamura, and Sophia Rosser, all of whom read a revised introduction on a tight deadline and offered insightful comments and critiques. We thank Leo Biehl for his feedback and significant assistance with the manuscript at two critically important points in the process and Nicole Adrian for crucial last-minute help with copy edits. We remain grateful for the support of our colleagues and deans at Claremont McKenna College and the University of Pennsylvania. We are also grateful to the Penn History Department and Chair Sophia Rosenfeld for generous financial assistance, which supported the creation of the volume's index by Amanda Cox. We thank all of our students who have shaped our thinking on this topic in a number of important ways and whose frustrations and anxieties about the institutions they are inheriting underscored its stakes.

Our children—Lucinda and Margot Cebul and Gabe and June Geismer—provided distraction and humor, consistently reminded us of what matters, and even joined in on the odd Zoom meeting. Finally, we especially thank our partners, Michael Kaufman and Katherine Treppendahl, for their endless patience for our collective endeavors—especially after we swore we would never do this again. Last one, promise!

NOTES

Introduction

1. Barbara Ehrenreich and John Ehrenreich, "The Professional-Managerial Class," *Radical America* 11, no. 7 (March–April 1977): 7–31.

2. Gabriel Winant, "Professional-Managerial Chasm," *N+1*, October 10, 2019, https://www.nplusonemag.com/online-only/online-only/professional-managerial-chasm; Catherine Liu, *Virtue Hoarders: The Case against the Professional Managerial Class* (Minneapolis: University of Minnesota Press, 2021); Matt Karp, "Is This the Future Liberals Want?," *Jacobin*, October 14, 2019, https://jacobin.com/2019/10/future-liberals-want-matt-karp-populism-class-voting-democrats.

3. We have pursued these questions in our previously co-authored and solo-authored projects. See Brent Cebul, Lily Geismer, and Mason B. Williams, *Shaped by the State: Toward a New Political History of the Twentieth Century* (Chicago: University of Chicago Press, 2019); Brent Cebul, *Illusions of Progress: Business, Poverty, and Liberalism in the American Century* (Philadelphia: University of Pennsylvania Press, 2023); Lily Geismer, *Don't Blame Us: Suburban Liberals and the Transformation of the Democratic Party* (Princeton, NJ: Princeton University Press, 2015); Lily Geismer, *Left Behind: The Democrats' Failed Attempt to Solve Inequality* (New York: PublicAffairs, 2022).

4. Elizabeth Popp Berman, *Thinking Like an Economist: How Efficiency Replaced Equality in U.S. Public Policy* (Princeton, NJ: Princeton University Press, 2022): 65.

5. In 1970, there were 6,682 women enrolled in law schools against 71,336 men. American Bar Association Approved Law School Enrollment and Degrees Awarded data, https://www.americanbar.org/groups/legal_education/resources/statistics/statistics-archives/. See also Thomas D. Snyder, ed., *120 Years of American Education: A Statistical Portrait* (Washington, DC: National Center for Education Statistics, US Department of Education, Office of Educational Research and Improvement, January 1993), https://nces.ed.gov/pubs93/93442.pdf.

6. David L. Chambers et al., "The Real Impact of Eliminating Affirmative Action in American Law Schools: An Empirical Critique of Richard Sander's Study," *Stanford Law Review* 57, no. 6 (2005): 1856. For more on affirmative action and the rise of the Black professional class in the 1970s and 1980s, see William Julius Wilson, *The Truly Disadvantaged: The Inner City, the Underclass, and Public Policy* (Chicago: University of Chicago Press, 1987).

7. While there have been parallel developments on the right, more recently professional class conservatives use their elite educations and professional status as populist evidence of their experience with the corruption and rot in elite institutions of education and government. See Evan Osnos, "Rules for the Ruling Class," *New Yorker*, January 29, 2024.

8. There has emerged a vast literature on the various components of neoliberalism and its historical emergence, as well as debates among scholars on its utility for the study of United States history. From an initial emphasis on "free markets," scholars have increasingly come to see neoliberalism as capturing historically specific approaches to governance emphasizing the protection of capital accumulation from popular, democratic publics. See, for example, Angus Burgin, *The Great Persuasion: Reinventing Free Markets since the Depression* (Cambridge, MA: Harvard University Press, 2012); Wendy Brown, *Undoing the Demos: Neoliberalism's Stealth Revolution* (New York: Zone Books, 2015); Melinda Cooper, *Family Values: Between Neoliberalism and the New Social Conservatism* (Princeton, NJ: Princeton University Press, 2017); David Harvey, *A Brief History of Neoliberalism* (New York: Oxford University Press, 2005); Jaime Peck, *Constructions of Neoliberal Reason* (New York: Oxford University Press, 2010); and Quinn Slobodian, *The Globalists: The End of Empire and the Birth of Neoliberalism* (Cambridge, MA: Harvard University Press, 2018). For discussions of historians' uses of neoliberalism, see Daniel Rodgers, "The Uses and Abuses of Neoliberalism," *Dissent* (Winter 2018); responses by Julia Ott et al., "Debating the Uses and Abuses of 'Neoliberalism': Forum," *Dissent*, January 22, 2018, www.dissentmagazine.org/online_articles/debating-uses-abuses-neoliberalism-forum; and Kim Phillips-Fein, "The History of Neoliberalism," in *Shaped by the State*, ed. Cebul, Geismer, and Williams, 347–62.

9. Lawyers and economists, of course, were essential actors in the Roosevelt and Kennedy administrations' "brain trusts." See Elliot A. Rosen, "Roosevelt and the Brains Trust: An Historiographical Overview," *Political Science Quarterly* 87, no. 4 (December 1972): 531–57; Robert Dallek, *Camelot's Court: Inside the Kennedy White House* (New York: HarperCollins, 2013).

10. On race and the concept of electoral capture, see especially Paul Frymer, *Uneasy Alliances: Race and Party Competition in America* (Princeton, NJ: Princeton University Press, 1999); Robert O. Self, "The Reagan Devolution: Movement Conservatives and the Right's Days of Rage, 1988–1994," in *Recapturing the Oval Office: New Historical Approaches to the American Presidency*, ed. Brian Balogh and Bruce J. Schulman (Ithaca, NY: Cornell University Press, 2015): 75–92. Recent victories such as *Dobbs* are the result, in effect, of decades of evangelical and Catholic conservative institution building that has, in effect, enabled the antiabortion Right to capture the Republican Party, a state of affairs further enabled by minoritarian constitutional structures such as the Electoral College, the Supreme Court, the Senate, and partisan gerrymandering. See Mary Ziegler, *Dollars for Life: The Anti-Abortion Movement and the Fall of the Republican Establishment* (New Haven, CT: Yale University Press, 2022). On the nationalization of US politics, see Daniel J. Hopkins, *The Increasingly United States: How and Why American Political Behavior Nationalized* (Chicago: University of Chicago Press, 2018).

11. According to the Bureau of Labor Statistics, professionals compose nearly a quarter of today's workforce—more than tripling their share of the labor force in the 1950s. "Household Data Annual Averages: Employed Persons by Detailed Occupation, Sex, Race, and Hispanic or Latino Ethnicity," Bureau of Labor Statistics, detailed occupation statistics tables, 2023, https://www.bls.gov/cps/cpsaat11.pdf; and John B. Judis and Ruy

Teixeira, *Where Have All the Democrats Gone: The Soul of the Party in the Age of Extremes* (New York: Henry Holt and Company, 2023): 19.

12. See, for instance, Amanda Seitz, "Majority of Americans Unhappy with Health Care System: AP- NORC Poll," *PBS NewsHour*, September 12, 2022, https://www.pbs.org/newshour/politics/majority-of-americans-unhappy-with-health-care-system-ap-norc-poll; "In Depth: Guns," Gallup, October 2, 2023, https://news.gallup.com/poll/1645/guns.aspx; Gregory Svirnovskiy, "Paid Leave Is Incredibly Popular—Even with Republicans," *Vox*, June 7, 2021, https://www.vox.com/2021/6/7/22380427/poll-paid-leave-popular-democrats-republicans-covid-19; Lydia Saad, "A Seven-Year Stretch of Elevated Environmental Concern," Gallup, April 5, 2022, https://news.gallup.com/poll/391547/seven-year-stretch-elevated-environmental-concern.aspx.

13. Eli Yokley, "America Has Become Less Liberal but Not Necessarily More Conservative," *Morning Consult*, August 18, 2022, https://morningconsult.com/2022/08/18/america-ideology-less-liberal-but-not-necessarily-more-conservative/.

14. See for example, Jonathan Cohn, *The Ten Year War: Obamacare and the Unfinished Crusade for Universal Coverage* (New York: St. Martin's Press, 2021); Daniel Béland, Philip Rocco, and Alex Waddan, *Obamacare Wars: Federalism, State Politics, and the Affordable Care Act* (Lawrence: University Press of Kansas, 2023); Barack Obama, *A Promised Land* (New York: Crown, 2020); Theda Skocpol and Vanessa Williamson, *The Tea Party and the Remaking of American Conservatism* (New York: Oxford University Press, 2012).

15. On liberal governance and the relationship between state and non-state actors see Cebul, *Illusions of Progress*, 9–10. The governing techniques and orientations toward politics explored in this volume are necessarily topical rather than comprehensive, though the influence of professional, technocratic governance extends well beyond policy areas and political issues explored here. On the evolution of liberalism in social and political domains less centrally covered in this volume, including mass incarceration and policing, second-wave feminism, environmentalism, the global war on terror, and industrial policy, see Elizabeth Hinton, *From the War on Poverty to the War on Crime* (Cambridge, MA: Harvard University Press, 2016); Marisa Chappell, *The War on Welfare: Family, Poverty, and Politics in Modern America* (Philadelphia: University of Pennsylvania Press, 2010); Katherine Turk, *The Women of NOW: How Feminists Built an Organization that Transformed America* (New York: Farrar, Straus and Giroux, 2023); Samuel P. Hays, *A History of Environmental Politics since 1945* (Pittsburgh, PA: University of Pittsburgh Press, 2000); Samuel Moyn, *Humane: How the United States Abandoned Peace and Reinvented War* (New York: Farrar, Straus and Giroux, 2021); Spencer Ackerman, *Reign of Terror: How the 9/11 Era Destabilized America and Produced Trump* (New York: Viking, 2021); Cebul, *Illusions of Progress*; and Nelson Lichtenstein and Judith Stein, *A Fabulous Failure: The Clinton Presidency and the Transformation of American Capitalism* (Princeton, NJ: Princeton University Press, 2023).We also do not focus in depth on the internal dynamics and structure of the Democratic Party itself. For more on the Democrats as a party, see Daniel Schlozman and Sam Rosenfeld, *The Hollow Parties: The Many Pasts and Disordered Present of American Politics* (Princeton, NJ: Princeton University Press, 2024) and Michael Kazin, *What It Took to Win: A History of the Democratic Party* (New York: Farrar, Straus and Giroux, 2022).

16. On these orientations toward policy design and the challenges they pose for electoral and constitutional democracy, see Suzanne Mettler, *The Submerged State: How Invisible Government Policies Undermine American Democracy* (Chicago: University of Chicago Press, 2011); and Karen Orren and Stephen Skowronek, *The Policy State: An*

American Dilemma (Cambridge, MA: Harvard University Press, 2017). See also Nicholas Bagley, "The Procedure Fetish," *Michigan Law Review* 118, no. 345 (2019).

17. Ehrenreich and Ehrenreich, "Professional-Managerial Class," 26.

18. Ehrenreich and Ehrenreich, "Professional-Managerial Class," 26.

19. In her state-of-the-field essay on US conservatism, Kim Phillips-Fein identified the need to explore the "emotional tone" of the conservative movement, a fruitful site of political-cultural investigation for historians of liberalism as well. See Kim Phillips-Fein, "Conservatism: A State of the Field," *Journal of American History* 98, no. 3 (2011): 723–43, at 736. This has also been central in the work of Thomas Frank. See Thomas Frank, *What's the Matter with Kansas: How Conservatives Won the Heart of America* (New York: Metropolitan Books, 2004); Thomas Frank, *Listen Liberal: Or, What Ever Happened to the Party of the People?* (New York: Metropolitan Books, 2016).

20. Daniel Rodgers, *Atlantic Crossings: Social Politics in a Progressive Age* (Cambridge, MA: Harvard University Press, 1998); Daniel Amsterdam, *Roaring Metropolis: Businessman's Campaign for a Civic Welfare State* (Philadelphia: University of Pennsylvania Press, 2016); Kenneth Feingold, *Experts and Politicians: Reform Challenges to Machine Politics in New York, Cleveland, and Chicago* (Princeton, NJ: Princeton University Press, 1995).

21. Walter Lippman, *Drift and Mastery: An Attempt to Diagnose the Current Unrest* (New York: M. Kennerly, 1914): 83 and 151.

22. David Brooks, "What If We're the Bad Guys Here?" *New York Times*, August 2, 2023.

23. Where political historians *did* train their attention on social politics, it was largely to understand the development of modern conservatism. See, for instance, Lisa McGirr, *Suburban Warriors: The Origins of the New American Right* (Princeton, NJ: Princeton University Press, 2001).

24. On these dynamics, see Michael Kazin, *American Dreamers: How the Left Changed the Nation* (New York: Knopf, 2011); and Douglas C. Rossinow, *Visions of Progress: The Left-Liberal Tradition in America* (Philadelphia: University of Pennsylvania Press, 2007).

25. Samuel Moyn, *Liberalism against Itself: Cold War Intellectuals and the Making of Our Times* (New Haven, CT: Yale University Press, 2023): 2–3.

26. While attempts at synthesis have been rare, they have also been notably ambivalent about liberalism's core commitments. Observers of twentieth-century politics have regularly described liberalism as "protean" and "plastic," emphasized its "capaciousness," and called it a "paradox" riven by "contradiction." See Gary Gerstle, "The Protean Character of American Liberalism," *American Historical Review* 99, no. 4 (October 1994): 1043–73; Robert Self, *American Babylon: Race and the Struggle for Postwar Oakland* (Princeton, NJ: Princeton University Press, 2003): 13–14.

27. Without downplaying the significance of the Wagner Act's enshrinement of labor's right to collectively bargain, that act, for instance, delegated the possibilities of improved wages and benefits to the vicissitudes of particular market formations and to the ability of workers to overcome obstruction by management and capital. See Gabriel Winant, *The Next Shift: The Fall of Industry and the Rise of Health Care in Rust Belt America* (Cambridge, MA: Harvard University Press, 2021) and Nelson Lichtenstein, *State of the Union: A Century of American Labor* (Princeton, NJ: Princeton University Press, 2002). Also delegated to market structures, in this case bond markets, was funding for "public" housing projects and a significant swathe of ostensibly public goods, from schools to critical infrastructure to the fiscal solvency of municipal governments. See, for instance, Michael R. Glass and Sean Vanatta, "The Frail Bonds of Liberalism: Pensions, Schools, and the

Unraveling of Fiscal Mutualism in Postwar New York," *Capitalism: A Journal of History and Economics* 2, no. 2 (2021): 427–72; Destin Jenkins, *The Bonds of Inequality: Debt and the Making of the American City* (Chicago: University of Chicago Press, 2021); Cebul, *Illusions of Progress*. Such ascriptive hierarchies were reinforced and created in other ways, too: white, male breadwinning was an essential component of the era's more equitable distribution of wealth, which simultaneously rendered invisible women's household labor upon which the entire system depended. In the case of LGBTQ citizens, the Cold War state was responsible for creating exclusionary practices that simultaneously rendered these subjects highly exploitable in private employment markets as well. See Alice Kessler-Harris, *In Search of Equity: Women, Men and the Quest for Economic Citizenship in Twentieth Century America* (New York: Oxford University Press, 2001); Robert Self, *All in the Family: The Realignment of American Democracy since the 1960s* (New York: Hill and Wang, 2013); Margot Canaday, *The Straight State: Sexuality and Citizenship in Twentieth-Century America* (Princeton, NJ: Princeton University Press, 2009); Margot Canaday, *Queer Career: Sexuality and Work in Modern America* (Princeton, NJ: Princeton University Press, 2023). One scholar suggests that the period of exceptional liberal governance in the New Deal rested upon a period of sharply limited immigration, which made exceptions for seasonal migration, the oversight of which liberals largely delegated to agricultural and other business interests. Jefferson Cowie, *The Great Exception: The New Deal and the Limits of American Politics* (Princeton, NJ: Princeton University Press, 2016). On New Deal liberalism and immigration, see Mae Ngai, *Impossible Subjects: Illegal Aliens and the Making of Modern America* (Princeton, NJ: Princeton University Press, 2004); Julie Wiese, *Corazón de Dixie: Mexicanos in the U.S. South since 1910* (Chapel Hill: University of North Carolina Press, 2015).

28. On the literature on corporate liberalism, see Ellis W. Hawley, "The Discovery and Study of a 'Corporate Liberalism,'" *Business History Review* 52, no. 3 (Autumn 1978): 209–320. See also Gerald Berk, "Corporate Liberalism Reconsidered: A Review Essay," *Journal of Policy History* 3, no. 1 (January 1991): 70–84.

29. On the "warfare state," see especially Michael J. Hogan, *A Cross of Iron: Harry S. Truman and the Origins of the National Security State, 1945–1954* (New York: Cambridge University Press, 2000); C. Wright Mills, *The Power Elite* (New York: Oxford University Press, [1956] 2000); and James T. Sparrow, *Warfare State: World War II Americans and the Age of Big Government* (New York: Oxford University Press, 2011).

30. Some scholars have identified the social unrest produced by such "contradictions" as responsible for New Deal or mid-century liberalism's collapse and demise—insinuating, in some instances, that minority-rights movements were ultimately the cause of liberalism's collapsing fortunes. On certain limitations of this framework, see Sophia Lee, "Rights in the New Deal Order and Beyond," in *Beyond the New Deal Order: U.S. Politics from the Great Depression to the Great Recession*, ed. Gary Gerstle, Nelson Lichtenstein, and Alice O'Connor (Philadelphia: University of Pennsylvania Press, 2019): 110–23.

31. For two paradigmatic examinations of how mid-century liberalism gave rise to each of these movements, see Thomas J. Sugrue, *Origins of the Urban Crisis Race and Inequality in Postwar Detroit* (Princeton, NJ: Princeton University Press, 1996); and Self, *American Babylon*.

32. Schlesinger certainly disparaged conservatives for being hopelessly out of step with the times. But he also fired caustic barbs at the Left, whose "progressivism," he charged in his seminal volume *The Vital Center: The Politics of Freedom* (1949), reflected a naïve and "sentimental belief in progress" that risked a return to the gulags or

the gas chambers. Arthur M. Schlesinger Jr., *The Vital Center: The Politics of Freedom* (Boston, MA: Houghton Mifflin, Co., 1949): 38. Cold War liberalism has been the subject of recent debate and reappraisal. See, for instance, Joshua L. Cherniss, *Liberalism in Dark Times: The Liberal Ethos in the Twentieth Century* (Princeton, NJ: Princeton University Press, 2011); Katrina Forrester, *In the Shadow of Justice: Postwar Liberalism and the Remaking of Political Philosophy* (Princeton, NJ: Princeton University Press, 2019); and Moyn, *Liberalism against Itself*. The anti-communism of liberals such as Schlesinger also abetted reactionary purges of leftists and non-heteronormative citizens from the civil service. See, especially, Landon R. Y. Storrs, *The Second Red Scare and the Unmaking of the New Deal Left* (Princeton, NJ: Princeton University Press, 2012); David K. Johnson, *The Lavender Scare: The Cold War Persecution of Gays and Lesbians in the Federal Government* (Chicago: University of Chicago Press, 2004); and Canaday, *Straight State*.

33. See Karen Tani, *States of Dependency: Welfare, Rights, and American Governance, 1935–1972* (Cambridge: Cambridge University Press, 2016); and Laura Kalman, *The Strange Career of Legal Liberalism* (New Haven, CT: Yale University Press, 1996).

34. On these political, intellectual, administrative, and philosophical developments, see especially S. M. Amadae, *Rationalizing Capitalist Democracy: The Cold War Origins of Rational Choice Liberalism* (Chicago: University of Chicago Press, 2003): "scrupulous individualism" at 4; Brian Balogh, *Chain Reaction: Expert Debate and Public Participation in American Commercial Nuclear Power, 1945–1975* (New York: Cambridge University Press, 1991); David Ciepley, *Liberalism in the Shadow of Totalitarianism* (Cambridge, MA: Harvard University Press, 2007); Reuel Schiller, *Forging Rivals: Race, Class, Law, and the Collapse of Postwar Liberalism* (New York: Cambridge University Press, 2015); and Forrester, *In the Shadow of Justice*. On mid-century liberalism and the politics of administrative procedure and regulatory restraint, see especially Joanna Grisinger, *The Unwieldy American State: Administrative Politics since the New Deal* (New York: Cambridge University Press, 2012); and Anne Kornhauser, *Debating the American State: Liberal Anxieties and the New Leviathan* (Philadelphia: University of Pennsylvania Press, 2015). On the relationship between the therapeutic ethos, state development, and social policy, see Ellen Herman, *The Romance of American Psychology: Political Culture in an Age of Experts* (Berkeley: University of California Press, 1994); Andrew Polsky, *The Rise of the Therapeutic State* (Princeton, NJ: Princeton University Press, 1991); Daryl Michael Scott, *Contempt and Pity: Social Policy and the Image of the Damaged Black Psyche* (Chapel Hill: University of North Carolina Press, 1997); Alice O'Connor, *Poverty Knowledge: Social Science, Social Policy and the Poor in Twentieth Century U.S. History* (Princeton, NJ: Princeton University Press, 2001). On the Progressive Era and ideas about efficiency and elite, expert leadership that anticipated later forms of technocratic liberalism, see Feingold, *Experts and Politicians*; Rodgers, *Atlantic Crossings*; Jennifer K. Alexander, *The Mantra of Efficiency: From Waterwheel to Social Control* (Baltimore, MD: Johns Hopkins University Press, 2008).

35. Legal scholar William Forbath has argued that perhaps mid-century liberalism's most enduring "legacy enshrine[d] the New Deal's expansion of national power, but not the new rights of national citizenship that warranted the expansion." See William E. Forbath, "The New Deal Constitution in Exile," *Duke Law Journal* 51, no. 165 (2001). See also Sparrow, *Warfare State*; Samuel Moyn, "The Second Bill of Rights: A Reconsideration," in *Human Rights, Democracy, and Legitimacy in a World of Disaster*, ed. Silja Voeneky and Gerald L. Neuman (New York: Cambridge University Press, 2018): 111–36.

36. Rodgers, *Atlantic Crossings*. Contemporary liberals' ambivalence about popular democratic engagement suggests the importance of future scholarship on democratic and civic capacity and their erosion—particularly as a key dynamic associated with neoliberalization. See, for instance, Theda Skocpol, *Diminished Democracy: From Membership to Management in American Civic Life* (Norman: University of Oklahoma Press, 2003); Caroline Lee, Michael McQuarrie, and Edward T. Walker, eds., *Democratizing Inequalities: Dilemmas of the New Public Participation* (New York: NYU Press, 2015). On popular democratic capacities in an earlier era, see Johann M. Neem, "Two Approaches to Democratization: Engagement versus Capacity," in *Practicing Democracy: Popular Politics in the United States from the Constitution to the Civil War*, ed. Daniel Peart and Adam I. P. Smith (Charlottesville: University of Virginia Press, 2015).

37. On neoliberalism and the eclipse of the welfare state, see Amy Zanoni, "Remembering Welfare as We Knew It: Understanding Neoliberalism through Histories of Welfare," *Journal of Policy History* 35, no. 1 (January 2023): 118–58.

38. On these dynamics, see Margaret O'Mara, *Cities of Knowledge: Cold War Science and the Search for the Next Silicon Valley* (Princeton, NJ: Princeton University Press, 2004); Fred Turner, *From Counterculture to Cyberculture: Stewart Brand, the Whole Earth Network, and the Rise of Digital Utopianism* (Chicago: University of Chicago Press, 2006); Fred Turner, *The Democratic Surround: Multimedia and American Liberalism from World War II to the Psychedelic Sixties* (Chicago: University of Chicago Press, 2013); Margaret O'Mara, *The Code: Silicon Valley and the Remaking of America* (New York: Penguin, 2019).

39. On liberals, deregulation, and the emergence of "self-regulation" within the financial sector, see Timothy A. Canova, "The Legacy of the Clinton Bubble," *Dissent* (Summer 2008).

40. See, for instance, Kenneth S. Baer, *Reinventing Democrats: The Politics of Liberalism from Reagan to Clinton* (Lawrence: University Press of Kansas, 2000); David Osborne and Ted Gaebler, *Reinventing Government: How the Entrepreneurial Spirit Is Reinventing the Public Sector* (Boston, MA: Addison-Wesley Publishing Company, 1992); Randall Rothenberg, *The Neoliberals: Creating the New American Politics* (New York: Simon and Schuster, 1984); E. J. Dionne, *Why Americans Hate Politics* (New York: Simon and Schuster, 1991). We are grateful to Mason Williams for these points.

41. For more on this practice, see Geismer, *Left Behind*, 19–26.

42. For the classic example of the Democrats' rightward shift, see Thomas Ferguson and Joel Rogers, *Right Turn: The Decline of the Democrats and the Future of American Politics* (New York: Hill and Wang, 1987).

43. Phillips-Fein, "Conservatism: A State of the Field." In the last decade, scholars of the right have turned their attention to its extreme and radical fringes. See for example, Kathleen Belew, *Bring the War Home: The White Power Movement and Paramilitary America* (Cambridge, MA: Harvard University Press, 2018); John S. Huntington, *Far-Right Vanguard: The Radical Roots of Modern Conservatism* (Philadelphia: University of Pennsylvania Press, 2021).

44. This argument builds on one of the key claims of our earlier edited volume; see Cebul, Geismer, and Williams, eds., *Shaped by the State*.

45. These developments have been reflected in other developed democracies, suggesting that deeper structural, economic, and generational forces have cut across and remade Western democratic capitalist societies. For accounts of these processes that emphasize the influence of rising professional classes, see Peter Maier, *Ruling the Void: The Hollowing of Western Democracy* (London: Verso, 2013); and Stephanie L. Mudge, *Liberalism*

Reinvented: Western Parties from Socialism to Neoliberalism (Cambridge, MA: Harvard University Press, 2018).

46. Schlesinger Jr., *Vital Center*, 48.

47. Lichtenstein and Stein, *Fabulous Failure*.

48. The classic expression of this position is E. E. Schattschneider, *Party Government* (New York: Farrar and Rinehart, 1942). See also Sam Rosenfeld, *Polarizers: Postwar Architects of Our Partisan Era* (Cambridge, MA: Harvard University Press, 2018).

Chapter One

1. See "GOP Senators Call on Sec. Tillerson to Investigate State Department Meddling," Mike Lee press release, March 14, 2017, https://www.lee.senate.gov/2017/3/gop-senators-call-on-sec-tillerson-to-investigate-state-department-meddling; and Isaac Arnsdorf, Andrew Hanna, and Kenneth Vogel, "GOP Takes Up Russia-Aligned Attack on Soros," *Politico*, March 22, 2017, https://www.politico.com/magazine/story/2017/03/george-soros-russia-republicans-214938/. Also see Emily Tamkin, *The Influence of Soros: Politics, Power, and the Struggle for Open Society* (New York: Harper, 2020): chapter 7. For Trump's final campaign ad, see "Donald Trump 'Donald Trump's Argument for America' | Campaign 2016," *Washington Post*, November 7, 2016, https://www.washingtonpost.com/video/politics/team-trump-donald-trumps-argument-for-america-campaign-2016/2016/11/06/218f32d4-a443-11e6-ba46-53db57f0e351_video.html. The Anti-Defamation League has characterized several of the attacks against Soros as peddling antisemitic tropes. See, for example, "The Antisemitism Lurking behind George Soros Conspiracy Theories," *ADL Blog*, October 11, 2018, https://www.adl.org/resources/blog/antisemitism-lurking-behind-george-soros-conspiracy-theories; and "Soros Conspiracy Theories and the Protests: A Gateway to Antisemitism," *ADL Blog*, June 2, 2020, https://www.adl.org/resources/blog/soros-conspiracy-theories-and-protests-gateway-antisemitism.

2. Nancy MacLean, *Democracy in Chains: The Deep History of the Radical Right's Stealth Plan for America* (New York: Viking, 2017); and Jane Mayer, *Dark Money: The Hidden History of the Billionaires Behind the Rise of the Radical Right* (New York: Anchor, 2016). Both books were reviewed in the *New York Times* and several other press outlets. On the Kochs' latest efforts to translate their philanthropic dollars into policy reform by capitalizing 501c4 organizations, see Matt Durot, "Charles Koch Has Given More Than $5 Billion of His Stock to Two Nonprofits," *Forbes*, October 10, 2023, https://www.forbes.com/sites/mattdurot/2023/10/10/exclusive-charles-koch-koch-industries-has-given-more-than-5-billion-of-his-koch-industries-stock-to-two-nonprofits/?sh=113386da7bd1. For campaigns against the Kochs, see Erica L. Green and Stephanie Saul, "What Charles Koch and Other Donors Got for Their Money," *New York Times*, May 5, 2018, https://www.nytimes.com/2018/05/05/us/koch-donors-george-mason.html; and John Schwartz, "Science Museum Urged to Cut Ties with Kochs," *New York Times*, March 24, 2015, https://www.nytimes.com/2015/03/24/science/science-museums-urged-to-cut-ties-with-kochs.html.

3. The formulation of twentieth-century American liberalism as an effort to balance between property rights and the public good draws on Duncan Bell, "What Is Liberalism?" *Political Theory* 42, no. 6 (December 2014): 682–715; Wendy Brown, *Regulating Aversion: Tolerance in the Age of Identity and Empire* (Princeton, NJ: Princeton University Press, 2008); Chiara Cordelli, *The Privatized State* (Princeton, NJ: Princeton University Press, 2020); Bonnie Honig, *Public Things: Democracy in Disrepair* (New York: Fordham

University Press, 2017); Laura Kalman, *The Strange Career of Legal Liberalism* (New Haven, CT: Yale University Press, 1996); John Rawls, *Political Liberalism*, expanded ed. (New York: Columbia University Press, 2005); and Michael Walzer, "The Communitarian Critique of Liberalism," *Political Theory* 18, no. 1 (February 1990): 6–23.

4. On New Deal and Great Society liberalism, see Alan Brinkley, *The End of Reform: New Deal Liberalism in Recession and War* (New York: Vintage Books, 1996); Jefferson Cowie, *The Great Exception: The New Deal and the Limits of American Politics* (Princeton, NJ: Princeton University Press, 2017); and Steve Fraser and Gary Gerstle, eds. *The Rise and Fall of the New Deal Order, 1930–1980* (Princeton, NJ: Princeton University Press, 1989).

5. On the dissolution of New Deal liberalism as fuel for what I am calling philanthropic governance, see Alan Brinkley, *Liberalism and Its Discontents* (Cambridge, MA: Harvard University Press, 1998); Angus Burgin, *The Great Depression: Reinventing Free Markets Since the Great Depression* (Cambridge, MA: Harvard University Press, 2012); Gary Gerstle, *The Rise and Fall of the Neoliberal Order: America and the World in the Free Market Era* (New York: Oxford University Press, 2022); and Kim Phillips-Fein, *Invisible Hands: The Businessmen's Crusade against the New Deal* (New York: Norton, 2010). On the financialized assumptions and structures that bolstered philanthropic governance, see Larry Bartels, *Unequal Democracy: The Political Economy of the New Gilded Age* (Princeton, NJ: Princeton University Press, 2008); Wendy Brown, *Undoing the Demos: Neoliberalism's Stealth Revolution* (New York: Zone Books, 2015); Gerald F. Davis, *Managed by the Markets: How Finance Re-Shaped America* (New York: Oxford, 2009); and Greta Krippner, *Capitalizing on Crisis: The Political Origins of the Rise of Finance* (Cambridge, MA: Harvard University Press, 2011).

6. Classic accounts of twentieth-century American liberalism generally make only cursory mention of philanthropy, usually by referring to the Ford Foundation, but offer little analysis of philanthropy as a political force. See, for example, Brinkley, *End of Reform*; Fraser and Gerstle, eds., *Rise and Fall of the New Deal Order*; and Allen Matusow, *The Unraveling of America: A History of Liberalism in the 1960s* (New York: Harper and Row, 1984). For the most comprehensive political history of philanthropy, see Olivier Zunz, *Philanthropy in America: A History* (Princeton, NJ: Princeton University Press, 2012). For two recent studies that extend Zunz's approach to more specific inquiries, see Lila Corwin Berman, *The American Jewish Philanthropic Complex: The History of a Multibillion-Dollar Institution* (Princeton, NJ: Princeton University Press, 2020); and Elisabeth Clemens, *Civic Gifts: Voluntarism and the Making of the American Nation-State* (Chicago: University of Chicago Press, 2020).

7. On the growth of American state power and the blurry lines between public and private, see Brian Balogh, *The Associational State: American Governance in the Twentieth Century* (Philadelphia: University of Pennsylvania Press, 2015); and William Novak, "The Myth of the 'Weak' American State," *American Historical Review* 113, no. 3 (June 2008): 752–72. On the importance of tracing political history beyond partisan divisions, see Matt Lassiter, "Political History beyond the Red-Blue Divide," *Journal of American History* 98, no. 3 (December 2011): 760–64. Wendy Brown's discussion of depoliticization as a mode that naturalizes power by stripping it of its history underlies this paragraph. See Wendy Brown, *Regulating Aversion: Tolerance in the Age of Identity and Empire* (Princeton, NJ: Princeton University Press, 2006): 15–18. Finally, for a discussion of the fuzziness endemic to American liberalism in the second half of the twentieth century, see Abby Whitaker, "*Sesame Street* and the Making of Fuzzy Liberalism" (PhD diss., Temple University, 2024).

8. Sarah Barringer Gordon, "The First Disestablishment: Limits on Church Power and Property Before the Civil War," *University of Pennsylvania Law Review* 162, no. 1 (December 2013): 317. Also see Jonathan Levy, "Altruism and the Origins of Nonprofit Philanthropy," in *Philanthropy in Democratic Societies: History, Institutions, Values*, ed. Rob Reich, Chiara Cordelli, and Lucy Benholz (University of Chicago Press, 2016): 28–29.

9. On global efforts, see Heather Curtis, *Holy Evangelicals: American Evangelicals and Global Aid* (Cambridge, MA: Harvard University Press, 2018): 109–20; and William Hutchison, *Errand to the World: American Protestant Thought and Foreign Missions* (Chicago: University of Chicago Press, 1987). On the expansion of benevolent work in the Progressive Era and its tie to state centralization, see Lori Ginzberg, *Women and the Work of Benevolence: Morality, Politics, and Class in the Nineteenth-Century United States* (New Haven, CT: Yale University Press, 1992); Michael McGerr, *A Fierce Discontent: The Rise and Fall of the Progressive Movement* (New York: Free Press, 2003); and Theda Skocpol, Marshall Ganz, and Ziad Munsoon, "A Nation of Organizers: The Institutional Origins of Civic Voluntarism in the United States," *American Political Science Review* 94, no. 3 (September 2000): 527–46.

10. W. Elliot Brownlee, *Federal Taxation in America: A Short History* (Cambridge: Cambridge University Press, 2004): 53–71; Vada Waters Lindsey, "The Charitable Contribution Deduction: A Historical Review and a Look to the Future," *Nebraska Law Review* 81, no. 3 (2002): 1056–96; and Ajay Mehrotra, *Making the Modern American Fiscal State: Law, Politics, and the Rise of Progressive Taxation, 1877–1929* (Cambridge: Cambridge University Press, 2013): chapter 3.

11. Rob Reich, *Just Giving: Why Philanthropy Is Failing Democracy and How It Can Do Better* (Princeton, NJ: Princeton University Press, 2018): 24. On the priorities of these longstanding American private foundations, see Inderjeet Parmar, *Foundations of the American Century: The Ford, Carnegie, and Rockefeller Foundations in the Rise of American Power* (New York: Columbia University Press, 2012).

12. Zunz, *Philanthropy in America*, 20–21.

13. On the establishment of the Social Science Research Council, see Dorothy Ross, *The Origins of American Social Science* (Cambridge: Cambridge University Press, 1990): 400–404. On Hoover and the Great Depression, see Zunz, *Philanthropy in America*, 127–28.

14. Zunz, *Philanthropy in America*, 127–28.

15. On the regressive nature of tax exemptions or deductions within a progressive system of taxation, see Stanley Surrey, "Tax Incentives as a Device for Implementing Government Policy: A Comparison with Direct Government Expenditures," *Harvard Law Review* 83, no. 4 (February 1970): 705–38.

16. See Clemens, *Civic Gifts*, 179 and 198.

17. On the philanthropic influence in New Deal health care and Social Security programs, see Jennifer Klein, *For All These Rights: Business, Labor, and the Shaping of America's Public-Private Welfare State* (Princeton, NJ: Princeton University Press, 2003): 120. On international American philanthropy, see Maribel Morey, *White Philanthropy: Carnegie Corporation's* An American Dilemma *and the Making of a White World Order* (Chapel Hill: University of North Carolina Press, 2021): especially chapter 5.

18. On the professionalization of philanthropy as early as the 1920s and 1930s, see Zunz, *Philanthropy in America*, 66. These same patterns appeared in the world of Jewish philanthropy. See Beth Wenger, "Federation Men: The Masculine World of New York

Jewish Philanthropy," *American Jewish History* 101, no. 3 (2017): 377–99. This connects to the rising cultural power of expertise and professionalization over the same period. See Sarah Igo, *The Averaged American: Surveys, Citizens, and the Making of a Mass Public* (Cambridge, MA: Harvard University Press, 2008).

19. The exact language from the hearings is described in Judith Kindell and John Francis Reilly, *Election Year Issues* (Washington, DC: Internal Revenue Service, 2002), https://www.irs.gov/pub/irs-tege/eotopic02.pdf; and see Roger Colinvaux, "The Political Speech of Charities in the Face of *Citizens United*: A Defense of Prohibition," *Case Western Reserve Law Review* 62, no. 3 (2012): 694–97 for a similar analysis. For the standard interpretation of the Johnson Amendment, see Patrick O'Daniel, "More Honored in the Breach: A Historical Perspective of the Permeable IRS Prohibition on Campaigning by Churches," *Boston College Law Review* 42 (July 2001): 733–69.

20. On congressional investigations prior to the Patman one in the 1960s, see Eleanor Brilliant, *Private Charity and Public Inquiry: A History of the Filer and Peterson Commission* (Bloomington: Indiana University Press, 2000): chapter 2; and Peter Dobkin Hall, *Inventing the Nonprofit Sector and Other Essays on Philanthropy, Voluntarism, and Nonprofit Organization* (Baltimore, MD: Johns Hopkins University Press, 1992): 66–71.

21. On the valuation of the Ford Foundation, see Karen Ferguson, *Top Down: The Ford Foundation, Black Power, and the Reinvention of Racial Liberalism* (Philadelphia: University of Pennsylvania Press, 2013): 5.

22. On Ford's international and domestic programs, see Sam Collings-Wells, "Developing Communities: The Ford Foundation and the Global Urban Crisis, 1958–66," *Journal of Global History* 16, no. 3 (November 2021): 336–54; Daniel Immerwahr, *Thinking Small: The United States and the Lure of Community Development* (Cambridge, MA: Harvard University Press, 2015): 75–77, chapter 5; Ferguson, *Top Down*, chapters 2 and 3; Alice O'Connor, "Community Action, Urban Reform, and the Fight Against Poverty: The Ford Foundation's Gray Areas Program," *Journal of Urban History* 22, no. 5 (July 1996): 586–625; and Alice O'Connor, "Foundations: Social Movements, and the Contradictions of Liberal Philanthropy," in *American Foundations: Roles and Contributions*, ed. Helmut K. Anheier and David Hammack (Washington, DC: Brookings Institution Press, 2010): 328–46. On the Ford Foundation and its connection to the CIA, see Alice O'Connor, "The Politics of Rich and Rich: Postwar Investigations of Foundations and the Rise of the Philanthropic Right," in *American Capitalism: Social Thought and Political Economy in the Twentieth Century*, ed. Nelson Lichtenstein. (Philadelphia: University of Pennsylvania Press, 2006): 230; and Zunz, *Philanthropy in America*, 151, 203.

23. On the links between the War on Poverty and foundation-assisted foreign-development programs, see Amy Offner, *Sorting Out the Mixed Economy: The Rise and Fall of Welfare and Development States in the Americas* (Princeton, NJ: Princeton University Press, 2019): chapter 6. On the rise of community development corporations and other nonprofits that absorbed federal and private charitable funds, see Claire Dunning, *Nonprofit Neighborhoods: An Urban History of Inequality and the American State* (Chicago: University of Chicago Press, 2022); Benjamin Holtzman, *The Long Crisis: New York City and the Path to Neoliberalism* (Oxford: Oxford University Press, 2021); and Andrew Morris, *The Limits of Voluntarism: Charity and Welfare from the New Deal to the Great Society* (Cambridge: Cambridge University Press, 2009).

24. Thomas Troyer, "The 1969 Private Foundation Law: Historical Perspective on Its Origins and Underpinnings," *Exempt Organization Tax Review* 27, no. 1 (2000): 52–65. On one of the most significant and novel tax strategies to emerge from the 1969 legislation,

see Lila Corwin Berman, "Donor Advised Funds in Historical Perspective," *Boston College Law Forum on Philanthropy and the Public Good* 1 (October 2015): 5–27.

25. On Patman's populism as part of the pre-1970s Democratic Party, see Matt Stoller, "How Democrats Killed Their Populist Soul," *Atlantic*, October 24, 2016, https://www.theatlantic.com/politics/archive/2016/10/how-democrats-killed-their-populist-soul/504710/.

26. For a discussion of the way that twentieth-century political orders "bend the opposition party to its will," see Gerstle, *Rise and Fall of the Neoliberal Order*, 2–3. For a history of the cultural discourse of family values and its political ramifications, see Robert Self, *All in the Family: The Realignment of American Democracy Since the 1960s* (New York: Hill and Wang, 2012). Also see Brent Cebul, Lily Geismer, and Mason B. Williams, "Beyond Red and Blue: Crisis and Continuity in Twentieth-Century U.S. Political History," in *Shaped by the State: Toward a New Political History of the Twentieth Century*, ed. Brent Cebul, Lily Geismer, and Mason B. Williams (Chicago: University of Chicago Press, 2019): 3–23.

27. Joanne Meyerowitz, *A War on Global Poverty: The Lost Promise of Redistribution and the Rise of Microcredit* (Princeton, NJ: Princeton University Press, 2021): 144.

28. For a discussion of the political nature and expansion of NGOs, see Jennifer Rubinstein, *Between Samaritans and States: The Political Ethics of Humanitarian INGOs* (Oxford: Oxford University Press, 2015); and Allison Schnable, *Amateurs without Borders: The Aspirations and Limits of Global Compassion* (Berkeley: University of California Press, 2021).

29. Meyerowitz, *War on Global Poverty*, 145.

30. For the multiple faces of America's imperial projects, which included human rights and economic projects, see Greg Grandin, *Empire's Workshop: Latin America, the United States, and the Rise of the New Imperialism* (New York: Metropolitan Books, 2006); Daniel Immerwahr, *How to Hide an Empire: A History of the Greater United States* (New York: Farrar, Straus and Giroux, 2019); and Samuel Moyn, *The Last Utopia: Human Rights in History* (Cambridge, MA: Belknap Press of Harvard University Press, 2010).

31. Meyerowitz, *War on Global Poverty*, 110–11.

32. Lily Geismer, *Left Behind: The Democrats' Failed Attempt to Solve Inequality* (New York: PublicAffairs, 2022): introduction. On the role of religious and ethnic actors in the delivery of social-welfare services, see Ram Cnaan, *The Invisible Caring Hand: American Congregations and the Provision of Welfare* (New York: New York University Press, 2002); and Axel Schaefer, *Piety and Public Funding: Evangelicals and the State in Modern America* (Philadelphia: University of Pennsylvania Press, 2012).

33. On the moderating effect philanthropy exercised over radical social movements in the civil rights era, see J. Craig Jenkins and Craig Eckert, "Channeling Black Insurgency: Elite Patronage and Professional Social Movement Organizations in the Development of the Black Movement," *American Sociological Review* 51, no. 6 (December 1986): 812–29; Benjamin Marquez, *The Politics of Patronage: Lawyers, Philanthropy, and the Mexican American Legal Defense and Educational Fund* (Austin: University of Texas Press, 2021); and Noliwe Rooks, *White Money/Black Power: The Surprising History of African American Studies and the Crisis of Race and Higher Education* (Boston, MA: Beacon Press, 2006).

34. Sam Collings-Wells, "From Black Power to Broken Windows: Liberal Philanthropy and the Carceral State," *Journal of Urban History* 48, no. 4 (July 2022): 739–59; Dunning, *Nonprofit Neighborhoods*, 179; Holtzman, *Long Crisis*, 37–39.

35. See Brent Cebul, "Supply-Side Liberalism: Fiscal Crisis, Post-Industrial Policy, and the Rise of the New Democrats," *Modern American History* 2, no. 2 (July 2019): 139–64; and Gerstle, *Rise and Fall of the Neoliberal Order*, chapter 5.

36. Jonathan Levy describes a fiscal triangle defined by government, for-profit, and nonprofit sectors and explains that in the neoliberal period, its vertices no longer held. See Jonathan Levy, "From Fiscal Triangle to Passing Through: Rise of the Nonprofit Corporation," in *Corporations and American Democracy*, ed. Naomi Lamoreaux and William Novak (Cambridge, MA: Harvard University Press, 2017). Others describe a similar dynamic as "sector blur." For an overview of different perspectives on this phenomenon, see *Stanford Social Innovation Review* 13, no. 3 (Summer 2015).

37. Lisa Levenstein, *They Didn't See Us Coming: The Hidden History of Feminism in the Nineties* (New York: Basic Books, 2020): 75–80. See also Lily Geismer, "Agents of Change: Microenterprise, Welfare Reform, the Clintons, and Liberal Forms of Neoliberalism," *Journal of American History* 107, no. 1 (June 2020): 107–31.

38. On the Clinton Foundation's health care work, see Jeremy Youde, "The Clinton Foundation and Global Health Governance," in *Partnerships in Foundations in Global Health Governance*, ed. Simon Rushton and Owen David Williams (New York: Palgrave Macmillan, 2011). On the Gates Foundation, see Linsey McGoey, *No Such Thing as a Free Gift: The Gates Foundation and the Price of Philanthropy* (New York: Verso, 2015).

39. David Fahrenthold, Tom Hamburger, and Rosalind Helderman, "The Inside Story of How the Clintons Built a $2 Billion Global Empire," *Washington Post*, June 2, 2015, https://www.washingtonpost.com/politics/the-inside-story-of-how-the-clintons-built-a-2-billion-global-empire/2015/06/02/b6eab638-0957-11e5-a7ad-b430fc1d3f5c_story.html?tid=HP_more.

40. Catherine Rottenberg, *The Rise of Neoliberal Feminism* (Oxford: Oxford University Press, 2018).

41. The organization INCITE! Women of Color Against Violence used this phrase first as the name of a 2004 conference and later a book that called out the "non-profit-industrial complex" for thwarting truly radical social movements. See INCITE! Women of Color Against Violence, *The Revolution Will Not Be Funded: Beyond the Non-Profit Industrial Complex* (Cambridge, MA: South End Press, 2007); and Levenstein, *They Didn't See Us Coming*, 86–87.

42. Anand Giridharadas, *Winners Take All: The Elite Charade of Changing the World* (New York: Knopf, 2018).

Chapter Two

This chapter is a modified version of Stephen Macekura, "Making the Contract State: Nathan Associates, Inc. and Foreign Aid Privatization," *Diplomatic History* 47, no. 2 (April 2023): 197–223.

1. Joseph J. Thorndike Jr., "Close Up—Bob Nathan," *Life*, April 13, 1942: 47–50.

2. On the term "contract state" or "contractor state," see Christopher D. McKenna, *The World's Newest Profession: Management Consulting in the Twentieth Century* (Cambridge: Cambridge University Press, 2006): 80–110; H. L. Nieburg, *In the Name of Science*, rev. ed. (Chicago: Quadrangle, 1970): 184. On the military-industrial complex, see Alex Roland, *Delta of Power: The Military-Industrial Complex* (Baltimore, MD: Johns Hopkins University Press, 2021); Michael Brenes, *For Might and Right: Cold War Defense Spending and the Remaking of American Democracy* (Amherst: University of Massachusetts Press,

2020). On Cold War strategy and state-building, see Aaron L. Friedberg, *In the Shadow of the Garrison State: America's Anti-Statism and its Cold War Grand Strategy* (Princeton, NJ: Princeton University Press, 2000).

3. Sheyda F. A. Jahanbani, "New Directions or Dead Ends? Democracy and Development in the 'Postwar,'" *Diplomatic History* 45, no. 1 (January 2021): 83–105; Michael E. Latham, *The Right Kind of Revolution: Modernization, Development, and U.S. Foreign Policy from the Cold War to the Present* (Ithaca, NY: Cornell University Press, 2011): 157–85; David Ekbladh, *The Great American Mission: Modernization and the Construction of an American World Order* (Princeton, NJ: Princeton University Press, 2010): 226–56.

4. On Cold War liberalism, see Doug Rossinow, *Visions of Progress: The Left-Liberal Tradition in America* (Philadelphia: University of Pennsylvania Press, 2008): 195–232.

5. For an overview of the historiography on international development, see Stephen Macekura and Erez Manela, "Introduction," in *The Development Century: A Global History*, ed. Stephen Macekura and Erez Manela (New York: Cambridge University Press, 2018): 1–20.

6. See, for example, Amy C. Offner, *Sorting Out the Mixed Economy: The Rise and Fall of Welfare and Developmental States in the Americas* (Princeton, NJ: Princeton University Press, 2019); Brent Cebul, *Illusions of Progress: Business, Poverty, and Liberalism in the American Century* (Philadelphia: University of Pennsylvania Press, 2023); Brent Cebul, Lily Geismer, and Mason B. Williams, "Beyond Red and Blue: Crisis and Continuity in Twentieth Century U.S. Political History," in *Shaped by the State: Toward a New Political History of the Twentieth Century*, ed. Brent Cebul, Lily Geismer, and Mason B. Williams (Chicago: University of Chicago Press, 2019): 3–26.

7. USAID Bureau for Management Office of Acquisition and Assistance, *Fiscal Year 2019 Progress Report* (Washington, DC: USAID, 2019): 2, https://2017-2020.usaid.gov/sites/default/files/documents/1868/2019-ProgressReport-02-20-2020_0.pdf.

8. Robert R. Nathan, "Robert R. Nathan Oral History Interview, June 22, 1989," interview by Niel M. Johnson, Harry S. Truman Library, https://www.trumanlibrary.gov/library/oral-histories/nathanrr; Thorndike, "Close Up—Bob Nathan."

9. Thorndike, "Close Up—Bob Nathan," 48; Adam Bernstein, "Robert R. Nathan Dies at 92," *Washington Post*, September 6, 2001; Nathan, "Robert R. Nathan Oral History Interview, June 22, 1989."

10. Mark R. Wilson, *Destructive Creation: American Business and the Winning of World War II* (Philadelphia: University of Pennsylvania Press, 2016): 4. See also Robert Nathan, "Robert Nathan Interview," interview by F. Duchêne, Washington, DC, May 15, 1987, Oral History Collections, European University Institute, Fiesole, Italy; Bernstein, "Robert R. Nathan Dies at 92"; Nathan, "Robert R. Nathan Oral History Interview, June 22, 1989"; Wilson, *Destructive Creation*, 47–49; Kenneth D. Durr, *The Best Made Plans: Robert R. Nathan and 20th Century Liberalism* (Rockville, MD: Montrose Press, 2013): 40–51.

11. Nathan, "Robert Nathan Interview."

12. Thorndike, "Close Up—Bob Nathan," 50.

13. Nathan, "Robert R. Nathan Oral History Interview, June 22, 1989."

14. Nathan, "Robert R. Nathan Oral History Interview, June 22, 1989."

15. Robert Nathan, "Good Old Days," *Washington Post*, December 8, 1974.

16. McKenna, *World's Newest Profession*, 82–87.

17. Durr, *Best Made Plans*, 63–74.

18. "A Big Business in Credibility," *Business Week*, March 7, 1977: 85.

19. Brian Balogh, *Chain Reaction: Expert Debate and Public Participation in American Commercial Nuclear Power 1945–1975* (New York: Cambridge University Press, 1991); Michael J. Hogan, *The Marshall Plan: America, Britain, and the Reconstruction of Western Europe, 1947–1952* (New York: Cambridge University Press, 1987): 1–25.

20. James T. Sparrow, *Warfare State: World War II Americans and the Age of Big Government* (New York: Oxford University Press, 2011).

21. Brenes, *For Might and Right*, 32.

22. McKenna, *World's Newest Profession*, 87–98; Paul C. Light, *The True Size of Government* (Washington, DC: Brookings Institution Press, 1999): 99–102.

23. On the origins of postwar foreign policy, see Melvyn P. Leffler, *A Preponderance of Power: National Security, the Truman Administration, and the Cold War* (Stanford, CA: Stanford University Press, 1992).

24. Stephen Macekura, "The Point Four Program and U.S. International Development Policy," *Political Science Quarterly* 128, no. 1 (2013): 138–48.

25. Vernon W. Ruttan, *United States Development Assistance Policy: The Domestic Politics of Foreign Economic Aid* (Baltimore, MD: Johns Hopkins University Press, 1996): 50, 54–58.

26. Murray Marder, "Draft of Legislation for 'Bold Program' Going to Congress within Few Weeks," *Washington Post*, April 17, 1949: M1.

27. Dean Acheson, "Point Four—A Revolution against Hunger, Disease, and Human Misery," *Department of State Bulletin* 669 (April 21, 1952): 608, 610.

28. US Congress, Senate, Committee on Foreign Relations, *Technical Assistance: Final Report of the Committee on Foreign Relations*, 85th Cong., 1st sess., S. Report 139, March 12, 1957: 305, 321–26.

29. On liberalism, foreign-aid policy, and modernization, see Ekbladh, *Great American Mission*, 42–113; Latham, *Right Kind of Revolution*.

30. For a longer discussion of Nathan's work in Burma, see Macekura, "Making the Contract State," 207–13.

31. Nathan, "Robert R. Nathan Oral History Interview, June 22, 1989."

32. Hugh Tinker, "Economic Development in Burma, 1951–1960: Book Review," *Pacific Affairs* 36, no. 3 (Autumn 1963): 327.

33. Durr, *Best Made Plans*, 131.

34. Tinker, "Economic Development in Burma, 1951–1960: Book Review," 327; Kenton Clymer, *A Delicate Relationship: The United States and Burma/Myanmar since 1945* (Ithaca, NY: Cornell University Press, 2015): 168–71.

35. Louis J. Walinsky, *Economic Development in Burma: 1951–1960* (New York: Twentieth Century Fund, 1962): xxvii.

36. Nathan, "Robert R. Nathan Oral History Interview, June 22, 1989."

37. Robert C. Albright, "ADA Urges Foreign Aid Continuance," *Washington Post*, December 31, 1955.

38. US Congress, Joint Committee on the Economic Report, *Hearings before the Subcommittee on Foreign Economic Policy of the Joint Committee on the Economic Report*, 84th Cong., 1st sess., 1955: 469, 473.

39. Robert R. Nathan, "Arise, Ye Prisoners of Plenty," *Washington Post*, September 27, 1959.

40. Durr, *Best Made Plans*, 141, 152–53.

41. Nathan, "Robert R. Nathan Oral History Interview, June 22, 1989." On Nathan's work in Afghanistan, see Timothy Nunan, *Humanitarian Invasion: Global Development in Cold War Afghanistan* (New York: Cambridge University Press, 2016): 68–82.

42. *Report of the Joint Economic Committee, Congress of the United States, on the January 1964 Economic Report of the President*, US Senate, 88th Cong., 2nd sess., 1964: 209.

43. Latham, *Right Kind of Revolution*, 57; Ruttan, *United States Development Assistance Policy*, 91–93.

44. Subsequent revisions reinforced the provision. See *Improvements and New Legislation Needed in AID's Contracting for Consultants and Advisors* (Washington, DC: Comptroller General, 1976): 1–2.

45. Contract Services Division, Department of State, "Current Technical Services Contracts as of September 30, 1964," USAID Development Experience Clearinghouse (DEC), 1964, https:/dec.usaid.gov.

46. *Improvements and New Legislation Needed in AID's Contracting for Consultants and Advisors*, 2.

47. Judith Tendler, *Inside Foreign Aid* (Baltimore, MD: Johns Hopkins University Press, 1975): 16.

48. On the private sector in Kennedy and Johnson's foreign and domestic development policies, see Offner, *Sorting Out the Mixed Economy*, 79–114; 175–213.

49. Durr, *Best Made Plans*, 143-146.

50. Robert Nathan, diary entry, August 21, 1963, box 1, folder 26, Robert R. Nathan papers, 1943–1975, Division of Rare and Manuscript Collections, Cornell University Library, Ithaca, NY (hereafter "Nathan papers").

51. Robert Nathan, diary entry, January 8, 1965, box 1, folder 32, Nathan papers; Robert Nathan, diary entry, August 18, 1963, box 1, folder 26, Nathan papers; USAID/San Jose to USAID/Washington Airgram, "Goal and Activity Progress Report," February 18, 1965: 3, USAID DEC, https:/dec.usaid.gov; *Country Program Digest*, Costa Rica, August 20, 1965: 6, USAID DEC, https:/dec.usaid.gov.

52. Durr, *Best Made Plans*, 145.

53. Harvey H. Segal, "D. C.'s 'Bull Market' in Brainpower," *Washington Post*, March 20, 1966; Harvey H. Segal, "Research-Shop Mortality High," *Washington Post*, March 21, 1966.

54. Durr, *Best Made Plans*, 186.

55. Jahanbani, "New Directions or Dead Ends?," 91–95.

56. Frank Church, "Farewell to Foreign Aid: A Liberal Takes Leave," *Congressional Record*, October 29, 1971: 38252–58.

57. Allison Stanger, *One Nation Under Contract: The Outsourcing of American Power and the Future of Foreign Policy* (New Haven, CT: Yale University Press, 2009): 119.

58. "The New Directions Mandate and the Agency for International Development," Congressional Research Service, July 13, 1981, in US Congress, House of Representatives, Committee on Government Operations, *AID's Administrative and Management Problems in Providing Foreign Economic Assistance*, 97th Cong., 1st sess., October 6, 1981: 298–307, 404–6; Robert R. Nathan Associates, Inc., "Liberia's Agricultural Program Development Project: Evaluation and Recommended Evolution," 1976, USAID DEC, https:/dec.usaid.gov.

59. Donald G. Gavin, "Government Requirement Contracts," *Public Contract Law Journal* 5 (1972): 234–73; Rubén Berríos, *Contracting for Development: The Role of For-Profit Contractors in U.S. Foreign Development Assistance* (Westport, CT: Praeger, 2000): 90.

60. Curt Tarnoff, *USAID: Background, Operations, and Issues*, report 7-5700 (Washington, DC: Congressional Research Service, July 21, 2015): 48.

Notes to Pages 47–50

61. Leon F. Hesser to Carl Fritz, "Request for Approval of a New IQC for Land Resource Inventory," October 20, 1976, USAID DEC, https://dec.usaid.gov.

62. Robert R. Nathan Associates, Inc., "An Economic Assessment of Crop Insurance for Small Farmers in Latin America," work order no.17, contract AID/afr-C-1134, August 1977, USAID DEC, https:/dec.usaid.gov; R. A. Sedjo, "A Framework for U.S. Assistance in Southern Africa; Country Resource Paper: Zambia," contract AID/afr-C-1134 1977, USAID DEC, https:/dec.usaid.gov; Robert R. Nathan Associates, Inc., "Report on Potential Collaborative Industrial Enterprises in the Near East Region," contract AID/afr-C-1134, January 1979, USAID DEC, https:/dec.usaid.gov; USAID, Resources for Development, "Directory of AID Indefinite Quantity Contracts (IQCs)," April 1981: 37, 72, 132, USAID DEC, https:/dec.usaid.gov.

63. Charles S. Rowe, Jr., "Nathan Giving Up Presidency of Firm," *Washington Post*, September 5, 1978.

64. Durr, *Best Made Plans*, 79–85.

65. Durr, *Best Made Plans*, 185–86.

66. Frank C. Porter, "Ma Bell Takes the Offensive, Cites Need to Lure Capital," *Washington Post*, June 8, 1966: D7.

67. "Big Business in Credibility," 84–85.

68. Durr, *Best Made Plans*, 186.

69. Robert R. Nathan, recorded interview by John F. Stewart, June 9, 1967, John F. Kennedy Library Oral History Program, https://www.jfklibrary.org/asset-viewer/archives/JFKOH/Nathan%2C%20Robert%20R/JFKOH-RRN-01/JFKOH-RRN-01.

70. Thomas J. Foley, "U.S. Must Finance Both War and Great Society," *Los Angeles Times*, August 7, 1966: J1.

71. "Interview with Robert Nathan: Advice to the Next President," *Challenge* (January–February 1976): 25.

72. Durr, *Best Made Plans*, 216.

73. Meyerowitz, *War on Global Poverty*, 160–62.

74. John D. Hanrahan, *Government by Contract* (New York: W. W. Norton and Company, 1983): 21.

75. Berríos, *Contracting for Development*, 47.

76. Lily Geismer, *Left Behind: The Democrats' Failed Attempt to Solve Inequality* (New York: PublicAffairs, 2022): 117; Nelson Lichtenstein and Judith Stein, *A Fabulous Failure: The Clinton Presidency and the Transformation of American Capitalism* (Princeton, NJ: Princeton University Press, 2023): 253–60.

77. Berríos, *Contracting for Development*, 1.

78. Tarnoff, *USAID: Background, Operations, and Issues*, 48.

79. Berríos, *Contracting for Development*, 47.

80. James Wallar, interview by Charles Stuart Kennedy, March 9, 2002, 139, Association for Diplomatic Studies and Training, Foreign Affairs Oral History Project, https://www.adst.org/OH%20TOCs/Wallar.James.pdf; Hugh 'Sher' Plunkett, interviewed by Charles Stuart Kennedy and Robin Matthewman, October 16, 2020: 115, Association for Diplomatic Studies and Training, Foreign Affairs Oral History Project, https://adst.org/OH%20TOCs/Plunkett.Sher.pdf.

81. David Segal, "A Dissent into the Maelstrom," *Washington Post*, March 16, 1998: 9.

82. "Nathan Associates, Inc.," USASpending.gov, accessed February 26, 2024, https://www.usaspending.gov/recipient/b0b92ee7-3959-856c-0f2d-223442b866f2-C/latest.

83. "Nathan Associates, Inc.," Nathan Associates, accessed February 26, 2024, https://www.nathaninc.com/.

84. Louis J. Walinsky, "Note for the Burma File," October 1, 1959, box 12, Robert Nathan Associates papers, Manuscript Division, Library of Congress, Washington, DC.

85. Robert Nathan, diary entry, August 20, 1963, box 1, folder 26, Nathan papers.

86. C. David Esch, interview by W. Haven North, August 19, 1988, Association for Diplomatic Studies and Training, Foreign Affairs Oral History Collection, https://adst.org/OH%20TOCs/Esch-C.-David.pdf.

87. Tarnoff, *USAID: Background, Operations, and Issues*, 47–49; Berríos, *Contracting for Development*, 123–26.

Chapter Three

1. Gallup Organization, Gallup poll # 861, question 8, USGALLUP.861.Q008A (Ithaca, NY: Cornell University, Roper Center for Public Opinion Research, 1972), https://doi.org/10.25940/ROPER-31087828.

2. Books examined for this chapter are Edward Cox, Robert Fellmeth, and John Schulz, *The Nader Report on the Federal Trade Commission* (New York: Baron, 1969, hereafter *FTC*); James S. Turner, *The Chemical Feast: The Ralph Nader Study Group Report on Food Protection and the Food and Drug Administration* (New York: Grossman, 1970, hereafter *CF*); Robert C. Fellmeth, *The Interstate Commerce Omission: The Ralph Nader Study Group Report on the Interstate Commerce Commission* (New York: Grossman, 1970, hereafter *ICO*); John C. Esposito, *Vanishing Air: The Ralph Nader Study Group Report on Air Pollution* (New York: Grossman, 1970, hereafter *VA*); David Zwick and Mary Benstock, *Water Wasteland: Ralph Nader's Study Group Report on Water Pollution* (New York: Grossman, 1971, hereafter *WW*); Mark Green, Beverly C. Moore Jr., and Bruce Wasserstein, *The Closed Enterprise System: Ralph Nader's Study Group Report on Antitrust Enforcement* (New York: Grossman, 1971, hereafter *CES*); Mark Green, James M. Fallows, and David Zwick, *Who Runs Congress? The President, Big Business or You?* (New York: Bantam Books, 1972, hereafter *WRC*); Mark Green, ed., *The Monopoly Makers: Ralph Nader's Study Group Report on Regulation and Competition* (New York: Grossman, 1973, hereafter *MM*); and Ralph Nader and Donald Ross, *Action for Change: A Student's Manual for Public Interest Organizing* (New York: Penguin, 1973, hereafter *AFC*).

3. Ralph Nader, *Unsafe at Any Speed: The Designed-In Dangers of the American Automobile* (New York: Grossman, 1965).

4. United States Congress, Senate Committee on Government Operations, Subcommittee on Executive Reorganization, *Federal Role in Traffic Safety: Hearings Before the United States . . . , Parts 1–4* (Washington, DC: Government Printing Office, 1965): 1381.

5. Morton Mintz, "GM's Goliath Bows to David," *Washington Post*, March 27, 1966: A7.

6. See, for example, Paul Sabin, *Public Citizens: The Attack on Big Government and the Remaking of American Liberalism* (New York: Norton, 2021); Reuel Schiller, "Regulation and the Collapse of the New Deal Order or How I Learned to Stop Worrying and Love the Market," in *Beyond the New Deal Order: U.S. Politics from the Great Depression to the Great Recession*, ed. Gary Gerstle, Nelson Lichtenstein, and Alice O'Connor (Philadelphia: University of Pennsylvania Press, 2019): 168–85.

7. See Laura Kalman, *Right Star Rising: A New Politics, 1974–1980* (New York: Norton, 2010): 319; Peter N. Carroll, *It Seemed Like Nothing Happened: America in the 1970s* (New Brunswick, NJ: Rutgers University Press, 1990): 98, 209, 322; William C. Berman,

America's Right Turn: From Nixon to Clinton, 2nd ed. (Baltimore, MD: Johns Hopkins University Press, 1998): 11, 25, 69; Dominic Sandbrook, *Mad as Hell: The Crisis of the 1970s and the Rise of the Populist Right* (New York: Anchor, 2012): 39, 43. On the consumer movement: Lawrence B. Glickman, *Buying Power: A History of Consumer Activism in America* (Chicago: University of Chicago Press, 2012): 256, 277–79, 281–82; Lizabeth Cohen, *A Consumer's Republic: The Politics of Mass Consumption in Postwar America* (New York: Vintage, 2003): 345–87. On the environmental movement: Samuel P. Hays, *Beauty, Health, and Permanence: Environmental Politics in the United States, 1955–1985* (New York: Cambridge University Press, 1989): 182, 304, 460–61; Richard J. Lazarus, *The Making of Environmental Law* (Chicago: University of Chicago Press, 2006): 48, 58, 76. On governmental reform: Michael Schudson, *Rise of the Right to Know: Politics and the Culture of Transparency, 1945–1975* (Cambridge, MA: Harvard University Press, 2018): 1, 91–92.

8. Kim Phillips-Fein, *Invisible Hands: The Businessmen's Crusade against the New Deal* (New York: Norton, 2009): 157–59; Alice O'Connor, "Financing the Counterrevolution," in *Rightward Bound: Making America Conservative in the 1970s*, ed. Bruce J. Schulman and Julian E. Zelizer (Cambridge, MA: Harvard University Press, 2008): 158–59; Glickman, *Buying Power*, 270–99; Benjamin C. Waterhouse, *Lobbying America: The Politics of Business from Nixon to NAFTA* (Princeton, NJ: Princeton University Press, 2014): 167–71; Jefferson Decker, *The Other Rights Revolution: Conservative Lawyers and the Remaking of American Government* (New York: Oxford University Press, 2016): 25–28, 41; Steven M. Teles, *The Rise of the Conservative Legal Movement: The Battle for Control of the Law* (Princeton, NJ: Princeton University Press, 2010): 74–75, 128, 225–27.

9. Michael McCann, *Taking Reform Seriously: Perspectives on Public Interest Liberalism* (Ithaca, NY: Cornell University Press, 1986); Sabin, *Public Citizens*; Martha Davis, *Brutal Need: Lawyers and the Welfare Rights Movement* (New Haven, CT: Yale University Press, 1993); Paul Adler, *No Globalization without Representation: US Activists and World Inequality* (Philadelphia: University of Pennsylvania Press, 2021).

10. McCann, *Taking Reform Seriously*, 21.

11. *AFC*, 4.

12. Ross Perlin, *Intern Nation: Earn Nothing and Learn Little in the Brave New Economy* (London: Verso, 2011): xiv, 33–34.

13. The Commission was consistently criticized for its ineffectiveness throughout the 1950s and 1960s. See, e.g., Committee on Independent Regulatory Commissions, *Task Force Report on Regulatory Commissions [Appendix N] Prepared for the Commission on Organization of the Executive Branch of the Government* (Washington, DC: Government Printing Office, 1949): 119–30; James Landis, *Report on Regulatory Agencies for the President-Elect* (Washington, DC: Government Printing Office, 1960): 48–52; and Carl A. Auerbach, "The Federal Trade Commission: Internal Organization and Procedure," *Minnesota Law Review* 48, no. 383 (1964).

14. "Meet Ralph Nader," *Newsweek*, January 22, 1968: 70; Edward F. Cox, "Reinvigorating the FTC: The Nader Report and the Rise of Consumer Advocacy," *Antitrust Law Journal* 73, no. 3 (2005): 899–901.

15. Veera Korhonen, "Share of Adult Population Enrolled in College or Other Higher Education in the United States from 1970 to 2020, by Age Group," *Statista*, June 2, 2023, https://www.statista.com/statistics/236093/higher-education-enrollment-rates-by-age-group-us/.

16. George Thayer, "A 'Masterful Expose': The Nader Report on the Federal Trade Commission," *Washington Post*, October 24, 1969: B11; "Abolish the FTC?" *Washington Post*, January 9, 1969: A18; Simon Lazarus, "The Nader Report," *New York Times*, October 19, 1969: BR3.

17. Ronald G. Shaffer, "'Nader's Raiders' Stir Bureaucratic Concern in Washington Again," *Wall Street Journal*, July 22, 1969: 1.

18. Sabin, *Public Citizens*, 26.

19. *Hearings before the Subcommittee on Executive Reorganization of the Senate Committee on Government Operations 97*, 91st Cong., 1969: 81.

20. *Hearings before the Subcommittee on Executive Reorganization of the Senate Committee*, 95.

21. *Hearings before the Subcommittee on Executive Reorganization of the Senate Committee*, 97.

22. William Greider, "Nader Marshals 5 Attorneys as 'Raiders,'" *Washington Post*, July 6, 1969: 7.

23. "The Irrelevant World," *Daily Princetonian*, March 11, 1969: 3.

24. Jack Tate, "Nader Slams Harvard Law School," *Harvard Law Record*, November 7, 1968: 1, 4.

25. Ronald Patterson, "Nader's 'Raiders' Plan Greater Invasion," *Harvard Law Record*, February 6, 1969: 2.

26. The National Air Pollution Control Administration and the Federal Water Quality Office were precursors to the Environmental Protection Agency, which was created as part of an executive reorganization at the end of 1970.

27. Ronald G. Shafer, "Nader's Raiders' Stir Bureaucratic Concern in Washington," *Wall Street Journal*, July 22, 1969.

28. The New World, New York, and Taconic Foundations bankrolled the 1969 cohort. Shafer, "Nader's Raiders' Stir Bureaucratic Concern in Washington."

29. William Greider, "Institutional Lone Ranger," *Washington Post*, December 5, 1971: A1, A22.

30. *AFC*, 95.

31. Julius Duscha, "Nader's Raiders Is Their Name and Whistle-Blowing Is Their Game," *New York Times*, March 21, 1971.

32. Jay Acton, *Ralph Nader: A Man and a Movement* (New York: Warner, 1972): 90.

33. *MM*, x.

34. Acton, *Ralph Nader*, 90.

35. Reuel Schiller, "The Curious Origins of Airline Deregulation: Economic Deregulation and the American Left," 93 *Business History Review* 729 (2019): 732–34. Interestingly, many thinkers on the right embraced this jaundiced view of the state as well. Schiller, "Enlarging the Administrative Polity: Administrative Law and the Changing Definition of Pluralism, 1945–1970," *Vanderbilt Law Review* 53, no. 1389 (2000): 1412.

36. For specific citations, see, for example, *CES*, 18n* (Mills), 439n25 (Kolko); *MM*, 366n1 (Kolko).

37. *CES*, ix.

38. *CES*, xii.

39. *CES*, ix.

40. See, e.g., *ICO*, 2–4, 15–22, 312–13, 339–49; *MM*, 14–16, *CES*, 330; *VA*, 185–87; *CF*, vi–vii, 16–17, 49–53, 209–13.

41. *CES*, 17.

42. Herbert Marcuse's *One-Dimensional Man* (Boston, MA: Beacon, 1964) is a canonical statement of this idea. See also C. Wright Mills, *The Power Elite*, 2nd ed. repr. (New York: Oxford University Press, 1999 [1956]): 298.

43. Charles McGarry, *Citizen Nader* (New York: Signet, 1972): 51; "The Playboy Interview: Ralph Nader," *Playboy*, October 1968: 76.

44. McGarry, *Citizen Nader*, 46, 50, 53, 54. Plate glass windows: "Hot in summer, cold in winter. Where do you suppose we got this system of perverted aesthetics?" McGarry, *Citizen Nader*, 54.

45. McGarry, *Citizen Nader*, 52.

46. *FTC*, 17–19. See also, *CF*, v–vi; and *VA*, 233.

47. "Ralph Nader Reports," *Ladies' Home Journal* (April 1974): 44.

48. *AFC*, 107–8.

49. Michael Kinsley, "My Life and Hard Times with Nader's Raiders," *Seventeen* (September 1971): 204.

50. "Playboy Interview: Ralph Nader," 221.

51. Kinsley, "My Life and Hard Times," 204.

52. Kinsley, "My Life and Hard Times," 148.

53. Schiller, "Enlarging the Administrative Polity," 1410–14.

54. Maurice Isserman and Michale Kazin, *America Divided: The Civil War of the 1960s* (New York: Oxford University Press, 2000): 165–86; Jefferson Cowie, *Stayin' Alive: The 1970s and the Last Days of the Working Class* (New York: New Press, 2010): 23–74; Felica Kornbluh, *The Battle for Welfare Rights: Politics and Poverty in Modern America* (Philadelphia: University of Pennsylvania Press, 2007).

55. *AFC*, 9, 13, 145.

56. Greider, "Institutional Lone Ranger," A22.

57. *AFC*, 22.

58. *AFC*, 22.

59. *AFC*, 22–23.

60. *FTC*, xi.

61. *WRC*, 249.

62. *WRC*, 249.

63. *WRC*, 249.

64. *WRC*, 258–59.

65. *WRC*, 260.

66. *WRC*, 263.

67. *WRC*, 263.

68. "Playboy Interview: Ralph Nader."

69. *WRC*, 277–78. For more on the relationship between civil rights and antiwar activism and the public-interest law movement, see Sabin, *Public Citizens*, 51–52.

70. The canonical texts are V. O. Key Jr., *Politics, Parties, and Pressure Groups* (New York: Crowell, 1942); David B. Truman, *The Governmental Process: Political Interests and Political Opinion* (New York: Knopf, 1951); and Robert A. Dahl, *A Preface to Democratic Theory* (Chicago: University of Chicago Press, 1956). See also Schiller, "Enlarging the Administrative Polity," 1398–410.

71. John Kenneth Galbraith, *American Capitalism: The Concept of Countervailing Power* (Cambridge, MA: Riverside, 1952), reprint (Mansfield Centre, CT: Martino, 2012): 115–39.

72. He called the Ontario native "Canada's gift to America" and a man of "mostly unfailing good judgment." Ralph Nader, "Galbraith—A Public-Spirited Economist," Nader.org, August 18, 2006, https://nader.org/2006/08/18/galbraith-a-public-spirited-economist/.

73. *FTC*, xi.
74. *MM*, xiii.
75. *AFC*, 9.
76. *AFC*.
77. Schiller, "Enlarging the Administrative Polity," 1399–401.
78. *CES*, 125, 129.
79. *FTC*, 150.
80. *FTC*, 150–58, 172.
81. See, for example, *CES*, 369–84; *VA*, 183–89; and *CF*, 188 and 197.
82. *CES*, 436.
83. *MM*, 26–27, 126–30, 160, 224, 253; *VA*, 121, 152; *CES*, 66–114, 321–33; *CF*, 3–4, 236–37; *ICO*, 1–9, 15–22, 36–39, 311; *FTC*, 130–40, 169–72.
84. *MM*, 27, 253–54; *VA*, 121, 152; *CES*, 124–29; *FTC*, 140–59, 172, 226–28; *ICO*, 13–15.
85. *VA*, 264, 309; *CES*, 129–30; *WW*, 401–6, 417–18.
86. *FTC*, 164–68; *CF*, 46–47; *MM*, 26, 125–26, 134–38, 142, 152, 222–23; *VA* 141, 164–67, 271; *CES*, 87–88, 112, 174–77, 207, 385; *ICO*, 257–73, 324.
87. *MM*, 97–99, 189; *VA*, 277, 300, 303, 305, 309; *CES*, 47–60, 308–18; *WW*, 397, 404–7; *CF*, 152.
88. *CF*, v; *VA*, 218, 302; *CES*, 122.
89. These two strategies are articulated most clearly in the introduction to *The Monopoly Makers* and in an article Nader and Mark Green published that same year in the *Yale Law Journal*. See *MM*, 3–31; Ralph Nader and Mark Green, "Economic Regulation vs. Competition: Uncle Sam the Monopoly Man," *Yale Law Journal* 82, no. 871 (1973).
90. See, for example, *CES*, 9, 313.
91. *CES*, 293–318, 398–412.
92. *CES*, 314–15.
93. *CES*, 347–48.
94. *CES*, xi.
95. *CES*, xiii.
96. This theme is central to both Moore and Wasserstein, *Closed Enterprise System*, and Green, *Monopoly Makers*. It is also proffered as a solution to environmental and transportation problems. See *VA*, 299–310; *ICO*, 119–35.
97. *VA*, 112–51, 234–58.
98. *VA*, 305.
99. *VA*, 306.
100. *VA*, 280–98.
101. The material in this paragraph is taken from Cox, "Reinvigorating the FTC: The Nader Report and the Rise of Consumer Advocacy," *Antitrust Law Journal* 73, no. 3 (2005): 899–900. See also Richard A. Harris and Sidney M. Milkis, *The Politics of Regulatory Change: A Tale of Two Agencies* (New York: Oxford University Press, 1989).
102. Justin Martin details these tactics in *Nader: Crusader, Spoiler, Icon* (New York: Basic, 2002): 92–96. See also Kinsley, "My Life and Hard Times," 148–49.

Notes to Pages 70–73

103. Ralph Nader, "Morton Mintz Turns 100—Investigative Nemesis of Corporate Criminals," Nader.org, January 25, 2022, https://nader.org/2022/01/25/morton-mintz-turns-100-investigative-nemesis-of-corporate-criminals/.

104. Ronald G. Shaffer, "Nader's Raiders Stir Bureaucratic Concern in Washington Again," *Wall Street Journal*, July 22, 1969: 1, 28.

105. John Mendeloff, *Regulating Safety: An Economic and Political Analysis of Occupational Safety and Health Policy* (Cambridge, MA: MIT Press, 1979): 18, 156–58; Charles Noble, *Liberalism at Work: The Rise and Fall of OSHA* (Philadelphia, PA: Temple University Press, 1968): 253n17; Thomas McGarity and Sidney A. Shapiro, *Workers at Risk: The Failed Promise of the Occupational Safety and Health Administration* (New York: Praeger, 1993): 51, 80; Michael Pertschuk, *When the Senate Worked for Us: The Invisible Role of Staffers in Countering Corporate Lobbies* (Nashville, TN: Vanderbilt University Press, 2017): 153, 155–56; Sam Archibald, "The Early Years of the Freedom of Information Act. 1955 to 1974," *PS: Political Science and Policy* 26 (December 1993): 730.

106. Greider, "Institutional Lone Ranger," A22.

107. See, for example, the treatment of Edmund Muskie (*VA*, 287–93; *WW*, 423–27, 428–29), John Blatnik (*WW*, 423–27), or Martha Griffiths. Mary Russell, "Nader Takes on Congress: 25,000-Page Critical Study Draws Outcry," *Washington Post*, October 1, 1972: A1, A16, A17.

108. "Action for a Change," Student PIRGs, accessed June 16, 2022, https://studentpirgs.org/.

109. Laura Foreman, "Carter's Raiders: The Outsiders are In," *New York Times*, April 20, 1977. See also Sabin, *Public Citizens*, 136–37.

110. Many Nader alums became leading public-interest lawyers. For example, Mark Green was elected to head New York City's Office of the Public Advocate. David Zwick became an environmental advocate and national director of Clean Water Action. Mary Benstock founded and directed the Clean Air Campaign. Lowell Dodge served in a variety of position including the director of the Center for Auto Safety, the executive assistant to the chair of the Consumer Products Safety Commission, and the executive director of two environmental organizations. Judith Areen and Robert Fellmeth served as law professors at Georgetown and Harvard, respectively.

111. Michael Kinsley, James Fallows, and Peter Lance are former Raiders who became well-known journalists.

Chapter Four

Epigraphs: "What Is a Populist Approach," in Steve Kest to Interested Parties, September 23, 1988, series M94-059, box 5, folder 35; testimony presented to Subcommittee on Financial Institutions, Supervision, Regulation, and Insurance of the Committee on Banking, Finance, and Urban Affairs on Issues of Financial Restructuring by George Butts, board member, Philadelphia ACORN, April 18, 1991, series 2001-170, box 16, folder 70; and "Talking Points about the Campaign," March 24, 1989, series M94-059, box 5, folder 34, all in ACORN records, Wisconsin Historical Society, Madison, WI (hereafter ACORN records). The author thanks the editors, Kara Ritzheimer, Nicole von Germeten, N. D. B. Connolly, the participants of the New Histories of Liberalism Workshop, and the anonymous readers for their thoughtful engagement and feedback; Oregon State University's School of History, Philosophy, and Religion and the Jefferson Scholars Foundation for travel support; and the archivists at the Wisconsin Historical Society for their assistance.

1. Testimony presented for ACORN by Irma Pernell, president of DC ACORN, to Hon. Dan Rostenkowski, chairman, Ways and Means Committee, US House of Representatives, March 9, 1989, series M94-059, box 5, folder 34, ACORN records, 1.

2. Testimony presented by Mildred Brown, president of ACORN, to Hon. Frank Annunzio, chairman, Financial Institutions Subcommittee, Committee on Banking, US House of Representatives, March 21, 1989, series M94-059, box 5, folder 34, ACORN records. Several scholars argue that the term "reregulation" is a more accurate label for policy changes that gave financial institutions a freer hand, since it entailed a "rewriting of rules to support changed priorities such as bank competition and inflation fighting, rather than the concept of 'security,' central to the New Deal financial regime." Rebecca Marchiel, *After Redlining: The Urban Reinvestment Movement in the Era of Financial Deregulation* (Chicago: University of Chicago Press, 2020): 16. I use these terms as my historical subjects used them; when ACORN members called for "reregulation" they meant reimposing New Deal-era restrictions on financial institutions.

3. Jefferson Cowie, *Stayin' Alive: The 1970s and the Last Days of the Working Class* (New York: New Press, 2010). A few historians have begun to chronicle labor activism and its increasingly intersectional approach in the 1970s, but these works focus largely on organized labor. See, for example, Jane Berger, *A New Working Class: The Legacies of Public-Sector Employment in the Civil Rights Movement* (Philadelphia: University of Pennsylvania Press, 2021); Lane Windham, *Knocking on Labor's Door: Union Organizing in the 1970s and the Roots of a New Economic Divide* (Chapel Hill: University of North Carolina Press, 2017); and Eileen Boris and Jennifer Klein, *Caring for America: Home Health Workers in the Shadow of the Welfare State* (New York: Oxford University Press, 2012).

4. Many scholars refer to the bipartisan commitment to a series of public-policy interventions designed to release the "free market" from constraints as neoliberalism. Others criticize the term, arguing that its logic and features were always inherent in twentieth-century liberalism, especially as it operated for people of color. See N. D. B. Connolly, "The Strange Career of American Liberalism" in *Shaped by the State: Toward a New Political History of the Twentieth Century*, ed. Brent Cebul, Lily Geismer, and Mason B. Williams (Chicago: University of Chicago Press, 2019): 62–95.

5. Connolly, "Strange Career of American Liberalism," 84.

6. Brent Cebul, "Supply-Side Liberalism: Fiscal Crises, Post-Industrial Policy, and the Rise of the New Democrats," *Modern American History* 2, no. 2 (2019): 139–64; Lily Geismer, *Left Behind: The Democrats' Failed Attempt to Solve Inequality* (New York: Public Affairs, 2022).

7. For an overview of banking deregulation, see João Rafael Cunha, "The Advent of a New Banking System in the United States," in *Financial Deregulation: A Historical Perspective*, ed. Alexis Drach and Yousef Cassis (Oxford: Oxford University Press, 2021): 24–46.

8. This perspective was a constitutive feature of New Deal liberalism that carried over into neoliberal policymaking. On liberal policymakers' effort to insulate financial decisions from democratic governance, see Destin Jenkins, *The Bonds of Inequality: Debt and the Making of the American City* (Chicago: University of Chicago Press, 2021).

9. Testimony presented by Mildred Brown, March 21, 1989, 1, 5.

10. John Anner, "A Red Lining in the Savings and Loan Cloud," *Minority Trendsetter* 4, no. 1 (Winter 1990–1991) (reprint), series M2001-170, box 16, folder 67, ACORN records. Reagan-era regulators also liberalized ownership restrictions, eliminated limits

Notes to Pages 77–79 323

on loan-to-value ratios, and opened thrifts to so-called brokered deposits. Daniel Immergluck, *Credit to the Community: Community Reinvestment and Fair Lending Policy in the United States* (New York: Routledge, 2015): 42; Alane Moysich, "The Savings and Loan Crisis and Its Relationship to Banking," in *History of the Eighties: Lessons for the Future, Vol. 1: An Examination of the Banking Crisis of the 1980s and Early 1990s* (Washington, DC: Federal Deposit Insurance Corporation, 1997): 173–75, 177–80; Lenny Glynn, "Who Really Made the S&L Mess?" *Dissent* (April 1991): 13; James M. Glassman, "The Great Banks Robbery," *New Republic* 203 (October 8, 1990), reprinted in Robert Emmett Long, *Banking Scandals: The S & Ls and BCCI*, The Reference Shelf 65, no. 3 (New York: H. W. Wilson, 1993): 28; David L. Mason, *From Buildings and Loans to Bailouts: A History of the American Savings and Loan Industry, 1831–1995* (Cambridge: Cambridge University Press, 2004): 226.

11. When it became clear that many thrifts were in trouble, regulators tried to minimize the problem by reducing capital requirements, liberalizing accounting rules, and offering forbearance, all of which allowed the problems to get worse. Moysich, "Savings and Loan Crisis," 180; Mason, *From Building and Loans to Bailouts*, 213, 228; Glynn, "Who Really Made the S&L Mess?" 19–20; Representative Henry B. Gonzalez, press release, August 23, 1990, series M98-059, box 7, folder 5, ACORN records.

12. Nathaniel C. Nash, "Bush Savings Plan Is Passed by House," *New York Times*, June 16, 1981: A1; Kevin Kelly, "Taxpayers Likely to Drown in Savings and Loan Bailout," *In These Times*, March 1–14, 1989 (reprint), series M94-059, box 5, folder 34, ACORN records.

13. Kest co-directed the campaign with Tom Schlesinger, director of the Southern Finance Project.

14. FDC flyer, "Now That the Party's Over, Why Should You Have to Pay for It?" 1989, series M98-059, box 5, folder 30, ACORN records.

15. FDC trifold, "Who Speaks for Us?" 1990, series M98-059, box 7, folder 5, ACORN records.

16. FDC press release, "Alliance Assesses Winners and Losers," August 7, 1989; and FDC press release, "The S&L Bailout: Winners and Losers," August 7, 1989; both in series M98-059, box 5, folder 30, ACORN records; FDC memo, "S&L Villains," n.d., series M2001-170, box 16, folder 70, ACORN records; Steve [Kest] to Field Operations, October 23, 1990, series M98-059, box 7, folder 5, ACORN records: 2.

17. ACORN and Public Citizen press release, "Citizen Groups Target Congressman Anthony in Campaign Finance Reform Ad," July 6, 1990, series M98-059, box 7, folder 4, ACORN records: 2.

18. Steve [Kest] to staff and board, April 6, 1989, series M94-045, box 5, unlabeled folder, ACORN records.

19. Untitled ACORN flyer and ACORN flyer, "The U.S. League Must Accept Responsibility for Causing the Savings and Loan Crisis," both in series M94-059, box 5, folder 37, ACORN records; John Anner, "A Red Lining in the Savings and Loan Cloud," *Minority Trendsetter* 4, no. 1 (Winter 1990–1991) (reprint), series M2001-170, box 16, folder 67, ACORN records; ACORN and Public Citizen press release, "Citizen Groups Target Congressman Anthony in Campaign Finance Reform Ad."

20. Tom Schlesinger and Mildred Brown, "Hittin' 'Em Where They Ain't," n.d., series M94-059, box 5, folder 35, ACORN records.

21. Testimony presented to Subcommittee on Financial Institutions, Supervision, Regulation, and Insurance of the Committee on Banking, Finance, and Urban Affairs on

Issues of Financial Restructuring by George Butts, board member, Philadelphia ACORN, April 18, 1991, series 2001-170, box 16, folder 70, ACORN records: 4.

22. Marla Dickerson, "Jackson, Kennedy Say S&L Plan Should Address Housing Issue," *American Banker*, April 6, 1989, series M94-045, box 5, unlabeled folder, ACORN records.

23. Testimony presented for ACORN by Arthur Cross, leader, Arkansas ACORN, to Hon. Henry Gonzalez, chairman, Committee on Banking, Finance, and Urban Affairs, US House of Representatives, San Antonio, TX, March 10, 1989, series M94-059, box 5, folder 34, ACORN records: 5; Arkansas Community Housing Corporation application for funding, Campaign for Human Development, 1991, series M2002-002, box 6, folder 10, ACORN records: 7.

24. In 1981, 78 percent of thrift lending went to residential mortgages. By 1986, mortgages accounted for only 56 percent of thrift investments, and many of those were for commercial rather than residential projects. Moysich, "Savings and Loan Crisis," 179.

25. Testimony submitted by Maude Hurd, Executive Committee member, ACORN, to Hon. Henry B. Gonzalez, chairman, Committee on Banking, Finance, and Urban Affairs, US House of Representatives, *Hearings on Domestic Economic Issues: Their Impact on Various Groups of Citizens, Financial Service Providers, and the Safety and Soundness of the U.S. Financial System* (Washington, DC: US Congress Committee on Banking, Finance, and Urban Affairs, January 24, 1989), series M98-059, box 4, folder 3, ACORN records: 10.

26. Testimony presented for ACORN by Ernest Brown, leader, Texas ACORN, to Hon. Henry B. Gonzalez, chairman, Committee on Banking, Finance, and Urban Affairs, US House of Representatives, San Antonio, TX, March 10, 1989, series M94-059, box 5, folder 34, ACORN records: 1, 4.

27. Testimony submitted by Maude Hurd, January 24, 1989, 2.

28. Testimony presented for ACORN by Ernest Brown, March 10, 1989, 1, 4.

29. The FDC proposed raising the top marginal tax rate to 33 percent, still below the top marginal rate before Congress cut it to 28 percent in the Tax Reform Act of 1986; increasing the alternative minimum corporate income tax rate; taxing foreign investors; and eliminating the mortgage interest tax deduction for second homes. FDC, "Who Do You Think You're Fooling?" flyer, series M98-059, box 5, folder 30, ACORN records.

30. FDC, "Who Do You Think You're Fooling?" Projected costs of the bailout vary significantly from source to source and depending on date.

31. Elena Hanggi, untitled statement given at press conference, circa April 5, 1989, Washington, DC, series M94-059, box 5, folder 35, ACORN records: 1–2.

32. FDC, "Alliance Appeals for Open Meeting on S&L Bailout," July 24, 1989, series M98-059, box 5, folder 30, ACORN records.

33. Lisabeth Weiner, "ACORN Demands Homes from FSLIC," *American Banker*, n.d. (reprint), series M94-059, box 5, folder 34, ACORN records.

34. Camille Walsh, *Racial Taxation: Schools, Segregation, and Taxpayer Citizenship, 1869–1973* (Chapel Hill: University of North Carolina Press, 2018): 36.

35. Andrew W. Kahrl, "The Short End of Both Sticks: Property Assessments and Black Taxpayer Disadvantage in Urban America," in *Shaped by the State: Toward a New Political History of the Twentieth Century*, ed. Brent Cebul, Lily Geismer, and Mason B. Williams (Chicago: University of Chicago Press, 2019): 189–217. On the 1970s tax revolt, see Josh Mound, "Stirrings of Revolt: Regressive Levies, the Pocketbook Squeeze, and the 1960s Roots of the 1970s Tax Revolt," *Journal of Policy History* 32, no. 2 (April 2020): 105–50;

Notes to Pages 81–84　　　325

Isaac William Martin, *The Permanent Tax Revolt: How the Property Tax Transformed American Politics* (Stanford, CA: Stanford University Press, 2008); Simon Hall, *American Patriotism, American Protest, Social Movements since the Sixties* (Philadelphia: University of Pennsylvania Press, 2011): chapter 5.

36. Hanggi used states rather than cities to locate her taxpayers and chose states (Iowa and Oregon) with overwhelmingly white populations. According to the 1980 Census, Iowa was the fourth whitest state and Oregon the thirteenth whitest. African Americans accounted for less than 2 percent of the population of both states.

37. Polls in February and March 1989 showed widespread opposition to a taxpayer-funded bailout. See FDC memo, "Talking Points about the Campaign," March 24, 1989, series M94-059, box 5, folder 34, ACORN records: 1; Lou Harris, "Public Reaction to S&L Bailout Negative," March 5, 1989 (reprint of syndicated column), series M94-059, box 5, folder 34, ACORN records.

38. FDC to Friend, June 30, 1989, and Marla Dickerson, "'Donahue' Wakes Up to S&L Crisis," *Banking Week*, May 22, 1989 (reprint), both in series M98-059, box 5, folder 30, ACORN records.

39. FDC Action Alert, June 23, 1989, and Steve [Kest] to interested parties, June 27, 1989, both in series M98-059, box 5, folder 30, ACORN records.

40. Kevin Kruse, *White Flight: Atlanta and the Making of Modern Conservatism* (Princeton, NJ: Princeton University Press, 2007).

41. Testimony presented for ACORN by Arthur Cross, leader, Arkansas ACORN to Hon. Henry Gonzalez, chairman, Committee on Banking, Finance, and Urban Affairs, US House of Representatives, San Antonio, TX, March 10, 1989, series M94-059, box 5, folder 34, ACORN records: 2.

42. Testimony presented by Mildred Brown, March 21, 1989, 5.

43. For example, the Housing Act of 1949 set the goal of "a decent home and a suitable living environment for every American family."

44. The National Housing Task Force detailed some of the contours of the affordable-housing crisis in its report *A Decent Place to Live* (Washington, DC: National Housing Task Force, March 1988), https://www.huduser.gov/Publications/pdf/HUD-5830.pdf.

45. Steve Kest to staff and board, February 17, 1989, series M94-045, box 5, folder "Savings and Loan Campaign Update FR: Steve Kest to: Staff and Board 3/9/89," ACORN records: 2.

46. Testimony presented by Mildred Brown, March 21, 1989, 4.

47. Rex Nelson, "ACORN Protesters Urge Plan to Provide Public Housing," *Arkansas Democrat*, n.d. (reprint), series M94-045, box 5, unlabeled folder, ACORN records.

48. Testimony presented by Mildred Brown, March 21, 1989, 3.

49. Steve Kest to staff and board, February 17, 1989, 2.

50. Steve Kest to board and staff, May 22, 1989, series M94-045, box 6, folder "Savings and Loan Campaign Update FR: Steve Kest 5/22/89," ACORN records: 1–2.

51. Nathaniel C. Nash, "In Savings Bill, a Populist Message," *New York Times*, June 17, 1989 (reprint), series M98-059, box 5, folder 30, ACORN records. In his first decade in Congress, Schumer was a sometime ally of ACORN. FDC, "More Winners: The Good, the Bad, and the Extremely Ugly: Awards Fit for a $300 Billion Bailout," n.d., series M98-059, box 5, folder 30, ACORN records: 2.

52. Steve Kest to board and staff, June 19, 1989, series M94-045, box 6, folder "Victories in the S&L Campaign 6/19/89," ACORN records.

53. Jay Rosenstein, "Jackson Calls for Low-Cost Mortgage Fund Backed by Industry," *American Banker*, March 3, 1989 (reprint), series M94-059, box 5, folder 34, ACORN records.

54. Nash, "In Savings Bill, a Populist Message."

55. ACORN's grassroots pressure enabled its House allies to win a bill that included substantive affordable-housing and anti-redlining provisions, though these were not included in the Senate bill. In the last week of debate, the Bush administration threatened to veto the bill if it included ACORN's measures, leading the Senate to reject the conference committee bill and forcing intense negotiation. Steve Kest to board and staff, June 19, 1989, series M94-045, box 6, folder "Victories in the S&L Campaign 6/19/89," ACORN records; Steve Kest to Friends of the Financial Democracy Campaign, August 8, 1989, series M98-059, box 5, folder 30, ACORN records.

56. Steve Kest to board and staff, May 3, 1989, series M94-045, box 6, folder "Savings and Loan Campaign Update Congressional Action 5/3/89 FR Steve Kest," ACORN records: 1.

57. Phil Gramm to colleagues, August 3, 1989, series M94-045, box 5, folder "Final Victory in the S&L Bailout Campaign FR: Steve Kest 8/8/89," ACORN records.

58. Steve Kest to board and staff, May 3, 1989, 1.

59. FDC, "More Winners."

60. Steve [Kest] to head organizers, March 15, 1991, series M2001-170, box 17, folder 70, ACORN records: 1.

61. In 1996, the Government Accounting Office put the price tag at nearly half a trillion dollars, "including more than $130 billion from taxpayers." Richard W. Stevenson, "G.A.O. Puts Cost of S&L Bailout at Half a Trillion Dollars," *New York Times*, July 13, 1996: 34.

62. "Summary of ACORN's Ten-Point Plan to Reform the Banking Industry," n.d., and ACORN press release, "ACORN Proposes 'People's Bank Reform' Alternative: Butts Calls for Bank 'Workfare,'" April 18, 1991, both in series M94-059, box 6, folder 41, ACORN records; testimony presented to Subcommittee on Financial Institutions, Supervision, Regulation, and Insurance of the Committee on Banking, Finance, and Urban Affairs on Issues of Financial Restructuring by George Butts, board member, Philadelphia ACORN, April 18, 1991, series 2001-170, box 16, folder 70, ACORN records.

Chapter Five

1. Bill D. Moyers, Ruth C. Streeter, and Perry Wolff, "CBS Reports, The Vanishing Family: Crisis in Black America," aired January 25, 1986, on CBS (New York: CBS Special News Report, 1986).

2. K. Johnson, "Celebrating the Black Family with Seminars and Songs," *Philadelphia Inquirer*, July 27, 1990: 40.

3. Johnson, "Celebrating the Black Family."

4. "New Help for Self-Help," *Wall Street Journal*, February 18, 1986: 1.

5. Michael Lomax, remarks at Democratic Leadership Council Platform Symposium, June 21, 1987, box 38, folder 9, Michael Lomax Papers, Stuart Rose Library, Emory University, Atlanta, Georgia.

6. Huey Newton, "Black Capitalism Re-Analyzed: June 5, 1971," in *To Die for the People: The Writings of Huey P. Newton* (New York: Vintage Books, 1972): 104–5.

7. Devin Fergus, *Liberalism, Black Power, and the Making of American Politics, 1965–1980* (Athens: University of Georgia Press, 2009); Karen Ferguson, *Top Down: The Ford Foundation, Black Power, and the Reinvention of Racial Liberalism* (Philadelphia: University of Pennsylvania Press, 2013).

8. See Lester K. Spence, *Knocking the Hustle: Against the Neoliberal Turn in Black Politics* (New York: Punctum, 2015); Michael C. Dawson and Megan Ming Francis, "Black Politics and the Neoliberal Racial Order," *Public Culture* 28, no. 1 (78) (2016): 23–62.

9. N. D. B. Connolly, "The Strange Career of American Liberalism," in *Shaped by the State: Toward a New Political History of the Twentieth Century*, ed. Brent Cebul, Lily Geismer, and Mason B. Williams (Chicago: University of Chicago Press, 2019): 86. See also Melinda Cooper, *Family Values: Between Neoliberalism and the New Social Conservatism* (New York: Zone Books, 2017).

10. Cooper, *Family Values*, 73–82.

11. See Robin D. G. Kelley, *Freedom Dreams: The Black Radical Imagination* (Boston, MA: Beacon Press, 2002); Christopher Alan Bracey, *Saviors or Sellouts: The Promise and Peril of Black Conservatism, from Booker T. Washington to Condoleezza Rice* (Boston, MA: Beacon Press, 2008); Irvin J. Hunt, *Dreaming the Present: Time, Aesthetics, and the Black Cooperative Movement* (Chapel Hill: University of North Carolina Press, 2022).

12. Elizabeth Hinton, "Roundtable: Defining the Black 1980s," *Journal of African American History* 108, no. 3 (2023): 360.

13. This volume's introduction, 6.

14. Rayford W. Logan, *The Negro in American Life and Thought: The Nadir, 1877–1901* (New York: Dial Press, 1954).

15. Michele Mitchell, *Righteous Propagation: African Americans and the Politics of Racial Destiny after Reconstruction* (Chapel Hill: University of North Carolina Press, 2004): 13.

16. See Evelyn Brooks Higginbotham, *Righteous Discontent: The Women's Movement in the Black Baptist Church, 1880–1920* (Cambridge, MA: Harvard University Press, 1994); Kevin Gaines, *Uplifting the Race: Black Leadership, Politics, and Culture in the Twentieth Century* (Chapel Hill: University of North Carolina Press, 1996); Touré F. Reed, *Not Alms but Opportunity: The Urban League and the Politics of Racial Uplift, 1910–1950* (Chapel Hill: University of North Carolina Press, 2008).

17. See James D. Anderson, *The Education of Blacks in the South, 1860–1935* (Chapel Hill: University of North Carolina Press, 1988); Tyrone McKinley Freeman, *Madam C. J. Walker's Gospel of Giving: Black Women's Philanthropy during Jim Crow* (Urbana-Champaign: University of Illinois Press, 2020); Maribel Morey, *White Philanthropy: Carnegie Corporation's* An American Dilemma *and the Making of a White World Order* (Chapel Hill: University of North Carolina Press, 2021).

18. Morey, *White Philanthropy*, 40. See also Eric Anderson and Alfred A. Moss, *Dangerous Donations: Northern Philanthropy and Southern Black Education, 1902–1930* (Columbia: University of Missouri Press, 1999).

19. Marybeth Gasman and Noah D. Drezner, "White Corporate Philanthropy and Its Support of Private Black Colleges in the 1960s and 1970s," *International Journal of Educational Advancement* 8, no. 2 (2008): 79–92.

20. Megan Ming Francis, "The Price of Civil Rights: Black Lives, White Funding, and Movement Capture," *Law and Society Review* 53, no. 1 (2019): 278.

21. See David M. Freund, *Colored Property: State Policy and White Racial Politics in Suburban America* (Chicago: University of Chicago Press, 2010); N. D. B. Connolly, *A World More Concrete: Real Estate and the Remaking of Jim Crow South Florida*

(Chicago: University of Chicago Press, 2014); Todd Michney and LaDale Winling, "New Perspectives on New Deal Housing Policy: Explicating and Mapping HOLC Loans to African Americans," *Journal of Urban History* 46, no. 1 (2020): 150–80.

22. See Claude A. Clegg III, "Philanthropy, Civil Rights Movement, and the Politics of Racial Reform," in *Charity, Philanthropy, and Civility in American History*, ed. Lawrence Jacob Friedman and Mark D. McGarvie (Cambridge: Cambridge University Press, 2004): 341–62; Ferguson, *Top Down*.

23. A. Philip Randolph and Bayard Rustin, *A "Freedom Budget" for All Americans: A Summary* (New York: A. Philip Randolph Institute, 1967); on the movement for full employment and a federal job guarantee, see Mathew Forstater, "From Civil Rights to Economic Security: Bayard Rustin and the African-American Struggle for Full Employment, 1945–1978," *International Journal of Political Economy* 36, no. 3 (2007): 63–74; David Stein, "'This Nation Has Never Honestly Dealt with the Question of a Peacetime Economy': Coretta Scott King and the Struggle for a Nonviolent Economy in the 1970s," *Souls* 18, no. 1 (2016): 80–105.

24. Ted Ownby, *Hurtin' Words: Debating Family Problems in the Twentieth-Century South* (Chapel Hill: University of North Carolina Press, 2018).

25. See Mitchell, *Righteous Propagation*, 218–39. See also Ula Taylor, *The Promise of Patriarchy: Women and the Nation of Islam* (Chapel Hill: University of North Carolina Press, 2017).

26. Margo Natalie Crawford, "Must Revolution Be a Family Affair? Revisiting the Black Woman," in *Want to Start a Revolution? Radical Women in the Black Freedom Struggle*, ed. Dayo F. Gore, Jeanne Theoharis, and Komozi Woodard (New York: New York University Press, 2009): 189–95; see also Michele Wallace, *Black Macho and the Myth of the Superwoman* (London: Verso Books, 1999).

27. Mitchell, *Righteous Propagation*.

28. See Khalil Gibran Muhammad, *The Condemnation of Blackness* (Cambridge, MA: Harvard University Press, 2010); Talitha LeFlouria, *Chained in Silence: Black Women and Convict Labor in the New South* (Chapel Hill: University of North Carolina Press, 2015); Saidiya Hartman, *Wayward Lives, Beautiful Experiments: Intimate Histories of Riotous Black Girls, Troublesome Women, and Queer Radicals* (New York: W. W. Norton, 2019); Tera Eva Agyepong, *The Criminalization of Black Children: Race, Gender, and Delinquency in Chicago's Juvenile Justice System, 1899–1945* (Chapel Hill: University of North Carolina Press, 2018).

29. This reading is informed by Melinda Cooper's analysis of the "ethic of family responsibility," which she argues united neoliberals and social conservatives behind a revival of poor laws in the neoliberal era. Cooper's argument, nonetheless, centers white families. Shifting the focus to African Americans reveals how black families were always already "responsibilized" in the United States. See Cooper, *Family Values*.

30. Daryl Michael Scott, *Contempt and Pity: Social Policy and the Image of the Damaged Black Psyche, 1880–1996* (Chapel Hill: University of North Carolina Press, 1997): 42–50, 74–76, 104–6, 148–50.

31. See Judith Stein, *Pivotal Decade: How the United States Traded Factories for Finance in the Seventies* (New Haven, CT: Yale University Press, 2010).

32. Forstater, "From Civil Rights to Economic Security," 71.

33. Craig Allan Kaplowitz, "Struggles of the First 'New Democrat': Jimmy Carter, Youth Employment Policy, and the Great Society Legacy," *Presidential Studies Quarterly* 28, no. 1 (1998): 201.

34. See Paul Friesema, "Black Control of Central Cities: The Hollow Prize," *Journal of the American Institute of Planners* 35, no. 2 (1969): 75–79; Jeffrey S. Adler, *African-American Mayors: Race, Politics, and the American City* (Urbana-Champaign: University of Illinois Press, 2001).

35. John Jacobs, "New Responsibilities for Blacks," *Pittsburgh Courier*, January 23, 1982: 4.

36. Ownby, *Hurtin' Words*, 156–58.

37. See Frances Beale, "Double Jeopardy: To Be Black and Female," in *The Black Woman: An Anthology*, ed. Toni Cade Bambara (New York: Washington Square, 2005): 109–22; Crawford, "Must Revolution be a Family Affair?"

38. On the welfare rights movement, see Premilla Nadasen, *Welfare Warriors: The Welfare Rights Movement in the United States* (New York: Routledge, 2005); Felicia Kornbluh, *The Battle for Welfare Rights: Politics and Poverty in Modern America* (Philadelphia: University of Pennsylvania Press, 2007); Marisa Chappell, *The War on Welfare: Family, Poverty, and Politics in Modern America* (Philadelphia: University of Pennsylvania Press, 2012).

39. "U.S. Woes Reflected in Black Family," *Jet* 53, no. 8 (November 24, 1977): 26.

40. "U.S. Woes Reflected in Black Family."

41. Natasha Zaretsky, *No Direction Home: The American Family and the Fear of National Decline, 1968–1980* (Chapel Hill: University of North Carolina Press, 2010): 8–12.

42. "NAACP to Hold Meet on 'Crisis' of Black Family," *Atlanta Daily World*, September 20, 1983: 1.

43. National Association for the Advancement of Colored People (NAACP) and the National Urban League (NUL), *Report on the Black Family Summit, May 3–5, 1984, Fisk University* (Baltimore, MD: NAACP, 1984).

44. NAACP and NUL, *Report on the Black Family Summit*.

45. NAACP and NUL, *Report on the Black Family Summit*.

46. NAACP and NUL, *Report on the Black Family Summit*.

47. NAACP and NUL, *Report on the Black Family Summit*.

48. Walter Fauntroy to Andy Young, January 3, 1985, box 278, folder 17, Andrew Young Papers, Auburn Avenue Research Library, Atlanta, GA.

49. Congressional Black Caucus, *The Black Leadership Family Plan: For the Unity, Survival, and Progress of Black People* (Washington, DC: Congressional Black Caucus, 1982, 1985).

50. William Julius Wilson, *Truly Disadvantaged: The Inner City, the Underclass, and Public Policy* (Chicago: University of Chicago Press, 1987): 56.

51. Congressional Black Caucus, *The Black Leadership Family Plan*.

52. Congressional Black Caucus, *The Black Leadership Family Plan*.

53. See Marcia Chatelain, *Franchise: The Golden Arches in Black America* (New York: Liveright, 2020).

54. See Julia Rabig and Laura Warren Hill, eds., *The Business of Black Power: Community Development, Capitalism, and Corporate Responsibility in Postwar America* (Rochester, NY: University of Rochester Press, 2012).

55. William Raspberry, "A Winning Lineup: Self-Help and Government Aid" *Orlando Sentinel*, August 1, 1986: A15.

56. "Coors and UL Host Black Family Awareness," *Atlanta Daily World*, October 14, 1984: 3.

57. Frank E. Moss, *Initiatives in Corporate Responsibility* (Washington, DC: US Government Printing Office, 1972): 115; Dwight Burlingame, *Philanthropy in America: A Comprehensive Historical Encyclopedia*, vol. 1 (Santa Barbara, CA: ABC-CLIO, 2004): 48.

58. "Photos of Black Americans Underscore Legacy at Family Reunion Celebration," *Atlanta Daily World*, October 6, 1987: 3; Sharon A. Morgan, "Family Reunions: Keeping Black Families Together," *Atlanta Daily World*, March 26, 1989: 2.

59. Jack Wilkinson, "Black Family Life Affirmed," *Atlanta Constitution*, June 14, 1987: B1.

60. Wilkinson, "Black Family Life Affirmed," B6.

61. Kimberly McLarin, "A Festive Celebration of Family," *Philadelphia Inquirer*, July 29, 1990: B2.

62. James T. Bennett, *Tax-Funded Politics* (New York: Taylor and Francis, 2017); Fred L. Pincus and Howard J. Ehrlich, *Race and Ethnic Conflict: Contending Views on Prejudice, Discrimination, and Ethnoviolence* (New York: Taylor and Francis, 2018).

63. NAACP and NUL, *Report on the Black Family Summit*.

64. Lily Geismer, *Left Behind: The Democrats' Failed Attempt to Solve Inequality* (New York: Public Affairs, 2022): 6.

65. James Forman Jr., *Locking Up Our Own: Crime and Punishment in Black America* (New York: Farrar, Straus and Giroux): 12.

66. Cooper, *Family Values*, 268.

67. Barack Obama, "Remarks by the President at a Father's Day Event," June 21, 2010, Office of the Press Secretary, The White House, https://obamawhitehouse.archives.gov/the-press-office/remarks-president-a-fathers-day-event.

68. Jesse Lee, "President Obama Promotes Responsible Fatherhood: 'No Excuses,'" Obama White House Archives, https://obamawhitehouse.archives.gov/blog/2010/06/21/president-obama-promotes-responsible-fatherhood-no-excuses.

69. This volume's introduction, 16.

Chapter Six

1. Ari Shapiro, "Obama Endorses Same-Sex Marriage," *Morning Edition*, aired May 10, 2012, on NPR, https://www.npr.org/2012/05/10/152396814/obama-endorses-same-sex-marriage; Ken Rudin, "Obama & Gay Marriage: 'Courageous' or Put into a Corner?," *NPR*, https://www.npr.org/sections/politicaljunkie/2012/05/14/152382635/obama-gay-marriage-courageous-or-put-into-a-corner-happy-300th-podcast; "Growing Public Support for Same-Sex Marriage," Pew Research Center, February 7, 2012, https://www.pewresearch.org/politics/2012/02/07/growing-public-support-for-same-sex-marriage/; Josh Levi, "Obama's Change on Same-Sex Marriage Comes After Voters Reach Turning Point," *CNN*, May 10, 2012, https://www.cnn.com/2012/05/10/politics/same-sex-marriage-polling/index.html.

2. Josh Earnest, "President Obama Supports Same-Sex Marriage," *White House Blog*, May 10, 2012, https://obamawhitehouse.archives.gov/blog/2012/05/10/obama-supports-same-sex-marriage; "President Obama ABC News Interview on Same-Sex Marriage," *C-Span*, May 9, 2012, https://www.c-span.org/video/?305933-1/president-obama-abc-news-interview-marriage.

3. I recognize that "LGBTQ" is an anachronistic way to reference queer politics before the very recent past. Part of the difficulty of discussing these movements in the abstract and across a large span of time is that conceptualizations of sexual difference shifted

radically even within the span of a few years. In most of this essay, I instead use "queer" as a shorthand to refer to a shifting terrain of social movements organized around the concerns of sexual and gender minorities. While "queer" is a more historically appropriate term than "LGBTQ," I also recognize that it also has its own etymology that does not perfectly equate with my usage.

4. For more on the social and legal history of queer identity and liberalism, see Margot Canaday, *The Straight State: Sexuality and Citizenship in Twentieth-Century America* (Princeton, NJ: Princeton University Press, 2011); Robert O. Self, *All in the Family: The Realignment of American Democracy since the 1960s* (New York: Hill and Wang, 2012); Carlos A. Ball, *From the Closet to the Courtroom: Five LGBT Rights Lawsuits That Have Changed Our Nation* (Boston, MA: Beacon Press, 2010); Joey L. Mogul, Andrea L. Ritchie, and Kay Whitlock, *Queer (In)Justice: The Criminalization of LGBT People in the United States* (Boston, MA: Beacon Press, 2012); Marc Stein, *Sexual Injustice: Supreme Court Decisions from Griswold to Roe* (Chapel Hill: University of North Carolina Press, 2010); David K. Johnson, *The Lavender Scare: The Cold War Persecution of Gays and Lesbians in the Federal Government* (Chicago: University of Chicago Press, 2004); Clay Howard, *The Closet and the Cul-de-Sac: The Politics of Sexual Privacy in Northern California* (Philadelphia: University of Pennsylvania Press, 2019); Christopher M. Elias, *Gossip Men: J. Edgar Hoover, Joe McCarthy, Roy Cohn, and the Politics of Insinuation* (Chicago: University of Chicago Press, 2023); Timothy Stewart-Winter, "The Fall of Walter Jenkins and the Hidden History of the Lavender Scare," in *Intimate States: Gender, Sexuality, and Governance in Modern US History*, ed. Margot Canaday, Nancy Cott, and Robert Self (Chicago: University of Chicago Press, 2021): 211–34; Amy L. Stone, *Gay Rights at the Ballot Box* (Minneapolis: University of Minnesota Press, 2012).

5. I am using "queer citizenship" as a shorthand to refer to the body of rights and obligations that queer people are entitled to, which has been debated for the past several decades. Ken Plummer's notion of sexual or "intimate" citizenship is also a helpful one here. He defines it as "the *control (or not) over* one's body, feelings, relationships; *access (or not) to* representation, relationships, public spaces, etc.; and *socially grounded choices (or not) about* identities, gender experiences" (quoted in Jeffrey Weeks, "The Sexual Citizen," *Theory, Culture and Society* 15, nos. 3–4 (1998): 37).

6. Nancy Cott, *Public Vows: A History of Marriage and the Nation* (Cambridge, MA: Harvard University Press, 2000): 1.

7. As FDR explained, the Depression involved "not only a further loss of homes, farms, savings and wages, but also a loss of spiritual values—the loss of that sense of security for the present and the future so necessary to the peace and contentment of the individual and his family." Franklin Delano Roosevelt, "Second Fireside Chat," May 7, 1933, online at *The American Presidency Project*, ed. Gerhard Peters and John T. Woolley, https://www.presidency.ucsb.edu/documents/second-fireside-chat.

8. See Self, *All in the Family*; Elaine Tyler May, *Fortress America: How We Embraced Fear and Abandoned Democracy* (New York: Basic Books, 2017).

9. "International Lesbian Conference," *Power of Women: Magazine of the International Wages for Housework Campaign* 5 (n.d., ~1975), https://bcrw.barnard.edu/archive/lesbian/Power_of_Women.pdf.

10. We can see similar dynamics at work across a range of leftist movements. The literature is too vast to cite comprehensively, but see Nancy MacLean, *Freedom Is Not Enough: The Opening of the American Workplace* (Cambridge, MA: Harvard University Press, 2008); Serena Mayeri, *Reasoning from Race: Feminism, Law, and the Civil Rights*

Revolution (Cambridge, MA: Harvard University Press, 2014); Lisa Levenstein, *A Movement without Marches: African American Women and the Politics of Poverty in Philadelphia* (Chapel Hill: University of North Carolina Press, 2009).

11. For an introduction, see Louise Milling, "The New Faith-Based Discrimination," *Boston Review*, December 14, 2022, https://www.bostonreview.net/articles/the-new-faith-based-discrimination/.

12. See, for instance, George Chauncey, *Why Marriage? The History Shaping Today's Debate over Gay Equality* (New York: Basic Books, 2004); William N. Eskridge Jr. and Christopher R. Riano, *Marriage Equality: From Outlaws to In-Laws* (New Haven, CT: Yale University Press, 2020); Evan Gerstmann, *Same-Sex Marriage and the Constitution* (Cambridge: Cambridge University Press, 2008); M. V. Lee Badgett, *When Gay People Get Married: What Happens When Societies Legalize Same-Sex Marriage* (New York: New York University Press, 2009).

13. A robust body of scholarship and activist writing exists that critiques these limits, but my aim here is not to examine that larger discussion. For reference, much of this scholarship begins with Cathy Cohen's groundbreaking 1997 essay "Punks, Bulldaggers, and Welfare Queens: The Radical Potential of Queer Politics?," *GLQ* 3, no. 4: 437–65. For more, see Lisa Duggan, "The New Homonormativity: The Sexual Politics of Neoliberalism," in *Materializing Democracy: Toward a Revitalized Cultural Politics*, ed. Russ Castronovo and Dana D. Nelson (Durham, NC: Duke University Press, 2002); Lisa Duggan, *The Twilight of Equality? Neoliberalism, Cultural Politics, and the Attack on Democracy* (Boston, MA: Beacon Press, 2003); Christina B. Hanhardt, *Safe Space: Gay Neighborhood History and the Politics of Violence* (Durham, NC: Duke University Press, 2013); Dean Spade, *Normal Life: Administrative Violence, Critical Trans Politics, and the Limits of Law* (Durham, NC: Duke University Press, 2015).

14. Amy Dru Stanley, *From Bondage to Contract: Wage Labor, Marriage, and the Market in the Age of Slave Emancipation* (Cambridge: Cambridge University Press, 1998).

15. Priscilla Yamin, "The Search of Marital Order: Civic Membership and the Politics of Marriage in the Progressive Era," *Polity* 41, no. 1 (January 2009): 86–112. It's important to note that the definition of consent in these cases hinged on mental health and disability rather than on age or other factors more common in contemporary uses of the term.

16. Nancy Cott, *Public Vows*, 156–58. See also Stephanie Coontz, *The Way We Never Were: American Families and the Nostalgia Trap* (New York: Basic Books, 2000); Coontz, *Marriage, a History: How Love Conquered Marriage* (New York: Penguin Books, 2005); Self, *All in the Family*.

17. Linda Gordon, *Pitied but Not Entitled: Single Mothers and the History of Welfare, 1890–1935* (New York: Free Press, 1994).

18. See Self, *All in the Family*; Brent Cebul, "Frugal Governance, Family Values, and the Intimate Roots of Neoliberalism," in *Intimate States*, ed. Canaday, Cott, and Self, 325–36.

19. Margot Canaday, *Queer Career: Sexuality and Work in Modern America* (Princeton, NJ: Princeton University Press, 2023): 7–9 (emphasis in original).

20. Gayle Rubin, "The Traffic in Women: Notes on the 'Political Economy' of Sex," in *The Second Wave: A Reader in Feminist Theory*, ed. Linda Nicholson (New York: Routledge, 1997): 28.

21. Christina Hanhardt, "The Radical Potential of Queer Political History?," *GLQ* 25, no. 1 (2019): 145–46.

22. Cohen, "Punks, Bulldaggers, and Welfare Queens," 437–65.

Notes to Pages 115–119

23. Alison Lefkovitz, *Strange Bedfellows: Marriage in the Age of Women's Liberation* (Philadelphia: University of Pennsylvania Press, 2018).

24. Felix Richter, "50 Years of US Wages, in One Chart," *World Economic Forum*, April 12, 2019, https://www.weforum.org/agenda/2019/04/50-years-of-us-wages-in-one-chart/. As of March 2022, the average wage had increased from the 2019 value by $0.74 in 2019 dollars. Data from the US Bureau of Labor Statistics, "Average Hourly Earnings of Production and Nonsupervisory Employees, Total Private," FRED, Federal Reserve Bank of St. Louis, accessed March 8, 2024, https://fred.stlouisfed.org/series/AHETPI; and the Consumer Price Index Inflation Calculator, accessed March 8, 2024, https://www.bls.gov/data/inflation_calculator.htm.

25. Kimberly Phillips-Fein, *Fear City: New York's Fiscal Crisis and the Rise of Austerity Politics* (New York: Macmillan, 2018); Destin Jenkins, *The Bonds of Inequality: Debt and the Making of the American City* (Chicago: University of Chicago Press, 2021).

26. Louis Hyman, *Debtor Nation: The History of America in Red Ink* (Princeton, NJ: Princeton University Press, 2011).

27. Spencer Headworth, *Policing Welfare: Punitive Adversarialism in Public Assistance* (Chicago: University of Chicago Press, 2021).

28. Canaday, *Queer Career*, 11–12. Canaday points out that few civil rights laws actually applied to queer workers (and this remains the case into the present), yet "the civil rights imaginary increasingly included gay people . . . even if civil rights laws did not."

29. William Orville Douglas and the Supreme Court of the United States, "U.S. Reports: Griswold v. Connecticut, 381 U.S. 479 (1965)," *U.S. Reports* 381 (October 1964), https://www.loc.gov/item/usrep381479/.

30. Lauren Gutterman, *Her Neighbor's Wife: A History of Lesbian Desire within Marriage* (Philadelphia: University of Pennsylvania Press, 2020): 12–17.

31. Canaday, Cott, and Self, eds., *Intimate States*, 12.

32. Bill Clinton, "How We Ended Welfare, Together," *New York Times*, August 22, 2006, https://www.nytimes.com/2006/08/22/opinion/22clinton.html.

33. Melinda Cooper, *Family Values: Between Neoliberalism and the New Social Conservatism* (Princeton, NJ: Princeton University Press, 2017); Emma Dowling, *The Care Crisis: What Caused It and How Can We End It?* (New York: Verso, 2021).

34. Anthony Kennedy and Supreme Court of the United States, *Obergefell v. Hodges*, 576 U.S. 644 (2015), https://supreme.justia.com/cases/federal/us/576/14-556/.

35. Tara Siegel Bernard and Ron Lieber, "The High Price of Being a Gay Couple," *New York Times*, October 2, 2009, https://www.nytimes.com/2009/10/03/your-money/03money.html.

36. Michael A. Ash and M. V. Lee Badgett, "Separate and Unequal: The Effect of Unequal Access to Employment-Based Health Insurance on Same-Sex and Unmarried Different-Sex Couples," *Contemporary Economic Policy* 24, no. 4 (October 2006): 582–99. Importantly, a significant part of this story that I do not dwell on here is the impact that the lack of universal health care has on the institution of marriage in the United States.

37. Louise Toupin, *Wages for Housework: A History of an International Feminist Movement, 1972–77* (London: Pluto Press, 2018); Silvia Federici and Arlen Austin, *Wages for Housework: The New York Committee 1972–1977, History, Theory, Documents* (Chico: AK Press, 2017); Emily Callaci, "Care Work in a Wageless World," *Boston Review*, March 2, 2022, https://www.bostonreview.net/articles/selma-james-care-work/; Christina

Rousseau, "Wages Due Lesbians: Visibility and Feminist Organizing in 1970s Canada," *Gender, Work, and Organization* 22, no. 4 (2015): 364–74.

38. Beth Capper and Arlen Austin, "'Wages for Housework Means Wages *Against* Heterosexuality': On the Archives of Black Women for Wages for Housework and Wages Due Lesbians," *GLQ* 24, no. 4 (2018): 446.

39. Silvia Federici, "Wages against Housework," pamphlet (April 1975), https://www.dropbox.com/s/30ndsy3vyir07y5/Wages%20Against%20Housework%20%281%29.pdf?dl=0, via Arlen Austin, Beth Capper, and Tracey Deutsch, "Wages for Housework and Social Reproduction: A Microsyllabus," *The Abusable Past*, April 27, 2020, https://www.radicalhistoryreview.org/abusablepast/wages-for-housework-and-social-reproduction-a-microsyllabus/.

40. Capper and Austin, "Wages for Housework," 449.

41. Quoted in Capper and Austin, "Wages for Housework," 445–46.

42. Quoted in Capper and Austin, "Wages for Housework," 445–46. See also literature on the broader welfare rights movement, including Felicia Kornbluh, *The Battle for Welfare Rights: Politics and Poverty in Modern America* (Philadelphia: University of Pennsylvania Press, 2007); Premilla Nadasen, *Welfare Warriors: The Welfare Rights Movement in the United States* (New York: Routledge, 2005); Annelise Orleck, *Storming Caesars Palace: How Black Mothers Fought Their Own War on Poverty* (Boston, MA: Beacon Press, 2005); Marisa Chappell, *The War on Welfare: Family, Poverty, and Politics in Modern America* (Philadelphia: University of Pennsylvania Press, 2010).

43. Quoted in Ryan Patrick Murphy, *Deregulating Desire: Flight Attendant Activism, Family Politics, and Workplace Justice* (Philadelphia: Temple University Press, 2016): 1–2.

44. Quoted in Murphy, *Deregulating Desire*, 8–15.

45. "What Is the Self-Sufficiency Standard?," Center for Women's Welfare, University of Washington School of Social Work, accessed March 8, 2024, https://selfsufficiencystandard.org/the-standard/overview/.

46. This literature is robust. To start, see Dowling, *The Care Crisis*.

47. Elizabeth Warren and Amelia Warren Tyagi, *The Two-Income Trap: Why Middle-Class Parents Are Going Broke* (New York: Basic Books, 2003).

48. Laura Briggs, *How All Politics Became Reproductive Politics: From Welfare Reform to Foreclosure to Trump* (Berkeley: University of California Press, 2018).

49. Juliana Menasce Horowitz, Nikki Graf, and Gretchen Livingston, "Marriage and Cohabitation in the U.S.," Pew Research Center, November 6, 2019, https://www.pewresearch.org/social-trends/2019/11/06/marriage-and-cohabitation-in-the-u-s/.

50. John D'Emilio, "Capitalism and Gay Identity," in *The Lesbian and Gay Studies Reader*, ed. Henry Abelove, Michèle Aina Barale, and David M. Halperin (New York: Routledge, 1993): 470.

51. D'Emilio, "Capitalism and Gay Identity," 473, 475.

52. Lawrence Hurley and Andrew Chung, "Analysis: 'Aggressively Conservative' Supreme Court Plunges into U.S. Culture Wars," *Reuters*, January 25, 2022, https://www.reuters.com/legal/government/aggressively-conservative-supreme-court-plunges-into-us-culture-wars-2022-01-25/.

53. Hannah Schoenbaum, "Republican States Aim to Restrict Transgender Health Care in First Bills of 2023," *PBS News Hour*, January 7, 2023, https://www.pbs.org/newshour/politics/republican-states-aim-to-restrict-transgender-health-care-in-first-bills-of-2023; Maham Javaid, "New State Bills Restrict Transgender Health Care—For

Adults," *Washington Post*, March 1, 2023, https://www.washingtonpost.com/nation/2023/02/28/anti-trans-bills-gender-affirming-care-adults/.

Chapter Seven

1. Margaret Sullivan, "The Media Didn't Want to Believe Trump Could Win. So They Looked the Other Way," *Washington Post*, November 9, 2016, https://www.washingtonpost.com/lifestyle/style/the-media-didnt-want-to-believe-trump-could-win-so-they-looked-the-other-way/2016/11/09/d2ea1436-a623-11e6-8042-f4d111c862d1_story.html.

2. Works that examine the idea of the "liberal media" tend to focus on conservatives instead of historicizing the changing nature of liberalism or the news industry as a whole. See Nicole Hemmer, *Messengers of the Right: Conservative Media and the Transformation of American Politics* (Philadelphia: University of Pennsylvania Press, 2016); and David Greenburg, "The Idea of 'The Liberal Media' and Its Roots in the Civil Rights Movement," *The Sixties: A Journal of History, Politics and Culture* 1, no. 2 (December 2008): 167–86. Commentators from the left argue the press is far from progressive, pointing to its close relationship with powerful institutions. See Edward S. Herman and Noam Chomsky, *Manufacturing Consent: The Political Economy of the Mass Media* (New York: Pantheon, 1988); and Eric Alterman, *What Liberal Media? The Truth about Bias and the News* (New York: Basic Books, 2003).

3. On the transformation of the Democratic Party in the late twentieth century, see Lily Geismer, *Left Behind: The Democrats' Failed Attempt to Solve Inequality* (New York: Public Affairs, 2022). For the relationship between politics and news media, see Bruce J. Schulman and Julian E. Zelizer, eds., *Media Nation: The Political History of News in Modern America* (Philadelphia: University of Pennsylvania Press, 2017).

4. Julia Guarneri, *Newsprint Metropolis: City Papers and the Making of Modern Americans* (Chicago: University of Chicago Press, 2017): 62–75; and David Paul Nord, *Communities of Journalism: A History of American Newspapers and Their Readers* (Champaign: University of Illinois Press, 2001): 225–77.

5. Guarneri, *Newsprint Metropolis*, 219, and "History of Ownership Consolidation," *Dirks, VanEssen, and April*, March 31, 2017, https://dirksvanessen.com/articles/history-of-ownership-consolidation-/.

6. Will Mari, *The American Newsroom: A History, 1920–1960* (Columbia: University of Missouri Press, 2021): 70–71.

7. Morton Sontheimer, *Newspaperman: A Book about the Business* (New York: McGraw Hill, 1941): 322.

8. Sam Roberts, "Arthur Gelb, Critic and Editor Who Shaped the Times, Dies at 90," *New York Times*, May 20, 2014; Mari, *American Newsroom*, 26–27.

9. Steven Greenhouse, "More Secure Jobs, Bigger Paychecks: The Reasons for Unionizing Haven't Changed Much in the Last 80 Years," *Columbia Journalism Review* (Spring/Summer 2018).

10. Shannan Clark, *The Making of the American Creative Class: New York's Culture Workers and Twentieth-Century Consumer Capitalism* (New York: Oxford University Press, 2021): 63–66, 68–69; Mari, *American Newsroom*, 209–13.

11. Even amidst the labor peace of the 1940s, media interests began to resist reformers' efforts to make media more democratic. See Victor Pickard, *America's Battle for Media Democracy: The Triumph of Corporate Libertarianism and the Future of Media Reform* (New York: Cambridge University Press, 2014): chapter 7.

12. Chris Lehmann, "The Eyes of Spiro Are upon You: The Myth of the Liberal Media," *Baffler* 14 (Spring 2001): 25–26; and Matthew Pressman, "The New York Daily News and the History of Conservative Media," *Modern American History* 4, no. 3 (Fall 2021): 219–38. For pre-WWII media critiques from the populist left, see Sam Lebovic, "When the 'Mainstream Media' Was Conservative: Media Criticism in the Age of Reform" in *Media Nation*, ed. Schulman and Zelizer, 63–76.

13. Mari, *American Newsroom*, 30–32.

14. See for example: *Washington Post* ad in "Career Planning & Placement Center Listings," *Stanford Daily*, October 20, 1972: 4.

15. John W. C. Johnstone, Edward J. Slawski, and William W. Bowman, *The News People: A Sociological Portrait of Journalists and Their Work* (Urbana: University of Illinois Press, 1976): 31–47; David H. Weaver, Lars Willnat, and G. Cleveland Wilhoit, "The American Journalist in the Digital Age: Another Look at U.S. News People," *Journalism and Mass Communication Quarterly* 96, no. 1 (March 2019): 104. Graduate-degree figure in Joshua Benton, "It's Time to Create an Alternative Path into a Journalism Career," *NiemanLab*, October 20, 2021, https://www.niemanlab.org/2021/10/its-time-to-create-an-alternative-path-into-a-journalism-career/#:~:text=About%2020%25%20of%20journalists%20have,master's%20in%20some%20other%20field.

16. Christopher R. Martin, *No Longer Newsworthy: How the Mainstream Media Abandoned the Working Class* (Ithaca, NY: Cornell University Press, 2019): 71–88.

17. On the "sectorial revolution," see Matthew Pressman, *On Press: The Liberal Values That Shaped the News* (Cambridge, MA: Harvard University Press, 2018): 115–19 and 127–32.

18. Felix Gutierrez and Clint C. Wilson II, "The Demographic Dilemma," *Columbia Journalism Review* (January/February 1979): 53.

19. Lorenzo Benet, "Life Is One Long Mass of Fine Print for Consumer Advocate Horowitz," *Chicago Tribune*, February 19, 1987; and Pressman, *On Press*, 184–218.

20. By 2014, only two of the top twenty-five newspapers employed full-time labor reporters. See Martin, *No Longer Newsworthy*, 49–52.

21. Nikki Usher, *News for the Rich, White, and Blue: How Place and Power Distort American Journalism* (New York: Columbia University Press, 2021): 51–54; Martin, *No Longer Newsworthy*, 109–119.

22. Martin, *No Longer Newsworthy*, 66.

23. Doug Underwood, *When MBAs Rule the Newsroom: How Marketers and Managers are Reshaping Today's Media* (New York: Columbia University Press, 1993): 8–9 and 14–25.

24. Martin, *No Longer Newsworthy*, 101–2.

25. Gutierrez and Wilson II, "Demographic Dilemma," 53.

26. Leo Bogart, *Preserving the Press: How Daily Newspapers Mobilized to Keep Their Readers* (New York: Columbia University Press, 1991): 158; Martin, *No Longer Newsworthy*, 65, 69–70.

27. On the underground press, see John C. McMillian, *Smoking Typewriters: The Sixties Underground Press and the Rise of Alternative Media in America* (New York: Oxford University Press, 2011): statistic on 4.

28. Harvey Wasserman, "The Power of Time," *Great Speckled Bird* 1, no. 10 (July 19, 1968): 11, 14, Great Speckled Bird collection, Digital Collections, Georgia State University, https://digitalcollections.library.gsu.edu/digital/collection/GSB/id/130/rec/3.

29. Joshua Clark Davis, *From Head Shops to Whole Foods: The Rise and Fall of Activist Entrepreneurs* (New York: Columbia University Press, 2017).

30. Calvin Trillin, "Alternatives," *New Yorker*, April 2, 1978: 118; and McMillian, *Smoking Typewriters*, 172–85.

31. Mary Ellen Schoonmaker, "Has the Alternative Press Gone Yuppie?," *Columbia Journalism Review*, November 1, 1987: 60.

32. Michael Wolff, "35 Years," *New York*, March 28, 2003.

33. See Edward Costikyan, "The Ten Most Powerful Men in New York," *New York*, January 5, 1970: 24–27.

34. Miriam Greenburg, "Branding Cities: A Social History of the Urban Lifestyle Magazine," *Urban Affairs Review* 36, no. 2 (November 2000): 244–45.

35. Pressman, *On Press*, 136–37.

36. Consumer Research Center, Conference Board, and US Bureau of the Census, *A Marketer's Guide to Discretionary Income* (New York: Conference Board, 1983), available at the Hagley Museum and Library, Wilmington, DE.

37. Joseph Turow, *Breaking Up America: Advertisers and the New Media World* (Chicago: University of Chicago Press, 1997): 65–68, quote on 66. On the history of *Ebony* and Black middle-class magazines, see Adam Green, *Selling the Race: Culture, Community, and Black Chicago, 1940–1955* (Chicago: University of Chicago Press, 2007).

38. For Hamill's biography, see Christopher Bonanos, "Pete Hamill Was One of Us, Only Better at It," *New York*, August 6, 2020, https://nymag.com/intelligencer/2020/08/pete-hamill-was-one-of-us-only-better-at-it.html; Alex Williams, "Pete Hamill 'Ain't Done Yet,'" *New York Times*, November 26, 2019.

39. Pete Hamill, "Brooklyn: The Sane Alternative," *New York*, July 14, 1969.

40. Pete Hamill, "The Revolt of the White Lower Middle Class," *New York*, April 14, 1969.

41. Pete Hamill, "The New Race Hustle," *Esquire*, September 1, 1990: quote on 78.

42. Pete Hamill, "Breaking the Silence: A Letter to a Black Friend," *Esquire*, March 1, 1988: 91–102, quote on 102.

43. On Mailer, see Alison Stine, "Reports of Norman Mailer's Cancellation Have Been Greatly Exaggerated," *Salon*, February 5, 2022, https://www.salon.com/2022/01/05/norman-mailer-cancelled. On Breslin, see "Rage & Outrage: Jimmy Breslin's Racist Newsroom Pique Provokes a Nationwide Furor," *Los Angeles Times*, May 15, 1990.

44. Pete Hamill, "Confessions of a Heterosexual," *Esquire*, August 1, 1990: 55–56.

45. This paragraph draws from Jacqueline Brandon, "Dead Center: The New Democrats and the Transformation of Liberalism" (PhD diss., Princeton University, 2023): chapter 2, http://arks.princeton.edu/ark:/88435/dsp017p88ck81v.

46. Mark Muro, "Hot *New Republic* Beams in Power Town," *Chicago Tribune*, June 21, 1985: 2; David A. Bell, "On 'The New Republic,'" *Los Angeles Review of Books*, December 29, 2014, https://lareviewofbooks.org/article/new-republic/.

47. See, for example, Charles Murray, "Affirmative Racism," *New Republic*, December 31, 1984: 17–23; Hendrik Hertzberg, "Up from Crisis," *New Republic*, December 10, 1984: 9–12.

48. Editorial, "The Case for the Contras," *New Republic*, March 24, 1986: 7–9; and Brandon, "Dead Center," 33.

49. Leon Wieseltier, "The Great Nuclear Debate," *New Republic*, January 10 and 17, 1983: 7–9.

50. Jay Rosen, "Why Political Coverage Is Broken," *PressThink*, August 26, 2011, https://pressthink.org/2011/08/why-political-coverage-is-broken/. See also Todd Gitlin, "Blips, Bites & Savvy Talk," *Dissent*, January 1990: 21–22.

51. Walter Lippmann, *Public Opinion* (New York: Harcourt, Brace & Co., 1922): 310.

52. While embraced in the 1970s by neoconservatives, including Daniel Patrick Moynihan and Norman Podhoretz, the term was originally coined by John Kenneth Galbraith in his 1958 *The Affluent Society*. For a sociological overview of the New Class debate, see Steven Brint, "'New-Class' and Cumulative Trend Explanations of the Liberal Political Attitudes of Professionals," *American Journal of Sociology* 90, no. 1 (July 1984): 30–71.

53. Irving Kristol, "Business and 'The New Class,'" *Wall Street Journal*, May 1, 1975.

54. S. Robert Lichter et al., *The Media Elite* (Bethesda, MD: Adler & Adler, 1986): 21 and 30. Also Edith Efron, *The News Twisters* (Los Angeles: Nash Publishing, 1971).

55. Pressman, *On Press*.

56. "Just Another Union?," *Columbia Journalism Review* (September/October 1972): 4.

57. Daniel Lazare, "Journalism's New Underclass?," *Columbia Journalism Review*, March 1, 1987: 11–13.

58. See Robert W. McChesney and Victor Pickard, eds., *Will the Last Reporter Please Turn Out the Lights: The Collapse of Journalism and What Can Be Done to Fix It* (New York: New Press, 2010).

59. Larry Hatfield, "1994 San Francisco News Strike Pushed Limits and Ushered In Online Media," *Pacific Media Workers Guild*, https://mediaworkers.org/1994-strike-set-a-sour-tone-for-a-new-era-in-newspapers/; David Margolick, "Strike Prevents Delivery of San Francisco Daily Newspapers," *New York Times*, November 3, 1994.

60. During the strike, management at the *Examiner* launched their own competing website, the *Gate*. Without an editorial team, it ran republished wire stories.

61. Carl Bialik, "Freeing the Press," *Wall Street Journal*, May 12, 2004; readership in Peter H. Lewis, "The News, Virtually," *New York Times*, November 13, 1994. On WELL, see Fred Turner, *From Counterculture to Cyberculture: Stewart Brand, the Whole Earth Network, and the Rise of Digital Utopianism* (Chicago: University of Chicago Press, 2010).

62. Bialik, "Freeing the Press."

63. Wendell Cochran, "Searching for Right Mixture," *Quill* (May 1995): 36.

64. Carol Pogash, "Cyberspace Journalism," *American Journalism Review*, June 1, 1996.

65. George Kamiya, "Ten Years of Salon," *Salon*, November 14, 2005, https://www.salon.com/2005/11/14/salon_history/; Laura Lippman, "Sultan of Salon," *Baltimore Sun*, March 13, 2000.

66. Pogash, "Cyberspace Journalism."

67. Jack Shafer and Tucker Doherty, "The Media Bubble Is Worse Than You Think," *Politico* (May/June 2017), https://www.politico.com/magazine/story/2017/04/25/media-bubble-real-journalism-jobs-east-coast-215048/.

68. Brent Cunningham, "Across the Great Divide—Class," *Columbia Journalism Review* (May/June 2004); "Salary Increase for Grads," *Quill* (October 1996): 7.

69. Usher, *News for the Rich, White, and Blue*, 58.

70. Howard Kutz, "The White Person for the Job," *Washington Post*, April 8, 1995.

71. Jonathan Wai and Kaja Perina, "Expertise in Journalism: Factors Shaping a Cognitive and Culturally Elite Profession," *Journal of Expertise* 10, no. 10 (March 2018): 9.

72. Michael Kinsley, "Welcome to Slate," *Slate*, June 25, 1996, https://slate.com/news-and-politics/1996/06/welcome-to-slate.html.

73. Michael Kinsley, "My History of Slate," *Slate*, June 18, 2006, https://slate.com/news-and-politics/2006/06/michael-kinsley-s-history-of-slate.html; Kinsley, "Slate on Paper at Starbucks," *Slate*, September 14, 1996, https://slate.com/news-and-politics/1996/09/slate-on-paper-at-starbucks.html; Ken Auletta, "The Reeducation of Michael Kinsley," *New Yorker*, May 13, 1996: 58–65.

74. "Roll Call: Who's for War, Who's against It, and Why," *Slate*, February 19, 2003, https://slate.com/news-and-politics/2003/02/who-s-for-war-who-s-against-it-and-why.html.

75. "Comment: Doing the Devil's Work," *Columbia Journalism Review* (January/February 1980): 22–23.

76. Reece Peck, *Fox Populism: Branding Conservatism as Working Class* (Cambridge: Cambridge University Press, 2019): 18, 51, 121–25.

77. Peck, *Fox Populism*, 134–35.

78. Timothy J. Lombardo, *Blue-Collar Conservatism: Frank Rizzo's Philadelphia and Populist Politics* (Philadelphia: University of Pennsylvania Press, 2018).

79. For an account of the regional and attitudinal divides among elites, see Melinda Cooper, "Family Capitalism and the Small Business Insurrection," *Dissent* (Winter 2022), https://www.dissentmagazine.org/article/family-capitalism-and-the-small-business-insurrection/.

Chapter Eight

This chapter contains material previously published in Timothy Shenk, *Left Adrift: What Happened to Liberal Politics* (New York: Columbia Global Reports, 2024).

1. Kevin Phillips, *The Emerging Republican Majority* (New York: Doubleday, 1969). On Phillips's background, see Garry Wills, *Nixon Agonistes: The Crisis of the Self-Made Man* (Boston, MA: Houghton Mifflin, 1969): 264–71.

2. On which see Lily Geismer, *Left Behind: The Democrats' Failed Attempt to Solve Inequality* (New York: Public Affairs, 2022): 17–48, 106–12.

3. "Excerpts from Jackson to Convention Delegates for Unity in Party," *New York Times*, July 18, 1984: A18.

4. Documented at length in Amory Gethin, Clara Martínez-Toledano, and Thomas Piketty, eds., *Political Cleavages and Social Inequalities: A Study of Fifty Democracies, 1948–2020* (Cambridge, MA: Harvard University Press, 2021).

5. For Inglehart's fullest views on the subject, see Ronald Inglehart and Pippa Norris, *Cultural Backlash: Trump, Brexit, and Authoritarian Populism* (Cambridge: Cambridge University Press, 2019).

6. See Ronald Brownstein, "Obama Buoyed by Coalition of the Ascendant," *National Journal*, November 8, 2008: 5.

7. On the making of political consulting, see Adam Sheingate, *Building a Business of Politics: The Rise of Political Consulting and the Transformation of American Democracy* (New York: Oxford University Press, 2016); and Dennis W. Johnson, *Democracy for Hire: A History of American Political Consulting* (New York: Oxford University Press, 2017): 129–235.

8. For instance, John Harwood, "Two Pollsters Embody Democratic Divide," *Wall Street Journal*, July 1, 1998: A20.

9. Napolitan explained and defended the new profession in *The Election Game and How to Win It* (New York: Doubleday, 1972).

10. Pew Research Center for the People and the Press, Don't Blame Us: The Views of Political Consultants (Washington, DC: Pew Research Center, June 17, 1998), http://www.people-press.org/1998/06/17/dont-blame-us/.

11. Molly Ball, "There's Nothing Better than a Scared, Rich Candidate," *Atlantic*, October 15, 2016, https://www.theatlantic.com/magazine/archive/2016/10/theres-nothing-better-than-a-scared-rich-candidate/497522/.

12. Lydia Saad, "Democrats' Identification as Liberal Now 54%, a New High," *Gallup*, January 12, 2023, https://news.gallup.com/poll/467888/democrats-identification-liberal-new-high.aspx.

13. For Greenberg's biography, see Stanley Greenberg, *Dispatches from the War Room: In the Trenches with Five Extraordinary Political Leaders* (New York: St. Martin's Publishing Group, 2009); and, for a more critical perspective, David Roediger, *The Sinking Middle Class: A Political History* (New York: Haymarket Books, 2022): 121–54. I thank Dr. Greenberg for confirming details of this account with me in an interview on April 13, 2022.

14. A revised version of Stanley Greenberg's dissertation was published as *Politics and Poverty: Modernization and Response in Five Poor Neighborhoods* (New York: John Wiley and Sons, Inc., 1974).

15. Stanley Greenberg, *Race and State in Capitalist Development: Comparative Perspectives* (New Haven, CT: Yale University Press: 1980): 29–30.

16. Greenberg, *Race and State in Capitalist Development*, 24.

17. Stanley Greenberg, *The Two Americas: Our Current Political Deadlock and How to Break It* (New York: St. Martin's Publishing Group, 2004): xi.

18. Stanley Greenberg, *Middle-Class Dreams: The Politics and Power of the New American Majority* (New York: Random House, 1995): 39–40.

19. Stanley Greenberg, "Interview 1 with Stanley Greenberg," interview by Russell Riley and Paul Freedman, January 27, 2005, https://millercenter.org/the-presidency/presidential-oral-histories/stanley-greenberg-oral-history-2005.

20. Greenberg, *Dispatches from the War Room*, 182.

21. Eleanor Clift and Tom Brazaitis, *War without Bloodshed: The Art of Politics* (New York: Scribner, 1997): 27.

22. Stanley Greenberg, "From Crisis to Working Majority," *American Prospect*, December 5, 1991, https://prospect.org/culture/books/crisis-working-majority/.

23. Greenberg, *Dispatches from the War Room*, 104, 20.

24. Stephen Smith, ed., *Preface to the Presidency: Selected Speeches of Bill Clinton, 1974–1992* (Fayetteville: University of Arkansas Press, 1996): 91; Marshall Ingwerson, "Transition Tests Clinton's Ability to Balance Competing Interests," *Christian Science Monitor*, November 9, 1992, https://www.csmonitor.com/1992/1109/09091.html.

25. Greenberg, *Dispatches from the War Room*, 37.

26. Greenberg, *Dispatches from the War Room*, 40.

27. This transition within the political team maps onto a larger shift in the Clinton administration, on which see Nelson Lichtenstein and Judith Stein, *A Fabulous Failure: The Clinton Presidency and the Transformation of American Capitalism* (Princeton, NJ: Princeton University Press, 2023).

28. "The Morris Meltdown," *Newsweek*, September 8, 1996, https://www.newsweek.com/morris-meltdown-177794.

29. On Schoen's life, see Douglas E. Schoen, *The Power of the Vote: Electing Presidents, Overthrowing Dictators, and Promoting Democracy around the World* (New York: Harper Collins, 2007). I thank Dr. Schoen for discussing elements of this account with me in an interview on April 26, 2022.

30. For Penn's early biography, see James Bennett, "The Guru of Small Things," *New York Times*, June 18, 2000, https://www.nytimes.com/2000/06/18/magazine/the-guru-of-small-things.html.

31. Richard M. Scammon and Ben J. Wattenberg, *The Real Majority* (New York: Primus, 1992 [1970]): 57.

32. Schoen, interview with author, April 26, 2022.

33. Scammon and Wattenberg, *Real Majority*, 58.

34. Mark Penn and Douglas Schoen, "Reagan's Revolution Ended?," *New York Times*, November 9, 1986: 23.

35. Dennis Farney, "Indiana Race for Governor Finds GOP Stumped by Democrat with a Fresh Face, Legendary Name," *Wall Street Journal*, October 24, 1988: A14.

36. Schoen, *Power of the Vote*, 232–33.

37. Schoen, *Power of the Vote*, 235.

38. *Guide to U.S. Elections*, 6th ed., vol. 1 (Washington, DC: SAGE Publications, 2010): 25, 798.

39. Theda Skocpol and Stanley Greenberg, "Popularizing Progressive Politics," in *The New Majority: Toward a Popular Progressive Politics*, ed. Stanley Greenberg and Theda Skocpol (New Haven, CT: Yale University Press, 1997): 4.

40. Schoen, *Power of the Vote*, 349.

41. Schoen, *Power of the Vote*, 225.

42. Schoen, *Power of the Vote*, 351.

43. "Taxes," "Immigration," and "Crime," *Gallup*, accessed April 8, 2024, https://news.gallup.com/poll/1714/taxes.aspx; https://news.gallup.com/poll/1660/immigration.aspx; and https://news.gallup.com/poll/1603/crime.aspx.

44. Greenberg, *Dispatches from the War Room*, 232.

45. "Gore's Next Move," *CBS News*, August 20, 2000, https://www.cbsnews.com/news/gores-next-move/.

46. John Harris, "Policy and Politics by the Numbers," *Washington Post*, December 31, 2000: A01.

47. Mark Penn with E. Kinney Zalesne, *Microtrends: The Small Forces behind Tomorrow's Big Changes* (New York: Twelve, 2007): xiii.

48. Penn with Zalesne, *Microtrends*, 139.

49. John Judis and Ruy Teixiera, *The Emerging Democratic Majority* (New York: Simon and Schuster, 2002).

50. See, for instance, Sasha Issenberg, *The Victory Lab: The Secret Science of Winning Elections* (New York: Broadway Books, 2012).

51. Mark Penn, "Weekly Strategic Review on Hillary Clinton for President Committee," *Atlantic*, March 19, 2007, https://www.theatlantic.com/politics/archive/2008/08/penn-strategy-memo-march-19-2008/37952/.

52. Greenberg, *Dispatches from the War Room*, 106.

53. Greenberg, *Dispatches from the War Room*, 107.

54. Andrew Malcolm, "The Ties that Bind," *Los Angeles Times*, June 7, 2010, available at https://www.latimes.com/archives/blogs/top-of-the-ticket/story/2010-06-07/opinion-the-ties-that-bind-remember-rahm-emanuels-rent-free-d-c-apartment-the-owner-a-bp-adviser.

55. Greenberg, *Dispatches from the War Room*, 419.

56. Greenberg, *Dispatches from the War Room*, 419.

57. Saad, "Democrats' Identification."

Chapter Nine

1. Lyndon Johnson, "Remarks upon Signing the Voting Rights Act," August 6, 1965, online at the Miller Center, https://millercenter.org/the-presidency/presidential-speeches/august-6-1965-remarks-signing-voting-rights-act.

2. On the fights over voting rights in the late twentieth century, see Ari Berman, *Give Us the Ballot: The Modern Struggle for Voting Rights in America* (New York: Picador, 2016); Alexander Keyssar, *The Right to Vote: The Contested History of Democracy in the United States* (New York: Basic Books, 2009); J. Morgan Kousser, *Colorblind Injustice: Minority Voting Rights and the Undoing of the Second Reconstruction* (Chapel Hill: University of North Carolina Press, 1999); and Steven F. Lawson, *In Pursuit of Power: Southern Blacks and Electoral Politics, 1965–1982* (New York: Columbia University Press, 1985).

3. On the relationship between disenfranchisement and democratic expansions (and a review of debates over the conditions under which elites extend the franchise), see David A. Bateman, *Disenfranchising Democracy: Constructing the Electorate in the United States, the United Kingdom, and France* (New York: Cambridge University Press, 2018).

4. For an important example of skepticism about democracy more generally, see, for example, Michel Crozier, Samuel Huntington, and Joji Watanuki, *The Crisis of Democracy: Report on the Governability of Democracies to the Trilateral Commission* (New York: New York University Press, 1975). Huntington and other "overload theorists" warned that the era's democratic "excesses" would trigger spiraling social-program costs, inflation, alienation, and ultimately political crisis.

5. See, for example, Adam Sheingate, *Building a Business of Politics: The Rise of Political Consulting and the Transformation of American Democracy* (New York: Oxford University Press, 2018); Takahito Moriyama, *Empire of Direct Mail: How Conservative Marketing Persuaded Voters and Transformed the Grassroots* (Lawrence: University Press of Kansas, 2022); Theda Skocpol, *Diminished Democracy: From Membership to Management in American Civic Life* (Norman: University of Oklahoma Press, 2003); and Matthew A. Crenson, *Downsizing Democracy: How America Sidelined Its Citizens and Privatized Its Public* (Baltimore, MD: Johns Hopkins University Press, 2002).

6. Wendy Brown, "We Are All Democrats Now . . . ," *Theory and Event* 13, no. 2 (2010), https://doi.org/10.1353/tae.0.0133.

7. Joe Soss and Vesla Weaver have called for political scientists to integrate the role of state surveillance and repression more comprehensively into their analyses in "Police Are Our Government: Politics, Political Science, and the Policing of Race–Class Subjugated Communities," *Annual Review of Political Science* 20, no. 1 (May 11, 2017): 565–91.

8. Michael McDonald and Samuel Popkin, "The Myth of the Vanishing Voter," *American Political Science Review* 95 (December 2001): 963–74. On percentages of ineligible voters, see "VAP v. V[E]P," United States Election Project, accessed March 15, 2024, https://www.electproject.org/election-data/faq/vap-v-vap.

9. Edmund Fawcett, *Liberalism: The Life of an Idea* (Princeton, NJ: Princeton University Press, 2018).

10. Aziz Rana, *The Two Faces of American Freedom* (Cambridge, MA: Harvard University Press, 2010).

11. See, for example, Mae M. Ngai, *Impossible Subjects: Illegal Aliens and the Making of Modern America* (Princeton, NJ: Princeton University Press, 2004).

12. One important exception was "whites only" primaries, which the Supreme Court struck down in Smith v. Allwright 321 U.S. 649 (1944). On the history of voter suppression, see Carol Anderson, *One Person, No Vote: How Voter Suppression Is Destroying Our Democracy* (New York: Bloomsbury Publishing, 2018).

13. See, for examples, Linda Gordon, *Pitied but Not Entitled: Single Mothers and the History of Welfare, 1890–1935* (New York: Free Press, 1994); Ira Katznelson, *When Affirmative Action Was White: An Untold History of Racial Inequality in Twentieth-Century*

America (New York: W. W. Norton and Company, 2006); Alice Kessler-Harris, *In Pursuit of Equity: Women, Men, and the Quest for Economic Citizenship in 20th-Century America* (Oxford: Oxford University Press, 2003); and Margot Canaday, *The Straight State: Sexuality and Citizenship in Twentieth-Century America* (Princeton, NJ: Princeton University Press, 2011).

14. Harper v. Virginia Bd. of Elections, 383 U.S. 663 (1966), available at Justia Law, https://supreme.justia.com/cases/federal/us/383/663/.

15. Oregon v. Mitchell, 400 U.S. 112 (1970), available at Oyez, https://www.oyez.org/cases/1970/43-orig.

16. Eli L. Levine, "Does the Social Contract Justify Felony Disenfranchisement? Note," *Washington University Jurisprudence Review* 1 (2009): 193–224; and "Disenfranchisement of Ex-Felons: Citizenship, Criminality, and the Purity of the Ballot Box, the Notes," *Harvard Law Review* 102 (1988–1989): 1300–17.

17. On the importance of the image of US democracy in Cold War diplomacy, see Mary L. Dudziak, *Cold War Civil Rights: Race and the Image of American Democracy*, new ed. (Princeton, NJ: Princeton University Press, 2011).

18. See John F. Kennedy, "Executive Order 11100—Establishing the President's Commission on Registration and Voting Participation," March 30, 1963, online at *The American Presidency Project*, ed. Gerhard Peters and John T. Woolley, http://www.presidency.ucsb.edu/ws/index.php?pid=59039; and "Outmoded Laws Blamed for U.S. Voter Apathy," *Hartford Courant*, January 7, 1964: 20a.

19. *Report of the President's Commission on Registration and Voting Participation* (Washington, DC: Government Printing Office, November 1963): 2–3, http://hdl.handle.net/2027/umn.31951d029875154.

20. Steven F. Lawson, *In Pursuit of Power: Southern Blacks and Electoral Politics, 1965–1982* (New York: Columbia University Press, 1985): 39–42; Bayard Rustin, "An Attack on the Black Vote," *New York Amsterdam News*, December 13, 1969: 18; and United States Commission on Civil Rights, *Political Participation: A Study of the Participation by Negroes in the Electoral and Political Processes in 10 Southern States since Passage of the Voting Rights Act of 1965* (Washington, DC: Commission on Civil Rights, 1968): 12–13.

21. Byrd quoted in Arlen J. Large, "Poverty War: Tightening the Strings," *Wall Street Journal*, October 26, 1967: 18. See also "Antipoverty Program Survives Assault, Gets $1.8 Billion," in *CQ Almanac 1967*, 23rd ed. (Washington, DC: Congressional Quarterly, 1968).

22. "The Real Black Power," *Time* 90, no. 20 (November 17, 1967): 23, https://time.com/vault/issue/1967-11-17/page/42/.

23. Laurence Stern and Richard Harwood, "Ford Foundation: Its Works Spark a Backlash," *Washington Post*, November 2, 1969: A1, A14. See also Frances Fox Piven, Lorraine Minnite, and Margaret Groarke, *Keeping Down the Black Vote: Race and the Demobilization of American Voters* (New York: New Press, 2009): 75–77.

24. See, for example, Roy Wilkins, "Says Reform Bills Are Anti-Black," *New Pittsburgh Courier*, August 23, 1969: 13; James T. Wooten, "Group Says Tax Bill Perils Black Vote," *New York Times*, November 19, 1969: 37; and Rustin, "Attack on the Black Vote," 18.

25. See Evan Faulkenbury, *Poll Power: The Voter Education Project and the Movement for the Ballot in the American South* (Chapel Hill: University of North Carolina Press, 2019): chapter 5; and Piven, Minnite, and Groarke, *Keeping Down the Black Vote*, 75. Foundations now had to spread voter registration work across five or more states. Voter registration campaigns were prohibited from having more than one-fourth of their funding come from a single tax-exempt group.

26. Statement of Hon. H. A. Boucher, lieutenant governor of the State of Alaska, "Voter Registration," Hearings before the Committee on Post Office and Civil Service on S. 352 and S. 472, United States Senate, 93rd Congress, February 7, 1973: 40.

27. "Voter Registration: Senate Rejects Nationwide Plan," CQ Almanac 1972, 28th ed. (Washington, DC: Congressional Quarterly, 1973).

28. "Postcard Voter Registration," CQ Almanac 1976, 32nd ed. (Washington, DC: Congressional Quarterly, 1977): 517–19.

29. Jimmy Carter, "Election Reform Message to the Congress," March 22, 1977, online at *The American Presidency Project*, ed. Gerhard Peters and John T. Woolley, http://www.presidency.ucsb.edu/ws/index.php?pid=721. Carter's post-presidency work with international election monitoring and domestic voting-reform commissions also reflect this commitment. After 1980, Carter joined with prominent Republicans to lead several high-profile, bipartisan inquiries into election reform. For example, he headed with James Baker the Commission on Federal Election Reform empaneled after the 2000 election. See Dan Balz, "Carter-Baker Panel to Call for Voting Fixes," *Washington Post*, September 19, 2005. On the Carter Center's international democracy projects, see "Democracy Program," Carter Center, accessed March 15, 2024, https://www.cartercenter.org/peace/democracy/index.html.

30. "Memoranda—Pat Caddell, 12/10/76–12/21/76," collection: Records of the White House Press Office; series: Jody Powell's Transition Files; folder: Memoranda—Pat Caddell, 12/10/76–12/21/76; container 4, Jimmy Carter Presidential Library, Atlanta, GA.

31. Dick Moe, "Memo re: Universal Voter Registration Proposal," February 21, 1977, collection: Office of Staff Secretary; presidential files; folder: 2/21/77; container 8, Jimmy Carter Presidential Library, Atlanta, GA.

32. David Broder, "Voting Plan: Has the GOP Gone Crazy? Leaders Back Easy-Registration Idea That Could Sink the Party—or Could It?," *Los Angeles Times*, March 29, 1977: C5.

33. See, for one example, Warren Weaver, "Carter's Voter Registration Plan Would 'Reform' an Older Reform," *New York Times*, March 29, 1977: 17.

34. Quoted in James F. Wolfe, "Instant Voter Registration," *Human Events*, May 21, 1977: 15, 19.

35. Victor Riesel, "How Aliens Could Use Instant Registration," *Human Events*, April 30, 1977: 16, 19.

36. Paul Houston and Grayson Mitchell, "Action on Voter Registration Bill Delayed," *Los Angeles Times*, May 20, 1977: 21.

37. Walter Mondale, "Voter Registration Bill," memo to the president, July 14, 1977, collection: Domestic Policy Staff; series: Steven Simmons' Subject Files; folder: Elections—Universal Voter Registration; container 52, Jimmy Carter Presidential Library, Atlanta, GA.

38. "Election Reforms: Delay and Defeat," CQ Almanac 1977, 33rd ed. (Washington, DC: Congressional Quarterly, 1978): 798–812.

39. Frances Fox Piven and Richard Cloward, *Why Americans Still Don't Vote: And Why Politicians Want It That Way* (Boston, MA: Beacon Press, 2000): chapters 7–8.

40. For chronicles of these campaigns, see Piven, Minnite, and Groarke, *Keeping Down the Black Vote*; and Piven and Cloward, *Why Americans Still Don't Vote*.

41. Richard Cloward and Frances Fox Piven, "Toward a Class-Based Realignment of American Politics: A Movement Strategy," *Social Policy* 13, no. 3 (Winter 1983): 3–14, at 4.

42. "Project Vote: Summary of Litigation (as of 11/15/1984)," Human SERVE records, box 12, folder 571, Rare Book and Manuscript Library, Columbia University Library, NY: 2.

43. Piven and Cloward, *Why Americans Still Don't Vote*, chapters 7–10. On the Reagan administration's obstruction, see 178–81.

44. Quoted in Piven and Cloward, *Why Americans Still Don't Vote*, 196–97.

45. See, for example, Jesse L. Jackson, "Hey, You Democrats: We'll All Benefit if a Black Runs for President," *Washington Post*, April 10, 1983; and Colin A. Moore, "Jesse, Candidate or Crusader?," *New York Amsterdam News*, October 8, 1983: 15.

46. Jesse Jackson, "You Got a Chance, and You Got a Choice," speech, January 16, 1984, Tendley Baptist Church, Philadelphia, PA, https://speakola.com/political/jesse-jackson-campaign-announcement-david-goliath-1984.

47. Rhodes Cook, "'Have-Not' Surge to Polls: Major Force in 1984 Elections," *Congressional Quarterly Weekly* (July 23, 1984): 1506.

48. William Greider, "The Ballot Box Revolution," *Rolling Stone*, October 13, 1984, https://www.rollingstone.com/politics/news/the-ballot-box-revolution-19840913; and Piven and Cloward, *Why Americans Still Don't Vote*, 150–52.

49. Thomas B. Edsall and Haynes Johnson, "High-Tech, Impersonal Computer Net Is Snaring Prospective Republicans," *Washington Post*, April 22, 1984: A1.

50. The DNC was mired in debt and had been outspent by the debt-free Republican Party in past races by almost five to one. "G.O.P. Outspends Democrats 5-1," *New York Times*, October 8, 1982: A27; and Jeff Gerth, "Democrats Set Up $27 Million Voting Drive," *New York Times*, August 29, 1984: A20, https://www.nytimes.com/1984/08/29/us/democrats-set-up-27-million-drive.html.

51. Joel Rogers, "The Politics of Voter Registration," *Nation* (July 21–28, 1984): 45–49.

52. Thomas B. Edsall, "Elections Can Hinge on Persuading Likely Opponents Not to Vote," *Washington Post*, April 29, 1984: A2.

53. William Gaston and Elaine Kamarck, *The Politics of Evasion: Democrats and the Presidency* (Washington, DC: Progressive Policy Institute, September 1989), http://www.progressivepolicy.org/wp-content/uploads/2013/03/Politics_of_Evasion.pdf.

54. On New Democrats' governing logics, see Lily Geismer, *Left Behind: The Democrats' Failed Attempt to Solve Inequality* (New York: PublicAffairs, 2022); and Brent Cebul, "Supply-Side Liberalism: Fiscal Crisis, Post-Industrial Policy, and the Rise of the New Democrats," *Modern American History* 2, no. 2 (July 2019): 139–64.

55. Margaret Groarke, "The Impact of Voter Fraud Claims on Voter Registration Reform Legislation," *Political Science Quarterly* 131, no. 3 (September 1, 2016): 571–95.

56. Piven and Cloward, *Why Americans Still Don't Vote*, 245–58.

57. Mitch McConnell, "Should US Simplify Voter Registration?," *Christian Science Monitor*, October 1, 1991, For the "auto-fraudo" quip, see "Bush Rejects 'Motor Voter' Legislation," *CQ Almanac*, 48th ed. (Washington, DC: Congressional Quarterly, 1992).

58. Senator Gramm quoted in Piven and Cloward, *Why Americans Still Don't Vote*, 252.

59. "Bush Rejects 'Motor Voter' Legislation."

60. Piven and Cloward, *Why Americans Still Don't Vote*, chapter 11.

61. Sasha Issenberg, *The Victory Lab: The Secret Science of Winning Campaigns* (New York: Crown, 2012).

62. Richard Cloward and Frances Fox Piven, "The Declining Significance of Class? The Case of the National Voter Registration Act of 1993," *Reflections: Narratives of Professional Helping* 8, no. 1 (Winter 2002): 23.

63. Royce Crocker, "The National Voter Registration Act of 1993: History, Implementation, and Effects," Congressional Research Service, September 18, 2013; and Laura Williamson, Pamela Cataldo, and Brenda Wright, "Toward a More Representative

Electorate," *Dēmos*, December 21, 2018, https://www.demos.org/research/toward-more-representative-electorate.

64. Oral History interview by Ruth Milkman, *Frances Fox Piven: Scholar and Activist* (Washington, DC: American Sociological Association, 2017): 75.

65. Keyssar, *Right to Vote*, 287–91.

66. On the fall of the rehabilitative ideal, see Julilly Kohler-Hausmann, *Getting Tough: Welfare and Imprisonment in 1970s America* (Princeton, NJ: Princeton University Press, 2017).

67. Mary Fainsod Katzenstein, Leila Mohsen Ibrahim, and Katherine D. Rubin, "The Dark Side of American Liberalism and Felony Disenfranchisement," *Perspectives on Politics* 8, no. 4 (December 2010): 1035–54, at 1041.

68. Katzenstein, Ibrahim, and Rubin, "Dark Side of American Liberalism and Felony Disenfranchisement," 1041.

69. See Toby Talbot, "In Just Two States, All Prisoners Can Vote. Here's Why Few Do," *Marshall Project*, June 11, 2019, https://www.themarshallproject.org/2019/06/11/in-just-two-states-all-prisoners-can-vote-here-s-why-few-do; and Edgar B. Herwick III, "How Massachusetts Prisoners (Recently) Lost the Right to Vote," *GHB News*, May 29, 2019, https://www.wgbh.org/news/local-news/2019/05/29/how-massachusetts-prisoners-lost-the-right-to-vote.

70. On the implications of the vote for broader civic standing, see Judith N. Shklar, *American Citizenship: The Quest for Inclusion* (Cambridge, MA: Harvard University Press, 1998).

71. See the discussion, grounded in democratic theory, of the ways that felon disenfranchisement is foundational for other "collateral consequences" in Andrew Dilts, *Punishment and Inclusion: Race, Membership, and the Limits of American Liberalism* (New York: Fordham University Press, 2014): 45–48. On the ways the criminal legal system produces a distinct category of citizenship, see Reuben Jonathan Miller and Forrest Stuart, "Carceral Citizenship: Race, Rights and Responsibility in the Age of Mass Supervision," *Theoretical Criminology* 21, no. 4 (November 1, 2017): 532–48.

72. On the particularities of neoliberalism embraced by the Democratic Party, see Geismer, *Left Behind*.

73. See N. D. B. Connelly, "The Strange Career of American Liberalism," and Brent Cebul and Mason B. Williams, "'Really and Truly a Partnership': The New Deal's Associational State and the Making of Postwar American Politics," in *Shaped by the State: Toward a New Political History of the Twentieth Century*, ed. Brent Cebul, Lily Geismer, and Mason B. Williams (Chicago: University of Chicago Press, 2019): 62–123.

74. See, for example, "Florida Voters Mistakenly Purged in 2000," *Tampa Bay Times*, June 14, 2012, https://www.tampabay.com/news/politics/stateroundup/florida-voters-mistakenly-purged-in-2000/1235456/; Gregory Palast, "Florida's Flawed 'Voter-Cleansing' Program," *Salon*, December 4, 2000, https://www.salon.com/2000/12/04/voter_file/; and Jeff Manza, *Locked Out: Felon Disenfranchisement and American Democracy* (New York: Oxford University Press, 2008).

Chapter Ten

Epigraphs: Hubert Humphrey, "Statement on Introduced Bills and Joint Resolutions," *Congressional Record* 525 (January 20, 1972); Judith Heumann, interviewed by Susan Olson, box 4, BANC MSS 2018/207, Susan M. Olson Disability Rights Litigation Collection, Bancroft Library, University of California, Berkeley.

Notes to Pages 185–187

1. James T. Sparrow, *Warfare State: World War II Americans and the Age of Big Government* (New York: Oxford University Press, 2011); Karen M. Tani, "Welfare and Rights before the Movement: Rights as a Language of the State," *Yale Law Journal* 122, no. 2 (2012): 314–521.

2. Unless quoting from a source, I tend to use the "identity-first" term "disabled people" rather than "people with disabilities." This usage appears to be more prevalent today among people who publicly identify as disabled. When referring to people with intellectual disabilities, I use the "people-first" term, because I think the norm is less clear.

3. Naomi Murakawa, *The First Civil Right: How Liberals Built Prison America* (New York: Oxford University Press, 2013): 3.

4. Important recent exceptions include David Pettinicchio, *Politics of Empowerment: Disability Rights and the Cycle of American Policy Reform* (Palo Alto, CA: Stanford University Press, 2019); Bess Williamson, *Accessible America: A History of Disability and Design* (New York: New York University Press, 2019); Aimi Hamraie, *Building Access: Universal Design and the Politics of Disability* (Minneapolis: University of Minnesota Press, 2017); Audra Jennings, *Out of the Horrors of War: Disability Politics in World War II America* (Philadelphia: University of Pennsylvania Press, 2016); Lennard J. Davis, *Enabling Acts: The Hidden Story of How the Americans with Disabilities Act Gave the Largest US Minority Its Rights* (Boston, MA: Beacon Press, 2016); and Jennifer Erkulwater, *Disability Rights and the American Social Safety Net* (Ithaca, NY: Cornell University Press, 2006).

5. This literature on the Americans with Disabilities Act is particularly rich. For a sampling, see Marta Russell, *Beyond Ramps: Disability at the End of the Social Contract* (Monroe, ME: Common Courage Press, 1998); Samuel R. Bagenstos, *Law and the Contradictions of the Disability Rights Movement* (New Haven, CT: Yale University Press, 2009); Linda Krieger, ed., *Backlash against the ADA: Reinterpreting Disability Rights* (Ann Arbor: University of Michigan Press, 2010).

6. See, e.g., Paul K. Longmore and Lauri Umanski, eds., *The New Disability History: American Perspectives* (New York: New York University Press, 2001); Catherine J. Kudlick, "Disability History: Why We Need Another 'Other,'" *American Historical Review* 108 (June 2003): 763–93; Kim E. Nielsen, *A Disability History of the United States* (Boston, MA: Beacon Press, 2012); Susan Burch and Michael Rembis, eds., *Disability Histories* (Urbana: University of Illinois Press, 2014).

7. Samuel Haber, *Efficiency and Uplift: Scientific Management in the Progressive Era 1890–1920* (Chicago: University of Chicago Press, 1964).

8. Cass R. Sunstein, *The Cost-Benefit State: The Future of Regulatory Protection* (Chicago: American Bar Foundation, 2002). On the tentacular spread of an "economic style" of reasoning in the late twentieth century, see Elizabeth Popp Berman, *Thinking Like an Economist: How Efficiency Replaced Equality in U.S. Public Policy* (Princeton, NJ: Princeton University Press, 2022). "Regulatory czar" refers to Sunstein's leadership of the Office of Information and Regulatory Affairs.

9. Cass R. Sunstein, *The Second Bill of Rights: FDR's Unfinished Revolution and Why We Need It More Than Ever* (New York: Basic Books, 2004).

10. Stephen R. Holmes and Cass Sunstein, *The Cost of Rights: Why Liberty Depends on Taxes* (New York: W. W. Norton and Co., 2000).

11. See Edward Shorter, *The Kennedy Family and the Story of Mental Retardation* (Philadelphia, PA: Temple University Press, 2000).

12. On these movements and their legacies, see Alison C. Carey, Pamela Block, and Richard K. Scotch, *Allies and Obstacles: Disability Activism and Parents of Children with Disabilities* (Philadelphia, PA: Temple University Press, 2020); and Fred Pelka, *What We*

Have Done: An Oral History of the Disability Rights Movement (Amherst: University of Massachusetts Press, 2021); Davis, *Enabling Acts*, 22–23, 39–40.

13. Brown v. Board of Education, 347 U.S. 483 (1954); Allison C. Carey, *On the Margins of Citizenship: Intellectual Disability and Civil Rights in Twentieth-Century America* (Philadelphia, PA: Temple University Press, 2010): 122.

14. Jennings, *Out of the Horrors of War*, 15.

15. See generally Davis, *Enabling Acts*, 13; Pelka, *What We Have Done*, 151–73, 183–96.

16. *The Mental Retardation Facilities and Community Mental Health Centers Construction Act of 1963*, Public Law 88-164, U.S. Statutes at Large 77 (1963): 282–99; *Maternal and Child Health and Mental Retardation Planning Amendments of 1963*, Public Law 88-156, U.S. Statutes at Large 77 (1963): 273–76.

17. Edward D. Berkowitz and Larry DeWitt, *The Other Welfare: Supplemental Security Income and U.S. Social Policy* (Ithaca, NY: Cornell University Press, 2013); Jennifer L. Erkulwater, "Social Security Disability Insurance and Supplemental Security Income," in *The Oxford Handbook of U.S. Social Policy*, ed. Daniel Béland, Christopher Howard, and Kimberly J. Morgan (New York: Oxford University Press, 2015): 434–50.

18. Mary E. Switzer, "The Expanding Program of the Vocational Rehabilitation Administration," *Hospital and Community Psychiatry* (March 1966): 80–83. Policymakers' interest in "rehabilitating" injured veterans, from pensioners to wage-earners, goes back to World War I. Over time, the program expanded to civilians. See Beth Linker, *War's Waste: Rehabilitation in World War I America* (Chicago: University of Chicago Press, 2017); Claire H. Liachowitz, *Disability as a Social Construct: Legislative Roots* (Philadelphia, PA: Temple University Press, 1988): 31–34.

19. On the embrace of work-focused "rehabilitation" within public-welfare policy during this period, see generally Jennifer Mittelstadt, *From Welfare to Workfare: The Unintended Consequences of Liberal Reform, 1945–1965* (Chapel Hill: University of North Carolina Press, 2005). See also Nancy E. Rose, "Gender, Race, and the Welfare State: Government Work Programs from the 1930s to the Present," *Feminist Studies* 19, no. 2 (1993): 318–42, 329–33; Harry J. Holzer, "Workforce Development Programs," in *Legacies of the War on Poverty*, ed. Martha J. Bailey and Sheldon Danziger (New York: Russell Sage Foundation, 2013); John Worsencraft, "Salvaging Marginalized Men: How the Department of Defense Waged the War on Poverty," *Journal of Policy History* 33, no. 4 (2021): 373–400.

20. John F. Kennedy, Special Message to the Congress on Public Welfare Programs, February 1, 1962, https://www.ssa.gov/history/jfkstmts.html#welfare.

21. *Vocational Rehabilitation Act Amendments of 1965*, Public Law 89-333, U.S. Statutes at Large 79 (1965): 1282–94.

22. See Richard K. Scotch, *From Good Will to Civil Rights: Transforming Federal Disability Policy*, 2nd ed. (Philadelphia, PA: Temple University Press, 2001): 43–45 (noting that in 1972, Senator Hubert Humphrey (D-MN) suggested amending Title VI of the 1964 Civil Rights Act to include disability).

23. *Amendments to the Elementary and Secondary Education Act of 1965*, Public Law 89-750, U.S. Statutes at Large 80 (1966): 1191–222. This legislation built on a 1958 law that offered grants to states for training special education teachers. *Act to Encourage Expansion of Teaching in the Education of Mentally Retarded Children*, Public Law 85-926, U.S. Statutes at Large 72 (1958): 1777.

24. *Education for All Handicapped Children Act*, Public Law 94-142, U.S. Statutes at Large 89 (1975): 773–96. Congress later retitled this law the Individuals with Disabilities Education Act.

25. *Architectural Barriers Act of 1968*, Public Law 90-480, U.S. Statutes at Large 82 (1968): 718–19. A raft of similar legislation already existed at the state level. Jacobus tenBroek, "The Right to Live in the World: The Disabled and the Law of Torts," *California Law Review* 54, no. 2 (1966): 841–919.

26. Pettinicchio, *Politics of Empowerment*, 59–61; tenBroek, "Right to Live in the World," 846.

27. *An Act to Provide Long-Term Financing for Expanded Urban Public Transportation Programs, and for Other Purposes*, Public Law 91-453, U.S. Statutes at Large 84 (1970): 962–69.

28. *Rehabilitation Act of 1973*, Public Law 93-112, U.S. Statutes at Large 87 (1973): 355–94, 394.

29. Joy Milligan, "Remembering: The Constitution and Federally Funded Apartheid," *University of Chicago Law Review* 89 (2022): 65–155, 73 (explaining "Spending Clause civil rights"); Robert A. Katzmann, *Institutional Disability: The Saga of Transportation Policy for the Disabled* (Washington, DC: Brookings Institution Press, 1986): 100 (documenting the vast reach of federal funding by 1973).

30. In this regard, Section 504 was very different from Title VI and Title IX. On Title VI, see Stephen C. Halpern, *On the Limits of the Law: The Ironic Legacy of Title VI of the 1964 Civil Rights Act* (Baltimore, MD: Johns Hopkins University Press, 1995). On Title IX, see Bernice Resnick Sandler, "Title IX: How We Got It and What a Difference It Made Symposium: Celebrating Thirty-Five Years of Sport and Title IX," *Cleveland State Law Review* 55, no. 4 (2007): 473–89. On the lack of external attention to Section 504, including by disability-focused groups, see Scotch, *From Good Will to Civil Rights*, 45–59.

31. Scotch, *From Good Will to Civil Rights*, 51–53. President Nixon did have concerns about the cost of the 1972 Rehabilitation Act, which is why he pocket-vetoed it in the fall of 1973. But in explaining his action, Nixon did not specifically mention the antidiscrimination guarantee. The Rehabilitation Act that finally became law—in the fall of 1973—was a "scaled-down version," but still included the provision now known as Section 504. Katzmann, *Institutional Disability*, 48.

32. Nik Edes, interview by Richard Scotch, October 23, 1980, on file with author.

33. Katzmann, *Institutional Disability*, 79.

34. It became HEW's responsibility to implement Section 504. Scotch, *From Good Will to Civil Rights*, 60–61. That, within HEW, the task went to the Office for Civil Rights was a natural choice. OCR had deep experience with Title VI and Title IX, and its staff members were more enthusiastic about accepting responsibility for Section 504 than were members of other HEW offices. Scotch, *From Good Will to Civil Rights*, 61–62.

35. Scotch, *From Good Will to Civil Rights*, 60–62; Katzmann, *Institutional Disability*, 100; John Wodatch, interview with author, December 10, 2021.

36. Martin Gerry, interview by Richard Scotch, January 5, 1981, on file with author; see also Sally Foley, interview by Richard Scotch, June 10, 1981, on file with author (stating that the "party line" within OCR was that, for a civil rights law, "cost can never be a consideration").

37. Gerry interview, January 5, 1981.

38. *Bilingual Education Act*, Public Law 90-247, U.S. Statutes at Large 81 (1968): 816–20.

39. J. Stanley Pottinger to School Districts with More Than Five Percent National Origin-Minority Group Children, May 25, 1970, memorandum, Department of Health, Education, and Welfare, https://www2.ed.gov/about/offices/list/ocr/docs/lau1970.html. On OCR's introduction to the issue in 1969 and the swift response from top

administrators, see Gareth Davies, "The Great Society after Johnson: The Case of Bilingual Education," *Journal of American History* 88, no. 4 (2002): 1405–29, 1417–21. On the history of language rights in this period, see also Ming Hsu Chen, "Language Rights as a Legacy of the Civil Rights Act," *SMU Law Review* 67 (2014): 247–56.

40. Gerry interview, January 5, 1981; Wodatch interview, December 10, 2021.

41. On foot-dragging by HEW leadership between 1974 and 1977, and the fierce response from disabled organizers and allies, see Scotch, *From Good Will to Civil Rights*, 82–120; Susan Schweik, "Lomax's Matrix: Disability, Solidarity, and the Black Power of 504," *Disability Studies Quarterly* 31, no. 1 (2011).

42. Katzmann, *Institutional Disability*, 103.

43. Karen M. Tani, "After 504: Training the Citizen-Enforcers of Disability Rights," *Disability Studies Quarterly* 42, nos. 3–4 (2023), https://doi.org/10.18061/dsq.v42i3-4.7558. To be clear, "pan-disability" does not mean "inclusive of all disabilities." For example, people with invisible disabilities and intellectual disabilities were not involved to the same degree.

44. Statement of John W. Adams, Director, Federal/State Relations, Council of Chief State School Officers, *Implementation of Section 504, Rehabilitation Act of 1973: Hearings before the Subcommittee on Select Education of the Committee on Education and Labor, US House of Representatives, 95th Congress, First Session, September 9, 13, and 16, 1977* (Washington, DC: US Government Printing Office, 1977): 7 (noting "no specific authorization for federal funds supporting compliance with Section 504"). But see Timothy M. Cook, "The Scope of the Right to Meaningful Access and the Defense of Undue Burdens under Disability Civil Rights Laws," *Loyola of Los Angeles Law Review* 20, no. 5 (1987): 1471–525, 1492 (noting that by 1979, Congress had authorized funds to assist with Section 504 compliance costs); Mary F. Smith, *Accessibility for the Physically Handicapped: The Statute and Its Implementation* (Washington, DC: Congressional Research Service, July 21, 1981) (noting the availability of tax breaks and the potential to use other pots of federal money).

45. See Beatrice Adler-Bolton and Artie Vierkant, *Health Communism* (New York: Verso, 2022).

46. On the "social model" of disability, which separates biological "impairments" from the societal judgments that give those impairments meaning, see Rabia Belt and Doron Dorfman, "Disability, Law, and the Humanities: The Rise of Disability Legal Studies," in *The Oxford Handbook of Law & the Humanities*, ed. Simon Stern, Maksymilian Del Mar, and Bernadette Meyler (New York: Oxford University Press, 2019).

47. See, e.g., Milliken v. Bradley, 418 U.S. 717 (1974).

48. Even at the height of Jim Crow, the Supreme Court said as much. See McCabe v. Atchison, Topeka, and Santa Fe Railway Co., 235 U.S. 151 (1914) (finding meritless the state's argument that a Black passenger's right to receive equal access to railway travel might turn on whether there was enough demand by Black passengers to make service provision profitable). The NAACP-Legal Defense Foundation's "equalization" strategy relied on this logic: if cost was no excuse for failing to provide "separate-but-equal" facilities and services, integration might seem more appealing.

49. Judith Welch Wegner, "The Antidiscrimination Model Reconsidered: Ensuring Equal Opportunity without Respect to Handicap under Section 504 of the Rehabilitation Act of 1973," *Cornell Law Review* 69, no. 3 (1983–1984): 401–516, 447. Some of the most quotable language comes from cases involving racial segregation. See, e.g., Palmer v. Thompson, 403 U.S. 217, 226 (1971) ("Citizens may not be compelled to forgo their constitutional rights because officials . . . desire to save money"). But similar statements also

appeared in other antidiscrimination contexts. See, e.g., Manhart v. City of Los Angeles, 435 U.S. 702 (1978) (rejecting the idea of a cost-justification defense to a sex discrimination claim); Plyler v. Doe, 457 U.S. 202, 230 (1982) (entertaining a state's arguments about the cost of educating undocumented children but deeming any savings "wholly insubstantial in light of the costs involved to these children, the State, and the Nation").

50. Executive Order 11821, November 28, 1974.

51. Charles W. Vernon II, "The Inflation Impact Statement Program: An Assessment of the First Two Years," *American University Law Review* 26, no. 4 (1977): 1138–68, 1155–56.

52. The consultant ultimately concluded that anticipated benefits "substantial[ly] offset" anticipated costs, but on the basis of calculations that were sometimes "no more than reasoned guesses." Dave M. O'Neill, Public Research Institute, "Discrimination against Handicapped Persons: The Costs, Benefits and Inflationary Impact of Implementing Section 504 of the Rehabilitation Act of 1973 Covering Recipients of HEW Financial Assistance," February 1976, reprinted in 41 Fed. Reg. 20312 (1976), Monday, May 17, 1976: 20151–388.

53. See, for example, Lloyd v. Illinois Regional Transp. Authority, 548 F.2d 1277 (7th Cir. 1977). On other major cases, see Susan M. Olson, *Clients and Lawyers: Securing the Rights of Disabled Persons* (Westport, CT: Greenwood Press, 1984).

54. On school boards, see, e.g., Kampmeier v. Nyquist, 553 F.2d 296 (2d. Cir. 1977); Kruse v. Campbell, 431 F.Supp. 180 (E.D. Va. 1977), vacated and remanded, 434 U.S. 808 (1977). On colleges and universities, see, e.g., Barnes v. Converse College, 436 F.Supp. 635 (D. S.C. 1977); Crawford v. Univ. of North Carolina, 440 F.Supp. 1047 (M.D.N.C. 1977). On health care facilities, see, e.g., National Association for the Advancement of Colored People v. Wilmington Medical Center, 453 F.Supp. 280 (D. Del. 1978); Doe v. Colautti, 454 F.Supp. 621 (E.D. Pa. 1978). On public employers, see, e.g., Gurmankin v. Costanzo, 411 F.Supp. 982 (E.D. Pa. 1977); Duran v. Tampa, 430 F.Supp. 75 (M.D. Florida 1977).

55. Vanko v. Finley, 440 F.Supp. 656, 661 n4 (N.D. Ohio 1977). On the "discourse of cost and proportion," see also Williamson, *Accessible America*, 129.

56. *Barnes*, 436 F.Supp. at 638.

57. Davis v. Southeastern Community College, 574 F.2d 115 (4th Cir. 1978); Southeastern Community College v. Davis, 439 U.S. 1065 (1979).

58. Brief of the American Council on Education, et al., Southeastern Community College v. Davis, no. 78-711, 1978 WL 265982, at *2.

59. Southeastern Community College v. Davis, 442 U.S. 397, 405–7, 409–11 (1979).

60. Popp Berman, *Thinking Like an Economist*, 68. On this "new economic style," see Popp Berman, *Thinking Like an Economist*, 35–37.

61. Congressional Budget Office, *Urban Transportation for Handicapped Persons: Alternative Federal Approaches* (Washington, DC: Government Printing Office, 1979), https://www.cbo.gov/sites/default/files/96th-congress-1979-1980/reports/1979_11_urban.pdf.

62. Congressional Budget Office, *Urban Transportation for Handicapped Persons*.

63. "Must Every Bus Kneel to the Disabled?," *New York Times*, November 19, 1979. "Kneel" was a reference to an accessibility function of the prototype buses that emerged from the Department of Transportation's Transbus project. Williamson, *Accessible America*, 135.

64. Neal R. Pierce, "The Great Wheelchair Flap," *Washington Post*, December 28, 1978. For additional examples of the cost narrative in the late 1970s, see Pettinicchio, *Politics of Empowerment*, 86–95; Williamson, *Accessible America*, 134–42.

65. Executive Order 12291 (February 17, 1981). On centralized regulatory review, see Jim Tozzi, "OIRA's Formative Years: The Historical Record of Centralized Regulatory Review Preceding OIRA's Founding," *Administrative Law Review* 63 (2011): 37–69. On cost-benefit analysis in modern American governance, see Theodore M. Porter, *Trust in Numbers: The Pursuit of Activity in Science and Public Life* (Princeton, NJ: Princeton University Press, 1995): 148–89. On the Reagan administration's efforts, see Tozzi, "OIRA's Formative Years," 63–66; Popp Berman, *Thinking Like an Economist*, 212–13.

66. Ronald Reagan, "Remarks Announcing the Establishment of the Presidential Task Force on Regulatory Relief," January 22, 1981, online at *The American Presidency Project*, ed. Gerhard Peters and John T. Woolley https://www.presidency.ucsb.edu/documents/remarks-announcing-the-establishment-the-presidential-task-force-regulatory-relief. On deregulation in the Reagan administration, see Larry N. Gerston, Cynthia Fraleigh, and Robert Schwab, *The Deregulated Society* (Pacific Grove, CA: Brooks/Cole Publishing Company, 1987).

67. Stephen L. Percy, *Disability, Civil Rights, and Public Policy: The Politics of Implementation* (Tuscaloosa: University of Alabama Press, 1989): 88.

68. Center for Independent Living, Inc., Disability Law Resource Center, final technical assistance report (February 15, 1981), folder 1, carton 16, Disability Rights Education and Defense Fund records, Bancroft Library, University of California, Berkeley (hereafter "DREDF Papers"). The Office of Management and Budget has historically played a key role in supervising federal agencies and, in doing so, implementing the president's preferences.

69. Both these developments occurred at the end of the Carter administration. Percy, *Disability, Civil Rights, and Public Policy*, 86.

70. Arlene B. Mayerson, "Disability Rights and the Status of the Federal Government: The Status of Section 504 and P.L. 94-182 in 1982," working paper, December 28, 1982, folder 44, carton 3, DREDF Papers.

71. Mayerson, "Disability Rights and the Status of the Federal Government."

72. Davis, *Enabling Acts*, 33.

73. Lloyd Burton, "On Computing the Cost of Freedom," working paper, ca. 1980–82, folder 31, carton 3, DREDF Papers; Gary Gill, "Application of Economics to Disability Rights Law and Policy," working paper, February 8, 1982, folder 33, carton 21, DREDF Papers.

74. American Public Transit Ass'n v. Lewis, 655 F.2d 1272, 1278 (D.C. Cir. 1981).

75. Katzmann, *Institutional Disability*, 176.

76. Alexander v. Choate, 469 U.S. 287, 301 (1985).

77. See, e.g., Alexander v. Choate, 469 U.S., 308.

78. See, for example, Marta Russell, "What Disability Civil Rights Cannot Do: Employment and Political Economy," *Disability and Society* 17, no. 2 (2002): 117–35; Samuel R. Bagenstos, "The Americans with Disabilities Act as Welfare Reform," *William and Mary Law Review* 44 (2003): 976–85; Mary Johnson, *Make Them Go Away: Clint Eastwood, Christopher Reeve, and the Case against Disability Rights* (Louisville, KY: Advocado Press, 2003): 11–21.

79. The ADA's definition of "discrimination" includes "not making reasonable accommodations to the known physical or mental limitations of an otherwise qualified individual with a disability who is an applicant or employee, *unless such covered entity can demonstrate that the accommodation would impose an undue hardship on the operation of the business of such covered entity.*" The terms "undue hardship" and "undue burden"

appear throughout the statute. *Americans with Disabilities Act of 1990*, Public Law 101-336, U.S. Statutes at Large 104 (1990): 327–78 (emphasis added).

80. Richard A. Epstein, "AIDS, Testing and the Workplace," *University of Chicago Legal Forum* 1988 (1988): 33–56. On employer responses to the AIDS epidemic and the applicability of antidiscrimination laws, see Margot Canaday, *Queer Career: Sexuality and Work in Modern America* (Princeton, NJ: Princeton University Press, 2023): 187–226.

81. Epstein, "AIDS, Testing and the Workplace," 47, 50–56. At the time, an economic approach to civil rights law was uncommon in legal academia. In economics, it had a somewhat larger footprint. See Gary S. Becker, *The Economics of Discrimination* (Chicago: University of Chicago Press, 1957).

82. Richard A. Epstein, *Forbidden Grounds: The Case against Employment Discrimination Laws* (Cambridge, MA: Harvard University Press, 1992).

83. Epstein, *Forbidden Grounds*, 494. For examples of high-profile outlets, see Ian Ayres, "Price and Prejudice," *New Republic* 207, no. 2 (July 6, 1992): 30–34; Calvin Woodard, "In Defense of Discrimination," *New York Times*, May 3, 1992; J. Houlte Verkerke, "Free to Search," *Harvard Law Review* 105 (1992): 2080–97; Thomas Sowell, "The Civil Rights Tax," *Forbes* 149, no. 8 (1992): 94.

84. Richard H. McAdams, "Epstein on Private Discrimination: Searching for Common Ground," *Journal of Legal Studies* 50 (June 2021): S293–S312, S296.

85. Mark Kelman, "Market Discrimination and Groups," *Stanford Law Review* 53 (2001): 833–96, 835. See also Mark Kelman, "Defining the Antidiscrimination Norm to Defend It," *San Diego Law Review* 43 (2006).

86. Michael Ashley Stein, "Same Struggle, Different Difference: ADA Accommodations as Antidiscrimination," University of Pennsylvania Law Review 153 (2004): 579–673, 586.

87. Scholars may have felt especially inclined to adopt this framing after prominent judges interpreted the requirement of "reasonable accommodation" as an instantiation of cost-benefit analysis. See especially the opinion of Judge Posner in *Vande Zande v. Wisconsin Department of Administration*, 44 F.3d 538 (7th Cir. 1995).

88. Christine Jolls, "Antidiscrimination and Accommodation," *Harvard Law Review* 642 (2001): 642–99 (asserting the descriptive similarity, but making no normative claims); Samuel R. Bagenstos, "'Rational Discrimination,' Accommodation, and the Politics of (Disability) Civil Rights," *Virginia Law Review* 89 (2003) (claiming a descriptive and normative similarity); Stein, "Same Struggle, Different Difference" (arguing that disability rights laws and other antidiscrimination laws address the same general problem and require similar types of expenditures on the part of targeted institutions).

89. See, e.g., Michael Ashley Stein, "The Law & Economics of Disability Accommodations," *Duke Law Journal* 53 (2003); Hoult Verkerke, "*Is the ADA Efficient?*," *UCLA Law Review* 50 (2003); Stein, "Same Struggle, Different Difference," 649.

90. Bagenstos, "Rational Discrimination," 902.

91. Benjamin Wallace-Wells, "Cass Sunstein Wants to Nudge Us," *New York Times*, May 13, 2010.

92. Another place to see this kind of movement—of market models into civil rights—is in federal court decisions interpreting the reach of "Spending Clause civil rights" statutes: starting in the 1980s, the Supreme Court began treating federal-state flows of money—a vital tool of modern governance—as akin to contracts between private

parties, which, in turn, resulted in weaker protection for federally guaranteed rights. See Katie Eyer and Karen M. Tani, "Disability and the Ongoing Federalism Revolution," *Yale Law Journal* 133 (2024): 3000–3091.

93. On congressional dysfunction and its relationship to executive-branch policymaking, see Jessica Bulman-Pozen, "Executive Federalism Comes to America," *Virginia Law Review* 102, no. 4 (2016): 953–1030, 959–62. On the importance of regulatory review to what happens within the federal administrative state, see Nicholas Bagley and Richard L. Revesz, "Centralized Oversight of the Regulatory State," *Columbia Law Review* 106 (2006): 1260–329.

94. See, e.g., Philip Shabecoff, "Reagan Order on Cost-Benefit Analysis Stirs Political and Economic Debate," *New York Times*, November 7, 1981.

95. Cass R. Sunstein, "Cost-Benefit Analysis and the Separation of Powers," *Arizona Law Review* 23 (1981): 1267–80; see also Dale Whittington and W. Norton Grubb, "Economic Analysis in Regulatory Decisions: The Implications of Executive Order 12291," *Science, Technology, and Human Values* 9, no. 1 (1984): 63–71, 69–70.

96. Executive Order 12866 (2013).

97. On the governing style of Clinton and other New Democrats, see Lily Geismer, *Left Behind: The Democrats' Failed Attempt to Solve Inequality* (New York: PublicAffairs, 2022). On some liberals' explicit embrace of cost-benefit analysis in prior years, see Duncan Kennedy, "Cost-Benefit Analysis of Entitlement Problems: A Critique," *Stanford Law Review* 33 (1981): 387–445.

98. See, e.g., Cass R. Sunstein, "Congress, Constitutional Moments, and the Cost-Benefit State," *Stanford Law Review* 48, no. 2 (1996): 247–309; Sunstein, *Cost-Benefit State*.

99. Sunstein, "Congress, Constitutional Moments, and the Cost-Benefit State," 291–92.

100. Daniel Farber, "God Bless Taxes," *New York Times*, April 19, 1999.

101. Cass R. Sunstein, *The Cost-Benefit Revolution* (Cambridge, MA: MIT Press, 2019).

102. Lisa Heinzerling, "Cost-Benefit Jumps the Shark," *Georgetown Law Faculty Blog*, June 13, 2012, https://gulcfac.typepad.com/georgetown_university_law/2012/06/cost-benefit-jumps-the-shark.html. See also Lisa Heinzerling, "Quality Control: A Reply to Professor Sunstein," *California Law Review* 102 (2014): 1457–67.

103. Cass R. Sunstein, "Costs, Benefits, and the Non-Political Nature of OIRA Review," *Regulatory Review*, September 13, 2013, https://www.theregreview.org/2013/09/13/13-sunstein-cost-benefit/.

104. "Nondiscrimination on the Basis of Sex in Education Programs or Activities Receiving Federal Financial Assistance," 34 CFR part 106, *Federal Register* 87, no. 132 (July 12, 2022), https://www.federalregister.gov/documents/2022/07/12/2022-13734/nondiscrimination-on-the-basis-of-sex-in-education-programs-or-activities-receiving-federal. See also "Nondiscrimination on the Basis of Race, Color, or National Origin in Programs or Activities Receiving Federal Financial Assistance," 31 CFR part 22, *Federal Register* 80, no. 133 (July 13, 2015), https://www.regulations.gov/document/TREAS-DO-2015-0006-0001 (proposing a revised interpretation of Title VI of the 1964 Civil Rights Act); "Nondiscrimination in Programs or Activities Conducted by the United States Department of Agriculture," 7 CFR part 15d, *Federal Register* 78, no. 249 (December 27, 2013), https://www.federalregister.gov/documents/2013/12/27/2013-30812/nondiscrimination-in-programs-or-activities-conducted-by-the-united-states-department-of-agriculture (proposing a change to the Department of Agriculture's regulation on nondiscrimination).

Notes to Pages 198–202   355

105. "Affirmatively Furthering Fair Housing," 24 CFR parts 5, 91, 92, 570, 574, 576, and 903, *Federal Register* 78, no. 139 (July 19, 2013), https://www.federalregister.gov/documents/2013/07/19/2013-16751/affirmatively-furthering-fair-housing.

106. I borrow this astute phrasing from Samuel Bagenstos; see Bagenstos, "'Rational Discrimination,'" 831.

107. Kennedy, "Cost-Benefit Analysis of Entitlement Problems," 445.

108. Barbara Young Welke, *Law and the Borders of Belonging in the Long Nineteenth Century United States* (New York: Cambridge University Press, 2010).

109. Robert O. Self, *All in the Family: The Realignment of American Democracy* (New York: Farrar, Straus and Giroux, 2012).

Chapter Eleven

1. Ethnographers have been attuned to the role of computers mediating experience of the welfare state. Virginia Eubanks, *Digital Dead End: Fighting for Social Justice in the Information Age* (Cambridge, MA: MIT Press, 2011); John Gilliom, *Overseers of the Poor: Surveillance, Resistance, and the Limits of Privacy* (Chicago: University of Chicago Press, 2001).

2. John Stevens and Robert McGowan, *Information Systems and Public Management* (New York: Praeger, 1985): 96–99.

3. David Burnham, *The Rise of the Computer State* (New York: Random House, 1983): 29–30; David Dery, *Computers in Welfare: The MIS-Match* (Beverly Hills, CA: SAGE Publications, 1981).

4. These changes also parallel federal funding to states for technological "modernization" of law enforcement. Elizabeth Hinton, *From the War on Poverty to the War on Crime: The Making of Mass Incarceration in America* (Cambridge, MA: Harvard University Press, 2016).

5. Recent scholarship on liberalism sees reliance on private-sector tools not as a rejection of the liberal project but as a core strategy for liberals in desperate need of state capacity for liberal policy aims. These tools corresponded to a shift to the conception of the citizen as client or customer. Brent Cebul, *Illusions of Progress: Business, Poverty, and Liberalism in the American Century* (Philadelphia: University of Pennsylvania Press, 2023); Claire Dunning, *Nonprofit Neighborhoods: An Urban History of Inequality and the American State* (Chicago: University of Chicago Press, 2022); Amy Offner, *Sorting out the Mixed Economy: The Rise and Fall of Welfare and Developmental States in the Americas* (Princeton, NJ: Princeton University Press, 2019); Lily Geismer, *Don't Blame Us: Suburban Liberals and the Transformation of the Democratic Party* (Princeton, NJ: Princeton University Press, 2015). For the infrastructural turn in histories of federalism, see Teal Arcadi, "Partisanship and Permanence: How Congress Contested the Origins of the Interstate Highway System and the Future of American Infrastructure," *Modern American History* 5, no. 1 (March 2022): 53–77; Mary Bridges, "The Infrastructural Turn in Historical Scholarship," *Modern American History*, April 18, 2023: 1–18.

6. On the role of federalism in welfare, including matching federal funds to coordinate state practices, see Karen Tani, *States of Dependency: Welfare, Rights, and American Governance, 1935–1972* (Cambridge: Cambridge University Press, 2016).

7. Margaret O'Mara, *The Code: Silicon Valley and the Remaking of America* (New York: Penguin Press, 2019); Lily Geismer, "Atari Democrats," *Jacobin*, February 8, 2016; Daniel Greene, *The Promise of Access: Technology, Inequality, and the Political Economy of Hope*

(Cambridge, MA: MIT Press, 2021): 29–58; Marc Aidinoff, "Centrists against the Center: The Jeffersonian Politics of a Decentralized Internet," in *Abstractions and Embodiments: New Histories of Computing and Society*, ed. Janet Abbate and Stephanie Dick (Baltimore, MD: Johns Hopkins University Press, 2022): 40–59.

8. The phrase "pragmatic idealism" comes from Charles Peters as part of his effort to remake and rebrand liberalism in "A Neo-Liberal's Manifesto," *Washington Post*, September 5, 1982. Lily Geismer, *Left Behind: The Democrats' Failed Attempt to Solve Inequality* (New York: PublicAffairs, 2022).

9. A key insight of Science and Technology Studies reveals how policymakers and technical experts alike conflate normative and descriptive claims about technologies. This chapter therefore reads claims about computers as an archive of what policymakers thought effective welfare administration ought to be. On the co-constitution of prescriptive and descriptive see Steven Shapin and Simon Schaffer, *Leviathan and the Air-Pump: Hobbes, Boyle, and the Experimental Life* (Princeton, NJ: Princeton University Press, 1985); Sheila Jasanoff, *The Fifth Branch: Science Advisers as Policymakers* (Cambridge, MA: Harvard University Press, 1994); and Eden Medina, *Cybernetic Revolutionaries: Technology and Politics in Allende's Chile* (Cambridge, MA: MIT Press, 2011).

10. Political scientist Eva Bertram concluded that in negotiations leading up to the Family Support Act of 1988 there was among liberals "a retreat from the New Deal notion of a welfare entitlement owed to recipients by government, to the concept of a 'reciprocal obligation.'" Eva Bertram, *The Workfare State: Public Assistance Politics from the New Deal to the New Democrats* (Philadelphia: University of Pennsylvania Press, 2015): 152; Nancy A. Naples, "The 'New Consensus' on the Gendered 'Social Contract': The 1987–1988 U.S. Congressional Hearings on Welfare Reform," *Signs* 22, no. 4 (1997): 907–45. On the power and the consequences of the contract metaphor see Nancy Fraser and Linda Gordon, "Contract versus Charity: Why Is There No Social Citizenship in the United States?," *Socialist Review* (January 1992).

11. New York senator Daniel Patrick Moynihan, US Congress, Senate, Committee on Finance: Hearings on Welfare Reform, part 1 of 3, 100th Cong., 1st sess., April 9, 1987: 33.

12. Felicia Kornbluh and Gwendolyn Mink, *Ensuring Poverty: Welfare Reform in Feminist Perspective* (Philadelphia: University of Pennsylvania Press, 2019): esp. 42–56; Libby Adler and Janet Halley, "'You Play, You Pay': Feminists and Child Support Enforcement in the United States," in *Governance Feminism: Notes from the Field*, ed. Janet Halley et al. (Minneapolis: University of Minnesota Press, 2019): 287–316.

13. Amy Dru Stanley, *From Bondage to Contract: Wage Labor, Marriage, and the Market in the Age of Slave Emancipation* (Cambridge: Cambridge University Press, 1998); Tera Hunter, *Bound in Wedlock: Slave and Free Black Marriage in the Nineteenth Century* (Cambridge, MA: Harvard University Press, 2017): esp. 238–39; Melinda Cooper, *Family Values: Between Neoliberalism and the New Social Conservativism* (Cambridge, MA: Zone Books, 2017): esp. 78–82.

14. While many liberals championed programs to promote marriage and "traditional" family values, their embrace of the debt contract can still be read as a retreat from marriage, or at least a begrudging conclusion that marriage as it existed by the end of the century was not a sufficiently effective resource for privatizing the costs of poverty reduction. On the push toward marriage as the primary interpretation for child support enforcement see Alison Lefkowitz's *Strange Bedfellows: Marriage in the Age of Women's Liberation* (Philadelphia: University of Pennsylvania Press, 2018): 127–29; Cooper, *Family Values*, 67–118.

15. Robert Sobel, *IBM: Colossus in Transition* (New York: Times Books, 1981): 82.

16. Linda Gordon, *Pitied but Not Entitled: Single Mothers and the History of Welfare, 1890–1935* (Cambridge, MA: Harvard University Press, 1994): 295.

17. Sarah Igo, *The Known Citizen: A History of Privacy in Modern America* (Cambridge, MA: Harvard University Press, 2018): 55–98; Daniel Bouk, *How Our Days Became Numbered: Risk and the Rise of the Statistical Individual* (Chicago: University of Chicago Press, 2015): 227–44.

18. For overviews see Amy Zanoni, "Remembering Welfare as We Knew It: Understanding Neoliberalism through Histories of Welfare," *Journal of Policy History* 35, no. 1 (January 2023): 118–58; and Michael Katz, *In the Shadow of the Poorhouse: A Social History of Welfare in America*, updated ed. (New York: Basic Books, 1996).

19. Gordon, *Pitied but Not Entitled*, 2.

20. Workers saw New Deal welfare programs as more than charity and often as an entitlement from the beginning. See Lizabeth Cohen, *Making a New Deal: Industrial Workers in Chicago, 1919–1939*, 2nd ed. (Cambridge: Cambridge University Press, 2008): 251–90.

21. *The Social Security Act*, Public Law 74-271 (49 Stat. 620), approved August 14, 1935, Title IV.

22. Tani, *States of Dependency*.

23. Felicia Kornbluh, *The Battle for Welfare Rights: Politics and Poverty in Modern America* (Philadelphia: University of Pennsylvania Press, 2007); Premilla Nadasen, *Welfare Warriors: The Welfare Rights Movement in the United States* (New York: Routledge, 2005); Annelise Orleck, *Storming Caesars Palace: How Black Mothers Fought Their Own War on Poverty* (Boston, MA: Beacon Press, 2005); Martha Davis, *Brutal Need: Lawyers and the Welfare Rights Movement, 1960–1973* (New Haven, CT: Yale University Press, 1993).

24. Premilla Nadasen, "From Widow to 'Welfare Queen': Welfare and the Politics of Race," *Black Women, Gender and Families* 1, no. 2 (2007): 52–77; Felicia Kornbluh, "Political Arithmetic and Racial Division in the Democratic Party," *Social Policy* 26, no. 3 (March 22, 1996): 49–64.

25. Both Jennifer Mittelstadt and Alice O'Connor attend to the ways the work of often well-intentioned liberal academics and policymakers repeatedly undermined the anti-poverty efforts and social rights. Jennifer Mittelstadt, *From Welfare to Workfare: The Unintended Consequences of Liberal Reform, 1945–1965* (Chapel Hill: University of North Carolina Press, 2005); Alice O'Connor, *Poverty Knowledge: Social Science, Social Policy, and the Poor in Twentieth-Century U.S. History* (Princeton, NJ: Princeton University Press, 2001).

26. Marisa Chappell argues that after 1972, "the antipoverty coalition—both middle-class liberals and grassroots antipoverty activists consciously neglected defending AFDC in its effort to keep white, working class voters in the Democratic fold." *War on Welfare: Family, Poverty, and Politics in Modern America* (Philadelphia: University of Pennsylvania Press, 2011): 17.

27. Austin Sarat, "The Law Is All Over: Power, Resistance and the Legal Consciousness of the Welfare Poor," *Yale Journal of Law and the Humanities* 2, no. 2 (1990): 343–80; Tani, *States of Dependency*, 8.

28. I treat code as enacting legal reforms, similar to but not synonymous with law. Lawrence Lessig, *Code: And Other Laws of Cyberspace* (New York: Basic Books, 1999); Cornelia Vismann and Markus Krajewski, "Computer Juridisms," *Grey Room* 29 (October 2007): 90–109.

29. "Sumrall Named to Post," *Daily Advertiser* (Lafayette, LA), January 18, 1979.

30. Donald C. Brown Jr., "State Computer System Had Very Human Habit," *Town Talk* (Alexandria, LA), March 13, 1974.

31. "Long Will Address Employment Meet," *Daily Review* (Morgan City, LA), September 14, 1979.

32. Bill Simmons, "Arkansas Pares Rolls of ADC Recipients," *Times* (Shreveport, LA), March 20, 1980.

33. Guy Coates, "Computer May Stop Cheaters," *Greenwood Commonwealth* (Baton Rouge, LA), December 30, 1980.

34. David Flaherty, *Protecting Privacy in Surveillance Societies* (Chapel Hill: University of North Carolina Press, 1992): 344–359; Igo, *Known Citizen*, 221–63.

35. Office of Technology Assessment, "Federal Government Information Technology: Electronic Record Systems and Individual Privacy" (Washington, DC: Government Printing Office, 1986), Princeton University Archive, Princeton, NJ: 43.

36. Christy Hoppe, "Welfare Is Spindled and Folded," *Corpus Christi Caller*, April 22, 1979.

37. Carole Lawes, "Welfare Workers in County Taste the Age of Computers," *Bolivar Commercial* (Cleveland, MS), March 18, 1987.

38. Mississippi Department of Human Services, "MAVERICS: Advance Planning Document," September 1991: 6, box 31530, folder: Management Information Services Correspondence, Mississippi Department of Archives and History, Jackson, MS (hereafter MDAH).

39. If scholars like Brian Balogh have turned our attention to the role of contractors as critical elements of state power, this chapter treats those contractors as vectors of expertise and as *agents* of federalism. They link state and federal capacity. Brian Balogh, *The Associational State: American Governance in the Twentieth Century* (Philadelphia: University of Pennsylvania Press, 2015).

40. James Cortada, *The Digital Hand Volume III: How Computers Changed the Work of American Public Sector Industries* (Oxford: Oxford University Press, 2008).

41. Kevin Whalen, "State Gets Lucky with Computer," *Bismarck Tribune*, July 19, 1984.

42. As Geraldo Con Diaz has noted in his history of intellectual property law, IBM effectively positioned itself as the expert on which regulators would rely in *Software Rights: How Patent Law Transformed Software Development in America* (New Haven, CT: Yale University Press, 2019).

43. Andrew Russell, *Open Standards and the Digital Age: History, Ideology, and Networks* (Cambridge: Cambridge University Press, 2014).

44. "Systems Network Architecture: Concepts and Products" (Durham, NC: IBM Corporation, 1984): 1–4.

45. Frank Stebbins, "'New Direction' for State Information System: Briefing for CDPA Employees," January 11, 1988: 3, series 1616: Policy and Planning Committee files, 1986–1994, box 6512, MDAH.

46. Rob Kling, "Automated Welfare Client-Tracking and Service Integration: The Political Economy of Computing," *Communications of the ACM* 21, no. 6 (June 1978): 488–89; and "Computerization and Social Transformations," *Science, Technology, and Human Values* 16, no. 3 (July 1991): 342–67.

47. Mississippi Department of Human Services, "MAVERICS," 61.

48. Moynihan had an ambivalent relationship with the label "liberal" as part of his electoral project. Patrick Andelic, "Daniel Patrick Moynihan, the 1976 New York Senate

Race, and the Struggle to Define American Liberalism," *Historical Journal* 57, no. 4 (December 2014): 1111–33; Daniel Patrick Moynihan, "The Liberals' Dilemma," *New Republic*, January 22, 1977.

49. For state experiments, in a punitive welfare, Julilly Kohler-Hausmann, *Getting Tough: Welfare and Imprisonment in 1970s America* (Princeton, NJ: Princeton University Press, 2017); and as sites of experimental reform to liberalism, Geismer, *Don't Blame Us*; David Osborne, *Laboratories of Democracy* (Boston, MA: Harvard Business School Press, 1988).

50. Clinton seemed to like the idea of a literal signed contract, a strategy deployed in some states like California. Clinton's prepared remarks only referenced a "binding contractual agreement." Arkansas governor Bill Clinton, US Congress, Senate, Committee on Finance: Hearings on Welfare Reform, part 1 of 3, 100th Cong., 1st sess., April 9, 1987: 17, 21.

51. Moynihan, Hearings on Welfare Reform, 33.

52. Office of Policy Planning and Research, *The Negro Family: The Case for National Action* (Washington, DC: US Department of Labor, March 1965).

53. On the social-scientific construction of the "broken family" see O'Connor, *Poverty Knowledge*; Chappell, *War on Welfare*; Mittelstadt, *From Welfare to Workfare*; Daniel Geary, *Beyond Civil Rights: The Moynihan Report and Its Legacy* (Philadelphia: University of Pennsylvania Press, 2015); Daryl Michael Scott, *Contempt and Pity: Social Policy and the Image of the Damaged Black Psyche, 1880–1996* (Chapel Hill: University of North Carolina Press, 1997); Ted Ownby, *Hurtin' Words: Debating Family Problems in the Twentieth-Century South* (Chapel Hill: University of North Carolina Press, 2018).

54. The absentee father has come in and out of focus as a primary public-policy problem and the object of sustained liberal ire. Ann Cammett, "Deadbeat Dads & Welfare Queens: How Metaphor Shapes Poverty Law," *Boston College Journal of Law and Social Justice* 34, no. 2 (2014): 233–66; Michael Willrich, "Home Slackers: Men, the State, and Welfare in Modern America," *Journal of American History* 87, no. 2 (September 2000): 460; Jocelyn Elise Crowley, *Defiant Dads: Fathers' Rights Activists in America* (Ithaca, NY: Cornell University Press, 2008); Irwin Garfinkel et al., eds., *Fathers under Fire: The Revolution in Child Support Enforcement* (New York: Russell Sage Foundation, 2001).

55. Clinton, Hearings on Welfare Reform, 17.

56. Chappell, *War on Welfare*, 173.

57. Brent Cebul, "Frugal Governance, Family Values, and the Intimate Roots of Neoliberalism," in *Intimate States: Gender, Sexuality and Governance in Modern US History*, ed. Margot Canaday, Nancy Cott, and Robert Self (Chicago: University of Chicago Press, 2021): 325–36.

58. Daniel Patrick Moynihan, *Family and Nation* (Orlando, FL: Harcourt Brace Jovanovich, 1986): 180.

59. Delaware governor Michael Castle, US Congress, Senate, Committee on Finance: Hearings on Welfare Reform, part 1 of 3, 100th Cong., 1st sess., April 9, 1987: 27.

60. Daniel Patrick Moynihan, *Miles to Go: A Personal History of Policy* (Cambridge, MA: Harvard University Press, 1996): 26–28.

61. Clinton, *My Life*, 345.

62. *Family Support Act of 1988*, Public Law 100-485. U.S. Statutes at Large 102 (1998): 2351–52.

63. Ed Tucker, "Fax of Draft Strategic Master Plan with Comments," November 13, 1990: 6, series 1616: Policy and Planning Committee files, 1986–1994, box 6512, folder: Policy and Planning Committee 1991, MDAH.

64. Tucker, "Fax of Draft Strategic Master Plan with Comments," 15.

65. Tucker, "Fax of Draft Strategic Master Plan with Comments," 2.

66. Joint Committee on Performance Evaluation and Expenditure Review, *Evaluation of the Department of Human Services, Child Support Enforcement Division's Accountability Information Systems* (Jackson: Mississippi Legislature, April 15, 1997), "Total Child Support Collection," FY2020, series 2740: Executive Directors' correspondence and files, box 33435, folder: Child Support–undistributed funds, MDAH.

67. "Division of Child Support Enforcement," 2001, series 2740: Executive Directors' correspondence and files, box: 33431, folder: MDHS' Divisions Accomplishments, MDAH.

68. Patricia Whitley, "Memo to Russell Ferguson; Re: Programming Services for Department of Human Services," February 10, 1994, series 160: Central Data Processing Authority Board minutes, box 6188, folder 146, MDAH.

69. Alsee McDaniel, "Memorandum to Janice Broome Brooks; Subject: Updates on Critical Issues," December 27, 2000, series 2740: Executive Directors' correspondence and files, box 33431, folder: MDHS Programmatic/Critical Issues, MDAH; Richard Harris and Edwin H. Henry, "Memorandum to County Directors; Subject: Child Support Clarifications," January 23, 1998, series 2740: Executive Directors' correspondence and files, box 33434, folder: Child Support Bulletins, MDAH.

70. Richard Harris, "Memorandum to County Directors; Subject: Procedures for Case Resolution and Treatment of Noncustodial Parents Referred without SSNs," April 17, 1998, series 2740: Executive Directors' correspondence and files, box 33434, folder: Child Support Bulletins, MDAH.

71. Harris and Henry, "Memorandum to County Directors; Subject: Child Support Clarifications."

72. Alsee McDaniel, "Financial Institution Data Match Policy," November 30, 2000, series 2740: Executive Directors' correspondence and files, box 33434, folder: Child Support Bulletins, MDAH.

73. Alsee McDaniel, "License Suspension," April 6, 2000, series 2740: Executive Directors' correspondence and files, box 33434, folder: Child Support Bulletins, MDAH.

74. Kaaryn S. Gustafson, *Cheating Welfare: Public Assistance and the Criminalization of Poverty* (New York: New York University Press, 2011); Tonya L. Brito, "Fathers behind Bars: Rethinking Child Support Policy toward Low-Income Noncustodial Fathers and Their Families," *Journal of Gender, Race and Justice*, no. 3 (2012): 617–74; Amanda Geller, Irwin Garfinkel, and Bruce Western, "Paternal Incarceration and Support for Children in Fragile Families," *Demography* 48, no. 1 (February 1, 2011): 25–47; Jessica Pearson, "Building Debt While Doing Time: Child Support and Incarceration," *Judges' Journal* 1 (2004): 4–11; Noah Zatz, "A New Peonage? Pay, Work, or Go to Jail in Contemporary Child Support Enforcement and Beyond," *Seattle Law Review* 39, no. 3 (February 2016): 927–55.

75. Bill Clinton, "The New Covenant: Responsibility and Rebuilding the American Community," speech, Georgetown University, Washington, DC, October 23, 1991.

76. Barbara Vobejda, "The Debates over Welfare," *Washington Post*, June 4, 1995.

77. Moynihan, *Miles to Go*, 34.

78. Moynihan addresses these critics at lengths in *Miles to Go*, 26–63.

79. Vobejda, "The Debates Over Welfare."

80. President William Jefferson Clinton, "Remarks on Signing the Personal Responsibility and Work Opportunity Reconciliation Act of 1996 and an Exchange with

Reporters," in *Public Papers of the President of the United States: Administration of William J. Clinton*, bk. 2 (Washington, DC: Government Printing Office, 1996): 1329.

81. Adler and Halley, "'You Play, You Pay,'" 288.

82. Clinton, "Remarks on Signing the Personal Responsibility and Work Opportunity Reconciliation Act," 1330.

Chapter Twelve

1. John Joseph Moakley, "John Joseph Moakley's Statement to Members of the Salvadoran Community in Los Angeles at El Rescate's 9th Annual Christmas Party for Central American Refugee Children, 20 February 1990," December 20, 1990, Moakley Archive and Institute (hereafter MA&I), Suffolk University, Boston, MA, https://moakleyarchive.omeka.net/items/show/8831.

2. Cameron Barr, "Salvadoran Refugees 'Protected,'" *Christian Science Monitor*, November 19, 1990: 8.

3. Moakley, "Statement to Members of the Salvadoran Community."

4. Maria Newman, "Salvadoran Woman Benefits from New Law," *Los Angeles Times*, December 1, 1990: 1.

5. Todd Howland, "To Some, Refuge Looks More Like a Trap," *Los Angeles Times*, June 5, 1991: B7.

6. Roberto Lovato, "Central Americans: A Savvy Bunch," *Los Angeles Times*, August 6, 2001: B11.

7. Roberto Lovato, "Too Many Immigrants Trapped in the Shadows of American Life," *Los Angeles Times*, January 9, 2004: B19.

8. Bradford Martin, *The Other Eighties: A Secret History of America in the Age of Reagan* (New York: Hill and Wang, 2011); Nick Witham, *The Cultural Left and the Reagan Era: US Protest and Central American Revolution* (London: I. B. Tauris, 2015); Barbara J. Keys, *Reclaiming American Virtue: The Human Rights Revolution of the 1970s* (Cambridge, MA: Harvard University Press, 2014); Vanessa Walker, *Principles in Power: Latin America and the Politics of US Human Rights Diplomacy* (Ithaca, NY: Cornell University Press, 2020); Sarah B. Snyder, "'A Call for US Leadership': Congressional Activism on Human Rights," *Diplomatic History* 37, no. 2 (April 2013): 372–97.

9. See, for example, Oscar Handlin, *The Uprooted: The Epic Story of the Great Migration that Made the American People* (Boston, MA: Little, Brown and Company, 1951); John Bodnar, *The Transplanted: A History of Immigrants in Urban America* (Bloomington: Indiana University Press, 1985). For a critique of this approach, see Donna Gabaccia, "Is Everywhere Nowhere? Nomads, Nations, and the Immigrant Paradigm of United States History," *Journal of American History* 86, no. 3 (December 1999): 1115–34.

10. See, for example, Mae Ngai, *Impossible Subjects: Illegal Aliens and the Making of Modern America* (Princeton, NJ: Princeton University Press, 2004); Kelly Lytle Hernández, *Migra!: A History of the U.S. Border Patrol* (Berkeley: University of California Press, 2010); S. Deborah Kang, *The INS on the Line: Making Immigration Law on the US-Mexico Border, 1917–1954* (New York: Oxford University Press, 2017); Adam Goodman, *The Deportation Machine: America's Long History of Expelling Immigrants* (Princeton, NJ: Princeton University Press, 2020); Sarah Coleman, *The Walls Within: The Politics of Immigration in Modern America* (Princeton, NJ: Princeton University Press, 2021).

11. See, for example, Cecilia Menjívar, "Liminal Legality: Salvadoran and Guatemalan Immigrants Lives in the United States," *American Journal of Sociology* 111, no. 4 (January

2006): 999–1037; Jennifer M. Chacón, "Producing Liminal Legality," *Denver Law Review* 92, no. 4 (January 2015): 709–67; María Cristina García, *Seeking Refuge: Central American Migration to Mexico, the United States, and Canada* (Berkeley: University of California Press, 2006). On the history of proceduralism, see Kunal Parker, *The Turn to Process: American Legal, Political, and Economic Thought, 1870–1970* (New York: Cambridge University Press, 2024).

12. John Joseph Moakley, interviewed by Robert Allison and Joseph McEttrick, John Joseph Moakley Oral History Project (hereafter JJMOHP), OH-001, April 2, 2001: 1–2, 7–13, 27, MA&I; Mark Robert Schneider, *Joe Moakley's Journey: From South Boston to El Salvador* (Boston, MA: Northeastern University Press, 2013): 16–18; roundtable discussion with John Joseph Moakley's family and staff, JJMOHP, OH-056, September 28, 2001: 4; Esther Cassidy, "Transcript of Enemies of War 56 Minute Rough Cut," 1997, MA&I, https://moakleyarchive.omeka.net/items/show/292.

13. Robert F. Moakley and Thomas J. Moakley, interviewed by Robert Allison and Joseph McEttrick, JJMOHP, OH-003, April 29, 2003: 14; Esther Cassidy, "Transcript of Esther Cassidy's Interview with Jim McGovern Regarding His Involvement with El Salvador," tape 43: 14–17, transcribed by author from digitized Betamax video provided by the MA&I, https://moakleyarchive.omeka.net/items/show/290.

14. Stephanie M. Huezo, "The Murdered Churchwomen in El Salvador," *Origins: Current Events in Historical Perspective* (December 2020), https://origins.osu.edu/milestones/murdered-churchwomen-el-salvador; Matt Eisenbrandt, *The Assassination of a Saint: The Plot to Murder Óscar Romero and the Quest to Bring His Killers to Justice* (Oakland: University of California Press, 2017): ix–xi; Thomas Buergenthal, "The U.S. Should Come Clean on 'Dirty Wars,'" *New York Times*, April 8, 1998: A19.

15. Huezo, "Murdered Churchwomen in El Salvador."

16. John Joseph Moakley, "DI-1237B Congressional Record Excerpt," December 8, 1981, *The People's Congressman: Joe Moakley's Mission for Peace and Justice in El Salvador*, https://moakleyandelsalvador.omeka.net/items/show/102.

17. Mark Danner, *The Massacre at El Mozote: A Parable of the Cold War* (New York: Vintage, 1994); Central American Solidarity Association, "DI-1224A CASA Press Release," February 9, 1982, *The People's Congressman: Joe Moakley's Mission for Peace and Justice in El Salvador*, https://moakleyandelsalvador.omeka.net/items/show/106.

18. John Joseph Moakley, "DI-1227 Moakley News Release on Reagan Certification," February 3, 1982, https://moakleyandelsalvador.omeka.net/items/show/105; and John Joseph Moakley, "DI-0127 Letter to President Ronald Reagan from Congressman John Joseph Moakley," February 1, 1982, https://moakleyandelsalvador.omeka.net/items/show/16, both from *The People's Congressman: Joe Moakley's Mission for Peace and Justice in El Salvador*.

19. Cassidy, "Transcript of Esther Cassidy's Interview with Jim McGovern," tape 40: 23–24.

20. Leonel Gómez, testimony on the "U.S. Policy Toward El Salvador," Hearings before the Subcommittee on Inter-American Affairs of the Committee on Foreign Affairs, US House of Representatives, 97th Congress, First Session, March 11, 1981, 201; Aryeh Never, executive director, Americas Watch, prepared statement for "Human Rights in El Salvador" Hearings before the Subcommittees on Human Rights and International Organizations and on Western Hemisphere Affairs, Committee on Foreign Affairs, US House of Representatives, 98th Congress, First Session, July 26, 1983: 30.

21. Jim McGovern, "For Joe Moakley, All Politics Was Personal," *Roll Call*, June 7, 2001.

22. Roundtable discussion with John Joseph Moakley's family and staff, September 28, 2001: 18.

23. Four other people signed the letter to Moakley: Sister Magee Cappelli, Catholic Connection; Dorothy Cox, JPCOCA; Father Joseph Gaudet, Church of the Blessed Sacrament; Dina Matthews, Comité Centroamericano. Jamaica Plain Committee on Central America, "Letter from Jamaica Plain Committee on Central America members to John Joseph Moakley, December 13, 1982," December 13, 1982, MA&I, https://moakleyarchive.omeka.net/items/show/743; Virginia Vogel Zanger, interviewed by Laura Fountaine, JJMOHP, OH-005, April 19, 2003: 8–9; Carol Pryor, interviewed by Christian Engler, JJMOHP, OH-008, May 9, 2003: 5; Fran Price, interviewed by Francis C. Weymouth Jr., JJMOHP, OH-007, May 7, 2003: 5, 21–22; Edmund G. Crotty, interviewed by Francis C. Weymouth Jr., JJMOHP, OH-006, April 21, 2003: 17; Ann Wheelock, "Residents Lobby Moakley about Central America Issues," *Jamaica Plain Citizen*, February 3, 1983; Jim Phillips, "A Copy of an Oxfam America Special Report on El Salvador Sent to Congressman John Joseph Moakley from a Constituent," February 21, 1982, MA&I, https://moakleyarchive.omeka.net/items/show/9333.

24. Miguel Satut, executive director of Jamaica Plain's Oficina Hispana and one of the people present at the January 1983 meeting with Moakley, estimated that as many as ten thousand Salvadoran refugees lived in Boston at the time. Ann Wheelock, "Residents Lobby Moakley about Central America Issues," *Jamaica Plain Citizen*, February 3, 1983; Fran Price, interviewed by Francis C. Weymouth Jr, JJMOHP, OH-007, May 7, 2003: 5, MA&I.

25. John Joseph Moakley, "Draft of a Dear Colleague Letter Regarding Extended Voluntary Departure Status for Salvadoran Refugees," circa 1982, MA&I, https://moakleyarchive.omeka.net/items/show/9377.

26. James P. McGovern, interviewed by Joseph McEttrick and Beth Anne Bower, JJMOHP, OH-013, August 15, 2003: 2–5; Carol Pryor, interviewed by Christian Engler, JJMOHP, OH-008, May 9, 2003: 11; Fran Price, interviewed by Francis C. Weymouth Jr., JJMOHP, OH-007, May 7, 2003: 21; Virginia Vogel Zanger, interviewed by Laura Fountaine, JJMOHP, OH-005, April 19, 2003: 10–12; James P. McGovern, "The Influx of Illegal Salvadoran Refugees: A Challenge to the State and Local Governments," December 5, 1983, MA&I, https://moakleyarchive.omeka.net/items/show/9181; Virginia Zanger, "DI-0184 Letter to Congressman Moakley from Virginia Zanger," March 30, 1983, https://moakleyandelsalvador.omeka.net/items/show/22, both in *The People's Congressman: Joe Moakley's Mission for Peace and Justice in El Salvador*.

27. John Joseph Moakley and Les AuCoin, "Dear Colleague Letter," June 2, 1983, MA&I, https://moakleyarchive.omeka.net/items/show/9378.

28. Moakley collaborated with Senator Dennis DeConcini (D-AZ), who introduced similar bills in the Senate. H.R. 4447, 98th Congress, 1st Session, November 17, 1983; H.R. 822, 99th Congress, 1st Session, January 30, 1985; H.R. 618, 100th Congress, 1st Session, May 20, 1987; H.R. 45, 101st Congress, 1st Session, October 19, 1989.

29. Patrick Scallen, "US State and Civil Society Responses to Salvadoran Refugees, 1980–1991," in *Refugee Crises, 1945–2000: Political and Societal Responses in International Comparison*, ed. Jan Jansen and Simone Lässig (Cambridge: Cambridge University Press, 2020): 226–27; David Edgar Fitz, "Congressional Policymaking: The Case of Temporary Protected Status for El Salvadorans, 1993" (PhD diss., University of Pittsburgh, 1993): 71–72, 107–8.

30. Hearing before the Committee on the Judiciary, US Senate, 101st Congress, 2nd Session, on the Proposed US Refugee Resettlement Admissions Program for Fiscal Year 1991, October 3, 1990: 10.

31. Francine Price and Mark Zanger, "Invisible Neighbors: Salvadoran Refugees in Boston," *Boston Globe*, October 6, 1985: SM13.

32. Stay of Deportation for Undocumented Salvadorans and Nicaraguans, Hearing before the Subcommittee on Immigration, Refugees, and International Law of the Committee on the Judiciary, US House of Representatives, 100th Congress, 1st Session, H.R. 618, May 20, 1987: 16; Central American Studies and Temporary Relief Act of 1989, US House of Representatives, 101st Congress, 1st Session, Report to Accompany H.R. 45, October 19, 1989: 3.

33. Laura J. Dietrich, deputy assistant secretary of state for Human Rights and Humanitarian Affairs, prepared statement before the Committee on the Judiciary, Subcommittee on Immigration Refugees and International Law, US House of Representatives, Washington, DC, November 7, 1985: 54.

34. Hearing before the Subcommittee on Immigration and Refugee Affairs of the Committee on the Judiciary of the United States Senate, 100th Congress, 1st Session, on S. 332, June 18, 1987: 187.

35. Bob Mitchell, "Moakley's Illegal Aliens Plan Attacked," *Taunton Daily Gazette*, June 4, 1987: 3.

36. Mitchell, "Moakley's Illegal Aliens Plan Attacked," 3.

37. Schneider, *Joe Moakley's Journey*, 162.

38. In June 1990, the House passed the bill to cut aid to the Salvadoran government. This development alarmed Salvadoran military authorities and prompted them to begin speaking with Moakley's task force. Their testimony confirmed his hunch that the order to kill the Jesuits had come from generals at the top. That fall the Senate passed the bill and Bush signed it into law, though he released the full amount of military aid in January 1991, arguing that the FMLN had violated a clause against attacking civilians and receiving outside military assistance. Schneider, *Joe Moakley's Journey*, 164–82; "U.S. Aid to El Salvador Slashed, Restored," in *CQ Almanac 1990*, 46th ed. (Washington, DC: Congressional Quarterly, 1991): 779–86.

39. Fitz, "Congressional Policymaking," 122–23; Schneider, *Joe Moakley's Journey*, 181–82; Moakley, interviewed by Allison and McEttrick, 45–46. On the Immigration Act of 1990, see Carly Goodman, *Dreamland: America's Immigration Lottery in an Age of Restriction* (Chapel Hill: University of North Carolina Press, 2023): 54–67.

40. Fitz, "Congressional Policymaking," 134.

41. Virginia Vogel Zanger, interviewed by Laura Fountaine, JJMOHP, OH-005, April 19, 2003: 16.

42. LeighAnna Hidalgo, "Interview of Rossana Pérez," part IV, March 28, 2017, UCLA Library Center for Oral History Research, Los Angeles, CA.

43. Cameron Barr, "Salvadoran Refugees 'Protected,'" *Christian Science Monitor*, November 19, 1990: 8.

44. Cecilia Menjívar, *Fragmented Ties: Salvadoran Immigrant Networks in America* (Berkeley: University of California Press, 2000): 88. See also Sarah J. Mahler, *Salvadorans in Suburbia: Symbiosis and Conflict* (Needham Heights, MA: Allyn and Bacon, 1995): 18–19.

45. Maria Newman, "INS 'Safe Haven' May Carry Risk of Deportation, Salvadorans Warned," *Los Angeles Times*, January 3, 1991: 6.

46. Ashley Dunn, "Federal Refugee Haven Program Gets Poor Response," *Los Angeles Times*, April 5, 1991: 34.

47. Tracy Wilkinson, "Haven's Price Is Called Too High," *Los Angeles Times*, January 17, 1991: 3; Bill Frelick, "New Lease on Life for Salvadorans, Guatemalans in the

United States," *Refugee Reports* 12, no. 1 (1991): 1–8; Ashley Dunn, "Suit Claims INS Overcharges Refugees from El Salvador," *Los Angeles Times* May 3, 1991: 35.

48. Carolyn Patty Blum, "The Settlement of *American Baptist Churches v. Thornburgh*: Landmark Victory for Central American Asylum-Seekers," *International Journal of Refugee Law* 3, no. 2 (1991): 347–56; Dunn, "Federal Refugee Haven Program Gets Poor Response"; National Immigration, Refugee and Citizenship Forum, "Call to Action," April 5, 1991, box 357, folder 14, collection M744, National Council on La Raza (hereafter NCLR) records, Stanford University Special Collections, Stanford, CA.

49. Dunn, "Federal Refugee Haven Program Gets Poor Response"; Robert Rubin to Bill Frelick, June 4, 1991, box 40, folder 7, US Committee for Refugees and Immigrants, Immigration History Research Center Archive, University of Minnesota, Minneapolis, MN; Ashley Dunn, "Salvadorans Rush to Beat Deadline for Legal Status," *Los Angeles Times*, June 18, 1991: 3; Sam Fulwood III, "House OKs Easing Deadline for Salvadoran Refugees," *Los Angeles Times*, June 26, 1991: 16; Ashley Dunn, "Thousands Apply for U.S. Haven as Deadline Nears," *Los Angeles Times*, October 31, 1991, 1; Tracy Wilkinson, "New Questions Arise for Salvadorans in Los Angeles," *Los Angeles Times*, January 12, 1992: 1.

50. Al Kamen, "U.S. Warns Salvadorans of Deportation," *Washington Post*, January 11, 1992: A12; Rose Apodaca, "Few Salvadorans Here Plan Return to Homeland Soon," *Los Angeles Times*, February 13, 1992: 1; Wilkinson, "New Questions Arise for Salvadorans in Los Angeles."

51. Apodaca, "Few Salvadorans Here Plan Return to Homeland Soon"; George H. W. Bush to Alfredo Cristiani, May 4, 1992; John Joseph Moakley to William P. Barr, January 9, 1992; John Joseph Moakley to James A. Baker, III, January 9, 1992, all found in box 359, folder 2, collection M744, NCLR records.

52. Angela Kelley to interested parties, June 9, 1992, box 359, folder 2, collection M744, NCLR records.

53. Edward J. Flynn, "ABCs of a Complex Immigration Policy," *Los Angeles Times*, November 19, 1992: 6; Patrick McDonnell and H. G. Reza, "Salvadorans Fear Deportations Future Uncertain for Refugees after Federal Decision," *Los Angeles Times*, December 3, 1994: 1; Susan Bibler Coutin, *Legalizing Moves: Salvadoran Immigrants' Struggle for U.S. Residency* (Ann Arbor: University of Michigan Press, 2000): xiv–8; Caryle Murphy, "Gift to Salvadoran Community," *Washington Post*, March 3, 2001: A8; information compiled by author from the *Federal Register*, 1990–2022.

54. Marcela Valdes, "Their Lawsuit Prevented 400,000 Deportations. Now It's Biden's Call," *New York Times Magazine*, April 7, 2021, https://www.nytimes.com/2021/04/07/magazine/immigration-el-salvador.html; Cecilia Menjívar and Leisy J. Abrego, "Legal Violence: Immigration Law and the Lives of Central American Immigrants," *American Journal of Sociology* 117, no. 5 (March 2012): 1380–421.

Chapter Thirteen

1. Ron Klain, Twitter post, April 29, 2022, 4:52 a.m., https://twitter.com/WHCOS/status/1520008171045150720?s=20&t=z-XL_h37lyOyQM66HpxCjQ.

2. Matt Henry, Twitter post, April 29, 2022, 5:24 a.m., https://twitter.com/MenryWY/status/1520016126675021824?s=20&t=z-XL_h37lyOyQM66HpxCjQ.

3. Joseph R. Biden, "Statement by President Biden on Senate Passage of the Inflation Reduction Act," White House, August 7, 2022, https://www.whitehouse.gov/briefing-room/statements-releases/2022/08/07/statement-by-president-biden-on-senate-passage-of-the-inflation-reduction-act/.

4. It is true that fiscal contraction would likely undermine inflation due to the removal of purchasing power from the economy, though much would depend on *how* the legislation would achieve its reduction. For example, one Congressional Budget Office analysis notes that the new regulations on drug pricing will reduce costs to Medicare and Medicaid and result in $237 billion in deficit reduction between 2022 and 2031. This provision would not necessarily have the deleterious impact on purchasing power that other kinds of deficit reduction would have. Similarly, reducing the deficit via stronger IRS enforcement of the wealthy would be unlikely to undermine purchasing power in significant ways. Accordingly, Biden's discussion of the deficit is an improvement to the one that reigned from the 1980s until 2020, which held: reduce the deficit irrespective of inflation. See Trevor Higgins, "The Inflation Reduction Act: A Year in Review," Center for American Progress, September 21, 2023, https://www.americanprogress.org/article/the-inflation-reduction-act-a-year-in-review/.

5. Leslie Kaufman, "A Year into Biden's Climate Agenda, the Price Tag Remains Mysterious," *Bloomberg.com*, August 16, 2023, https://www.bloomberg.com/news/articles/2023-08-16/total-cost-of-joe-biden-s-inflation-reduction-act-is-rising-one-year-later.

6. Robert Edward Rubin and Jacob Weisberg, *In an Uncertain World: Tough Choices from Wall Street to Washington* (New York: Random House, 2003): 354.

7. John B. Judis, "Old Master: Robert Rubin's Artful Role," *New Republic*, December 13, 1992: 21–28. Rubin and Weisberg, *In an Uncertain World*, 361–67.

8. Ruth Wilson Gilmore, "Fatal Couplings of Power and Difference: Notes on Racism and Geography," *Professional Geographer* 54, no. 1 (February 1, 2002): 21.

9. Rubin and Weisberg, *In an Uncertain World*, 355–56.

10. Seymour E. Harris, "A Liberal Economic Program," in *Saving American Capitalism: A Liberal Economic Program*, ed. Seymour E. Harris (New York: Alfred A. Knopf, 1948): 372.

11. On Godley and sectoral-balance analysis, see Wynne Godley, *Seven Unsustainable Processes* (Annandale-on-Hudson, NY: Jerome Levy Economics Institute of Bard College, 1999), https://www.levyinstitute.org/publications/seven-unsustainable-processes.

12. Stephanie Kelton, *The Deficit Myth: Modern Monetary Theory and the Birth of the People's Economy*, 1st edition (New York: PublicAffairs, 2020): 106.

13. Alan Sweezy, "The Keynesians and Government Policy, 1933–1939," *American Economic Review* 62, nos. 1/2 (1972): 118.

14. Julian E. Zelizer, "The Forgotten Legacy of the New Deal: Fiscal Conservatism and the Roosevelt Administration, 1933–1938," *Presidential Studies Quarterly* 30, no. 2 (2000): 331–58.

15. Jason Scott Smith, "The Triumph of the Mixed Economy: The New Deal Order, Keynes, and the Genius of American Liberalism," in *Capitalism Contested: The New Deal and Its Legacies*, ed. Romain Huret, Nelson Lichtenstein, and Jean-Christian Vinel (Philadelphia: University of Pennsylvania Press, 2020): 59.

16. Influential historians have also embraced Clinton's surpluses as a triumph. Gary Gerstle, *The Rise and Fall of the Neoliberal Order: America and the World in the Free Market Era* (New York: Oxford University Press, 2022): 158; Kevin Michael Kruse and Julian E. Zelizer, *Fault Lines: A History of the United States Since 1974*, 1st edition (New York: W. W. Norton and Company, 2019): 210.

17. Joe Weisenthal, "The Untold Story of How Clinton's Budget Destroyed the American Economy," *Business Insider*, September 5, 2012, https://www.businessinsider.com/how-bill-clintons-balanced-budget-destroyed-the-economy-2012-9.

18. Kelton, *Deficit Myth*, 111.

19. See, for example, Richard V. Gilbert, George H. Hildebrand Jr., Arthur W. Stuart, Maxine Yaple Sweezy, Paul M. Sweety, Lorie Tarshis, and John D. Wilson, *An Economic Program for American Democracy* (New York: Vanguard Press, 1938): 42–43, 56–62; Henry A. Wallace, *Sixty Million Jobs* (New York: Reynal and Hitchcock; Simon and Schuster, 1945): 214–15; Leon Keyserling, "Deficiencies of Past Programs and the Nature of New Needs," in *Saving American Capitalism: A Liberal Economic Program*, ed. Seymour E. Harris (New York: Alfred A. Knopf, 1948): 81–94.

20. Wahneema Lubiano, "Black Ladies, Welfare Queens, and State Minstrels: Ideological War by Narrative Means," in *Race-Ing Justice, En-Gendering Power: Essays on Anita Hill, Clarence Thomas, and the Construction of Social Reality*, 1st ed. (New York: Pantheon Books, 1992).

21. Daniel HoSang and Joseph E. Lowndes, *Producers, Parasites, Patriots: Race and the New Right-Wing Politics of Precarity* (Minneapolis: University of Minnesota Press, 2019): 27–28.

22. Al From interview, April 27, 2006, William J. Clinton Presidential History Project, Miller Center, University of Virginia, Charlottesville, https://millercenter.org/the-presidency/presidential-oral-histories/al-oral-history-2006.

23. I am grateful to Nelson Lichtenstein for emphasizing this point.

24. Elizabeth Popp Berman, *Thinking Like an Economist: How Efficiency Replaced Equality in U.S. Public Policy* (Princeton, NJ: Princeton University Press, 2022): 37–41, 221–25.

25. K. Sabeel Rahman, "Building the Administrative State We Need," *Yale Journal on Regulation*, June 29, 2023, https://www.yalejreg.com/nc/building-the-administrative-state-we-need-by-k-sabeel-rahman/.

26. "1972 Democratic Party Platform," July 12, 1976, online at *The American Presidency Project*, ed. Gerhard Peters and John T. Woolley, https://www.presidency.ucsb.edu/documents/1972-democratic-party-platform.

27. "1984 Democratic Party Platform," July 16, 1984, online at *The American Presidency Project*, ed. Gerhard Peters and John T. Woolley, http://www.presidency.ucsb.edu/ws/index.php?pid=29608.

28. Alan S. Blinder and Jeremy B. Rudd, "The Supply-Shock Explanation of the Great Stagflation Revisited," in *The Great Inflation: The Rebirth of Modern Central Banking*, ed. Michael D. Bordo and Athanasios Orphanides, National Bureau of Economic Research conference report (Chicago: University of Chicago Press, 2013): 138–39; Gregory Brew, "Chapter 8: The Geopolitics of Oil: The United States in the Twentieth Century," in *Handbook on Oil and International Relations*, ed. Roland Dannreuther and Wojciech Ostrowski (Northampton, MA: Edward Elgar Publishing, 2022): 122.

29. Andrew Yamakawa Elrod, "Stabilization Politics in the Twentieth-Century United States: Corporatism, Democracy, and Economic Planning, 1945–1980" (PhD diss., University of California, Santa Barbara, 2021): 541–60, https://www.proquest.com/dissertations-theses/stabilization-politics-twentieth-century-united/docview/2597777571/se-2.

30. Edgar R. Fiedler, "On Practicing That Old-Time Religion," remarks before the 11th annual forecasting conference co-sponsored by the Chicago chapter of the American Statistical Association, the College of Business Administration, University of Illinois, and the Chicago Association of Commerce and Industry, Chicago, IL, June 11, 1974, reprinted in *Press Releases of the United States Department of the Treasury*, vol. 190 (Washington,

DC: US Department of the Treasury, May 1, 1974–June 29, 1974), https://fraser.stlouisfed.org/title/6111/item/587033.

31. Gerstle, *Rise and Fall of the Neoliberal Order*, 62.

32. Alan S. Blinder, *A Monetary and Fiscal History of the United States, 1961–2021*, 1st ed. (Princeton, NJ: Princeton University Press, 2022): 80; Alfred S. Eichner, *Toward a New Economics: Essays in Post-Keynesian and Institutionalist Theory* (London: Macmillan, 1986): 113–14.

33. Alfred S. Eichner, "Introduction," in *A Guide to Post-Keynesian Economics*, ed. Alfred S. Eichner (New York: M. E. Sharpe; distributed by Pantheon Books, 1979): 17.

34. Joan Robinson, "What Has Become of the Keynesian Revolution?," *Challenge* 16, no. 6 (January 1974): 9; Joan Robinson, "The Age of Growth," *Challenge* 19, no. 2 (June 1976): 6, 9.

35. Gar Alperovitz and Jeff Faux, "Missing the Point: A Reply," *Challenge* 23, no. 6 (January 1981): 49, https://doi.org/10.1080/05775132.1981.11470661.

36. Gar Alperovitz, "Consumers Opposed to Inflation in the Necessities," interview by author, August 16, 2019.

37. John F. Kennedy, "Commencement Address at Yale University, June 11, 1962," John F. Kennedy Presidential Library and Museum, June 11, 1962, https://www.jfklibrary.org/archives/other-resources/john-f-kennedy-speeches/yale-university-19620611.

38. Eichner, *Toward a New Economics*, 135–36.

39. Eichner, "Introduction," 17.

40. For creative thinking along these lines, I am informed by Fred Lee's emphasis on the social construction of resources and the capacity of the state to direct their creation. I am also indebted to conversations with Nathan Tankus on this point, as well as Lee's overall thought. See Frederic S. Lee and Tae-Hee Jo, *Microeconomic Theory: A Heterodox Approach* (New York: Routledge, 2018): 64, 208.

41. Robert M. Collins, *The Business Response to Keynes, 1929–1964* (New York: Columbia University Press, 1981): 169.

42. Quinn Slobodian, *Globalists: The End of Empire and the Birth of Neoliberalism* (Cambridge, MA: Harvard University Press, 2018): 6.

43. Jimmy Carter, *Keeping Faith: Memoirs of a President* (New York: Bantam Books, 1982): 21.

44. Iwan W. Morgan, *The Age of Deficits: Presidents and Unbalanced Budgets from Jimmy Carter to George W. Bush* (Lawrence: University Press of Kansas, 2009): 47.

45. Jimmy Carter, *White House Diary*, 1st ed. (New York: Farrar, Straus and Giroux, 2010): 37, 45–46, 317.

46. Carter, *Keeping Faith*, 73.

47. Carter, *Keeping Faith*, 81.

48. Benjamin C. Waterhouse, "Mobilizing for the Market: Organized Business, Wage-Price Controls, and the Politics of Inflation, 1971–1974," *Journal of American History* 100, no. 2 (September 2013): 454–78.

49. Charles Schultze, *Slaying the Dragon of Debt: Fiscal Politics and Policy from the 1970s to the Present: A Project of the Walter Shorenstein Program in Politics, Policy and Values*, conducted by Martin Meeker in 2010 (Berkeley: Regional Oral History Office, Bancroft Library, University of California, Berkeley, 2011): 27, https://digitalassets.lib.berkeley.edu/roho/ucb/text/schultze_charles.pdf.

50. James D. Savage, *Balanced Budgets and American Politics* (Ithaca, NY: Cornell University Press, 1988): 162.

51. Sandra Bush et al., eds., *Official Proceedings of the 1984 Democratic National Convention* (Washington, DC: Democratic National Committee, July 16, 1984): 489.

52. Augustus Hawkins, statement, in *The 1984 Economic Report of the President, Hearings before the Joint Economic Committee*, 98th Cong. 48, 1984.

53. Robert Eisner, "Will the Real Deficit Please Stand Up?," *New York Times*, September 25, 1983.

54. Leon Keyserling, statement, in *The 1984 Economic Report of the President, Hearings before the Joint Economic Committee*, 98th Cong. 67, 1984.

55. William H. Miller, "On the Campaign Trail," *Industry Week*, June 25, 1984.

56. Rubin and Weisberg, *In an Uncertain World*, 93, 355–56, 363, 119–120.

57. Rubin and Weisberg, *In an Uncertain World*, 356.

58. Daniel Schlozman and Sam Rosenfeld, "The Politics of Listlessness: The Democrats since 1981," October 8, 2019: 55–58, https://static1.squarespace.com/static/540f1546e4b0ca60699c8f73/t/5e6005bdd383da153fb4d2d5/1583351230480/SchlozmanRosenfeld+Politics+of+Listlessness+-+Oct+8.pdf.

59. Bruce Reed interview, February 19–20, 2004, William J. Clinton Presidential History Project, Miller Center, University of Virginia, Charlottesville, VA.

60. Robert E. Rubin, *Slaying the Dragon on Debt: Fiscal Politics and Policy since the 1970s*, conducted by Martin Meeker in 2011 (Berkeley: Regional Oral History Office, Bancroft Library, University of California, Berkeley, 2011), https://digitalassets.lib.berkeley.edu/roho/ucb/text/rubin_robert.pdf; Alan Blinder interview, June 27, 2003, William J. Clinton Presidential History Project, Miller Center, University of Virginia, Charlottesville, VA.

61. Al From interview, April 27, 2006.

62. Rubin, *Slaying the Dragon on Debt*, 2011.

63. Jane Seaberry, "Conservative Democrats Set New Agenda," *Washington Post*, November 9, 1986, https://www.washingtonpost.com/archive/business/1986/11/09/conservative-democrats-set-new-agenda/6365918e-2ebb-44e3-8c85-cd95fff88d8a/.

64. Berman, *Thinking Like an Economist*, 217.

65. Rubin and Weisberg, *In an Uncertain World*, 107.

66. Gwen Ifill, "Clinton Says He's Met Pledge to Cut Staff by 25%," *New York Times*, October 1, 1993, https://www.nytimes.com/1993/10/01/us/clinton-says-he-s-met-pledge-to-cut-staff-by-25.html.

67. Rubin and Weisberg, *In an Uncertain World*, 117.

68. Christopher Edley, *Slaying the Dragon of Debt: Fiscal Politics and Policy from the 1970s to the Present: A Project of the Walter Shorenstein Program in Politics, Policy and Values*, conducted by Martin Meeker in 2010 (Berkeley: Regional Oral History Office, Bancroft Library, University of California, Berkeley, 2012), https://digitalassets.lib.berkeley.edu/roho/ucb/text/edley_christopher.pdf.

69. On the concept of monetary silencing, I am informed by Jakob Feinig. See Jakob Feinig, *Moral Economies of Money: Politics and the Monetary Constitution of Society*, Currencies (Stanford, CA: Stanford University Press, 2022).

70. Alice Rivlin, *Slaying the Dragon of Debt: Fiscal Politics and Policy from the 1970s to the Present: A Project of the Walter Shorenstein Program in Politics, Policy and Values*, conducted by Martin Meeker with Patrick Sharma in 2011 (Berkeley: Regional Oral History Office, Bancroft Library, University of California, Berkeley, 2011), https://digitalassets.lib.berkeley.edu/roho/ucb/text/rivlin_alice.pdf.

71. Rubin and Weisberg, *In an Uncertain World*, 121.

72. Rivlin, *Slaying the Dragon of Debt*, 2011; Edley, *Slaying the Dragon of Debt*, 2012; Nelson Lichtenstein, "A Fabulous Failure: Clinton's 1990s and the Origins of Our Times," *American Prospect*, January 29, 2018, https://prospect.org/health/fabulous-failure-clinton-s-1990s-origins-times/.

73. Rubin and Weisberg, *In an Uncertain World*, 121.

74. Edley, *Slaying the Dragon of Debt*, 2012.

75. Robert Rubin, Peter R. Orszag, and Allen Sinai, "Sustained Budget Deficits: Longer-Run U.S. Economic Performance and the Risk of Financial and Fiscal Disarray," paper presented at the American Economics Association–North American Economics and Finance Association Joint Session, Allied Social Science Associations annual meetings, Andrew Brimmer Policy Forum, "National Economic and Financial Policies for Growth and Stability," San Diego, CA, January 4, 2004, https://www.brookings.edu/wp-content/uploads/2016/06/20040105.pdf: 12.

76. Peter Orszag, quoted in Scott T. Fullwiler, "Interest Rates and Fiscal Sustainability," *Journal of Economic Issues* 41, no. 4 (December 2007): 1006–7.

77. Rubin, Orszag, and Sinai, "Sustained Budget Deficits."

78. Joseph E. Stiglitz, *The Roaring Nineties: A New History of the World's Most Prosperous Decade*, 1st ed. (New York: W. W. Norton, 2003): 53.

79. Elaine Kamarck, "Lessons for the Future of Government Reform," Brookings Institution, June 18, 2013, https://www.brookings.edu/testimonies/lessons-for-the-future-of-government-reform/.

80. Dimitri B. Papadimitriou and L. Randall Wray, *What to Do with the Surplus: Fiscal Policy and the Coming Recession* (Annandale-on-Hudson, NY: Levy Economics Institute of Bard College, June 1998): 1.

81. US Bureau of Economic Analysis, "Personal Saving Rate [PSAVERT]," FRED, Federal Reserve Bank of St. Louis, accessed February 14, 2023, https://fred.stlouisfed.org/series/PSAVERT. Board of Governors of the Federal Reserve System (US), "Household Debt Service Payments as a Percent of Disposable Personal Income [TDSP]," FRED, Federal Reserve Bank of St. Louis, accessed February 14, 2023, https://fred.stlouisfed.org/series/TDSP.

82. James K. Galbraith, "Review: Economic Report of the President, Transmitted to the Congress February 2000," *Challenge* 43, no. 6 (November–December 2000): 116–17.

83. Louis Uchitelle, "Union Critical of Obama's Top Economics Aide," *New York Times*, June 12, 2008, https://www.nytimes.com/2008/06/12/business/12econ.html.

84. Monica Langley, "Volcker Makes a Comeback as Part of Obama Brain Trust," *Wall Street Journal*, October 21, 2008, https://www.wsj.com/articles/SB122454498635252109.

85. Reed Hundt, *A Crisis Wasted: Barack Obama's Defining Decisions* (New York: RosettaBooks, 2019): 57.

86. US Bureau of Labor Statistics, "Unemployment Rate [UNRATE]," FRED, Federal Reserve Bank of St. Louis, accessed October 17, 2022, https://fred.stlouisfed.org/series/UNRATE.

87. Hundt, *Crisis Wasted*, 131–32.

88. Noam Scheiber, "EXCLUSIVE: The Memo That Larry Summers Didn't Want Obama to See," *New Republic*, February 21, 2012, https://newrepublic.com/article/100961/memo-larry-summers-obama.

89. Ryan Grim, *We've Got People: From Jesse Jackson to Alexandria Ocasio-Cortez, the End of Big Money and the Rise of a Movement* (Washington, DC: Strong Arm Press, 2019): 127.

90. Hundt, *Crisis Wasted*.

91. US Bureau of Labor Statistics, "Unemployment Rate [UNRATE]," FRED, Federal Reserve Bank of St. Louis, accessed October 17, 2022, https://fred.stlouisfed.org/series/UNRATE; US Bureau of Labor Statistics, "Unemployment Level [UNEMPLOY]," FRED, Federal Reserve Bank of St. Louis, accessed October 17, 2022, https://fred.stlouisfed.org/series/UNEMPLOY.

92. Grim, *We've Got People*, 128.

93. Barack Obama, "Address Before a Joint Session of the Congress," February 24, 2009, online at *The American Presidency Project*, ed. Gerhard Peters and John T. Woolley, https://www.presidency.ucsb.edu/documents/address-before-joint-session-the-congress-1.

94. US Bureau of Labor Statistics, "Unemployment Level [UNEMPLOY]," FRED, Federal Reserve Bank of St. Louis, accessed September 26, 2022, https://fred.stlouisfed.org/series/UNEMPLOY.

95. Barack Obama, "Remarks by the President in State of the Union Address," White House, January 27, 2010, https://obamawhitehouse.archives.gov/the-press-office/remarks-president-state-union-address.

96. US Bureau of Labor Statistics, "Unemployment Rate [UNRATE]," FRED, Federal Reserve Bank of St. Louis, accessed September 27, 2022, https://fred.stlouisfed.org/series/UNRATE; US Bureau of Labor Statistics, "Unemployment Level [UNEMPLOY]," accessed September 26, 2022.

97. Ethan Pollack, "Two Years into Austerity and Counting . . . ," *Working Economics: The Economic Policy Institute Blog*, October 19, 2011, https://www.epi.org/blog/years-austerity-counting/.

98. Lawrence Summers, "Executive Summary of Economic Policy Work," December 15, 2008:16, originally linked in Noam Scheiber, "EXCLUSIVE: The Memo That Larry Summers Didn't Want Obama to See," *New Republic*, February 21, 2012, https://newrepublic.com/article/100961/memo-larry-summers-obama.

99. Hundt, *Crisis Wasted*, 133.

100. "'Lost Decade' Casts a Post-Recession Shadow on State Finances," issue brief, Pew Charitable Trusts, June 4, 2019, https://www.pewtrusts.org/en/research-and-analysis/issue-briefs/2019/06/lost-decade-casts-a-post-recession-shadow-on-state-finances.

101. Felicia Wong and Michael Tomasky, "Podcast Episode 8: Making Meaning from the Midterms," November 10, 2022, in *How to Save a Country*, produced by Jocelyn Gonzalez, Alli Rodgers, and Cara Shillenn, podcast, MP3 audio, 28:45, https://rooseveltinstitute.org/2022/11/10/podcast-episode-8-making-meaning-of-the-midterms/.

102. Bob Woodward, *The Agenda: Inside the Clinton White House* (New York: Simon and Schuster, 2014): 158–61.

103. James D. Savage, "Deficits and the Economy: The Case of the Clinton Administration and Interest Rates," *Public Budgeting and Finance* (Spring 1994): 108.

104. Labor/Community Strategy Center, *Reconstructing Los Angeles from the Bottom Up* (Los Angeles: Labor/Community Strategy Center, 1993): 36, 15, 8.

105. Labor/Community Strategy Center, *Reconstructing Los Angeles from the Bottom Up*, 37.

106. K. Sabeel Rahman, "Saving Bidenomics," *Boston Review*, January 4, 2024, https://www.bostonreview.net/articles/saving-bidenomics/.

107. Paul Waldman, "Joe Biden Has Launched an Economic Policy Revolution," *Washington Post*, December 21, 2022, https://www.washingtonpost.com/opinions/2022/12/21/biden-industrial-policy-economic-revolution/.

108. The phrasing "high-care, low-carbon" derives from the Roosevelt Institute's Felicia Wong. See Ezra Klein, "Transcript: Ezra Klein Interviews Felicia Wong," *Ezra Klein Show* podcast transcript, *New York Times*, September 16, 2022, https://www.nytimes.com/2022/09/16/podcasts/ezra-klein-interviews-felicia-wong.html.

Chapter Fourteen

1. Barack Obama, keynote address at the Democratic National Convention, Boston, MA, July 27, 2004.

2. Chris Matthews, *Tip and the Gipper: When Politics Worked* (New York: Simon and Schuster, 2013).

3. Peter Beinart, "The New Liberal Order," *Time*, November 24, 2008: 30–32; Michael Grunwald, *The New New Deal: The Hidden Story of Change in the Obama Era* (New York: Simon and Schuster, 2012).

4. See, for instance, Tim Alberta, *American Carnage: On the Front Lines of the Republican Civil War and the Rise of President Trump* (New York: Harper, 2019).

5. Sam Rosenfeld, *The Polarizers: Postwar Architects of Our Partisan Era* (Chicago: University of Chicago Press, 2017); Robert Mason and Iwan Morgan, eds., *The Liberal Consensus Reconsidered: American Politics and Society in the Postwar Era* (Gainesville: University Press of Florida, 2017).

6. "H.R. 7152 Passage," Senate roll call vote no. 409, 88th Congress, June 19, 1964, https://www.govtrack.us/congress/votes/88-1964/s409; "To Pass S. 1564, the Voting Rights Act of 1965," Senate roll call vote no. 78, 89th Congress, May 26, 1965, https://www.govtrack.us/congress/votes/89-1965/s78.

7. Nicole Hemmer, *Messengers of the Right: Conservative Media and the Transformation of American Politics* (Philadelphia: University of Pennsylvania Press, 2016); Matthew Dallek, *Birchers: How the John Birch Society Radicalized the American Right* (New York: Basic Books, 2023).

8. Daniel Bell, *The End of Ideology: On the Exhaustion of Political Ideas in the Fifties* (New York: Free Press, 1960).

9. Hemmer, *Messengers of the Right*, chapter 10.

10. David S. Broder, "The Reagan-O'Neill Understanding," *Washington Post*, October 10, 1983.

11. Thomas F. Schaller, *The Stronghold: How Republicans Captured Congress but Surrendered the White House* (New Haven, CT: Yale University Press, 2015): 100.

12. Steve Kornacki, *The Red and the Blue: The 1990s and the Birth of Political Tribalism* (New York: Ecco, 2018); Steven M. Gillon, *The Pact: Bill Clinton, Newt Gingrich, and the Rivalry that Defined a Generation* (New York: Oxford University Press, 2008); Nicole Hemmer, *Partisans: The Conservative Revolutionaries Who Remade American Politics in the 1990s* (New York: Basic Books, 2022).

13. Suzanne Mettler, *The Submerged State: How Invisible Government Policies Undermine American Democracy* (Chicago: University of Chicago Press, 2011): esp. chapter 1.

14. Danielle Wiggins, this volume, chapter 5; Janny Scott, "In 2000, a Streetwise Veteran Schooled a Young Bold Obama," *New York Times*, September 9, 2007: 1, 26.

15. Timothy Shenk, *Realigners: Partisan Hacks, Political Visionaries, and the Struggle to Rule American Democracy* (New York: Farrar, Straus and Giroux, 2022): 306.

16. Fredrick Harris, *The Price of the Ticket: Barack Obama and the Rise and Decline of Black Politics* (New York: Oxford University Press, 2012).

17. On the limits of elite diversification, see, for instance, Olúfẹ́mi O. Táíwò, *Elite Capture: How the Powerful Took Over Identity Politics (and Everything Else)* (Chicago: Haymarket Books, 2022).

18. Sheryl Sandberg with Nell Scovell, *Lean In: Women, Work, and the Will to Lead* (New York: Knopf, 2013).

19. Valerie Jarrett, *Finding My Voice: My Journey to the West Wing and the Path Forward* (New York: Viking, 2019): 178–82.

20. "Obama's Ratings Slide Across the Board," news release, Pew Research Center, July 30, 2009, https://www.pewresearch.org/wp-content/uploads/sites/4/legacy-pdf/532.pdf; Shirley Sherrod, *The Courage to Hope: How I Stood Up to the Politics of Fear* (New York: Atria Books, 2012); Daniel Q. Gillion, *Governing with Words: The Political Dialogue on Race, Public Policy, and Inequality in America* (Cambridge: Cambridge University Press, 2016).

21. Sarah Milov and Reuel Schiller, this volume, chapter 3; Barack Obama, *The Audacity of Hope: Thoughts on Reclaiming the American Dream* (New York: Crown, 2006): 83.

22. Barack Obama, "Executive Order 13684—Establishment of the President's Task Force on 21st Century Policing," December 18, 2014, online at *The American Presidency Project*, ed. Gerhard Peters and John T. Woolley, https://www.presidency.ucsb.edu/documents/executive-order-13684-establishment-the-presidents-task-force-21st-century-policing.

23. Barack Obama, "Executive Order 13688—Federal Support for Local Law Enforcement Equipment Acquisition," January 16, 2015, online at *The American Presidency Project*, ed. Gerhard Peters and John T. Woolley, https://www.presidency.ucsb.edu/documents/executive-order-13688-federal-support-for-local-law-enforcement-equipment-acquisition; see also Law Enforcement Equipment Working Group, *Recommendations Pursuant to Executive Order 13688* (Washington, DC: Law Enforcement Equipment Working Group, May 2015), https://obamawhitehouse.archives.gov/sites/default/files/docs/le_equipment_wg_final_report_final.pdf.

24. President's Task Force on 21st Century Policing, *Implementation Guide: Moving from Recommendations to Action* (Washington, DC: President's Task Force on 21st Century Policing, 2015), https://cops.usdoj.gov/RIC/Publications/cops-p341-pub.pdf.

25. "FACT SHEET: White House Police Data Initiative Highlights New Commitments," White House Office of the Press Secretary, April 21, 2016, https://obamawhitehouse.archives.gov/the-press-office/2016/04/22/fact-sheet-white-house-police-data-initiative-highlights-new-commitments.

26. Glenn Thrush, "Exclusive: Obama on Iowa, Clinton, Sanders and 2016," *Politico*, January 25, 2016, https://www.politico.com/story/2016/01/obama-iowa-2016-sanders-off-message-218166.

27. Brian Stelter, "The Facebooker Who Befriended Obama," *New York Times*, July 7, 2008: C1; Chris Hughes, *Fair Shot: Rethinking Inequality and How We Earn* (New York: St. Martin's Press, 2018).

28. Cecilia Kang and Juliet Eilperin, "Why Silicon Valley Is the New Revolving Door for Obama Staffers," *Washington Post*, February 8, 2015, https://www.washingtonpost.com/business/economy/as-obama-nears-close-of-his-tenure-commitment-to-silicon-valley-is-clear/2015/02/27/3bee8088-bc8e-11e4-bdfa-b8e8f594e6ee_story.html.

29. Richard H. Thaler and Cass R. Sunstein, *Nudge: Improving Decisions about Health, Wealth, and Happiness* (New Haven, CT: Yale University Press, 2008).

30. Michael Cooper, "From Obama, the Tax Cut Nobody Heard Of," *New York Times*, October 19, 2010.

31. Karen Tani, this volume, chapter 10; Council of Economic Advisors, *Economic Perspectives on Incarceration and the Criminal Justice System* (Washington, DC: Council of Economic Advisors, April 23, 2016), https://obamawhitehouse.archives.gov/the-press-office/2016/04/23/cea-report-economic-perspectives-incarceration-and-criminal-justice.

32. Wilson, "How Do You Transform a Nation? Nudge, Shove, Shoot," *GlennBeck.com*, September 23, 2013, https://www.glennbeck.com/2013/09/23/how-do-you-transform-a-nation-nudge-shove-shoot/; "Glenn Beck: From Nudge to Shove," transcript from the *Glenn Beck* radio show, September 27, 2010, posted on *Fox News*, September 28, 2010, https://www.foxnews.com/story/glenn-beck-from-nudge-to-shove.

33. Alberta, *American Carnage*; Eric Cantor, Paul Ryan, and Kevin McCarthy, *Young Guns: A New Generation of Conservative Leaders* (New York: Threshold, 2010).

34. E. J. Dionne, "The Reformicons," *Democracy* (Summer 2014), https://democracyjournal.org/magazine/33/the-reformicons/.

35. Keeanga Yamahtta-Taylor, *From #BlackLivesMatter to Black Liberation* (Chicago: Haymarket Books, 2016): esp. chapter 5. Rushing is quoted on 162.

Chapter Fifteen

1. See for example Tim Snyder, *On Tyranny: Twenty Lessons from the Twentieth Century* (New York: Tim Duggan, 2017); Heather Cox Richardson, "Letters from an American," newsletter, https://heathercoxrichardson.substack.com/.

2. Michael Scherer, Ashley Parker, and Tyler Pager, "Historians Privately Warn Biden that America's Democracy Is Teetering," *Washington Post*, August 10, 2022; "As a Historian, I Want to Hear It All," *BC News*, March 2022, https://www.bc.edu/bc-web/bcnews/humanities/history/heather-cox-richardson-talks-about-interview-with-president-biden.html.

3. On some of the basic contours of this debate, see Walter Johnson, "On Agency," *Journal of Social History* 37, no. 1 (Autumn 2003): 113–24; Geoff Eley and Keith Nield, *The Future of Class in History: What's Left of the Social?* (Ann Arbor: University of Michigan Press, 2007).

4. As this crisis dawned, many of Marxist historiography's own participants and fellow travelers had begun to observe the failure of the supposedly inevitable to eventuate. See for example Eric Hobsbawm, "The Forward March of Labour Halted," *Marxism Today* (September 1978): 279–86; Gareth Stedman Jones, *Languages of Class: Studies in English Working-Class History, 1832–1982* (New York: Cambridge University Press, 1984).

5. The classic critique was developed by Joan W. Scott in the essays in *Gender and the Politics of History* (New York: Columbia University Press, 1988).

6. Nell Irvin Painter, "The New Labor History and the Historical Moment," *International Journal of Politics, Culture, and Society* 2, no. 3 (Spring 1989): 367–70.

7. Alan Brinkley, "The Problem of American Conservatism," *American Historical Review* 99, no. 2 (April 1994): 409, 412–13.

8. Eley and Nield, *Future of Class in History*; William H. Sewell, "The Political Unconscious of Social and Cultural History, Or, Confessions of a Former Quantitative Historian," in *Logics of History: Social Theory and Social Transformation* (Chicago: University of Chicago Press, 2009): 22–80.

9. Ira Katznelson, "The 'Bourgeois' Dimension: A Provocation about Institutions, Politics, and the Future of Labor History," *International Labor and Working-Class History* 46 (Fall 1994): 13–16.

10. On the organizational synthesis, see Louis Galambos, "The Emerging Organizational Synthesis in Modern American History," *Business History Review* 44, no. 3 (1970): 279–90; Brian Balogh, "Reorganizing the Organizational Synthesis: Federal-Professional Relations in Modern America," *Studies in American Political Development* 5, no. 1 (1991): 119–72. Polanyi's classic is *The Great Transformation: The Political and Economic Origins of Our Time* (Boston, MA: Beacon Press, 1944); for an account of the Polanyi renaissance, see Fred Block and Margaret R. Somers, *The Power of Market Fundamentalism: Karl Polanyi's Critique* (Cambridge, MA: Harvard University Press, 2016). On neo-institutionalism, see Peter B. Evans, Dietrich Rueschemeyer, and Theda Skocpol, eds., *Bringing the State Back In* (New York: Cambridge University Press, 1985).

11. Stephanie L. Mudge, *Leftism Reinvented: Western Parties from Socialism to Neoliberalism* (Cambridge, MA: Harvard University Press, 2018): 260–364; Elizabeth Popp Berman, *Thinking Like an Economist: How Efficiency Replaced Equality in U.S. Public Policy* (Princeton, NJ: Princeton University Press, 2022).

12. On production, see Michael J. Piore and Charles F. Sabel, *The Second Industrial Divide: Possibilities for Prosperity* (New York: Basic Books, 1986); Fred Block, *Postindustrial Possibilities: A Critique of Economic Discourse* (Berkeley: University of California Press, 1990). On consumption, see Lizabeth Cohen, *A Consumer's Republic: The Politics of Mass Consumption in Postwar America* (New York: Vintage, 2003); Meg Jacobs, *Pocketbook Politics: Economic Citizenship in Twentieth-Century America* (Princeton, NJ: Princeton University Press, 2005); Lawrence B. Glickman, *Buying Power: A History of Consumer Activism in America* (Chicago: University of Chicago Press, 2009). On monopoly and antimonopoly, see Charles Postel, *The Populist Vision* (New York: Oxford, 2007); Richard White, *Railroaded: The Transcontinentals and the Making of Modern America* (New York: Norton, 2011).

13. Gary Gerstle and Steve Fraser, eds., *Ruling America: A History of Wealth and Power in a Democracy* (Cambridge, MA: Harvard University Press, 2005); White, *Railroaded*.

14. Sheri Berman, *The Primacy of Politics: Social Democracy and the Making of Europe's Twentieth Century* (New York: Cambridge University Press, 2006); Ira Katznelson, *Fear Itself: The New Deal and the Origins of Our Times* (New York: Liveright, 2013); Michael Kazin, *What It Took to Win: A History of the Democratic Party* (New York: Farrar, Straus and Giroux, 2022).

15. Paul Potter, "Name the System!," in *Debating the 1960s: Liberal, Conservative, and Radical Perspectives*, ed. Michael W. Flamm and David Steigerwald (Lanham, MD: Rowman and Littlefield, 2008): 95.

16. Richard R. John, "The State Is Back In," *Journal of the Early Republic* 38, no. 1 (Spring 2018): 118.

17. Gary Gerstle, *Liberty and Coercion: The Paradox of American Government from the Founding to the Present* (Princeton, NJ: Princeton University Press, 2017): 351.

18. George Lipsitz, "The Struggle for Hegemony," *Journal of American History* 75, no. 1 (June 1988): 147.

19. Barrington Moore Jr., *Social Origins of Dictatorship and Democracy: Lord and Peasant in the Making of the Modern World* (Boston, MA: Beacon, 1966). For a summary and application of the corporate liberal tradition, see James Weinstein, *The Corporate Ideal in the Liberal State, 1900–1918* (Boston, MA: Beacon, 1969). The classic Gramsci edition is *Selections from the Prison Notebooks*, Quintin Hoare and Geoffrey Nowell Smith, eds. and trans. (New York: International, 1971).

20. For examples see Ralph Miliband, *The State in Capitalist Society* (New York: Basic, 1969); Nicos Poulantzas, *Political Power and Social Classes* (London: New Left Books, 1973); James O'Connor, *The Fiscal Crisis of the State* (New York: St. Martin's, 1973); Göran Therborn, *What Does the Ruling Class Do When It Rules?* (London: New Left Books, 1978); Jürgen Habermas, *Legitimation Crisis*, trans. Thomas McCarthy (Boston, MA: Beacon, 1975); Claus Offe, *Contradictions of the Welfare State*, ed. John Keane (Cambridge, MA: MIT Press, 1984).

21. Fred Block, "The Ruling Class Does Not Rule," *Socialist Revolution* 33 (May–June 1977): 15.

22. For empirical examples, see David Stein, "Containing Keynesianism in an Age of Civil Rights: Jim Crow Monetary Policy and the Struggle for Guaranteed Jobs, 1957–1979," in *Beyond the New Deal Order: U.S. Politics from the Great Depression to the Great Recession*, ed. Gary Gerstle, Nelson Lichtenstein, and Alice O'Connor (Philadelphia: University of Pennsylvania Press, 2019): 124–41; Tim Barker, "Cold War Capitalism: The Political Economy of American Military Spending, 1947–1990" (PhD diss., Harvard University, 2022), https://dash.harvard.edu/handle/1/37372276.

23. Leo Panitch, "The Impoverishment of State Theory," *Socialism and Democracy* 13, no. 2 (1999): 29. Thanks to Tim Barker for this example.

24. See for example Daniel Carpenter, *The Forging of Bureaucratic Autonomy: Reputations, Networks, and Policy Innovation in Executive Agencies, 1862–1928* (Cambridge, MA: Harvard University Press, 2002).

25. Nicos Poulantzas, *State, Power, Socialism*, trans. Patrick Camiller (London: Verso, 2014): 184–85.

26. See Colin Gordon, *Dead on Arrival: The Politics of Health Care in Twentieth Century America* (Princeton, NJ: Princeton University Press, 2003). On path dependency, see Paul Pierson, "When Effect Becomes Cause: Policy Feedback and Political Change," *World Politics* 45, no. 4 (1993): 595–628.

27. Theda Skocpol and Eric Schickler, "A Conversation with Theda Skocpol," *Annual Review of Political Science* 22, no. 1 (2019): 2; Theda Skocpol, "A Critical Review of Barrington Moore's *Social Origins of Dictatorship and Democracy*," *Politics and Society* 4, no. 1 (1973): 18.

28. Ira Katznelson, "Measuring Liberalism, Confronting Evil: A Retrospective," *Annual Review of Political Science* 24, no. 1 (2021): 7.

29. Paul Buhle, "Madison Revisited," *Radical History Review* 57 (1993): 248. See also Todd Gitlin, *The Sixties: Years of Hope, Days of Rage* (New York: Bantam, 1987); Max Elbaum, *Revolution in the Air: Sixties Radicals Turn to Lenin, Che and Mao* (New York: Verso, 2002): 9.

30. Rafael Khachaturian, "Bringing What State Back In: Neo-Marxism and the Origin of the Committee on States and Social Structures," *Political Research Quarterly* 72, no. 3 (2019): 721.

31. Evans, Rueschemeyer, and Skocpol, eds., *Bringing the State Back In*; Peter A. Hall, ed., *The Political Power of Economic Ideas: Keynesianism across Nations* (Princeton, NJ: Princeton University Press, 1989).

32. Theda Skocpol and Kenneth Finegold, "State Capacity and Economic Intervention in the Early New Deal," *Political Science Quarterly* 97, no. 2 (Summer 1982): 260–61.

33. Indeed, more recent historical work does tackle American political development from exactly this premise. Elizabeth Sanders, *The Roots of Reform: Farmers, Workers, and the American State, 1877–1917* (Chicago: University of Chicago Press, 1999); Monica

Prasad, *The Land of Too Much: American Abundance and the Paradox of Poverty* (Cambridge, MA: Harvard University Press, 2012); Ariel Ron, *Grassroots Leviathan: Agricultural Reform and the Rural North in the Slaveholding Republic* (Baltimore, MD: Johns Hopkins University Press, 2020).

34. Mike Davis, *Prisoners of the American Dream* (New York: Verso, 1986): 12.

35. Theda Skocpol, *Social Policy in the United States: Future Possibilities in Historical Perspective* (Princeton, NJ: Princeton University Press, 1995): 218.

36. Theda Skocpol, "Political Response to Capitalist Crisis: Neo-Marxist Theories of the State and the Case of the New Deal," *Politics and Society* 10, no. 1 (1980): 200, quoted in Brian Waddell, "When the Past is Not Prologue: The Wagner Act Debates and the Limits of American Political Science," *New Political Science* 34, no. 3 (2012): 346–48.

37. Skocpol and Schickler, "Conversation with Theda Skocpol," 7.

38. Ira Katznelson, "Lenin or Weber? Choices in Marxist Theories of Politics," *Political Studies* 29, no. 4 (December 1981): 639.

39. Lily Geismer, *Left Behind: The Democrats' Failed Attempt to Solve Inequality* (New York: PublicAffairs, 2022); Nelson Lichtenstein and Judith Stein, *A Fabulous Failure: The Clinton Presidency and the Transformation of American Capitalism* (Princeton, NJ: Princeton University Press, 2023).

40. Robert Reich, Robert Kuttner, and Paul Starr, "Reclaim a Tradition," 1989, original *American Prospect* prospectus, reposted on the *American Prospect*, October 27, 2015, https://prospect.org/power/reclaim-tradition/.

41. Robert Kuttner, interview with Anita Hecht, July 9, 2011, Senator William Proxmire Collection, Wisconsin Historical Society, Madison, WI: 1–3.

42. Lichtenstein and Stein, *Fabulous Failure*.

43. Stanley B. Greenberg, "From Crisis to Working Majority," *American Prospect*, December 5, 1991.

44. Theda Skocpol and Stanley Greenberg, "A Politics for Our Time," in *The New Majority: Toward a Popular Progressive Politics*, ed. Stanley Greenberg and Theda Skocpol (New Haven, CT: Yale University Press, 1997): 10; Margaret Weir and Marshall Ganz, "Reconnecting People and Politics," in *New Majority*, ed. Greenberg and Skocpol, 151–56. Skocpol's frequent collaborator Kenneth Finegold, along with Alan Weil, cautiously praised welfare reform as a potential "virtuous circle" in 2002. See Weil and Finegold, eds., *Welfare Reform: The Next Act* (Washington, DC: Urban Institute Press, 2002): xxii–xxiii.

45. Alan Brinkley, *Voices of Protest: Huey Long, Father Coughlin, and the Great Depression* (New York: Vintage, 1983): 290.

46. Brinkley, "Problem of American Conservatism"; Alan Brinkley, *The End of Reform: New Deal Liberalism in Recession and War* (New York: Vintage, 1996).

47. Tony Judt, "A Clown in Regal Purple: Social History and the Historians," *History Workshop Journal* 7, no. 1 (Spring 1979): 66–94; Geoff Eley and Keith Nield, "Why Does Social History Ignore Politics?," *Social History* 5, no. 2 (May 1980): 249–71.

48. Carroll Moody and Alice Kessler-Harris, eds., *Perspectives on American Labor History: The Problems of Synthesis* (DeKalb: Northern Illinois University Press, 1990); Lenard R. Berlanstein, ed., *Rethinking Labor History: Essays on Discourse and Class Analysis* (Urbana: University of Illinois Press, 1993); Geoff Eley and Keith Nield, "Farewell to the Working Class?," *International Labor and Working-Class History* 57 (2000): 1–30.

49. Melvyn Dubofsky, *The State and Labor in Modern America* (Chapel Hill: University of North Carolina Press, 1994): xi–xii, 236.

50. See Steve Fraser and Gary Gerstle, "Epilogue," in *The Rise and Fall of the New Deal Order, 1930–1980*, ed. Steve Fraser and Gary Gerstle (Princeton, NJ: Princeton University Press, 1989): 296; Jefferson Cowie, *The Great Exception: The New Deal and the Limits of American Politics* (Princeton, NJ: Princeton University Press, 2016); David Brody, "The Breakdown of Labor's Social Contract," *Dissent* (Winter 1992): 38.

51. Hugh Heclo, *Modern Social Politics in Britain and Sweden: From Relief to Income Maintenance* (New Haven, CT: Yale University Press, 1974): 305.

52. E. P. Thompson, *The Making of the English Working Class* (New York: Vintage, 1966): 12.

53. "A New Vision for a Celebrated History Series," Princeton University Press, March 28, 2022, https://press.princeton.edu/ideas/a-new-vision-for-a-celebrated-history-series.

54. Margot Canaday, *The Straight State: Sexuality and Citizenship in Twentieth-Century America* (Princeton, NJ: Princeton University Press, 2009): 5.

55. Laura McEnaney, *Civil Defense Begins at Home: Militarization Meets Everyday Life in the Fifties* (Princeton, NJ: Princeton University Press, 2000); Mae Ngai, *Impossible Subjects: Illegal Immigrants and the Making of Modern America* (Princeton, NJ: Princeton University Press, 2004); Jacobs, *Pocketbook Politics*; Jennifer Klein, *For All These Rights: Business, Labor, and the Shaping of America's Public-Private Welfare State* (Princeton, NJ: Princeton University Press, 2003).

56. Ngai, *Impossible Subjects*, 19.

57. Stanley B. Greenberg, "Popularizing Progressive Politics," in *The New Majority: Toward a Popular Progressive Politics*, ed. Stanley Greenberg and Theda Skocpol (New Haven, CT: Yale University Press, 1997): 287.

58. Thomas B. Edsall, "Trump Won't Let America Go. Can Democrats Pry It Away?," *New York Times*, December 8, 2021.

59. Ruth Wilson Gilmore, *Golden Gulag: Prisons, Surplus, Crisis, and Opposition in Globalizing California* (Berkeley: University of California Press, 2007); Vesla Weaver, "Frontlash: Race and the Development of Punitive Crime Policy," *Studies in American Political Development* 21, no. 2 (2007): 230–65; Naomi Murakawa, *The First Civil Right: How Liberals Built Prison America* (New York: Oxford University Press, 2014); Elizabeth Hinton, *From the War on Poverty to the War on Crime: The Making of Mass Incarceration in America* (Cambridge, MA: Harvard University Press, 2016); Julilly Kohler-Hausmann, *Getting Tough: Welfare and Imprisonment in 1970s America* (Princeton, NJ: Princeton University Press, 2017).

60. Gilmore, *Golden Gulag*, 245.

61. Ira Katznelson, *When Affirmative Action Was White: An Untold History of Racial Inequality in Twentieth Century America* (New York: Norton, 2005); Katznelson, *Fear Itself*.

62. Kim Phillips-Fein, *Fear City: New York's Fiscal Crisis and the Rise of Austerity Politics* (New York: Metropolitan, 2017); Keeanga-Yamahtta Taylor, *Race for Profit: How Banks and the Real Estate Industry Undermined Black Homeownership* (Chapel Hill: University of North Carolina Press, 2019); Destin Jenkins, *The Bonds of Inequality: Debt and the Making of the American City* (Chicago: University of Chicago Press, 2021): 3.

63. See Jacob S. Hacker and Paul Pierson, *Let Them Eat Tweets: How the Right Rules in an Age of Extreme Inequality* (New York: Liveright, 2020).

64. E. P. Thompson, "Agendas for Radical History," *Radical History Review* 36 (1986): 41–42, quoted in Jonathan M. Wiener, "Radical Historians and the Crisis in American History, 1959–1980," *Journal of American History* 76, no. 2 (September 1989): 434.

CONTRIBUTORS

Editors

BRENT CEBUL is associate professor of history at the University of Pennsylvania. He is the author of *Illusions of Progress: Business, Poverty, and Liberalism in the American Century* (University of Pennsylvania Press, 2023) and co-editor of *Shaped by the State: Toward a New Political History of the Twentieth Century* (University of Chicago Press, 2019). His work has been published in scholarly publications including the *Journal of American History* and *Modern American History* as well as popular outlets including the *Atlantic*, the *Washington Post*, and the *New Republic*.

LILY GEISMER is professor of history at Claremont McKenna College, the author of *Left Behind: The Democrats' Failed Attempt to Solve Inequality* (PublicAffairs, 2022) and *Don't Blame Us: Suburban Liberals and the Transformation of the Democratic Party* (Princeton University Press, 2015), and the co-editor of *Shaped by the State: Toward a New Political History of the Twentieth Century* (University of Chicago Press, 2019). Her work has appeared in the *Journal of American History*, the *New York Times*, the *Washington Post*, the *Nation*, *Dissent*, *Jacobin*, and *New Republic*.

Contributors

MARC AIDINOFF is a postdoctoral researcher at the Institute for Advanced Study in Princeton, NJ, and an incoming assistant professor of the history of technology at Harvard University. He recently served as the chief of staff and senior advisor in the White House Office of Science and Technology Policy. He is currently working on a book titled *Rebooting Liberalism: The Computerization of the Social Contract from 1974 to 2004*.

B. ALEX BEASLEY is assistant professor at the University of Texas at Austin. His work has been published in *Diplomatic History*, *Radical History*

Review, and the *Urban History Review*. He is currently working on a book titled *Expert Capital: Houston and the Making of a Service Empire* (Harvard University Press, under contract).

LILA CORWIN BERMAN is the Paul and Sylvia Steinberg Professor of American Jewish History at New York University. She is the author of *The American Jewish Philanthropic Complex: The History of a Multibillion-Dollar Institution* (Princeton University Press, 2020), *Metropolitan Jews: Politics, Race, and Religion in Postwar Detroit* (University of Chicago Press, 2015), and *Speaking of Jews: Rabbis, Intellectuals, and the Creation of an American Public Identity* (University of California Press, 2009). She has published work in the *Journal of American History*, *American Historical Review*, and the *AJS Review* as well as in the *Washington Post*. She is currently writing a book about American Jews and citizenship.

MARISA CHAPPELL is associate professor of history at Oregon State University. She is the author of *The War on Welfare: Family, Poverty, and Politics in Modern America* (University of Pennsylvania Press, 2009). Her writing has appeared in the *Journal of Policy History*, the *Journal of Women's History*, and the *Washington Post*. She is currently completing a book on the history of ACORN.

ADAM GOODMAN is associate professor of history at the University of Illinois Chicago. He is the author of *The Deportation Machine: America's Long History of Expelling Immigrants* (Princeton University Press, 2022). His work has appeared in the *Journal of American History*, the *Nation*, and the *Washington Post*.

DYLAN GOTTLIEB is assistant professor of history at Bentley University. His writing has been published in the *Journal of American History*, *Enterprise and Society*, the *Washington Post*, and the *Journal of Urban History*. He is currently working on his first book, titled *Yuppies: Wall Street and the Remaking of New York* (Harvard University Press, forthcoming).

NICOLE HEMMER is associate professor of history at Vanderbilt University. She is the author of *Partisans: The Conservative Revolutionaries Who Remade American Politics in the 1990s* (Basic Books, 2022) and *Messengers of the Right: Conservative Media and the Transformation of American Politics* (University of Pennsylvania Press, 2016). Her work has been published in several edited volumes as well as in the *New York Times*, *US News and World Report*, the *Washington Post*, and *CNN*, where she is a columnist. She has hosted and produced several historically focused podcasts.

JULILLY KOHLER-HAUSMANN is associate professor of history at Cornell University. She is the author of *Getting Tough: Welfare and Imprisonment in 1970s America* (Princeton University Press, 2017). Kohler-Hausmann's writing has appeared in the *Journal of American History*,

Journal of Urban History, Journal of Social History, and the *New York Times*. She is currently working on a book about the history of US democracy since the 1965 Voting Rights Act.

STEPHEN MACEKURA is professor of international studies at Indiana University. He is the author of *The Mismeasure of Progress: Economic Growth and Its Critics* (University of Chicago Press, 2020) and *Of Limits and Growth: The Rise of Global Sustainable Development in the Twentieth Century* (Cambridge University Press, 2015). His work has appeared in the *Journal of Global History, History of Political Economy,* and *Political Science Quarterly*. His current research focuses on the history of privatization in US foreign relations.

SARAH MILOV is associate professor of history at the University of Virginia. She is the author of *The Cigarette: A Political History* (Harvard University Press, 2019). Her scholarly work has appeared in the *Journal of Policy History, Osiris,* and the *Business History Review*. Her writing has also appeared in the *New York Times*, the *Washington Post*, *Time*, and the *Atlantic*. She is currently writing a biography of nuclear whistleblower Karen Silkwood.

REUEL SCHILLER is the Honorable Roger J. Traynor Chair and professor of law at the University of California College of the Law, San Francisco. He is the author of *Forging Rivals: Race, Class, Law, and the Collapse of Postwar Liberalism* (Cambridge University Press, 2015). His scholarly writing has appeared in the *Law and History Review*, the *Journal of Policy History*, the *New Labor Forum*, and the *Business History Review*, as well as a variety of law reviews and edited volumes.

TIMOTHY SHENK is assistant professor of history at George Washington University. He is the author of *Realigners: Partisan Hacks, Political Visionaries, and the Struggle to Rule American Democracy* (Farrar, Straus and Giroux, 2022) and *Left Adrift: What Happened to Liberal Politics* (Columbia Global Reports, 2024). His writing has appeared in *Modern Intellectual History*, the *New York Times*, the *Guardian*, *London Review of Books*, the *Nation*, *New Republic*, and *Dissent*, where he is co-editor.

DAVID STEIN is assistant professor of history at the University of California, Santa Barbara, and a fellow at the Roosevelt Institute. His work has appeared in scholarly and news publications such as *Souls, Social Justice*, the *Washington Post*, the *Intercept*, and the *Nation*. He is currently completing his first book, *Fearing Inflation, Inflating Fears: The Civil Rights Struggle for Full Employment and the Rise of the Carceral State, 1929–1986* (University of North Carolina Press, under contract).

KAREN M. TANI is Seaman Family University Professor at the University of Pennsylvania, where she holds appointments in the law school and history department. She is the author of *States of Dependency: Welfare,*

Rights, and American Governance, 1935–1972 (Cambridge University Press, 2016). She has published in scholarly journals including the *California Law Review*, the *Law and History Review*, and the *Yale Law Journal*, and has also appeared in the *Los Angeles Times* and the *New Rambler*. Her current research focuses on the history of disability law in the late twentieth century.

DANIELLE WIGGINS is assistant professor of history at the California Institute of Technology. Her writing has been published in the *Journal of Urban History*, the *Journal of African American History*, and *Black Perspectives*, as well as in the *Washington Post*. Her first book is forthcoming from the University of Pennsylvania Press and explores black liberal politics in Atlanta during the post–Civil Rights era.

GABRIEL WINANT is associate professor of history at the University of Chicago. He is the author of *The Next Shift: The Fall of Manufacturing and the Rise of Health Cares in Rust Belt America* (Harvard University Press, 2021). His work has appeared in the *Radical History Review*, the *Journal of Social History*, and the *Journal of American History*, as well as in *Dissent*, *n+1*, the *Nation*, and the *New Republic*. He is currently working on a book exploring capitalist development and class formation in the early twentieth century.

INDEX

AAPC (American Association of Political Consultants), 148
abortion, 300n10
Abrego, Leisy, 235
Acheson, Dean, 40–41
ACORN (Association of Community Organizations for Reform Now): bill by, 326n55; Black Freedom Movement and, 74; Mildred Brown and, 73–74; civil rights and, 84; criticism of, 76; FDC and, 77–78, 80–81; financial policymaking and, 75–76; FIRREA and, 85; Housing Opportunity Fund and, 82; liberalism and, 6, 74–76, 82, 83–84, 85, 86; New Deal and, 75, 78–79; Populist uprising and, 74; professional-class liberals and, 6; reregulation and, 322n2; "Sunshine, Safety and Service" campaign, 79; taxpayer politics and, 81; US League of Savings Institutions and, 78; voter registration and, 177
ADA (Americans with Disabilities Act), 194–95, 196, 352n79
ADC (Aid to Dependent Children), 205
AFDC (Aid to Families with Dependent Children): antipoverty coalition and, 357n26; black family and, 99; black feminists and, 97; computerized case management and, 203; opponents of, 183; political failure of, 201
affirmative-action programs, 3, 141, 299n6

AFL-CIO (American Federation of Labor and Congress of Industrial Organizations), 138
Aid to Dependent Children. *See* ADC (Aid to Dependent Children)
Aid to Families with Dependent Children. *See* AFDC (Aid to Families with Dependent Children)
Ailes, Roger, 143
Alexander v. Choate, 194
Alinsky, Saul, 74
Allen, James B., 174
Alperovitz, Gar, 243
American Association of Political Consultants (AAPC), 148
American Baptist Churches v. Thornburgh, 231
American Civil Liberties Union, 226
American Council on Education, 192
American Federation of Labor and Congress of Industrial Organizations (AFL-CIO), 138
American Friends Service Committee, 226
American Newspaper Guild (ANG), 128–29, 138–39
American Prospect, 288–89
American Recovery and Reinvestment Act, 254
Americans for Democratic Action, 43
Americans with Disabilities Act (ADA), 194–95, 196, 352n79
ANG (American Newspaper Guild), 128–29, 138–39

Architectural Barriers Act, 188
Argueta, Gloria, 231–32
Arroyo, Felix, 225
Association of Community Organizations for Reform Now. *See* ACORN (Association of Community Organizations for Reform Now)
AT&T, 48
Atlanta Magazine, 134
Atlantic, 141
Atwater, Lee, 86

Bagenstos, Samuel, 196
Baker, James, 344n29
Bale, Frances, 97
Balogh, Brian, 39, 358n39
Bambara, Toni Cade, 97
Barak, Ehud, 159
Barr, William P., 232
Bartlett, Steve, 81
Beck, Glenn, 274
Bell, Daniel, 262
Ben & Jerry's, 133
Bentsen, Lloyd, 249
Bethune-Cookman College, 102
Biden, Joe, 182, 237, 257–58, 366n4
Billingsley, Andrew, 97, 98
Black Collegian, 134
Black Enterprise, 134
black family: AFDC and, 99; Black Family Awareness conference and, 101, 102; "Black Leadership Family Plan for the Unity, Survival, and Progress of Black People" and, 100; black leaders on, 95, 97–101, 103–5; Coca-Cola and, 101; Ford Foundation and, 101; Humphrey-Hawkins Full Employment Act and, 99; IBM and, 101; Keynesian liberalism and, 96; MacArthur Foundation and, 101; Nation of Islam and, 94–95; Barack Obama and, 105; Philip Morris and, 101; Progressive Era and, 95; Responsible Fatherhood Initiative and, 105–6; "Summit on the Black Family" and, 98–100. *See also* black liberals
Black Freedom Movement, 74, 84
"Black Leadership Family Plan for the Unity, Survival, and Progress of Black People," 100–101

black liberals: black American history and, 91; black family and, 91–92, 95, 97, 99, 103, 105; black full employment and, 96; black professional class, 299n6; black state skepticism and, 90–91; Bill Clinton and, 104; DLC and, 104; Ford Foundation and, 91; James Forman Jr. and, 105; Freedom Budget and, 90, 94; Great Society and, 90; Humphrey-Hawkins Full Employment Act and, 96; John E. Jacobs and, 96–97; Jim Crow and, 90; John M. Olin Foundation and, 103; Marshall Plan and, 105; National Center for Neighborhood Enterprise and, 103; neoliberalism and, 92, 106; New Deal and, 90, 93–94, 95–96; professional-class liberals and, 91; Reconstruction and, 90; Sarah Scaife Foundation and, 103; self-help initiatives and, 101; social welfare and, 89; state skepticism and, 96; tradition of, 89; War on Poverty and, 94
Black Lives Matter, 8, 275
Black Panther Party, 89
Black Women for Wages for Housework, 110, 120
Blair, Tony, 159
Block, Fred, 283–84
Boston Globe, 131
Boston Globe's Spotlight, 130
Breslin, Jimmy, 136
Brinkley, Alan, 279, 288–89, 290
Broder, David, 175, 263
Broder, Jonathan, 140
Brody, David, 290–91
Brown, Michael, 268–69
Brown, Mildred, 73–74, 78–79, 81–83
Brown, Wendy, 307
Brown, Wilmette, 110, 120
Brown v. Board of Education, 187
Buckley, William F., Jr., 262
Buffet, Warren, 253
Burma, 41–42
Burton, Philip, 70
Bush, George H. W., administration: bailout bill of, 79–81; DED and, 232–33; New Democrats and, 30; private enterprise and, 49–50; Resolution Trust Corporation and, 80; small

businesses and, 49–50; thrift industry and, 77, 78; TPS and, 232; voter registration and, 181
Bush, George W., 183–84, 264
Business Roundtable, 75, 246
Buttigieg, Pete, 1
Butts, George, 79
Byrd, Robert, 173

Caddell, Pat, 175
Campaigns Inc., 148
Canaday, Margot, 114, 117, 292
Cantor, Eric, 274
Cappelli, Magee, 363n23
CARECEN (Central American Refugee Center), 227
Carnegie Corporation, 23, 92
Carnegie Foundation, 25, 27, 29–30, 93, 101
Carter, Jimmy, administration: James Baker and, 344n29; Commission on Federal Election Reform and, 344n29; deficit reduction and, 245–46; El Salvador and, 223; Gerald Ford and, 245; Humphrey-Hawkins Full Employment Act and, 96; Walter Mondale and, 174, 176; Nader's Raiders and, 71; Tip O'Neill and, 245; William Simon and, 245–46; Paul Volcker and, 246; voter registration and, 174–75
Castle, Mike, 212
Catholicism, 300n10
CBA (cost-benefit analysis), 197–98, 353n87
CBO (Congressional Budget Office), 192
Center for the Study of Responsive Law, 53, 58–63, 65–69, 70
Central American Refugee Center (CARECEN), 227
Chacón, Óscar, 220
Chatelain, Marcia, 101
Chemonics International, 50
Chicago *Reader*, 133
Chicago *Tribune*, 131
child support, 211–15
Church, Frank, 46
Church World Services, 226
CIO (Congress of Industrial Organizations), 48, 129

Civil Rights Act, 188
civil rights legislation, 2–3
Clark, Kenneth, 95
Clarke, Maura, 223
Clean Air Act, 68, 70
Clean Water Act, 68
Climate Data Initiative, 273
Clinton, Bill, administration: big government and, 104; bipartisanship and, 264; black liberals and, 104; Clinton Foundation and, 31–32; computerized case management and, 203; contractual agreements and, 359n50; crime bill and, 264; DED and, 233; deficit reduction and, 248–49, 252, 256; economic policy of, 251; financial deregulation and, 86; fiscal surpluses and, 239–40; Stan Greenberg and, 153–55, 161; Illegal Immigration Reform and Immigrant Responsibility Act and, 233; indefinite quantity contracts and, 50; Dick Morris and, 155; NAFTA and, 263–64; NEC and, 249; neoliberalism and, 37; New Covenant and, 215; Mark Penn and, 155, 157–59; Personal Responsibility and Work Opportunity Act and, 215–16; political strategists and, 147; presidency of, 7; professional-class liberals and, 50; reelection campaigns of, 153–55, 157–59; Republican leadership and, 263; Douglass Schoen and, 155, 157–59; USAID and, 50; vision of, 30–31; voter registration and, 181; welfare and, 117, 207, 210–11, 215–17
Clinton, Hillary, 1–2, 160–61
Clinton Foundation, 31–32
Cloward, Richard, 177–78, 181
Coca-Cola, 101
Cohen, Cathy, 115
COIN (Consumers Opposed to Inflation in the Necessities), 243
Cold War: conservative partners since, 16; contract state and, 36; economic development and, 41; end of, 7; LGBTQ citizens and, 303n27; liberalism and, 11, 25, 304n32; professional-class liberals and, 11; "warfare state" and, 39–40
Commentary, 136

Committee in Solidarity with the People of El Salvador, 226
Committee on States and Social Structures, 286
Community Action Agencies, 173
community-development corporations, 30
Community Reinvestment Act, 76, 82–83, 85
Con Diaz, Geraldo, 358n42
Congressional Black Caucus, 100, 104
Congressional Budget Office (CBO), 192
Congress of Industrial Organizations (CIO), 48, 129
Congress of Racial Equality (CORE), 173
conservatives: Catholics and evangelicals, 300n10; emotional tone of, 302n19; power of, 15; professional class and, 14, 300n7; voting rights and, 168; welfare and, 205
Consumer Price Index (CPI), 242
Consumers Opposed to Inflation in the Necessities (COIN), 243
contract state: Cold War and, 36; foreign-policy commitments and, 40; growth of, 37–38, 45; history of, 42; John F. Kennedy and, 51; military-industrial complex and, 36; Nathan Associates and, 35–36, 38, 51; New Deal and, 40; New Directions reforms and, 36; Harry S. Truman and, 51; "wartime state" and, 40
Cook, Tim, 272
Coors, Adolph, IV, 102
Coors, William, 101
Coors Brewing Company, 101
CORE (Congress of Racial Equality), 173
Cosby, Bill, 87–88
Cosby, Camille, 87–88
cost-benefit analysis (CBA), 197–98, 353n87
Cott, Nancy, 109, 113, 117
Cox, Dorothy, 363n23
CPI (Consumer Price Index), 242
Cristiani, Alfredo, 232
Cross, Arthur, 79–80, 81
Crotty, Ed, 225
Currie, Lauchlin, 38, 239

DACA (Deferred Action for Childhood Arrivals), 221
Data-Driven Justice Initiative, 273
David, Troy, 275
Davis, Francis, 192
Davis, Mike, 256–57, 286–87
Davis, Ossie, 102
DeConcini, Dennis, 227, 230
DED (Deferred Enforced Departure), 232–33
Deferred Action for Childhood Arrivals (DACA), 221
Deferred Enforced Departure (DED), 232–33
deficit hawks, 237–38, 240, 241, 256–58
DeLauro, Rosa, 152
D'Emilio, John, 122–23
Democratic Leadership Council (DLC): alumni of, 14; black liberals and, 104; economic policy and, 241; founding of, 180; Al From and, 241; mass politics and, 168; New Democrats and, 75; racial politics and, 153
Democratic National Committee (DNC), 153
Democratic Party: criticism of, 177, 262; debt of, 345n50; dynamics of, 301n15; electoral prospects of, 4; full employment and, 241; LGBTQ rights and, 107; liberalism and, 4, 84, 146, 150; mass politics and, 168–69; neoliberalism and, 112; policymakers of, 15; Silicon Valley and, 15; structure of, 301n15; transformation of, 2; voter registration and, 179–81; Wall Street and, 15
Department of Agriculture, 59
Department of Health, Education, and Welfare (HEW), 189, 190, 191, 349n34
Department of Housing and Urban Development (HUD), 198
Department of Transportation, 192
Dietrich, Laura J., 228
disability language, 190, 347n2, 350n43
disability rights: *Brown v. Board of Education* and, 187; CBO and, 192; cost arguments and, 191–94, 351n52; discrimination and, 191, 195–96; Kennedy family and, 187; liberalism

and, 187; litigation of, 191–92; Thurgood Marshall and, 194; movement of, 12, 187; *Southeastern Community College v. Davis* and, 192
Disability Rights Education and Defense Fund, 193–94
Dixon, Paul Rand, 69
DLC. *See* Democratic Leadership Council (DLC)
DNC (Democratic National Committee), 153
Dodd, Chris, 152
Donahue, Phil, 81
Donovan, Jean, 223
Douglas, Paul, 43
Douglas, William O., 116
Dubofsky, Melvyn, 290

Earnest, Josh, 107
Easterbrook, Gregg, 142
Eastman-Kodak, 101
Edley, Chris, 249–51
Edsall, Thomas, 178, 290–91
Ehrenreich, Barbara, 1, 5
Ehrenreich, John, 1, 5
Eichner, Alfred, 243, 244
Eisenhower, Dwight, administration, 49, 261
Eisner, Robert, 247
Electoral College, 175
Elementary and Secondary Education Act, 188, 189
Elman, Philip, 69
El Rescate, 227, 231, 232
Emanuel, Rahm, 1, 161
Emerge, 134
Environmental Protection Agency (EPA), 71, 318n26
Epstein, Richard, 195
Equal Rights Amendment, 174
Esquire, 135
evangelicalism, 300n10
Evans, Peter, 286
Excel, 134

Fair Lending Oversight and Enforcement Act, 83, 84
Fallows, James, 142, 321n111
Family Assistance Program, 205

Family Support Act, 212–13, 356n10
Fauntroy, Walter, 100
FDC. *See* Financial Democracy Campaign (FDC)
Federal Home Loan Banks, 76–77, 82
Federal Savings and Loan Insurance Corporation (FSLIC), 76, 77
Federal Trade Commission (FTC), 56–57, 66–70
Federal Water Quality Office, 59, 318n26
Federici, Silvia, 119
Felker, Clay, 133
Fellmeth, Robert, 321n110
Fifteenth Amendment, 171
Financial Democracy Campaign (FDC), 77–78, 80–81, 83, 85, 324n29
Financial Institution Data Match program, 214
Financial Institutions Reform, Recovery, and Enforcement Act (FIRREA), 85–86
Finegold, Kenneth, 286–87
Fisher, Robert, 265–66
FMLN (Frente Farabundo Martí para la Liberación Nacional), 223
Food and Drug Administration, 59, 67
Forbath, William, 304n35
Ford, Gerald, 245
Ford, Harold, Sr., 212
Ford, Ita, 223
Ford Foundation: black economic power and, 101; black family and, 101; black liberals and, 91; community-development corporations and, 30; CORE and, 173; Gray Areas program and, 26; Kennedy administration and, 26; Wright Patman and, 26–27; philanthropy and, 26, 307; War on Poverty and, 27; "Women's Funds" and, 31; work of, 29–30
Fordist model of media, 126, 127, 128, 138–39
Foreign Assistance Act, 28, 29
Forman, James, Jr., 105
Fox News, 15, 142–43
Francis, Megan Ming, 93
Frazier, E. Franklin, 95
Freedom Budget, 94

Freedom Bureau, 92
Freedom of Information Act, 70
Frente Farabundo Martí para la Liberación Nacional (FMLN), 223
Friedman, Milton, 37
From, Al, 241, 248
FSLIC (Federal Savings and Loan Insurance Corporation), 76, 77
FTC (Federal Trade Commission), 56–57, 66–70
Furman, Jason, 253

Galbraith, James, 252–53
Galbraith, John Kenneth, 65–67, 338n52
Gamble, James, 102
Gamble, James Norris, 102
Garland Fund, 93
Garvey, Marcus, 88–89
Gate, 338n60
Gates, Bill, 19
Gates, Henry Louis, 267–68
Gates Foundation, 32
Gelb, Arthur, 128
General Motors, 54
Genovese, Eugene, 277
George, 137
Gerstle, Gary, 282, 291–92
Gilmore, Ruth Wilson, 293
Gingrich, Newt, 215–16, 263–64
Gingrich Congress, 15
Giovanni's Room, 133
Giridharadas, Anand, 33
Gitlin, Todd, 288–89
GNP (Gross National Product), 38
Godley, Wynne, 239
Goldwater, Barry, 262
Gonzalez, Henry, 80, 83, 85
Goodwyn, Lawrence, 277
Gordon, Colin, 285
Gordon, Linda, 204, 205
Gordon, Sarah Barringer, 22
Gore, Al, 159–60
Graham, Phil, 38
Gramm, Phil, 84–85, 181
Gramsci, Antonio, 283
Gray Areas program, 26
Great Depression, 10
Great Society, 14, 20, 29, 90, 112
Great Speckled Bird, 132–33

Green, Mark, 321n110
Greenberg, Stan: associates of, 152, 159–61; Bill Clinton and, 153–55, 158, 161, 289; Democratic coalition and, 147; life of, 150–52; mass incarceration and, 293; New Democrats and, 153; racial politics and, 153; work of, 6, 151–55, 161–62
Greenspan, Alan, 250–51
Grim, Ryan, 253
Griswold v. Connecticut, 116
Gross National Product (GNP), 38

Hamill, Pete, 135–36
Hanggi, Elena, 80, 81
Hannity, Sean, 143
Harper's, 141
Harris, Kamala, 1
Hatch Act, 175
Hawkins, Augustus, 96, 247, 257
Heclo, Hugh, 291
Height, Dorothy, 87–88, 94, 102
Heinzerling, Lisa, 197–98
Henderson, Leon, 38
Heritage Foundation, 75
Hertzberg, Hendrik, 136
HEW (Department of Health, Education, and Welfare), 189, 190, 191, 349n34
Hightower, Jim, 77
Hinton, Elizabeth, 91
Holder, Eric, 266, 268
Home Mortgage Disclosure Act (HMDA), 76, 85
Hooks, Benjamin, 98
Hoover, Herbert, 24, 39, 40
Hopkins, Harry, 38
Horowitz, David, 131, 140
HotWired, 140
Housing Act, 325n43
Housing Opportunity Fund, 82
HUD (Department of Housing and Urban Development), 198
Hughes, Chris, 271–72
Huguley, Garnett, 103
Human SERVE (Human Service Employees Registration and Voter Education Fund), 177, 180
Humphrey, Hubert, 96

Humphrey-Hawkins Full Employment Act, 96, 99
Hundt, Reed, 253
Hurd, Maude, 79

IBM (International Business Machines), 101, 204, 208–9, 358n42
Illegal Immigration Reform and Immigrant Responsibility Act, 233
Immigration Act, 221, 229
Immigration and Naturalization Service (INS), 230–31
indefinite quantity contracts, 47, 50
Inflation Reduction Act, 237, 257
Inglehart, Ronald, 146
initiatory democracy, 55, 63, 64, 68, 71
INS (Immigration and Naturalization Service), 230–31
institutionalism, 277, 280–81, 287–88. *See also* neo-institutionalism
International Business Machines. *See* IBM (International Business Machines)
International Typographical Union, 128
Interreligious Task Force, 226
Interstate Commerce Commission, 59
Isserman, Maurice, 290–91

Jackson, Jesse, 77, 84, 178
Jacobs, John E., 96–97, 98, 104
Jacobs, Meg, 292
Jamaica Plain Committee on Central America (JPCOCA), 220, 225, 226
Janis, Madeline, 230
Japanese Automobile Manufacturer's Association, 48
Jarrett, Valerie, 267
Jenkins, Destin, 293–94
Jim Crow: African American civic participation and, 92; black liberals and, 90; black passengers and, 350n48; conditional citizenship and, 171; New Deal and, 93–94; segregation and, 4, 10
Jive, 134
John, Richard, 282
John Birch Society, 262
John M. Olin Foundation, 103
Johnson, Lyndon B., administration, 15, 25–26, 27, 167

Jordan, Vernon, 94
journalism, online, 126
JPCOCA (Jamaica Plain Committee on Central America), 220, 225, 226
Judis, John, 160
Justice Department's Antitrust Division, 66–67

Kamarck, Elaine, 252
Katznelson, Ira, 279–80, 285, 286, 293
Kazel, Dorothy, 223
Kazin, Michael, 290–91
Keating, Charles, 78
Kelman, Mark, 196
Kelton, Stephanie, 239
Kennedy, Anthony, 118
Kennedy, Duncan, 199
Kennedy, John F., administration: brain trust of, 300n9; contract state and, 51; Ford Foundation and, 26; Keynesian economics of deficits and, 244; Robert Nathan and, 43; praise of, 49; transformation of liberalism and, 15; vocational rehabilitation and, 187; voter registration and, 172
Kennedy, Joseph, 81, 83, 84, 85
Kennedy, Ted, 157
Kennedy family, 187
Kest, Steve, 77, 83, 84
Keynesianism, 96, 243. *See also* post-Keynesianism
Keyserling, Leon, 48–49, 247
Khachaturian, Rafael, 286
King, Coretta Scott, 257
Kinsley, Michael, 141–42, 321n111
Kirk, Paul, 153
Kirkpatrick, Jeane, 223
Klain, Ron, 237
Klein, Jennifer, 292
Kling, Rob, 209
Koch, Charles, 19, 306
Koch, David, 19, 306
Koch, Ed, 156
Kolko, Gabriel, 60
Koon, Bruce, 139
KPMG Peat Marwick, 50
Krauthammer, Charles, 136–37
Kristol, Irving, 137–38
Krugman, Paul, 141

Kuttner, Robert, 288–89
Kuznets, Simon, 38

Labor/Community Strategy Center (LCSC), 256–57
Ladner, Joyce, 97
Landauer, Jerry, 69
Lasch, Christopher, 277
law enforcement, 355n4
law school, 299n5
LCSC (Labor/Community Strategy Center), 256–57
Leach, Jim, 84
League of Women Voters, 180
Left, 8, 9, 11, 16, 63, 109–10, 303n32
Lemann, Nicholas, 142
Lewis, Michael, 142
LGBTQ community: employment and, 114, 115, 116, 333n28; queer citizenship and, 108, 110–11, 123, 331n5; rights and, 107–8, 110, 111, 115, 116, 123, 331n5; same-sex marriage and, 107–8, 117–18, 121–22, 123
liberalism: abandonment of, 8; absentee fathers and, 359n54; ACORN and, 6, 74–76, 82, 83–84, 85, 86; allies of, 12; alternative visions of, 6; anticommunism of, 304n32; arguments of, 13; causes and social aspirations of, 4–5, 9; Cold War and, 25, 304n32; collapsing fortunes of, 303n30; core commitments of, 302n26; corporate liberalism and, 10; debt contract and, 356n14; democratic engagement and, 305n36; Democratic Party and, 84, 146, 150; disability rights and, 187; end of, 10; evolution of, 2, 4, 6, 11–12, 14–16, 301n15; Great Depression and, 10; Great Society and, 14, 112; historiography and, 277–78; journalism and, 127, 135; Left and, 9, 16; LGBTQ rights and, 107–8, 111; liberal elite and, 1; liberal media and, 127; liberal policy and, 355n5; liberal Republicans and, 4; marriage and, 109, 112, 117; media and, 138; mid-century liberalism and, 37, 303, 304; Ralph Nader and, 71; neoliberalism and, 2, 14, 15; New Deal and, 4, 10, 12, 14, 76, 112–13, 136, 322n8; *New Republic* and, 127; news industry and, 335n2; newspapers and, 129; philanthropy and, 21–22; politicians and, 12; problem solving by, 15; professional-cultural characteristic and, 5; Progressive Era and, 4; queer employees and, 114; queer marriage and, 115; rapprochement with, 8; Reagan era and, 3; reliance of upon philanthropy, 12; scholarship of, 13; sober governance and, 15; social benefits and, 12; social imagination of, 8; tensions of, 5, 6, 20, 21, 22; triangulation and, 14–15; Vietnam War and, 10; voting rights and, 13, 168; welfare and, 205–6. *See also* black liberals; professional-class liberalism
Life magazine, 132
Lippmann, Walter, 7, 137
Lomax, Michael, 6, 88
Long, Russell, 206
Lorde, Audre, 97
Los Angeles Times, 130, 132, 141
Lovato, Robert, 220
Lowi, Theodore, 60
Lynd, Staughton, 277

MacArthur Foundation, 101
MacLaine, Shirley, 135
Maddox, Lester, 133
Magnuson, Warren, 70
Mailer, Norman, 136
Manchin, Joe, 237
Mandela, Nelson, 159
Marcus Garvey movement, 94–95
marriage: autonomy and, 115; Black Women for Wages for Housework and, 110; consent and, 332n15; economic transformation of, 117–18; evolution of, 115–16; family wage and, 117, 121; liberalism and, 109, 112, 117; New Deal and, 109–10, 113, 115; *Obergefell v. Hodges* and, 121; oppression and, 115; Progressive Era and, 112–13; same-sex, 107–8, 110, 115, 117–18, 121–22, 123; status quo of, 121; universal health care and, 333n36
Marshall, Thurgood, 194
Marshall Plan, 105
Martin, Trayvon, 268
Marxism, 283, 286–88. *See also* neo-Marxism

Matthews, Dina, 363n23
Matthews, Forrest David, 191
Maung, U Hla, 41
McConnell, Mitch, 180–81, 182
McDonald's, 101
McEnaney, Laura, 292
McGovern, George, 138
McGovern, Jim, 224, 226
McNary, Gene, 230
McWhorter, John, 142
Meany, George, 243
Mears, Tracey L., 269
Menjívar, Cecilia, 230, 235
Merrill Lynch, 78
Mettler, Susan, 264
Meyerowitz, Joanne, 29
Meyers, Michael, 229
Microsoft, 141
military-industrial complex, 36
Miller, Michelle, 272
Mills, C. Wright, 60
Milov, Sarah, 11, 129–30
Moakley, Joe, 219, 221–23, 225–29
Moakley-DeConcini bills, 227
Mondale, Walter, 70, 174, 176, 179, 246–47
Monnet, Jean, 38
Moore, Barrington, 283
Moore, Melba, 102–3
Morgenthau, Henry, 239
Morris, Dick, 155, 158
Morrison, Bruce, 83, 84
Moss-Magnuson Act, 69, 70
Mount, John, 130
Moyers, Bill, 87
Moynihan, Daniel Patrick: black family and, 94; black poverty and, 211; computerized case management and, 203; Family Support Act and, 212–13; "liberal" label and, 358n48; New Class and, 338n52; welfare reform and, 210–11, 212
Moynihan Report, 94, 97
Multimedia Gulch, 140
Murakawa, Naomi, 185
Murdoch, Rupert, 142
Murphy, Ryan Patrick, 120
Murray, Charles, 136
Murray, Phil, 48
Muskie, Edmund, 69

NAACP (National Association for the Advancement of Colored People), 88, 93, 94, 98, 180
Nader, Ralph: activism and, 55, 63–64; associates of, 56–57, 65–66, 69–70; Center for the Study of Responsive Law and, 53, 70; civil rights and, 65; class upscaling and, 129–30; consumer society and, 61–62; corporate socialism and, 61; countervailing power and, 65–66, 70; FTC and, 56, 57, 68, 69–70; General Motors and, 54; influence of, 70; initiatory democracy and, 55, 63, 71; Justice Department and, 68; leadership of, 70; liberalism and, 55–56, 68, 71; Nader's Raiders and, 53, 54, 57, 69, 70–71; Nixon administration and, 69; PIRGs and, 59, 66, 70; political vision of, 55–56; Public Citizen group and, 70; Ronald Reagan and, 55; Upper West Side Air Pollution Campaign and, 64; work of, 6, 53–54
NAFTA (North American Free Trade Agreement), 263–64
Napolitan, Joseph, 148
Napolitano, Janet, 266
Nashville Urban League, 101
Nathan, Robert: Americans for Democratic Action and, 43; associates of, 41–43, 48–49; AT&T and, 48; CIO and, 48; Cold War and, 41; foreign aid and, 43; GNP and, 38; Japanese Automobile Manufacturer's Association and, 48; John F. Kennedy and, 43; liberal elites and, 38; life of, 38; New Deal and, 39; President's Committee on Economic Security and, 38; professional-class liberalism and, 48; Roosevelt administration and, 39; Truman administration and, 39; USAID and, 44; war mobilization and, 39; work of, 6, 35–37
Nathan Associates: Burma and, 41–42; contracts of, 46, 47; contract state and, 35–36, 38, 51; evolution of, 49–50; foreign aid and, 44; Planning Ministry and, 41–42; USAID and, 49–50
National Air Pollution Control Administration, 59, 318n26

National Association for the Advancement of Colored People (NAACP), 88, 93, 94, 98, 180
National Association of Newsweeklies, 133
National Black Family Reunion, 87–88, 102, 103
National Center for Neighborhood Enterprise, 103
National Council of Negro Women (NCNW), 87, 102, 103
National Council on La Raza, 226
National Economic Council (NEC), 249
National Governors Association, 210
National Highway Transportation Safety Administration, 71
National Immigration, Refugee, and Citizenship Forum, 226
National Pollution Control Administration, 67
National Urban League, 94, 98
National Welfare Rights Organization, 63, 74
Nation of Islam, 94–95
NBC's Los Angeles TV affiliate, 131
NCNW (National Council of Negro Women), 87, 102, 103
NEC (National Economic Council), 249
Nelson, Alan, 228
neoconservatives, 138
neo-institutionalism, 285, 286
neoliberalism: black American history and, 91; black liberals and, 92, 106; Bill Clinton and, 37; Democratic Party and, 112; fiscal triangle and, 311n36; Milton Friedman and, 37; governance and, 300n8; liberalism and, 2, 14, 15; professional-class liberalism and, 3, 14, 16; public-policy interventions and, 322n4; queer politics and, 111–12; Ronald Reagan and, 37
neo-Marxism, 285, 286. *See also* Marxism
New Class, 137–38, 143, 338n52
New Deal: ACORN and, 75, 78–79; black liberals and, 90, 93–94, 95–96; Carnegie Foundation and, 25; collapse of liberalism, 303n30; computerization and, 204; contract state and, 40; failures of, 29–30; family-based economic security and, 114; federal income tax and, 24; Fordist model of media and, 128; Great Society and, 20; Jim Crow and, 93–94; leftist movements and, 11; liberalism and, 4, 10, 12, 14, 15, 76, 112, 136, 303n30; marriage and, 109–10, 113–14; Robert Nathan and, 39; policy of, 113; reputation of, 48; Rockefeller Foundation and, 25; Franklin D. Roosevelt and, 24; Soviet communism and, 40; state-building practices of, 39
New Democrats: George H. W. Bush and, 30; deficit reduction and, 251; DLC and, 75; Stan Greenberg and, 153; inequality and, 104; policy goals of, 30; Ronald Reagan and, 30; reciprocal responsibility and, 183; voter registration and, 180; work of, 29–30
New Directions, 46–47
New Left, 126, 132–33, 138, 283
New Republic, 126, 127, 136–37, 141
newspapers: ANG and, 128–29; Black newspapers, 134; consumption of, 131; content of, 130–31; International Typographical Union and, 128; organized labor and, 128; professional class and, 131; readership of, 131–32; rural white subscribers and, 132; social class and, 127, 131, 138
New Times, 134
Newton, Huey P., 89
New York, 126, 133–34, 135
New Yorker, 141
New York *Post*, 135, 142
New York Review of Books, 141
New York Times, 128, 130–32, 134, 140
Nextdoor, 270
Ngai, Mae, 292
Nicaraguan Adjustment and Central American Relief Act, 233
Nineteenth Amendment, 171
Nixon, Richard, administration, 28–29, 69, 242–43, 262, 349n31
nongovernmental organizations (NGOs), 28, 29
North American Free Trade Agreement (NAFTA), 263–64
Nu, U, 41–42
Nuclear Regulatory Commission, 71

Index

Obama, Barack, administration: black family and, 91–92, 105; black liberalism and, 265–66; Black Lives Matter and, 275; CBA and, 197–98; choice architecture and, 273–74; diversification and, 266–67; economic policy and, 253–56; Henry Louis Gates and, 267–68; immigration policy and, 276; Occupy Wall Street and, 275; PDI and, 270; polarization and, 271; policies of, 7; policing and, 268–69; political circumstances of, 260; presidential campaign of, 265; professional-class liberalism and, 268; recession and, 254–56; Responsible Fatherhood Initiative and, 105–6; Rubinomics and, 253–54; same-sex marriage and, 107–8; technology and, 270–73; 1033 Program and, 269; theory of politics of, 259–60; universalist policies of, 265–66
Obamacare, 5
Obergefell v. Hodges, 108, 117–18, 121, 123
Ocasio-Cortez, Alexandria, 257
Occupational Safety and Health Act, 70
Occupy Wall Street, 8, 275
Office for Civil Rights (OCR), 189, 191, 349n34
Office of Information and Regulatory Affairs (OIRA), 197
Office of Management and Budget (OMB), 71, 193, 249–50
Onassis, Jacqueline Kennedy, 135
O'Neill, Tip, 224–25, 245, 263
OPEC (Organization of Petroleum Exporting Countries), 242
Operation Big Vote, 177
Oregon v. Mitchell, 171
O'Reilly, Bill, 143
Organization of Petroleum Exporting Countries (OPEC), 242
Orszag, Peter, 251

Packnett, Brittney, 269
Painter, Nell, 279
Panetta, Leon, 249
Panitch, Leo, 284
Papadimitriou, Dimitri, 252
participatory democracy, 63
Patman, Wright, 26–27

PDI (Police Data Initiative), 270
Peabody Fund, 92
Pearce, Diana, 120–21
Peck, Reece, 143
Penn, Mark, 147, 155, 156–59, 160, 161
Perelman, Ron, 77
Peretz, Marty, 136
Pérez, Rossana, 229–30
Perot, Ross, 248
Personal Responsibility and Work Opportunity Reconciliation Act, 117
Phelps Stokes Fund, 93
philanthropy: Carnegie Foundation and, 25; Ford Foundation and, 26, 307; Anand Giridharadas and, 33; governance and, 20–21, 28–32; history of, 20; Lyndon B. Johnson and, 25–26; liberalism and, 21–22, 33–34; professional-class liberalism and, 27; Revenue Act and, 24; Sackler family and, 33; tax reform and, 27; Third World nations and, 26; Donald Trump and, 32–33; Vietnam War and, 29
Philip Morris, 101
Phillips, Kevin, 145, 175
Phillips-Fein, Kim, 293
Piven, Frances Fox, 177–78, 181
Podhoretz, Norman, 338n52
Pod Save America, 137
Point Four program, 40–41
Police Data Initiative (PDI), 270
policy design, 301n15
political consultants, 148–50
Politico, 137
Popular Front, 11
Populist uprising, 74
post-Keynesianism, 243. *See also* Keynesianism
Potter, Paul, 281
Poulantzas, Nicos, 284–85
Pratt, Richard, 78
Precision Medicine Initiative, 273
President's Committee on Economic Security, 38
Pressman, Matthew, 138
print journalism, 126
Procter and Gamble, 87–88, 102, 103
professional and graduate training, 2, 3

professional-class liberalism: ACORN and, 6; autonomy of, 8; beliefs of, 2, 9, 13–14; black liberals and, 91; capitalism and, 3; Center for the Study of Responsive Law and, 68; choice architecture and, 273; Cold War and, 3, 11; computerized government systems and, 202–3; conservatism and, 14; democracy and, 3, 12; economic crises and, 4; electoral politics and, 2; governance and, 3, 9, 88; Pete Hamill and, 136; historians and, 277; liberal-Democratic electoral coalition and, 4; mid-century liberalism and, 3; Ralph Nader and, 68; Robert Nathan and, 48; neoliberalism and, 3, 14, 16; New Deal and, 3; Obama administration and, 268; philanthropy and, 27; polarization and, 271; political crises and, 4; professional-class formation and, 92; professional middle class and, 4; rise of, 8, 11–12; Daniel Rodgers and, 12; skepticism of, 11; Cass Sunstein and, 186; trust of, 12; universalism and, 13

professional-managerial class, 1–2

Progressive Era: black family and, 95; liberalism and, 4; marriage and, 112–13; reformers of, 12; social-welfare services and, 22–23; values of, 7

Project Vote, 177

Pryor, Carol, 225

Public Citizen group, 70

Public Interest, 136

Public Interest Research Groups (PIRGs), 59, 70

Pulido, Laura, 256–57

queer community. *See* LGBTQ community

Rainbow Coalition, 178

Ralph Nader's Public Citizens, 11

Ramsey, Charles, 269

Randolph, A. Philip, 94

Rathke, Wade, 74

Rauh, Joe, 38

Reagan, Ronald, administration: black full employment and, 96; deportations of Salvadorans and, 226; disenfranchisement and, 178; Ralph Nader and, 55; neoliberalism and, 37; New Democrats and, 30; Tip O'Neill and, 263; private enterprise and, 49–50; Regulatory Impact Analyses and, 193; Salvadoran funding and, 224; Salvadoran refugees and, 221; small businesses and, 49–50; thrift industry and, 78

Reconstruction, 88, 90

Reed, Bruce, 248

refugees, 226–27, 230–33

Regan, Don, 78

Rehabilitation Act, 349n31. *See also* Section 504

Reich, Rob, 23

Reich, Robert, 248, 288–89

Republican Party: abortion and, 300n10; anti-statism of, 15; budgets and, 15; consensus politics and, 261–62; criminal-justice reform and, 270; free-market ideologues and, 75; power of, 15; George Soros and, 19; voter registration and, 179

Resolution Trust Corporation, 80, 85–86

Responsible Fatherhood Initiative, 105–6

Revenue Act, 24

Ribicoff, Abraham, 57–58, 69, 70

Rieder, Jonathan, 290–91

Riesel, Victor, 176

Riesman, David, 137

Rivlin, Alice, 249, 250

Robinson, Joan, 243

Robinson, Laurie, 269

Robinson-Patman Act, 67–68

Rockefeller Foundation: black Americans and, 92; Black Family Summit and, 101; funding by, 23; Great Depression and, 24; New Deal and, 25; schemes of, 23; War on Poverty and, 27; "Women's Funds" and, 31

Rodezno, Guillermo, 231

Rodgers, Daniel, 12

Rogers, Joel, 179

Romer, Christina, 253–55

Romero, Óscar, 223

Roosevelt, Franklin D., administration, 24, 25, 39, 300n9

Rosen, Jay, 137

Rosenthal, Abe, 134

Rosenwald Fund, 92

Rubin, Gayle, 115

Rubin, Robert, 6, 237–38, 247–51

Index

Rubinomics, 247–49, 253, 254, 257
Rubio, Marco, 274
Rueschemeyer, Dietrich, 286
Ruiz, Jorge, 232
Rushing, Michael, 275
Russell Sage Foundation, 24
Rustin, Bayard, 94
Ryan, Paul, 274

Sackler family, 19, 33
Safe Software, 270
Salon, 126, 140
Salvadoran government, 364n38
Salvadoran military, 223–24
Sandberg, Sheryl, 32, 267
Sanders, Bernie, 1, 2, 8
San Francisco *Bay Guardian*, 133
San Francisco Chronicle, 139, 140
San Francisco Examiner, 126, 139, 140, 338n60
San Francisco Free Press, 139
Sarah Scaife Foundation, 103
Satut, Miguel, 225, 363n24
Sauls, Rommie, 78
Savage, James, 246
Savvy, 134–35
Schaller, Thomas, 263
Schiller, Reuel, 11, 129–30
Schlesinger, Arthur, Jr., 11, 15
Schoen, Douglass, 147, 155–61
Schröder, Gerhard, 159
Schultz, George, 226
Schumer, Chuck, 83
Scovell, Nell, 267
Second Bill of Rights, 186
Section 504, 188–89, 191–95, 349n34
Self, 134–35
Self, Robert, 117
Self-Sufficiency Standard, 120–21
Senate Banking Committee, 73
Shah, Mohammed Zahir, 43
Sharry, Frank, 219, 229
Sherrod, Shirley, 268
Silicon Valley, 15
Simon, William, 245–46
Simpson, Alan, 228
Sixteenth Amendment, 23
Skocpol, Theda, 285, 286–87
Skrondal, Beth, 120
Sky News, 142

Slate, 141–42
Smith, "Shep," 143
Smith, William French, 226
social history, 278–79
socialism, corporate, 61
Social Science Research Council (SSRC), 24, 286
Social Security, 204, 205
Social Security Act, 204–5
Sontheimer, Morton, 128
Soros, George, 19
Sotomayor, Sonia, 266
Southeastern Community College v. Davis, 192, 194
Sparrow, James, 39–40
Squier, Robert, 179
SSRC (Social Science Research Council), 24, 286
Standby Job Corps, 96
Starr, Paul, 288–89
Stein, Herbert, 142
Stevenson, Bryan, 269
Stiglitz, Joseph, 251–52
Stokes, Carl, 173
Student Nonviolent Coordinating Committee, 63
Students for Democratic Society, 63
Sullivan, Andrew, 142
Sullivan, Margaret, 125
Summers, Larry, 238, 253–55
Sumrall, Herb, 206–7
"Sunshine, Safety and Service" campaign, 79
Sunstein, Cass: CBA and, 197–98; choice architecture and, 273; civil rights and, 196; cost-benefit state and, 186, 197; discrimination and, 194; professional-class liberalism and, 186; Second Bill of Rights and, 186; work of, 6
Sweezy, Alan, 239

Talbot, David, 126, 140
Talese, Gay, 136
TANF (Temporary Assistance for Needy Families), 183
Tapper, Jake, 140
Task Force on 21st Century Policing, 268–69
Tax Offset Program, 214
Tax Reform Act, 174, 324n29

Taylor, Keeanga-Yamahtta, 275, 277, 293
Teixeira, Ruy, 160
Temporary Assistance for Needy Families (TANF), 183
Temporary Protected Status (TPS), 219–21, 229–32, 235
1033 Program, 269
Third World, 26, 41
Thompson, E. P., 291, 295
Thorndike, Joseph, Jr., 35
Tillerson, Rex W., 19
Toxic Substances Control Act, 70
TPS (Temporary Protected Status), 219–21, 229–32, 235
Transport Workers Union, 120
triangulation, 14–15
Trillin, Calvin, 133
Truman, Harry S., administration, 39, 40, 51
Trump, Donald, administration, 32–33, 125, 157, 256
Tsongas, Paul, 249
Tuskegee Model, 93

United Negro College Fund, 102
Upper West Side Air Pollution Campaign, 64
Upscale, 134
US Agency for International Development (USAID), 28, 43–44, 45–46, 47, 49–50
USA Today, 140
US Department of Justice, 193
US Full Employment Service, 96
US League of Savings Institutions, 78

Vietnam War, 10, 11, 29
Village Voice, 135
Villaseñor, Roberto, 269
vocational rehabilitation, 187, 348n18
Volcker, Paul, 246, 253
Voter Education Project, 173
voter registration, 169–70, 174
Voting Rights Act, 13, 167, 171, 173
Vox, 137

Wages for Housework (WfH), 118–20
Wagner Act, 302n27
Walinsky, Lou, 42, 51

Wallace, Guy, 103
Wall Street, 15
Wall Street Journal, 138
Walsh, Camille, 80
"warfare state," 39–40
War on Poverty, 27, 94
War on Terror, 8
Warren, Elizabeth, 1
Washington, Booker T., 93
Washington Monthly, 126, 136, 137
Washington Office on Latin America, 226
Washington Post, 125, 131, 132
Wealth Tax, 25
Wegner, Judith, 190–91
welfare, 201–2, 204–9, 211–12, 215–16, 356n9
Welfare Rights Organization, 109–10
welfare system, attacks on, 205
WELL (Whole Earth 'Lectronic Link), 139
White, Lawrence, 81
Whiting, Ernestine, 80
Whitten, Jamie, 40
Whitworth, William, 141
Whole Earth Catalog, 139
Whole Foods, 133
Wieseltier, Leon, 137
Wilkins, Roger, 88
Wilkins, Roy, 88, 94
Wilson, William Julius, 100–101, 288–89
Win, Ne, 41–42
Wolff, Michael, 133–34
Woodson, Robert, 103
Working Mother, 134–35
Working Woman, 134–35
World War I, 24
World War II, 24
Wray, Randall, 252

Xerox, 101

Young, Whitney, 94

Zanger, Virgina Vogel, 225
Zimmerman, George, 268
Zuckerberg, Mark, 19